Historical Linguistics

HISTORICAL LINGUISTICS
AN INTRODUCTION

FOURTH EDITION

Lyle Campbell

The MIT Press
Cambridge, Massachusetts

Published in the United States and Canada by the MIT Press 2020

First published in Great Britain by Edinburgh University Press Ltd

Typeset in 11/13 Baskerville by
Servis Filmsetting Ltd, Stockport, Cheshire, and
printed and bound in Great Britain

Library of Congress Control Number: 2020946922

ISBN 978-0-262-54218-0

CONTENTS

LIST OF TABLES

LIST OF FIGURES AND MAPS

PREFACE

A number of historical linguistics textbooks exist, but this one is different. Most others talk *about* historical linguistics; they may illustrate concepts and describe methods, and perhaps discuss theoretical issues, but they do not focus on how *to do* historical linguistics. A major goal of this book is to present an accessible, hands-on introduction to historical linguistics which does not just talk about the topics, but shows how to apply the procedures, how to think about the issues, and, in general, how to do what historical linguists do. To this end, this text contains abundant examples and exercises to which readers can apply the principles and procedures in order to learn for themselves how to 'do' historical linguistics. This text differs also by integrating several topics now generally considered important to the field but which are often lacking in other historical linguistics textbooks; these include areal linguistics, linguistic prehistory, distant genetic relationships (how to show that languages are related), quantitative methods, and others. Also, the range of examples is greater and the number of languages from which examples are presented is much broader. Many examples are selected from the history of English, French, German, and Spanish to make the concepts which they illustrate more accessible, since these are languages with which more readers have some acquaintance, but examples from many non-Indo-European languages are also presented; these show the depth and richness of the various concepts and methods, and sometimes provide clearer cases than those available in the better-known languages. In short, this text differs in its emphasis on accessibility, its 'how-to' orientation, its range of languages and examples, and its inclusion of certain essential but often neglected topics.

This book is intended as an introduction to historical linguistics, and assumes only that readers will have had an introduction to linguistics. It is hoped that linguists in general and others interested in language-related matters will find things of interest to them in this book, though it is primarily intended for students of historical linguistics who have little background.

Historical linguistic practice today is linked with theories of general linguistics, particularly with regard to attempts to explain 'why' language changes. In this book, an attempt is made to keep to a minimum the complications for under-standing and applying historical linguistics that diverse theories often occasion, though basic linguistic terminology is employed. Readers who have had some prior introduction to linguistics will fare better; in particular, some familiarity with phonetic symbols may be useful. (Symbols of the International Phonetic Alphabet are used extensively in this text; see the Phonetic Symbols Chart (below) for a list of these and other symbols utilized in this book.) However, one can understand much of historical linguistics even without getting bogged down in theoretical details, phonetic notation, or the mass of general linguistic terms utilized in talking about language. For more detail on the topics covered here, the references cited throughout the book and the sources given in the general bibliography at the end, which contains references to most of the introductory works on historical linguistics, can be consulted.

I believe it is important for students to have some sense of the general thinking concerning the various topics discussed, and to this end I occasionally mention how matters are typically presented in other textbooks or how they are gener-ally seen by practising historical linguists. At the same time, I do not necessarily accept everything that is talked about and so feel some obligation to argue for what (I hope) is the best understanding of some topics. In such instances, I have attempted to present a reasonably unbiased account of opposing opinions. It is important for students to understand how historical linguists think and the sorts of arguments and evidence that would be necessary to resolve such issues. Many of these involve areas where the differences of opinion can be decided only on the basis of substantive evidence which is not currently available but is hoped for from future research. Seeing the different sides of these issues should provide a basis for students to reach their own conclusions when the evidence becomes available, although it is not appropriate or possible in an introductory text to go into intricate detail concerning controversies and unresolved issues of the field.

A concern is the question of how to present complex notions. Definitions and descriptions without examples are usually not clear, but examples with no prior understanding of the concepts involved are also not clear. So, what should be presented first, contextless definitions or contextless examples? I present first the concepts and then the examples to illustrate them. In several cases in the text, it will prove valuable for clarity's sake to read the definitions, description, and discussion, then the examples, and then to reread the general description and discussion – this may be true of many things, but is especially relevant in some contexts here.

Using This Book

As is appropriate in introductory textbooks generally, for the most part each suc-ceeding chapter of this one builds on previous chapters. Nevertheless, different readers and different instructors will have different interests and backgrounds, and so there are abundant cross-references to other chapters and sections throughout the book which make it possible to adjust the sequence in which different chapters are approached. Different readers and instructors can tailor the order to their needs and to the specific objectives of their courses. There is sufficient coverage in this textbook so that it can be adapted for shorter or longer courses, or for more introductory courses or somewhat more advanced ones.

The following presents outline plans of possible organization for courses of different lengths. It is arranged by weeks. It is assumed that the number of class contact hours is roughly the same each week – 3 hours (or 2 hours 30 minutes per week, taking into account 10-minute breaks after each hour). That is, courses generally meet three times per week for 50 minutes for each class, or they meet twice per week for 1 hour 20 minutes each. (Courses can also meet once per week for 2 hours 30 minutes; however, students prefer more class meetings of shorter lengths.) One of the possible course plans below is designed for a semester-long course at American universities, typically 15 weeks long. The other plan is for quarter-length courses, usually 10 weeks long, and for semester-long courses in the UK and many other Commonwealth countries that are 10–12 weeks long.

Sample plan I (15-week course)
Week 1 Chapter 1 Introduction
Week 2 Chapter 2 Sound Change
Week 3 Chapter 3 Loanwords (Borrowing)
Week 4 Chapter 4 Analogical Change
Week 5 Chapter 5 Lexical Change and Chapter 6 Semantic Change
Weeks 6-7 Chapter 7 The Comparative Method and Linguistic Reconstruction
Week 8 Chapter 8 Internal Reconstruction
Week 9 Chapter 9 Language Classification and Models of Linguistic Change
Week 10 Chapter 10 Language Contact
Week 11 Chapter 11 Change in Syntax and Morphology
Week 12 Chapter 12 Explanation of Language Change
Week 13 Chapter 13 Distant Genetic Relationship
Week 14 Chapter 14 Writing and Philology and Chapter 15 Linguistic
    Prehistory
    Alternatively for week 14: Chapter 16 Quantitative Approaches to
    Historical Linguistics and Technical Tools (and not Chapters 14 and 15)
Week 15 Wrap up (might include course review, final examination, or pres-
    entation of student papers)

Sample plan II (10-week course)
Week 1 Chapter 1 Introduction
Week 2 Chapter 5 Lexical Change and Chapter 6 Semantic Change
Week 3 Chapter 2 Sound Change
Week 4 Chapter 3 Loanwords (Borrowing) and Chapter 10 Language Contact
Weeks 5 Chapter 4 Analogical Change and Chapter 11 Change in Syntax
    and Morphology
Week 6 Chapter 7 The Comparative Method and Linguistic Reconstruction
Week 7 Chapter 8 Internal Reconstruction
Week 8 Chapter 9 Language Classification and Models of Linguistic Change
    and Chapter 13 Distant Genetic Relationship

Week 9 Chapter 12 Explanation of Language Change
Week 10 Wrap up (might include course review, final examination, or presentation of student papers)
    Alternatively for week 10: Chapter 14 Writing and Philology and Chapter 15 Linguistic Prehistory

Alternative sample plan II presupposes less in-depth treatment of several topics than is possible in sample plan I. An alternative to that is to eliminate some topics in order to spend more time on more centrally important ones.

Alternative sample plan II (10-week course)
Week 1 Chapter 1 Introduction
Week 2 Chapter 5 Lexical Change and Chapter 6 Semantic Change
Week 3 Chapter 2 Sound Change
Week 4 Chapter 3 Loanwords (Borrowing) and Chapter 10 Language Contact
Weeks 5 Chapter 4 Analogical Change
Week 6 Chapter 7 The Comparative Method and Linguistic Reconstruction and Chapter 9 Language Classification and Models of Linguistic Change
Week 7 Chapter 8 Internal Reconstruction
Week 8 Chapter 11 Change in Syntax and Morphology
Weeks 9 Chapter 12 Explanation of Language Change
Week 10 Wrap up (might include course review, final examination, or presentation of student papers)

Other orders and choices, of course, are possible in any of these plans.
There are exercises at the end of chapters (except for Chapters 10, 12, and 16) and these can easily be incorporated into lesson plans.
Unlike some other textbooks, this one has no glossary. That is because most of the terms for which a glossary would be useful are in fact the topics that are defined and exemplified in the various chapters and sections of this book, making a glossary redundant. For a more official glossary of historical linguistics, see Campbell and Mixco (2007) or Trask (2000).

ACKNOWLEDGEMENTS

This is the fourth edition of this book, and different colleagues and friends have contributed in different ways to the different editions, some in the beginning with comments on a manuscript version of the first edition and many in response to various questions that I have asked them regarding specific examples and issues in the various editions, and with helpful comments, information, and corrections. I am very grateful to them all and thank them all here in alphabetical (not in chronological) order: Rich Alderson, Cynthia Allen, Raimo Anttila, Robert Blust, Claire Bowern, Matthias Brenzinger, William Bright, Una Canger, Andrew Carstairs-McCarthy, Antony Deverson, Mark Donohue, Nicholas Evans, Jan Terje Faarlund, Andrew Garrett, Russell Gray, Simon J. Greenhill, Verónica Grondona, Harald Hammarström, Sharon L. Hargus, Alice C. Harris, Bernd Heine, Jan Henrik Holst, Laszlo Honti, John Huehnergard, Jay Jasanoff, Haowen Jiang, Brian Joseph, John Justeson, Harold Koch, Johanna Laakso, Roger Lass, Adrienne Lehrer, Yaron Matras, Terence M. Neary, Elisabeth Norcliffe, Victor Parker, Timothy J. Pulju, Heidi Quinn, Don Ringe, Malcolm Ross, Tapani Salminen, Pekka Sammallahti, Seija Tiisala, Sarah G. Thomason, Brent Vine, Michael Weiss, and Marc Zender. It goes without saying that none of these scholars is responsible for any misuse or disregard of some of their comments and information. (Not all their recommendations could be implemented, due in part to limitations of space, and sometimes to mutually incompatible recommendations they made.) I am extremely grateful to these scholars for their input and help.

I am especially grateful to Marc Zender for the figures (illustrations) in Chapter 14, for the cover illustration, and for clarifications concerning writing systems. I am deeply grateful to Simon J. Greenhill for the figures in Chapter 16 and clarification of matters there. Finally, I thank Kevin Cowan, cartographer of the Department of Geography, Australian National University, for making most of the maps.

Also, two basic references have been employed extensively in examples cited in this book. For Indo-European forms, I have relied primarily on Calvert

Watkins' *The American Heritage Dictionary of Indo-European Roots* (1985; 3rd edn, 2011), a consistent, accurate, and readily available basic reference. I have also frequently consulted information in Mallory and Adams (1997), *Encyclopedia of Indo-European Culture*. For the history of words in English, I have used the *Oxford English Dictionary* (Oxford University Press, 1989) extensively, supplemented by several online sources.

PHONETIC SYMBOLS AND CONVENTIONS

The conventions for presenting examples used in this book are widely utilized in linguistics, but it will be helpful to state the more important of these for readers unfamiliar with them.

Most linguistic examples are given in italics and their glosses (translations into English) are presented in single quotes, for example: Finnish *rengas* 'ring'.

In instances where it is necessary to make the phonetic form clear, the phonetic representation is presented in square brackets ([]), for example: [sĩŋ] 'sing'. In instances where it is relevant to specify the phonemic representation, this is given between slashed lines (/ /), for example German *Bett* /bɛt/ 'bed'. The convention of angled brackets (< >) is utilized to show that the form is given just as it was written in the original source from which it is cited, for example: German <Bett> 'bed'.

A hyphen (-) is used to show the separation of morphemes in a word, as in *jump-ing* for English *jumping*. Occasionally, a plus sign (+) is used to show a morpheme boundary in a context where it is necessary to show more explicitly the pieces which some example is composed of.

It is standard practice to use an asterisk (*) to represent reconstructed forms, as for example Proto-Indo-European **penkwe* 'five'.

A convention in this text (not a general one in linguistics) is the use of ✘ to represent ungrammatical, non-occurring, or erroneous forms. Outside of historical linguistics, an asterisk is used to indicate ungrammatical and non-occurring forms; but since in historical linguistic contexts an asterisk signals reconstructed forms, to avoid confusion ✘ is used here for ungrammatical or non-occurring forms.

It is standard in historical linguistics to use the symbol > to mean 'changed into', for example: **p* > *b* (original *p* changed into *b*), and < to mean 'changed from, comes from', for example: *b* < **p* (*b* comes from original *p*).

To show an environment (context) where something occurs or in which a change takes place, the notation that combines / and __ is used, where / means in the context, and where __ indicates the location of the material that changes, much as in the idea of 'fill in the blank'. Thus, a change in which *p* became *b* between vowels is represented as: p > b / V__V. A change conditioned by something in the context before the segment which changes is represented as, for example, in: k > č / __i, meaning that *k* became *č* (IPA [ʧ)] in the context before *i*). A change conditioned by something in the environment after the segment which changes is represented as, for example, in: k > č /i__ (meaning *k* became *č* in the context after *i*). The symbol # means 'word boundary', so that / __# means 'word-finally' and /#__ means 'word-initially'.

To avoid notational (and theoretical) complications, when whole classes of sounds change or when only a single phonetic feature of a sound or class of sounds changes, sometimes just individual phonetic attributes (features) are mentioned, for example: *stops* > *voiced*, meaning 'all the stop consonants change by becoming voiced'. Distinctive feature notation and other theoretical apparatus are not used in this text, in order to make the examples more accessible.

Finally, there are traditions of scholarship in the study of different languages and language families which differ significantly from one another with respect to the phonetic notation that they use. For example, vowel length is represented by a 'macron' over the vowel in some (as for example, [ā]), as a colon (or raised dot) after the vowel in others (as [a:], [a·]), and as a repetition of the vowel in still others (as [aa]). In this book, for the presentation of some of the examples cited, some of these different notational conventions commonly used for the various languages involved have been kept – common practice in historical linguistics – though in cases where difficulty of interpretation might result, forms are also given in IPA symbols.

PHONETIC SYMBOLS CHART

	Bilabial	Labiodental	Dental	Alveolar	Postalveolar	Retroflex	Palatal	Velar	Uvular	Pharyngeal	Glottal
Voiceless stops	p			t		ʈ		k	q		ʔ
Voiced stops	b			d				g		ɢ	
Voiceless affricates				ts	č						
Voiced affricates				dz	ǰ						
Voiceless fricatives	ɸ	f	θ	s	ʃ	ʂ	ç	x	χ	ħ	h
Voiced fricatives	β	v	ð	z	ʒ	ʐ		ɣ	ʁ	ʕ	
Nasals	m			n		ɳ	ɲ	ŋ	N		
Approximants	w			ɹ			j		ʀ		
Laterals			l								

	Front		Central		Back
High					
close (tense)	i	y	ɨ	ʉ	u
open (lax)	i	y			u
Mid					
close (tense)	e	ø	ə		o
open (lax)	ɛ	œ			ɜ
Low	æ		a		ɑ

Cʰ	aspirated consonant
C̩	dental consonant
C'	glottalized consonant
Cʷ	labialized consonant
Cʲ, Cʸ	palatalized consonant
V̥, C̥	voiceless sound
tɬ	voiceless lateral affricate
ɫ	velarized or pharyngealized lateral approximant
l̥	voiceless lateral approximant (sometimes symbolized as ɬ)
ɓ	voiced imploded bilabial stop
ʃ, š	voiceless postalveolar fricative
ʧ, č	voiceless postalveolar affricate
ʤ, ǰ	voiced postalveolar affricate
ʒ, ž	voiced postalveolar fricative
s̪	voiceless apical alveolar fricative
ṣ̌	voiceless laminal retroflex fricative
č̣	voiceless laminal retroflex affricate
ć	voiceless prepalatal affricate (IPA [tɕ])
ɕ	voiceless prepalatal (alveolo-palatal) fricative
r (or r̃)	voiced alveolar trill
ɾ	voiced alveolar flap (tap)
lʲ, lʸ	voiced palatalized alveolar lateral approximant, palatal "l" (IPA [ʎ])
ḥ	voiceless pharyngeal fricative (used in Arabic sources)
ḍ, ṭ, ṣ	pharyngealized consonants (as in Arabic)
Ç̣	retroflex consonants as represented in Sanskrit, South Asian and Native American sources
i̯	voiced high front semivowel (second vowel in some diphthongs, not the nucleus of the syllable)
ʍ	voiceless rounded labiovelar approximant (devoiced w)
Ṽ, Ṿ	nasalized vowel
V:, V̄	long vowel (vowel length)
C:	long consonant (geminate consonant)
ñ, nʲ, nʸ	palatalized alveolar nasal, palatal nasal (IPA [ɲ])
x̟	fronted velar fricative
ṇ	symbol for retroflex nasal used in Sanskrit and other sources
ń	postalveolar nasal (Sanskrit)
ś	voiceless postalveolar fricative (used in Sanskrit and other sources) (IPA [ʃ]); also:
ś	voiceless prepalatal fricative (IPA [ɕ])
*ḱ, *ĝ, *ĝh	'palatal' stops in Indo-European

Note that usually no distinction is made between [a] and [ɑ], and *a* is used to symbolize both.

1

INTRODUCTION

3e [ye] knowe eek [also] that in fourme of speche [speech] is chaunge [change],
  [You know also, that there is change in the form of speech,]
With-inne [within] a thousand 3eer [years], and wordes tho [then]
  [In a thousand years, and words then]
That hadden pris [value], now wonder nyce [stupid] and straunge
  [That had value, now wonderfully stupid and strange]
Us thenketh hem [them]; and 3et thei spake [spoke] hem [them] so,
  [They seem to us; and yet they spoke them so,]
And spedde [succeeded] as wel in loue as men now do.
  [And succeed as well in love as men do now.]

(Geoffrey Chaucer [1343–1400],
Troilus and Criseyde, c. 1381–6, book II, lines 22–6)

1.1 Introduction

What is historical linguistics? Historical linguists study language change. The scads of popular books, websites and blogs, newspaper columns, media broadcasts, and magazine articles about the history of words show that there is a lot of public interest in language change and language history. People want to know about the origins of words; they want explanations for what is unusual or weird in their languages; and they typically have strong opinions about changes that are going on in the languages they speak. The mission of this book is to provide an understanding of language change.

If you were to ask practising historical linguists why they study change in language, they would give you lots of different reasons, but certainly included in their answers would be that it is fun, exciting, and intellectually engaging, that it involves some of the hottest topics in linguistics, and that it has important contributions to make to linguistic theory and to the understanding of human nature.

There are many reasons why historical linguists feel this way about their field. For one, a grasp of the ways in which languages can change provides a much better understanding of language in general, of how languages work, how their pieces fit together, and in general what makes them tick. For another, historical linguistic methods have been looked to for models of rigour and excellence in other fields. Historical linguistic findings have been utilized to solve historical problems of concern to society that extend far beyond linguistics. Those dedicated to the humanistic study of individual languages would find their fields much impoverished without the richness provided by historical insights into the development of these languages – just imagine the study of any area of non-modern literature in English, French, German, Italian, Spanish, or other languages without insights into how these languages have changed. A very important reason why historical linguists study language change and are excited about their field is because historical linguistics contributes significantly to other subareas of linguistics and to linguistic theory. For example, human cognition and the human capacity for language learning are central research interests in linguistics, and historical linguistics contributes significantly to this goal. As we determine more accurately what can change and what cannot change in language, and what the permitted versus impossible ways are in which languages can change, we contribute significantly to the understanding of universal grammar, language typology, and human cognition in general – fundamental to understanding our very humanity.

More linguists list historical linguistics as one of their areas of specialization (not necessarily their first or primary area of expertise) than any other subfield of linguistics (with the possible exception of sociolinguistics). That is, it is clear that there are many practising historical linguists, though this may seem to be in contrast to the perception one might get from a look at the lists of required courses in linguistics programmes, from the titles of papers at many professional linguistic conferences, and from the tables of contents of most linguistics journals. Nevertheless, historical linguistics is a major, thriving area of linguistics, as well it should be, given the role it has played and continues to play in contributing towards the primary goals of linguistics in general.

1.1.1 What historical linguistics isn't

Let's begin by clearing away some possible misconceptions, by considering a few things that historical linguistics is *not* about, though sometimes some non-linguists think it is. Historical linguistics is not concerned with the *history of linguistics*, though historical linguistics has played an important role in the development of linguistics – being the main kind of linguistics practised in the nineteenth century – and indeed historical linguistic notions had a monumental impact in the humanities and social sciences, far beyond just linguistics. For example, the development of the comparative method (see Chapter 7) is heralded as one of the major intellectual achievements of the nineteenth century.

Another topic not generally considered to be properly part of historical linguistics is the ultimate *origin of human language* and how it may have evolved from non-human primate call systems, gestures, or whatever, to have the properties we now associate with human languages in general. Many hypotheses abound, but it is very difficult to gain solid footing in this area. Historical linguistic methods and theory are very relevant for research here, and can provide checks and balances in this field where speculation often exceeds substantive findings, but this is not a primary concern of historical linguistics itself.

Finally, historical linguistics is also not about determining or preserving pure, 'correct' forms of language or attempting to prevent change. The popular attitude towards change in language is generally negative, encountered with surprising frequency in newspaper columns and letters to the editor, books, English classes, seemingly countless blogs and other internet sites, and even in ordinary conversations. The changes are often seen as corruption, decay, degeneration, deterioration, as due to laziness or slovenliness, as a threat to education, to morality, and even to national security. We read laments in letters to newspapers stating that our language is being destroyed, deformed, and reduced to an almost unrecognizable remnant of its former and rightful glory. These are of course not new sentiments; laments like these are found throughout history. For example, even from Jakob and Wilhelm Grimm (1854: iii), of fairytale fame and founding figures in historical linguistics, we read:

> The farther back in time one can climb, the more beautiful and more perfect he finds the form of language, [while] the closer he comes to its present form, the more painful it is to him to find the power and adroitness of the language in decline and decay.

The complaint has even spawned poetry:

> Coin brassy words at will, debase the coinage;
> We're in an if-you-cannot-lick-them-join age,
> A slovenliness provides its own excuse age,
> Where usage overnight condones misusage,
> Farewell, farewell to my beloved language,
> Once English, now a vile orangutanguage.

(Ogden Nash,
Laments for a Dying Language, 1960)

However, change in language is inevitable, and this makes complaints against language change both futile and silly. All languages change all the time (except dead ones). Language change is just a fact of life; it cannot be prevented or avoided. All the worries and fears notwithstanding, life always goes on with no obvious ill-effects in spite of linguistic change. The language of today is just as able to meet our communicative needs as the language of former times. Indeed, the changes going on today which so distress some in our society are exactly the same in kind and character as many past changes about which there was much complaint and worry as they were taking place, but the results of which today are considered to have enriched the language as we know it now. Languages are always changing, adapting to accommodate the needs of its users. That is why we have such new words as *bling, blog, cyberstalking, to google, to manspain, meh, road rage, selfie, sexting, turducken, unfriend, wannabe,* and many others. As users' needs and interests change, language change follows. The beauty (or lack thereof) that comes from linguistic change may be in the eye (better said, in the ear) of the beholder, but language change is not really good or bad; mostly it just is. Since it is always taking place, those who oppose ongoing changes would do their stress-levels well just to make peace with the inevitability of language change. Of course, society can assign negative or positive value to things in language (be they new changing ones or old ones), and this can have an impact on how or whether these things change. This sociolinguistic conditioning of change is an important part of historical linguistics (see Chapters 9 and 12).

1.2 What is Historical Linguistics About?

As already mentioned, historical linguistics deals with language change. Historical linguistics is sometimes called *diachronic* linguistics (from Greek *dia-* 'through' + *khronos* 'time' + *-ic*), since historical linguists are concerned with change in language or languages over time. This is contrasted with *synchronic* linguistics (from Greek *sun-* 'together, with' + *khronos* 'time' + *-ic*), which deals with a language at a single point in time. For example, linguists may attempt to write a grammar of present-day English as spoken in some particular speech community, and that would be a synchronic grammar. Similarly, a grammar written of Old English intended to represent a single point in time would also be a synchronic grammar. There are various ways to study language *diachronically*. For example, historical linguists may study changes in the history of a single language, for instance the changes from Old English to Modern English, or between Old French and Modern French, to mention just two examples. Modern English is very different from Old English, as is Modern French from Old French. Often the study of the history of a single language is called *philology*, for example English philology, French philology, Hispanic philology, and so on. (The term *philology* has several other senses as well, as will be seen in Chapter 14.)

The historical linguist may also study changes revealed in the comparison of related languages, often called *comparative* linguistics. We say that languages are related to one another when they descend from (are derived from) a single original language, a common ancestor: for example, the modern Romance languages (which include Italian, French, Spanish, Portuguese, and others) descend from earlier spoken Latin (see Chapters 7 and 9).

In the past, many had thought that the principal domain of historical linguistics was the study of 'how' languages change, believing that answers to the question of 'why' they change were too inaccessible. However, since about the 1960s, great strides have been made also to understand 'why' languages change (see Chapter 12). Today, historical linguistics is dedicated to the study of both 'how' and 'why' languages change, both to the methods of investigating linguistic change and to the theories designed to explain these changes.

Some people imagine that historical linguists mostly just study the history of individual words – and many people are fascinated by word histories, as shown by the number of popular books, newspaper columns, websites, blogs, and podcasts, and the many pronouncements from the many pseudointellectual self-appointed language pundits dedicated to the topic, more properly called *etymology* (derived from Greek *etumon* 'true' [neuter form], that is, the 'true or original meaning of a word'). The primary goal of historical linguistics is *not* etymologies, but accurate etymology is an important product of historical linguistic work. Let us, for illustration's sake, consider a couple of examples and then see what the real role of etymology in historical linguistics is. Since word histories have a certain glamour about them for many people, let's check out the history of the word *glamour* itself. Surprisingly, it connects with a main concern of linguistics, namely *grammar*.

Glamour is a changed form of the word *grammar*, originally in use in Scots English; it meant 'magic, enchantment, spell', found especially in the phrase 'to cast the glamour over one'. It did not acquire its sense of 'a magical or fictitious beauty or alluring charm' until the mid-1800s. The word *grammar* has its own interesting history. It was borrowed from Old French *grammaire*, itself from Latin *grammatica*, ultimately derived from Greek *gramma* 'letter, written mark'. In Classical Latin, *grammatica* meant the methodical study of literature broadly. In the Middle Ages, it came to mean chiefly the study of or knowledge of Latin and hence came also to be synonymous with learning in general, the knowledge peculiar to the learned class. Since this was popularly believed to include also magic and astrology, French *grammaire* (inherited from Latin *grammatica*) came to be used sometimes for the name of these occult 'sciences'. It is in this sense that it survived in *glamour*, and also in earlier English *gramarye*, as well as in French *grimoire* 'conjuring book, unintelligible book or writing'. English *gramarye*, *grammary* meant 'grammar, learning in general, occult learning, magic, necromancy', a word revived in literary usage by later writers; it is clearly archaic, an example of the vocabulary loss discussed in Chapter 5.

What is of greater concern to historical linguists is not the etymology of these words per se, but the kinds of changes they have undergone and the techniques or methods we have at our disposal to recover this history. Thus, in the history of the words *glamour* and *grammar* we notice various kinds of change: borrowing from Greek to Latin and ultimately from French (a descendant of Latin) to English, shifts in meaning, and the sporadic change in sound (*r* to *l*) in the derived word *glamour*. Changes of this sort are what historical linguistics is about, not just the individual word histories. These kinds of changes that languages can and do undergo and the techniques that have been developed in historical linguistics to recover them are what the chapters of this book are concerned with.

Let's take *goodbye* as a second example. This everyday word has undergone several changes in its history. It began life in the late 1500s as *god be with you* (or *ye*), spelled variously as *god be wy ye*, *god b'uy*, and so on. The first part changed to *good* either on analogy (see Chapter 4) with such other greetings as *good day*, *good morning*, and *good night*, or as a euphemistic deformation to avoid the blasphemy of saying *god* (taboo avoidance, see Chapter 6) – or due to a combination of the two. The various independent words in *god be with you* were amalgamated (see Chapter 5) into one, *goodbye*, and ultimately even this was shortened (clipped, see Chapter 5) to *bye*.

In large part, then, a word's etymology is the history of the linguistic changes it has undergone. Therefore, when we understand the various kinds of linguistic change dealt with in the chapters of this book, the stuff that etymologies are made of and based on becomes clear. Historical linguists are concerned with all these things broadly and not merely with the history behind individual words. For that reason, etymology is not the primary purpose of historical linguistics, but rather the goal is to understand language change in general; and when we understand this, then etymology, one area of historical linguistics, is a by-product of that understanding.

1.3 Kinds of Linguistic Changes: An English Example

As seen in these sample etymologies, there are many kinds of linguistic change. A glance at the chapter titles of this book reveals the major ones. In effect, any aspect of a language's structure can change, and therefore we are concerned with learning to apply accurately the techniques that have been developed for dealing with these kinds of changes, with sound change, grammatical change, semantic change, borrowing, analogy, and so on, and with understanding and evaluating the basic assumptions upon which these historical linguistic methods are based.

We can begin to get an appreciation for the various sorts of changes that are possible in language by comparing a small sample from various stages of English. This exercise compares the verse in Matthew 26:73 from translations of the Bible at different time periods, starting with the present and working back to Old English. This particular example was selected in part because it talks about language and in part because in translations of the Bible we have comparable texts from the various time periods which can reveal changes that have taken place:

1.   Modern English (*The New English Bible*, 1961):
     Shortly afterwards the bystanders came up and said to Peter, 'Surely you are another of them; your accent gives you away!'
2.   Early Modern English (*The King James Bible*, 1611):
     And after a while came vnto him they that stood by, and saide to Peter, Surely thou also art one of them, for thy speech bewrayeth thee.
3.   Middle English (*The Wycliff Bible*, fourteenth century):
     And a litil aftir, thei that stooden camen, and seiden to Petir, treuli thou art of hem; for thi speche makith thee knowun.
4.   Old English (*The West-Saxon Gospels*, c. 1050):
     þa æfter lytlum fyrste genēalǣton þa ðe þær stodon, cwædon to petre. Soðlice þu eart of hym, þyn spræc þe gesweotolað.
     [Literally: then after little first approached they that there stood, said to Peter. Truly thou art of them, thy speech thee makes clear.]

In comparing the Modern English with the Early Modern English (1476–1700) version, we note several kinds of changes. (1) *Lexical*: in Early Modern English *bewrayeth* we have an example of lexical replacement. This word was archaic already in the seventeenth century and has been replaced by other words. It meant 'to malign, speak evil of, to expose (a deception)'. In this context, it means that Peter's way of speaking, his accent, gives him away. (2) *Grammatical* (syntactic and morphological) change: from *came vnto* [unto] *him they* to the Modern English equivalent, *they came to him*, there has been a syntactic change. In earlier times, English, like other Germanic languages, had a rule which essentially inverted the subject and verb when preceded by other material (though this rule was not obligatory in English as it is in German), so that because *and after a while* comes first in the sentence, *they came* is inverted to *came they*. This rule has for the most part been lost in Modern English. Another grammatical change is seen in the difference between *thou . . . art* and *you are*. Formerly, *thou* was 'you (singular familiar)' and contrasted with *ye/you* 'you (plural or singular formal)', but this distinction was lost. The *-eth* of *bewray-eth* was the 'third person singular' verb agreement suffix; it was replaced in time by *-(e)s* (*giveth > gives*). (3) *Sound change*: Early Modern English was not pronounced in exactly the same way as Modern English, but it will be easier to show examples of sound changes in the earlier texts (below). (4) *Borrowing*: the word *accent* in Modern English is a loanword from Old French *accent* 'accent, pronunciation' (see Chapter 3 on borrowing). (5) *Changes in orthography* (spelling conventions): while differences in orthography (spelling conventions) are not of central concern in historical linguistics, we do have to be able to interpret what the texts represent phonetically in order to utilize them successfully (this is part of philology; see Chapter 14). In *vnto* for modern *unto* we see a minor change in orthographic convention. Earlier in many European languages, there was in effect no distinction between the letters *v* and *u* (the Latin alphabet, upon which most European writing systems are based, had no such difference); both could be used to represent either the vowel /u/ or the consonant /v/ or in other cases /w/, though for both /v/ and /u/ usually *v* was used initially (<vnder> 'under') and *u* medially (<haue> 'have'). One could tell whether the vowel or consonant value was intended only in context – a *v* between consonants, for example, would most probably represent /u/. More revealing examples of changes in orthography are seen (below) in the Old English text. In *thou* (formerly pronounced /θuː/) we see the influence of the French scribes – French had a monumental influence on English after the Norman French conquest of England in 1066. The *ou* was the French way of spelling /u/, as in French *nous* /nu/ 'we'; later, English underwent the Great Vowel Shift (a sound change, mentioned below; see Chapter 2) in which /uː/ became /au/, which explains why words such as *thou, house,* and *loud* (formerly /θuː/, /huːs/, and /luːd/ respectively) no longer have the sound /uː/ that the French orthographic *ou* originally represented.

Examples of kinds of changes seen in the comparison of the Middle English (1066–1476) text with later versions include the following, among others. (1) *Sound change*: final *-n* was lost by regular sound change under certain conditions, as seen in the comparison of Middle English *stooden, camen,* and *seiden* with modern English *stood, came,* and *said*. (2) *Grammatical change* (morphological and syntactic): the forms *stooden, camen,* and *seiden* ('stood', 'came', and 'said') each contain the final *-n* which marked agreement with the third person plural subject (in this case 'they', spelled *thei*). When final *-n* was lost by sound change, the grammatical change was brought about that verbs no longer had this agreement marker (-*n*) for the plural persons. (3) *Borrowing*: the *hem* is the original third person plural object pronoun, which was replaced by *them*, a borrowing from Scandinavian, which had great influence on English.

Between Old English (c. 450–1066) and Modern English we see many changes. Some of the kinds of change represented in this text include:

1. *Lexical change*: there are instances of loss of vocabulary items represented by the words in this short verse, namely *genēaldǣton* 'approached', *cwǣdon* 'said' (compare archaic *quoth*), *soðlice* 'truly' (*soothly*, compare *soothsayer* 'one who speaks the truth'), and *gesweotolað* 'shows, reveals'.

2. *Sound change*: English has undergone many changes in pronunciation since Old English times. For example, the loss of final -*n* in certain circumstances mentioned above is also illustrated in *þyn* 'thy' (modern 'your') (in *þyn sprǣc* 'thy speech' [translated in the Modern English version as 'your accent']). A sporadic change is seen in the loss of *r* from *sprǣc* 'speech' (compare the German cognate *Sprache* 'language, speech', where the *r* is retained). English vowels underwent a number of changes. In the Great Vowel Shift (mentioned above), long vowels raised and long high vowels /iː/ and /uː/ became diphthongs, /ai/ and /au/, respectively. This is seen in the comparison of some of the Old English words with their Modern English equivalents:

Old English	*Modern English*
stodon /stoːd-	stood /stʊd/
petre /peːter/	Peter /pitər/
soðlice /soːθ-/	soothly /suθ-/ ('soothly, truly')
þu /θuː/	thou /ðau/
þyn /θiːn/	thy /ðai/
þe /θeː/	thee /ði/

3. *Grammatical*: the change mentioned above, the loss of the subject–verb inversion when other material preceded in the clause, is seen in a comparison of *genēalǣton þa* 'approached they' with the modern counterpart 'they approached'. The loss of case endings is seen in *æfter lytlum*, where the -*um* 'dative plural' is lost and no longer required after prepositions such as *after*. The same change which was already mentioned above in the Middle English text is seen again in the loss of the -*n* 'third person plural' verbal agreement marker, in *genēalǣton* '(they) approached', *stodon* '(they) stood', and *cwǣdon* '(they) said'. Another change is the loss of the prefix *ge-* of *genēalǣton* 'approached' and *gesweotolað* 'shows'. This was reduced in time from [je] to [j] to [i] and finally lost, so that many perfect forms ('has done', 'had done') were no longer distinct from the simple past ('did'); that is, in the case of *sing/sang/have sung*, these remain distinct, but in the case of *bring/brought/have brought* they are not distinct, though formerly the *have brought* form would have borne the *ge-* prefix (Old English *gebroht*), distinguishing it from the *brought*

('past') (Old English *brōhte*) form without the prefix, which is now lost from the language.

4. *Orthographic*: there are many differences in how sounds are represented. Old English *þ* 'thorn' and *ð* 'eth' (as in *þa* 'then', *þær* 'there', *soðlice* 'truly', *þu* 'thou', *þyn* 'thy', *þe* 'that', and *gesweotolað* 'makes clear' in the verse above) have been dropped and are spelled today with *th* for both the voiceless (θ) and voiced (ð) dental fricatives. The *æ* (called 'ash', from Old English *æsc*, its name in the runic alphabet) (as in *æfter* 'after', *genēalǣton þær* 'there', *cwædon* 'said', and *spræc* 'language' in the verse cited above) is also no longer used.

The various sorts of changes illustrated in this short text are the subject matter of the chapters of this book.

1.4 Exercises

Exercise 1.1

This exercise is about attitudes towards language change.

1. Try to find letters to newspapers or columns in newspapers or magazines, or on blogs or on YouTube, which express opinions about changes that are taking place in English now. What do you think they reveal about attitudes towards language change?
2. Ask your friends, family, and associates what they think about language today; do they think it is changing, and if so, is it getting better or worse?
3. Find books, articles, or web pages on 'proper' English (prescriptive grammar); what attitudes if any do they reveal towards changes that are going on in today's language?
4. Consider the many things that schoolteachers or school grammar books and would-be language pundits warn you against as being 'wrong' or 'bad grammar'. Do you think any of these involve changes that are taking place in the language?
5. Compare books on etiquette written recently with some written forty years ago or more. Find the sections which deal with appropriate ways of speaking and use of language. What changes have taken place between the recommendations made then and more recent ones? Do these differences reveal anything about change in the language or in language use, or about attitudes towards language changes?

Exercise 1.2

Observe the language you hear around you, and write down any changes you notice that are going on now or have taken place in your lifetime. For example, if you are old enough, you might observe that earlier *attitude* meant simply 'point of view, way of thinking about someone or something, a position' but for younger people it has shifted its meaning to 'antagonistic manner, resentful, uncooperative behaviour', giving rise also to slang *'tude* 'an arrogant attitude'. You might notice that former *passed away* (or *passed on*) as a euphemistic alternative to *died* has changed now to just *passed* for younger speakers, with no *away* or *on* needed with it any more to get the sense of *died*. Slang often changes at a rather fast pace; what observations might you make about recent slang versus earlier slang? Can you find examples of ongoing change in other areas of the language besides just vocabulary?

Exercise 1.3

Changes in spelling and occasional misspellings are sometimes used to make inferences about changes in pronunciation. This can, of course, be misleading, since spellings are sometimes used for other purposes than just to represent pronunciation. Try to find examples of recent differences in spelling or of misspellings and then try to imagine what they might mean, say, to future linguists looking back trying to determine what changed and when it changed. For example, you might compare the spelling *lite* with *light, gonna* with *going to, wannabee* with *want to be*, or *alright* and *alot* with *all right* and *a lot* respectively. In particular, variations in spellings can be very revealing; see if you can find examples which may suggest something about language change.

Exercise 1.4

A number of examples from Shakespeare's plays (Shakespeare lived 1564 to 1616), written in the Early Modern English period (roughly 1500 to 1800), are presented here which illustrate differences from how the same thing would be said today. Think about each example and attempt to state what changes have taken place in the language that would account for the differences you see in the constructions mentioned in the headings, in the negatives, auxiliary verbs, and so on. For example, in the first one we see: *Saw you the weird sisters?* The Modern English equivalent would be *Did you see the weird sisters?* Had the heading directed your attention to yes/no questions, you would attempt to state what change had taken place, from former *saw you* (with inversion from *you saw*) to the modern version which no longer involves inversion but requires a form of *do* (*did you see*) which was not utilized in Shakespeare's version.

Treatment of negatives:

1. Saw you the weird sisters? . . . Came they not by you? (*Macbeth* IV, i)
2. I love thee not, therefore pursue me not (*A Midsummer Night's Dream* II, i)
3. I know thee not, old man: fall to thy prayers (*Henry V* V, v)
4. Let not thy mother lose her prayers, Hamlet: I pray thee, stay with us; go not to Wittenberg (*Hamlet* I, ii)
5. But yet you draw not iron (*A Midsummer Night's Dream* II, i)
6. Tempt not too much the hatred of my spirit (*A Midsummer Night's Dream* II, i)
7. And I am sick when I look not on you (*A Midsummer Night's Dream* II, i)
8. I will not budge for no man's pleasure (*Romeo and Juliet* III, i)
9. I cannot weep, nor answer have I none (*Othello* IV, ii)
10. I am not sorry neither (*Othello* V, ii)

Treatment of auxiliary verbs:

1. Macduff is fled to England (*Macbeth* IV, i) = 'has fled'
2. The king himself is rode to view their battle (*Henry V* IV, iii) = 'has ridden'
3. Thou told'st me they were stolen into this wood (*A Midsummer Night's Dream* II, i) = 'had stolen away/had hidden'

Treatment of comparatives and superlatives:

1. She comes more nearer earth than she was wont (*Othello* 5, 2)
2. This was the most unkindest cut of all (*Julius Caesar* 3, 2)
3. What worser place can I beg in your love (*A Midsummer Night's Dream* II, i)

Differences in verb agreement inflections (endings on the verbs which agree with the subject):

1. The quality of mercy is not strain'd
   It dropp**eth** as the gentle rain from heaven
   Upon the place beneath: it is twice blessed;
   It bless**eth** him that give**s** and him that take**s**
   (*The Merchant of Venice* IV, i)
2. The one I'll slay, the other slay**eth** me
   (*A Midsummer Night's Dream* II, i)
3. O, it offend**s** me to the soul to
   Hear a robostious periwig-pated fellow tear
   A passion to tatters
   (*Hamlet* III, i)
4. And could of men distinguish, her election
   Hath seal'd thee for herself: for thou ha**st** been
   As one, in suffering all, that suffer**s** nothing
   (*Hamlet* III, i)

Exercise 1.5

The following is a sample text of Middle English, from Chaucer c. 1380. It is presented in sets of three lines: the first line is from Chaucer's text; the second is a word-by-word translation, with some of the relevant grammatical morphemes indicated; and the third line is a modern translation. Compare these lines and report the main changes you observe in morphology, syntax, semantics, and lexical items. (Do not concern yourself with the changes in spelling or pronunciation.)

The Tale of Melibee, Geoffrey Chaucer (c. 1380)

Upon a day bifel that he for his desport is went into the feeldes hym to pleye.
On one day befell that he for his pleasure is gone to the fields him to play.
'One day it happened that for his pleasure he went to the fields to amuse himself.'
   [NOTE: *is went* = Modern English 'has gone'; with verbs of motion the auxiliary used was a form of the verb 'to be', where today it has a form of 'to have']

His wif and eek his doghter hath he laft inwith his hous,
his wife and also his daughter has he left within his house,
'His wife and his daughter also he left inside his house,'
   [NOTE: *wif* = 'wife, woman']

of which the dores wer-en faste y-shette.
of which the doors were-PLURAL fast PAST.PARTICIPLE-shut
'whose doors were closed firmly.'

Thre of his old foos ha-n it espied, and sett-en laddres to the walles of his hous,
three of his old foes have-PLURAL it spied, and set-PLURAL ladders to the walls of his house,
'Three of his old enemies saw this, and set ladders to the walls of his house,'

and by wyndowes ben entred, and betten his wyf,
and by windows had entered, and beaten his wife,
'and had entered by the windows, and beat his wife,'
   [NOTE: *ben entred* = 'have entered', a verb of motion taking 'to be' as the auxiliary]

and wounded his doghter with fyve mortal woundes in fyve sondry places –
and wounded his daughter with five mortal wounds in five sundry places –
'and wounded his daughter with five mortal wounds in five different places –'

this is to sey-n, in hir feet, in hir handes, in hir erys, in hir nose, and in hir
  mouth, –
this is to say-INFINITIVE, in her feet, in her hands, in her ears, in her nose,
  and in her mouth, –
'that is to say, in her feet, in her hands, in her ears, in her nose, and in her
  mouth –'

and left-en hir for deed, and went-en awey.
and left-PLURAL her for dead, and went-PLURAL away
'and left her for dead, and went away.'

(Lass 1992: 25–6)

Exercise 1.6

The text in this exercise is a sample of Early Modern English, from William
Caxton, *Eneydos* (c. 1491). As in Exercise 1.5 just above, three-line sets are
presented: the first line is from Caxton's text; the second is a word-by-word
translation, with some of the relevant grammatical morphemes indicated;
the third is a more colloquial modern translation. Compare these lines and
report the main changes you observe in morphology, syntax, semantics, and
lexical items. (Again, do not concern yourself with the changes in spelling or
pronunciation.)

And that commyn englysshe that is spoken in one shyre varyeth from a
  nother. In so moche
and that common English that is spoken in one shire varies from another.
  In so much
'And the common English that is spoken in one county varies so much from
  [that spoken in] another. In so much'

that in my days happened that certayn marchauntes were in a ship in
  tamyse
that in my days happened that certain merchants were in a ship in
  Thames
'that in my time it happened that some merchants were in a ship on the
  Thames'

for to haue sayled ouer the see to zelande/ and for lacke of wynde thei
  taryed atte forlond;
for to have sailed over the sea to Zeeland. And for lack of wind they tarried
  at.the coast;
'to sail over the sea to Zeeland. And because there was no wind, they stayed
  at the coast'
[NOTE: Zeeland = a province in the Netherlands]

and wente to land for to refreshe them. And one of theym, named sheffelde
  a mercer
and went to land for to refresh them. And one of them, named Sheffield,
  a mercer,
'and they went on land to refresh themselves. And one of them, named
  Sheffield, a fabric-dealer,'

cam in to an hows and axed [aksed] for mete, and specyally he axyd after
  eggys.
came into a house and asked for meat, and especially he asked after eggs.
'came into a house and asked for food, and specifically he asked for "eggs".'

And the goode wyf answerede. that she coude no frenshe.
and the good woman answered that she could no French.
'And the good woman answered that she knew no French.'

And the marchaunt was angry. for he also coude speke no frenshe.
and the merchant was angry, for he also could speak no French,
'And the merchant was angry, because he couldn't speak any French
  either.'
  [NOTE: *coude* = 'was able to, knew (how to)']

but wolde haue hadde egges/and she vnderstode hym not/
but would have had eggs; and she understood him not.
'but he wanted to have eggs; and she did not understand him.'
  [NOTE: *wolde* = 'wanted', the source of Modern English *would*]

And thenne at laste a nother sayd that he wolde haue eyren/
and then at last an other said that he would have eggs.
'and then finally somebody else said that he wanted to have eggs.'

then the good wyf said that she understod him wel/
then the good woman said that she understood him well.
'Then the good woman said that she understood him well.'
                (Source of Caxton's text: Fisher and Bornstein 1974: 186–7)

2

SOUND CHANGE

The real cause of sound-change seems to be organic shifting – failure to hit the mark, the result of either carelessness or sloth.

(Henry Sweet 1900: 20)

A sound-law may be regarded as simply a statement of the fact that in a certain period of a certain language its speakers got into the habit of mispronouncing a certain word.

(Henry Sweet 1900: 24)

2.1 Introduction

The most thoroughly studied area of historical linguistics is sound change. Over time, the sounds of languages tend to change. The study of sound change has yielded very significant results, and important assumptions that underlie historical linguistic methods, especially the comparative method (see Chapter 7), are based on these findings. An understanding of sound change is very important for historical linguistics in general, and this needs to be stressed – it plays an extremely important role in the comparative method and hence also in linguistic reconstruction, in internal reconstruction (see Chapter 8), in detecting loanwords (see Chapter 3), and in determining whether languages are related to one another (see Chapters 9 and 13). This chapter is about how sounds change. (As we will see, the reasons for sound change offered by Henry Sweet in the quotations at the outset of this chapter are not among those today's linguists accept.)

Sound change is often the major concern of books on the history of individual languages – it is extremely important to historical linguistics. Typically, sound changes are classified, often in long lists of different kinds of sound changes, each with its own traditional name (some with more than one name). To be at home with sound change, it is valuable to know the most frequently used of these names and to be familiar with the kinds of changes they represent. The most commonly

recurring kinds of sound changes in the world's languages are listed and exemplified in this chapter. They are organized in a representative classification of
sound changes, but there is nothing special about this particular arrangement,
and different textbooks present a variety of other classifications of kinds of sound
change. To understand these categories, it will be helpful to read the description
of them first, then look at the examples, and then read the definitions again.

2.2 Kinds of Sound Change

Regular sound changes are accorded great amounts of attention in historical
linguistics, and rightly so – they are extremely important to the methods and
theories about language change. In fact, the most important basic assumption
in historical linguistics is that sound change is regular, a fundamental principle
with far-reaching implications for the methods considered in later chapters. To
say that a sound change is regular means that the change takes place whenever
the sound or sounds which undergo the change are found in the circumstances
or environments that condition the change. For example, original *p* regularly
became *b* between vowels in Spanish (p > b /V__V); this means that in this
context between vowels, every original *p* became a *b*; it is not the case that some
original intervocalic *p*'s became *b* in some words, but became, say, *ŋ* in some other
words, and *ε* in still other words, in unpredictable ways. If a sound could change
in such arbitrary and unpredictable ways, the change would not be regular; but
sound change is regular (though as we will see in other chapters, some other kinds
of change can also affect sounds, so that the results may not appear regular when
they are subject to other kinds of explanations).

This is called 'the *regularity principle*' or 'the *Neogrammarian hypothesis*'. The
Neogrammarians, beginning in about 1876 in Germany, became extremely
influential in general thinking about language change, and about sound change
in particular. The Neogrammarians were a group of younger scholars who
antagonized the leaders of the field at that time by attacking older thinking and
loudly proclaiming their own views. The early Neogrammarians included such
well-known linguists as Karl Brugmann, Berthold Delbrück, August Leskien,
Hermann Osthoff, Hermann Paul, and others. They were called *Junggrammatiker*
'young grammarians' in German, where *jung-* 'young' had the sense of 'young
Turk', originally intended as an unflattering nickname for the rebellious circle
of young scholars, although they adopted the term as their own name. English
Neogrammarian is not a very precise translation. Their slogan was: *sound laws suffer
no exceptions* ('die Lautgesetze erleiden überhaupt keine Ausnahme') (Osthoff and
Brugmann 1878). The notion of the 'regularity of the sound laws' became fundamental to the comparative method (see Chapter 7). By 'sound laws' they meant
merely 'sound changes', but they referred to them as 'laws' because these scholars
linked linguistics with the rigorous sciences which dealt in laws and law-like statements. We return to the regularity principle in more detail in Chapters 7 and 9.

Sound changes are typically classified according to whether they are *unconditioned* or *conditioned*. When a sound change occurs generally and is not dependent
on the phonetic context in which the sound occurs, that is, not dependent on or

restricted in any way by neighbouring sounds, it is *unconditioned*. Unconditioned sound changes modify the sound in all contexts in which it occurs, regardless of what other sounds may be found in words containing the changing sound: that is, the change happens irrespective of the phonological context in which the sound that changes may be found. When a change takes place only in certain contexts (when it is dependent upon neighbouring sounds, upon the sound's position within words, or on other aspects of the grammar), it is *conditioned*. Conditioned changes are more restricted and affect only some of the sound's occurrences, those in particular contexts, but not other occurrences which happen to be found in environments outside the restricted situations in which the change takes effect. For example, the Spanish change of *p* to *b* intervocalically (mentioned above) is conditioned; only those *p*'s which are between vowels become *b*, while *p*'s in other positions (for example, at the beginning of words) do not change. On the other hand, most varieties of Latin American Spanish have changed palatalized *l* to *y*, that is, *ʎ* > *y* (IPA *ʎ* > *j*) unconditionally, as for example in *calle* 'street' /kalʸe/ > /kaye/ – every instance of an original *ʎ* has changed to *y* regardless of the context in which the *ʎ* occurred.

The distinction between *phonemic* and *non-phonemic* changes is present in some fashion in most treatments of sound change. It has to do with the recognition of distinct levels of phonological analysis in linguistic theory – the phonetic level and the phonemic level. There is sometimes disagreement about how the second level is to be understood, that is, about how abstract phonemes may be (how different or distant they can be from the phonetic form) and how they are to be represented. Naturally, if there were full agreement in phonological theory about the 'phonemic' level, there would be more of a consensus in historical linguistics on how to talk about the aspects of sound change which relate to it. However, for our purposes, a definitive characterization is not crucial, so long as we recognize that talk about sound change makes reference to two distinct levels. In general, it is helpful to think of phonetics as representing the actually occurring physical sounds, and of phonemes as representing the speakers' knowledge or mental organization of the sounds of their language. A non-phonemic change (also called *allophonic* change) does not alter the total number of phonemes in the language or change one phoneme into another phoneme. Some call the non-phonemic changes *shifts*, referring to the shift in pronunciation (at the phonetic level) with no change in the number of distinctive sounds, though this can be misleading, since some major sound changes are also sometimes called shifts, meaning just sound change. A *phonemic* change results in a change in the phonemes (the basic sounds that native speakers hold to be distinct) of a language by adding to the number of phonemes of the language, or deleting from that number, or by changing one phoneme into a different phoneme.

2.3 Non-phonemic (Allophonic) Changes

Non-phonemic changes have not been considered to be as important as pho-nemic changes (below), perhaps because they do not have consequences for the overall phonemic inventory of a language.

2.3.1 Non-phonemic unconditioned changes

(1) In varieties of English, *u* > *ʉ* (high central rounded vowel), and in some dialects the change even went on to *y* (high front rounded vowel), as in 'shoe' [ʃu] > [ʃʉ], and in some even [ʃy].

(2) Pipil (a Uto-Aztecan language of El Salvador): *o* > *u*. Proto-Nahua, Pipil's immediate ancestor, had the vowel inventory /i, e, a, o/. When Pipil changed *o* to *u*, this did not change the number of distinctive vowels, and therefore it is a non-phonemic change. Since the change affected all instances of *o*, turning them all into *u* regardless of other sounds in the context, it is an unconditioned change.

(3) Guatemalan Spanish: *r* > *š̬*. The 'trilled' *r* found in most Spanish dialects has become the so-called 'assibilated' *r* (in this case phonetically a voiceless laminal retroflex fricative) in rural Guatemalan Spanish. Since *r* becomes *š̬* in all contexts, without restrictions that depend upon neighbouring sounds, this is an unconditioned change. In this change, one sound, *š̬*, is switched for another, for *r*, but this is just the change in pronunciation of this sound, not a change in its phonemic status in the language.

2.3.2 Non-phonemic conditioned changes

(1) Many English dialects have undergone a change in which a vowel is phonetically lengthened before voiced stops, for example, /bɛd/ > [bɛˑd] 'bed', but not lengthened before voiceless stops, as in /bɛt/ > [bɛt] 'bet', a change that left [ɛ] and [ɛˑ] as allophones of a single phoneme /ɛ/.

(2) Spanish dialects: n > ŋ /__#. In many dialects of Spanish, final *n* has changed so that it is no longer pronounced as [n], but rather as a velar nasal [ŋ], as in *son* 'they are' [son] > [soŋ], *bien* 'well, very' [byen] > [byeŋ] (IPA [bjeŋ]). This is a conditioned change, since *n* did not change in all its occurrences, rather only where it was at the end of words. It is non-phonemic, since the change results in no change at the phonemic level. Before the change, the phoneme /n/ had one phonetic form (allophone), [n]; after the change, /n/ came to have two non-contrastive variants (allophones), predictable from context, with [ŋ] word-finally and [n] when not in final position.

2.4 Phonemic Changes

Two principal kinds of phonemic changes are *mergers* and *splits*.

2.4.1 Merger (A, B > B, or A, B > C)

Mergers are changes in which, as the name suggests, two (or more) distinct sounds merge into one, leaving fewer distinct sounds (fewer phonemes) in the phonological inventory than there were before the change.

(1) Most varieties of Latin American Spanish: *ľ* (spelled 'll') and *y* merge, *ľ*, *y* > *y* (IPA *ʎ, j* > *j*). Spanish used to contrast the two sounds and this contrast is still maintained in some dialects of Spain and in the Andes regions of South America;

2.6.1.3 Partial contact regressive assimilation

(1) Proto-Indo-European *swep-no- > Latin *somnus* 'sleep'. This change is *partial* because *p* only takes on some of the features of the conditioning *n*, namely, it becomes more like the *n* by taking on its feature of nasality, becoming *m*. Because the *p* is next to the *n*, this is a *contact* change; it is regressive because the *p* is before the *n* which conditions the change.

(2) In Spanish (in the non-careful pronunciations of most dialects), *s* > *z* /___ voiced C, as in: *mismo* > [mizmo] 'same', *desde* > [dezde] 'since'.

(3) The assimilation of nasals in point of articulation to that of following stops, extremely frequent in the world's languages, is illustrated in English by the changes in the morpheme /in-/ 'not', as in *in-possible* > *im*possible; *in-tolerant* > *in*tolerant; *in-compatible* > *iŋ*compatible (in the last case, the change of *n* to *ŋ* is optional for many speakers).

2.6.1.4 Partial contact progressive assimilation

(1) The English suffixes spelled *-ed* formerly had a vowel, but after the change which eliminated the vowel, the *d* in many contexts came to be adjacent to a preceding consonant, and it became voiceless if that preceding consonant was voiceless (and not an alveolar stop), as in /wɔkt/ 'walked', /træpt/ 'trapped' (d > t /voiceless C__).

(2) English suffixes spelled with *-s* also assimilated, becoming voiced after a preceding voiced (non-sibilant) consonant, as in /dɔgz/ 'dogs', /rɪbz/ 'ribs'.

2.6.1.5 Distant (non-adjacent) assimilation

Assimilation at a distance (non-adjacent or non-contact) is not nearly as common as contact assimilation, though some changes having to do with vowels or consonants in the next syllable are quite common. Distant assimilations can be partial or total, and regressive or progressive. These are illustrated in the following examples.

(1) Umlaut (see the example above illustrating phonemic split in English) is a well-known kind of change which involves distant assimilation in which a vowel is fronted under the influence of a following front vowel (or a *j*), usually in the next syllable. Umlaut has been important in the history of most Germanic languages.

(2) Proto-Indo-European *penkʷe > Latin kʷinkʷe (spelled *quinque*) 'five' (total distant regressive assimilation); Proto-Indo-European *pekʷ- > Italic *kʷekʷ- 'to cook, ripen' (compare Latin /kokʷ-/ in *coquere* 'to cook').

(3) Proto-Indo-European *penkʷe > pre-Germanic *penpe 'five' (compare German *fünf*) (total distant progressive assimilation).

(4) Distant assimilations are seen also in the various sorts of harmonies known to hold in various languages, for example, vowel harmony (where vowels within a word must agree with one another in some of their features, for instance only back vowels vs. only front vowels); sibilant harmony (for example in Chumash

where if the right-most sibilant in a word is /ʃ/, other sibilants before it in the word must change to /ʃ/ as well); nasal harmony; etc.

2.6.2 Dissimilation

Dissimilation, the opposite of assimilation, is change in which sounds become less similar to one another. Assimilation is far more common than dissimilation; assimilation is usually regular throughout the language, though sometimes it can be sporadic. Dissimilation is much rarer and is usually not regular (is sporadic), though dissimilation can be regular. Dissimilation often happens at a distance (is non-adjacent), though contact dissimilations are not uncommon. The following examples illustrate these various sorts of dissimilatory changes.

(1) Some English dialects dissimilate the sequence of two nasals in the word *chimney* > *chim(b)ley*.

(2) Instances of multiple occurrences of *r* within a word are often sporadically dissimilated in Romance languages; for example, sequences of /r . . . r/ often become /l . . . r/, sometimes /r . . . l/: Latin *peregrīnus* 'foreigner, alien' > Italian *pellegrino* 'foreigner, pilgrim, traveller'; French *pèlerin* (compare Spanish *peregrino* which retained the two *r*'s; English *pilgrim* is a loanword from Old French *pelegrin*); Latin *arbor* > Spanish *árbol* 'tree'. This Spanish change is a case of distant progressive dissimilation. In a more regular dissimilation involving these sounds, the Latin adjectival ending -*al* dissimilated to -*ar* when attached to a root ending in *l*; this is illustrated in the following Latin loans in English, *alveolar*, *velar*, *uvular*, which have dissimilated due to the preceding *l*; these can be contrasted with forms in which -*al* remains unchanged because there is no preceding *l*, for example, *labial*, *dental*, *palatal*. Some examples from Spanish which illustrate this suffix (though with a different meaning) in both its original and dissimilated form are: *pinal* 'pine grove' (based on *pino* 'pine'), *encinal* 'oak grove' (compare *encino* 'oak'), but *frijolar* 'bean patch' (compare *frijol* 'bean'), *tular* 'stand of reeds' (see *tule* 'reed, cattail'), *chilar* 'chilli patch' (based on *chile* 'chilli pepper'), with *l* > *r* because of a preceding *l* in the root.

(3) *Grassmann's Law*, a famous sound change in Indo-European linguistics, is a case of regular dissimilation in Greek and Sanskrit where in words with two aspirated stops the first dissimilates to an unaspirated stop. These are voiced aspirated stops in Sanskrit and voiceless aspirated stops in Greek:

> Sanskrit *bhabhūva* > *babhūva* 'became' (reduplication of root *bhū-*).
> Greek *phépūka* > *péphūka* 'converted' (reduplication of *phú-* 'to engender').

A frequently cited Greek example which show Grassmann's Law in action involves the following:

> *trikh-ós* 'hair'(genitive singular) / *thrík-s* (nominative singular).
> *tréphō* 'I rear (nourish, cause to grow)' / *thrép-s-ō* 'I will rear'.
> *trekh-ō* 'I walk'/ *threk-s-ō* 'I will walk'.

Greek *trikhós* 'hair' (genitive singular) comes from earlier *thrikh-ós, to which Grassmann's Law has applied to dissimilate the *th* due to the following aspirated *kh* (*th ... kh > t ... kh); similarly, *tréphō* 'I rear' is from *thréph-ō, where *th ... ph > t ... ph. In *thríks* 'hair (nominative singular)', from *thrikh-s, the *kh* lost its aspiration before the immediately following *s* (the nominative singular ending) (*khs > ks), and thus Grassmann's Law did not apply in this form as the second aspirated stop had already lost its aspiration before Grassmann's Law took place. This left initial *th* still aspirated in this word, since there was no longer a sequence of two aspirates which would cause the first to dissimilate and lose its aspiration. Similarly, in *thrépsō* 'I will rear' (from *thréph-s-ō) *phs > ps, and with no second aspirated consonant (no longer a *ph* but now only *p*), the *th* remained aspirated in this word. These changes are seen more clearly in Table 2.3 (*nom* = nominative, *gen* = genitive, *sg* = singular).

TABLE 2.3: Grassmann's Law and its interaction with other Greek changes

	'hair' nom sg	'hair' gen sg	'I will rear'	'I rear'
Pre-Greek	*thrikh-s	*thrikh-os	*threph-s-ō	*threph-ō
deaspiration before s	thriks	—	threpsō	—
Grassmann's Law	—	trikhos	—	trephō
Greek forms	thriks	trikhos	threpsō	trephō

Most of the examples presented so far have been cases of distant dissimilations; some additional examples of both contact and distant dissimilation follow.

(4) Finnish *k > h/__t, d*, as in, for example, /tek-dæ/ > *tehdæ* 'to do' (spelled *tehdä*) (compare *teke-e* 'he/she does'); /kakte-na/ > *kahtena* 'as two' (compare *kaksi* 'two') from /kakte-/ to which other changes applied, e > i / __# (*kakte* > *kakti*) and t > s / __i (*kakti* > *kaksi*); since as a result of these changes the *k* no longer appeared before a *t* or *d* in *kaksi*, it remained *k* and so it did not change to *h* (as in *kahtena* 'as two', where it did change to *h*). This is a regular change; all *kt* and *kd* clusters in native Finnish words changed to *ht* and *hd* respectively.

(5) In K'iche' (Mayan), the velar stops (*k, k'*) were palatalized when the next consonant after an intervening non-round vowel was a uvular (*q, q', χ*): kaq > *kʸaq* 'red'; iš*k'aq* > *išk'ʸaq* 'fingernail, claw' (*š* = IPA [ʃ] *kʸ* = IPA [kʲ]); *k'aq* > *kʸ'aq* 'flea'; *ke:χ* > *kʸe:χ* 'horse'. The difference between a velar and a uvular stop in the same word is difficult both to produce and to perceive, and for this reason words with *k(')Vq(')* have palatalized the velar (*k, k'*) in order to make them more distinguishable from the uvular (*q, q'*) in these words. This is a regular change (Campbell 1977; see also section 10.2.5 on borrowed rules and Map 10.1).

(6) Dahl's Law is a sound change which took place in a number of East African Bantu languages in which two voiceless consonants in a word dissimilate so that the first becomes voiced. For example, in Kikuyu the change affects only /k/, as in: *gikuyu* 'Kikuyu' < *kikuyu*; *githaka* 'bush' < *kithaka*; *gukua* 'die' < *kukua* (Newman 2000: 268). The change is commonly stated in several of the languages as involving the dissimilation of aspiration, where an aspirated stop when followed by

another aspirated stop in the next syllable loses its aspiration and becomes voiced, as in Nyamwezi: -*kʰatʰi* 'in the middle' > *gatʰi*, -*pʰitʰ*- 'to pass' > -*bitʰa*, etc. (Mutaka 2000: 253; see also Collinge 1985: 280).

While several of the examples just presented involve dissimilation in regular sound changes, sporadic dissimilations are more frequent on the whole. Another example of sporadic dissimilation is:

(7) In Old French *livel* 'level' (from which English borrowed *level*), the sequence of two *l*'s dissimilated, giving *nivel*, which became Modern French *niveau* 'level' through subsequent sound changes which affected the final *l*.

2.7 Kinds of Common Sound Changes

The following is a list of the names for various kinds of sound changes that are used in the literature on language change. In parentheses after each name is a visual representation based on nonsense forms which shows what happens in the change. Several examples of each kind of change are presented.

2.7.1 Deletions

2.7.1.1 Syncope (*atata* > *atta*)

The loss (deletion) of a vowel from the interior of a word (not initially or finally) is called *syncope* (pronounced [sínkəpi], from Greek *sunkopé* 'a cutting away', *sun*- 'with, together' + *kopé* 'cut, beat'); such deleted vowels are said to be 'syncopated'. Syncope is a frequently used term. Syncope changes can be regular or sporadic.

(1) The change in many varieties of English which omits the medial unstressed vowel of words such as *fam(i)ly* and *mem(o)ry* illustrates syncope, seen also in words such as *asp(i)rin*, *cam(e)ra*, *choc(o)late*, *rest(au)rant*, etc.

(2) Starting in Vulgar Latin and continuing in the Western Romance languages, the short unstressed vowels other than *a* were lost in the interior of words three syllables long or longer, as in *pópulu*- 'people' (*pópulu*- > *poplV*-), reflected by French *peuple* 'people' and Spanish *pueblo* 'people, town' (English *people* is borrowed from French). Latin *fābulare* 'to talk' became *hablar* 'to speak' in Spanish (*fābulare* > *fablar(e)* > *hablar* /ablar/). (English *fable* comes from this same root, borrowed from Old French *fable* 'story, fable, tale, drama, fiction, falsehood', which is inherited from the Latin word *fābula* 'story, talk, play, fable'.)

While syncope is normally reserved for loss of vowels, some people sometimes speak of 'syncopated' consonants. However, it is more common in the case of consonants just to speak of *loss* or *deletion*.

2.7.1.2 Apocope *(tata > tat)*

Apocope (pronounced [əpókəpi], from Greek *apokopé* 'a cutting off', *apo*- 'away' + *kopé* 'cut, beat') refers to the loss (apocopation, deletion) of a sound, usually a vowel, at the end of a word, said to be 'apocopated'. Apocope is a frequently used term.

(1) In words which had final *e* in Latin, this *e* was regularly deleted in Spanish in the environment VC__# if the consonant was a dental or alveolar (*l, r, n, s, θ*) or *y* [j], as in *pane* > *pan* 'bread', *sōle* > *sol* 'sun', *sūdāre* > *sudar* 'to sweat'.

(2) A comparison of the following Old English nouns (shown in their nominative singular form) with their modern counterparts shows the apocope of the final vowels in these words:

Old English	Modern English
sticca	stick
sunu	son
mōna	moon

(3) Estonian (a Uralic language) lost final vowels in words where this vowel was preceded either by a long vowel and a single consonant or by two consonants:

*hooli > hool [ho:l] 'care, worry'
*leemi > leem [lɛ:m] 'broth'
*jalka > jalg [jalk] 'foot, leg'
*härkä [hærkæ] > härg [hærk] 'bull'

However, the vowel was not lost when preceded by a short vowel and a single consonant, as in *kala* > *kala* 'fish', *lumi* > *lumi* 'snow'.

2.7.1.3 Aphaeresis (or apheresis) *(atata > tata)*

Aphaeresis (pronounced [əfɛɹəsis], from Greek *aphairesis* 'a taking away') refers to changes which delete the initial sound (usually a vowel) of a word. Aphaeresis can be regular or sporadic. Commonly cited English examples include the likes of *'bout* < *about*, *'tis* < *it is*, *'twas* < *it was*, and *specially* < *especially*.

(1) The sporadic change where the initial vowel that was present in Latin *apotēca* 'storehouse, wine-store' was lost in Spanish *bodega* 'wine cellar, storeroom, warehouse' illustrates aphaeresis. In Spanish, intervocalic -*p*- from Latin became -*b*-, but initial *p*- remained *p*-; the *b* of *bodega* shows that the initial vowel (*a*-) was still present when *p* > *b* and was deleted (by aphaeresis) after this change, *apotēka* > *abodega* > *bodega*.

(2) Spanish dialects show many cases of sporadic aphaeresis: *caso* < *acaso* 'perhaps, by chance'; *piscopal* < *episcopal* 'episcopal', 'of the bishop'; *ahora* > *hora* 'now' (especially frequent in *horita* < *ahorita* 'right now').

(3) The Sapaliga dialect of Tulu (Dravidian) provides an example of regular aphaeresis, where the loss can be seen in comparison with the Shivalli dialect, which has not lost the original vowel. (Here, <c> = [č], IPA [ʧ]; in the convention in the Indian linguistic tradition the consonants with dots under them are retroflexed: <ḍ> = IPA [ɖ], <!> = IPA [ɭ]):

Sapaliga Tulu	*Shivalli Tulu*	
dakki	aḍakki	'throw'
lappu	aḷappu	'plough'
latti	eḷatti	'tender'
laccilɨ	oḷoccilɨ	'stumble'
dattɨ	eḍattɨ	'left'

(Bhat 2001: 66)

Aphaeresis is a rarely used term; many just speak of initial vowel loss or deletion.

2.7.2 Epentheses or insertions (asta > asata)

Epenthesis inserts a sound into a word. (*Epenthesis* is from Greek *epi-* 'in addition' + *en* 'in' + *thesis* 'placing'.) In sound change, sounds can be inserted in several different ways; several of these have their own names and are considered in the sections that follow, though it is common to refer to them all simply as kinds of epenthesis or insertion.

2.7.2.1 Prothesis *(tata > atata)*

Prothesis (from Greek *pro-* 'before' + *thesis* 'placing') is a kind of epenthesis in which a sound is inserted at the beginning of a word. This is not a particularly frequent term, and such changes are also referred to as word-initial epentheses.

(1) Starting in the second century, Latin words beginning with *s*+ STOP (*sp*, *st*, *sk*) took on a prothetic short *i*. The following examples trace the development to modern French and Spanish. The prothetic *i* became *e*, and later in French the *s* was lost when it occurred before other consonants. (a) Latin *schola* [skóla] 'school' > *iskola* > *eskola* > Old French *escole* [eskole] > Modern French *école* [ekol]; for Spanish: *scola* [skóla] > *iskola* > *escuela* [eskuéla]. (b) Latin *scūtum* [skŭtum] 'shield' > *iskutu* > *eskutu* > Old French *escu* > Modern French écu [eky] 'shield, coin (of gold or silver)'; the sequence in Spanish was from Latin *scūtum* [skŭtum] > *iskutu* > *eskutu* > *escudo* 'shield'. (c) Latin *stabulum* [stábulum] 'stall, stable' > *istabula* > *estabula* > Old French *estable* > Modern French étable [etábl] 'stable, barn, shed'; for Spanish: *stabulum* [stábulum] > *istabulo* > *estabulo* > Spanish *establo* 'barn, stall, cowshed'.

(2) In Nahuatl, forms which came to have initial consonant clusters, due to the loss of a vowel in the first syllable, later changed to take on a prothetic *i*: **kasi* > *kši* > *ikši* 'foot' (compare *no-kši* 'my foot', where no epenthetic *i* occurs because there is no word-initial consonant cluster) (here *š* = IPA [ʃ]).

2.7.2.2 Anaptyxis *(anaptyctic) (VCCV > VCV̆CV)*

Anaptyxis (from Greek *ana-ptussō* 'unfold, open up, expand') is a kind of epenthesis in which an extra vowel is inserted between two consonants (also called a 'parasitic' vowel or '*svarabhakti*' vowel). This term is used very infrequently, since epenthesis covers this sort of change.

(1) Examples of sporadic anaptyxis are the pronunciation in some dialects of English of *athlete* as [ˈæθəlit] and of *film* as [ˈfiləm] with the extra vowel. In varieties of Spanish, Standard Spanish *Inglaterra* 'England' > *Ingalaterra*, *crónica* 'chronicle' > *corónica*.

(2) In Finnish dialects of eastern Finland, after the first syllable (which bears the stress), a short copy of the preceding vowel is added regularly between consonants of a consonant cluster which begins with *l* or *r*. (The *ä* of Finnish spelling represents [æ].) For example:

Eastern dialects	Standard Finnish	
nelejä	neljä	'four'
kolome	kolme	'three'
pilikku	pilkku	'comma, dot'
jalaka	jalka	'foot, leg'
kylymä	kylmä	'cold'
silimä	silmä	'eye'

(Kettunen 1930: 120; 1969: map 199)

2.7.2.3 Excrescence *(amra > ambra; anra > andra; ansa > antsa)*

Excrescence (from Latin *ex* 'out' + *crēscentia* 'growth') is a type of which refers to a consonant being inserted between other consonants; usually the change results in phonetic sequences which are somewhat easier to pronounce than the original clusters would be without the excrescent consonant.

(1) Old English *θunrian* > Modern English *thunder* (compare the German cognate *Donner* 'thunder'); Old English *θȳmel* > Modern English *thimble* (compare *humble/humility*). The example of *chimney* > *chimbley* in English dialects was already mentioned above; its *b* is excrescent.

(2) Proto-Indo-European **n̥-mr̥t-os* > Greek *ambrotos* 'immortal' (seen in English in *ambrosia* 'food of the gods' (what makes you immortal), also a 'fruit and coconut dish', is a loan with its origin ultimately in Greek.

(3) Spanish *hombre* [ombre] 'man' is from Latin *hominem*, which became *homne* through regular sound changes (syncope, *hominem* > *homne(m)*, then *homre* through dissimilation of the adjacent nasals (*mn* > *mr*), and then *b* was inserted – an example of excrescence – to make the transition from *m* to *r* easier to pronounce ([omre] > [ombre]). Contrast French *homme* 'man', which shows a different history, where at the *homne* stage, the *n* assimilated to the preceding *m* (*homne* > *homme*). Latin *fēmina* 'woman' became *femna* through syncope of the middle vowel; Old French assimilated the *n* to the adjacent *m*, ultimately giving *femme* 'woman'; Spanish, however, dissimilated the two nasals (*femna* > *femra*), and this then underwent excrescence, inserting a *b* between the *m* and *r*, giving modern Spanish *hembra* /embra/ 'female' (in Spanish, *f-* > *h-* > Ø, though <h> remains in the orthography). Another example is Latin *nomināre* 'to name' > *nomnar* > *nomrar* > *nombrar* in Spanish; French assimilated *mn* to *mm* in this word, giving *nommer* 'to name'. In a similar example French did undergo excrescence: Latin *numerus* 'number' > Old French *numere* > *numre* > *numbre* borrowed into English as *number*

(Modern French *nombre* 'number'; compare *numerous*, a loan from Latin, which lacks the excrescent *b*).

(4) French *chambre* 'room' comes from Latin *camera* 'arched roof'; when the *mr* cluster was created because of the regular syncope of the medial *e* (*camera* > *camra*) the *b* was added between the two consonants (this is the source of the loanword *chamber* in English, from French *chambre* 'room').

(5) Greek *andros* 'man (GENITIVE SINGULAR)' comes from earlier *anr-os*; compare Greek *anēr* 'man (NOMINATIVE SINGULAR)'.

2.7.2.4 Paragoge *(tat > tata)*

Paragoge (from Greek *paragōgé* 'a leading past') adds a sound (usually a vowel) to the end of a word.

(1) Dialects of Spanish sometimes add a final *-e* (sporadically) to some words that end in *-d*: *huéspede* < *huésped* 'guest'; *rede* < *red* 'net'.

(2) Arandic languages (a branch of Pama-Nyungan, in Australia) regularly added a final *ə* at the end of words that end in a consonant (Ø > ə / C__#), as in **nuŋkam* > *ŋkwərnə* 'bone' (Koch 1997: 281–2).

Paragoge is a rarely used term; there are few examples of this kind of change. Mention of the insertion of a final vowel covers these changes.

2.7.3 Compensatory lengthening (tast > ta:t)

In changes of compensatory lengthening, something is lost and another segment, usually a vowel, is lengthened, as the name implies, to compensate for the loss.

(1) In the history of English, a nasal was lost before a fricative with the simultaneous compensatory lengthening of the preceding vowel, as in the following from Proto-Germanic to English: **tonθ* > *tōθ* (> Modern English /tuθ/) 'tooth'; **fimf* > *fīf* (> Modern English /faiv/) 'five'; **gans* > *gōs* (> Modern English /gus/) 'goose' (compare the German cognates, which retain the *n*: *Zahn* [tsa:n] 'tooth', *fünf* 'five', and *Gans* 'goose').

(2) An often-cited example is that of the compensatory lengthening which took place in the transition from Proto-Celtic to Old Irish, as in:

Proto-Celtic	Old Irish	
*magl	ma:l	'prince'
*kenetl	cene:l	'kindred', 'gender'
*etn	e:n	'bird'
*datl	da:l	'assembly'

(Arlotto 1972: 89)

(3) Old Norse compensatorily lengthened vowels together with the loss of *n* before *s* or *r* (n > Ø /__s, r), as in Proto-Scandinavian **gans* > *gōs* 'goose', **ons* > *ōs* 'us', **þunra-* 'thunder' > *þōr* 'thunder, Thor' (the Scandinavian god *Thor*, god of thunder and lightning, is the source of *Thursday*, literally 'Thor's

day'; compare English *thunder* and German *Donner* 'thunder', cognates of these Scandinavian forms; English *thunder* underwent excrescence) (Wessén 1969: 48).

(4) Middle Indo-Aryan sequences of vowel–nasal–consonant changed to a long nasalized vowel–consonant (VNC > Ṽ:C) in modern Indo-Aryan languages, as seen in the following examples:

Middle-Indo-Aryan	Hindi	Bengali	Gujarati	
kampa-	kã:p-	kã:p-	kã:p-	'tongue'
gaṇṭhi	gã:ṭh	gã:ṭh	gã:ṭh	'knot'
bandha	bã:dh	bã:dh	bã:dh	'bond, dam'
sañjha	sã:jh	sã:jh	sã:jh	'twilight'

(Masica 1991: 188)

2.7.4 Rhotacism (VsV > VrV)

Rhotacism (from Greek *rhotakismos* 'use of *r*') refers to a change in which *s* (or *z*) becomes *r*; usually this takes place between vowels or glides. Some assume that cases of rhotacism often go through an intermediate stage *-s-* > *-z-* > *-r-*, where *s* is first voiced and then turned into *r* later. The best-known examples of rhotacism come from Latin and Germanic languages.

(1) In the oldest Latin, *s* > *r* / V_V, as seen in *honōr-is* 'honour (GENITIVE SINGULAR)' and *honōr-i* 'honour (DATIVE SINGULAR)'; *honōs* 'honour (NOMINATIVE SINGULAR)' retains *s*, since *s* is not between vowels in this form. (In later Latin, *honōs* 'NOMINATIVE SINGULAR' became *honor*, due to analogy with the other forms which contain the intervocalic *r* due to rhotacism; see Chapter 4.)

(2) In West Germanic and North Germanic, **z* > *r*. Proto-Germanic **hauzjan* 'hear' > Old High German *hōren* (Modern German *hören*), Old English *hieran* (Modern English *hear*); contrast the Gothic cognate *hausjan* 'hear' which did not undergo the change (Gothic is East Germanic). Proto-Germanic **maizōn* 'greater' (from Proto-Indo-European **meh₁-is*, comparative of **meh₁-* 'big') underwent rhotacism to become Old English *māra* 'greater', modern English *more*. (*Most* is from Old English *mǣst*, Germanic **maista-* 'most', from Proto-Indo-European **meh₁-isto-*, the superlative of 'big'.)

While changes involving rhotacism are relatively rare, the term is a frequent one in linguistics, due no doubt to the fact that examples of rhotacism in Latin and Germanic are so well known.

2.7.5 Metathesis (asta > atsa; asata > atasa)

Metathesis (from Greek *metathesis* 'transposition, change of sides') is the transposition of sounds; it is a change in which sounds exchange positions with one another within a word. Metathesis is often thought to be found mostly only in sporadic changes, but metathesis can also be a regular change.

(1) Sporadic examples of metathesis occur in the history of English: Old English *brid* > Modern English *bird*; Old English *hros* > *horse* (rV > Vr).

(2) Spanish has sporadic cases of *l*/*r* metathesis, as in *palabra* 'word' < Latin *parabola* 'explanatory illustration, comparison' (r . . . l > l . . . r).

(3) Spanish has undergone a reasonably regular change of metathesis in which sequences of *dl*, which were created by vowel loss, shifted to *ld*, as in *tilde* 'tilde, tittle' (the 'swung dash' on *ñ*) < Latin *titulus* 'label, title' (through a series of regular changes: *titulus* > *tidulo* > *tidlo* > *tildo* [metathesis *dl* > *ld*] > *tilde*); *molde* 'mould, pattern' < Latin *modulus* 'small measure' (*modulus* > *modlo* > *moldo* > *molde*). (Cf. English *module*, a borrowing ultimately from the same Latin source via Middle French *module* 'module'.)

(4) Some examples of sporadic metatheses in various Spanish dialects are: *probe* < *pobre* 'poor'; *sequina* < *esquina* 'corner'; *naide* < *nadie* 'nobody'; *Grabiel* < *Gabriel* 'Gabriel'.

2.7.6 Haplology (tatasa >tasa)

Haplology (from Greek *haplo-* 'simple, single') is the name given to the change in which a repeated sequence of sounds is simplified to a single occurrence. For example, if the word *haplology* were to undergo haplology (were to be haplologized), it would reduce the sequence *lolo* to *lo*, so *haplology* > *haplogy*. Some real examples are:

(1) English *humbly* was *humblely* in Chaucer's time, pronounced with three syllables, but has been reduced to two syllables (only one *l*) in modern standard English. English has numerous examples involving adverbs with *-ly*, for example *ably* < *able* + *-ly*, *gently* < *gentle* + *-ly*, etc.

(2) Some other English examples include *pacifism* < *pacificism* (this contrasts with *mysticism* < *mysticism*, where the repeated sequence is not reduced and does not end up as *mystism*), and *urinalysis* < *urine analysis*. Some varieties of English reduce *library* to '*libry*' [laibri] and *probably* to '*probly*' [prɔbli].

(3) Modern German *Zauberin* 'sorceress, female magician' < *Zaubererin* (*Zauber* 'magic, enchantment, charm' + *-er* 'one who does' (like *-er* in English) + *-in* 'female agent' (like *-ess* in English)).

2.7.7 Breaking

Breaking refers to the diphthongization of a short vowel in particular contexts. While changes which diphthongize vowels are common (see below), the term 'breaking' is most commonly encountered in Germanic linguistics, used for example in discussions of the history of Afrikaans, English, Frisian, and Scandinavian.

(1) For example, Old English underwent the breaking of **i* > *io*, **e* > *eo*, **a* > *ea* before *l* or *r* followed by a consonant, or before *h*, as in **kald-* > *ceald* 'cold', **erθe* > *eorþe* 'earth', **nǣh* > *nēah* 'near', **sæh* > *seah* 'saw' (compare Beekes 1995: 275; Hogg 1992: 102–3). (The history of breaking in English is complex and the phonetic interpretation is disputed; the spelling <ea> probably represented [æa].)

(2) Old Norse *e* > *ea* (then later > *ia*) before *a* of the next syllable, which is then syncopated, as in **heldaz* > *healdar* < *hialdar* < *hialdr* 'battle', and *e* > *eo* > *io* > *iɔ̄* before *u* of the next syllable (which also later underwent syncope), as in **erþu* > *iɔ̄rþu* > *jɔrð* [jɔrð] 'earth' (cf. Beekes 1995: 67).

2.7.8 Other frequent sound changes

There are several other kinds of sound change which are frequently found in discussions of the history of various languages, even though they are usually not included in typical lists of kinds of sound changes. Some of the most common of these kinds of changes follow, described in less detail and with fewer examples. This is by no means an exhaustive listing.

2.7.8.1 Final-devoicing

A very common change is the devoicing of stops or obstruents word-finally; some languages devoice final sonorants (*l*, *r*, *w*, *j*, nasals) and some devoice final vowels. In some languages, the devoicing takes place both word-finally and syllable-finally (as in German). In Kaqchikel (Mayan), the sonorants l, r, w, y > VOICELESS /__#. The sounds *l*, *r*, *w*, *y* (*y* = IPA [j]) underwent the change in which they became voiceless at the end of words, for example, *a:l* 'child' [aːl] > [aːl̥], *kar* 'fish' [kar] > [kar̥], *kow* 'hard' [kow] > [kow̥], *xa:y* 'house' [xaːy] > [xay̥].

2.7.8.2 Intervocalic voicing (and voicing generally)

It is also very common for various sounds to become voiced between vowels (or between voiced sounds). This affects just stops in some languages, fricatives in others, and all obstruents in others. Often the voicing is not just between vowels, but also occurs in the environment of the glides *w* and *y* (IPA *j*) and liquids. Many languages also voice stops (some also voice other consonants) after nasals or after any voiced sound; some also voice other sounds when they come before voiced sounds. For example, in the transition from Latin to Spanish (and this includes other Western Romance languages as well), the voiceless stops become voiced between vowels, as illustrated in *lupu-* > *lobo* 'wolf' (*p* > *b*), *vīta* > *vida* 'life' (*t* > *d*), and *ficu-* > *higo* 'fig' (*k* > *g*).

2.7.8.3 Nasal assimilation

It is extremely common for nasals to change to agree with the point of articulation of following stops (in some languages with any following consonant): *np* > *mp*, *mt* > *nt*, *nk* > *ŋk*, and so on.

To see this in English, consider the various forms of the negative morpheme *in-* determined by the consonant the follows it, as in *im*possible, *in*tolerant, and *iŋ*considerate (for the last of these a non-assimilated alternative pronunciation is also available, *in*considerate).

2.7.8.4 Palatalization

Palatalization often takes place before or after *i* and *j* or before other front vowels, depending on the language, although unconditioned palatalization can also take place. Two common kinds of changes are called 'palatalization'. One is the typical change of a velar or alveolar sound to a palato-alveolar sound, as in $k > č$, $t > č$, $s > š$, and so on ($č$ = IPA [ʧ], $š$ = IPA [ʃ]). For example, in colloquial English, there are sequences of $t + y$ (IPA [j]) > $č$ (IPA [ʧ]) and $d + y$ (IPA [j]) > $ǰ$ (IPA [dʒ]), as in examples such as *whatcha doin'* ['what are you doing?'], *I betcha* ['I bet you'], *didja go* ['did you go?'], seen also in English varieties where *ty* [tj] word-internal sequences have changed to $č$ [ʧ], as in *nature, picture, literature, lecture, fortune*, and *dy* [dj] sequences changed to $ǰ$ [dʒ], in *module, grandeur*, etc. English has undergone many changes involving palatalizations of this kind throughout its history. For example, Old English *cinn* [kɪn:] 'chin' > *chin* [čɪn] ([ʧɪn]) illustrates the palatalization of k before front unrounded vowels (compare the German cognate *Kinn* 'chin, jaw'). In another example, in the history of Spanish the sequence *kt* became *it* (where *i* was the second element of a diphthong), and then the *t* further became palatalized because of the *i*, producing $č$, as in *lakte > laite > leite > leiče > leče* 'milk' (spelled *leche*) and *okto > oito > oičo > očo* 'eight' (spelled *ocho*).

Unconditioned changes of this sort of palatalization can also occur, not conditioned by front vowels. For example, the change of $k > č$ spread among several languages of the Northwest Coast linguistic area (see Chapter 10); in Cholan as well as in a few other Mayan languages, $*k > č$ in general.

In a second kind of change called palatalization, a consonant becomes palatalized by taking palatalization as a secondary manner of articulation, as in eastern dialects of Finnish, where consonants are palatalized before *i*, *susi > susʲi* (and later *susʲ*) 'wolf', *tuli > tulʲi (tulʲ)* 'fire'. Slavic languages are well known for a number of palatalization changes.

2.7.8.5 Diphthongization

Diphthongization refers to any change in which an original single vowel changes into a sequence of two vowel segments which together occupy the nucleus of a single syllable. For example, earlier (in the discussion of splits) we saw the change in English in which original long high vowels /ī/ and /ū/ became /ai/ and /au/ respectively, in /mīs/ > /mais/ 'mice' and /mūs/ > /maus/ 'mouse' (a part of the Great Vowel Shift; see section 2.9, below). In Spanish, the Proto-Romance vowels *ɛ and *ɔ diphthongized to *ie* and *ue* respectively when in stressed position, as in *petra > piedra* 'stone', *bɔno > bueno* 'good'. In French, by the ninth century, $e > ei$, and $o > ou$. These later changed further; $ou > eu > ø$ (dolor > dolour > doleur > dolør <doleur> 'pain'); $ei > oi > oe > we > wa$ (me > mei > moi > moe > mwe > mwa <moi> 'me'; lei > [lwa] <loi> 'law', rei > [rwa] <roi> 'king') (Darmsteter 1922: 96–7, 142–3). The ī and ū of Middle High German became *ai* and *au* respectively in Modern German, as in *īs > Eis* /ais/ 'ice' and *hūs > Haus* /haus/ 'house'. In Finnish, original long mid vowels diphthongized by raising the first portion of the vowel: $e: > ie$ (long vowels in Finnish are spelled orthographically with a double vowel, *tee > tie* 'road'); $o: > uo$ (too > tuo 'bring'); $ø: > yø$ (tøø > tyø [spelled *työ*] 'work'). *Breaking* (above) is a kind of diphthongization.

2.7.8.6 Monophthongization

In monophthongization, a former diphthong changes into a single vowel, as in the change from Classical Latin to Vulgar Latin of *au* to *o* which shows up as *o* in the modern Romance languages, as in *auru-* > Spanish *oro*, French *or*, Italian *oro* 'gold'; *tauru-* > Spanish *toro*, French *toreau* [toro], Italian *toro* 'bull'; *causa-* 'cause, case, thing' > Spanish *cosa* 'thing', French *chose* [ʃoz] 'thing', Italian *cosa* 'thing'. An example from English is the monophthongization of /ai/ to /a:/ before *r* in some dialects, as in [fa:(r)] 'fire', [ta:(r)] 'tire' (cf. Wells 1982: 239). Another case is the Sanskrit change of **ai* > *e* and **au* > *o*, as in the first syllable of *kekara* 'squinting' < Proto-Indo-European **kaiko-* 'one-eyed, squinting' (compare Latin *caecus* 'blind').

An instance of monophthongization in the history of French is somewhat complicated by several other changes and by the orthographic conventions with which it is represented. At the end of the twelfth century, French changed *al* > *au* before consonants, as in *altre* > *autre* 'other'; then later *au* monophthongized to *o*, [otR] (still spelled *autre*) 'other'. Thus, *cheval* [ʃəvál] 'horse' retained *al*, since no consonant follows it, but *chevals* 'horses', on the other hand, changed to *chevaux* [ʃəvó], undergoing the changes *als* > *aus* > *os* > *o*, because in this case a consonant, *s*, did follow the original *al*. Such forms are spelled in Modern French with *x*, which stems from the practice in the Middle Ages of using *x* to abbreviate *-us* (for example, <nox> for *nous* 'we, us'); this gave the spelling <chevax> for 'horses,' which ended in [aus], and when the use of the abbreviation ceased, <x> came to be understood as a substitute for <s>, and so the *u* heard at that time in the *au* diphthong was reinstated in the writing of such words, hence the modern spelling *chevaux* 'horses' (Darmesteter 1922: 151–2).

2.7.8.7 Vowel raising

Changes in which low vowels change to mid (or high) vowels, or mid vowels move up to high vowels, are quite common. In particular, long or tense vowels frequently rise. Sometimes these changes can involve rather wholesale changes in much of the vowel system, known as vowel shifts, as in the Great Vowel Shift in English (see section 2.9 below). One environment in which raising is not uncommon is at the ends of words, such as the Finnish change of *e* to *i* word-finally (for example, *vere-* > *veri* 'blood'). William Labov (1994, 2001) argues that in vowel shifts, long (or tense, or peripheral) vowels tend to rise, seen in several vowel shifts in English and other languages.

2.7.8.8 Vowel lowering

Vowel lowering, the opposite of raising, results in high vowels becoming mid or low vowels, or mid vowels becoming low. For example, vowels are often lowered before uvular and pharyngeal consonants, or when a lower vowel occurs in the next syllable, to mention a few common environments. Also, nasalized vowels are frequently lowered. For example, Proto-Dravidian **i* and **u* were lowered before *a in the next syllable in South Dravidian languages, as in *ilay > elay 'leaf', *pukay > pokay 'smoke' (y = IPA j) (Zvelebil 1990: 5–6). However, vowel lowering does not necessarily need to be conditioned.

2.7.8.9 Nasalization

In nasalization, vowels become nasalized; this usually happens in the environment of nasal consonants. The typical scenario is for the nasalized vowels to become phonemic (contrastive) when later in time the nasal consonant is lost that originally conditioned the nasalization of the vowel, as in French bon > [bõn] > [bõ] 'good' (spelled bon).

2.7.8.10 Lenition (weakening)

Lenition is a reasonably loose notion applied to a variety of kinds of changes in which the resulting sound after the change is conceived of as somehow weaker in articulation than the original sound. Lenitions thus typically include changes of stops or affricates to fricatives, of two consonants to one, of other consonants to glides (j or w), of voiceless consonants to voiced in various environments, and so on. Lenition is sometimes considered to include any kind of reduction in length, magnitude, or even absence of a sound; thus it can also include the complete loss of sounds. An example of lenition is the change of the intervocalic stops which were voiceless in Latin (p, t, k) to voiced stops (b, d, g) in Spanish, as in lupus > lobo 'wolf', natāre 'to swim, float' > nadar 'to swim', lacus 'lake, tank, vat' > lago 'lake'.

2.7.8.11 Strengthening (fortition)

The variety of changes which are sometimes referred to as 'strengthening' (also sometimes called 'fortition') share a loosely defined notion that, after the change, the resulting sound is somehow 'stronger' in articulation than the original sound was. For example, in the change in Q'eqchi' (Mayan) of w > kw (as in winq > kwi:nq 'person') and y > ty (IPA [j] > [tj]) (as in iyax > ityax 'seed'), the kw and ty are perceived as being stronger than the original w and y.

2.7.8.12 Gemination

Gemination (from Latin geminātiŏn-em 'doubling', related to geminus 'twin', seen in the astrological sign Gemini) means, as the name suggests, the doubling of consonants, that is, the change which produces a sequence of two identical consonants, as in t > tt. For example, in certain Finnish dialects in a sequence of short vowel–short consonant–long vowel (VCV:) the consonant is regularly geminated (long vowels and long or geminate consonants are written double: /aa/ = [a:], /ss/ = [s:]), as in osaa > ossaa 'he/she knows', pakoon > pakkoon 'into flight (fleeing)'. Geminate consonants can also result from assimilations, as for example in the case of Italian kt > tt (as in Latin octō > Italian otto 'eight', seen above).

2.7.8.13 Degemination

When a sequence of two identical consonants is reduced to a single consonant (sometimes called a *singleton* or *singleton consonant*), the change is often called *degemination*. An example is the change from Latin *pp*, *tt*, *kk* to Spanish *p*, *t*, *k* respectively, as in: *mittere > meter* 'to put', *peccātum* [pekka:tum] 'mistake, fault, sin' > *pecado* /pekado/ 'sin, offence'.

2.7.8.14 Affrication

Affrication refers to changes in which a sound, usually a stop, sometimes a fricative, becomes an affricate; for example, *k* > *č* /__*i, e* (*č* = IPA [ʧ]) is quite a common change; *t* > *ts* /__*i* is not as common, but it is well represented in the world's languages.

2.7.8.15 Spirantization (fricativization)

In spirantization, a sound changes to a fricative. Not uncommonly, an affricate will be weakened (lenited) to a fricative, or a stop will become a fricative. In Cuzco Quechua, syllable-final stops became fricatives, as for example in **rapra > raɸra* 'leaf, wing'; **suqta > soχta* 'six'. A common change is the spirantization of stops between vowels, a frequent change in Dravidian languages (for example, Proto-Dravidian **tapu* 'to perish' > Kannada *tavu* 'to decrease') (Zvelebil 1990: 8). Finnic languages (earlier called Balto-Finnic) underwent a similar change in closed syllables (that is, in /__CC or /__C#, as in Finnish *tavan* 'custom, manner, way' [ACCUSATIVE SINGULAR]' < **tapa-n*).

2.7.8.16 Deaffrication

Most cases of deaffrication involve affricates leniting to fricatives; however, any change in which an original affricate would change into some non-affricate sound can also be called deaffrication. Though less common than an affricate becoming a fricative, a former affricate can also change to a stop or a glide or some other non-affricate sound. An example is *č* > *š* (IPA ʧ > ʃ) in the Spanish of areas of Chile and Panama (in the speech of younger people, varying according to sociolinguistic conditions) (Canfield 1982: 33, 69). Another example, in Chiltiupán Pipil (a Uto-Aztecan language of El Salvador), is *ts* > *s*, as in *tsutsukul > susukul* 'water jug'.

2.7.8.17 Lengthening

Lengthening refers to the change in which some sound, usually a vowel, is lengthened in some context. For example, in Q'eqchi' (Mayan), vowels are lengthened before a consonant cluster which begins with a sonorant (*l*, *r*, *m*, or *n*): *kenq' > ke:nq'* 'bean', *ɓalk > ɓa:lk* 'brother-in-law'. Cases of lengthening are quite common. (Compensatory lengthening, seen above in section 2.7.3, is one kind of lengthening, among others.)

2.7.8.18 Shortening

Sounds, particularly vowels, often undergo changes which shorten them in a variety of contexts, such as word-finally, before consonant clusters, when unstressed, and so on. Long vowels also often merge with short vowels. For example, in Middle English, long vowels were shortened before a consonant cluster, as in Old English *cēpte* > Middle English *kepte* 'kept' (compare modern *kept* with a short vowel, but related *keep* reflecting the earlier long vowel not before a consonant cluster, *pt* in this case), and shortened also in trisyllabic forms, when followed by two or more syllables, as in *hōliday* > *holiday* 'holiday', from *holy day*; contrast modern *holy* (that has the reflex of the long vowel) with the first part of the compound *holiday* (that reflects the shortened vowel). Some other examples illustrating these are *leave/left, sleep/slept, feel/felt, weep/wept*, and *serene/serenity, grateful/gratitude, divine/divinity, pronounce/pronunciation, provoke/provocative*, etc. Cases such as *south/southern* illustrate trisyllabic shortening (also called trisyllabic laxing) because formerly *southern* was *southerne*, with three syllables.

2.7.8.19 Tonogenesis and prosodic changes

Numerous kinds of changes can affect prosody. Prosody refers to phonetic things that are not segmental (not consonants or vowels), for example stress, tone, and intonation.

Stress can change from non-predictive stress (phonemic stress) to stress fixed on a particular syllable or determined by syllable weight, as for example in the shift in Proto-Germanic to stress fixed on the first syllable of the root, from Proto-Indo-European that did not have fixed stress.

Tonogenesis involves the development of tonal contrasts in languages. Tonal contrasts often develop on vowels in connection with the merger or loss of adjacent consonants. Voiced consonants typically cause following vowels to have a lower pitch. In the history of a number of languages, Mandarin (Chinese) being a well-known example, as voiced and voiceless stops merged, the following vowels ended up with contrasting tones: low tone on the vowels that formerly followed voiced stops and high tone on the vowels that were after voiceless stops. In many other languages, tonal contrasts arose as sequences of *Vh* or *Vʔ* lost the laryngeal (the *h* or *ʔ*) and changed the vowel to one with falling tone or low tone, contrasting with the tone of other vowels. In some languages, however, sequences of *Vh* or *Vʔ* have had the opposite result, becoming vowels with high or rising tone in contrast with the tones of other vowels. Tones in particular contexts often undergo various sorts of language-specific changes, frequently influenced by the presence of other tones in the word, by a tone's location in the word or utterance, or by the kinds of syllables in which they are found.

2.8 Relative Chronology

A sound change takes place at a particular time in the history of a language. This means that in a particular language some sound changes may take place at some earlier time and then cease to be active, whereas others may take place at some later stage in the language's history. Often in the case of different changes from different times, evidence is left behind which provides clues about the relative chronology of the changes, that is, the temporal order in which the changes took place. (For those who are familiar with rule ordering in synchronic phonology, it may be helpful to point out that relative chronology is similar to rule ordering in phonology, but in historical linguistics relative chronology refers to the historical sequence in which different changes took place, not their phonological status.) Part of working out the phonological history of a language is determining the relative chronology of the changes which have affected the language. A couple of straightforward examples show what is involved.

(1) In the history of Swedish, the change of umlaut took place before syncope, in the sequence:

umlaut: a > e /__(C)Ci.
syncope: i > Ø/V(C)C__r after a root syllable (approximate form of the changes; they are more general, but only the portions affecting this example are presented here).

From Proto-Germanic to Modern Swedish: *gasti-z > Proto-Scandinavian *gastiz > gestir > Old Norse gestr > Modern Swedish gest 'guest' (spelled gäst) (Wessén 1969: 10–11). We can be reasonably certain that these changes took place in this chronological order with umlaut before syncope since if syncope had taken place first (gastir > gastr), then there would have been no remaining i to condition the umlaut and the form would have come out as the non-existent ✗gast. (Note that ✗ is the symbol used in this book to signal ungrammatical and incorrect forms, distinguished from * which signals reconstructed forms.)

(2) Finnish underwent the two changes:

(1)   e > i /__#
(2)   t > s /__i

In words such as Proto-Uralic *wete 'water' which became vesi in Finnish, clearly (1) (e > i /__#) had to change final e into i before (2) (t > s /__i) took place, since (2) only applied with i, and the i of vesi would not have been present in this word until after (1) had applied. In vete-nä (ä = [æ]) 'as water', the root vete- retained its e because it is not in word-final position, followed here by the ESSIVE SINGULAR case suffix -nä; since there is no final i in vete-nä, the t did not become s by sound change (2). (Examples involving relative chronology come up again in several places in this text, especially in Chapters 2, 7, and 8.)

2.9 Chain Shifts

Sometimes multiple sound changes seem to be interrelated, with far-reaching impact on the overall phonological system of the language. These changes do not happen in isolation from one another, but appear to be connected, dependent upon one another in some way. Such interconnected changes are called *chain shifts*. Several reasons have been put forward for why chain shifts occur, and the final word about this is surely yet to come, though the connectedness of the changes involved has often been attributed to notions such as 'symmetry in phonemic inventories', 'naturalness' or 'markedness', 'maximum differentiation', and 'a tendency for holes in phonological patterns to be filled'. (See Chapter 12.) In some cases it is probably as simple as just one change taking place earlier, and then some other change taking place later that affects some of the sounds involved in the earlier change in some way that makes the changes seem to be connected.

It is believed that the sounds of a sound system are integrated into a whole whose parts are so interconnected that a change in any one part of the system can have implications for other parts of the system. The general idea behind chain shifts is that sound systems tend to be symmetrical or natural, and those that are not, that is, those that have a 'gap' in the inventory, tend to change to make them symmetrical or natural (to fill in the gap). However, a change which fills one gap may create other gaps elsewhere in the system, which then may precipitate other changes towards symmetry/naturalness to rectify its effects, thus setting off a chain reaction.

There are two types of chain shifts, *pull chains* (often called *drag chains*) and *push chains*. In a *pull chain*, one change may create a hole in the phonemic pattern (an asymmetry, a gap), which is followed by another later change which fills that hole (gap) by 'pulling' some sound from somewhere else in the system and changing that sound to fit the needs of symmetry/naturalness so that it fills the gap in the phonemic inventory, and, if the sound which shifted to fill the original hole in the pattern leaves a new hole elsewhere in the pattern, then some other change may 'pull' some other sound in to fill that gap.

Behind a *push chain* is the notion that languages (or their speakers) want to maintain differences between sounds in the system in order to keep contrasting words phonetically distinct, to facilitate understanding, the processing of what is heard. If a sound starts changing by moving into the articulatory space of another sound, in the push-chain view, this can precipitate a change where the sound moves away from the encroaching one in order to maintain distinctions important to meaning differences. If the fleeing sound is pushed towards the articulatory space of some other sound, then that encroached-upon sound too may shift to avoid the encroachment, thus setting off a chain reaction called a push chain.

Sometimes the notion of '*maximum differentiation*' is called upon in these instances. The idea behind maximum differentiation is that the sounds in a sound system tend to be distributed so as to allow as much perception difference between them as the articulatory space can provide. Thus, if a language has only three vowels, we expect them to be spread out, with *i* (high front unrounded), *u* (high back rounded), and *a* (low central or back unrounded); we do not expect them to be bunched up, for example, all in the high front area (say, *i, ɪ,* and *y*), and this expectation is confirmed by the languages of the world, where most of the three-vowel systems have /i, u, a/ or /i, o, a/. If a language has four stops, we do not expect them to be bunched at one point of articulation, say all labials (*p, b, p', pʰ*) with none at other points of articulation; rather, we expect them to be spread across labial, alveolar, velar, and perhaps other points of articulation (see Martinet 1970).

A look at some specific examples will give these abstract notions some substance.

(1) Attic Greek (the Classical Greek dialect of ancient Athens) underwent two changes: $\bar{u} > \bar{y}$ and $\bar{o} > \bar{u}$. This series of events would be seen as a pull change if the fronting of $\bar{u}$ to $\bar{y}$ took place first, 'pulling' ('dragging') original $\bar{o}$ after it into the phonetic space vacated by original $\bar{u}$ in the change $\bar{o} > \bar{u}$. Alternatively, if the raising of $\bar{o} > \bar{u}$ began first, followed by $\bar{u}$ to $\bar{y}$, the series of changes would be seen as a push chain, where the move of $\bar{o}$ towards $\bar{u}$ 'pushed' former $\bar{u}$ out of its slot and towards $\bar{y}$ to avoid merger with the $\bar{o}$ which was encroaching on the space of $\bar{u}$.

(2) Grimm's Law is an extremely important set of sound changes in historical linguistics; it is intimately involved in the history of the comparative method and the regularity hypothesis (and so we come back to it in more detail again in Chapter 7). Grimm's Law covers three interrelated changes in the series of stops from Proto-Indo-European to Proto-Germanic:

voiceless stops > voiceless fricatives:

*p	>	f
*t	>	θ
*k, *k̂	>	h (x)
*kʷ	>	hw

voiced stops > voiceless stops

*b	>	p
*d	>	t
*g, *ĝ	>	k
*gʷ	>	kw

voiced aspirated (or murmured) stops > plain voiced stops

*bh	>	b
*dh	>	d
*gh, *ĝh	>	g
*gʷh	>	gw, w

(The sounds *k̂, *ĝ, and *ĝh represent the 'palatal' series in Indo-European. See also section 7.4.1 in Chapter 7.)

This means that words in modern Germanic languages, because they inherit the results of these changes from Proto-Germanic, show the effects of the changes, but cognate words from other Indo-European languages (not from the Germanic branch) do not show the results of these changes. Some examples which illustrate the effects of Grimm's Law are given in Table 2.4, which compares words from English (Germanic) with cognates from Spanish and French (Romance languages, not Germanic).

In some cases, Spanish and French have undergone other changes of their own, making the correspondences expected from Grimm's Law not as obvious today, though the connections are clear when we take the full history of these

TABLE 2.4: Grimm's Law in English, Spanish, and French comparisons

	Spanish	French	English
*p > f	pie	pied	foot
	padre	père	father
	por	per	for
*t > θ	tres, tu	trois, tu	three, thou
*k > h	(can)	chien (< kani-)	hound (< hūnd)
	ciento	cien (< kent-)	hundred
	corazón	cœur	heart
*b > p	[NOTE: *b was rare in PIE; many think it was missing]		
*d > t	diente	dent	tooth (< tanθ)
	dos	deux	two
*g > k	—	genou	knee
	grano	grain	corn

	Sanskrit	Latin	English
*bh > b	bhrǎtar	frāter	brother
	bhára-	fer-	bear
		(f < *bh)	
*dh > d	dhā-	facere	do, did, deed
		(f < dh)	
*gh > g	haṃsá (<*ĝh)	(h)anser	goose
	[hə̃sə]		

languages into account – this is particularly true of the voiced aspirated sounds, for which examples from Sanskrit and Latin are substituted instead.

Grimm's Law can be interpreted as either a pull chain or a push chain (where *t, d,* and *dh* here represent all the stops of these series). If the temporal sequence were

(1)   t > θ, (2) d > t, (3) dh > d,

it would be a pull chain. It would be assumed that (1) *t* > θ took place first, leaving the language with the three series, voiceless fricatives (*f, θ, h*), voiced stops (*b, d, g*), and voiced aspirates (*bh, dh, gh*), but no plain voiceless stops (no *p, t, k*). This would be an unnatural situation which would tend to pull in the voiced stops to fill the gap where the voiceless stops had been ((2) *d* > *t*); however, this would leave the language with voiced aspirates but no plain voiced stops, also an unnatural arrangement, and so the voiced aspirates would be pulled in to fill the slot vacated by the plain voiced stops ((3) *dh* > *d*), making a more symmetrical sound system.

In the push-chain scenario, the voiced aspirates first started to move towards the plain voiced stops, a natural change towards easier articulation ((3) *dh* > *d*), but the approach of *dh* into the space of *d* forced original **d* to move towards *t* ((2) *d* > *t*), which in turn pushed original **t* to θ in order to maintain a distinction between these series of sounds ((1) *t* > θ).

(3) Classical Latin had three series of stops intervocalically, the geminates (*pp*, *tt*, *kk*), the single voiceless (*p*, *t*, *k*), and the voiced (*b*, *d*, *g*). These three original series of stops changed from Latin to Spanish in an interrelated fashion:

- Geminate (double) stops became single voiceless stops: *pp* > *p*, *tt* > *t*, *kk* > *k*, as in Latin *cuppa* [kuppa] 'cup, cask, barrel' > Spanish *copa* [kopa] 'cup'; *gutta* > *gota* 'drop'; *bucca* [bukka] 'puffed-out cheek, jowl' > *boca* [boka] 'mouth'.
- Plain voiceless stops became voiced stops: *p* > *b*, *t* > *d*, *k* > *g*, as in Latin *sapere* 'to understand, have sense' > Spanish *saber* 'to know'; *vīta* [wi:ta] > *vida* 'life'; *amīka* [ami:ka] > *amiga* 'female friend'.
- Voiced stops (except *b*, which remained) were lost: *d* > Ø, *g* > Ø, (*b* > *b*), as in Latin *cadere* > *caer* 'to fall', *crēdere* 'to trust, believe' > *creer* 'to believe'; *rēgīna* > *reina* 'queen', *vāgīna* 'sheath, scabbard, husk, vagina' > *vaina* 'sheath, scabbard'.

The series of changes in the intervocalic stops in the development from Latin to Spanish has been interpreted as a push chain (let *tt*, *t*, and *d* represent all the stops in the three respective series), having taken place in the order:

(1)   *tt* > *t*, (2) *t* > *d*, (3) *d* > Ø.

In this view, as the geminates began to simplify, (1) *tt* > *t* put pressure on the plain voiceless series to get out of the way, (2) *t* > *d*, which in turn put pressure on the voiced series, causing it to be lost (except for *b*), (3) *d* > Ø. It would also be possible to interpret this series of changes as a pull chain, applying in the temporal sequence:

(3)   *d* > Ø, (2) *t* > *d*, (1) *tt* > *t*.

In this possible scenario, the loss of the intervocalic voiced stops, (3) *d* > Ø, left a gap in the inventory, which was filled by the shift of the plain voiceless stops to voiced, (2) *t* > *d*; but this then left a gap for the voiceless stops, and a language with voiceless geminates but no plain voiceless stops would be unexpected, so (1) *tt* > *t* took place.

(4) Mamean shift: chain shifts of various sorts, some more complex, some involving only a couple of changes, are known from numerous languages, not just from Indo-European. One example is the chain shift in Mamean languages (a branch of the Mayan family) in which:

*r > t (for example, Mam *ti:x* < **ri:x* 'old man', *t-* < **r-* 'his, hers, its' (a prefix).

*t > č (*čap* < **tap* 'crab', *čeʔw* < **teʔw* 'cold').

*č > ç̌; *č' > ç̌' (*ç̌o:ç̌'* < **čohč'* 'earth', *ç̌'am* < **č'am* 'sour'). (The [ç̌] is a laminal retroflex grooved affricate; [ç̌'] is its glottalized (ejective) counterpart. IPA has no symbol for these sounds, as IPA's retroflex sounds are apicals.)

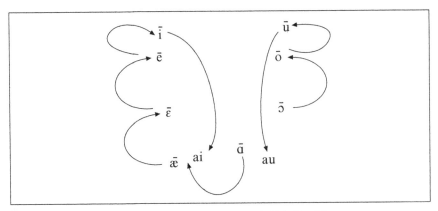

FIGURE 2.1: The Great Vowel Shift in English

(5) The English Great Vowel Shift, mentioned in examples above, is one of the best known of all chain shifts. Between Chaucer (born 1343) and Shakespeare (born 1564), English underwent a series of interrelated vowel changes known as the Great Vowel Shift, in which long vowels systematically raised, and the highest long vowels diphthongized, as seen in Figure 2.1.

These changes are seen in the following words:

Middle English	Chaucer	Shakespeare		Modern English
bite(n)	/bītə/	/bəit/	/bait/	'bite' (ī > ai)
tide	/tīd/	/təid/	/taid/	'tide'
bete	/bētə/	/bīt/	/bi(:)t/	'beet' (ē > i)
mete	/mēt/	/mēt/	/mi(:)t/	'meat'(ɛ̄ > ē > i)
bete 'strike'	/bǣt/	/bēt/	/bit/	'beat' (ǣ > i)
name	/nāmə/	/nǣm/	/neim/	'name' (ā > ei)
hous	/hūs/	/həus/	/haus/	'house' (ū > au)
boote	/bōt/	/būt/	/bu(:)t/	'boot' (ō > u)
boat	/bɔ̄t/	/bōt/	/bout/	'boat' (ɔ̄ > ou)

Vowel shifts are also found in a good number of other languages, and have continued in various dialects of English. William Labov has proposed general principles of chain shifting for vowels. Earlier, he argued that (1) long vowels rise, (2) short vowels fall, and (3) back vowels move to the front. This would fit the changes seen in the Great Vowel Shift in English. Later he revised this to (1) tense vowel nuclei rise, (2) lax vowel nuclei fall, and (3) back vowel nuclei move to the front, again illustrated by the English Great Vowel Shift. However, there are exceptions. For example, the short, lax front vowels /æ/ (as in *trap*) and /ɛ/ (as in *dress*) were raised in New Zealand English (æ towards ɛ, and ɛ towards *i*), not lowered, as predicted by Labov's principles (see Gordon et al. 2004).

Later, Labov revised the principles further, referring to the peripherality or non-peripherality of vowels. Labov (1994: 172) explains:

the term *peripherality* was introduced to describe the path of the high vowels in the Great Vowel Shift . . . I will use the term non-peripheral and the feature [-peripheral] to describe any type of vowel nucleus that is plainly more distant from the periphery in its mean and distribution than another vowel of the same height.

Labov sees as a central principle that 'in chain shifts, peripheral vowels become more open [lower] and non-peripheral vowels become less open [higher]' (Labov 1994: 601). This is stated later as the principles (1) tense nuclei rise along a peripheral track, and (2) lax nuclei fall long a non-peripheral track (see Labov 2010: 145–50 for details). The definition of peripherality was somewhat imprecise (Labov 1994: 173, 212, 285; 2010: 145–9; cf. Gordon et al. 2004: 271). In each of these formulations of the principles, it is sometimes difficult to determine whether particular vowels are long or short, tense or lax, or peripheral or non-peripheral. Nevertheless, even if exceptions may exist, Labov's chain shift principles do reflect the fact that very often in vowel shifts, long or tense or peripheral vowels rise and short or lax or non-peripheral vowels fall.

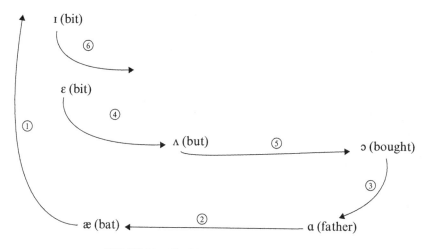

FIGURE 2.2: The Northern Cities Vowel Shift

(6) In the Northern Cities Vowel Shift six vowels rotate, as in Figure 2.2: (1) the tensing, raising, and fronting of /æ/ (as in *bat*); (2) the fronting of /ɑ/ (as in *got* or *father*); (3) the lowering and fronting of /ɔ/ (as in *bought*); (4) the lowering and backing of /ɛ/ (as in *bet*); (5) the backing of /ʌ/ (as in *cut* or *but*); and (6) the lowering and backing of /ɪ/ (as in *bit*). This chain shift involves a broad area of the US called the Inland north, around the Great Lakes. William Labov hypothesizes that the shift started in the early nineteenth century during the construction of the Erie Canal, with the migration to the Great Lakes area of workers from the East Coast representing different varieties of American English. (See Labov 2010; Labov et al. 2006.)

2.10 Exercises

Exercise 2.1 Sound change – Proto-Germanic to Old English

Compare the Proto-Germanic forms with their descendants in Old English and determine what sound changes involving vowels have taken place. Write out the sound change involved, and identify (by name) the kind of change found. Ignore changes involving second syllables. (Note that ī, ō, and ū are long vowels.)

	Proto-Germanic	Old English	gloss
1.	*fimf	fīf	'five'
2.	*gans-	gōs	'goose'
3.	*grinst	grīst	'a grinding', 'grist'
4.	*hanh-	hōh	'heel, hock'
5.	*linθj(az)-	līθe	'mild, lithe'
6.	*munθ-	mūθ	'mouth'
7.	*tanθ-	tōθ	'tooth'
8.	*gang-	gang	'a going'
9.	*grind-	grind	'grind'
10.	*hlink-	hlink	'ridge, links'
11.	*hund-	hund	'dog, hound'
12.	*land-	land	'land'
13.	*sing-	sing-	'sing'
14.	*slink-	slink-	'slink'
15.	*sund-	sund-	'swimming, sea, sound'
16.	*swing-	swing-	'swing'
17.	*θingam	θing-	'assembly

Exercise 2.2 Sound change – Old English to Modern English

Compare the Old English words with their counterparts in Modern English and determine what sound change or changes explain the changes that affect the word-initial consonant clusters in these words. Write out the sound change or changes involved. Ignore changes involving any other sounds in these words. (Note that ī, ē, ā, ō, and ū are long vowels.)

	Old English	Modern English
1.	hlūd 'noisy'	loud
2.	hlāf	loaf
3.	hreaw 'raw, uncooked'	raw
4.	hring 'ring, circle'	ring
5.	hnutu	nut

	Old English	Modern English
6.	hnitu 'louse egg'	nit
7.	cnīf [kn-]	knife [n-]
8.	cnāwan [kn-]	know [n-]
9.	cnēo [kn-]	knee [n-]
10.	cnotta [kn-]	knot [n-]
11.	gnætt [gn-]	gnat [n-]
12.	gnagan [gn-]	gnaw [n-]
13.	slāw 'inactive, sluggish'	slow
14.	slīdan	slide
15.	snāw	snow
16.	snaca	snake
17.	flēon	flee
18.	flæx	flax
19.	fretan 'devour, consume'	fret
20.	frogga	frog

Exercise 2.3 Sound change – Sanskrit to Pali

Compare the Sanskrit forms with their descendants in later Pali. Determine what sound changes have taken place. Write out the changes, and identify (by name) the kind of changes where possible.

NOTE: Sanskrit *s* = [s], *ś* = [ʃ], *ṣ* = [ṣ]. Each set is in effect a separate sound change exercise, though some changes may be illustrated in the examples of more than one set.

Set I

	Sanskrit	Pali	gloss
1.	śaśa	sasa	'hare'
2.	kēśa	kesa	'hair'
3.	dēśa	desa	'country'
4.	dōṣa	dosa	'fault'
5.	dāṣa	dasa	'slave'
6.	śiṣya	sissa	'pupil'
7.	sasya	sassa	'grain'

Set II

	Sanskrit	Pali	gloss
8.	snāna	sināna	'bathing'
9.	sneha	sineha	'friendship'
10.	snihyati	sinihyati	'is fond of'
11.	snigdha	siniddha	'oily'

Set III

	Sanskrit	Pali	gloss
12.	āuṣadha	ōsadha	'herbs, medicine'
13.	kāuśika	kōsika	'owl'
14.	gaura	gōra	'pale'
15.	mauna	mōna	'silence'
16.	augha	ōgha	'flood'
17.	tāila	tēla	'oil'
18.	vāira	vēra	'enmity'
19.	śāila	sēla	'rocky'
20.	aikya	ekka	'oneness'

Set IV

	Sanskrit	Pali	gloss
21.	pariṣat	parisā	'assembly'
22.	matimant	matimā	'wise'
23.	ārakāt	ārakā	'from afar'
24.	dharmāt	dhammā	'merit (ablative)'
25.	arthāt	atthā	'that is'
26.	bhagavant	bhagavā	'venerable'
27.	mitravant	mittavā	'having friends'

(Bhat 2001: 67, 68, 70; Masica 1991: 168)

Exercise 2.4 Sound change – Sanskrit to Prakrit

Compare the Sanskrit forms with their descendants in later Prakrit. Determine what sound changes have taken place. Write out the changes, and identify (by name) the kind of changes where possible.

NOTE: Consonants with subscript dots are retroflex; Sanskrit ṣ = [ṣ], ś = [ʃ], ṣ = [ʂ]. The *dh* in examples 3 and 6 is a single segment (not a consonant cluster); it is a breathy voiced (or murmured) stop, traditionally called a voiced aspirate. Each set is in effect a separate sound change exercise, though some changes may be illustrated in the examples of more than one set.

Set I

	Sanskrit	Prakrit	gloss
1.	sapta	satta	'seven'
2.	dugdha	duddha	'milk'
3.	udgāra	uggāla	'spit out'
4.	tikta	titta	'pungent'
5.	mudga	mugga	'mung bean'
6.	ardha	addha	'half'
7.	karpaṭa	kappaḍa	'rag, cloth'
8.	kurkura	kukkura	'dog'

	Sanskrit	Prakrit	gloss
9.	darpa	dappa	'arrogance'
10.	parṇa	paṇṇa	'leaf'
11.	karma	kamma	'work'

Set II

	Sanskrit	Prakrit	gloss
12.	saras	sara	'lake'
13.	śara	sara	'arrow'
14.	sapta	satta	'seven' (repeated from example 1)
15.	śakta	satta	'able'
16.	sarva	savva	'all'
17.	śava	sava	'corpse'
18.	sīsa	sīsa	'lead'
19.	śīla	sīla	'conduct'

Set III

	Sanskrit	Prakrit	gloss
20.	káśmīra	kamhīra	'Kashmir'
21.	grīṣma	grimha	'summer'
22.	vismaya	vimhaya	'surprize
23.	ūṣman	umhā	'heat'
24.	viṣṇu	viṇhu	'Visnu'
25.	praśna	paṇha	'question'
26.	snāna	ṇhāṇa	'bath'

(Bhat 2001: 6–7, 32, 83)

Exercise 2.5 Sound change – Proto-Slavic to Russian

What sound changes that have taken place in Russian since Proto-Slavic times are illustrated in the following data? Write sound change rules to account for the palatalization of consonants, the change in the stem vowels, loss of vowels, and change in voicing of consonants. Do not attempt to write sound changes for the changes in the consonant clusters (*bl, tl, dl*) in examples 1, 2, and 3. More than one change has applied to some forms; for these, state the relative chronology of these changes (the order, temporal sequence) in which the different changes took place.

(The breve /ˇ/ over vowels means 'short'.)

NOTE: Many find this exercise difficult, though easy to understand once the changes are discovered. HINT: Consider the influence of vowels upon other vowels.

	Proto-Slavic	Russian	gloss
1.	*greblŏ	grʲop	'rowed'
2.	*metlŏ	mʲol	'swept'

	Proto-Slavic	Russian	gloss
3.	*vedlŏ	vʲol	'led'
4.	*nesŏ	nʲos	'carried'
5.	*pĭsŏ	pʲos	'dog'
6.	*domŏ	dom	'house'
7.	*grobŏ	grop	'coffin'
8.	*nosŏ	nos	'nose'
9.	*rodŏ	rot	'gender'
10.	*volŏ	vol	'bull'
11.	*dĭnĭ	dʲenʲ	'day'
12.	*konĭ	konʲ	'horse'
13.	*vĭsĭ	vʲesʲ	'all'

(The verb forms in these data are 'THIRD PERSON MASCULINE PAST TENSE'.)

Exercise 2.6 Sound change – dialects of Tulu (Dravidian)

The forms in the Sapaliga dialect correspond to those of the oldest stage of the language; therefore, compare the forms in the other dialects to those of Sapaliga and determine what sound changes have taken place in each of the other dialects of Tulu. Write out and list the sound changes for each dialect, and identify (name) the kind of change involved in each instance, wherever this is possible. Do you imagine that some of the dialects went through more than one change in intermediate stages to arrive at some of the individual sounds they now have? If so, what might the intermediate stages have been?

NOTE: <c> = [č] (IPA [ʧ]); consonants with dots beneath are retroflex.

	Sapaliga	Holeya	Setti	Jain 1	Jain 2	gloss
1.	tare	care	sare	hare	are	'wear off'
2.	tali	cali	sali	hali	ali	'sprinkle'
3.	tavḍu	cavḍu	savḍu	havḍu	avḍu	'bran'
4.	tōjɨ	cōjɨ	sōjɨ	hōjɨ	ōjɨ	'appear'
5.	tinɨ	cinɨ	sinɨ	hinɨ	inɨ	'eat'
6.	tudɛ	cudɛ	sudɛ	hudɛ	–	'river'
7.	tōḍu	cōḍu	sōḍu	hōḍu	ōḍu	'stream'
8.	tanɛ	canɛ	sanɛ	hanɛ	anɛ	'conceiving' (of cattle)
9.	tappu	cappu	sappu	happu	appu	'leaf'
10.	tay	cay	say	hay	ay	'die'
11.	tavtɛ	cavtɛ	savtɛ	havtɛ	avtɛ	'cucumber'
12.	tuttu	cuttu	suttu	huttu	uttu	'wear'
13.	tumbu	cimbu	sumbu	humbu	umbu	'carry on head'
14.	tū	cū	sū	hū	ū	'see'

(Bhat 2001: 51)

Exercise 2.7 Sound change – Proto-Indo-European (PIE) to Latin

What sound changes have taken place in the transition from Proto-Indo-European to Latin? Try to formulate the most general, most inclusive statements possible to describe these changes. Concentrate on the sounds at the beginning of roots. (The sounds h_1, h_2, and h_3 refer to the laryngeals reconstructed for Proto-Indo-European; do not be concerned with their phonetic value but just treat them as consonants of a general sort. Conventionally *h_1 is considered 'neutral, perhaps /h/ or /ʔ/; *h_2 is 'a-colouring', perhaps /x/ or /ħ/; and *h_3 is 'o-colouring', perhaps /ʕ/. There is still not complete agreement among specialists about the Indo-European laryngeals.)

NOTE: Consonants with small circles beneath them (ḷ and ṛ) are syllabic.

	Proto-Indo-European		Latin	gloss
1.	*pórḱos	'piglet'	porcus /porkus/	'pig, hog'
2.	*pótis	'capable'	potis	'able'
3.	*bʰébʰrus	'beaver'	fiber	'beaver'
4.	*bʰréh₂tēr	'brother'	frāter	'brother'
5.	*bʰér-o	'carry'	ferō	'I carry'
6.	*tauros	'bull'	taurus	'bull'
7.	*tréyes	'three'	trēs	'three'
8.	*dḷkus	'sweet'	dulcis /dulkis/	'sweet'
9.	*dóh₃nom	'gift'	dōnum	'gift, offering'
10.	*dʰeh₁lus	'nourishing'	fēlīx /feːliːks/	'fruitful, fortunate'
11.	*dʰúh₂mos	'smoke'	fūmus	'smoke, steam'
12.	*dʰeh₁-	'to place, set'	faciō /fakioː/	'I do, make'
13.	*ḱm̥tóm	'hundred'	centum /kentum/	'hundred'
14.	*ḱ(u)wōn	'dog'	canis /kanis/	'dog'
15.	*ĝénu	'jaw'	gena	'cheek'
16.	*ĝus-tu-	'taste'	gustus	'taste'
17.	*kápr̥	'penis'	caper /kaper/	'goat'
18.	*kom	'near, by, with'	cum /kum/	'with'

	Proto-Indo-European		Latin	gloss
19.	*genh₁os	'race, kind'	genus	'race, kind'
20.	*g̥lh₁is	'mouse'	glīs	'dormouse'
21.	*gʰaidos	'goat'	haedus /haedus/	'kid, young goat'
22.	*gʰóstis	'stranger, guest'	hostis	'enemy, stranger'
23.	*kʷis	'who'	quis /kwis/	'who'
24.	*kʷétwor-	'four'	quattuor /kwattuor/	'four'
25.	*gʷemyo	'come'	veniō /wenio:/	'I come'
26.	*gʷih₃wos	'living'	vīvus /wi:wus/	'alive'
27.	*gʷʰermno-	'warm'	furnus	'oven'
28.	*gʷʰén-	'repel'	(dē-)fen(-dō)	'I repel'
29.	*gʷʰér-	'wild beast'	ferus	'wild, uncivilized'

Exercise 2.8 Sound change – Portuguese

Make the most general statements you can to account for the sound changes which took place intervocalically in the transition from Late Latin to Modern Portuguese, based on the following examples. (Do not attempt to explain changes in vowels that you see.)

	Late Latin		Modern Portuguese	gloss
1.	lupu-		lobo	'wolf'
2.	sapore		sabor	'flavour, taste'
3.	mutu-		mudo /mudu/	'dumb, mute, silent'
4.	latu-		lado /ladu/	'side'
5.	pacare /pakare/	'pacify'	pagar	'to pay'
6.	focu /foku/		fogo /fogu/	'fire'
7.	nebula		névoa	'mist'
8.	debere		dever	'to owe'
9.	caballu		cavalo /kavalu/	'horse'
10.	gradu		grau	'degree'
11.	nuda		nua	'nude' (FEMININE)
12.	regale		real	'royal'
13.	cogitare	'to think'	cuidar	'to take care'

	Late Latin	Modern Portuguese	gloss
14.	palu	pau	'stick'
15.	filu	fio /fiu/	'thread'
16.	salute	saúde	'health'
17.	luna	lua	'moon'
18.	corona	coroa	'crown'
19.	moneta	moeda	'coin'

Exercise 2.9 Sound change – Greek

What happened to the former labiovelar sounds (k^w, g^w, g^{wh}) and to w in Attic Greek? Formulate the most general (most inclusive) statement of the sound change(s) involving these sounds from Proto-Indo-European (PIE) to Attic Greek that you can based on the following data.

	PIE	Attic Greek	gloss
1.	*$k^w$is	tis	'who'
2.	*k^we	te	'and'
3.	*k^wetwóres	tettares	'four'
4.	*pénk^{w}e	pente	'five'
5.	*k^wóti- 'how much'	pósis	'how much, how many'
6.	*k^wóteros 'which of two'	póteros	'which'
7.	*leik^{w}o-	leipō	'leave'
8.	*yēk^{w}r̥	hēpar	'liver'
9.	*g^welb^{h}us	delp^{h}ús	'womb'
10.	*g^wous	bous	'cow'
11.	*g^wm̥ti-	basis	'going'
12.	*g^wm̥ye- 'come'	bainō	'I walk, come'
13.	*g^wabh-	bap-t [p < ph]	'I dip in'
14.	*g^{wh}aidrós 'bright, shining'	p^{h}aidrós	'beaming, cheerful'
15.	*g^{wh}ren- 'think'	p^{h}renéō	'I think'
16.	*snig^{wh}-s	nip^{h}a	'snow'
17.	*g^{wh}ermós	t^{h}ermós	'warm'
18.	*g^{wh}el- 'wish, want'	t^{h}élō	'I want, wish'
19.	*g^{wh}en- 'strike'	t^{h}eínō	'I strike'
20.	*g^{wh}ónos 'striking down'	p^{h}ónos	'murder'

	PIE	Attic Greek	gloss
21.	*woiк̂- 'clan'	oikía	'household'
22.	*wóghos 'carrier'	okhos	'wagon'
23.	*dhewo- 'run'	theō	'I run'

Exercise 2.10 Sound change – Finnic to Finnsh and Estonian

Determine what sound changes affecting the vowels have taken place in Finnish and Estonian. Write out these changes and specify under what conditions they took place in each of the two languages. Identify (name) the changes, where possible, one set of changes for Finnish, another set for Estonian.

NOTE: *ä* = [æ], *ö* = [ø], *ü* = [y] (*y* = also [y]), *õ* = [ɨ]. Double vowels (for example *aa, oo,* and so on) are long vowels. Orthographic <b, d, g> in Estonian are represented here as [p, t, k] respectively, although these sounds are between voiced and voiceless, described sometimes as 'semi-voiceless' or 'half-voiced'.

	Proto-Finnic	Finnish	Estonian	gloss
1.	*maa	maa	maa	'land'
2.	*noori	nuori	noor	'young'
3.	*koori	kuori	koor	'bark, peel'
4.	*hooli	huoli	hool	'care, worry'
5.	*jooni	juoni	joon	'line, direction'
6.	*leemi	liemi	leem	'broth'
7.	*mees	mies	mees	'man'
8.	*meeli	mieli	meel	'mind'
9.	*keeli	kieli	keel	'tongue, language'
10.	*reemu	riemu	rõõm [riːm]	'joy'
11.	*meekka	miekka	mõõk [miːkː]	'sword'
12.	*peena	piena	põõn [piːn]	'slat, rail, cross-piece'
13.	*veeras	vieras	võõras [viːras]	'foreign'
14.	*luu	luu	luu	'bone'
15.	*hiiri	hiiri	hiir	'mouse'
16.	*kyynärä	kyynärä	küünar	'ell' (measure)
17.	*töö	työ	töö	'work'
18.	*möö-	myö-	möö-	'along, by'
19.	*kala	kala	kala	'fish'
20.	*lapa	lapa	laba [lapa]	'blade'
21.	*kylä	kylä	küla	'village'
22.	*ikä	ikä	iga [ika]	'age'
23.	*isä	isä	isa	'father'
24.	*joki	joki	jõgi [jiki]	'river'

	Proto-Finnic	Finnish	Estonian	gloss
25.	*hiki	hiki	higi [hiki]	'sweat'
26.	*kivi	kivi	kivi	'stone'
27.	*lumi	lumi	lumi	'snow'
28.	*läpi	läpi	läbi [læpi]	'through, hole'
29.	*suku	suku	sugu [suku]	'family'
30.	*ilma	ilma	ilm 'world'	'weather, world'
31.	*jalka	jalka	jalg [jalk]	'foot, leg'
32.	*kalma	kalma	kalm	'grave (mound)'
33.	*nälkä	nälkä	nälg [nælk]	'hunger'
34.	*härkä	härkä	härg [hærk]	'ox, bull'
35.	*silmä	silmä	silm	'eye'
36.	*marja	marja	mari	'berry'
37.	*karja	karja	kari	'cattle'
38.	*orja	orja	ori	'slave'
39.	*lintu	lintu	lind [lint]	'bird'
40.	*hullu	hullu	hull	'crazy'
41.	*mänty	mänty	mänd [mænʲtʲ]	'pine'
42.	*synty	synty	sünd [synʲtʲ]	'birth'
43.	*hanki	hanki	hang [haŋk]	'crust of snow'
44.	*kurki	kurki	kurg [kurk]	'crane'
45.	*nahka	nahka	nahk	'leather'
46.	*lehmä	lehmä	lehm	'cow'
47.	*lehti	lehti	leht	'leaf, sheet'
48.	*hauta	hauta	haud [haut]	'grave'
49.	*lauta	lauta	laud [laut]	'board'
50.	*lava	lava	lava	'platform, frame'
51.	*haava	haava	haav	'wound'
52.	*hinta	hinta	hind [hint]	'price'
53.	*into	into	ind [int]	'passion'
54.	*halko	halko	halg [halk]	'piece/block of wood'
55.	*kylmä	kylmä	külm	'cold'
56.	*kylki	kylki	külg [kylk]	'side'
57.	*kirppu	kirppu	kirp [kirp:]	'flea'
58.	*verkko	verkko	võrk [vɨrk:]	'net'
59.	*onsi	onsi	õõs [ɨːs]	'a hollow place'
60.	*kansi	kansi	kaas	'cover'
61.	*kynsi	kynsi	küüs	'fingernail, claw'
62.	*mesi	mesi	mesi	'honey'
63.	*kuusi	kuusi	kuus	'six'
64.	*kusi	kusi .	kusi	'urine'
65.	*tosi	tosi	tõsi [tɨsi]	'true'

	Proto-Finnic	Finnish	Estonian	gloss
66.	*mato	mato 'worm'	madu [matu]	'snake'
67.	*elo	elo	elu	'life/building'
68.	*hako	hako	hagu [haku]	'evergreen sprig, brushwood'
69.	*ilo	ilo 'joy'	ilu	'beauty'
70.	*himo	himo	himu	'lust, desire'
71.	*iho	iho	ihu	'skin, hide'
72.	*vesa	vesa	võsa [vɪsa]	'sprout, brush, weed'
73.	*helma	helma	hõlm [hɪlm]	'skirt, frock'
74.	*terva	terva	tõrv [tɪrv]	'tar'
75.	*velka	velka	võlg [vɪlk]	'debt'
76.	*perna	perna	põrn [pɪrn]	'spleen'
77.	*leuka	leuka	lõug [lɪuk]	'jaw, chin'
78.	*solki	solki	sõlg [sɪlk]	'buckle, brooch'
79.	*sormi	sormi	sõrm [sɪrm]	'finger'
80.	*pohja	pohja	põhi [pɪhi]	'bottom, base'
81.	*poski	poski	põsk [pɪsk]	'cheek'
82.	*korpi	korpi	kõrb [kɪrp]	'dark woods, wilderness'
83.	*metsä	metsä	mets	'woods'
84.	*leppä	leppä	lepp [lep:]	'alder'

For additional sound change exercises with solutions, see Blust (2018: 30–86, 222–96).

3

LOANWORDS (BORROWING)

Fällt von ungefähr ein Fremdwort in den Brunnen einer Sprache, so wird
    es so lange darin umgetrieben, bis es ihre Farbe annimmt.
    [If a foreign word falls by accident into the spring of a language, it will be
    driven around in there until it takes on that language's colour.]
                            (Jakob Grimm, *Deutsches Wörterbuch*, 1854, p. xxvi)

3.1 Introduction

It is common for one language to take words from another language and
make them part of its own vocabulary: these are called *loanwords* or just
loans. The process is called linguistic *borrowing*, and the loanwords themselves
are also often called borrowings. Borrowing, however, is not restricted to
just lexical items taken from one language into another. Any linguistic material – sounds, phonological rules (or patterns or constraints), grammatical
morphemes, syntactic patterns, semantic associations, discourse strategies, or
whatever – can be borrowed, that is, can be taken over from a foreign language so that it becomes part of the borrowing language. Borrowing normally
implies a certain degree of bilingualism for at least some people in both the
language which borrows (typically called the *recipient* language) and the language which is borrowed from (called the *donor* language). In this chapter, we
are concerned with answering the questions: (1) what are loanwords?; (2) why
are words borrowed?; (3) what are the methods for determining that something is a loanword and for identifying the source languages from which words
are borrowed?; (4) how are words borrowed and what happens to borrowed
words when they are taken into another language?; and (5) how do loanwords
help reveal past history? (Other aspects of linguistic borrowing are treated in
Chapters 10 and 11.)

3.2 What is a Loanword?

A loanword is a lexical item (a word) which has been 'borrowed' from another language, a word which originally was not part of the vocabulary of the recipient language but was adopted from some other language and made part of the borrowing language's vocabulary. For example, Old English did not have the word *pork*; this became an English word only after it was adopted from French *porc* 'pig, pork', borrowed in the late Middle English period – so we say, as a consequence, that *pork* is a French loanword in English. French, in turn, has also borrowed words from English, for example *bifteck* 'beefsteak', among many others. Loanwords are extremely common; some languages have many. There are extensive studies of the many Scandinavian and French loans in English; Germanic and Baltic loans in Finnish; Basque, German, and Arabic loans in Spanish; loanwords from Native American languages in Spanish and Spanish loans in various Native American languages (called *hispanisms*); Turkic in Hungarian; English in Japanese; Sanskrit in Malay and other languages of Indonesia; Arabic in various languages of Africa and Asia; and so on, to mention just a few cases which have been studied. Too mention a much consulted source, Haspelmath and Tadmor (2009) gives case studies involving the loanwords in forty-one languages.

A quick glance at the origins of the names of many common foods we eat will begin to give an appreciation of the impact of loanwords on English vocabulary and indeed on our lives:

cake < Old Norse *kaka* 'cake'

catsup, ketchup < apparently originally from Amoy Chinese *kôe- chiap*, *kè-tsiap* 'brine of pickled fish or shellfish', borrowed into Malay as *kēchap*, taken by Dutch as *ketjap*, the probable source from which English acquired the term

cherry < Anglo-Norman French *cherise* (compare Modern French *cerise* 'cherry') (from Vulgar Latin *ceresia*, which was borrowed from late Greek *kerasian* 'cherry')

chocolate < Nahuatl (Mexico, the language of the Aztecs) *čokolātl* 'a drink made from the seeds of the cacao tree', borrowed into Spanish as *chocolate*, from which many other languages of the world obtained the term, for example Arabic *shukulata*, Basque *txokolatea*, Chinese *qiǎokèlì*, Finnish *suklaa*, German *Schokolade*, Greek *sokoláta*, Hawaiian *kaloka*, Hindi *chokalet*, Hungarian *csokoládé*, Italian *cioccolato*, Japenese *chokorēto*, Khmer *saukaula*, Korean *chokollis*, Russian *shokolad*, Somali *shukulaato*, Tagalog *tsokolate*, Turkish *çikolata*, Welsh *siocled*, Zulu *ushokoledi*, etc.

Coca-Cola < *coca* < Quechua *kuka* 'coca leaves, coca bush', borrowed via Spanish *coca*, and *cola* < languages of West Africa *kola* 'cola nut' (for example Temne *kola*, Mandingo *kolo* 'cola (tree species)'

coffee < Turkish *kahveh* 'coffee', itself borrowed earlier from Arabic *qahwah* 'coffee, wine', from an earlier meaning connected with 'dark'. Words for 'coffee' are widely borrowed around the world, for example Chinese *kāfēi*, Czech *káva*, French *café*, Finnish *kahvi*, German *Kaffee*, Greek *kafés*,

Hindi *kofee*, Hungarian *kávé*, Indonesian *kopi*, Italian *caffè*, Japanese *kōhī*, Korean *keopi*, Māori *kawhe*, Polish *kawa*, Russian *kofe*, Swahili *kahawa*, Zulu *ikhofi*, etc.

cookie (American English) < Dutch *koekje* 'little cake', diminutive of *koek* [kuk] 'cake'

flour < Old French *flour* 'flower' (compare French *fleur de farine* 'flower of meal/flour', that is, the 'best or finest of the ground meal')

hamburger < German *Hamburger* 'person or thing native to Hamburg'

juice < French *jus* 'broth, sauce, juice of plant or animal'

macaroni < southern Italian dialect *maccaroni* (Standard Italian *maccheroni*), the plural of *maccarone*, a pasta made of flour, cheese, and butter

pantry < Old French *paneterie* 'bread-room, bread-closet', based ultimately on Latin *pānis* 'bread'

pepper < ultimately of ancient oriental origin (compare Sanskrit *pippalī* 'long pepper'); it came early to Germanic peoples via Latin *piper*, borrowed from Greek *piperi*

pie < Medieval Latin *pie* 'a pastry with meat of fish'; earlier in English *pie* meant 'pastry'

pizza < Italian *pizza* that earlier meant 'cake, tart, pie'; it is attested in English since 1935

potato < Taino (Cariban language of Haiti) *patata* 'sweet potato', borrowed through Spanish *batata*, *patata* to many other languages

pumpkin < earlier meant 'pumpkin, melon', from Middle French *pompom* < Latin *peponem* 'large melon'

rice < ultimately from an Indo-Iranian language, via Latin *oryza*, where Latin had borrowed it from Greek *oríza*

sausage < French (see Modern French *saucisse*), inherited from Vulgar Latin *salsica* 'sausage', derived from *salsicus* 'seasoned with salt' (cf. Latin *sal* 'salt')

spaghetti < Italian *spaghetti*, plural of *spaghetto* 'small thread', the diminutive of *spago* 'string, twine'

squash < Narraganset (Algonquian) *askutasquash* 'the things that can be eaten raw'

sugar < from Arabic *sukkar*, through Old French *çucre*. Arabic *sukkar* itself is a borrowing from Persian *shakar*, apparently originally from Sanskrit *śarkarā* 'ground or candied sugar, sugar' (originally 'grit, gravel'). The Arabic word was borrowed in various other European languages (Spanish *azúcar*, Italian *zucchero*, German *zucker*, among others).

tea < ultimately from Chinese. Chinese languages have two predominant forms for 'tea'; in Mandarin and Cantonese it is *chá*; in Hokkien varieties of the southern cost of China and southeast Asia it is *teh*. *Tea* in English is from Amoy *tê* (southern Fujian province). The word was brought to Europe by the Dutch; it may have come into Dutch directly from Amoy Chinese, or Dutch may have got it from Malay *te/teh*, which had borrowed the Chinese word first. The *cha* form comes from Cantonese *chàh* 'tea', spread from ports of Hong Kong and Macau especially by the

Portuguese. The *chai* form is from the northern Chinese *chá* version; it spread overland to central Asia and Persia. In Persian it took on a suffix, becoming *chay*, and this *chay* was borrowed in Russian, Arabic, Turkish, etc., and also in India. English gets *chai* (meaning not just regular 'tea' but 'a drink made by blending black tea, honey and spices, and milk') from Hindi *chāy* 'tea'.

tomato < Nahuatl *tomatl*, through Spanish *tomate*

waffle < Dutch *wafel* 'waffle'.

These are but a few of the borrowed words involving English foodstuffs. Languages borrow words from other languages primarily because of *need* and *prestige*. When speakers of a language acquire some new item or concept from elsewhere, they *need* a name for the new acquisition; often a foreign name is borrowed along with the new concept. This explains, for example, why so many languages have similar words for 'automobile' (as in German *Automobil*, *Auto*, Russian *avtomobil'*, Finnish *auto*, Swedish *bil* – from the last syllable of *automobil*, Uzbek *avtomobil*); 'coffee' (Russian *kofe*, Finnish *kahvi*, Japanese *kōhii*); 'tobacco' (Finnish *tupakka*, Indonesian *tembakau* [təmbakau], Japanese *tabako* 'cigarette, tobacco', Spanish *tabaco* 'tobacco'); and *Coca-Cola*, for example, since languages presumably needed new names for these new concepts when they were acquired. Of course, most examples of loanwords are not so widespread as these.

The other main reason why words are taken over from another language is for *prestige*, because the foreign term for some reason was highly esteemed. For example, English could have done perfectly well with only native terms for 'pig flesh/pig meat' and 'cow flesh/cow meat', but for reasons of prestige, *pork* (from French *porc* 'pig') and *beef* (from French boeuf 'beef, ox, steer') were borrowed, as well as many other terms of 'cuisine' from French – *cuisine* itself is from French *cuisine* 'kitchen' – because French had more social status and was considered more prestigious than English during the period of Norman French dominance in England (1066–1300). Some examples are *bacon* (from Old French *bacon*, itself earlier borrowed from Germanic), *lettuce* (< Old French *laitues*, plural of *laitue* 'lettuce'), *mutton* (< Old French *moton*, cf. Modern French *mouton* 'sheep'), *salad* (< Old French *salade*, from Vulgar Latin *salata* 'salted', ultimately from older *herba salata* 'salted vegetables', vegetables seasoned with brine being a popular Roman dish), *veal* (< Old French *veel* 'calf', cf. Modern French *veau*), and so many more.

Udmurt (aka Votyak, a Uralic language) borrowed from Tatar (a Turkic language) words for such things as 'mother', 'father', 'grandmother', 'grandfather', 'husband', 'older brother', 'older sister', 'uncle', and 'human', among other things. Since Udmurt had native terms for 'father' and 'mother' and these other kin before contact with Tatar, need was not the motivation for these borrowings, rather prestige was. Similarly, Finnish borrowed words for 'mother' (*äiti*, from Germanic; compare Gothic *aiþei* [ɛ̄θ̄ī], Old High German *eidī*, Proto-Germanic *aiþī*); 'daughter' (*tytär*, from Baltic; compare Lithuanian *dukteř̃s* (GENITIVE)); 'sister' (*sisar*, from Baltic; compare Lithuanian *seseř̃s* (GENITIVE)); and 'bride', 'navel', 'neck', 'thigh', and 'tooth', among many other borrowings from Baltic and Germanic (compare Anttila 1989: 155). Clearly, Finnish had previously had terms for close female kin and for these body parts before borrowing these terms from neighbouring Indo-European languages, and thus it is prestige that accounts for these borrowings and not need.

Some loans involve a third, much rarer (and less important) reason for borrowing, the opposite of prestige: borrowing due to negative evaluation, the adoption of the foreign word to be *derogatory*. Here are a few examples, all borrowed presumably with derogatory intentions. French *hâbler* 'to speak a lot with exaggeration and bragging' is borrowed from Spanish *hablar* 'to speak'. Finnish *koni* 'nag' [old horse], with negative connotations, is borrowed from Russian *kon^j*, a neutral term for 'horse', with no negative connotations in the donor language. More examples can be found in negative names for ethnic groups, such as unfavourable *kraut* for 'German', from German *Kraut* 'herb, plant', shortened from *Sauerkraut* 'sauerkraut (pickled cabbage)'. In some cases it is not so clear where the negative associations come from, as in the case of English *hausfrau* with the pejorative meaning of 'frumpy, overly domesticated woman', borrowed from German *Hausfrau* 'housewife, home-maker', which has neutral connotations in German. Loanwords of English origin in other languages can also reflect less than positive attitudes, as in the case of Japanese *wan-man* 'the type of leader who wants to make all decisions without consulting anyone' from English *one man*, and Japanese *bosu*, from English *boss*, where in Japanese *bosu* almost always implies a boss involved in clandestine activities. The Russian loanwords *bíznes* 'business' and *biznesmén* 'businessman' are also often considered pejorative. Korean *hɔstis*, borrowed from English *hostess*, has a negative connotation, referring to the woman who works at nightclubs and bars that serve mainly male customers. It is possible, of course, that some examples of this sort were not borrowed with derogatory purposes in mind at all, but rather merely involve things which have low status or negative connotations.

3.3 How do Words get Borrowed?

Borrowed words are usually remodelled to fit the phonological and morphological structure of the borrowing language, at least in early stages of language contact. The traditional view of how words get borrowed and what happens to them as they are assimilated into the borrowing language holds that loanwords that are introduced to the borrowing language by bilinguals may contain sounds which are foreign to the receiving language, but due to *phonetic interference* the foreign sounds are changed to conform to native sounds and phonetic constraints. This is frequently called *adaptation* (or *phoneme substitution*). In adaptation, a foreign sound in borrowed words which does not exist in the receiving language is replaced by the nearest phonetic equivalent to it in the borrowing language. For example, formerly Finnish had no voiced stops *b, d, g*; in loans borrowed into Finnish from Germanic languages which contained *b, d, g*, voiceless stops (*p, t, k*), the closest phonetic counterparts in Finnish, replaced these voiced sounds, as seen in, for example, *parta* 'beard' (from Germanic **bardaz*) and *humpuuki* 'humbug' (ultimately from English *humbug*). Similarly, in Sayula Popoluca (a Mixe-Zoquean language of southern Mexico), which had no native *l* or *r*, the foreign *l* and *r* of borrowed words were replaced by native *n*, as in Sayula Popoluca *kúnu:š* (IPA *kúnu:ʃ*) 'cross', borrowed from Spanish *cruz* [krus], *mu:na* 'mule' from Spanish *mula*, and *puná:tu* 'plate, dish' from Spanish *plato*. Occasionally in borrowings, substitutions may spread the phonetic features of a single sound of the donor language across two segments in the borrowing language; for example, Finnish had no native *f*, so intervocalic *f* in loanwords was replaced by the sequence *hv*, as in *kahvi* 'coffee' (from Swedish *kaffe*), and *pihvi* 'beef' (from English *beef*). In this instance, some of the features of foreign *f* are represented on the first segment – *h* conveys 'voiceless' – and other features on the second segment – *v* conveys 'labiodental' – and both *h* and *v* signal 'fricative'.

Non-native phonological patterns are also subject to *accommodation*, where loanwords which do not conform to native phonological patterns are modified to fit the phonological combinations that are permitted in the borrowing language. This is usually accomplished by deletion, addition or recombination of certain sounds to fit the phonological structure of words in the borrowing language. For example, Mayan languages do not permit initial consonant clusters, and consequently Spanish *cruz* /krus/ 'cross' was borrowed as *rus* in Chol (Mayan), where the initial consonant of the donor form was simply left out, and as *kurus* in Tzotzil (another Mayan language), where the consonant cluster was broken up by the insertion of a vowel between *k* and *r*. Similarly, in the Sayula Popoluca example above, since the language did not have initial consonant clusters, the *kr* and *pl* of Spanish were broken up by the insertion of *u* in, for example, *kúnu:š* 'cross' (< Spanish *cruz*, just mentioned) and *puná:tu* 'plate' (< Spanish *plato*). Similarly, Finnish, with no initial consonant clusters in native words, eliminated all but the last consonant of initial consonant clusters in loanwords, for example *Ranska* 'French' (< Swedish *Franska* 'French'), *risti* 'cross' (< Old Russian *kristĭ*), *ruuvi* 'screw' (< Swedish *skruv* 'screw').

However, there are many different kinds of language-contact situations, and the outcome of borrowing can vary according to the length and intensity of the contact, the kind of interaction, and the degree of bilingualism in the population. In situations of more extensive, long-term or intimate contact, new phonemes can be introduced into the borrowing language together with borrowed words which contain these new sounds, resulting in changes in the phonemic inventory of the borrowing language; this is sometimes called *direct phonological diffusion*. For example, before intensive contact with French, English had no phonemic /ʒ/. This sound became an English phoneme through the many French loans that contained it which came into English, such as *rouge* /ruʒ/ (< French *rouge* 'red') (and added to by the palatalization in the eighteenth century of /zj/ > /ʒ/, as in *vision, Asia*, and so on). In the case of *v*, formerly English had only an allophonic [v] that occurred in native English words only as the intervocalic variant (allophone) of /f/, but no phonemic /v/. A remnant of this situation is still seen in alternations such as *leaf–leaves, wife–wives*, and so on, where the suffix *-es* used to have a vowel in the spoken language, putting the *f* between vowels. Later, *v* became phonemic due in part to French loans containing *v* in environments where [v] was not formerly permitted in English. Borrowed words with initial *v* of French origin – such as *very* from French *vrai* 'true' and *valley* < Old French *valée* – caused /v/ to become a separate phoneme in its own right, no longer just the allophonic variant of /f/ that occurred only between vowels. The phonological patterns (phonotactics, syllable structure) of a language can also be altered by the acceptance in more intimate language contact of loans which do not conform to native patterns. For example, while native Finnish words permit no initial consonant clusters, now through intimate contact and the introduction of many borrowings from other languages, especially from Swedish and later from English, Finnish phonology permits loans with initial clusters, as seen in, for example, the more recent loans *krokotiili* 'crocodile', *kruunu* 'crown' (compare Swedish *krona*), *presidentti* 'president', *smaragdi* 'emerald' (from Swedish *smaragd*), and so on.

While there may be typical patterns of substitution for foreign sounds and phonological patterns, substitutions in borrowed words in a language are not always uniform. The same foreign sound or pattern can sometimes be borrowed in one loanword in one way and in another loanword in a different way. This happens for the following reasons.

Sometimes different words are borrowed at different times, so that older loans reflect sound substitutions before intimate contact brought new sounds and patterns into the borrowing language, while more recent borrowings may exhibit the newer segments or patterns acquired after more intensive contact. (The extent to which the source language is known by speakers of the borrowing language is relevant here.) An example is Sayula Popoluca *turu* 'bull' (recently borrowed from Spanish *toro*), with *r*, where earlier loans would have substituted *n* for this foreign sound (mentioned above). Another example is seen in the comparison of Tzotzil (Mayan) *pulatu* 'dishes' (from Spanish *plato* 'plate, dish'), borrowed earlier when Tzotzil permitted no initial consonant clusters, and Tzotzil *platu* 'plate', borrowed later from the same Spanish source, now containing the initial consonant cluster which was formerly prohibited.

In most cases, borrowings are based on pronunciation, as illustrated in the case of Finnish *meikkaa-* 'to make up (apply cosmetics)', based on the English pronunciation of *make* /meik/. However, in some cases, loans can be based on written versions ('spelling pronunciations'), as seen in the case of Finnish *jeeppi* [jɛːpːi] 'jeep', which can only be based on a spelling pronunciation of English 'jeep', not on the English pronunciation (/ǰip/ [IPA /dʒip/]) – Finnish has /i/ and /iː/ and so if the loan were based on pronunciation and not spelling, it would have /iː/ or /i/ in the first syllable of a loan for 'jeep' (note that borrowed nouns that end in a consonant add *i* in Finnish). In the case of English *quixotic* [kwɪkˈsɒtɪk] 'pursuing ideals without thought of practicality' (that is, exhibiting behaviour like that of Don Quixote), a loan from Spanish, based on *Don Quixote*, the [ks] in English is due to a spelling pronunciation of the <x>. In older Spanish, <x> represented [ʃ]; this sound later changed to [x] (voiceless velar fricative) in Spanish and came to be spelled as <j> (compare Spanish *quijotesco* [kixoˈtɛsko] 'quixotic', with <j> [x]). The Spanish source for this loan never had [ks] in its pronunciation. In contrast, the original [ʃ] pronunciation is reflected in the *Don Quichotte* of French novels and operas based on Miguel de Cervantes' Don Quijote, also reflected in the title of Salman Rushdie's novel *Quichotte*.)

Another example is English *machismo*. This is borrowed from Spanish *machismo* 'exaggerated masculinity'. In North America it follows Spanish pronunciation with [tʃ] ([maˈtʃizmou]), but it is pronounced by many in British Commonwealth countries as [makízmou], a pronunciation based on Italian spelling, where <chi> represents [ki], the <h> showing that the 'c' is not pronounced as [tʃ] as it would be if spelled in Italian as <ci>. For example, contrast the pronunciation of such loans in English from Italian as *cappuccino*, *ciao*, and *capriccio* that have [tʃi] with *gnocchi*, *macchiatto* 'strained' (as in *caffè macchiato* 'strained coffee'), *Machiavellian*, and *zucchini* that have [ki].

In another case, Spanish *élite* [ˈɛlite] 'elite' was borrowed from French <élite> [eˈlit] 'elite' but Spanish placed stress on the first syllable due to a misunderstanding of French spelling; Spanish speakers misinterpreted the acute accent mark on the <é> as representing stress, as it does in Spanish; however, in French orthography <é> has nothing to do with stress but rather signals a close front mid vowel [e], which contrasts with <e> (with no diacritic) representing an open front mid vowel [ɛ].

It is good to remember that words can be borrowed into some particular language and then borrowed further by other languages, so that some borrowed words do not come directly from their ultimate source but rather via intermediate languages. For example, English borrowed *tofu* 'bean curd' from Japanese, but Japanese had borrowed it earlier from Chinese *doufu* (*dou* 'beans + *fu* 'rotten'). English got many terms for things encountered in the New World from Spanish, which in turn had borrowed them from indigenous American languages. English has a large number of loanwords that it took from Spanish but which came into Spanish first as loanwords from Nahuatl (language of the Aztecs): *coyote* < Spanish *coyote* < Nahuatl *coyotl* 'coyote'; *avocado* < Spanish *aguacate* < Nahuatl *āwaka-tl* 'avocado'; *chilli* < Spanish *chile* < Nahuatl *chīl-li* 'chilli, chilli pepper, red'; *chipotle* < Spanish *chipotle* < Nahuatl *chīl-pōk-tli* 'type of chilli pepper' (*chīl-* 'chilli pepper' + *-pōk* 'smoke' + *-tli* 'a noun suffix'); *chocolate* < Spanish *chocolate* < Nahuatl *čokolā-tl* 'chocolate'; *cocoa, cacao* < Spanish *cacao* < Nahuatl *kakawa-tl* 'cacao, chocolate bean'; *mezcal (mescal)* < Spanish *mezcal* < Nahuatl *meškal-li* 'mescal, distilled alcoholic beverage made from any type of agave'; *ocelot* < Spanish *ocelote* < Nahuatl *ōsēlō-tl* 'ocelot'; *tomato* < Spanish *tomate* (*jitomate* in Mexico) < Nahuatl *toma-tl* 'tomato'; among others.

In some cases a loan can be passed from one language to another and on to others in a chain of successive borrowings. For example, Finnish *suklaa* 'chocolate' was borrowed from Swedish *choklad* [ɧuklád], which was taken from French *chocolat* [ʃok(o)lá], borrowed earlier into French from Spanish *chocolate* [ʧokoláte], which is borrowed from Nahuatl *chocola-tl* [ʧokólatl] 'chocolate'.

Loan words are not only remodelled to accommodate aspects of the phonology of the borrowing language; they can also be adapted to fit the morphological patterns of the borrowing language. For example, Spanish and French borrowings into some varieties of Arabic have been made to fit Arabic morphological paradigms, which involve alternations in the vowels to signal different grammatical morphemes, such as 'singular' and 'plural' difference, as in:

resibo 'receipt' (singular), but *ruāseb* (plural) < Spanish *recibo* 'receipt'
bābor 'a steamship, steamer', but plural *buāber* < Spanish *vapor* /bapor/
'steam, steamship' (see Vendryes 1968: 95). (Compare Modern Arabic
bābūr 'steamship, locomotive' (singular), *bwābīr* (plural).)

Chiricahua Apache often has verbs where European languages have adjectives, and as a consequence the Spanish adjectives *loco* 'crazy' and *rico* 'rich' were borrowed but adapted to the Apache verb paradigm, as in:

lô:gò	'he/she is crazy'	*žî:gò*	'he/she is rich'
lô:šgò	'I am crazy'	*žî:šgò*	'I am rich'
lóngò	'you are crazy'	*žíngò*	'you are rich'

(*š* = IPA [ʃ], *ž* = IPA [ʒ].)

Here, as might be expected, it is the third person verb form ('he is crazy/rich') which phonetically matches the form of the original Spanish adjectives most closely (where Apache lacks *r*, and substituted *ž* instead; the diacritics on the vowels indicate tones and are required by Chiricahua Apache for verbs such as these) (Anttila 1989: 158).

Western Subanon, an Austronesian language of the Philippines, has the loanword *pinilitu* 'fried food,' borrowed from Spanish *frito* 'fried'. Morphologically it is (*p<in>ilitu*) derived from a basic form *pilitu* 'fry' with the native verbal infix *-in-* that crossreferences the noun that is the theme (focus) of the clause. Some younger speakers and more educated people say *piniritu*, with an *r* more like that of the Spanish source, *frito*.

(See Poplack 2018 for a more detailed study of how foreign items are introduced and adapted into recipient languages.)

3.4 How do we Identify Loanwords and Determine the Direction of Borrowing?

An important question is: how can we tell if something is a loanword or not? In dealing with borrowings, we want to ascertain which language is the source (donor) and which the recipient (borrower). The following criteria, rough rules of thumb, address these questions (compare Haas 1969a: 79; Sapir 1949 [1916]). The strongest evidence for loanword identification and the direction of borrowing comes from phonological criteria.

(1) Phonological patterns of the language. Words containing sounds which are not normally expected in native words are candidates for loans. For example, in the Chiricahua Apache example just mentioned, the fact that *žî:gò* 'he is rich' has an initial *ž* and that *lô:gò* 'he is crazy' has an initial *l* makes these strong candidates for loans, since neither *ž* nor *l* occurs word-initially in native words. In another example, native Nahuatl words are not expected to begin with *p*, since Proto-Uto-Aztecan initial **p-* was lost through regular sound change in Nahuatl (**p* > *h* > Ø, for example Proto-Uto-Aztecan **pa:* > Nahuatl *a:-* 'water'). For this reason, Nahuatl roots such as *petla-* 'woven mat', *po:čo:-* 'silk-cotton tree (ceiba)',

and *pak-* 'to cure'/*paʔ-* 'medicine' violate expectations for sounds in native words, making them candidates for possible loans. On further investigation, the sources of these borrowings are found in neighbouring languages: *petla-* comes from Mixe-Zoquean **pata* 'woven mat' (Nahuatl changed *a* > *e* in this environment, and *t* > *tl* before *a*); *po:čo:-* is from Totonac *pu:ču:t* 'silk-cotton tree (ceiba)'; *pak-/paʔ-* is from Totonac *paʔk* 'to cure, get well'. It is the aberrant initial *p-* of these forms which suggests that they may be loans and which prods us to look for their sources in other languages.

Words which violate the typical phonological patterns (canonical forms, syllable structure, phonotactics) of a language are likely to be loans. For example, Mayan languages typically have only monosyllabic roots (of the form CVC); the polysyllabic morphemes found in Mayan languages, which violate this monosyllabic pattern, turn out mostly to be loanwords (or from earlier compounds). For example, the polysyllabic monomorphemic *tinamit* 'town' of Kaqchikel (Mayan) is a loanword from Nahuatl (Uto-Aztecan). Since this polysyllabic form violates the typical monosyllabic structure of Mayan roots, the inference is that it is probably a loan, and indeed its source is found in Nahuatl (the language of the Toltecs and Aztecs) *tena:mi-tl* 'fence or wall of a town/city', 'fortified town'.

(2) Phonological history. In some cases where the phonological history of the languages of a family is known, information concerning the sound changes that they have undergone can be helpful for determining loans, the direction of borrowing, and what the donor language was.

English underwent the sound change in which *sk* > *ʃ*, as for example in Proto-Germanic **skipaz* 'ship' > Modern English *ship*. English borrowed a number of words with /sk/ from Old Norse and Scandinavian languages which have /sk/, and they are readily identified as loanwords because *sk* was not possible in native English words after the sound change. For example, *shirt* underwent the *sk* > *ʃ* change; it comes from Old English *scyrte* 'skirt, tunic', inherited from Proto-Germanic **skurtjon* 'a short garment'. However, *skirt* is borrowed from Old Norse *skyrta* 'shirt, a kind of kirtle', and is also from that same Proto-Germanic **skurtjon*. This unchanged *sk* of *skirt* indicates that this is a loanword in English, contrasting with native *shirt*, which did undergo the change. Some other examples are:

> sky < Old Norse *sky* 'sky'
> skin < Old Norse *skinn* 'animal hide, fur' (the Anglo-Saxon word was *hide*)
> scale (for weighing) < *skal* 'bowl, drinking cup' (used also as the cup or pan for weighing)
> scant < Old Norse *skamt, skammr* 'short, brief'
> scathe < Old Norse *skaða* 'to hurt, injure, harm, damage'
> score < Old Norse *skor* 'mark, notch, incision' (in Icelandic 'twenty')
> scrap < Old Norse *skrap* 'scraps, trifles'
> scrape < Old Norse *skrapa* 'to scrape, erase, scratch out'
> skill < Old Norse *skil* 'distinction, discernment, ability to make out'
> skull < Old Norse *skalli* 'skull, bald head'

In the Mayan family, a number of languages have borrowed from Cholan (Mayan), since Cholan speakers were the principal bearers of Classic Maya civilization. Cholan, however, underwent a number of sound changes which languages of the other branches of the family did not, and this makes it fairly easy to identify many of these Cholan loans. For example, Cholan underwent the sound change *o: > u. Yucatec did not undergo this sound change, although some borrowings from Cholan into Yucatec show the results of this Cholan change; for example, Yucatec kùts 'turkey'< Cholan kuts (from Proto-Mayan *ko:ts); Yucatec tù:n 'stone, year, stela (monument)' < Cholan tun 'stone' (compare Proto-Mayan *to:ŋ 'stone'). Since these words in Yucatec show the results of a sound change that took place in Cholan but which native Yucatec words did not undergo (compare for example Cholan suts', Yucatec sò:ts' < Proto-Mayan *so:ts' 'bat'), it is clear in these cases that Yucatec borrowed the words and Cholan is the donor language (Justeson et al. 1985: 14).

3.4.1 Morphological complexity

The morphological make-up of words can help determine the direction of borrowing. In cases of borrowing, when the form in question in one language is morphologically complex (composed of two or more morphemes) or has an etymology which is morphologically complex, but the form in the other languages has no morphological analysis, then usually the donor language is the one with the morphologically complex form and the borrower is the one with the monomorphemic form. For example, English *alligator* is borrowed from Spanish *el lagarto* 'the alligator'; since it is monomorphemic in English, but based on two morphemes in Spanish, *el* 'the' + *lagarto* 'alligator', the direction of borrowing must be from Spanish to English. *Crocodile* is similar, ultimately from Greek *krókē* 'pebbles, gravel' + *dreilos* 'worm, dragon'. Latin borrowed it from Greek as *crocodīlus*; English borrowed it from Old French. It is monomorphemic in Latin (and English), but has a polymorphemic etymology in Greek, indicating that the word was borrowed from Greek. *Vinegar* in English is a loan from French *vinaigre*, which is from *vin* 'wine' + *aigre* 'sour'; since its etymology is polymorphemic in French but monomorphemic in English, the direction of borrowing is clearly from French to English. *Slogan* is revealed as a loan from Scottish Gaelic *sluagh-ghairm* 'war-cry'; it is morphologically complex in Gaelic but not in English, from the compound *sluagh* 'army' + *ghairm* 'shout'. Another case is *whisky*, earlier as *whiskybae* in English, from Scottish Gaelic *uisge beatha* 'water of life' (*uisge* 'water' + *bethu* 'life').

Spanish borrowed many words from Arabic, starting in 711, during the period of Moorish domination in Spain (711–1492). Many Arabic loans in Spanish include what was originally the Arabic definite article *al-* but are monomorphemic in Spanish. A few examples of this are:

> albañil 'mason' (Arabic banná 'builder, mason')
> albóndiga 'meat ball' (Arabic bunduq 'bullet, hazelnut')
> alcalde 'mayor' (compare Arabic qāḍī 'judge')

alcoba 'bedroom, alcove' (Arabic *qobbah* 'vault, dome, cupola'; French borrowed its *alcôve* 'alcove, recess, cubicle, niche' from Spanish, and English borrowed *alcove* from French)

alcohol 'alcohol' (Arabic *al-kohl* 'fine powder (used to stain the eyelids)' – obtained by crushing and by heating to high temperatures or distillation; the meaning was extended to include distillation of wine)

algodón 'cotton' (Arabic *qutn, qutun* 'cotton'; English *cotton* is also ultimately from Arabic, borrowed through Old French *coton* 'cotton')

alguacil 'constable, bailiff, peace officer' (Arabic *wazīr* 'minister, vizier, viceroy', also the ultimate source of English *vizier*, from Turkish *vezir* 'counsellor', a loan from Arabic *wazīr*)

almacén 'storehouse' (Arabic *maxzan* singular [plural *maxazīn*] 'storeroom, depository, magazine', derived from *m-* 'nominalizing prefix' + *xazana* 'to store up'; English *magazine* is ultimately from the same source).

Since these are polymorphemic in Arabic, composed of the article *al-* + root, but each is monomorphemic in Spanish, the direction of borrowing is seen to be from Arabic to Spanish.

In another example, frequently the early loans from Spanish into indigenous languages (called *hispanisms*) were based on the Spanish plural forms of nouns, borrowed as singular in meaning. A few examples from some Mayan languages are:

Jakalteko *kaplaš* 'goat' (< Spanish *cabra-s* 'goats' – with *-s* 'PLURAL')
Huastec *pa:tuš*, Tzotzil *patoš* (< Spanish *pato-s* 'ducks'), K'iche' *pataš* (< Spanish *pata-s* 'female ducks') 'duck'
Mocho' *ko:liš* 'cabbage' (< *col-es* 'cabbages', compare *col* 'cabbage')
Chol *wakaš* 'bull, cow', Tojolabal *wakaš* 'cattle, beef' (< *vaca-s* 'cows')
(/š/ = IPA [ʃ] in these examples.)

In sixteenth-century Spanish, the sound represented orthographically as <s> was phonetically [s̺], an apico-alveolar fricative; it was taken by speakers of these indigenous languages as being phonetically closer to their /š/ (IPA [ʃ]) than to their /s/, which accounts for the /š/ seen in these (monomorphemic) borrowings which corresponds to the polymorphemic Spanish plural forms, in *-(e)s*.

This is a very strong criterion, but not fool proof. It can be complicated by cases of folk etymology (see Chapter 4), where a monomorphemic loanword comes to be interpreted as containing more than one morpheme, though originally that was not the case. For example, Old French monomorphemic *crevice* 'crayfish' was borrowed into English and then later replaced by folk etymology with *crayfish*, on analogy with *fish*. Now it appears to have a complex morphological analysis, with *fish* as one of its components, but this is not original. Such cases, however, are rare.

3.4.2 Clues from cognates

When a word in two (or more) languages is suspected of being borrowed, if it has legitimate cognates (with regular sound correspondences; see Chapter 7) across sister languages of one language family, but is found in only one language (or a few languages) of another family, then the donor language is usually one of the languages for which the form in question has cognates in its sister languages. For example, Finnish *tytär* 'daughter' has no cognates in the non-Finnic branches of the Uralic family, while cognates of Proto-Indo-European **dhugh₂ter* 'daughter' are known from most Indo-European languages, including ones as geographically far apart as Sanskrit and English (Sanskrit *duhitṛ* and English *daughter*). Therefore, the direction of borrowing is from one of these Indo-European languages (actually from Baltic) to Finnish.

Spanish and Portuguese have *ganso* 'goose', borrowed from Germanic **gans*; Germanic has cognates, for example German *Gans*, Afrikaans *gans*, English *goose*, from Proto-Germanic **gans-*, but this Spanish and Portuguese word lacks true cognates in most other Romance languages. Rather, they have such things as French *oie*, Italian *oca*, Catalan *oca*, and others reflecting Latin *auca* 'goose'. (Latin also has *ānser* 'goose' which is cognate with Proto-Germanic **gans* 'goose', from Proto-Indo-European **ghans-*; however, this is not the source of Spanish and Portuguese *ganso*, borrowed from Germanic.) Thus, the direction of borrowing is from Germanic to Spanish and Portuguese.

3.4.3 Geographical and ecological clues

The geographical and ecological associations of words suspected of being loans can often provide clues helpful to determining whether they are borrowed and what the identity of the donor language is. For example, the geographical and ecological remoteness from earlier English-speaking territory of *aardvark*, *gnu*, *impala*, and *zebra* – animals found natively only in Africa – makes these words likely candidates for loanwords in English. Indeed, they were borrowed from local languages in Africa with which speakers of European languages came into contact when they entered the habitats where these animals are found – *aardvark* is from Afrikaans *aardvark* (also morphologically complex, *aard* 'earth' + *vark* 'pig'), *gnu* from a Khoe language, *impala* from Zulu, and *zebra* from a Congo language (*zebra* perhaps being borrowed first into Portuguese or Spanish or Italian from an African language and then from one of them borrowed into English).

Nahuatl (the language of the Aztecs and Toltecs) started out in the region of northwestern Mexico and migrated from there into central Mexico and on to Central America. Since cacao (the source of chocolate, cocoa) did not grow in the original Nahuatl desert homeland, the Nahuatl word *kakawa-* 'cacao' is likely to be a loan. Indeed, it was borrowed from Mixe-Zoquean (Proto-Mixe-Zoquean **kakawa* 'cacao'), spoken in the zone from where cacao trees spread in early times. Several other loans in Nahuatl reflect the adoption of names for plants and animals not encountered before the migration into lower Mexico, where previously unknown items endemic to the more tropical climate were encountered. In Nez Perce (a Sahaptian language of the northwestern USA), *lapatá:t* 'potato' is borrowed from Canadian French *la patate*; it is clearly a loan and clearly from French, not only because it is morphologically analysable in French (*la* 'the' + *patate* 'potato') and not in Nez Perce, but also because we know that potatoes were introduced to this area after European contact (Callaghan and Gamble 1997: 111). Knowledge of this history suggests that the term could be a borrowing. Further investigation shows this to be the case, a borrowing from French into Nez Perce.

Inferences from geography and ecology are not as strong as those from the phonological and morphological criteria mentioned above; however, when coupled with other information, the inferences which they provide can be useful.

3.4.4 Other semantic clues

A still weaker kind of inference, related to the last criterion, can sometimes be obtained from the semantic domain of a suspected loan. For example, English words such as *squaw, papoose, powwow, tomahawk, wickiup*, and so on have paraphrases involving 'Indian'/'Native American', that is, 'Indian woman', 'Indian baby', 'Indian house', etc.; this suggests possible borrowing from American Indian languages. Upon further investigation, this supposition proves true; these words are borrowed from Algonquian languages into English. In another example, in Xinkan (a small family of four languages in Guatemala) most terms for cultivated plants are known to be borrowed from Mayan; this being the case, any additional terms in this semantic domain that we encounter may be suspected of also being borrowings. This criterion is only a rough indication of possibilities. Sources for the borrowing must still be sought, and it is necessary to try to determine the exact nature of the loans, if indeed borrowings are involved.

3.5 Loans as Clues to Linguistic Changes in the Past

Evidence preserved in loanwords may help to document older stages of a language before later changes took place. An often-cited example is that of early Germanic loans in Finnish which document older stages in the development of Germanic. These loans bear evidence of things in Germanic which can be reconstructed only with difficulty from the evidence retained in the Germanic languages themselves – some of these reconstructed things are confirmed only through comparisons of Germanic with other branches of Indo-European. For example, Finnish *rengas* 'ring' (borrowed; see Proto-Germanic **hreng-az*) reveals two things about Germanic. First, it documents Germanic at the stage before the sound change of *e* to *i* before *n* (*e > i /__n*) – all attested Germanic languages show only the forms with *i*, the result after this change, as in English *ring*. A comparison of Finnish *rengas* with *kuningas* 'king' (also borrowed from Germanic, Proto-Germanic **kuning-az*) shows that Germanic originally contrasted *i* and *e* in the position before *n*, which is not seen in Germanic after the two sounds merged before *n*. Second, both these loans document the Proto-Germanic ending *-az, suggested by comparative Germanic evidence (but lost in most Germanic languages, seen as -s in Gothic). It is only by confirming *-az through comparisons from other branches of Indo-European (compare the cognates, Latin -us and Greek -os 'NOMINATIVE SINGULAR') and from borrowings such as these from earlier Germanic into Finnish that we can be certain of the Germanic reconstructions.

In another case, some loans in Finnish document Germanic before the umlaut change took place. For example, Finnish *patja* 'mattress' (borrowed from Germanic, see Proto-Germanic *badja* 'bed') documents Germanic before umlaut in which a > e when followed in the next syllable by j or i (as seen in English *bed*, German *Bett* – later the *-ja was lost through a series of changes, *badja* > *bedja* > *bed*). The pre-umlaut stage can be reconstructed from other considerations, in particular in comparisons with cognate words from related languages outside of the Germanic branch of Indo-European. In the umlaut context, words in modern Germanic languages show that they have undergone the change; Gothic is the only Germanic language which did not undergo the umlaut change. The loans which bear evidence of the earlier forms before the changes took place, such as these examples from Finnish, help to confirm the accuracy of the reconstructions.

In another example, Spanish used to contrast bilabial stop *b* and labiodental fricative *v*, although these are fully merged in modern Spanish (though still spelled differently, <b> and <v>, which are no longer distinct phonemes). The stop *b* came from Latin initial *b* and intervocalic *p*, whereas fricative *v* came from late Latin initial *v* and from intervocalic *v* and *b*; these two phonemes, /b/ and /v/, merged in Spanish to the single /b/ of modern Spanish. However, early loanwords from Spanish into American Indian languages (hispanisms) show clearly that the contrast persisted at least long enough to arrive in America, although soon afterwards the merger took place and later hispanisms reflect only the merged sound. In the early hispanisms, /v/ was borrowed typically as *w*, since most Native American languages lacked *v* (*w* being their sound which is nearest phonetically to *v*), whereas the /b/ of earlier Spanish was borrowed as /b/ or /p/, depending on the sounds available in the particular borrowing language which could be considered the closest phonetic equivalent to Spanish *b* in each recipient language. The following are a few early hispanisms in some Mayan languages which show the earlier contrast in Spanish before these sounds later merged. (Here /š/ = IPA [ʃ]; /ṣ̌/ is a retroflex laminal post alveopalatal fricative, equivalent to a retroflexed version of [ʃ]; IPA has no symbol for this sound.) Forms (1–3) show original intervocalic /b/ (borrowed as *p*, *b* or *ɓ*):

1. Spanish *jabón* 'soap' (phonetically [šabón] in the sixteenth century), borrowed as: Chol *šapum*, Huastec *šabuːn*, Q'anjobal *šapon*, Mocho' *šaːpuh*, K'iche' *šɓon*, Tzeltal *šapon*.
2. Spanish *nabo* 'turnip': K'iche' *napuš*, Tzotzil *napuš* (< *nabos* 'turnips', from the Spanish plural form).
3. Spanish *sebo* 'tallow, grease': Q'anjobal *šepuʔ*, K'iche' *šepu*, Tzotzil *šepu*.

Forms (4–6) show original intervocalic /v/ (borrowed as *w* or *v*):

4. *navaja* 'knife, razor': Akateko *nawaš*, Q'anjobal *nawuš*, Chol *ñawašaš*, Tzotzil *navašaš* (< *navaja-s*, 'PLURAL' form in Spanish, in the last two).
5. *clavo* 'nail': Akateko *lawuš*, Chol *lawuš*, K'iche' *klawuš*, Tzeltal *lawuš*, Tojolabal *lawuš* ('nail', 'spur'), Tzotzil *lavuš* (< *clavo-s* 'nails', borrowed from the Spanish plural form).
6. Old Spanish *cavallo* < Latin *cavallus* 'work horse'): Akateko *kawayú* 'horse, beast of burden', Chol *kawayu*, Q'anjobal *kawayo*, Q'eqchi' *kawaːy*, Mocho' *kwaːyuh* 'horse, mule', Tzeltal *kawu*, Tzotzil *kawayú* 'beast of burden'. (Cf. Modern Spanish *caballo* 'horse'.)

These loans demonstrate, first, the distinction between original /b/ and /v/ of Spanish, and, second, the fact that this merger of /b/ and /v/ had not yet taken place in the mid-sixteenth century when these languages began to borrow from Spanish.

Evidence from loanwords can also sometimes contribute to understanding the *relative chronology* of changes in a language (introduced in Chapter 2, and discussed again in Chapter 8). For example, Proto-Indo-European **rēǵ-* 'king' underwent the change of **ē* > **ī* in Proto-Celtic (branch of Indo-European). Then Celtic **rīg-* 'king' was borrowed into pre-Proto-Germanic as **rīg-*. Since Germanic would have inherited Proto-Indo-European **ē* as *ē* (which remained *ē* in Gothic, but later becoming *ā* in the other Germanic languages), this Germanic word has to have been borrowed from a language in which **ē* had become *ī*. Celtic is the only logical candidate for that. Then after the borrowing, the Germanic form underwent Grimm's Law (the voiced stop > voiceless stop part of Grimm's Law), giving Proto-Germanic **rīk-*. From this we establish the relative chronology:

1. First Proto-Indo-European **ē* > *ī* in Proto-Celtic (**rēǵ-* > **rīg-*);
2. then Celtic **rīg-* was borrowed into pre-Proto-Germanic as **rīg-*;
3. and finally, voiced stops > voiceless by Grimm's Law (**rīg-* > **rīk-*) in Germanic.

(Ringe 2009)

In another example, Mocho' (Mayan, Q'anjobalan branch) *čoːŋ* 'to sell' is borrowed from Cholan (a different branch of Mayan, the Cholan subgroup) *čon* (compare Proto-Mayan **koːŋ*). Cholan was the principal language of Classic Maya civilization, and as such contributed numerous loans to languages of the region. (Note that /č/ = IPA [ʧ].) Cholan underwent two changes: **k* > *č* and **ŋ* > *n*, though both original **k* and **ŋ* remained unchanged in Mocho' (as seen, for example, in *koŋob* 'market', which retains the native form, from **koːŋ* 'to sell' + *-oɓ* 'place of, instrumental suffix'). Therefore, loanwords of Cholan origin such as Mocho' *čoːŋ* reveal that in Cholan the change of **k* > *č* took place earlier than the change of **ŋ* > *n*, since from the form of the loan in Mocho' we conclude that Mocho' borrowed *čoːŋ* at the stage when **k* > *č* had already taken place in Cholan, but before Cholan had undergone the change of **ŋ* > *n*. Thus loans such as this one reveal the relative chronology of Cholan changes, first *k > $\check{c}$, followed later by *η > n.

3.6 Calques (Loan Translations, Semantic Loans)

In loanwords, aspects of both the phonetic form and the meaning of the word in the donor language are transferred to the borrowing language, but it is also possible to borrow, in effect, just the meaning, and instances of this are called *calques* or *loan translations*. This is illustrated by the often-repeated example of *black market*, which owes its origin in English to a loan translation of German *Schwarzmarkt*, composed of *schwarz* 'black' and *Markt* 'market'. Other examples follow.

(1) The word for 'railway' ('railroad') is a calque based on a translation of 'iron' + 'road/way' in a number of languages: Finnish *rautatie* (*rauta* 'iron' + *tie* 'road'); French *chemin de fer* and Italian *estrada de ferro* (literally 'road of iron'); German *Eisenbahn* (*Eisen* 'iron' + *Bahn* 'path, road'); Spanish *ferrocarril* (*ferro-* 'iron' in compound words + *carril* 'lane, way'); Swedish *järnväg* (*järn* 'iron' + *väg* 'road'); Irish *iarnród* (*iarn* 'iron' + *ród* 'roadway'); Turkish *demiryolu* (*demir* 'iron' + *yolu* 'way'); etc.

(2) English has a number of early calques based on loan translations from Latin, for example: *almighty* < Old English *ælmihtig*, based on Latin *omnipotēns* (*omni-* 'all' + *potēns* 'powerful, strong'), and *gospel* < *gōdspell* (*gōd* 'good' + *spel* 'news, tidings'), based on Latin *ēvangelium* which is borrowed from Greek *eu-aggelion* 'good-news/message' (<gg> is the normal transliteration for Greek [ŋg]).

(3) A number of languages have calques based on English *skyscraper*, as for example: French *gratte-ciel* (*gratte* 'grate, scrape' + *ciel* 'sky'); German *Wolkenkratzer* (*Wolken* 'clouds' + *kratzer* 'scratcher, scraper'); Spanish *rascacielos* (*rasca* 'scratch, scrape' + *cielos* 'skies, heavens'); and Russian *neboskrebo* (*nebo* 'sky' + *skrebo* 'scraper'); etc.

(4) Some Spanish examples include: *manzana de Adán* 'Adam's apple' in some American varieties of Spanish, a loan translation from the English name (compare Peninsular Spanish *nuez (de la garganta)*, literally 'nut (of the throat)'); *cadena* 'chain' now used also for 'chain of stores'; *estrella* 'star' and now also 'star celebrity, outstanding performer'; *guerra fría* 'cold war'; *tercer mundo* 'Third World'; *aire acondicionado* 'air conditioning'; *desempleo* 'unemployment'; *supermercado* 'supermarket'; etc.

(5) A number of calques are shared widely among the languages of the Mesoamerican linguistic area (see Chapter 10); these translate the semantic equations illustrated in the following: 'boa' = 'deer-snake', 'door' = 'mouth of house', 'egg' = 'bird-stone', 'knee' = 'leg-head', 'lime' = 'stone(-ash)', 'wrist' = 'hand-neck' (Campbell et al. 1986).

3.7 Emphatic Foreignization

Sometimes, speakers go out of their way to make borrowed forms sound even more foreign by substituting sounds which seem to them more foreign than the actual sounds of the donor language in particular loanwords. These examples of further 'foreignization' are somewhat akin to hypercorrection (see Chapter 4), sometimes called also 'hyper-foreignization'. The phenomenon is illustrated in examples such as the frequent pronunciations of *Azerbaijan* and *Beijing* with the somewhat more foreign-sounding *ʒ* and final-syllable stress [azərbaiˈʒan] and [beiˈʒɪŋ], rather than the less exotic but more traditional pronunciation with *ǰ* (IPA [dʒ]), [azərˈbaiǰan] and [beiˈǰɪŋ] (with penultimate stress in the first of these). The English borrowing from French *coup de grace* (literally, 'blow of grace/ hit of grace') is usually rendered without the final *s*, as /ku de gra/, not as /ku de gras/. Many English speakers expect French words spelled with *s* to lack *s* in the pronunciation and so they have extended this to eliminate the /s/ of *grace*, though in French this is pronounced, [gʁas]. Apparently it is also expected that many words of French origin will end in a stressed final /e/ (as in for example *café*, *ballet*, *protégé*), leading to pronunciations in English ending in /ei/, as in for example *lingerie* pronounced as [lɒndʒəˈrei] (compare French [lɛ̃ʒʁi]) and *repartee*, borrowed from French *repartie* 'rejoinder, spirited response' (pronounced in French as /ʁəpɑːʁˈtiː/), sometimes pronounced [ɹəpaɹˈtei] in English.

In borrowings in Finnish slang, sounds which match native Finnish sounds are often replaced with less native-sounding segments; for example, in *bonjata* 'to understand', from Russian *ponjatʲ*, and in *bunga-ta* 'to pay for, to come up with the money for', from Swedish *punga*, the native Finnish sound was further 'foreignized' by the substitution of more foreign-sounding *b*, a sound not found in native Finnish words, for the *p* of the donor languages.

(See Chapter 15 for other examples of how borrowing can contribute to an understanding of the prehistory of peoples. See Chapter 10 for examples and discussion of borrowing of things other than lexical items.)

3.8 Exercises

Exercise 3.1

Find ten examples of loanwords (not already mentioned in this chapter) in any language you like, including English. You can consult dictionaries and websites that give historical sources of lexical items or sources on the history of particular languages, or various websites that deal with loanwords in various languages, if you wish. Try to identify the form and meaning of the word in the donor language.

Exercise 3.2   Loans into English from various languages

In the history of English, large numbers of loans entered the language in earlier times, but many words have also been borrowed more recently, from many different languages. Here are a few examples. Look up twenty of these (or more if you like) either in good dictionary sources for English which indicate where the words come from or in dictionary sources on the language from which particular words are borrowed. Try to determine the original meaning and form in the donor language and note any changes (in meaning or form) that the word has undergone as it was adapted to English. The original meanings of many of these may surprize you.

Chinese: chow mein, dim sum, kowtow, kung fu
Czech: robot
French: boutique, camouflage, chassis, cinema, fuselage, sabotage
German: angst, blitz, flak, Nazi, snorkel, strafe
Hawaiian: aloha, lei, ukulele, wiki
Hebrew: jubilee, kibbutz, messiah
Italian: ciabatta, fascism, pasta, pizza
Japanese: anime, emoji, kamikaze, karaoke, karate, manga,
              Pokémon
Russian: cosmonaut, gulag, intelligentsia, rouble, soviet, sputnik,
              vodka
Spanish: burrito, cilantro, macho, nacho, vanilla
Swedish   (or Scandinavian generally): moped, ombudsman, slalom
Yiddish: klutz, maven, putz, schmooze, tush

Exercise 3.3   Māori and English loanwords

1. Based on the criteria for establishing loanwords and the direction of borrowing, determine from the following lists of words which are borrowed into Māori from English and which are borrowed into English from Māori. Note that Māori has the following inventory of sounds: /p, t, k, ɸ, h, r, m, n, ŋ, r, i, e, a, o, u/. In the traditional orthography, /ɸ/ (voiceless bilabial fricative) is spelled <wh>; /ŋ/ is spelled <ng>. Also, native Māori words permit no consonant clusters, rather only syllables of the shape CV (a single consonant followed by a single vowel), or word-initially also syllables that begin in a vowel (that is, some initial syllables have the shape of just V).

2. Can you say anything about the dialect of English from which Māori took its English loans (based on the pronunciation reflected in the borrowings into Māori)?

3. What can you say about the social or cultural nature of the contact between speakers of Māori and English? Can you identify semantic domains (fields of meaning) most susceptible to borrowing in either of the languages?

4. How were words from one language modified to fit the structure of the other?

1.	hāhi	'church'
2.	haina	'China; sign'
3.	haka	'haka, Māori dance'
4.	haki	'flag' (< Union *Jack*)
5.	hāma	'hammer'
6.	hānara	'sandal'
7.	hāngi	'hangi, oven' (hole in the ground with wrapped food placed on heated stones in the pit with fire)
8.	hānihi	'harness'
9.	hāpa	'harp'
10.	hāte	'shirt'
11.	hēmana	'chairman'
12.	hereni	'shilling'
13.	heti	'shed'
14.	hipi	'sheep'
15.	hiraka	'silk'
16.	hiriwa	'silver'
17.	hoeha	'saucer'
18.	hohipere	'hospital'
19.	hopa	'job'
20.	hōro	'hall'
21.	hū	'shoe'
22.	hui	'meeting for discussion'
23.	huka	'sugar'
24.	hūka	'hook'
25.	hupa	'soup'
26.	hūri	'jury'
27.	iāri	'yard'
28.	ihipa	'Egypt'
29.	ingarangi	'England'
30.	ingarihi	'English'
31.	inihi	'inch'
32.	iota	'yacht'
33.	iwi	'iwi, Māori tribe'
34.	kāka	'cork'
35.	kānara	'colonel'
36.	kapa	'copper, penny'
37.	kāpara	'corporal'
38.	kāpata	'cupboard'
39.	kara	'collar'
40.	karaehe	'grass; glassware, tumbler; class'
41.	karāhi	'glass'
42.	karahipi	'scholarship'
43.	karaka	'clock; clerk'
44.	karauna	'crown'

45.	kāreti	'college; carrot; carriage'
46.	kāta	'cart'
47.	kātaroera	'castor oil'
48.	kātipa	'constable'
49.	kaumātua	'kaumatua, Māori elder'
50.	kauri	'kauri tree'
51.	kāwana	'governor'
52.	kea	'kea' (mountain parrot)
53.	kihi	'kiss'
54.	kirihimete	'Christmas'
55.	kiwi	'kiwi bird'
56.	kōmihana	'commission'
57.	kōti	'court (of law); goat'
58.	kuihipere	'gooseberry'
59.	kūmara	'kumara, sweet potato'
60.	kura	'school'
61.	māhi	'mast'
62.	mana	'mana, influence, prestige'
63.	māori	'Māori, native people' (in Māori *māori* means 'clear, ordinary, native New Zealander')
64.	marae	'marae, enclosed meeting area'
65.	marahihi	'molasses'
66.	moa	'moa' (very large extinct flightless bird)
67.	mokopuna	'mokopuna, grandchild'
68.	motokā	'car, automobile' (< motor car)
69.	nēhi	'nurse'
70.	ngaio	'ngaio, coastal shrub'
71.	ōkiha	'ox'
72.	ōriwa	'olive'
73.	otimira	'oatmeal'
74.	pā	'pa, stockaded village'
75.	pahi	'bus'
76.	paihikara	'bicycle'
77.	paitini	'poison'
78.	pāka	'box'
79.	pākehā	'pakeha, European, non-Māori'
80.	pāmu	'farm'
81.	pāoka	'fork'
82.	parakuihi	'breakfast'
83.	parama	'plumber'
84.	pāua	'paua, abalone shell'
85.	pāuna	'pound'
86.	perakēhi	'pillowcase'
87.	pereti	'plate'
88.	pī	'bee'
89.	pirihi	'priest'

90.	pirihimana	'police(man)'
91.	piriniha	'prince'
92.	piriti	'bridge'
93.	pōkiha	'fox'
94.	pōro	'ball'
95.	pukapuka	'book'
96.	pūkeko	'pukeko, swamp hen'
97.	pune	'spoon'
98.	purū	'blue'
99.	pūru	'bull'
100.	rare	'lolly, sweets'
101.	rata	'doctor'
102.	reme	'lamb'
103.	rērewē	'railroad, railway'
104.	rēwera	'devil'
105.	rīhi	'dish; lease'
106.	rimu	'rimu, red pine'
107.	rōre	'lord' (title)
108.	rori	'road'
109.	takahē	'takahe, bird species' (*Notoris mantelli*)
110.	tana	'ton'
111.	tangi	'tangi, Māori mourning, wailing' (associated with funerals)
112.	tāone	'town'
113.	taonga	'taonga, heritage, Māori treasure, possessions'
114.	tāra	'dollar'
115.	taraiki	'strike'
116.	tauiwi	'tauiwi, non-Māori'
117.	tēpu	'table'
118.	tiā	'jar'
119.	tiaka	'jug'
120.	tiamana	'chairman; German' (cf. hēmana)
121.	tiāti	'judge'
122.	tīhi	'cheese'
123.	tōtara	'totara' (tree species, *Podocarpus totara*)
124.	tui	'tui, parson bird'
125.	waka	'waka, canoe'
126.	wātene	'warden'
127.	weka	'weka, woodhen'
128.	wētā	'weta, large insect species' (*Hemideina megacephala*)
129.	whakapapa	'whakapapa, genealogy'
130.	whānau	'whanau, extended family' (community of close fellows)
131.	whatura	'vulture'
132.	whira	'violin, fiddle'
133.	whīra	'field'

134.	whurū	'flu'
135.	whurutu	'fruit'
136.	whutupaoro	'football' (rugby)
137.	wihara	'whistle'
138.	wīra	'wheel'
139.	wōro	'wall'
140.	wuruhi	'wolf'

Exercise 3.4 Loanwords in Japanese

The following is a list of some of the loanwords into Japanese, primarily from English (though some other European languages may be involved as the source of a few of these).

1. How has Japanese modified the foreign sounds in these loans to fit its phonology?
2. What arguments can you make for particular cases here to show that the direction of borrowing is indeed from English into Japanese? State your evidence.

NOTE: Japanese does not permit syllable-final or word-final consonants other than -*n*; it does not tolerate word-initial or word-final consonant clusters, and medially allows only -*nC*-, though geminates (double consonants) are allowed. In Japanese, /t/ is [ts] before *u*, [č] (IPA [ʧ]) before *i*, and [t] elsewhere; similarly, /s/ is [š] (IPA [ʃ]) before *i*. Japanese has no *l* or *v*, and no *h* before *u* (but has *f* instead of *h* before *u*), and it has no *ə*.

1.	aidoru	'idol' (celebrity)
2.	aisukurīmu	'ice cream'
3.	amachua	'amateur'
4.	bā	'bar'
5.	bāgen	'bargain, sale'
6.	baiburu	'Bible'
7.	baiorin	'violin'
8.	baitaritī	'vitality'
9.	baketsu	'bucket'
10.	barēbōru	'volleyball'
11.	basuketto	'basket'
12.	batā	'butter'
13.	beruto	'belt'
14.	bifuteki	'beefsteak'
15.	bīru	'beer'
16.	bīrusu	'virus' (cf. uirusu)
17.	bitamin	'vitamin'

18.	bōi sukauto	'Boy Scout'
19.	borantia	'volunteer'
20.	bōru	'ball'
21.	boru	'bowl' (stadium)
22.	borutto	'bolt' (headed metal pin)
23.	burajā	'bra' (< brassiere)
24.	burausu	'blouse'
25.	buresuretto	'bracelet'
26.	burondo	'blond'
27.	chātā	'charter'
28.	chansu	'chance'
29.	gyamburu	'gamble'
30.	gyaroppu	'gallop'
31.	hādo-weā	'hardware' (computer)
32.	hambāgā	'hamburger'
33.	handoru	'handle, steering wheel'
34.	herumetto	'helmet'
35.	hotto doggu	'hotdog'
36.	hyūzu	'fuse'
37.	indekkusu	'index'
38.	īsuto	'yeast'
39.	jakketto	'jacket'
40.	jampā	'jumper'
41.	jigu-zagu	'zigzag'
42.	jīnzu	'jeans'
43.	jippā	'zipper'
44.	kādo	'card'
45.	kāru	'curl'
46.	kōhī	'café, coffee'
47.	komāsharu	'commercial'
48.	kompyūta	'computer'
49.	kurabu	'club'
50.	kyabetsu	'cabbage'
51.	kyampu	'camp'
52.	kyandī	'candy'
53.	kyaputen	'captain' (chief, leader)
54.	manējā	'manager'
55.	membā	'member'
56.	miruku	'milk'
57.	mishin	'sewing machine'
58.	morutaru	'mortar'
59.	myūjikaru	'musical' (play)
60.	napukin	'napkin'
61.	nattsu	'nut'
62.	nikkeru	'nickel'
63.	nyūsu	'news'

64.	ōba	'overcoat'
65.	ōbun	'oven'
66.	ōkē	'OK'
67.	ōkesutora	'orchestra'
68.	omuretsu	'omelette'
69.	oribu	'olive(s)'
70.	painappuru	'pineapple'
71.	paionia	'pioneer'
72.	panchi	'punch' (fruit punch) (cf. also ponchi, ponsu)
73.	panfuretto	'pamphlet'
74.	pantsu	'underpants, shorts, drawers'
75.	pāsento	'percent'
76.	pasupōto	'passport'
77.	pātī	'party'
78.	paturōru	'patrol'
79.	pēsuto	'paste'
80.	pikunikku	'picnic'
81.	pisutoru	'pistol'
82.	poketto	'pocket'
83.	posutā	'poster'
84.	posuto	'mailbox, post box'
85.	purasuchikku	'plastic'
86.	rādo	'lard'
87.	raifuru	'rifle'
88.	rajiētā	'radiator'
89.	rajio	'radio'
90.	rantan	'lantern'
91.	rejisutā	'register'
92.	rekōdo	'record'
93.	repōto	'report'
94.	resuringu	'wrestling'
95.	retasu	'lettuce'
96.	risuto	'list'
97.	rizōto	'resort'
98.	rosuto chikin	'roast chicken'
99.	sākasu	'circus'
100.	sararī	'salary'
101.	sāroin	'sirloin'
102.	shaberu	'shovel'
103.	shatsu	'shirt' (cf. waishatsu 'dress shirt' < white shirt)
104.	shiroppu	'syrup'
105.	shisutā	'sister'
106.	shīzun	'season'
107.	shōru	'shawl'
108.	sokkusu	'socks'
109.	suchimu	'steam'

110.	suchuwādesu	'stewardess' (aeroplane)
111.	sukurīn	'screen' (movie screen)
112.	sukyandaru	'scandal'
113.	sukāto	'skirt'
114.	sumāto	'smart' (fashionable)
115.	supaisu	'spice'
116.	supīkā	'speaker' (loud speaker)
117.	supurē	'spray'
118.	supurinkurā	'sprinkler'
119.	surakkusu	'slacks'
120.	surangu	'slang'
121.	surōgan	'slogan'
122.	sutā	'star' (film star)
123.	sutairu	'style'
124.	sutēki	'steak'
125.	sutenresu	'stainless steel'
126.	sutōbu	'stove' (heating stove)
127.	sutoraiki	'strike' (by employees)
128.	sutoraiku	'strike' (in baseball)
129.	sūtsukēsu	'suitcase'
130.	sutsūru	'stool'
131.	tairu	'tile'
132.	taiya	'tire'
133.	tēburu	'table'
134.	terebi(jon)	'television'
135.	torakku	'truck'
136.	torikku	'trick'
137.	tōsuto	'toast'
138.	tsuīdo	'tweed'
139.	ueitoresu	'waitress'
140.	uesuto	'waist'
141.	uīkuendo	'weekend'
142.	uinku	'wink'
143.	uirusu	'virus' (cf. bīrusu)
144.	wain	'wine'
145.	wakuchin	'vaccine'
146.	wanisu	'varnish'
147.	yādo	'yard (measure)'
148.	yotto	'yacht'
149.	yunifōmu	'uniform'

4

ANALOGICAL CHANGE

They have been at a great feast of languages, and stolen the scraps.

(Shakespeare [1564–1616],

Love's Labour's Lost V, 1, 39)

4.1 Introduction

Sound change, borrowing, and analogy have traditionally been considered the three most important (most basic) types of linguistic change. In spite of the importance of analogy, linguistics textbooks seem to struggle when it comes to offering a clear definition. Some do not even bother, but just begin straight away by presenting examples of analogical change. Some of the definitions of analogy that have been offered run along the following lines: analogy is change modelled on the example of other words or forms; analogy is a linguistic process involving generalization of a relationship from one set of conditions to another set of conditions; and analogy is a historical process which projects a generalization from one set of expressions to another. Arlotto (1972: 130), recognizing the problem of offering an adequate definition, gives what he calls 'a purposely vague and general definition': '[analogy] is a process whereby one form of a language becomes more like another with which it is somehow associated'. The essential element in all these definitions, vague and inadequate though this may sound, is that *analogical change involves a relation of similarity* (compare Anttila 1989: 88).

In analogical change, one pattern or piece of the language changes to become more like another pattern or piece of the language, where speakers perceive the changing part as similar to the pattern or piece that it changes to be more like. Analogy is sometimes described as 'internal borrowing', the idea being that in analogical change a language may 'borrow' influence from some of its own pieces to change other pieces to make them more similar.

For the Neogrammarians, sound change was considered regular, borrowings needed to be identified, and analogy was, in effect, everything else that was left over. That is, almost everything that was not regular sound change or borrowing was considered analogy. Analogy became the default (or wastebasket) category of changes. Some scholars do not find this very satisfying. Some see analogy as mostly only about changes in morphological paradigms (see for example Bybee 2015: 93); Robert Blust (personal communication) would limit analogy to only cases of proportional analogy (described below). The definition of proportional analogy is not vague like those offered for analogy in general, and, indeed, many of the other kinds of analogy discussed below are also in fact proportional.

Unsatisfying though the traditional broad concept of analogy may be, here we nevertheless consider the wider range of things that have traditionally been considered kinds of analogical change.

In spite of vague definitions, analogy is rather straightforward and is easily understood through examples, to which we now turn. We will look into the main kinds of analogical change, though let's start with one that is less commonly talked about: examples of analogical changes involving spelling.

The *s* of *island* was not originally part of the word, but was added to the spelling of it on analogy with *isle*, a word with a different origin. 'Island' in Old English was *igland*, which became *iland* with sound change. The spelling was modified to add the *s* in the sixteenth century, influenced by the spelling of *isle*. *Island* is a Germanic word; *isle*, however, is borrowed from early French *isle* 'island' (inherited from Latin *insula* 'island'). After English borrowed *isle*, French lost the *s* in sound change, now spelling the word as *île* in Modern French; English also lost the *s* from pronunciation but kept the old *s* in the spelling of *isle* ([ail]). Thus, *island* and *isle* are from entirely different sources, but by analogy with *isle*, *island* was influenced to add an *s* to its spelling, though no *s* was ever pronounced in this word.

In another example, the *l* in the spelling of *could* was also added by analogy. The past tense of *will* was *would* and that of *shall* was *should*, where the *l* of *would* and *should* was inherited as part of the root. *Could*, however, comes from *can*, whose past tense in Old English was *cuðe* (the *ð* was pronounced like 'th' in *this*), from the infinitive *cunnan* 'to be able'. We would expect *cunðe* for its past tense, but *n* was lost before fricative sounds (*s*, *f*, *ð*, etc.), *cunðe* > *cuðe* > /kud/, to which *l* was added in spelling (but not in pronunciation) due to the analogy with the spelling of *would* and *should*. (We see other examples of this loss of *n* before the fricatives in *us* from *uns* (compare German *uns* 'us'), *goose* (from Proto-Germanic **gans* 'goose', compare *gander*, cf. German *gans* 'goose'), *tooth* (from Proto-Germanic **tanþ* 'tooth', see Swedish *tand* 'tooth'), and so on.)

A straightforward example of a common sort of analogy involves the history of *sorry*. Originally, *sorry* and *sorrow* were quite distinct, but in its history *sorry* changed under influence from *sorrow* to become more similar to it. *Sorry* is from the adjective form of *sore*, Old English *sārig* 'sore, pained, sensitive' (derived from the Old English noun *sār* 'sore'). The original *ā* of *sārig* changed to *ō* in a regular sound change but then was shortened to *o* under influence from *sorrow* (Old English *sorh* 'grief, deep sadness, regret'), which had no historical connection to *sorry*.

In this chapter, we explore the different types of analogical changes and the role of analogy in traditional treatments of linguistic change, and we see how analogy interacts with sound change and to a more limited extent with grammatical change.

Some equate analogical change with morphological change, though this is misleading. While it is true that many analogical changes involve changes in morphology, not all do, and many changes in morphology are not analogical. In this book, aspects of morphological change are seen not only in this chapter, but also in Chapters 2, 7, 10, and 11.

4.2 Proportional Analogy

Traditionally, analogical changes are discussed as being either *proportional* or *non-proportional*, although the distinction is not always clear or relevant. Proportional analogical changes are those which can be represented in an equation of the form, a : b = c : x, where one solves for 'x' – a is to b as c is to what? (x = 'what?') For example: *ride* : *rode* = *dive* : x, where in this instance x is solved with *dove*. In this analogical change, the original past tense of *dive* was *dived*, but it changed to *dove* in North American English under analogy with the class of verbs which behave like *drive* : *drove*, *ride* : *rode*, *write* : *wrote*, *strive* : *strove*, and so on. (Today, both *dived* and *dove* are considered acceptable in Standard English, though the use of these forms varies regionally; *dove* is most common in North America but rare elsewhere, where it remains *dived*.) The four-term analogy of the form a : b = c : x is also sometimes presented in other forms, for example as: *a : b :: c : x*; or as:

$$\frac{a}{c} = \frac{b}{x}$$

Not all cases considered to involve proportional analogies can be represented easily in this proportional formula. In the end, the distinction between proportional and non-proportional analogy may not be especially important, so long as the general notion of analogy is understood. Many of the types of analogy discussed in this chapter can be viewed as cases of proportional analogy.

Let us consider some examples of four-part proportional analogy, which will make the concept clearer.

(1) A famous example comes from Otto Jespersen's observation of a Danish child 'who was corrected for saying *nak* instead of standard and expected *nikkede* 'nodded', [and] immediately retorted "stikker, stak, nikker, nak," thus showing on what analogy he had formed the new preterit' (Jespersen 1964: 131). That is, the child produced the proportional formula: *stikker* 'sticks' : *stak* 'stuck' = *nikker* 'nods' : *nak* 'nodded'.

(2) In English a number of verbs with the pattern of *sweep/swept*, where the past tense illustrates vowel shortening before consonant clusters (seen in Chapter 2), have changed by analogy to the regular verbs (so-called 'weak' verb pattern) such as *seep/seeped*, *heap/heaped*, etc. that do not have a different vowel in the past tense form that differs from that of the present tense form. In some cases the past

tense with the shorter vowel has been lost; in others both forms of the past tense still remain as alternates in the language, though in some cases these are now infrequent. Some examples are: *dreamed* (with *dreamt*), *kneeled* (with now infrequent *knelt*), *leaped* (with *leapt*), *weeped* (with *wept*), and *creeped* (with *crept*) (but only *creeped someone out* now, not ✗ *crept someone out*).

(3) In English, the pattern of the verb *speak/spoke/spoken* ('present tense'/'past tense'/'past participle') developed through remodelling on analogy with verbs of the pattern *break/broke/broken*. In Old English, the forms of the verb 'to speak' were *sprec/spræc/gesprecen* (and compare the *spake* 'past tense' of Early Modern English with present-day *spoke*).

(4) Finnish formerly had *laksi* 'bay, gulf (NOMINATIVE SINGULAR)'; its possessive form ('GENITIVE SINGULAR') was *lahde-n*, just as words such as *kaksi* (NOMINATIVE SINGULAR) : *kahde-n* (GENITIVE SINGULAR) 'two'. However, under the weight of other Finnish words with a different nominative–genitive pattern, as in *lehti* : *lehde-n* 'leaf', *tähti* : *tähde-n* 'star', the *laksi* NOMINATIVE SINGULAR of 'bay' changed to *lahti*, as in the proportional formula: *lehden : lehti :: lahden : lahti* (< *laksi*). The past tense form of the verb 'to leave' had the same fate: originally the pattern was *lähte-* 'leave' : *läksi* 'left', but this alternation was shifted by the same analogical pattern to give *lähti* 'left' (PAST TENSE) in Standard Finnish.

(5) An example of proportional analogical change that involves more grammar is found in some Spanish dialects in the non-standard pronoun pattern called *laísmo*. Standard Spanish has distinct masculine and feminine third person pronominal direct object forms, but the indirect object pronominal forms do not distinguish gender, as in:

> *lo vi* 'I saw him' [him I.saw], *la vi* 'I saw her' [her I.saw]
> *le di* 'I gave him/her (something)' [him/her I.gave].

In the dialects with *laísmo*, the change created a gender distinction in the indirect object pronoun forms by analogy that matched the gender contrast in the direct object pronouns, adding *la* for feminine third person pronominal in direct objects:

> *le di* 'I gave him (something)', ***la*** *di* 'I gave her (something)'.

The proportional analogy in the formula would be:

> *lo vi* 'I saw him' : *la vi* 'I saw her' :: *le di* 'I gave him (something) : x

where x is solved for *la di* 'I gave her (something).'

(6) Proto-Nahua had a single verbal prefix to signal reflexives, **mo-*, still the basic pattern in a majority of the modern varieties of Nahua, as in Pipil *ni-**mu**-miktia* 'I kill myself', *ti-**mu**-miktia-t* 'we kill ourselves', and ***mu**-miktia* 'he/she kills himself/herself'. However, on analogy with the subject pronominal verbal prefixes (*ni-* 'I', *ti-* 'we', and so on), Classical Nahuatl has created distinct reflexive pronouns, *-no-* 'myself', *-to-* 'ourselves', and *(-)mo-* 'himself/herself', as in: *ni-**no**-miktia* 'I kill myself', *ti-**to**-miktiaʔ* 'we kill ourselves', and ***mo**-miktia* 'he/she kills himself/herself'.

4.3 Analogical Levelling

Many of the proportional analogical changes are instances of analogical levelling. (Numerous others are extensions; see below.) Analogical levelling reduces
the number of allomorphs a form has; it makes paradigms more uniform. In
analogical levelling, forms which formerly underwent alternations (had more
allomorphs) no longer do so after the change.

(1) For example, in English the former 'comparative' and 'superlative' forms
of *old* have been levelled from the earlier pattern *old/elder/eldest* to the non--
alternating pattern *old/older/oldest*. Here, *o* had been fronted by umlaut due to the
presence of a front vowel in the second syllable of *elder* and *eldest*, but the effects
of umlaut were levelled out, to modern *old/older/oldest*. Now the words *elder* and
eldest remain only in restricted contexts, not as the regular 'comparative' and
'superlative' forms of *old*.

(2) There are numerous cases throughout the history of English in which strong
verbs (with stem alternations, as in *sing/sang/sung* or *write/wrote/written*) have been
levelled to weak verbs (with a single stem form and *-ed* or an equivalent for 'past'
and 'past participle', as in *bake/baked/baked* or *live/lived/lived*). Thus *cleave/clove/*
cloven (or *cleft*) 'to part, divide, split' has become *cleave/cleaved/cleaved* for most
speakers, while *strive/strove/striven* for many speakers has changed to *strive/strived/*
strived. (*Strive* is a borrowing from Old French *estriver* 'to quarrel, contend', but
came to be a strong verb early in its history in English, now widely levelled to a
weak verb pattern.)

(3) Some English strong verbs have shifted from one strong verb pattern to
another, with the result of a partial levelling. For example, in earlier English the
'present'/'past'/'past participle' of the verb *to bear* was equivalent to *bear/bare/*
born(e), and *break* was *break/brake/broke(n)*. They have shifted to the *fight/fought/*
fought, *spin/spun/spun* pattern, where the root of the 'past' and 'past participle'
forms is now the same, *bear/bore/born(e)*, and *break/broke/broken*.

(4a) *Near* was originally a 'comparative' form, meaning 'nearer', but it became
the basic form meaning 'near'. If the original state of affairs had persisted for
'near'/'nearer'/'nearest', we should have had *nigh/near/next*, from Old English
nēah 'near'/*nēarra* 'nearer'/*nēahsta* 'nearest'. However, this pattern was levelled
out; *nearer* was created in the sixteenth century, then *nearest* substituted for *next*.
Both *nigh* and *next* remained in the language, but with more limited, shifted meanings, not as the comparative and superlative forms of *near*.

(4b) Similarly, *far* was also comparative in origin (originally meaning 'farther'),
but this became the basic form meaning 'far', which then gave rise to the new
comparative *farrer*, which was replaced by *farther* under the influence of *further*
'more forward, more onward, before in position'.

(4c) The pattern *late/later/latest* is also the result of an analogical levelling
without which we would have had instead the equivalent of *late/latter/last*, with
the 'comparative' from Old English *lætra* and the 'superlative' from Old English
latost. (In this case, *later* replaced *latter*, which now remains only in restricted
meaning; and *last*, though still in the language, is no longer the 'superlative'
of *late*.)

(5) In Greek, *k^w became *t* before *i* and *e*, but became *p* in most other environments. By regular sound change, then, the verb 'to follow' in Greek (from Proto-Indo-European *sek^w-'to follow') should have resulted in forms such as: *hépomai* 'I follow', *hétēi* 'you follow', *hétetai* 'he/she/it follows' (*s > *h* in Greek). However, by analogy, the *p* (from original *k^w before *o* in this case) spread throughout the paradigm, levelling all the forms of 'to follow': *hépomai* 'I follow', *hépēi* 'you follow', *hépetai* 'he/she/it follows' (Beekes 1995: 73).

(6) Many verbs which have the same form in the singular and plural in Modern German once had different vowels, which were levelled by analogy. Thus, for example, Martin Luther (1483–1546) still wrote *er bleyb* 'he stayed'/*sie blieben* 'they stayed' and *er fand* 'he found'/*sie funden* 'they found', where Modern German has *er blieb/sie blieben* and *er fand/sie fanden* for these (Polenz 1977: 84).

4.4 Analogical Extension

Analogical extension extends the already existing alternation of some pattern to new forms which did not formerly undergo the alternation. An example of analogical extension is seen in the case mentioned above of *dived* being replaced by *dove* in North American English on analogy with the 'strong' verb pattern as in *drive/drove*, *ride/rode*, and so on, an extension of the alternating pattern of the strong verbs. Other examples follow.

(1) Modern English *wear/wore*, which is now in the strong verb pattern, was historically a weak verb which changed by extension of the strong verb pattern, as seen in earlier English *werede* 'wore', which would have become modern *weared* if it had survived.

(2) Other examples in English include the development of the non-standard past tense forms which show extension to the strong verb pattern which creates alternations that formerly were not there, as in: *squeeze/squoze* (Standard *squeeze/squeezed*) and *arrive/arrove* (Standard English *arrive/arrived*).

(3) In some Spanish verbs, *e* (unstressed) alternates with *ie* (when in stressed positions), as in *pensár* 'to think', *piénso* 'I think'. In some rural dialects, this pattern of alternation is sometimes extended to verbs which formerly had no such alternating pairs, for example: *aprendér* 'to learn'/*apriéndo* 'I learn', where Standard Spanish has *aprendér* 'to learn'/*apréndo* 'I learn'. Others include *compriendo* 'I understand' for *comprendo*, *aprieto* 'I tighten' for *apreto*. This also extends to such forms as *diferiencia* for *diferencia* 'difference'.

(4) Where Standard Spanish has no alternation in the vowels in forms such as *créa* 'he/she creates'/*creár* 'to create', many Spanish dialects undergo a change which neutralizes the distinctions between *e* and *i* in unstressed syllables, resulting in alternating forms as seen in *créa* 'he/she creates'/*criár* 'to create'. This alternation has been extended in some dialects to forms which would not originally have been subject to the neutralization. Thus, for example, on analogy with forms of the *créa/criár* type, illustrated again in *menéa* 'he/she stirs'/*meniár* 'to stir', some verbs which originally did not have the same stress pattern have shifted to this pattern, as seen in dialectal *cambéa* 'he/she changes'/*cambiár* 'to change', replacing Standard Spanish *cámbia* 'he/she changes'/*cambiár* 'to change'; *vacéo* 'I empty'/

vaciár 'to empty', replacing Standard Spanish *vácio* 'I empty'/*vaciár* 'to empty'. (Stress is indicated in these words here although no stress is marked in them in standard spelling.)

In both analogical levelling and analogical extension the speaker is making some patterns in the language more like other patterns that exist in the language.

4.5 The Relationship between Analogy and Sound Change

The relationship between sound change and analogy is captured reasonably well by the slogan (sometimes called 'Sturtevant's paradox') *sound change is regular and causes irregularity; analogy is irregular and causes regularity* (Anttila 1989: 94). That is, a regular sound change can create alternations, or variant allomorphs. For example, umlaut was a regular sound change in which back vowels were fronted due to the presence of a front vowel or glide in a later syllable, as in *brother* + *-en* > *brethren* (where *-en* was 'plural'). As a result of this regular sound change, the root for 'brother' came to have two variants, *brother* and *brethr-*. Earlier English had many alternations of this sort. However, an irregular analogical change later created *brothers* as the plural form, on analogy with the non-alternating singular/plural pattern in such nouns as *sister/sisters*. This analogical change is irregular in that it applied only now and then, here and there, to individual alternating forms, not across the board to all such alternations at the same time. This analogical change in the case of *brethren* in effect resulted in undoing the irregularity created by the sound change, leaving only a single form, *brother*, as the root in both the singular and plural forms; that is, analogy levelled out the alternation left behind by the regular sound change (*brethren* survives only in a restricted context with specialized meaning).

It should be noted that although analogical changes are usually not regular processes (which would occur whenever their conditions/environments are found), they can sometimes be regular.

A more complicated but informative example is seen in Table 4.1. (See also section 2.7.4 in Chapter 2.)

TABLE 4.1: Latin rhotacism and the interaction of analogy with sound change

Stage 1: Latin before 400BC		
honōs 'honour'	labōs 'labour'	nominative singular
honōsem	labōsem	accusative singular
honōsis	labōsis	genitive singular
Stage 2: rhotacism: s > r /V__V		
honōs	labōs	nominative singular
honōrem	labōrem	accusative singular
honōris	labōris	genitive singular
Stage 3: after 200BC, analogical reformation of nominative singular		
honor	labor	nominative singular
honōrem	labōrem	accusative singular
honōris	labōris	genitive singular

In this example, the regular sound change of rhotacism (s > r / V__V) in Stage 2 created allomorphy (*honōs/honōr-*), that is, it introduced irregularity into the paradigm. Later, irregular analogy changed *honōs* and *labōs* (nominative singular forms) to *honor* and *labor*, both now ending in *r*, matching the *r* of the rest of the forms in the paradigm. Thus irregular analogy has regularized the form of the root, eliminating the allomorphic alternations involving the final consonant of the root that were created by the regular sound change of rhotacism.

4.6 Immediate and Non-immediate Analogical Models

It is common to distinguish between *immediate models* and *non-immediate models* for some analogical changes. These models have to do with the place in the language where we find the 'relation of similarity' which is behind the analogical change. Cases involving *non-immediate models* are, like those of the Latin *labōs* > *labor* of Table 4.1, due to the influence of whole classes of words or paradigms which in actual connected speech do not normally occur in the near vicinity of the form that changes. In a case such as *honōs* > *honor* under analogy with other forms in the paradigm, such as *honōrem, honōris*, and so on, in normal discourse these forms would not typically occur adjacent to (or close to) one another. For the majority of analogical changes no immediate model exists, but rather the model is a class of related forms.

An *immediate model* refers to a situation in which the 'relation of similarity' upon which the analogical change is based is found in the same speech context as the thing that changes. This refers to instances where the thing that changes and the thing that influences it to change are immediately juxtaposed to one another or are located very near each other in speech. Thus, analogical changes based on an immediate model are typically found in frequently recited routines, such as sequences of basic numbers, days of the week, or months of the year, or in phrases used so frequently they can almost be taken as a unit, sometimes called formulaic language. For example, month names are frequently said together in sequence; as a result, for many English speakers, because of the immediate model of *January*, *February* has changed to *Febuary* [fɛbjuwɛɹi], becoming more like *January* [dʒænju-wɛɹi]. Some dialects go even further, changing *January* to '*Jenuary*' on analogy to the first vowel of following *February*.

(1) In English, *female* ['fimeil] was earlier *femelle* [fɛˈmɛl]; however, in the immediate model of *male and female*, frequently uttered together, the earlier *femelle* (the Middle English form) changed to *female* to be more similar to *male*.

(2) Modern Spanish has the following days of the week which end in *s*: *lunes* 'Monday', *martes* 'Tuesday', *miércoles* 'Wednesday', *jueves* 'Thursday', *viernes* 'Friday'; however, *lunes* and *miércoles* come from forms which originally lacked any final *s*, but took it by analogy to other day names which ended in *s* in this immediate context where the days of the week are commonly recited as a list. The Spanish day names are derived from shortened versions of the Latin names which originally contained *dies* 'day', as in the following, where the last sound in these compounds reveals which forms contained the original final *s* and which lacked it: Spanish *lunes* < Latin *dies lunae* 'moon's day' [no final -*s*], *martes* < *dies*

martis 'Mars' day', *miercoles* < *dies mercurī* 'Mercury's day' [no final *-s*], *jueves* < *dies jovis* 'Jupiter's day', *viernes* < *dies veneris* 'Venus' day'.

(3) Many examples of analogical changes based on an immediate model are found in numbers. For example, (1) Proto-Indo-European had *k^wetwor-* 'four', *$penk^w$e-* 'five'; *p became *f in Germanic by Grimm's law, and *k^w should have become *h^w, but we get *four* (with *f*, not expected *whour*) by influence from the *f* of following *five*. (2) In some Greek dialects, the sequence *hepta* 'seven', *oktō* 'eight' has become *hepta, hoktō*; in others, *oktō* has become *optō* 'eight', becoming more like the preceding *hepta* 'seven'. (3) In Slavic, originally 'nine' began with *n-* and 'ten' with *d-*, but they shifted so that 'nine' now begins with *d-*, making it more similar to following 'ten', as in Russian *d'ev'at'* 'nine' (< Proto-Indo-European *newn̥*), *d'es'at'* 'ten'(< Proto-Indo-European *dekm̥*).

The numbers in several Mayan languages illustrate this tendency for numbers counted in sequence to influence one another, as immediate models for analogical change. For example, Poqomchi' numbers have come to have the same vowel in *kiʔi:ɓ* 'two', *iŝi:ɓ* 'three', *kixi:ɓ* 'four', from earlier forms with distinct vowels: Proto-K'ichean *kaʔi:ɓ* 'two', *oŝi:ɓ* 'three', *kaxi:ɓ* 'four'. In Q'eqchi', 'ten' has been influenced by 'nine': *beleheb* 'nine', *laxe:b* 'ten', from Proto-K'ichean *be:lexeɓ* 'nine', *laxux̱* 'ten'. The Proto-Mayan forms *waq-* 'six' and *huq-* 'seven' have influenced each other in several Mayan languages: for example, the *w* of 'six' has influenced 'seven' to take *w* instead of its original *h*, as seen in Teco *wu:q* 'seven' and Tzotzil *wuk* 'seven'.

(4) An often-repeated example from Latin is Cicero's *senātī populīque Romanī* 'of the Roman senate and people', where *senātūs* 'senate (GENITIVE SINGULAR)' is expected. In this case, different noun classes are involved, which had different 'genitive singular' forms:

'NOMINATIVE SINGULAR':	animus 'soul, heart'	senātus 'senate'
'GENITIVE SINGULAR':	animī	senātūs

The *senātus* class was small, and only a few nouns belonged to it. The class to which *animus* belonged was much larger. A frequent phrase, in the nominative case, was *senātus populusque romanus* 'the Roman senate and people' (the clitic *-que* means 'and'). When Cicero put it in the genitive case, he did not say the expected *senātūs* 'senate (GENITIVE SINGULAR)', but *senātī* based on the immediate model of *populī* 'people (GENITIVE SINGULAR)' in this phrase (see Paul 1920: 106).

4.7 Other Kinds of Analogy

Many different kinds of change are typically called analogy; some of these have little in common with one other. It is important to have a general grasp of these various kinds of changes which are all lumped together under the general heading of analogy, for these terms are used frequently in historical linguistic works. As pointed out above, the proportional analogical changes which involve levelling and extension, though often irregular, can in some instances be regular and systematic. Most of the other kinds of analogy are mainly irregular and sporadic (and many of these can be interpreted as proportional, too). There is nothing particularly compelling about the classification of kinds of analogical changes given here. The names are standard, but one type is not necessarily fully distinct from another, so that some examples of analogical changes may fit more than one of these kinds of change.

4.7.1 Hypercorrection

Hypercorrection involves awareness of different varieties of speech which are attributed different social status. An attempt to change a form in a less prestigious variety to make it conform with how it would be pronounced in a more prestigious variety sometimes results in overshooting the target and coming up with what is an erroneous outcome from the point of view of the prestige variety being mimicked. That is, hypercorrection is the attempt to correct things which are in fact already correct and which already match the form in the variety being copied, resulting in overcorrection and thus getting the form wrong.

(1) Some English dialects in the western United States have: *lawnd* < *lawn*; *pawnd* (*shop*) < *pawn*; *drownd* (present tense)/*drownded* (past tense) < *drown*/*drowned*; and *acrost* (or *acrossed*) < *across*. These changes came about by hypercorrection in an overzealous attempt to undo the effects of final consonant cluster simplification found to one extent or another in most varieties of English, for example the loss of final *d* after *n*, as in *han'* for *hand* (common, for example, in *han(d)made*, *han(d) grenade* [often pronounced [hæŋɡrəneid], etc.); *fin'* for *find*; *roun'* for *round*; and loss of final *t* after *s* in consonant clusters, as in *firs'* for *first* (for example, in *firs(t)born*, *firs(t) person*, *firs(t) base*) and *las'* for *last* (as in *las(t) night*, *las(t) day*, *las(t) thing*).

(2) The frequently heard instances in English of things like *for you and **I*** for what in Standard English is *for you and **me*** involve hypercorrection. Schoolteachers have waged war on the non-standard use of *me* in subject positions, in instances such as ***me** and Jimmy watched 'Star Trek'* and ***me** and him ate popcorn*, and such like. Speakers, in attempting to correct cases such as these to *I*, sometimes go too far and hypercorrect instances of *me* to *I* that are direct or indirect objects and thus correctly have ***me*** in Standard English, as in *Maggie gave it to Kerry and **I*** or *Captain Kirk saved Spock and **I** from Klingons* (where Standard English requires *Maggie gave it to Kerry and **me*** and *Captain Kirk saved Spock and **me** from Klingons*).

(3) Some English dialects in the southern United States have *umbrellow* for 'umbrella' and *pillow* for 'pillar', a hypercorrection based on the less prestigious pronunciations of words such as *fella* and *yella*, changing to match to more formal (more prestigious) *fellow* and *yellow*.

(4) In many rural Spanish dialects, *d* before *r* has changed to *g* (d > g / __r), as in: *magre* 'mother' (< *madre*), *pagre* 'father' (< *padre*), *piegra* 'stone' (< *piedra*), *Pegro* 'Pedro'. Sometimes speakers of these dialects attempt to change these *gr* pronunciations to match the standard and prestigious *dr* counterpart; however, in doing this, they sometimes hypercorrect by changing instances of *gr* to *dr* where the standard language in fact does have *gr*, as for example *suedros* 'parents-in-law', where Standard Spanish has *suegros*, and *sadrado* 'sacred' instead of Standard Spanish *sagrado*.

(5) Standard Finnish has /d/, but many regional dialects do not; several have /r/ instead. An attempt to correct dialectal *suren* 'wolf (ACCUSATIVE SINGULAR)' to Standard Finnish *suden* would work out well through the replacement of dialect *r* by standard *d*. However, this sort of substitution leads to some hypercorrections such as *suuden* 'big' (ACCUSATIVE SINGULAR) where Standard Finnish actually does have /r/, *suuren* (Ravila 1966: 57).

(6) In regional dialects of Spanish, *f* has become *x* (a velar fricative) before *u*, and this leads to the following sorts of hypercorrections, since the standard language preserves *f* in these cases before *u* followed by another vowel (the historical *f* > *x* in other contexts in Standard Spanish), but Standard Spanish also has other legitimate instances of *xu* as well (where [x] is spelled in Spanish with <j>): non-standard *fueves* < Standard *jueves* 'Thursday', *fuicioso* < *juicioso* 'judicious', *fugo* < *jugo* 'juice'.

4.7.2 Folk etymology (popular etymology)

We could think of folk etymologies as cases where linguistic imagination finds meaningful associations in the linguistic forms which were not originally there and, on the basis of these new associations, either the original form ends up being changed somewhat or new forms based on the new associations are created.

(1) An often-cited example is that of English *hamburger*, whose true etymology is from German *Hamburg* + *-er*, 'someone or something from the city of Hamburg'. While hamburgers are not made of 'ham', speakers have folk-etymologized *hamburger* as having something to do with *ham* and on this basis have created such new forms as *cheeseburger, chilliburger, fishburger, veggieburger* or *veggie burger*, and so on.

(2) In Spanish, *vagabundo* 'vagabond, tramp' has also given rise to *vagamundo* (same meaning), associated by speakers in some way with *vagar* 'to wander, roam, loaf' and *mundo* 'world', since a tramp wanders about in the world, or so it may seem.

(3) The original name of the city of *Cuernavaca* in Mexico was *kwāwnawak* in Nahuatl, but it was folk-etymologized by the Spanish as *cuernavaca*, based on *cuerno* 'horn' + *vaca* 'cow', though the place had no connection with either 'horns' or 'cows'. Its true etymology is Nahuatl *kwaw-* 'tree' + *nāwak* 'near, adjacent to', that is, 'near the trees'.

(4) (*Beef*) *jerky, jerked beef* in English comes from Spanish *charqui* 'dried salted meat', which Spanish borrowed from Quechua *č'arqi* – nothing is 'jerked' in its preparation, as the folk etymology seems to assume.

(5) *Handiwork* comes from Old English *hanďǧeweorc*, composed of *hand* 'hand' + *ǧeweorc* 'work (COLLECTIVE formation)', where *ǧe* > *y* (IPA [j]) or *i* in Middle English, and then was lost elsewhere but not in this word. The word was reformulated by folk etymology in the sixteenth century on the basis of *handy* + *work* (compare Palmer 1972: 240).

(6) Some dialects of English have *wheelbarrel* for *wheelbarrow*, folk-etymologizing it as having some association with *barrel*. A similar example is the saying applied to things requiring two parties, *it takes two to tangle*, folk-etymologized from *it takes*

two to tango, made popular from the 1952 song 'Takes Two to Tango', recorded independently by Pearl Bailey and Louis Armstrong.

(7) Some speakers have changed *cappuccino* to *cuppacino*, influenced analogically by the word *cuppa* 'cup of tea', unknown in American English but widely used elsewhere, from *cup of* (*tea*). A seven-year-old boy thought *cappuccino* was *caffeccino* (based on *coffee*).

(8) Old Spanish *tiniebras* 'darkness' changed to Modern Spanish *tinieblas* through the folk-etymological assumption that it had something to do with *niebla* 'fog' (cf. the related Spanish word *tenebroso* 'dark, gloomy' < Latin *tenebrōsus*).

(9) The true etymology of English *outrage* has nothing to do with *out* or *rage* (as folk etymology might have us believe). Rather, *outrage* is in origin a borrowing from French *outrage* 'outrage, insult', which is based on Latin *ultrā* 'beyond' + the nominalizing suffix *-agium* (cf. the suffix *-age*).

(10) One of the glosses of the *Appendix Probi*, which warns against what the author considered improper pronunciations in Latin (see Exercise 14.1 in Chapter 14), says one should say *effeminatus* 'effeminate' (derived from *fēmina* 'woman, female') rather than the folk-etymologized version *infiminatus* (based on *infimus* 'lowest, below').

4.7.3 Back formation

In back formation (*retrograde* formation), a type of *folk etymology*, a word is assumed to have a morphological composition which it did not originally have, usually a root plus affixes, so that when the assumed affixes are removed, a new changed root is created. For example, children, confronted with a plate of pieces of cheese, may say 'can I have a chee?', assuming that *cheese* is the plural form, and therefore creating the logical-seeming singular root, *chee*, by removing the final *s*, which they associate with the *s* of plural. Similar examples which result in permanent changes in languages are quite common.

(1) *Cherry* entered English as a loan from Anglo-Norman French *cherise* (Modern French *cerise*) where the *s* was part of the original root, but was interpreted as representing the English 'plural', and so in back formation this *s* was removed, giving *cherry* in the singular.

(2) English *pea* is from Old English *pise* 'pea' [SINGULAR]/*pisan* 'peas' [PLURAL] (in Middle English *pease* 'singular'/*pesen* 'plural'); later the final *s* of the singular was reinterpreted as 'plural' and the form was backformed to *pea* when singular. Compare *pease-pudding* and *pease porridge* (an archaism preserved in the nursery rhyme, 'Pease porridge hot, pease porridge cold, . . .'), which retain the *s* of the earlier singular form.

(3) A number of new English verb roots have been created by back formations based on associations of some sounds in the original word with *-er* 'someone who does the action expressed in the verb': *to burgle* based on *burglar, to edit* from *editor, to escalate* based on *escalator, to letch* from *lecher, to orate* backformed from *orator, to peddle* based on *pedlar, to sculpt* from *sculptor,* etc.

(4) Many non-American varieties of English have a verb *to orientate*, backformed from *orientation* (competing with or replacing *to orient*). *Disorientated* is

less established, but is sometimes said, derived analogically on the model of *orientated*.

(5) Swahili *kitabu* 'book' is originally a loanword from Arabic *kitāb* 'book'. However, on analogy with native nouns such as *ki-su* 'knife'/*vi-su* 'knives' (where *ki-* and *vi-* represent the noun-class prefixes for which Bantu languages are well known), Swahili has backformed *kitabu* by assuming that its first syllable represents the *ki-* singular noun-class prefix, and thus created a new plural in *vitabu* 'books'.

(6) Setswana, another Bantu language (in Botswana and northern South Africa), has *sekole* 'school', borrowed from English (Setswana does not permit initial *sk-* consonant clusters); however, since *se-* is also a noun-class prefix for 'singular', this word has undergone the back formation *dikole* 'schools', where *di-* is the 'plural' prefix for this class of nouns (cf. Janson 2002: 48).

(7) *Donostia* is the Basque name of the famous city called in Spanish *San Sebastián*. Young Basque speakers have begun calling it *Donosti*, assuming the final *a* is the Basque article *-a* 'the'; however, this is a back formation. Its etymology appears to be from *done* 'saint, lord' (borrowed from Latin *dominus* 'lord') + *Sebastián*, which with time underwent several changes, Done Sebastián > Donestabian > Donestabia > Donastia > Donostia.

4.7.4 Metanalysis (reanalysis)

Traditionally, two things are treated under the title of metanalysis: *amalgamation* and *metanalysis proper* (today more often called *reanalysis*). Since amalgamation is also a kind of lexical change, it is treated in Chapter 5.

Metanalysis is from Greek *meta* 'change' + *analysis* 'analysis', and as the name suggests, metanalysis involves a change in the structural analysis, in the interpretation of which phonological material goes with which morpheme in a word or construction.

(1) English provides several examples: *adder* is from Old English *nǽddre*; the change came about through a reinterpretation (reanalysis) of the article–noun sequence *a + nǽddre* as *an + adder* (compare the German cognate *Natter* 'adder, viper'). English has several examples of this sort. *Auger* is from Middle English *nauger, naugur*, from Old English *nafo-gār* (*nafo-* 'nave [of a wheel]' + *gār* 'piercer, borer, spear', literally 'nave-borer'). *Apron* is from Middle English *napron*, originally a loan from Old French *naperon*, a diminutive form of *nape, nappe* 'tablecloth'. The related form *napkin* (from the French *nape* 'tablecloth' + *-kin* 'a diminutive suffix', apparently ultimately from Dutch) still preserves the original initial *n-*. *Umpire* < *noumpere* (originally a loanword from Old French *nonper* 'umpire, arbiter', *non* 'no' + *per* 'peer'). Finally, *newt* is from Middle English *ewt* (*an + ewt* > *a + newt*).

(2) Shakespeare (in *King Lear* I, 4, 170) had *nuncle* 'uncle', a form which survives in some dialects today. It is derived from a metanalysis based on the final *-n* of the possessive pronouns *mine* and *thine*. In earlier English the form of these possessive pronouns with the final nasal was required when the following word began in a vowel (as in *mine eyes*) but the form lacking final *-n* was employed before words beginning in a consonant (*my lips*). In *nuncle* the original *mine uncle* was reanalysed

so that the -*n* was no longer seen as just the end of the possessive pronoun *mine* but as the beginning of the following word, hence *mine* + *uncle* > *my nuncle*.

(3) Latin *argent-um* 'silver' and *argent-ārius* 'silversmith' respectively became in French *argent* [aʁʒã] 'silver, money' and *argentier* [aʁʒãtje] (with the analysis *argent* + *ier*); however, a reanalysis of this form as *argen*+*tier* is the basis of the -*tier* of newer words such as *bijoutier* 'jeweller', based on *bijou* 'jewel' + -*tier*; another example is the addition of -*tier* to *café* to create *cafetier* 'coffee house keeper', influenced by *cabaretier* 'cabaret owner, publican, innkeeper', which bears what was originally the -*ier* suffix. *Cafetier* was construed with -*tier* from comparison with *cabaret* [kabaʁe] 'cabaret, tavern, restaurant' / *cabaretier* 'cabaret owner'.

(4) Swedish *ni* 'you' (plural, formal) comes from Old Swedish *I* 'you [PLURAL]' (cognate with English *ye*), where it often came after verbs that ended in -*n* 'verbal plural agreement' (cognate with the -*n* that marked agreement with the third person plural subject of Old and Middle English, seen in Chapter 1), and the -*n* + *I* combination was reinterpreted as together being the pronoun *ni*, as in *veten I* > *veten ni* > *vet ni* 'you know', *vissten I* > *visten ni* > *visste ni* 'you knew' (Wessén 1969: 219).

Reanalysis is one of the most important mechanisms of syntactic change, and is treated in more detail in Chapter 11.

Blending is sometimes included with analogy, though here it is treated with kinds of lexical change (in Chapter 5).

4.8 Exercises

Exercise 4.1

Observe the language of your friends and associates, and of newspapers, television, social media, and other online resources, and attempt to find examples of your own of various sorts of analogy.

Exercise 4.2 Identifying analogical changes

Determine what kind of analogical change is involved in the following examples. Name the kind of change, and attempt to explain how it came about, if you can.

1. In some non-standard dialects of English, the pattern *bring/brought/brought* has become *bring/brang/brung*.
2. Where Standard English has *drag/dragged/dragged*, some varieties of English have *drag/drug/drug*. It appears in this case that the Standard English pattern, *drag/dragged/dragged*, is older.
3. Old Spanish *siniestro* 'left' changed from Latin *sinister* 'the left, on the left' to take on *ie* under the influence of the Spanish antonym *diestro* 'right,

right-handed'; *diestro and siniestro* frequently occurred together in speech. (In Modern Spanish *siniestro* means 'sinister, grim, ominous'.)

4. In many Spanish dialects, an intervocalic *d* is regularly lost, as in *mercado >   mercao* 'market'. In some instances, however, there are changes of the following sort: dialect *bacalado* but Standard Spanish *bacalao* 'codfish'; dialect *Bilbado* but Standard Spanish *Bilbao* (a place name).

5. In the Dominican Republic, forms such as Standard Spanish *atras* 'behind' are sometimes pronounced *astras*. In this variety of Spanish, preconsonantal *s* is often lost, as in *ata < asta* (spelled <hasta>) 'until'.

6. English *Jerusalem artichoke* (a kind of sunflower, with some similarities to an artichoke) is in origin from Italian *girasóle articiocco*, where Italian *girasóle* / dʒirasóle/ contains *gira-* 'turn, rotate' + *sole* 'sun', and *articiocco* 'artichoke', with nothing associated with *Jerusalem* originally.

7. In English, *Key West* (Florida) comes from the Spanish name *cayo hueso*, where *cayo* is 'key, small island' and *hueso* is 'bone'.

8. Colloquial and regional varieties of Spanish have *haiga* where Standard Spanish has *haya* (SUBJUNCTIVE, 'there may be') and *vaiga* where Standard Spanish has *vaya* (SUBJUNCTIVE, 'may go'). These have been influenced by Standard Spanish verb forms such as *traiga* (subjunctive of *traer* 'to bring', 'may bring') and *caiga* (subjunctive of *caer* 'to fall', 'may fall').

9. Middle English had *help-* 'present tense', *holp* 'past tense'; Modern English has *help, helped* for these.

10. English to *emote* is derived from *emotion*; to *enthuse* is derived from *enthusiastic*.

11. Many varieties of English have a new verb *to liaise* based on *liaison*.

12. English *to diagnose* is derived from *diagnosis*.

13. English *hangnail* is derived from Old English *angnægl* 'painful corn (on foot)'. When *ang* 'pain' as an independent word was lost (though later reintroduced in *anguish*, borrowed from Old French *anguisse* 'distress, anxiety, choking sensation'), the *angnægl* form was reinterpreted as having something to do with 'hanging', associated with painful detached skin of toes and then also hands.

5

LEXICAL CHANGE

All big changes of the world come from words.

(Marjane Satrapi,
quoted in Cavna 2012)

5.1 Introduction

Where do new words come from, and how do words get lost from a language? Though ordinary people – that is, non-linguists – may be mostly unaware of other sorts of changes going on in their languages, they do tend to notice changes in words (lexical change) and in their meanings (semantic change, taken up in Chapter 6). People want to know how words such as *ditz*, *dork*, *dweeb*, *geek*, *nerd*, *twit*, *wimp*, *wuss*, and *yutz* get added to the language so fast, and whatever happened to the *groovy* of late 1960s love songs, anyway? People are curious about recently added words to some English-language dictionaries, such as:

> *bling* 'expensive, ostentatious jewellery or clothing'.
> *blog* 'a regularly updated website, typically done by an individual or small group'.
> *butt-dial* 'to place a call unintentionally from a mobile phone because the send button was accidentally pressed while the phone was being carried in a rear pocket'.
> *emoji* 'small icon or digital image, sometimes called 'ideograms' or 'pictographs', used to express an idea or concept with a symbol instead of spelled-out words'.
> *MacGyver* 'to make or repair something in an improvised or inventive way, making use of whatever is at hand'.
> *selfie* 'a photograph of oneself taken with a mobile phone or hand-held digital camera'.

twerk 'a dance or dance move involving rapid, repeated thrusting hip movements and a low, squatting stance; to dance performing such movements'.
vape 'to inhale and exhale the aerosol vapour produced by an electronic cigarette or similar device'.

And people wonder why other words just drop out of use and get lost. Ready examples can be seen in the casual language or slang that older readers grew up with but that are now no longer in common use with these meanings:

bread 'money'
cat 'term for any hip person'
daddy-o 'a generally cool guy'
fuzz 'police, police officer'
gnarly 'difficult, dangerous, challenging, unpleasant, unattractive'
grody 'very unpleasant, disgusting, gross'
groovy 'enjoyable, exciting, excellent, fashionable'
the Man 'authority, the government, those in power'

Vocabulary change can be a matter of alarm and deep concern to some. We see this in the creation of language academies and the appointment of language commissions to protect the purity of languages such as French and Spanish, also seen, for example, in letters to newspaper editors in Australia, Great Britain, New Zealand, and South Africa, on the one hand denouncing the assumed invidious Americanisms forcing their way into vocabulary, and on the other hand decrying the degeneration of young people's all-too-limited vocabulary into nothing but slang (so they claim), holding up writers of famous literature as models of how we all should talk in order to be considered proper human beings who uphold our moral and linguistic obligations to the language. This chapter cuts past all that, showing what linguists think about lexical change, about how and why vocabulary changes.

5.2 Lexical Change and New Words

There are many kinds of lexical change. Several sources of new vocabulary have been seen already in the treatment of various kinds of analogy (Chapter 4) and borrowing (Chapter 3), and aspects of lexical change also involve semantic change, the subject of Chapter 6. We concentrate here on the other sources of *neologisms* (new words in a language), presenting a more or less traditional classification of kinds of lexical change together with examples. Abundant examples involving the more productive sources of neologisms are found especially in slang, advertising, and political discourse.

5.2.1 Creations from nothing (root creations)

Creations of new words from nothing, out of thin air, are rare, but examples exist. Examples of such creations that are sometimes cited include:

blurb coined by Gelett Burgess (American humourist) in 1907.

gas coined by Dutch chemist J. B. van Helmont in 1632, inspired by Greek *khāos* 'chaos', where the letter *g* of Dutch is pronounced [x] (a voiceless velar fricative), corresponding to the pronunciation of the Greek letter *X*, the first of the Greek word <χάος> [xaos] 'chaos'.

paraffin invented by Karl Reichenbach in 1830, based on Latin *parum* 'too little, barely' + *affinis* 'having affinity'.

It might be objected that in most cases of this sort, the creation isn't really fully out of 'nothing'; for example, *gas* has Greek 'chaos' lying in some way behind it; the creation of *paraffin* utilized pieces from Latin. Probably better examples of creations from nothing could be found in terms with slang origins such as *bling*, *pizzazz*, *zilch*, and in product names (see below).

Some *expressive words* seem to develop mostly out of nothing, for example *bodacious* 'remarkable, fabulous', *hellacious* 'remarkable, astonishing', *humongous* (also *humungous*) 'very large'. While the origin of these words is uncertain, it is possible that *bodacious* is connected in some way to *bold* and *audacious*, and that *humongous* perhaps reflects in some way *huge* together with associations from something like *tremendous* or *enormous*, or *monstrous*. *Hellacious* involves *hell* and some ending that probably has some analogical connection with words that inspired the similar ending on *bodacious*.

A related source of new words is *literary coinage*, new words created by (or at least attributed to) authors and famous people, for example:

blatant from Edmund Spenser (between 1590 and 1596).

blurb (seen above, from Gelett Burgess, 1907).

boojum from Lewis Carroll.

chortle from Lewis Carroll (a blend of *chuckle* + *snort*).

pandemonium 'the abode of all the demons, the capital of Hell', from John Milton's *Paradise Lost*, 1667 (the pieces from which this was created are Greek).

yahoo from Jonathan Swift's *Gulliver's Travels*, the name created for an imaginary race of brutes with human form.

5.2.2 From personal names and names of peoples

From names of individuals – some fictional or mythical – we have examples such as:

bloomers named for Amelia Jenks Bloomer (1818–94), US feminist activist who promoted this undergarment.

cereal from Latin *cereālis* 'of grain', derived from *Cerēs*, the Roman goddess of agriculture.

chauvinism, chauvinist from *Nicolas Chauvin*, a character in the Cogniard brothers' *La Cocarde Tricolore* of 1831, about a soldier in Napoleon's army who loyally idolized Napoleon and the Empire long after Napoleon abdicated.

dunce originally a term applied to followers of John Duns Scotus (1265–1308), Scottish scholar of philosophy and theology.

guillotine borrowed from French *guillotin*, named after the French physician Joseph-Ignace Guillotin (1738–1814), who suggested that the instrument be used in executions in 1789.

mesmerize from Austrian physician Franz Anton Mesmer (1734–1815), whose experiments induced trance-like states in his subjects.

nicotene from Jean Nicot (1530–1600), French ambassador in Portugal, who sent samples of a new 'tobacco' to the French queen Catherine de Medici in 1560. In his honour, plants of the genus are all called *nicotiana*; nicotene, the addictive alkaloid, comes from *nicotiana* plants.

panic from the Greek god *Pan*.

quixotic from Miguel de Cervantes' (1547?–1616) *Don Quixote*.

sandwich said to be named after John Montagu, the Fourth Earl of Sandwich (1718–92), who spent twenty-four hours gambling with no other food than slices of cold meat between slices of toast.

saxophone named for its Belgian inventor, Antoine 'Adolphe' Sax (1814–94).

volt named after Alessandro Volta, Italian scientist and physician (1745–1827).

There are also words which originate from names of groups of people:

cannibal, first recorded by Christopher Columbus, as *caniba*, an alternative form of the name for the feared Carib Indians, who, Columbus reports, were called *Carib* on Hispaniola. English borrowed the word from Spanish *canibal* 'cannibal'. (Thus *Caribbean* and *cannibal* come from the same original source.)

gothic from the Goths (Germanic tribes).

to gyp 'to cheat, swindle' from 'Gypsy' (today considered an improper, racist word).

to jew (a price down) from 'Jew' (no longer to be used because of its negative stereotyping).

vandal, *vandalize* from the Vandals (another Germanic tribe).

welch, *welsh* 'to cheat by avoiding payment of bets', said to be from 'Welsh'.

5.2.3 From place names

bedlam 'scene of uproar and confusion', from the common pronunciation of *St Mary of Bethlehem*, London's first psychiatric hospital.

bikini 'woman's two-pieced bathing suit', named for *Bikini Atoll*, Marshall Islands, destroyed by atom bomb testing in 1946; the bikini was so named supposedly because of its explosive impact on men.

byzantine 'excessively complicated or difficult to understand, involving excessive administrative detail', from *Byzantine Empire*, reflecting the complex and devious character of the royal court of Constantinople.

canary from *Canary Islands*.

caucasian 'the "white race", coined by anthropologist Johann Blumenbach (1752–1840), based on the *Caucasus Mountains*, the supposed original homeland of this 'race' of people.

champagne from *Champagne*, the name of a province in northern France for which the wine produced there is named.

currant ultimately from *Corinth*, a loan from Old French *raisins de Corauntz* (Modern French *raisins de Corinthe*) 'raisins of Corinth'.

denim ultimately from French *serge de Nîmes* 'serge (a woollen fabric) of Nîmes' (a manufacturing town in southern France).

frank from the *Franks*, Germanic conquerors of Gaul, whose name is seen in the name *France*.

geyser from *Geysir*, place in Iceland known for its famous geyser and thermal activity.

gypsy 'nomadic, free-spirited', from *Egypt*. The Rom (Romani people, also called 'gypsies', a term now avoided) were erroneously thought to have come from Egypt.

jeans from *Genoa* (for a twilled cotton cloth associated with Genoa).

lesbian from *Lesbos* island in Greece. Sappho, lyric poet, was from Lesbos; her erotic and romantic verse embraced women as well as men and became associated with homosexual relations among women.

meander from the *Maeander River*, Turkey (through Greek *maíandros*, which came to mean 'winding course').

muslin from *Mosul*, Iraq, where fine cotton fabric was made (from Arabic *mūslin*).

pheasant named for the Phasis River in the Caucasus, where in legend pheasants come from.

peach from *Persia*. English *peach* is a loan from French *pêche*, which derives from Latin *mālum persicum* 'Persian apple'. 'Persia' as the source of words for 'peach' is more visible in Dutch *perzik*, German *Pfirsich*, and Swedish *persika*, for example.

sherry from *Jerez*, a place in Spain associated with this fortified Spanish wine

sodomy from *Sodom*. Sexual relations considered inappropriate in medieval Europe were attributed to the inhabitants of this biblical town.

spa from *Spa*, a place in Belgium celebrated for the curative properties of its mineral water.

tangerine from *Tangier*, Morocco.

turkey from *Turkey*, shortened from *turkeycock*, *turkeyhen*, originally a guinea-fowl imported through Turkey, later applied erroneously to the bird of American origin. Names for 'turkey' in numerous European languages reflect often erroneous beliefs about where these birds come from. For example, 'India' is involved in Basque *indioilar*, Catalan *gall dindi* (*gall* 'rooster'), French *dinde* (female turkey), *dindon* (male turkey) (from *de* 'from' + *inde* 'India'), Polish *indyk*, Russian *indyuk*, Turkish *hindi*; Lithuanian *kalakutas*, Danish *kalkun*, Finnish *kalkkuna*, (from 'Calicut' in Kerala, now called *Kozhikode*, via Dutch *kalkoen*). In Portuguese it is *peru* reflecting 'Peru', seen also in Croatian *purica*.

5.2.4 From brand (trade) names

aspirin < Bayer's trademark for Acetylsalicylic acid.

breathalyzer < trademark owned by the Indiana University Foundation, for the invention by Rolla N. Harger, Indiana University professor, originally called 'Drunk-O-Meter'.

coke 'coca-cola, cola (drink)' < Coca-Cola. Words based on *coca-cola* are found in languages around the world, many in shortened forms to refer to Coca-Cola or similar drinks, for example English *coke*.

dumpster started as a brand name, from the Dempster Brothers Inc., that joined the name *Dempster* with the word *dump*, creating the *Dempster Dumpster*.

fridge, frigidaire < Frigidaire for 'refrigerator' (in the USA).

hoover (vacuum cleaner) < Hoover.

jello (jelly crystals, a gelatin dessert in North America) < Jell-O brand.

kleenex (tissue) < Kleenex brand tissues.

levis, levi jeans < Levi Strauss, their first manufacturer.

to google < Google.

uzi < the trademark of an Israeli submachine gun designed by Israeli Uziel Gal.

xerox < Xerox.

zipper < a B. F. Goodrich trademark, originally for use in rubber boots (that had a zipper).

5.2.5 Acronyms

Acronyms are words derived from the initial letters or syllables of each of the successive parts of a compound term or words in a phrase: *ASAP* < 'as soon as possible'; ASL 'American Sign Language'; *BS* < 'bullshit'; *CD* < 'compact disc'; *CIA* < 'Central Intelligence Agency'; *DJ* < 'disc jockey'; *emcee* < 'master of ceremonies'; *Gestapo* < from German *Geheime Staatspolizei* 'secret state's police', borrowed into English; *Hummer* < HMMWV 'High Mobility Multipurpose Wheeled Vehicle' (an abbreviation of which was pronounced *Humvee*, which General Motors changed to *hummer* when it bought the rights to make the vehicle, in order to market it better); *LOL* 'laughing out loud'; *MP* < 'military police', *MP* < 'member of parliament'; *OJ* < slang for 'orange juice'; *PDQ* 'fast' < 'pretty damned quick'; *radar* 'radio direction and ranging'; *SCUBA* < 'self-contained underwater breathing apparatus'; SIM card < 'subscriber identification module' card; *UK* 'United Kingdom'; *yuppie* < 'young urban professional'; and many more.

Some forms are turned into acronym-like words even though they do not originate as such. These usually involve sequences of letters from principal syllables in the word, for example: *TV* < television, *PJs* < pyjamas.

5.2.6 Compounding

Compounds are words (lexical items) formed from pieces or units that are (or were) themselves distinct lexical roots (words). Compounding is a productive process in English and many other languages. A number of examples of compounds that are relatively new in English include the following: *all-nighter* (*to pull an all-nighter* 'to stay up all night long, usually to study for exams'); *badass*; *bag lady*; *binge-watch*; *cashflow*; *couch potato* 'lazy person, someone who just lies around'; *cyberbullying*; *downmarket* 'less expensive, less sophisticated'; *downside*; words containing *-head* (as in *airhead, butthead, deadhead, dickhead, doughhead*); *knee-jerk* (adjective); *meltdown*; *motormouth*; words containing *-person* (as in *busperson, chairperson, clergyperson, minutepersons*); *red-eye* 'cheap whisky', *red-eye* 'late-night or early-morning flight'; *scumbucket*; *shareware*; *skateboard*; *slamdunk*; *stargaze*; *studmuffin* 'a muscular or attractive male'; *superpower*; *tummytuck*; *waterboarding*; and so on.

   In the case of older compounds, later changes can often make the original components of the compound no longer recognizable, as for example in:

> *elbow* < Proto-Germanic **alinō* 'forearm' + **bugōn* 'bend, bow' (compare Old English *eln* 'forearm, cubit').
>
> *gamut* < low G, the lowest note in the medieval musical scale, from a contraction of the Greek letter *gamma*, + Latin *ut* 'that', introduced in the Middle Ages to represent a note on the musical scale one note lower than *A*, which began the scale.
>
> *gossip* < Old English *godsibb* (*God* + *sib* 'related') 'one who has contracted spiritual affinity with another by agreeing to act as sponsor at a baptism', which came to mean 'family acquaintance, friend' and 'a woman's female friends invited to be present at a birth', and on to 'someone, usually a woman, of light and trifling character', changed further to mean 'the conversation of such a person', 'idle talk'.
>
> German *Elend* 'misery, miserable' < Old High German *elilenti* 'sojourn in a foreign land, exile' (compare Gothic *alja-* 'other' + *land* 'land').

   In others, the source of the compounding is only partially perceived today: *cobweb* < Middle English *coppe* 'spider' + *web*; *nickname* < *an* 'an + *eke* 'additional' + *name* 'name'; *werewolf* < Old English *wer* 'man' (cognate with Latin *vir* 'man') + *wolf*.

5.2.7 Other productive word-formation and derivational devices

In addition to compounding, new words are derived more or less productively through the employment of various derivational affixes in word-formation processes. The most productive kinds of morphological derivation that can give new words are not discussed here (they can be considered better treated as belonging to the generative capacity of synchronic grammars). Others involve what have been called 'neoclassical' compounds (involving elements from Greek or Latin, such as *auto-*, *trans-*, *bio-*, and so on); some of these are semi-productive. A few examples illustrating these processes are:

auto- (autoalign, autocorrect, autohypnotic, autoimmune, autopilot, autopopulate, autorelease, autosuggestion).
-belt (banana belt, Bible belt, cow belt, rustbelt, snowbelt, sunbelt).
mega- (megabyte, megachurch, megadeal, megahit, megapixel, megaproject, megastar).
micro- (microbiotic, microbrewery, microchip, microclimate, microenvironment, micromanage, microprocessor, microsurgery).
mini- from *miniskirt*, first attested in 1965 (minibar, minibike, minicam, minicomputer, minigun, minimart, mini-series, minivan).
pan- (Pan-Asian, pandemic, pandialectal, pan-ethnic, pangalactic, panglobal, pan-national).
pseudo- (pseudo-friend, pseudo-intellectual, pseudopsychological, pseudoscientific).
trans- (transgender, transmigration, transnationals, transpacific).
ultra- (ultracritical, ultrahazardous, ultrahot, ultraleftist, ultraliberal, ultramodern, ultraradical, ultrasensitive).

Some of these overlap with blends (see below, section 5.2.9), such as:

bio- (biochemical, biodegradable, biodiversity, bioenginering, biofeedback, biosphere, bioterrorism).
eco- (ecocentric, ecofascist, ecofreak, eco-friendly, ecosphere, ecoterrorists, ecotourism).

5.2.8 Amalgamation: hybrid words

Amalgamations are forms which were formerly composed of more than one free-standing word (which occurred together in some phrase), which as a result of the change get bound together into a single word. For example, English *nevertheless* and *already* are now single words, but come from the amalgamation of separate words, of *never* + *the* + *less* and *all* + *ready*, respectively. English has many words of this sort in whose background lies the amalgamation of earlier separate words into a single lexical item.

Amalgamation is often considered a kind of analogy. (Similarly, cases of blending [sometimes called contamination] are sometimes treated as a kind of lexical change, as discussed in Chapter 4.) We can see amalgamation under way in the frequent (mis)spellings of *alright* for *all right* (probably influenced by analogy with *already*), *alot* for *a lot* meaning 'many, much', and *no-one* (or *noone*) for *no one*. Some examples of amalgamations follow:

English *almost* < *all most*, *alone* < *all one*, *altogether* < *all together*, *always* < *all ways*, *however* < *how ever*, *without* < *with out*.
English *don* < *do on*; *doff* < *do off*.

English *wannabe* < *want to be* (of slang origin, 'someone who tries to be accepted by a group, adopting its appearance and manners').

Spanish *usted* 'you (plural, formal)' < *vuestra merced* 'your grace'.

Spanish *también* 'also' < *tan bene* 'as well', *todavía* 'still, yet' < *tota via* 'all way(s)'.

Latin *dē mānē* (*dē* 'of' + *mānus* 'good [ABLATIVE]'), meaning 'in good time', is behind amalgamated forms meaning 'morning, tomorrow' in some of the Romance languages, for example French *demain* 'tomorrow' and Italian *domani* 'morning, tomorrow'. Later, French underwent further amalgamations: *en demain* ('in' + 'tomorrow') > *l'endemain* (*l(e)* 'the' + *endemain*) > *le lendemain* 'tomorrow, the next day'.

Latin *hodie* 'today' should have ended up in French as *hui*, but this was further amalgamated, first to *jour d'hui* (from *jour* 'day' + *d(e)* 'of' + *hui* 'today') and then on to *aujourd'hui* 'today, nowadays' (from *au* 'to the' + *jour d'hui* – and *au* is also an amalgam of *a* 'to' + *le* 'the').

Spanish *hidalgo* 'noble', Old Spanish *fijodalgo*, comes from *fijo* 'son' (Latin *filiu-*; compare Modern Spanish *hijo* 'son') + *d(e)* 'of' + *algo* 'something'/'wealth'.

French *avec* 'with' comes from Latin *apud* 'with, by, beside' + *hoc* 'this, it', literally 'with/by this'.

Spanish *nosotros* 'we' comes from *nos otros* 'we others', *vosotros* 'you (familiar plural)' from *vos otros* 'you others'.

Note that many of the cases today called *grammaticalization* (see Chapter 11) are instances of amalgamation, where formerly independent words are amalgamated and in the process end up becoming grammatical affixes. Some examples follow:

In Spanish and other Romance languages, forms of the verb *haber* 'have' (from Latin *habēre*) were amalgamated with infinitives to give the 'future' and 'conditional' morphological constructions of today, for example Spanish *cantar he* > *cantar-hé* > *cantaré* 'I will sing' (*he* 'FIRST PERSON SINGULAR' of the auxiliary verb *haber*), *cantar has* > *cantar-has* > *cantarás* 'you will sing' (*has* 'SECOND PERSON SINGULAR' of *haber*); *cantar habías* > *cantarías* 'you would sing' (*habías* 'you had' [SECOND PERSON SINGULAR IMPERFECTIVE derived from *haber*]).

In another example, *mente* 'in mind' (from the ablative of Latin *mēns* 'mind') was grammaticalized in Romance languages as an adverbial clitic (in Spanish) or suffix (in French). From *absoluta mente* 'in absolute mind' we get Spanish *absolutamente* and French *absolument* 'absolutely'. (For discussion and other examples, see Chapter 11.)

5.2.9 Blending (contamination)

Blends are similar to amalgamations, though here it is not whole words but parts of some words that are involved. (Blending, often considered a kind of analogy [see Chapter 4] is treated here with lexical change.) In *blends*, pieces of two (or more) different words are combined to create new words. Usually the words which contribute the pieces that go into the make-up of the new word are semantically related in some way, sometimes as synonyms for things which have the same or a similar meaning. Some blends are purposefully humorous or sarcastic in their origin; others are more accidental, sometimes thought to originate as something like slips of the tongue that combine aspects of two related forms, which then catch on. The following English examples illustrate these various origins and outcomes.

1. Often-cited examples include: *smog* < *smoke* + *fog*; *brunch* < *breakfast* + *lunch*; *motel* < *motor* + *hotel*; *splatter* < *splash* + *spatter*; *flush* < *flash* + *blush*.
2. *bit* (computer bit) < *binary digit*.
3. *Brexit* < *British* + *exit* (for United Kingdom withdrawal from the European Union).
4. It is popular to create blends based on *cappuccino*, for example *mochaccino/mocaccino*, *muggaccino*, *frappaccino*, *cyberccino* (involving an internet coffee shop), *skinniccino/skinnyccino* (small black coffee), *skimmuccino* (cappuccino made with skim milk), *decafaccino* (cappuccino made of decaffeinated coffee), *soyaccino*, *kiddiccino*, and others.
5. A suffix-like element was created on the basis of a portion of *marathon*: *telethon*, *walkathon*, *bik(e)athon*, *danceathon*, and so on.
6. *newscast* < *news* + *broadcast*; also *podcast*, *sportscast*, *sportscaster*, *telecast*, *webcast*.
7. Based on a part of *alcoholic*: *workaholic*, *chocaholic*, *foodaholic*, *shoppaholic*, *talkaholic*, *blogaholic*, and so on.
8. *sexting* < *sex* + *texting*.
9. From combinations based on *hijack*: *skyjack(ing)* and *car-jack(ing)*.
10. *not* < an Old English compound composed of *ne* 'NEGATIVE' + *ōwiht* 'anything'; *neither* < Old English *nāhwæther*, composed of *nā* 'not' + *hwæther* 'whether', with influence from *either*.
11. *-gate* (a new suffix-like element created on the basis of *Watergate*, from the Richard Nixon Watergate scandal):

    Camillagate, involving a telephone call between Prince Charles and his then intimate friend and later spouse, Camilla Parker Bowles, now Duchess of Cornwall.
    Contragate, referring to the political scandal during the Ronald Reagan administration involving illegal US sales of arms to Iran to fund Contras (right-wing rebels) in Nicaragua.
    emailgate, about Hillary Clinton's private email server, which opponents to her 2016 candidacy for the US presidency claimed she had used illegitimately to send emails containing classified information, though she was exonerated.
    Monicagate, in reference to Monica Lewinsky, made famous by US President William J. Clinton's indiscretions involving her.
    nipplegate (also called *boobgate*), involving Janet Jackson's breast in a wardrobe malfunction during the Thirty-eighth Super Bowl halftime show.

Several more recent ones come from Donald Trump:

pussygate, about Trump's lewd comments about women on an *Access Hollywood* tape in which he said 'When you're a star . . . you can do any-thing . . . grab them by the pussy.'

sharpiegate, about Trump's altering of a weather map with a sharpie to suggest that Hurricane Dorian (2019) would hit Alabama, as he had inaccurately said earlier, though no official account of the hurricane had indicated it would reach Alabama.

shitholegate, from a meeting with law-makers about immigration in which Trump asked, 'Why are we having all these people from shithole coun-tries come here?'

towergate and *Russiagate*, about attempted cover-up of Russian involvement in Trump's 2016 candidacy for US president.

12. *bridezilla*, an extremely rude or demanding bride-to-be < *bride* + *godzilla*.
13. *gaydar*, the assumed ability to determine by intuition whether someone is homosexual, a blend of *gay* + *radar*.
14. *webinar*, for web-based seminar, a seminar, workshop, lecture, or presenta-tion that is transmitted over the internet, a blend of *web* + *seminar*.
15. A few other English examples are *heliport* < *helicopter* + *airport*; *snazzy* < *snappy* + *jazzy*; *jumble* < *jump* + *tumble*
16. Names of languages which borrow extensively from others or are highly influenced by others are the sources of such blends as *Spanglish* < *Spanish* + *English*, *Finnglish* < *Finnish* + *English*; *manglish* (created in feminist discourse to reflect male biases in English) < *man* + *English*; *Franglais* < *français* 'French' + *anglais* 'English'; *portuñol* (*portunhol*) 'an unsystematic mix of Portuguese and Spanish'; *Singlish* 'the variety of English spoken in Singapore'; etc.

There are also syntactic blends, a kind of reanalysis (see Chapter 11).

5.2.10 Clipping (compression, shortening)

Often, new words or new forms of old words come from 'clipping', that is, from shortening longer words. The several examples from English which follow show this process: *ad* < advertisement, *app* < application, *bike* < bicycle, *burger* < hamburger, *bus* < Latin *omnibus* 'for everyone' (-*bus* DATIVE PLURAL case ending; cf. Latin *omni-* 'all' – this is a much-cited example), *condo* < condominium, *decaf* < decaffeinated coffee, *dis(s)* (*dissing*) < disrespect, *fan* < fanatic, *gas* < gasoline, *gator* < alligator, *grad* < graduate (as in *grad school*, *undergrad*), *gym* < gymnasium, *jock* ('athlete') < jockstrap, *limo* < limousine, *math/maths* < mathematics, *mod* < modern, *nuke* (*nukes*, *to nuke*) < nuclear (weapons), *perp* < perpetrator, *perv* < pervert, *phone* < telephone, *prep* < prepare, preparation, *pro* < professional, *psycho* < psychotic, *pub* < public house, *rad* < radical, *schizo* [skɪtso] < schizophrenic, *stats* < statistics, *sub* < substitute ('a substitute, to substitute'), *sub* < submarine, *veg*, *to veg out* < vegetate, among many more.

5.2.11 Expressive creations

1. Onomatopoeia is another source of new words, created to mimic sounds in nature, as in *buzz, chirp, meow, moo, peep, whizz*.
2. Interjections (ejaculations) are another source: words such as *ah, oh, oops, ouch, whoop-de-doo, woo-hoo, wow, yadda yadda yadda, yuck*.
3. Phonesthemes (cases of sound symbolism) are often involved in the creation of new words, although what is phonesthemic can be difficult to pin down. A phonestheme is a particular sound or sequence of sounds that directly suggests a certain meaning, typically expressive. Though associated with particular meanings, phonesthemes are not themselves morphemes. A commonly cited example in English is the initial *fl*, said to be expressive of movement in air or water, in words such as *flail, flap, flash, flicker, fling, flip, flit, flitter, flop, flurry, flutter, fly*. Thus, given the assumed phonestheme of *wh-* in English thought to be associated with sounds involving rapid movement of or through the air (as in *whew, whir, whirl, whoop, whoosh*), perhaps it is not surprising to find that *wham* has no history in the language before 1923.

5.3 Obsolescence and Loss of Vocabulary

Those who think about lexical change are interested not only in the adoption of new vocabulary, but also in the question of why vocabulary items become archaic and sometimes disappear altogether from a language. Use of particular words can fade for a number reasons, but a main reason is just that the thing the word refers to ceases to be talked about by the speakers of the language. That is, changes in what a society deals with can lead to vocabulary loss as well as to semantic shifts (see Chapter 6). For example, there used to be a fairly large, active vocabulary for talking about armour, feudal society, falconry, and other things central to life in the Middle Ages which has mostly been forgotten as these things faded from modern life. Replacement of one word by another for the same meaning is another frequent means by which words can be lost. A few examples of older words now essentially lost to modern English vocabulary are the following (though some are occasionally resurrected for special purposes in historical fiction or fantasy literature, and in games reflecting medieval themes):

dorbel: a dull-witted pedant, a foolish pretender to learning; from Nicholas Dorbellus, a fifteenth-century professor of scholastic philosophy at Poitiers, similar to how followers of John Duns Scotus gave us *dunce* (see above).

dousabell: a common name in sixteenth-century poetry for a sweetheart, especially an unsophisticated country girl < French *douce et belle* 'sweet and beautiful'.

fribbler: a trifler; one who professes rapture for a woman yet dreads her consent.

jarkman: a vagabond counterfeiter of licences, certificates, passes (the seal of the falsified documents were called *jarks*).

kelchyn: a fine paid by one guilty of manslaughter, generally to the kindred of the person killed.

kexy: dry, brittle, withered.

mulligrubs: a twisting of the guts, so called from the symptomatic fever attending it.

palliard: a vagabond who slept on the straw in barns, hence a dissolute rascal, a lecher < Middle French *palliard* 'tramp, beggar, vagabond' (derived from French *paille* 'straw').

parnel: a punk, a slut; the diminutive of Italian *petronalla*; a priest's mistress.

rogitate: to ask frequently.

thural: of or pertaining to incense.

towrus: among hunters a roebuck eager for copulation is said to 'go to his towrus'.

tyromancy: divining by the coagulation of cheese.

wittol: a husband who knows of and endures his wife's unfaithfulness; a contented cuckold; from *woodwale*, a bird whose nest is invaded by the cuckoo, and so has the offspring of another palmed off on it for its own.

yelve: dung-fork; garden-fork; to use a garden fork.

5.4 Suppletion

Suppletion involves an intersection of lexical, semantic, and morphological change. It is the convergence of what were in origin two or more different lexical items so that the two or more originally unconnected roots (or stems) come to be used in the inflectional paradigm of a single lexical item. An example is *go/went*. Originally *went* had nothing to do with the past tense of *go*, but rather was the past tense of the verb *wend*, which was taken over as the past of 'to go' and incorporated into the inflectional paradigm of *to go*.

Standard suppletion involves complete replacement of one lexical form by another in a set of paradigmatically related forms. Suppletive forms are not frequent in most languages, but when they do occur they often involve quite frequent words in the language, as in the case of *go/went* and *be/am/is/are/was* in English. The suppletive nature of these verbs is highlighted when compared to the paradigmatically related forms of regular verbs, such as *bake*:

bake	*go*	*be*
I bake	I go	I am
we bake	we go	we are
she bakes	she goes	she is
he baked	he went	he was
they baked	they went	they were
have baked	have gone	have been

Some examples of suppletion in some other languages are:

> Finnish: *hyvä* 'good'/*parempi* 'better'/*paras* 'best'.
> French: *avoir* 'to have'/*eu* 'had' (PAST PARTICIPLE).
> German: *gut* 'good'/*besser* 'better'/*best* 'best'.
> Spanish: *ir* 'to go'/*va* '(he/she/it) goes'/*fue* '(he/she/it) went'.
> Nivaclé: (Matacoan language, Argentina and Paraguay) verb root /-ak/ 'to go' (as in *x-ak* 'I go')/*y-ič* [he/she/it-go] 'he goes'/*niʔ-ma* 'you don't go'/*meʔ-* 'go!'; and the verb root /-aw/ 'be, live' (as in *x-aw* [I-am] 'I am (at), I live (here)'/*y-iʔeʔ* [he/she/it-is] 'she is, she lives (here)'.

Not just any two lexical items can converge to create a single one involving suppletion. To explain suppletive changes, it would be necessary to be able to answer the question: what might cause two (or more) lexical items to converge? Answers that have been offered include frequency, semantic factors, and phonological reasons, where the relationship of the two (or more) lexical elements before the change is crucial. In some cases, sheer *phonetic similarity* may be enough to bring about changes that result in suppletion, as for example in the ongoing change in the English of Australia, New Zealand, and the UK in which *brought* is being replaced by *bought*, phonetically similar to *bought*, the past tense form of 'to buy', resulting in an even stranger strong-verb pattern with suppletion: *bring/bought/bought*.

It is sometimes said that when forms become too small phonetically to be perceived easily, a suppletion helps remedy the picture. For example, several of the forms of the Latin verb *īre* 'to go' that regular sound changes reduced to monosyllables in Romance languages were replaced through suppletion by polysyllabic forms derived from the Latin verb *vādere* 'to walk, rush', so for example forms from Classical Latin *īre* remained in Spanish when polysyllables were still in play:

Classical Latin	*Old Spanish*	
imus	imos	'we go'
itis	ides	'you (PLURAL) go'

However, forms of *īre* were replaced with forms from *vādere* in the instances where monosyllabic forms of *īre* were involved:

Classical Latin	*Old Spanish*	
eō (became *jo*)	vo (modern Spanish *voy*) < vado	'I go'
īs	vas < vadis	'you (PLURAL) go'
īt	va < vadit	'he/she goes'
eunt (became *junt*)	van < vadunt	'they go'

This is an interesting hypothesis, though it would be difficult to demonstrate conclusively that this assumed motivation for the change comes from the perceptual difficulty because of the small phonological size of the words, compensated for by the recruitment of longer forms from a semantically similar verb. (See Börjars and Vincent 2011.)

In other suggested explanations, it has been thought that *frequency* can be a factor determining which forms are recruited to replace others in a paradigm, presumably with forms from less frequent lexical items being imported into the paradigms of more frequent ones that are semantically similar, as in *went* from less frequent *wend* being taken over as the past tense of *go*. This does not, however, offer much to help in explaining why a form of *go* would be replaced at all. *Semantic scope* has also been mentioned as a possible factor, involving the difference in generality between the meanings of the forms involved, where, in the example just cited, *īre* 'to go' has a broader, more general meaning than narrower *vādere* 'to walk, rush', allowing the *īre* paradigm with its broader sense to import forms from *vādere*, more narrow in its meaning, but not permitting the paradigm of *vādere* to take over forms from semantically broader *īre*.

It is to be noted also that suppletion of this sort involves *semantic loss*, where forms of one lexical item lose some of their original meaning as they are substituted into the paradigm of another lexical item, whose broader meaning wins out in the change. So, for example, now *went* no longer has anything to do with *wend* 'to go in a specific direction, typically slowly or by an indirect route', but rather is just the past tense form of 'to go'.

This is the most common interpretation of suppletion, though irregular forms that have other sorts of origins are also sometimes talked about as suppletion. For example, sometimes forms which originally come from a single source are left seeming to be irregular or unrecognizable due to phonological or analogical change (see Chapter 4). An example is English *was/were*, forms which today are irregular but come from a single Old English lexical item, *wǣs/wǣron*, where the *r* of the plural came about through rhotacism (*s* to *r* between vowels; see Chapter 2), and is not due to the convergence of separate lexical roots in a single verb paradigm. Analogical extension can make new irregularities of the *dive/dove* sort (mentioned in Chapter 4), on analogy with the pattern in strong verbs such as *drive/drove*, from the former single verb root *dive/dived*, still the standard form for most English speakers outside of North America. Another popular example is *snuck* (replacing former regular *sneaked*), which appears to have become the past tense of *sneak* for a good number of English speakers, apparently extending the past tense form by analogy based on similarities with verbs such as *strike/struck*, *stick/stuck*, and *dig/dug*. Though these examples do not involve suppletion in the sense of formerly independent lexical items coming to be used in the inflectional paradigm of a single lexical item, sometimes, nevertheless, they are also called suppletive.

Not only do languages acquire new words and sometimes lose old ones, but the meanings of words also can change – the topic of the next chapter.

5.5 Exercises

Exercise 5.1 New words

Attempt to find examples of your own of new vocabulary items which represent some of the categories of lexical change considered in this chapter. Try to name or identify the categories involved. You can find them by listening for words that you think are new in the speech of your friends, family, and associates or by asking others if they can think of examples. Slang is often a fertile area for new vocabulary.

Exercise 5.2 Lexical change

The following are a few of the many new words (neologisms) that have been added to English dictionaries recently. Can you determine where these come from, that is, how they came into being? What processes of vocabulary creation or other kinds of linguistic change do you think lie behind the creation of these new words? (You may need to look some of these up to find their meanings, or ask your friends who might know what they mean.)

app	bae
blogosphere	buzzword
frenemy	guesstimate
mansplain	sexting
swole	to gaslight
woke (ADJECTIVE)	

6

SEMANTIC CHANGE

They that dally nicely with words may quickly make them wanton.
(Shakespeare, *Twelfth Night* III, i, 12–13)

6.1 Introduction

People are often curious about, even fascinated by, changes in the meaning of words. They wonder why *bloody* and *bugger* are obscene in Britain but not in America – the words don't even mean the same thing in the two places – and why *pissed* means 'angry' in the US but 'drunk' in the UK, and why *pissed* is so much less obscene and more tolerated than it was a generation ago in both countries. Some find a certain delight (some would say a twisted satisfaction) in the seeming irony in the semantic history of *to bless*, from Old English *blēdsian* (earlier *blōdsian)*, which originally meant 'to mark with blood' in an act of consecration in pagan sacrifice. With umlaut in mind, it is easy to see the connection between *blood* and the *blēd-* part of *blēdsian* (just think *to bleed* to see the connection more clearly). Some are charmed (perhaps perversely so) by a favourite example of handbooks, the story behind *cretin*. English *cretin* is borrowed from French *crétin* 'idiot'. It comes, to the surprize and delight of some etymology-lovers, ultimately from Latin *christiānum* 'Christian'. In Romance languages, the term for 'Christian' was used also for 'human being' to distinguish people from beasts; the semantic shift which gives the modern sense of *cretin* 'a stupid person' apparently came about in Swiss French dialects especially in reference to a class of dwarves and physically deformed idiots in certain valleys of the Alps, used euphemistically to mean that even these poor beings were human, and from this came the semantic shift from 'Christian' to 'idiot'. Those who learn other languages often ask how true cognates can come to have such different meanings in related languages, as in the English–German cognates *town/Zaun* 'fence', *timber/Zimmer* 'room', *bone/Bein* 'leg', and *write/reissen* 'to tear, rip'.

Languages are constantly changing the meaning of some words and, as seen in the last chapter, adding new words and losing others. This is illustrated 'nicely' in a comment about language in Shakespeare's *Twelfth Night*, in the quotation at the head of this chapter. Shakespeare wrote *They that dally nicely with words may quickly make them wanton*. To understand what he meant in today's language, we have to unpack the changes in meaning that several of the words in this line have undergone: *dally* meant 'chat', *nicely* meant 'foolishly', and *wanton* shifted from its original meaning of 'unmanageable' to 'sexually immodest or promiscuous, especially of a woman'. What Shakespeare was saying in this comment on semantic change was: 'They who chat foolishly with words may quickly make them unmanageable.' Let's look a bit more in detail at the history of the words in this line whose meanings have changed.

Dally came on the scene in English around 1300 as *dalien* 'to speak seriously', meaning in the late fourteenth century 'to talk intimately, converse politely'. The sense of 'to waste time' came about by the late fourteenth century; then the meaning turned to 'to play, frolic, flirt, engage in amorous exchanges' in the mid-fifteenth century; the meaning 'to linger, loiter, delay' is first attested from the 1530s, and hence the meaning of today's *dally* 'waste time, flirt'.

For *nicely* we follow the historical path of *nice*. In the late thirteenth century *nice* meant 'foolish, stupid, senseless', borrowed from Old French *nice* 'simple, stupid, silly, foolish, careless, clumsy, weak, poor, needy'. French inherited it from Latin *nescius* 'ignorant, unaware', derived from *ne-* 'not' + *scire* 'to know' (*scire* is also the root behind *science*). The word *nicely* itself is known from the fourteenth century in the meaning 'foolishly'; by around 1600 it had taken the meaning 'scrupulously', and it is first attested in 1714 with the sense of 'in an agreeable fashion'.

Wanton's story starts in the early fourteenth century as *wan-towen* 'resistant to control, wilful'. It contains the Middle English element *wan-* 'wanting, lacking, deficient', which alternated with *un-*. The *towen* part comes from Old English *togen*, past participle of *teon* 'to pull, draw' (compare *tug*). The basic meaning may have been 'ill-bred, poorly brought up' (that is, 'unpulled'). The sense of sexual indulgence comes from the late fourteenth century.

So how do languages change their meaning? This chapter is about meaning change and how it is dealt with in linguistics. In linguistics (also in anthropology, philosophy, and psychology), there are many approaches to semantics, the study of meaning. Unfortunately, these various approaches to semantics and the traditional historical linguistic treatments of change in meaning have typically had little in common, though clearly we would be in a better position to explain semantic change if we could base our understanding of change in meaning on a solid theory of semantics. Some recent approaches do attempt to reconcile the differences. Given the importance of semantic change, this chapter presents both a traditional classification of kinds of semantic changes and some thinking concerning tendencies in meaning change. Semantic change deals with change in meaning, understood to be a change in the concepts associated with a word, and has nothing to do with change in the phonetic form of the word (sound change). Note that aspects of semantic change are associated with some of the lexical changes seen in the previous chapter.

6.2 Traditional Notions of Semantic Change

Until recently nearly all work in semantic change has been almost exclusively concerned with lexical semantics (change in the meaning of individual words), and that is the focus in this chapter. Semantic change is mostly concerned with the meaning of individual lexical items, whereas much of semantic theory involves logical relations among items in longer strings. There are various classifications of types of semantic change, and there is nothing special about the classification presented here. Some of the categories overlap with others, and some are defined only vaguely, meaning that some instances of semantic change will fit more than one type. It is probably best to consider this classification as offering a sort of broad scheme for organizing kinds of semantic change, but with no pretensions to being particularly complete or adequate, only (it is hoped) useful.

6.2.1 Widening (generalization, extension, broadening)

In semantic changes involving widening, the range of meanings of a word increases so that the word can be used in more contexts than were appropriate for it before the change. Changes from more concrete to more abstract meanings fit here.

(1) *Bird* in Old English times and until about 1400 meant 'young bird, nestling'; later its meaning broadened to 'bird' in general.

(2) *Salary*. Latin *salārium* was a soldier's allotment of salt (based on Latin *sal* 'salt'), which then came to mean a soldier's wages in general, and then finally, as in English, wages in general, not just a soldier's pay. English borrowed *salary* from Anglo-French *salarie* (Old French *salaire*) 'wages, pay'.

(3) *Cupboard*. In Middle English times, *cupboard* meant 'a table ("board") upon which cups and other vessels were placed, a piece of furniture to display plates, a sideboard', whose meaning then became 'a closet or cabinet with shelves for keeping cups and dishes', and finally in America it changed to mean any 'small storage cabinet'. In parts of Canada, *cupboard* has been extended to mean also what others call a 'wardrobe' or 'clothes closet'. Spanish *armario* 'cupboard, cabinet, closet' was borrowed from Latin in the Middle Ages where it had to do with 'arms', 'weapons', and meant 'armoury'; later its meaning widened to include present-day 'clothes closet, cupboard, cabinet'. French *armoire* 'wardrobe, locker, cabinet' (also borrowed into English from French) has the same history.

(4) *Town*. Old English *tūn*, from which we get modern *town*, meant 'enclosure, garden, field, yard, farm, manor; homestead, dwelling, house', then later 'a group of houses, village, farm', and eventually 'town'. Cognates in other Germanic languages mean 'fence, hedge, field', as for example German *Zaun* 'fence'.

(5) Spanish *caballero*, originally 'rider, horseman', expanded to include 'gentleman, man of higher society' (since only men of means could afford to be riders of horses).

(6) Spanish *estar* 'to be' (especially 'to be in a location') < Latin *stāre* 'to stand'.

(7) Spanish *pájaro* 'bird' < Latin *passer* 'sparrow'.

(8) Finnish *raha* 'money' originally meant 'a fur-bearing animal' and its 'pelt'. The skins were an important means of exchange in the past, and *raha* came to mean 'skin used as medium of exchange'; when new means of exchange took the place of the old ones, *raha* shifted its meaning to 'money', its only meaning today (Ravila 1966: 105).

A few examples of recent changes involving widening of meaning follow.

(9) *Ghost*. *Ghost* has added a recent meaning as a verb of 'to cut off all contact abruptly with someone, such as a former romantic partner, by no longer accepting or responding to phone calls or messages'. Formerly *ghost* was just a noun, 'the spirit or soul of a dead person, an apparition of a dead person, typically as a nebulous image'.

(10) *Shade*. *Shade* has added a recent meaning of 'insult or disrespect', as in *throw shade* 'to express contempt or disrespect for someone publicly, particularly by subtle or indirect insult or criticism'. This meaning expanded from *shade's* earlier meaning of 'shadow, relative darkness and coolness caused by shelter from sunlight'.

(11) *Troll*. In the case of *troll* a change now includes the meaning of someone who purposely tries to antagonize others online by posting inflammatory or insulting comments; also as a verb, 'to troll.' Earlier, it meant only 'a dwarf or giant in Scandinavian folklore inhabiting caves or hills'.

(12) *Tweet*. Now *tweet* includes the added meaning 'to make a posting on the social media website Twitter'. Formerly, it referred just to 'a chirping sound, especially of a young bird; to make such a sound'.

6.2.2 Narrowing (specialization, restriction)

In semantic narrowing, the range of meanings is decreased so that a word can be used appropriately in fewer contexts than it could be before the change. Changes of more abstract meanings to more concrete ones fit this category.

(1) *deer* narrowed its sense from Old English *dēor* 'animal' (compare the German cognate *Tier* 'animal').

(2) *fowl* 'bird (especially edible or domestic)' has narrowed its sense from Old English *fugol*, which meant 'bird' in general (compare the German cognate *Vogel* 'bird').

(3) *girl* meant 'child or young person of either sex' in Middle English; it narrowed its referent in Modern English to 'a female child, young woman'.

(4) *hound* 'a species of dog (long-eared hunting dog which follows its prey by scent)' comes from Old English *hund* 'dog' in general.

(5) *meat* originally meant 'food' in general and later narrowed its meaning to 'meat' ('food of flesh'); this original meaning is behind the English compound *sweetmeat* 'candy'. The earlier meaning of *meat* as 'food' generally is seen also in the King James Bible (from 1611), for example in Genesis 1:29: 'And God said, Behold, I have given you every herb bearing seed, which is upon the face of all the earth, and every tree, in the which is the fruit of a tree yielding seed; to you it shall be for meat.' (Compare the Swedish cognate *mat* 'food'.)

(6) *starve* 'to suffer or perish from hunger' is from Old English *steorfan* 'to die'. (Compare the German cognate *sterben* 'to die'.)

(7) *wife* meant 'woman' in Old English times (as in the original sense of a *midwife*, literally a 'with-woman'). *Wife* narrowed to mean 'woman of humble rank or of low employment, especially one selling commodities of various sorts'. The first of these former meanings is preserved in *old wives' tales* and the second meaning in *fishwife*. Finally the meaning of *wife* shifted to 'married woman, female spouse'.

(8) French *soldat* 'soldier' comes from *solder* 'to pay' and thus meant 'a paid person'; it underwent a narrowing from 'any paid person' to 'someone in the military'.

(9) Spanish *rezar* 'to pray' is from Old Spanish *rezar* 'to recite, say aloud', from Latin *recitāre* 'to recite, say aloud', the source from which *recite* in English is borrowed. It narrowed from its earlier broader sense of 'to recite, say aloud' to the more restricted sense of 'to pray'.

As will be seen in Chapter 11, many examples of grammaticalization involve semantic narrowing, from a broader lexical meaning to a narrower grammatical function.

6.2.3 Degeneration (pejoration)

In degeneration (often called *pejoration*), the sense of a word takes on a less positive, more negative evaluation in the minds of the users of the language – an increasingly negative value judgement. A famous, oft-cited example is English *knave* 'a rogue', from Old English *cnafa* 'a youth, child', which was extended to mean 'servant' and then ultimately to the modern sense of *knave* 'rogue, disreputable fellow' (compare the German cognate *Knabe* 'boy, lad').

Some other examples of semantic changes involving degeneration follow.

(1) *attitude* originally involved the meaning 'position, pose', then shifted to mean 'mental state, mode of thinking' (as in a mental posture or position taken, holding an opinion, later a set or settled opinion). It deteriorated when in more casual speech it took on the meaning of 'an antagonistic, uncooperative, or confrontational stance' (where what was earlier *she's got a bad attitude* came to be expressed by simply *she's got an attitude*). In slang in the 1970s a to *tude*, 'an unpleasant, cocky, or arrogant way of behaving towards someone', arose.

(2) *bully* was originally like 'sweetheart, darling', a term of endearment applied to either sex. In the seventeenth century its meaning shifted to 'fine fellow', with positive senses of 'worthy, jolly, admirable' attested in the 1680s (see, for example, Shakespeare's *bully-rook* for 'jolly comrade'), preserved, for instance, in *bully for you!* The meaning later deteriorated to 'blusterer' and then 'harasser of the weak'.

(3) *dilettante* did not originally have a negative connotation, but meant 'devoted amateur, one with love of a subject'; it shifted its meaning to 'a dabbler, amateur who lacks the understanding of professionals', and then to 'one with superficial interest in an area of knowledge'. *Amateur* is similar, originally a lover of a topic (a French loan into English, from Latin *amator* 'lover, one who loves'), then it

acquired the meaning of 'a non-professional who engages in an activity for pleasure', and eventually shifted to the negative meaning of 'an incompetent person'.

(4) *evil* had the original sense of 'uppity, exceeding due limits', related etymologically to *up* and to *over*.

(5) *silly* 'foolish, stupid' comes from Middle English *sely* 'happy, innocent, pitiable', from Old English *sǣlig* 'blessed, blissful' (compare the German cognate *selig* 'blissful, happy').

(6) *villain* 'criminal, scoundrel' was borrowed from French *villein* 'person of the villa/farm/homestead, serf, farm worker', and in Middle English it meant 'low-born, base-minded rustic, a man of ignoble ideas or instincts', but later came to mean 'unprincipled or depraved scoundrel' and 'a man naturally disposed to criminal activities'.

(7) Spanish *siniestro* 'sinister' < Old Spanish *siniestro* 'left'; it is from Latin *sinister* 'left', the source of the loanword *sinister* in English.

Examples of degeneration involving terms for women are well known and are often cited as examples in works dealing with sexism in society. For example, in colloquial German, *Weib* means 'ill-tempered woman' or has a sort of macho feel to it when used by men, rather like *broad* in American English; however, in older German it just means 'woman' or 'a woman of the common people'. The English cognate *wife*, seen above, also formerly meant 'woman'. Many terms for women which were initially neutral (or at least not so negative) degenerated so that today they are quite negative in connotation:

> *bimbo* is borrowed from Italian *bimbo*, a variant of *bambino* 'baby (boy)'; in 1919 in the US it referred to 'a stupid or brutish man', and in the late 1920s came also to be associated with women, taking on the meaning of 'an attractive though unintelligent woman, often blonde and with sensual figure and large breasts, possibly wearing revealing clothing'.
>
> *harlot* originally meant 'tramp, beggar' (borrowed from Old French *harlot*, *herlot* 'vagabond').
>
> *madam* 'the female head of a house of prostitution' is from 'a title of courtesy used as a polite form of address to a woman' (from *Madame*, borrowed from Old French *ma dame* 'my lady').
>
> *mistress*, a borrowing from Old French *maistresse* 'a woman who rules or has control'; earlier in English it meant 'a woman who employs others in her service, a woman who has the care of or authority over servants or attendants'. The change to 'a woman having an extramarital sexual relationship, especially with a married man' is a degeneration in meaning.
>
> *spinster* 'unmarried older woman' is a degeneration from 'one who spins'.
>
> Italian *putta* and Spanish *puta* 'whore', quite obscene, earlier meant just 'girl'. Compare Old Italian *putta* 'girl', *putto* 'boy, from Latin *puta* 'girl', *putus* 'boy'. Italian *putto* 'figure in a work of art depicted as a chubby male child, usually naked and sometimes winged' is also from Latin *putus* 'boy'; it is more commonly seen in the plural, *putti*, also used in English discussions of Renaissance art.

Spanish *ramera* 'prostitute' earlier meant 'innkeeper's wife, female inn-keeper'.

6.2.4 Elevation (amelioration)

Meaning changes in the direction of more positive value judgements are cases of elevation (also called amelioration). The process is seen in the history of the following words.

(1) *dude* 'guy, person' was elevated in meaning from what was in 1883 a word of ridicule for 'a man who affects an exaggerated fastidiousness in dress, speech and deportment, concerned with what is aesthetically considered "good form", a dandy'.

(2) *fond* is from the past participle of Middle English *fonnen* 'to be foolish, silly'.

(3) *knight* 'mounted warrior serving a king' comes from Old English *cniht* 'boy, servant', which shifted to 'servant', then 'military servant', and finally to the modern senses of 'warrior in service of the king' and 'lesser nobility'. (Compare the German cognate *Knecht* 'servant, farm hand'.)

(4) *nice* (seen above) originally meant 'foolish, stupid, senseless'.

(5) *pretty* < Old English *prættig* 'crafty, sly'.

(6) The *villa* of the Middle Ages meant 'farm, homestead', but was elevated in French *ville* to 'city, town', and in Spanish *villa* to 'village, town, country house' (compare Italian *villa* 'country house').

(7) Spanish *caballo* 'horse' < Latin *caballus* 'nag, workhorse'.

(8) Spanish *calle* 'street' < Latin *calle* '(cattle-)path'.

(9) Spanish *casa* 'house' < Latin *casa* 'hut, cottage'.

(10) Spanish *corte* 'court' < Latin *cohortem, cortem* 'farmyard, enclosure', which came to mean 'division of a Roman military camp', which was extended to include 'body of troops (belonging to that division)' to 'imperial guard' and then further to 'palace' (see English *court*, a loan from Old French *court*, Modern French *cour* 'court (legal, royal), courtship' with the same Latin origin as the Spanish forms).

6.2.5 Taboo replacement and avoidance of obscenity

People frequently express delight or repulsion, depending on their dispositions, upon learning the history of changes involving taboo, obscenity, and euphemism. Many of these cases involve degeneration or metaphor, or other kinds of semantic changes discussed in this chapter. We also encounter cases where a meaning may remain but a different word which had other denotations before the change is substituted for it – lexical replacement. For instance, in English, *ass* 'long-eared animal related to a horse' has essentially been replaced in America by *donkey* (or *burro*) because *ass* with this meaning causes discomfort arising from homophony with obscene *ass* 'arse, butt, derriere'. Similarly, *cock* 'adult male chicken' is replaced by *rooster* due to the associations of *cock* with 'penis' – probably *rooster*, the favoured word in America, has entirely lost its original association with a bird that 'roosts'. In places where English *bloody* is obscene, what is in North

America a *bloody nose* becomes *blood nose* or *bleeding nose* in order to avoid the taboo word *bloody*.

In *euphemisms*, words regarded as unpleasant get replaced or changed. We see this in the many euphemistic replacements of words meaning 'toilet'. Terms for 'toilet' come to feel indelicate and so less distressing substitutions are made. The room where indoor toilets were installed was called a *water closet* (abbreviated *WC*) in Britain; this was soon replaced by *toilet*, originally a loan from French *toilette* 'small cloth' (diminutive of *toile* 'cloth, towel', the source of *towel* in English), which then shifted its meaning to 'a cloth cover for a dressing table', then 'articles used in dressing', 'furniture of the toilet', 'toilet-table', 'toilet service', and then to 'the table upon which these articles are placed', 'the action or process of dressing', 'a dressing room with bathing facilities', and finally to the 'toilet' fixture itself for bodily needs. This word is replaced in many parts of the English-speaking world by such other euphemisms as *bathroom, commode, john, lavatory, loo, restroom, washroom, ladies' room/men's room*, and so on. Similar euphemisms to avoid the discomfort of words meaning 'toilet' or 'bathroom/restroom' are found in other languages. For example, French has *petit coin* (literally 'small corner') for *toilettes* 'bathroom/restroom', *cabinets* 'toilet, bathroom/restroom' (from 'cabinet'), etc. Spanish has such things as *aseo* (etymologically from 'to tidy up'), *baño* 'bathroom, toilet' (from *baño* 'bath'), *inodoro* 'toilet' (etymologically NEG + 'odor'), *sanitario* 'bathroom/restroom' (etymologically from Latin *sānitās* 'health'), among others.

A few more examples from languages other than English of replacements due to taboo and euphemism follow.

(1) Spanish *huevo* 'egg' came to mean both 'egg' and 'testicle', but because of the word's obscene associations with 'testicle', in colloquial Mexican Spanish *huevo* as 'egg' came to be often avoided and replaced by *blanquillo* 'egg', originally 'small white thing' (*blanco* 'white' + *-illo* 'diminutive').

(2) Latin American Spanish *pájaro* 'bird' also came to be associated as an obscenity with 'penis', and for this reason *pajarito* is usually substituted for 'bird', from *pájaro* 'bird' + *-ito* 'diminutive'. This taboo avoidance is carried even further in Kaqchikel and K'iche' (Mayan languages of Guatemala), where in many dialects the native term *ts'ikin* 'bird' has become taboo due to influence from Spanish *pájaro* 'penis, bird' (Spanish is the dominant language of the region), and therefore *ts'ikin* has been replaced by *čikop* (IPA [tʃikop]) '(small) animal'. Thus the meaning of *čikop* has been extended to include both '(small) animal' and 'bird', while that of *ts'ikin* has been restricted now to only or predominantly 'penis', with its meaning of 'bird' either eliminated or now very recessive.

(3) Spanish *embarazada* 'pregnant' (originally meaning 'encumbered') has replaced earlier *preñada* 'pregnant'. (English *embarrass* also earlier meant 'to encumber, impede, hamper [movements, actions]', a borrowing from French *embarrasser* 'to block, to obstruct'.)

Not only are words often replaced to avoid obscenities and taboo, but their pronunciation can also be modified to give more acceptable, euphemistic outcomes. For example, *pee* originated as an abbreviated, deflected form of more obscene *piss*. English has many such 'deflected' (or 'distorted') euphemistic forms, for example: *dadnabbit, dang, dog-gone, friggin', fudge, gadzooks, gosh, jeez, shucks, zounds* (expression of surprize or anger, deflected from *God's wounds!, by God's wounds!,* in reference to Christ's wounds on the Cross), and many more.

Varieties of Spanish have examples such as *pucha, puchis, púchica,* and the like as euphemistic replacements for *puta* 'whore' (very obscene); *chin* in Mexican Spanish replaces the obscene *chingar* 'to screw, shag (have sexual intercourse)'. Examples of this sort are found in many languages. (Other cases of avoidance of taboo and obscenity are also seen in the discussion of *avoidance of homophony*, Chapter 12.)

6.2.6 Metaphor

Definitions of 'metaphor' (from Greek *metaphorā* 'transference') vary and are often vague; that is, it is often difficult to determine whether something fits the definition or not. Metaphor involves understanding or experiencing one kind of thing in terms of another kind of thing thought somehow to be similar in some way. Metaphor in semantic change involves extensions in the meaning of a word that suggest a semantic similarity or connection between the new sense and the original one. Metaphor is considered a major factor in semantic change. It has been likened to analogy where one thing is conceptualized in terms of another, with a leap across semantic domains. The semantic change of *grasp* 'seize' to 'understand' can thus be seen as such a leap across semantic domains, from the physical domain ('seizing') to the mental domain ('comprehension') (see Traugott and Dasher 2002: 28). A much-repeated example is English *bead*, now meaning 'small piece of (decorative) material pierced for threading on a line'. It comes from Middle English *bede* 'prayer, prayer bead', which in Old English was *beode, gebed* 'prayer' (compare the German equivalent *Gebet* 'prayer'). The semantic shift from 'prayer' to 'bead' came about through the metaphoric extension from the 'prayer', which was kept track of by the rosary bead, to the rosary bead itself, and then eventually to any 'bead', even including 'beads' of water.

(1) The notion 'to kill' often attracts metaphoric alternatives, as in English: *to blow away, bump off, dispatch, dispose of, do in, eliminate, erase, ice (someone), knock off, liquidate, off (someone), polish off, put down, put to sleep, rub out, slaughter, smoke (someone), stiff (someone), take care of, take out, terminate, waste, whack,* and others.

(2) In slang, there are many metaphoric meaning changes to refer to 'drunk' based on forms whose original meaning is associated with being 'damaged' in some way: *bashed, blasted, blitzed, bombed, hammered, obliterated, ploughed, ripped, shredded, smashed, tattered, totalled, wasted, zonked.* Another area of metaphor for 'drunk' involves being saturated with liquid: *besotted, flushed, juiced, pickled, pissed, sauced, sloshed, soaked, soused, tanked (tanked up),* etc.

Some other examples of metaphoric change are:

(3) *chill* 'to relax, calm down' of slang origin by metaphoric extension of the original meaning of *chill* 'to cool'.

(4) *stud* 'good-looking, sexy man' of slang origin, derived by metaphor from *stud* 'a male animal (especially a horse) used for breeding'.

(5) *mouse* by metaphor came also to be applied to a computer mouse, thought to resemble a mouse in size and shape.

(6) *thrill*, whose original meaning was 'to make a hole in, to pierce', shifted metaphorically to 'to pierce with emotion', and then later 'to fill with pleasure'.

(7) French *feuille* 'leaf, sheet of paper' from the original meaning of 'leaf (of plant)' only; also Spanish *hoja* 'leaf, sheet of paper' from 'leaf' (both from Latin *folium* 'leaf').

(8) Spanish *sierra* 'saw' was applied by metaphor to 'mountain range'; now there is *sierra* 'saw' and *sierra* 'mountain range'.

(9) Spanish *pierna* 'leg' < Latin *perna* 'ham'.

(10) French *fermer* 'to close' originally meant 'to fix, make firm or fast'. Spanish *firmar* 'to sign (with one's signature)' has the same source, both inherited from Latin *firmāre* 'to strengthen, fortify, confirm, prove'.

(11) French *chapeau* 'hat, bonnet' originally meant 'garland'.

6.2.7 Metonymy

Metonymy (from Greek *metōnumia* 'transformation of the name, change of name', from *meta* 'change' + *onuma* 'name') is a change in meaning where a word comes to have additional senses that are associated with the word's original meaning, although the conceptual association between the old and new meanings may not be especially precise. Metonymic changes typically involve some contiguity in the real world, a shift in meaning from one thing to another that is present in the context, although being present may be a conceptual judgement call that is not always readily apparent. Metonymy might be thought to involve conceptual shifts within the same semantic domain (Traugott and Dasher 2002: 28–9).

Some examples of metonymic change follow.

(1) *cheek*. A much-repeated example is that of English *cheek*. Old English *cēace* meant 'jaw, jawbone', but over time shifted to the sense of Modern English *cheek*, 'fleshy side of the face below the eye'.

(2) *tea*. *Tea* originally meant only 'tea', the beverage, but has shifted its meaning to apply also to 'the evening meal' in Britain and many Commonwealth countries; that meal was often accompanied by tea drinking.

(3) *elope*. *Elope* originally applied to a married woman running off with a lover, and later shifted to apply to a couple running away from home to get married without parents' permission (related etymologically to *leap*).

(4) Spanish *mejilla* 'cheek' < Latin *maxilla* 'jaw'.

(5) French *jument* 'mare' < 'pack horse'.

(6) Spanish *cadera* 'hip' < 'buttocks', ultimately from Latin *cathedra* 'armchair, easy chair'. (Compare the French cognate *chaise* 'chair', from earlier *chaire*, from the same Latin source.) *Cathedral* ultimately comes from this same Latin source. In the 1580s *cathedral* meant 'church of a bishop', taken from the phrase *cathedral church*, translating Late Latin *ecclesia cathedralis* 'church of a bishop's seat'. Latin had borrowed *cathedra* from Greek *kathedra* 'seat, bench' (from *kata* 'down' + *hedra* 'seat, base').

(7) Spanish *plata* 'silver' has been extended to mean 'money' also.

(8) Spanish *timbre* 'bell (as a doorbell)' and 'postage stamp' originally meant 'drum'. By metonymy this was extended to include a 'clapperless bell' (struck on the outside with a hammer), then 'the sound made by this sort of bell', and then 'the sonorous quality of any instrument or of the voice', then 'tone' (of a sound). From the round shape of a bell, it also extended to mean 'helmet-shaped', then 'the crest of a helmet', 'the crest in heraldry' (the ornament placed above the shield), and from this the meaning was extended to include 'the official mark stamped on papers', to 'the mark stamped by the post office upon letters', and finally to 'postage stamp'. (French *timbre* 'tone, postage stamp' has the same history of semantic changes; English *timbre* 'the distinctive quality of a sound' is borrowed from French.)

A common sort of metonymy, sometimes thought to be connected with *clipping* or *ellipsis* (see Chapter 5), is the use of the name of the place for a product characteristic of it, as in French *champagne* 'champagne', from the name of the region, *Champagne*. (For other examples, see Chapter 5.)

Traugott and Dasher (2002) give metonymy a more important role in semantic change than is traditionally the case. They do not believe that metaphor and metonymy in principle exclude each other, since easily understood metaphors can also be seen as typical associations – in some instances the notion of a leap across semantic domains (metaphor) and change within the same domain (metonymy) may not be clear or even relevant. Traugott and Dasher believe that it must be possible for the target (the semantic concept after the change) and/or the source (before the change) of a potential metaphor to be understood or conceptualized metonymically for metaphor to be possible (2002: 29).

6.2.8 Synecdoche

Synecdoche (from Greek *sunekdokhē* 'inclusion' [*sun-* 'with' + *-ek* 'out + *dekhestai* 'to receive']), often considered a kind of metonymy, involves a part-to-whole relationship, where a term with more comprehensive meaning is used to refer to a less comprehensive meaning or vice versa; that is, a part (or quality) is used to refer to the whole, or the whole is used to refer to a part, for example *hand*, which was extended also to 'hired hand, employed worker'. Some cases often found in various languages are 'tongue' > 'language', 'sun' > 'day', 'moon' > 'month'. Other examples follow.

(1) *Mail* was originally borrowed from Old French, meaning 'bag, pouch' (see modern French *malle* 'bag'), and then narrowed to mean 'bag for carrying letters', then changed to 'letters carried in that bag', and then on to mean 'mail' generally. *Email* is a step further removed from the original 'bag' meaning.

(2) *Paper* also took on the new meanings of a 'newspaper' and an 'article' in a journal or book.

(3) Spanish *boda* 'wedding' comes from Latin *vōta* 'marriage vows', where the term for a part of the ceremony, namely the 'vows', came to mean the whole thing, in this case the 'wedding'.

(4) German *Bein* 'leg' originally meant 'bone' (cognate with English *bone*).

(5) French *tableau* 'picture, panel, board' < Latin *tabula* 'board' (compare English *table*, a loanword ultimately from this same source).

If shocking examples, such as obscene or off-colour ones, can help make a concept memorable, then some of the following examples of synecdoche should help to make it unforgettable.

(6) *asshole* (from *arsehole*) formerly meant just 'anus', a body part with unpleasant associations; it changed its meaning to include *asshole* as 'a contemptible or stupid person', the part coming to represent the whole.

(7) *prick* 'penis' extended to 'despicable, contemptible male'. (*Prick* with the meaning 'penis' illustrates an earlier metaphoric extension from *prick* 'small puncture, sharp point' to 'penis')

(8) English *schmuck* 'contemptible person', comes from Yiddish *schmuck* 'penis, fool, stupid person', where it originally meant 'jewel' (compare German *Schmuck* 'jewel, ornament'), but it shifted to mean 'penis' (roughly analogous to jocular English *the family jewels*), and then *schmuck* as 'penis' extended its meaning to 'fool, stupid person', and along the way lost the original meaning of 'jewel'.

6.2.9 Displacement (ellipsis)

Displacement (sometimes called *ellipsis*) involves changes where one word absorbs part or all of the meaning of another word with which it is linked in a phrase, usually an adjective + noun). A frequently mentioned example is *private* from *private soldier*, where *private* after the change came to mean 'ordinary/regular soldier' (contrasted with 'officer'), taking on the meaning of the whole earlier phrase. Displacement is sometimes considered a special kind of synecdoche, sometimes called phrasal synecdoche. Some other examples are:

(1) *capital* < *capital city*.
(2) *contact(s)* < *contact lens(es)*.
(3) *intercourse* < *sexual intercourse*.
(4) *proposal, to propose* < *marriage proposal, to propose marriage*.
(5) *salad* < Old French *salade*, from Vulgar Latin *salata* meaning 'salted', a displacement from older *herba salata* 'salted vegetables' to just *salata*. Vegetables seasoned with brine were a popular Roman dish.
(6) French *succès* 'success' comes from *succès favorable* 'favourable issue, event' (derived from *succéder* 'to follow, transpire'; compare Latin *successus* 'advance uphill, result', derived from *succēdere* 'to go under, take on, go up, climb'). (French is the source of borrowed *success* in English.)
(7) French *journal* 'newspaper' is a displacement from *papier journal* 'daily paper' (*papier* 'paper' + *journal* 'daily'). In English, *a daily* (from *daily paper*) has the same meaning and has developed in the same way.
(8) French *foie* 'liver' and Spanish *hígado* 'liver' < Latin *iecur ficātum* 'fig-stuffed liver' by ellipsis so that only the reflex of *ficātum* 'fig-stuffed' remains with the meaning 'liver'.
(9) Finnish *yskä* 'cough' comes from original *yskä tauti*, literally 'chest sickness', *yskä* 'breast, lap' + *tauti* 'sickness', where *yskä* now no longer has the connotation of 'breast, chest' (Ravila 1966: 106).

6.2.10 Hyperbole (exaggeration by overstatement)

Hyperbole (from Greek *huperbolē* 'excess' [*huper* 'over, beyond' + *bolē* 'a throwing, casting']) involves shifts in meaning due to exaggeration by overstatement. Some examples of this kind of change in meaning are:

(1) *awesome*. In the 1590s *awesome* meant 'profoundly reverential'; by 1690 it had acquired the meaning of 'inspiring dread or awe'. Today's sense of 'impressive, very good' was attested by 1961 and was very much in use by the 1980s. To say a word meaning 'inspiring dread' when the intended meaning is 'very good' is an exaggeration by overstatement.

(2) *quell*. Old English *cwellan*, the source of Modern English *quell*, meant 'to kill, murder, slay'. The milder sense of 'suppress, extinguish' developed around 1300 by change due to hyperbolic usage of the word. The German cognate *quälen* 'to torment, torture' has a similar history of semantic shift by hyperbole. It, like English *quell*, comes from Proto-Germanic *k^waljan* 'to kill'.

(3) *spill*. The Old English source of *spill* was *spillan* 'to destroy, kill, mutilate'. By late Old English times it came to mean also 'to waste'. By the early fourteenth century it was used to mean 'to shed blood', and by the mid-foruteenth century it had developed the sense 'to let liquid fall or run out'.

(4) *terribly, horribly, awfully*. These and similar words today mean little more than 'very' (a generic intensifier); by overstatement they have lost their original semantic connections with *terror*, *horror*, and *awe*.

(5) German *sehr* 'very' < 'sorely' (cognate with English *sore*).

6.2.11 Litotes (exaggeration by understatement)

Litotes (from Greek *litótēs* 'smoothness, plainness') is exaggeration by understatement (such as 'of no small importance' when 'very important' is meant). Such exaggerations by understatement are frequently behind permanent changes in meaning. Some examples are:

(1) *battle*. *Battle* ultimately is from Latin *battuere* with the meaning 'to beat, to strike' (also the same ultimate source as for English *batter*). In Late Latin times *battualia*, the noun derived from *battuere*, meant 'exercise of soldiers and gladiators in fighting and fencing'. English got *to battle* from French *batailler* 'to fight' and the noun *battle* from Old French *bataille* 'single combat, battle' (descended from the Latin words). Saying 'beat, strike' while meaning 'battle (fight with opposing forces)' was an understatement.

(2) *bereaved, bereft*. These words that today mean 'deprived by death' earlier meant just 'robbed' (from Old English *bereafian* 'to rob, take away by violence, deprive', composed of *be-* 'about, around' + *reafian* 'to rob, plunder').

(3) *kill*. *Kill* originally meant 'to hit, strike, beat, knock'. Around 1300 it came to acquire the meaning of 'to deprive of life, to put to death'. Examples of litotes are found in many languages involving verbs meaning 'to kill'. If you say *hit* but intend it to mean 'kill', that is an understatement.

(4) *poison*. *Poison* involves change by litotes in French, reflected in English *poison*, borrowed from French. It comes from Latin *potiōnem* 'a drink, drinking' (derived

from *pōtāre* 'to drink'), which around the twelfth century gave Old French *poison*, *puison* 'a drink', especially 'a medical drink'. Later, around the fourteenth century, it came to mean 'a potion, a magic potion, poisonous drink', from which English borrowed *poison*. This, then, gives us the irony of *poison*, something bad, and *potable*, something good, coming from the same root, both ultimately derived from Latin *pōtāre* 'to drink'.

We can add German *Gift* 'poison' to this story – it is no accident that it is identical to English *gift*: the original meaning of German *Gift* was 'gift, present'. While in Johann Wolfgang von Goethe's time (1749–1832) *Gift* still included the 'gift, present' meaning, that sense has now disappeared from Modern German. The change from 'gift' towards 'deadly gift, poison' had already begun in Old High German, later influenced by the Greek and Medieval Latin word *dosis* 'gift, a giving, a specified amount of medicine' (the ultimate source of English *dose*, borrowed from French, ultimately based on Proto-Indo-European *doh_3-* 'to give'). The apparent euphemistic saying of 'a gift' to mean a 'poisonous gift, poison' is exaggeration by understatement.

(5) *venom*. *Venom* came into English from Old French *venim* 'poison, malice', which is from Latin *venēnum* 'poison', but which earlier meant 'drug, medical potion' and 'charm, seduction', presumably also 'love potion', from the Proto-Indo-European root *wen-* 'to desire, strive for'. This is likely to be an exaggeration by understatement, to go from a 'love potion, drug' to 'deadly poison'.

Proto-Indo-European *wen-* 'to desire' is also the source of *Venus*, the Roman goddess of love and beauty, from whence we get *venerable* 'commanding respect', *venerate* 'to treat with reverence', *venereal* 'description of an infection or disease that is caught or transmitted through sexual intercourse', and *venial* 'excusable, forgivable, pardonable'. And that is how the goddess of love (*Venus*), poison (*venom*), respect (*venerable*, *venerate*), and STDs, socially transmitted diseases (*venereal*), can all be related and come from the same root.

(6) French *meurtre* 'murder, homicide'. This comes via litotes from its earlier meaning of 'bruise', still seen in the etymologically related verb *meurtrir* 'to bruise' (compare the Spanish cognate *moretón* 'bruise, black-and-blue spot').

6.2.12 Semantic shift due to contact

Although usually not included in traditional classifications of semantic change, examples of semantic shift due to foreign contacts are occasionally encountered in the history of specific languages. The following are a few examples.

(1) Spanish *pavo* originally meant 'peacock'; however, when the Spanish came to the New World, they called the newly discovered turkey *pavo* also. Eventually, to distinguish the two birds, *pavo* remained with the meaning of 'turkey', while 'peacock' became *pavo real*, literally 'real turkey' (also 'royal turkey').

(2) In K'iche' (Mayan), *kye:x* originally meant 'deer'; however, with the introduction of horses after European contact, *kye:x* was applied to these animals and so *kye:x* also came to mean 'horse'. Eventually, to distinguish 'deer' from 'horse', the term for 'deer' became *k'i:če? kye:x*, literally 'forest horse', and *kye:x* ended up with only the meaning of 'horse'. (NOTE: *y* = IPA [j], [kje:x]; *č* = IPA [ʧ].)

(3) With the introduction of European guns, the Lake Miwok (of the Utian [Miwok-Costanoan] family, California) word *kó:no*, which originally meant 'bow', shifted its meaning to include 'gun'. The 'gun' meaning then extended so fully that 'bow' came to be called *hintí:l kó:no*, literally 'old-time gun' (*hintí:l* is a borrowing from Spanish *gentil* 'pagan, gentile', originally used to refer to un-Christianized Indians) (Callaghan and Gamble 1997: 112). See also calques, in Chapter 3.

6.2.13 Summary of traditional classification

As is easy to see, the categories of semantic change in this classification are not necessarily distinct from one another; rather, some of them overlap and intersect. For this reason, some scholars consider 'narrowing' and 'widening' to be the principal kinds of semantic change, with others as mere subtypes of these two. Some emphasize the tendency for change to be in the direction from *concrete* to *abstract*. Instances of overlapping and intersection are easily found in the examples listed here. For example, a semantic change could involve widening, degeneration, and metonymy all at once, as in the examples seen above where terms for male genitals have taken on negative meanings for a man of negative character, often obscene.

6.3 Attempts to Explain Semantic Change

General classifications of semantic change such as the one just seen seem to offer little in the way of explaining how and why these changes take place in the ways they do. Nevertheless, many scholars have called for a search for regularities and explanations in semantic change, and some general tendencies have been discussed and some generalizations proposed. It is important to see what understanding they may offer. The more traditional classifications of kinds of semantic change are generally thought to be useful for showing what sorts of changes might occur, but some of the generalizations that have been based on them amount to little more than restating the kind of change itself. Others point out that semantic change cannot be explained in a vacuum, but will require appeal to and coordination with analogy, syntax (especially in the form of grammaticalization; see Chapter 11), pragmatics, discourse analysis, and social history. Because sociocultural historical facts are often relevant in semantic change, some people insist that it is useless to seek generalizations to explain it, although most would admit that some general statements about how and why meanings change may be possible even if not all semantic changes are regular or predictable.

Some earlier work on semantic change did attempt to generalize. A general mechanism of semantic change was believed to be the associative patterns of human thought, and thus traditional approaches to meaning change typically had a psychological-cognitive orientation, though social context and pragmatic factors were emphasized by others. All of these factors play a role in more recent work on semantic change.

Although in the past it was rarely asked how semantic change might come about and how it was to be explained, many now recognize that semantic change must go through a stage of *polysemy*, where a word comes to have more than one meaning. Thus in a historical shift a word might expand its sphere of reference to take on additional meanings, becoming polysemous. Alternatively in a semantic change, a polysemous form may lose one (or more) of its meanings. A view which some have of semantic change combines both these situations: the word starts out with an original meaning, then acquires additional, multiple meanings, and then the original sense is lost, leaving only the newer meaning. Schematically this can be represented in three stages, beginning with form *a* which has meaning 'A':

Stage 1: *a* 'A'
Stage 2: *a* 'A', 'B' ('A' > 'A', 'B')
Stage 3: *a* 'B'   ('A', 'B' > 'B')

Some examples to show this will be helpful.

(1) English *timber*, German *Zimmer* 'room'. In Stage 1, form *a* = Germanic **temra-n*, with meaning 'A' = 'building, building material' (from Proto-Indo-European **dem-* 'house, household'; compare Latin *dom-us* 'house' and Old English *timrian* 'to build'). In Stage 2, English *a* = *timber*, 'A' = 'building', 'B' = 'material for building', 'wood which supplies building material'. Similarly in Stage 2, German *a* = *Zimmer*, 'A' = 'building, building material', 'B' = 'room'. In Stage 3, English *a* = *timber*, 'B' = 'material for building', 'wood which supplies building material' (meaning *A* 'building' was lost). Also in Stage 3, German *a* = *Zimmer*, 'B' = 'room' (meaning 'A' 'building, building material' was lost).

(2) English *write*. In Stage 1, *write* meant 'to cut, score' (compare the German cognate *reissen* 'to tear, split'). In Stage 2, the meaning was extended to include both 'to cut, scratch' and 'to write'; the connection is through runic writing, which was carved or scratched on wood and stone (compare Old Norse *rīta* 'to scratch, to write'). This stage is attested in Old English *wrītan* 'to write', 'to cut'. Stage 3 is illustrated by modern English *write* meaning 'to write' only, where the sense of 'to cut' or 'to scratch' has been lost.

(3) Spanish *alcalde* 'mayor'. When first borrowed from Arabic *qāḍī* this meant 'judge (in Islamic law)' ('A'), but was later broadened to mean 'an official who is magistrate and mayor' ('B', added with 'A'), and then eventually the term was restricted in meaning to only 'mayor' (only 'B'; meaning 'A' was lost).

This view recognizes (at least implicitly, and often explicitly) an intervening stage of polysemy as necessary in semantic changes. Other scholars do not emphasize this view so much; rather, they recognize that lexical items typically have a core meaning (or group of related core concepts) but also have various less central, more peripheral senses when used in a variety of discourse contexts, and they see semantic change as happening when a less central sense becomes more central or when the original core concept recedes to be more peripheral, often eventually being lost altogether. Still other scholars see meaning as a network or semantic map, where items within a semantic domain and from other domains are related by various overlappings in the polysemous choice which each lexical item has. Semantic change in this view follows paths of connections in the network, selecting and emphasizing different senses which an item has in different contexts. These are not really different approaches, but rather just more realistic versions of the view that holds that polysemy is a necessary intermediate step in semantic change.

Most linguists, past and present, have looked to structural (linguistic) and psychological factors as a primary cause of semantic change; however, historical factors outside of language have also been considered important causes of semantic change. Changes in technology, society, politics, religion, and in fact in all spheres of human life can lead to semantic shifts. Thus, for example, *pen* originally meant 'feather, quill' (a loan into English from Old French *penne* 'feather, writing quill'; compare Latin *penna* 'feather'), but as times changed and other instruments for writing came into use, the thing referred to by the word *pen* today is not remotely connected with 'feather'. As guns replaced older hunting implements and weapons, terms meaning 'bow' (or 'arrow') shifted to mean 'gun' in many languages. Thus in the Lake Miwok example mentioned above, *kó:no* 'gun' originally meant 'bow'. The word for 'blowgun' in K'iche' (Mayan), *uɓ*, shifted its meaning to include 'shotgun'. In the wake of automobiles and aeroplanes, *drive* and *fly* have taken on new meanings.

There are countless such examples of words whose meanings have changed due to sociocultural and technological change in the world around us, and several of the examples presented here in the classification of kinds of semantic changes are of this sort. For example, changes in religion and society are behind the shift from *blēdsian* 'to mark with blood in an act of consecration in pagan sacrifice' to modern *to bless*; and, as 'pelts' were replaced as a medium of exchange, Finnish *raha* shifted its meaning from 'pelt' to 'money'. In the historical events that brought English speakers to America, Australia, New Zealand, South Africa, and so on, new plants and animals were encountered, and sometimes native English words which originally referred to very different species were utilized to refer to these new species, leading to semantic shifts in the meaning of these words. Thus, for example, *magpie* and *robin* refer to totally different species of birds in North America, in the UK, and in Australia and New Zealand. *Magpie* in Europe is *Pica caudata* (of the family of *Corvidae*); the American magpie is *Pica pica hudsonia*; and the Australian and New Zealand magpie is *Gymnorhina tibicen* (of the *Cracticidae* family). *Robin* in England is of the genus *Erithacus*; in North America *robin* refers to *Turdus migratorius*; the New Zealand robin is *Petroica australis* (of the family *Muscicapidae*). The American *possum* (or *opossum*) (*Didelphis virginiana*) and Australian *possum* (*Trichosurus vulpecula* and other species) are very different animals. Many Spanish words have undergone semantic changes as the result of similar historical events; for example, *gorrión* means 'sparrow' in Spain, but shifted its meaning to 'hummingbird' in Central America; *tejón* means 'badger' in Spain, but 'coatimundi' in Mexico; *león* refers to 'lion' in Spain, but has shifted to 'cougar, mountain lion' in the Spanish of many areas of Latin America; similarly, Spanish *tigre*, originally 'tiger', means 'jaguar' in much of Latin America.

This sort of shift in meaning makes it difficult to generalize about semantic change. Since changes in society and technology are for the most part unpredictable, their affects on semantic change are also not predictable. Recent work concentrates on the general directionality observed for some kinds of semantic changes, and attempts based on these are being made to elaborate a more explanatory approach, one which might predict possible and impossible changes or directions of change. Eve Sweetser's and Elizabeth Closs Traugott's work in this area has been influential (see Sweetser 1990; Traugott 1989; Traugott and Dasher 2002; Traugott and Heine 1991; Traugott and König 1991; see also Hopper and Traugott 2003). Some general claims about semantic change that have been formulated are the following.

1. Semantically related words often undergo parallel semantic shifts. For example, various words which meant 'rapidly' in Old English and Middle English shifted their meaning to 'immediately', as with Old English *swifte* 'rapidly' and *georne* 'rapidly, eagerly', both of which changed the meaning to 'immediately' in about 1300 (Traugott and Dasher 2002: 67).
2. Phonetic similarity (especially cases of phonetic identity, homophony) can lead to shifts which leave the phonetically similar forms semantically more similar (sometimes identical). Note the confusion and lack of contrast many English speakers have with such sets of related words as *lie/lay* and *sit/set*. Standard English has *lie/lay/lain* as opposed to *lay/laid/laid*, but many speakers do not make these distinctions.
3. Spatial/locative words may develop temporal senses: *before, after, behind*. Also, spatial terms often develop from body-part terms, as in *ahead of*, North American *in back of, at the foot of*.
4. Some common semantic shifts typically (though not always) go in one direction and not the other; cases which recur and are found in numerous languages include the following.

(1) Words having to do with the sense of touch may typically develop meanings involving the sense of taste: *sharp, hot* ('spicy').

(2) Words involving the sense of taste may develop extended senses involving emotions in general: *bitter, sour, sweet*.

(3) Obligation > possibility/probability – more precisely, *root* senses of modals, also called *deontic* senses, by which is meant real-world forces, such as obligation, permission, and ability, typically develop *epistemic* meanings (where epistemic means 'speaker's assessment' and denotes necessity, probability, and possibility involving reasoning). For example, in the history of *may*, the meaning was first physical ability (*Elizabeth may come* = 'Elizabeth is able to come'); then the sense of social permission developed ('Elizabeth is allowed to come'); finally the epistemic, logical possibility sense came about ('it is perhaps the case that Elizabeth will come'). The history of *must* is similar: first, *Bess must sing* had the root meaning ('it is a requirement that Bess sing'); second, an epistemic sense was added ('that Bess must sing is a reasoned conclusion based on the evidence that her father and mother and brothers and sisters all sing, so it is likely that she, too, sings'). In these examples, the root senses are original and the epistemic senses developed later.

(4) Propositional > textual – things with propositional meanings tend to develop textual and later expressive meanings. For example, *while* in modern English means (1) 'a period of time' (propositional, a specific temporal situation), (2) 'during the time that', and (3) 'although' (textual, connecting clauses); however, *while* comes from Old English *þa hwīle þe* [that.ACCUSATIVE while/time.ACCUSATIVE SUBORDINATE.PARTICLE] 'at the time that', which had only the propositional sense, not the later textual one. This phrase was reduced by late Old English times to a simple conjunction, later *while* (Traugott and König 1991: 85).

(5) 'see' > 'know, understand'.

(6) 'hear' > 'understand', 'obey'.

(7) Physical-action verbs (especially with hands) > mental-state verbs, speech-act verbs. For example, verbs such as 'grasp', 'capture', 'get a hold on', 'get', 'catch on to' very commonly come to mean 'understand'; thus, *feel* goes from 'touch, feel with hands' to 'feel, think, have sympathy or pity for'; Spanish *captar*, originally 'capture, seize', added the sense 'to understand'; Finnish *käsittää* 'to comprehend' is derived from *käsi* 'hand'; Spanish *pensar* 'to think' comes from Latin *pēnsāre* 'to weigh'. English *fret* 'worry, be distressed' formerly meant 'to eat, gnaw' (compare the German cognate *fressen* 'to eat, devour, consume (of animals, or rudely of people)').

(8) Mental-state verbs > speech-act verbs (*observe* 'to perceive, witness' > 'to state, remark').

(9) 'man' > 'husband' (German *Mann* 'man, husband' < 'man').

(10) 'woman' > 'wife'.

(11) 'body' > 'person' (compare *somebody*).

(12) 'finger' > 'hand'.

(13) 'left(-handed, left side)' > 'devious, evil, foreboding' (English *sinister*, a borrowing from Latin *sinister* 'left').

(14) animal names > inanimate objects. For example, Spanish *gato* 'jack (for raising cars)' < *gato* 'cat'; in Central American Spanish *mico* 'jack'< *mico* 'monkey'; Spanish *grúa* '(construction) crane' < Old Spanish *grúa* 'crane' (bird) (compare Modern Spanish *grulla, grúa* 'crane (bird)') (compare English *crane* 'crane (a bird)', 'building crane').

Traugott speaks of broad explanatory tendencies:

1. Meanings based on the external situation > meanings based on the internal situation (evaluative/perceptual/cognitive). This would cover, for example, the cases called degeneration and elevation, which involve value judgements on the part of the users of the language. It would also include many of the examples from (5–7) above.

2. Meanings based on external or internal situations > meanings based on textual or (meta)linguistic situations. This would include many instances from (4), (7), and (8) above.

3. Meanings tend to become increasingly based on speakers' subjective beliefs, states, or attitudes towards the proposition. Instances of (1), (2), and especially (3) above illustrate the change of meaning involving increase in

subjective reaction. Many metonymic semantic changes fall under this. (See Traugott 1989.)

It is frequently claimed that semantic shifts typically go from more *concrete* to more *abstract*. For example, there are many semantic changes which extend body-part notions to more abstract meanings, but not the other way around, as with German *Haupt* originally meaning only 'head' (body part; concrete), which was later extended to mean 'main' or 'principal', as in *Hauptstadt* 'capital' (*Haupt* 'head' + *Stadt* 'town, city') and *Hauptbahnhof* 'central station' (*Haupt* 'head' + *Bahnhof* 'railway station'), and then later still *Haupt* lost its primary original meaning of 'head' in most contexts. While this is an important claim, a number of the traditional classes of semantic change, particularly narrowing, often involve change towards more concreteness, and therefore the claim needs to be understood as only a broad general tendency which can easily have exceptions.

In their explanatory treatment of semantic change, Traugott and Dasher (2002) emphasize the typical direction of certain kinds of semantic change. They identify 'regular' tendencies in semantic change, that is, changes that are encountered frequently across languages and also repeatedly within single languages. They propose an 'Invited Inferencing Theory of Semantic Change'. Polysemy is central in this theory, and it typically arises out of the pragmatic forces of *invited inferences* and *subjectification*. *Invited inferences* arise in the pragmatic use of language in given contexts. For example, *as long as* and *so long as* formerly had only spatial and temporal meanings, as in *King Alfred's long ships were almost twice **as long as** the other ships* (spatial) and *Squeeze the medication through a linen cloth onto the eye **as long as** he needs* (temporal). But such temporal sentences could invite the inference that *as/so long as* might also mean conditional ('provided that'), 'squeeze the medication on the eye for the length of time that he needs it' or 'if/on the condition that he still needs it'. Later, in some contexts the conditional sense became the only one possible, as in *He told the jury that it is proper for police to question a juvenile without a parent present **so long as** they made a reasonable effort to notify the parent.*

In *subjectification*, speakers come to develop meanings for words 'that encode or externalize their perspectives and attitudes as constrained by the communicative world of the speech event, rather than by the so-called "real-world" characteristics of the event or situation referred to' (Traugott and Dasher 2002: 30). For example, an increase in subjectivity is seen in semantic changes involving *indeed*: first as *in dede* 'in action', then 'certainly, in actuality'; second, *indeed* changed to include 'in truth' (subjective, reflecting speaker's attitude) in its meaning; third, *indeed* changed to add 'what's more', 'adding to that' (a discourse marker). Another example is the verb *promise*. Its original sense was as 'a directive imposing obligation on oneself as speaker', as in *I promise to do my best.* Semantic change added later the sense 'speaker's high degree of certainty' (more subjective, internalizing the speaker's perspective/attitude), as in *She promises to be an outstanding student.*

Now that we have seen phonological, lexical, and semantic change, it would be possible to continue directly on to syntactic change, grouping consideration of changes that affect the major components of the grammar. However, there are other sorts of changes that do not fit easily in these categories and that also need to be dealt with. It is especially important to understand the comparative method and internal reconstruction, which are the principal methods of historical linguistics, before turning to these other topics. This is, in fact, the traditional sequence followed by most textbooks in historical linguistics – that is, syntactic change, if considered at all, is usually presented later.

6.4 Exercises

Exercise 6.1

Attempt to find examples of your own of semantic changes. Try to name or identify the kinds (categories) of semantic change involved. You can consult internet resources to find some examples. Slang is an area where semantic shifts are frequently found.

Exercise 6.2

Look up the following words in a dictionary or on a website that provides etymologies for words. Determine what change in meaning has taken place in each word. State which type of semantic change is involved (from among the types discussed in this chapter).

For example, if you were to see *villain* in the list, you would look it up and find out that it originally meant 'person of the villa/farm' but has changed its meaning to 'criminal, scoundrel', and you would state this shift in meaning together with the identification of this change as an example of *degeneration* (or *pejoration*).

bug (in a computer program)	crafty
crazy	disease
fame	gaudy
journey	pretty
science	surf (the internet)
thing	vulgar
weird	

Exercise 6.3

In the following examples of semantic change, identify the kind of semantic change involved (widening, narrowing, metonymy, and so on).

1. English *lousy* 'worthless, bad' < 'infested with lice'.
2. English *gay* 'homosexual' is the result of a recent semantic shift, where the original sense, 'cheerful, lively', has become secondary; the shift to the 'homosexual' sense perhaps came through other senses, 'given to social pleasures', which the word had.
3. Spanish *pariente* 'relative' < Old Spanish *pariente* 'parent'.
4. Spanish *segar* 'to reap (to cut grain, grass with a scythe)' < Latin *secāre* 'to cut'.
5. Old Spanish *cuñado* 'relation by marriage' shifted to 'brother-in-law' in Modern Spanish. (This Spanish word comes ultimately from Latin *cognātus* 'blood-relation'.)
6. French *viande* 'meat' formerly meant 'food' in general. (This change parallels English *meat*, which originally meant 'food'.)
7. French *cuisse* 'thigh' < Latin *coxa* 'hip'.
8. Spanish *ciruela* 'plum' < Latin *prūna cēreola* 'waxy plum' (*prūna* 'plum' + *cēreola* 'of wax').
9. Spanish *depender* 'to depend' < Latin *dēpendēre* 'to hang down'.
10. Modern German *Dirne* 'prostitute' < Middle High German *dierne* 'maiden, servant girl' < Old High German *diorna* 'young maiden, girl'.

THE COMPARATIVE METHOD AND LINGUISTIC RECONSTRUCTION

Sprachgeschichte ist im Grunde die schwärzeste aller 'schwarzen' Künste, das einzige Mittel die Geister verschwundener Jahrhunderte zu beschwören. Mit der Sprachgeschichte reicht man am weitesten zurück ins Geheimnis: Mensch.

[Linguistic history is basically the darkest of the dark arts, the only means to conjure up the ghosts of vanished centuries. With linguistic history we reach furthest back into the mystery: humankind.]

(Cola Minis 1952: 107)

7.1 Introduction

The comparative method is central to historical linguistics, the most important of the various methods and techniques we use to recover linguistic history. In this chapter the comparative method is explained, its basic assumptions and its limitations are considered, and its various uses are demonstrated. The primary emphasis is on learning how to apply the method, that is, on how to reconstruct. The comparative method is also important in language classification (see Chapter 9), in linguistic prehistory (see Chapter 15), in research on distant genetic relationships (see Chapter 13), in detecting borrowings (see Chapters 3 and 10), and in other areas.

We say that languages which belong to the same language family are *genetically related* to one another (some prefer to say *phylogenetically* related): this means that these related languages derive from (that is, 'descend' from) a single original language, called a *proto-language*. In time, dialects of the proto-language develop through linguistic changes in different regions where the language was spoken, and then later through further changes some dialects become so different from others that they are no longer mutually intelligible and so are considered distinct languages.

The aim of reconstruction by the comparative method is to recover as much as possible of the ancestor language (the proto-language) from a comparison of the related languages, the descendants of the original language, and to determine what changes have taken place in the various languages that developed from the proto-language. The work of reconstruction usually begins with phonology, with an attempt to reconstruct the sound system; this leads in turn to reconstruction of the vocabulary and grammar of the proto-language. As can be seen from the way languages are classified, we speak of linguistic relationships in terms of kinship; we talk about 'sister languages', 'daughter languages', 'parent languages', and 'language families'. If reconstruction is successful, it shows that the assumption that the languages are related is warranted. (See Chapter 9 for other aspects of language classification, and for methods for determining whether languages are related see Chapter 13.)

With the genealogical analogy of your family tree in mind, we can see how modern Romance languages have descended from spoken Latin (better said, from Proto-Romance, which is reconstructed via the comparative method), illustrated in the family tree for the Romance languages in Figure 7.1. The biological kinship terms added here under the language names in Figure 7.1 don't belong there – they are just a trick to reveal the pedigree of the languages; in this case the focus is on Spanish. Not all Romance languages are present in this tree diagram of the family.

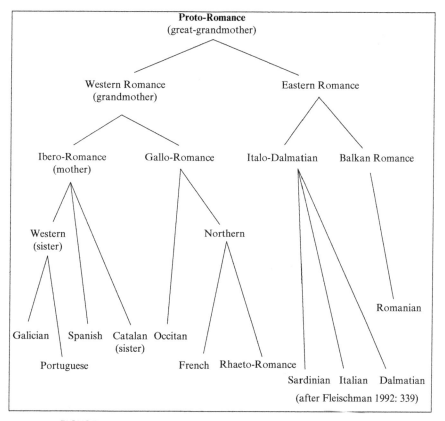

(after Fleischman 1992: 339)

FIGURE 7.1: Proto-Romance family tree (and genealogy of Spanish)

It should be noted that status of Catalan is controversial; some scholars classify it as belonging to Ibero-Romance and others as part of Gallo-Romance, depending on which compared linguistic features they emphasize. (See Maiden 2018: 27 for discussion of this.)

By comparing what these sister languages inherited from their ancestor, we attempt to reconstruct the linguistic traits which Proto-Romance possessed. (Proto-Romance is equivalent to the spoken language at the time when Latin began to diversify and split up into its descendant branches, essentially the same as Vulgar Latin at the time. The 'Vulgar' of Vulgar Latin means 'of the people'.) If we are successful, what we reconstruct for Proto-Romance by the comparative method should be similar to the Proto-Romance which was actually spoken at the time before it split up into its daughter languages. Of course, success is dependent upon the extent to which evidence of the original traits is preserved in the descendant languages (daughter languages) which we compare and upon how astute we are at applying the techniques of the comparative method, among other things. In this case, since Latin is abundantly documented, we can check to see whether what we reconstruct by the comparative method accurately approximates the spoken Latin we know about from written sources. However, the possibility of checking our reconstructions in this way is not available for most language families, for whose proto-languages we have no written records. For example, for Proto-Germanic (from which English descends), there are no written attestations at all, and Proto-Germanic is known only from comparative reconstruction.

Currently existing languages that have relatives all have a history which classifies them into language families. By applying the comparative method to related languages, we can postulate what that common earlier ancestor was like – we can reconstruct that language. Thus, comparing English with its relatives, Dutch, Frisian, German, Danish, Swedish, Icelandic, and so on, we attempt to understand what the proto-language, in this case called 'Proto-Germanic', was like. Thus, English is, in effect, a much-changed 'dialect' of Proto-Germanic, having undergone successive linguistic changes to make it what it is today, a different language from Swedish and German and its other sisters, which underwent different changes of their own. Therefore, every proto-language was once a real language, regardless of whether we are successful at reconstructing it or not.

7.2 The Comparative Method Up Close and Personal

To understand the comparative method, we need first to know the meaning and uses of some concepts and technical terms:

Cognate: a word (or morpheme) which is related to a word (morpheme) in sister languages by reason of these forms having been inherited by these sister languages from a common word (morpheme) of the proto-language from which the sister languages descend.

Cognate set: a set of words (morphemes) that are related to one another across sister languages because they are inherited and descend from a single word (morpheme) of the proto-language.

Comparative method: a method (or set of procedures) which compares forms from related languages, *cognates*, which have descended from a common ancestral language (the *proto-language*), in order to postulate, that is *to reconstruct*, the form in the ancestral language.

Proto-language: (1) the once spoken ancestral language from which daughter languages descend; (2) the language reconstructed by the comparative method which represents the ancestral language from which the compared languages descend. (To the extent that the reconstruction by the comparative method is accurate and complete, (1) and (2) should coincide.)

Reflex: the descendant in a daughter language of something the proto-language had. For example, a sound in a daughter language that comes from a sound of the proto-language is said to be a *reflex* of that original sound; the original sound of the proto-language is said to be *reflected* by the sound which descends from it in a daughter language. When speaking of reflexes, often it is sounds that are involved; however, anything – an affix, word, construction – in a daughter language that is inherited from its proto-language is also a reflex of that thing in the parent language.

Sister language: languages which are related to one another by virtue of having descended from the same common ancestor (proto-language) are sisters; that is, languages which belong to the same family are sisters to one another.

Sound correspondence (also called *correspondence set*): in effect, a set of 'cognate' sounds; the sounds found in the related words of cognate sets which correspond from one related language to the next because they descend from a common ancestral sound. (A sound correspondence is assumed to recur in various cognate sets.)

To illustrate the application of the comparative method, let's begin by applying it briefly in a simplified fashion to some Romance languages. (There are many more Romance languages, but for illustration's sake, this miniature introduction is limited to just a few of the better-known of these.) First, consider some data, the words compared among Romance languages given in Table 7.1. (The first line represents conventional spelling; the second is phonemic.)

Latin is *not* a Romance language; the Latin forms in Table 7.1 are presented only so that ultimately we can check the reconstructions which we postulate for Proto-Romance to see how close they come to the forms in the actual spoken proto-language, which was very nearly the same as Latin in this case.

For ease of description, we will talk about 'steps' in the application of the comparative method. Strictly speaking, though, it is not always necessary to follow all these steps in precisely the sequence described here. In practice, the comparative linguist typically jumps back and forth among these steps.

Step 1: Assemble cognates

To begin to apply the comparative method, we look for potential cognates among related languages (or among languages for which there is reason to suspect

TABLE 7.1: Some Romance cognate sets

Italian	Spanish	Portuguese	French	(Latin)	English gloss
1. capra	cabra	cabra	chèvre	capra	'goat'
/kapra/	/kabra/	/kabra/	/ʃevr(ə)/		
2. caro	caro	caro	cher	caru	'dear'
/karo/	/karo/	/karu/	/ʃer/		
3. capo	cabo	cabo	chef	caput	'head, top'
/kapo/	/kabo/	/kabu/	/ʃef/		
'main, chief'	'extremity'	'extremity'	'main, chief'		
4. carne	carne	carne	chair	carō/carn-	'meat, flesh'
/karne/	/karne/	/karne/	/ʃer/		
			(cf. Old French charn /čarn/)		
5. cane	can (archaic)	cão	chien	canis	'dog'
/kane/	/kan/	/kãw̃/	/ʃjẽ/		

relatedness) and list them in some orderly arrangement (in rows or columns). In Table 7.1, this step has already been done for you for the few Romance cognates considered in this exercise. In general, it is convenient to begin with cognates from 'basic vocabulary' (body parts, close kinship terms, low numbers, common geographical terms), since they resist borrowing more than other sorts of vocabulary, and for the comparative method we want to compare only true cognates, words which are related in the daughter languages by virtue of being inherited from the proto-language. For successful reconstruction, we must eliminate all other sets of similar words which are not due to inheritance from a common ancestor, such as those which exhibit similarities among the languages because of borrowing, chance (coincidence), and so on (for details, see Chapter 10; see also Chapter 13). Ultimately, it is the systematic correspondences which we discover in the application of the comparative method (in the following steps) that demonstrate true cognates.

Step 2: Establish sound correspondences

Next, we attempt to determine the sound correspondences. For example, in the words for 'goat' in cognate set 1 in Table 7.1, the first sound in each language corresponds in the way indicated in SOUND CORRESPONDENCE 1 (here we concentrate on the phonemic representation of the sound and not on the conventional spelling):

> *Sound correspondence* 1:
> Italian *k-*: Spanish *k-*: Portuguese *k-*: French *ʃ-*

Note that historical linguists often use the convention of a hyphen after a sound to indicate initial position, as *k-* here signals initial *k*; a preceding hyphen indicates that the sound is word-final (for example, *-k*); and a hyphen both before and after refers to a medial sound, one found somewhere in the middle of a word but neither initially nor finally (for example, *-k-*).

It is important to attempt to avoid potential sound correspondences that are due merely to chance. For example, languages may have words which are similar only by accident, by sheer coincidence, as in the case of Kaqchikel (Mayan) *mes* 'mess, disorder, garbage': English *mess* 'disorder, untidiness'. To determine whether a sound correspondence such as that of SOUND CORRESPONDENCE 1 is real (reflecting sounds inherited in words from the proto-language) rather than perhaps just an accidental similarity, we need to determine whether the correspondence recurs in other cognate sets. In looking for further examples of this particular Romance sound correspondence, we find that it does recur in the other cognate sets (2–5) of Table 7.1, all of which illustrate SOUND CORRESPONDENCE 1 for their first sound. However, if we were to attempt to find recurrences of the seeming *m-: m-* correspondence between Kaqchikel and English seen in the comparison of their words meaning 'mess', we would soon discover that there are no other instances of it, that it does not recur. This is illustrated by the compared words of Table 7.2, where the English words in the top part begin with *m* but the Kaqchikel words begin with various sounds, and the Kaqchikel words in the bottom part begin with *m* but the English words begin with various sounds.

TABLE 7.2 Kaqchikel–English comparisons

English	*Kaqchikel*
man	ači
moon	qati?t
mouse	č'oy
mother	nan

Kaqchikel	*English*
ma:n	no
mu:x	shade
maw	century plant
mušu?š	navel

Of course, in principle in a situation such as this, it is possible that the compared languages could be related but that we accidentally chose the few words to compare (in Table 7.2) where one or the other of the related languages has not retained the cognate due to borrowing, lexical replacement, or something else. To be certain that this is not the case, we would need to look at many comparisons (not just the handful presented in Table 7.2 for illustration's sake). However, in the case of English and Kaqchikel lexical comparisons, we will never find more than one or two which exhibit what initially might have been suspected of being an *m-: m-* correspondence based on the words meaning 'mess' in the two languages, and this is precisely because these two languages are not genetically related and therefore the *m: m* matching does not recur systematically and is not a true correspondence.

Similarly, we need to attempt to eliminate similarities found in borrowings which can seem to suggest sound correspondences. Usually (though not always), loanwords do not exhibit the sort of systematic sound correspondences found in the comparison of native words among related languages, and loans involving basic vocabulary are much rarer than borrowings of other kinds of vocabulary (see Chapter 13 for details).

Given that SOUND CORRESPONDENCE 1 recurs frequently in cognates among the Romance languages, as seen in the forms compared in Table 7.1, we assume that this sound correspondence is genuine. It is highly unlikely that a set of systematically corresponding sounds such as this one could come about by sheer accident in a large number of words so similar in sound and meaning across these languages.

Step 3: Reconstruct the proto-sound

There is no fixed rule about what should be done next. We could go on and set up other sound correspondence sets and check to see that they recur; that is, we could repeat step 2 over and over until we have found all the sound correspondences in the languages being compared. Or we could go on to step 3 and attempt to reconstruct the proto-sound represented in SOUND CORRESPONDENCE 1 from which the sound in each of the daughter languages descended. In the end, to complete the task, we must establish all the correspondences and reconstruct the proto-sound from which each descends, regardless of whether we do all of step 2 for each set first and then do step 3 for all the sets, or whether we do step 2 followed by step 3 for each set and then move on to the next set, repeating step 2 followed by step 3.

In either case, as we shall soon see, the initial reconstructions which we postulate based on these sound correspondences must be assessed in steps 5 and 6, when we check the fit of the individual reconstructed sounds which we initially postulate in step 3 against the overall phonological inventory of the proto-language and its general typological fit. It is often the case that some of the initial reconstructions for sounds postulated in step 3 need to be modified in steps 5 and 6.

The different sounds (one for each language compared) in the sound correspondence reflect a single sound of the proto-language which is inherited in the different daughter languages; sometimes the sound is reflected unchanged in some daughters, though often it will have undergone sound changes in some (or even all) of the daughter languages which make it different from the original proto-sound from which it descends. We reconstruct the proto-sound by postulating what the sound in the proto-language most likely was on the basis of the phonetic properties of the descendant sounds in the various languages in the correspondence set. The following are the general guidelines that linguists rely on to help them in the task of devising the best, most realistic reconstruction.

Directionality

The known directionality of certain sound changes is a valuable clue to reconstruction (see Chapter 2). By 'directionality' we mean that some sound changes that are found independently in languages typically go in one direction ($A > B$)

but are usually not (sometimes are never) found in the other direction (B > A). Some speak of this as 'naturalness', some changes 'naturally' taking place with greater ease and frequency cross-linguistically than others. For example, many languages (Greek, for instance) have changed s > h, but change in the other direction, h > s, is almost unknown. In cases such as this, we speak of 'directionality'. If we find in two sister languages the sound correspondence s in Language$_1$: h in Language$_2$, we reconstruct *s and postulate that in Language$_2$ *s > h. The alternative with *h and the change *h > s in Language$_1$ is highly unlikely, since it goes against the known direction of change. Usually, the directionality has some phonetic motivation. Some idea of the typical direction of many of the more commonly recurring sound changes can be gathered from a look at the examples considered in Chapter 2.

In the case of SOUND CORRESPONDENCE 1, we know that the direction of change from k to f is quite plausible and has been observed to occur in other languages, but that f essentially never changes to k. Actually, even more typical would be for k to change to f by first going through the intermediate stage with the affricate ʧ, that is, k > ʧ > f; documentary evidence shows that the sound change in French did go through this intermediate ʧ stage. In Old French the words in Table 7.1 were pronounced: ʧevr(ə) 'goat', ʧɛr 'dear', ʧɛf 'head', ʧarn 'meat', and ʧjɛŋ 'dog'. This intermediate stage is preserved in many English loans from French from that time, for example, *chief* and *Charles* with [ʧ], where more recent loans from the same French sources have [ʃ], the result of the later French change of ʧ > ʃ, as in *chef* and *Charlene*, with /ʃ/.

In another example of the way in which directionality aids in reconstruction, we know that very often voiceless stops (p, t, k) become voiced (b, d, g) between vowels. If we compare two related languages, Language$_1$ and Language$_2$, and we find intervocalic -b- in Language$_1$ corresponding to intervocalic -p- in Language$_2$, then we reconstruct *-p- and assume that Language$_1$ underwent the common sound change of intervocalic voicing of stops (p > b /V__V, in this case). If we tried to reconstruct *-b- in this situation, we would have to assume that Language$_2$ had changed -b- to -p-, but this goes against the direction most commonly taken in changes involving these sounds between vowels. This example comes up in SOUND CORRESPONDENCE 2 (below).

The phonetic motivation for the directionality in this case is clear. It is easy to voice stops between vowels, since vowels are inherently voiced, and therefore the change (1) p > b /V__V is very common, while it is not so easy to make stops voiceless between vowels, which makes the change (2) b > p /V__V very rare indeed – for (2) the vocal cords would be vibrating for the first vowel, then we would need to stop them from vibrating in order to produce the voiceless [p], and then start the vocal-cord vibration up again for the second vowel; for (1) we merely leave them vibrating for all three segments, the two vowels and the intervening [b]. The known directionality, then, with (1) encountered frequently across languages and (2) hardly at all, is natural and phonetically motivated. As a beginning linguist's experience with language changes and phonological systems increases, a stronger understanding of the directionality of changes develops.

Economy

What is meant by the criterion of economy is that when multiple alternatives are available, the one which requires the fewest independent changes is most likely to be right. For example, if for SOUND CORRESPONDENCE 1 we were to postulate */, this would necessitate three independent changes from */ > k, one each for Italian, Spanish, and Portuguese; however, if we postulate *k for the Proto-Romance sound, we need assume only one sound change, *k > / in French. The criterion of economy rests on the assumption that the odds are greater that a single change took place than that three independent changes took place. Of course, sometimes independent changes do take place, so that the criterion does not always guarantee correct results; but all else being equal, the chances of a reconstruction which embodies more economical assumptions being correct are greater than for a reconstruction which assumes less economical developments. (See below for other examples of the use of the economy criterion.)

Majority wins

Another guiding principle is that, all else being equal, we let the majority win – that is, unless there is evidence to the contrary, we tend to pick for our reconstructed proto-sound the particular sound in the correspondence set which shows up in the greatest number of daughter languages. Since in SOUND CORRESPONDENCE 1, Italian, Spanish, and Portuguese all have k, and only French diverges from this, with /, we would postulate *k for the Proto-Romance sound, under the assumption that the majority wins, since the majority of the languages have k in this correspondence set. This reconstruction assumes that French underwent the sound change *k > /, but that the other languages did not change at all, *k remaining k. The underlying rationale behind the majority-wins principle is that it is more likely that one language would have undergone a sound change (in this case, French *k > /) than that several languages would independently have undergone a sound change. In this case, if */ were postu-lated as the proto-sound, it would be necessary to assume that Italian, Spanish, and Portuguese had each independently undergone the change of */ > k. The majority-wins guideline and the economy criterion are clearly related to one another and not fully distinct.

Caution is necessary, however, in the use of the majority-wins guideline to reconstruction. Some sound changes are so common (and languages undergo them so easily) that several languages might undergo one of these kind of changes inde-pendently of one another (for example, loss of vowel length, nasalization of vowels before nasal consonants, and so on). It is also possible that only one of the daughter languages might have preserved the original sound unchanged while the others changed it in some way, or that all the daughter languages might have undergone various changes so that none reflects the proto-sound unchanged. Clearly, in these situations there is no majority to do the winning. Moreover, majority rule may not work if some of the languages are more closely related to one another. If some of the languages belong to the same branch (subgroup) of the family (see Chapter 9), then they have a more immediate ancestor which itself is a daughter of the proto-language. This intermediate language (a parent of its immediate descendants but itself a daughter of the proto-language) could have undergone a change and then later split up into its daughters, the members of the subgroup, and each of these daughters would then inherit the changed sound that their immediate common ancestor (itself earlier a single daughter of the proto-language) had undergone. For example, French, Spanish, and Portuguese all share some sounds which are the results of sound changes that took place in Western Romance before it split up further into French, Spanish, and Portuguese. Italian does not share reflexes of these changes because Italian comes from a separate branch of Romance. For example, Western Romance changed syllable-final *k* to *i̯* (a glide) seen in Spanish, Portuguese, and French, which separated from one another only after this change in Western Romance had taken place, as in *lakte > la̯ite 'milk', which gives us French *lait*, Portuguese *leite*, and Spanish *leche* (where later changes were *ai > ei > e* in these languages, and *i̯t > č* [IPA *tʃ*] in Spanish); Italian (not a Western Romance language) underwent a different change, *kt > tt*, giving *latte* 'milk' – we see the results of these changes in choices of kinds of coffee on menus, with *cafe au lait* (sometimes spelled *café au lait,* from French), *café con leche* (Spanish), and *cafe latte* (Italian). Now if we compare Italian *tt* with the *i̯t* of Portuguese, French, and formerly also of Spanish, 'majority wins' would seem to suggest * *i̯* as the reconstruction, with **i̯ > t /__t* in Italian; but knowing that Portuguese, Spanish, and French are closely related, all members of the Western Romance branch, we no longer need to compare three separate instances of *i̯t* to one of *tt*, but only one *i̯t* case (the result of the single change, **k > i̯ /__t*, that is, **kt > i̯t*, in Western Romance) to one *tt* case, in Italian. It is only with the aid of other information that we discover that the best reconstruction is *kt, from which both the Italian and Western Romance languages departed due to their separate sound changes. As will be seen in Chapter 9, it is the results of the comparative method which provide the basis for arriving at the classification that tells us which of the related languages belong to the same branches of the family.

So, 'majority wins' is an important principle, but it is easily overridden by other considerations. Still, it seems to work in the case of SOUND CORRESPONDENCE 1 above, suggesting *k as the best reconstruction, since it is found in a majority of the languages compared.

Factoring in features held in common

We attempt to reconstruct the proto-sound with as much phonetic precision as possible; that is, we want our reconstruction to be as close as possible to the actual phonetic form of the sound as it was pronounced when the proto-language was spoken. We can never know for sure how accurately our reconstructed sound matches the actual sound of the formerly spoken proto-language, but in general, the more information available upon which to base the reconstruction, the more likely it is that we may be able to achieve a reasonably accurate reconstruction. We attempt to obtain as much phonetic realism as possible by observing what phonetic features are shared among the reflexes seen in each of the daughter languages in the sound correspondence. We determine which phonetic features are common to the reflexes in the daughter languages (and features which can be derived by the known direction of sound changes, in step 2), and then we attempt to reconstruct the proto-sound by building into it these shared phonetic features.

To illustrate this, let us consider another sound correspondence from Table 7.1, seen to recur here in the words for (1) 'goat' and (2) 'head' (and in many other cognates not given in Table 7.1):

> *Sound correspondence* 2:
> Italian -*p*-: Spanish -*b*-: Portuguese -*b*-: French -*v*-

The reflexes in all four languages share the feature 'labial'; the Spanish, Portuguese, and Italian reflexes share the feature 'stop' (phonemically). Factoring the features together, we would expect the proto-sound to have been a 'labial stop' of some sort, a *p* or *b*. Given that the reflex in Spanish, Portuguese, and French is 'voiced', under the principle of 'majority wins' we might expect to reconstruct a 'voiced bilabial stop' (**b*). In this case, however, other considerations – especially directionality – override the majority-wins principle. The directionality is that it is easy for *p* to become voiced between voiced sounds (between vowels in cognate set 3 and between a vowel and *r* in cognate set 1 in Table 7.1), but the reverse is very rare. Therefore, by directionality, **p* is a better choice for the reconstruction, phonetically more plausible; Italian maintained *p* while the others underwent the change to voicing (**p* > *b* in Spanish and Portuguese; **p* > *v* in French, actually **p* > *b* > *v*). From directionality, we also know that stops frequently become fricatives between vowels (or between continuant sounds), but that fricatives rarely ever become stops in this environment. Thus, it is very likely that the French reflex *v* is the result of this sort of change. Taking these considerations into account, for correspondence set 2, we reconstruct **p* and postulate that in Spanish and Portuguese **p* > *b*, and French **p* > *v* (or **p* > *b* > *v*). SOUND CORRESPONDENCE 2, then, illustrates how the comparative linguist must balance the various rules of thumb for reconstruction, majority wins, directionality, and factoring in the features shared among the reflexes. Ultimately, we find out that Western Romance underwent the change of **p* > *b* in this position, and then after Western Romance split up, the change of *b* > *v* in French took place. That is, taking the degree of relatedness (the subgrouping; see Chapter 9) into account, there is no longer a majority with the reflex *b*, but rather only Western Romance *b* as opposed to Italian *p*.

The other two general considerations (rules of thumb) which linguists use in reconstructing sounds involve checking to see whether the individual sounds postulated to represent the various sound correspondences fit the overall phonological pattern of the proto-language, and to see whether this reconstructed pattern is consistent with linguistic universals and typological expectations. These are *phonological fit* and *typological fit* respectively (steps 5 and 6, below). These two considerations come into play mostly after the full set of sound correspondences has been dealt with and the overall inventory of reconstructed sounds that are being postulated can be considered. For this reason, let's deal first with the other correspondences of Table 7.1, and then come back to these two considerations later.

Let us then continue steps 2 and 3 for the other forms in Table 7.1, and establish the remaining sound correspondences illustrated in these forms and set up reconstructions for them. It does not matter in which order we investigate the sound correspondences. We could first look only at initial consonants for all of the cognate sets, then medial consonants, then final consonants, and finally the various vowels; or we could proceed by investigating the sound correspondence representing the next sound (the second) in the first cognate set, then go on to the third sound in that set, and so on until all the sounds of the words in that cognate set have been addressed, and then proceed to the next cognate set, dealing with each of the sound correspondences for each of the sounds found in that set in sequence (though some of these may recur in other cognate sets and thus may already have been established in the consideration of the previous cognate sets already dealt with). We continue in this way until all the recurring sound correspondences have been examined and proto-sounds to represent them have been postulated. In this way, we will eventually come to reconstruct the full inventory of sounds in the proto-language.

In the example in Table 7.1, let us continue with the corresponding sounds in cognate set 1, for 'goat'. The first vowel (the second sound) in the forms in cognate set 1 shows SOUND CORRESPONDENCE 3:

> *Sound correspondence* 3:
> Italian *a:* Spanish *a:* Portuguese *a:* French *ɛ*

We check this to see if it recurs, and we see that it is also found in other cognate sets of Table 7.1, for 'dear', 'head', and 'meat'. (It is also found again, in effect, in the last vowel of cognate set 1 for 'goat', though we must deal with the later change in French of final *ɛ* to *ə*/*Ø*.) Under the principles of economy and majority wins, for this sound correspondence we reconstruct **a* for the Proto-Romance sound, assuming that French has undergone the sound change **a* > *ɛ*.

The third sound in cognate set 1 'goat' has, in fact, already been dealt with in SOUND CORRESPONDENCE 2 (where we reconstructed **p* for the correspondence set Spanish *-b-:* Portuguese *-b-:* French *-v-:* Italian *-p-*).

The next sound in the sequence of sounds in the 'goat' cognates gives correspondence set 4:

> *Sound correspondence* 4:
> Italian *r:* Spanish *r:* Portuguese *r:* French *r*

SOUND CORRESPONDENCE 4 also recurs, in 'dear' and 'meat' (in Table 7.1). For it, we postulate Proto-Romance **r*, under 'majority wins', since all the languages have this reflex. (To be absolutely accurate, we would have to deal with the fact that in Standard French the *r* became a uvular, but for now we ignore this detail.)

The last sound in 'goat' in effect repeats SOUND CORRESPONDENCE 3, although French later changed final *ɛ* further (to *ə* or *Ø*). Though technically this must be considered a separate sound correspondence, to make it easier we will just assume here that we would readily discover that the two correspondence sets, for the first and last vowel in the 'goat' cognate set, belong together due to a later conditioned change in French (*a* > *ɛ* >, and then *ɛ* > *ə* > Ø word-finally).

To complete the task, we would need to establish the sound correspondences for all the cognate sets and reconstruct sounds to represent them. For example, we would find:

> *Sound correspondence 5:*
> Italian -*o:* Spanish -*o:* Portuguese -*u:* French -*Ø*.

This recurs, as in 'dear' and 'head'. For SOUND CORRESPONDENCE 5, we would reconstruct *o (economy, majority wins), assuming that Portuguese changed final *o to *u*, and that French lost final *o.

With more extensive data (many more cognate sets than presented in Table 7.1), we would confirm these reconstructions, with their attendant sound changes and the conditions under which they took place in the various languages, and we would eventually find all the sound correspondences and postulate reconstructions for all the sounds of the proto-language, and work out its phonemic inventory and phonological patterns.

Step 4: Determine the status of similar (partially overlapping) correspondence sets

Some sound changes, particularly conditioned sound changes, can result in a single proto-sound being associated with more than one correspondence set. These must be dealt with to achieve an accurate reconstruction. To see how this is done, we will work through an example. For this, let us consider some additional cognate sets in Romance languages, those of Table 7.3 (numbered to follow those of Table 7.1).

TABLE 7.3: Some additional Romance cognate sets

	Italian	Spanish	Portuguese	French	(Latin)	English gloss
6.	colore	color	côr	couleur	colōre	'colour'
	/kolore/	/kolor/	/kor/	/kulœr/		
7.	correre	correr	correr	courir	currere	'to run'
	/korere/	/kořer/	/korer/	/kuri(r)/		
8.	costare	costar	costar	coûter	co(n)stāre	'to cost'
	/kostare/	/kostar/	/kostar/	/kuter/	['stand firm']	
9.	cura	cura	cura	cure	cūra	'cure'
	/kura/	/kura/	/kura/	/kyr/	['care']	

Based on the cognates of Table 7.3, we set up a sound correspondence for the initial sound in these forms:

Sound correspondence 6:
Italian *k-:* Spanish *k-:* Portuguese *k-:* French *k-*

For SOUND CORRESPONDENCE 6, since all the languages have the same sound, *k*, we would naturally reconstruct **k*. However, SOUND CORRESPONDENCE 6 is quite similar to SOUND CORRESPONDENCE 1 (in Table 7.1), for which we also tentatively reconstructed **k*, repeated here for comparison with SOUND CORRESPONDENCE 6:

Sound correspondence 1:
Italian *k-:* Spanish *k-:* Portuguese *k-:* French *ʃ-*

The two sets overlap partially, since they share some of the same sounds. In fact, the only difference between the two is in French, which has *k* in SOUND CORRESPONDENCE 6 but *ʃ* in SOUND CORRESPONDENCE 1. In cases such as this of similar (partially overlapping) correspondence sets, we must determine whether they reflect two separate proto-sounds or only one which split into more than one sound in one or more of the languages. In the case of SOUND CORRESPONDENCE 1 and 6, we must determine whether both sets reflect **k*, or whether we must reconstruct something distinct for each of the two. Because we assume that sound change is regular, the options for possible solutions here are restricted to essentially only two. One possible solution would be for us to find evidence to show that the two correspondence sets are different today but represent only a single proto-sound. To show this, it would be necessary to explain away the difference between the two sets, that is, to show how a single original sound could change in ways that would result in the two different correspondence sets. For this, we would need to show that a single original sound ended up as *ʃ* in certain specific environments in French but as *k* in other circumstances – since the other languages all have only the single reflex, *k*, the most likely candidate is a **k* assumed not to have changed in these languages, but, under this hypothesis, changed to *ʃ* in French only in specific instances. If we cannot succeed in showing this – in being able to predict where the postulated original **k* became *ʃ* and where it remained *k* in French – then we cannot reconstruct a single sound for the two sets and we are forced to consider the other possible solution. In this other possible solution, the two correspondence sets represent two distinct sounds in the proto-language which merged to *k* in all contexts in Italian, Spanish, and Portuguese, but remained distinct in French.

In this case, we are able to determine the context in which French changed **k* to *ʃ* and the different contexts in which **k* remained unchanged in French. We notice that in the cognate sets of Table 7.1 which exhibit SOUND CORRESPONDENCE 1, this sound comes before *ɛ* in French and *a* in the other languages (SOUND CORRESPONDENCE 3), while in SOUND CORRESPONDENCE 6, illustrated by the cognate sets in Table 7.3, the initial sound is not before *a* or *ɛ* (as in SOUND CORRESPONDENCE 1), but before *o* or *u* (French *u* or *y*). Therefore, we determine that French underwent a conditioned sound change, that **k > ʃ* before the vowel of correspondence set 3 (*a* which became *ɛ* in French), but retained *k* unchanged before the round vowels seen in the cognates of Table 7.3.

So, in spite of two distinct sound correspondences (1 and 6), we reconstruct a single proto-sound and show that one of these (SOUND CORRESPONDENCE 1) is the result of a conditioned change which affected only some of the instances of original *k* in French (those before original *a*) but not the other cases of *k* (those before round vowels).

In some cases, however, we are forced to reconstruct separate proto-sounds in instances of similar, partially overlapping correspondence sets. Consider for example the two sound correspondences illustrated by the initial sounds in additional cognates in Table 7.4.

TABLE 7.4: Further Romance cognate sets

	Italian	Spanish	Portuguese	French	(Latin)	English gloss
10.	battere	batir	bater	battre	battuere	'to beat'
	/battere/	/batir/	/bater/	/batr/		
11.	bolla	bola	bola	boule	bulla	'ball, bubble'
	/bolla/	/bola/	/bola/	/bul/		
12.	bontà	bondad	bondade	bonté	bonitāte	'goodness
	/bonta/	/bondad/	/bõdadʒi/	/bõte/		
13.	bev-	beber	beber	boire	bibere	'to drink'
	/bev-/	/beber/	/beber/	Old French beivre		
14.	venire	venir	vir	venir	venīre	'to come'
	/venire/	/benir/	/vir/	/vənir/		
15.	valle	valle	vale	val	valle	'valley'
	/valle/	/baʎe/	/vale/	/val/		
16.	vestire	vestir	vestir	vêtir	vestīre	'to dress'
	/vestire/	/bestir/	/vestir/	/vetir/		

Cognate sets 10 to 13 show SOUND CORRESPONDENCE 7:

> *Sound correspondence 7:*
> Italian *b:* Spanish *b:* Portuguese *b:* French *b*

Cognate sets 14 to 16 show SOUND CORRESPONDENCE 8:

> *Sound correspondence 8:*
> Italian *v:* Spanish *b:* Portuguese *v:* French *v*

Clearly the best reconstruction for SOUND CORRESPONDENCE 7 would be *b*, since all the languages have *b* as their reflex. SOUND CORRESPONDENCE 8 partially overlaps with this in that Spanish also has *b* for its reflex in this set, corresponding to *v* of the other languages. As in the case of Proto-Romance *k* (above), either we must be able to explain the difference in these two correspondence sets by showing that those languages with *v* changed an original *b* to *v* under some clearly defined circumstances, or we must reconstruct two separate sounds in the proto-language, presumably *b and *v, where Spanish would then be assumed to have merged its original v with b. In this case, to make a long story short, if we look for factors which could be the basis of a conditioned change in Italian, Portuguese, and French, to explain how a single original *b could become v in certain circumstances but remain b in others in these languages, we are unable to find any. We find both b and v at the beginnings of words before all sorts of vowels, and with more extensive data we would find that both sounds occur quite freely in the same environments in these languages. Since no conditioning factor can be found, we reconstruct *b for the cognates in correspondence set 7 and *v for those in correspondence set 8, two distinct proto-sounds. From this, it follows that *v merged with *b in Spanish, accounting for why b is the Spanish reflex in both cognate sets 14–16 and 10–13 of Table 7.4.

A somewhat more revealing example of the problem of overlapping correspondence sets which prove to contrast and thus require separate sounds to be reconstructed is seen in the example in Table 7.5, from Mayan languages (of which only a few, each representing a major branch of the family, are represented).

TABLE 7.5: Some Mayan cognate sets

K'iche'	Tzeltal	Yucatec	Huastec	Proto-Mayan	English gloss
1. ra:h	ya	yah	yah-	*ra:h	'hot, spicy'
2. ri?x	yix	yi?ih	yeh-	*ri?ix	'old (old man)'
3. r-	y-	y-	—	*r-	'his/her/its'
4. raš	yaš	ya?aš	yaš-	*ra?aš	'green'
5. war	way	way	way	*war	'to sleep'
6. ya:x	yah	yah	ya?	*ya:h	'sick'
7. yaš	yaš	—	—	*yaš	'crab, pincers'
8. k'ay-	k'ay-	k'ay-	č'ay-	*k'ay	'to sell'
	['sing']	['sing, sell']	['buy']		

(NOTE: y = IPA [j], š = [ʃ], č = [tʃ], C' = glottalized (ejective) consonants.)

Note that the 'dash' (–) is the convention used by linguists to mean that either no cognate is known or the data are unavailable. In such instances, we must rely on information from other cognate sets in order to determine features of the languages where the forms are missing.

Cognate sets 1–5 show SOUND CORRESPONDENCE 1:

Sound correspondence 1:
K'iche' *r:* Tzeltal *y:* Yucatec *y:* Huastec *y*

Cognate sets 6–8 show SOUND CORRESPONDENCE 2:

Sound correspondence 2:
K'iche' *y:* Tzeltal *y:* Yucatec *y:* Huastec *y*

Clearly, by our standard criteria, the best Proto-Mayan reconstruction for SOUND CORRESPONDENCE 2 would be *y, preserved unchanged in all the languages. However, all the languages except K'iche' also have y as their reflex in SOUND CORRESPONDENCE 1, whereas K'iche' has r in this case. As in the discussion of the Proto-Romance *k case (above), we must either explain how the difference in these two sets arose by showing that K'iche' had changed original *y to r in some clear set of phonetic circumstances but not in others, or we must reconstruct two separate sounds in the proto-language. In this case, to make a long story short, if we look for factors which could be the basis of a conditioned change in K'iche', we are unable to find any. We find both r and y at the beginning and end of words, before all sorts of vowels, and so on, and basically either sound can occur in any context without restrictions. Since no conditioning factor can be found, we reconstruct *r for SOUND CORRESPONDENCE 1 and *y for SOUND CORRESPONDENCE 2, two distinct proto-sounds. From this, it follows that *r merged with y in Tzeltal, Yucatec, and Huastec, accounting for why they have y as the reflex in cognate sets 6–8 of Table 7.5. When we look at still other Mayan languages, we find the decision to reconstruct something different for the two correspondence sets further supported, since, for example, Mam has t and Mocho' has č where the languages of the K'ichean branch have r in the cognates that illustrate SOUND CORRESPONDENCE 1, but they both have y in cognates where K'iche' and its sisters have y in SOUND CORRESPONDENCE 2. That is, K'iche' turns out not to be the only witness of the distinction between the two sounds of these correspondence sets (Campbell 1977).

Step 5: Check the plausibility of the reconstructed sound from the perspective of the overall phonological inventory of the proto--language

Steps 5 and 6 are related. The rule of thumb in step 5 takes advantage of the fact that languages tend to have symmetrical sound systems with congruent patterns. For example, in the reconstruction of sounds for the individual sound correspondences in step 3, we can reconstruct each sound of the proto-language with little regard for how these sounds may relate to one another or to how they may fit together in the language to form a coherent sound system. Often in step 5 when we consider these sounds in the context of the overall inventory, we refine and correct our earlier proposals for reconstructing sounds in the proto-language. For example, if two related languages have the correspondence set Language$_1$ d: Language$_2$ r, we might initially reconstruct *r and assume *r > d in Language$_1$, since r > d is known to take place in languages, though the alternative of *d with the assumption that Language$_2$ underwent the change *d > r is just as plausible, since the change d > r is also found in languages. Suppose, however, that in step 5 we discover that we have reconstructed sounds based on other sound correspondences which would give the following phonological inventory for the proto-language:

```
*p  *t  *k
*b      *g
    *r
    *l
```

There is a gap in this inventory where *d would be expected to complete the voiced stop series, where the voiceless stops (*p, *t, *k) would each be matched by a voiced counterpart (*b, *d, *g), if a *d existed, which would make the series of stops symmetrical, the pattern congruent. The proto-language as tentatively reconstructed so far, with both *r and *l and with *b and *g, but with no *d, would be unusual and unexpected, with its gap in the voiced stop series (with no *d). However, by revising our earlier tentative reconstruction of *r for the d: r sound correspondence to the equally plausible *d (assuming *d > r in Language₂), we arrive at a much more coherent and likely set of sounds for the sound inventory of the proto-language, where the two stop series are now congruent:

```
*p  *t  *k
*b  *d  *g
    *l
```

While this instance is presented as a hypothetical possibility, it is in fact encountered in a number of real language families, for example in branches of Austronesian. It is important, however, to keep in mind that while languages tend to be symmetrical and have pattern congruity, that is, tend not to have gaps in the inventory, this is by no means always the case.

Let's consider one other hypothetical instance, also actually found in real language families. If in a family of two languages we encounter the correspondence set Language₁ s: Language₂ ʃ, either we could reconstruct *s (assuming *s > ʃ in Language₂) or we could postulate *ʃ (and assume *ʃ > s in Language₁). Both of these possible changes (*s > ʃ, and *ʃ > s) are found in languages. Suppose, however, that in step 5 we discover that the other sound correspondences justify the reconstruction of several proto-sounds in the alveolar series, including *ts, but no other palato-alveolar sound. This would give a proto-language with alveolar *ts but with palato-alveolar *ʃ and no *s, but this system would be asymmetrical and odd. However, a proto-language with *ts and *s together in the alveolar series but lacking *ʃ would be normal and not at all unusual. Therefore, in step 5 we would revise the preliminary reconstruction of step 3 to reconstruct *s for the s: ʃ correspondence set (assuming *s > ʃ in Language₂) to ensure a more plausible overall phonological inventory for the proto-language that we reconstruct. A real example which matches this situation precisely comes from Mixe-Zoquean (a family of languages from southern Mexico), where the languages of the Zoquean branch have s corresponding to ʃ of the Mixean languages. So, for Proto-Mixe-Zoquean, *s is a better reconstruction for the s: ʃ correspondence set.

Of course, languages do not have to be symmetrical or fully natural, though they tend to be. Also, it is conceivable that a proto-language might have gaps (such as the missing *d in the voiced stops in the first example) and asymmetries (*ts and *f rather than *ts and *s in the second example). However, unless there is strong evidence to compel us to accept a less expected reconstruction, a less symmetrical, less natural one, we are obliged to accept the reconstructions motivated by pattern congruity, symmetry, and naturalness. That is, languages in general have symmetrical (natural) systems much more often than not. Therefore, in the case of two possibilities, one with a more expected inventory of sounds and the other with a less expected, less normal inventory, the possibility that the reconstruction with the symmetrical, natural system accurately reflects the structure of the formerly spoken proto-language has a much higher probability of being right than the asymmetrical one does. Given the greater odds of the first being right, we choose it for our reconstruction, not the second, which is less likely to have existed.

Step 6: Check the plausibility of the reconstructed sounds and sound system from the perspective of linguistic universals and typological expectations

Certain inventories of sounds are found with frequency among the world's languages while some others are found not at all or only very rarely. When we check our postulated reconstructions for the sounds of a proto-language, we must make sure that we are not proposing a set of sounds which is never found in human languages. For example, we do not find any languages which have no vowels whatsoever. Therefore, a proposed reconstructed language lacking vowels would be ruled out by step 6. There are no languages with only glottalized (ejective) consonants and no plain counterparts, and therefore a reconstruction which claimed that some proto-language had only glottalized consonants with no non-glottalized counterparts would be false. Languages do not have only nasalized vowels with no non-nasalized vowels, and so we never propose a reconstruction which would result in a proto-language in which there are only nasalized vowels and no plain, non-nasalized ones.

Let us look at an actual case. The Nootkan family has the sound correspondences seen in Table 7.6.

TABLE 7.6: Nootkan correspondences involving nasals

Makah	Nitinat	Nootka (Nuu-chah-nulth)
1. b	b	m
2. d	d	n
3. b'	b'	m̓
4. d'	d'	n̓

Since the other guidelines do not help here, we might be tempted, based on the majority-wins principle, to reconstruct voiced stops for Proto-Nootkan for these four correspondence sets and postulate that these changed to the nasal counterparts in Nuu-chah-nulth (Nootka). However, only a very few languages of the world lack nasal consonants; therefore, we do not expect a nasal-less proto-language, and any postulated proto-language which lacks nasals altogether must be supported by very compelling evidence. In this case, Nitinat and Makah belong to the area of the Northwest Coast of North America where languages of several different families lack nasal consonants. The lack of nasals in these languages is due to the influence of other nasal-less languages in the linguistic area (see Chapter 10); Proto-Nootkan had nasals, as Nuu-chah-nulth (Nootka) still does, but Makah and Nitinat lost nasality – their former nasals became corresponding voiced oral stops (*m > b, *n > d, *m̓ > b', *n̓ > d'). The knowledge of universals and typological expectations in this case would direct us to reconstruct proto-Nootkan with nasals and to assume a subsequent change in Makah and Nitinat. Of course, in step 5, we also relied on general typological patterns in language and evaluated proposed proto-inventories on this basis; that is, steps 5 and 6 are related.

Step 7: Reconstruct morphemes

When we have reconstructed the proto-sounds from which we assume that the sounds in the sound correspondences descend, it is possible to go on to reconstruct lexical items and grammatical morphemes. For example, from the cognate set for 'goat' in Table 7.1, the first sound (in SOUND CORRESPONDENCE 1) was reconstructed as *k (based on the k: k: k: ʃ correspondence set); for the second sound in the cognates for 'goat', we reconstructed *a, as in SOUND CORRESPONDENCE 3 (with a: a: a: ɛ); the third sound is represented by SOUND CORRESPONDENCE 2 (p : b: b: v), for which we reconstructed *p; the next sound in cognate set 1, as represented by SOUND CORRESPONDENCE 4, reflects Proto-Romance *r (based on the r: r: r: r correspondence set); and the last sound in the 'goat' cognates reflects SOUND CORRESPONDENCE 2 (or actually a modification of it involving final vowels in French) which was reconstructed as *a. Putting these reconstructed sounds together following the order in which they appear in the cognates for 'goat' in set 1, we arrive at *kapra. That is, we have reconstructed a word in Proto-Romance, *kapra 'goat'. For cognate set 2 'dear' in Table 7.1, we would put together *k (SOUND CORRESPONDENCE 1), *a (SOUND CORRESPONDENCE 3), *r (SOUND CORRESPONDENCE 4) – all seen already in the reconstruction of 'goat' – and *o (SOUND CORRESPONDENCE 5, with o: o: u: Ø), giving us the Proto-Romance word *karo 'dear'. For cognate set 3 'head', we have combinations of the same correspondence sets already seen in the reconstructions for 'goat' and 'dear', SOUND CORRESPONDENCES 1, 3, 2, and 5, giving the Proto-Romance reconstructed word *kapo 'head'. In this way, we can continue reconstructing Proto-Romance words for all the cognate sets based on the sequence of sound correspondences that they reflect, building a Proto-Romance lexicon.

The reconstruction of a sound, a word, or large portions of a proto-language is, in effect, a hypothesis (or better said, a set of interconnected hypotheses) concerning what those aspects of the proto-language must have been like. Aspects of the hypothesized reconstruction can be tested and proven wrong, or can be modified, based on new insights. These insights may involve new interpretations of the data already on hand, or new information that may come to light. The discovery of a previously unknown language that is a member of the family may provide new evidence, a different testimony of the historical events which transpired between the proto-language and its descendants, which could change how we view the structure and content of the proto-language. There are a number of well-known cases where this has happened, including the famous case where Leonard Bloomfield's (1925; 1928) discovery of Swampy Cree confirmed his reconstruction in Proto-Central Algonquian of distinct sounds based on different sound correspondences that involved only sounds already involved in other correspondence sets, but in different arrangements in the different languages. This example was taken as proof of the regularity of sound change and as a demonstration of the comparative method's legitimate application to unwritten languages. With the discovery and decipherment of Hittite (or better said, the languages of the Anatolian branch of Indo-European), the picture of Proto-Indo-European phonology changed dramatically; this included clearer evidence of several new proto-sounds, the laryngeals.

7.3 A Case Study

Let us apply the comparative method in a somewhat more complex example (though still simplified) which illustrates what we have until now been considering mainly through a simplified comparison of Romance languages. The forms in Table 7.7 are cognates found in Finnish, Hungarian, and Udmurt (aka Votyak).

These languages belong to the Finno-Ugric branch of the Uralic family, but since there are also many other languages in this family (see Figure 9.2 in Chapter 9), the data in this example are far from complete enough to offer a full perspective on the proto-language – these three are compared here only for illustration's sake. These languages separated from one another a very long time ago, which explains why some of these cognates are not immediately apparent based on mere superficial similarity. The languages have undergone many changes and are now quite different from one another, and we would need much more information than presented here to be able to reconstruct all the sounds of Proto-Finno-Ugric. Therefore, here we concentrate only on the word-initial sounds in these data.

Step 1 is already done; the cognates have been assembled in Table 7.7. In step 2, we compare these cognates and set up sound correspondences. It is helpful to keep a good record of what we have looked at, by noting with each sound correspondence either the numbers which identify the cognate sets in which the sound correspondence is found, or if we do not use numbers, then the glosses. This is just a matter of bookkeeping – a means of being able to go back to check things without having to search back through all the data to find the examples of cognates which exhibit the correspondence in question, particularly useful, for example, in steps 5 and 6.

TABLE 7.7: Some Finno-Ugric cognate sets

Finnish	Hungarian	Udmurt (Votyak)	gloss
Set I			
1. pää [pæ:]	fej [fej]	pum, puŋ	'head, end'
2. pata [pata]	fazék [fɔze:k]	—	'pot'
3. pato 'dam, wall'	fal [fɔl] 'wall'	—	
4. pääsky- [pæ:sky]	fecske [fečke]	poɕki-	'swallow' (bird)
5. pelkää- [pelkæ:-]	fél [fe:l]	puli-	'to fear'
6. pesä [pesæ]	fészek [fe:sek]	puz-	'nest'
7. pii [pi:] 'tooth of rake'	fog [fog]	pinʲ	'tooth'
8. pilvi [pilvi]	felhő [felhø:]	piľʲem	'cloud'
9. poika [poika]	fiú [fiu:]	pi	'boy'
10. puno- [puno-]	fon [fon]	pun-	'spin, braid'
11. puu [pu:]	fa [fɔ]	pu	'tree'
Set II			
12. tä- [tæ-]	té- [te:-] (cf. tétova 'here and there')	ta	'this'
13. täi [tæi]	tetű [tety:]	tei	'louse'
14. talvi [talvi]	tél [te:l]	tol	'winter'
15. täyte- [tæyte-]	tel- [tel-] (in derived forms)	—	'full'
16. tunte- [tunte-]	tud [tud]	tod	'to know, sense'
17. tyvi [tyvi]	tő [tø:]	[dinʲ]	'base'
Set III			
18. kala [kala]	hal [hɔl]	—	'fish'
19. kalime- [kalime-]	háló [ha:lo:]	[Komi *kulem*]	'fishnet'
20. kamara [kamara]	hám- [ha:m-]	kəm	'peel'
21. koi [koi]	haj- [hɔj-]	[Komi *kɨa*]	'dawn'
22. kolme [kolme]	három [ha:rom]	kuinʲm-	'three'
23. kota [kota]	ház [ha:z]	kwa-/-ko/-ka 'summer hut'/ 'house'	'hut'
24. kunta [kunta] 'community, group, society'	had [hɔd] 'army'	—	
25. kuole- [kuole-]	hal [hɔl]	kul-	'to die'
26. kusi [kusi]	húgy [hu:dʲ]	kiʐ	'urine'
Set IV			
27. käte- [kæte-]	kéz [ke:z]	ki	'hand'
28. keri [keri]	kér [ke:r]	kur	'(tree-) bark'
29. kerjää- [kerjæ:]	kér [ke:r]	kur-	'to beg'

TABLE 7.7: continued

Finnish	Hungarian	Udmurt (Votyak)	gloss
30. kii- [ki:-] 'rut, mating'	kéj [ke:j] '(carnal) pleasure'	[Komi koj-] 'to make mating call'	
31. kivi [kivi]	kő [kø:]	kə 'mill stone'	'stone'
32. kyynel [ky:nel]	könny [kønnj]	-kiʎi- (in çin-kiʎi; çin(m)- 'eye')	'tear' (noun)
33. kytke- [kytke-]	köt [køt]	kɨtk-ɨ 'to harness'	'to tie'
34. kyy [ky:] 'adder'	kígyó [ki:dʲo:]	kɨj	'snake'
35. kyynär [ky:nær]	könyök [kønʲøk]	[gir-]	'elbow'
Set V			
36. salava [salava] 'willow'	szil [sil] 'elm'	—	
37. sarvi [sarvi]	szarv [sɔrv]	ɕur, ɕir	'horn'
38. sata [sata]	száz [sa:z]	ɕu	'hundred'
39. silmä [silmæ]	szem [sem]	ɕinm-	'eye'
40. suu [su:]	szá(j) [sa:j]	ɕu- (?) (in compounds)	'mouth'
41. sydäme- [sydæme-]	szív [si:v]	ɕulem	'heart'
Set VI			
42. sappi [sappi]	epe [epe]	sep	'gall'
43. sää [sæ:] 'weather'	ég [e:g] 'sky' <'weather'	[Komi sinəd] 'sunshine haze, mist'	
44. säynä- [sæynæ-]	őn [ø:n]	son- (son-tɕorig, tɕorig 'fish')	'fish (*Leucis-cus idus*)'
45. sula-[sula]	olva- [olvɔ-]	sɨlm-	'to melt'
46. suoni [suoni]	ín [i:n]	sin	'sinew'
47. syksy [syksy]	ősz [ø:s]	sizʲil	'autumn'
48. syli [syli]	öl [øl]	sul, sɨl	'lap, bosom'

Sound correspondences found in the cognates of Table 7.7 are:

1. Finnish *p-*: Hungarian *f-*: Udmurt *p-* (in set I, nos. 1–11)
2. Finnish *t-*: Hungarian *t-*: Udmurt *t-* (in set II, nos. 12–17)
3. Finnish *k-*: Hungarian *h-*: Udmurt *k-* (in set III, nos. 18–26)
4. Finnish *k-*: Hungarian *k-*: Udmurt *k-* (in set IV, nos. 27–35)
5. Finnish *s-*: Hungarian *s-*: Udmurt *ɕ-* (in set V, nos. 36–41)
6. Finnish *s-*: Hungarian *Ø-*: Udmurt *s-* (in set VI, nos. 42–48)
   (NOTE: ɕ = voiceless alveolo-palatal fricative (between [s] and [ʃ]); z = its voiced counterpart. Finnish and Hungarian forms are given in the standard orthography followed by their IPA equivalents in parentheses.)

In step 3 we attempt to reconstruct the proto-sound which we believe is reflected in each of these correspondence sets. For SOUND CORRESPONDENCE 1 (p : f: p) our choices are: (1) reconstruct *p and assume Hungarian changed to f; (2) reconstruct *f and assume Finnish and Udmurt changed this to p; or (3) reconstruct some third thing (say *pʰ) and assume that it changed in all three languages, that Hungarian changed in one way to give f while Finnish and Udmurt changed in another to give p. From directionality of change as a guideline, we conclude that possibilities (1) (*p) and (3) (some third thing, like *pʰ) are plausible, but (2) (with *f) is not a viable possibility, since in sound changes familiar from languages around the world we see that voiceless bilabial stops (p, pʰ) frequently become f, but extremely rarely do we find instances of f changing to p or pʰ. The guideline of economy urges us towards possibility (1) (*p). With *p (as in [1]), we would need to postulate only a single change, *p > f in Hungarian; in choice (2) (with *f) we would have to assume the change of *f > p twice, in Finnish and again in Udmurt. Choice (3) (with *pʰ) would require us to postulate the change *pʰ > p twice, in Finnish and Udmurt, and another change, *pʰ > f, in Hungarian. In the majority-wins guideline, since Finnish and Udmurt both have p, against Hungarian alone with f, this principle suggests *p as a more likely reconstruction than *f. In the guideline of factoring in features held in common, we may conclude from the sounds p and f in the sound correspondence that the proto-sound was voiceless and a labial of some kind, but this is consistent with all three of the possibilities (1–3). In this case, then, factoring in the common features provides no basis for choosing among the alternatives. Steps 4 and 5 can help us resolve which of these possibilities is the best reconstruction; however, we have sufficient reason now for selecting option (1), with *p, based on these considerations from directionality of change, economy, and majority wins.

SOUND CORRESPONDENCE 2 (t-: t-: t-) appears to reflect *t- (where none of the languages has changed).

SOUND CORRESPONDENCES 3 (k-: h-: k-) and 4 (k-: k-: k-) could present more of a challenge. In SOUND CORRESPONDENCE 4 we reconstruct *k-, since all three languages have k- and thus none of them appears to have changed. However, if SOUND CORRESPONDENCE 4 were not present to complicate the picture, then SOUND CORRESPONDENCE 3 would also seem to be best reconstructed as *k-. Directionality of change would support this possibility, since the change k > h (as would be required for Hungarian in this hypothesis) is very common and not unusual, whereas a change h- > k- is all but unknown. The criteria of economy and majority wins also support *k-, with k- in two languages but h- in only one.

We move to step 4 to attempt to resolve the difficulty of the partially overlapping SOUND CORRESPONDENCES 3 and 4. If we can show that both sound correspondence sets reflect the same original sound because one of the languages has undergone a conditioned change, where that sound changed in some environments but not in others, then we can reconstruct a single sound, the same one for both correspondence sets 3 and 4. We would explain the difference between the two sound correspondences by pointing out the conditions under which one of the languages changed and thus resulted in two different outcomes from the single original sound. If we cannot explain the difference in this way, then we are obligated to reconstruct two distinct proto-sounds, a distinct one to represent each of the two sound correspondences, with the assumption that these two originally distinct sounds merged to *k*- in Finnish and Udmurt. This, then, requires us to take a closer look at the cognates in question (those of sets III and IV). We notice that in the cognates of set III the *h* of Hungarian appears only before back vowels (*u, o, a*), whereas in the cognates of set IV Hungarian's *k* occurs only before front vowels. We conclude that Hungarian had a single original sound which changed to *h* before back vowels (as in set III) but remained *k* before front vowels (as in set IV). We reconstruct **k*, together with the change in Hungarian of **k* > *h* / __back vowel.

Someone might wonder whether the proto-language could not have had an **h* which then changed to *k* before front vowels in Hungarian and to *k* in all environments in Finnish and Udmurt. First, directionality argues against this possibility (since the change *h* > *k* is essentially unknown anywhere). Second, the criterion of economy also goes against this alternative; it is more likely that only one change took place, **k* > *h* before back vowels in Hungarian, than that several independent changes occurred, one of **h* > *k* before front vowels in Hungarian and, independently of the Hungarian development, changes of **h* > *k* in all contexts in Finnish and in Udmurt.

SOUND CORRESPONDENCES 5 (*s-: s-: ɛ-*) and 6 (*s-: Ø-: s-*) present a similar problem of partially overlapping correspondence sets. However, the partial overlap in this instance is not like that seen in SOUND CORRESPONDENCES 3 and 4, both of which come from a single original sound (**k*) in different positions due to conditioned sound change. Both SOUND CORRESPONDENCES 5 and 6 in the cognates of sets V and VI occur essentially in the same environments: both before the various vowels, front and back, and both before the same sorts of consonants in the following syllable (for example, before *l*, of 36, 45, and 48), which would be clearer if we had more cognates in the data than are presented here. Careful scrutiny in this case eventually shows that it is not possible to explain the difference between the two sound correspondence sets as conditioned sound change in some environment, given that both occur in essentially the same environments. This being the case, we have no choice but to reconstruct a different proto-sound to represent each of these two sound correspondences. Let us see how the general guidelines for reconstruction fare in these partially overlapping but ultimately contrastive cases, first applied to SOUND CORRESPONDENCE 5, then to 6, with the results then compared.

By *directionality*, for SOUND CORRESPONDENCE 5 (*s-: s-: ɛ-*) we might assume either **s* which became *ɛ* in Udmurt, or **ɛ* which became *s* in Finnish and Hungarian. Both are known changes, though *s* > *ɛ* is not common without some conditioning environment, say before front vowels. While not compellingly strong, *directionality* in this instance gives a slightly stronger vote for **ɛ* than for **s*, and thus for a change of **ɛ* > *s* being the most likely. On the other hand, *economy* clearly favours **s*, since this would require only one change, **s* > *ɛ* in Udmurt; the postulation of **ɛ* would require the change of *ɛ* > *s* twice, once in Finnish and once again in

Hungarian. *Majority wins* clearly votes for *s, since two languages have s (Finnish and Hungarian) and only one has ɕ (Udmurt). The criterion of examining the *features held in common* avails little in this instance, since s- and ɕ- share all their features except point of articulation, meaning the proto-sound presumably had all these same shared features – some kind of s-like sound. In sum, the guidelines do not all unanimously point in the same direction, but do favour *s for SOUND CORRESPONDENCE 5, which presumes the change *s > ɕ in Udmurt.

However, the existence of SOUND CORRESPONDENCE 6 (s-: Ø-: s-) complicates this picture, since it, too, appears to point to *s as the best probable reconstruction, and yet we were unable to combine 5 and 6 as possibly coming from the same original sound with some conditioned changes in particular contexts. *Directionality* clearly favours *s for SOUND CORRESPONDENCE 6, since s > Ø is a relatively frequent change (often through the intermediate stage of s > h > Ø), but Ø > s is not known and there is no phonetic motivation for why such a change should take place. *Majority wins* also clearly favours *s, given the two cases with s (Finnish and Udmurt) but only one with Ø (Hungarian). Similarly, the *features held in common* suggest *s, since s is the sound in two of the languages, and the features of Ø do not contribute insight here. Finally, *economy* also supports *s for SOUND CORRESPONDENCE 6, since this would require only the single change of *s > Ø in Hungarian. Postulation of *Ø, for example, because that is the reflex in Hungarian, would require the change Ø > s in Finnish and again in Udmurt (although stating the conditions under which this could have taken place would be next to impossible). Postulation of some third alternative, say *ʃ, would require even more changes, *ʃ > s in Finnish and in Udmurt, and *ʃ > Ø in Hungarian. In sum, then, the guidelines support *s for SOUND CORRESPONDENCE 6, with the presumed change *s > Ø in Hungarian.

However, this cannot be right. As already indicated, the two SOUND CORRESPONDENCES 5 and 6 occur in contrastive environments and apparently cannot be combined as separate outcomes from the same original sound due to conditioned change. This means that we cannot, then, reconstruct *s both for 5 and for 6, since sound change is regular and such a reconstruction would afford no means of explaining why the proposed single original *s behaves differently in the two different correspondence sets, why in Hungarian it is sometimes s (in set V cognates) and sometimes Ø (in set VI cognates), why in Udmurt it is sometimes ɕ, sometimes s, and so on. We must reconstruct a separate sound for each of these distinct correspondence sets. While the decision about what to reconstruct for each is not as straightforward as we might like, all the guidelines clearly suggest *s for SOUND CORRESPONDENCE 6 (s-: Ø: s), where for SOUND CORRESPONDENCE 5 (s-: s-: ɕ-) there was not such agreement – directionality favours *ɕ slightly. Let us then propose these reconstructions: *ɕ for 5 (postulating the sound changes *ɕ > s in Finnish and in Hungarian), and *s for 6 (with the change *s > Ø in Hungarian). In fact, with the aid of much additional evidence from other Finno-Ugric languages, Uralic specialists reconstruct *ś (IPA [sʲ] or alveolo-palatal [ɕ]) for SOUND CORRESPONDENCE 5 and *s for 6 (Sammallahti 1988).

Let us return to SOUND CORRESPONDENCES 1, 2, 3, and 4 and apply steps 5 and 6. Not enough cognate sets are given in the data here to reconstruct the full phonological inventory of Proto-Finno-Ugric, so that we are unable to apply steps 5 and 6 fully. However, for now let us assume that we at least have available in the cognates of Table 7.7 the evidence for the voiceless stops, and apply step 5 to these to illustrate the procedures. Our tentative reconstructions to this point based on the sound correspondences were:

*p (1) Finnish *p-*: Hungarian *f-*: Udmurt *p-* (in set I, nos. 1–11)
*t (2) Finnish *t-*: Hungarian *t-*: Udmurt *t-* (in set II, nos. 12–17)
*k (before back vowels) (3) Finnish *k-*: Hungarian *h-*: Udmurt *k-* (in set III, nos. 18–26)
*k again (before front vowels) (4) Finnish *k-*: Hungarian *k-*: Udmurt *k-* (in set IV, nos. 27–35).

We check these in step 5 to see how plausible the resulting inventory of voiceless stops would be with these sounds in the proto-language. A language with the stops *p, t, k* would be quite normal, with an internally consistent pattern of voiceless stops. If we did attempt to reconstruct possibility (3) (some third thing from which to derive *p* and *f* plausibly, say *p^h) for SOUND CORRESPONDENCE 1, we would no longer have a natural, symmetrical phonemic inventory of voiceless stops (*p, *t, *k), but rather the unlikely *p^h, *t, *k. In step 5, we would see that this would result in a series of stops which is not internally consistent, where the presence of aspirated *p^h (with no plain *p) is incongruent with *t* and *k* (with no *t^h and *k^h). In step 6, we would check this pattern to see how well it fits typologically with what we know of the sound systems of the world's languages. Here we would find that languages with only the stops *p^h, *t, *k* (but no *p* and no other aspirated stops) are very rare, while a large majority of languages have a stop series with *p, t, k*. For possibility (2) (which would reconstruct *f*), step 5 tells us a language with *f, t, k* (but no *p) is also internally not as consistent as one with *p, t, k*, and therefore not as good a reconstruction. Step 6 tells us the same thing; in looking at the sound systems of the world's languages, we find extremely few with *f, t, k* (and no *p*), but hundreds with *p, t, k*. Putting these considerations of directionality, economy, internal consistency, and typological realism together, we conclude that the reconstruction of *p is the best of the alternatives for SOUND CORRESPONDENCE 1. In turn, we apply steps 5 and 6 to the reconstructions with *t and *k and we find these to be supported in similar fashion in these steps. We find that the possible alternative with *h for SOUND CORRESPONDENCES 3 and 4, which might have been considered, would be inconsistent internally and typologically (leaving a system with *p, t, h*, but no *k*) not to mention being against economy, the known directionality of change, and the majority-wins guidelines.

7.4 Indo-European and the Regularity of Sound Change

The development of historical linguistics is closely associated with the study of Indo-European. *Grimm's Law, Grassmann's Law*, and *Verner's Law* are major milestones in the history of Indo-European and thus also in historical linguistics, and traditionally all linguists have learned these laws – indeed, knowledge of them is helpful for understanding the comparative method and the regularity hypothesis. (These laws were considered in preliminary form in Chapter 2.) In this section, each is taken up individually and, based on these laws, the development of the claim that sound change is regular is considered.

7.4.1 Grimm's Law

The forms of Table 7.8 illustrate Grimm's Law, a series of changes in the stops from Proto-Indo-European to Proto-Germanic:

voiceless stops > voiceless fricatives:

*p	>	f
*t	>	θ
*k, *ḱ	>	h (x)
*kw	>	hw

voiced stops > voiceless stops

*b	>	p
*d	>	t
*g, *ĝ	>	k
*gʷ	>	kw

voiced aspirated (murmured) stops > plain voiced stops

*bh	>	b
*dh	>	d
*gh, *ĝh	>	g
*gʷh	>	gw, w

Note here that some scholars believe that the voiced aspirates did not become plain voiced stops directly, but rather went through an intermediate stage of becoming voiced fricatives, which then later hardened to voiced stops (or became *w* in the case of **gʷh*): **bh > β > b, *dh > ð > d, *gh > ɣ > g, *ĝh > yʲ > ĝ, *gʷh > ɣʷ > w.* (The sounds **ḱ, *ĝ,* and **ĝh* represent the 'palatal' series in Indo-European. In many descriptions of Grimm's Law, the palatal series of stops is not distinguished from the velar series in Table 7.8.) In Table 7.8, the Gothic and English forms show the results of these changes in Germanic, while the Sanskrit, Greek, and Latin forms did not undergo Grimm's Law as the Germanic forms did. (An Old High German (OHG) form is sometimes substituted when no Gothic cognate is available; OE = Old English.)

Grimm's Law embodies systematic correspondences between Germanic and non-Germanic languages, the results of regular sound changes in Germanic. So, for example, as a result of the change **p > f* in the examples in set Ia of Table 7.8, Gothic and English (the Germanic languages) have the reflex *f* corresponding to *p* in Sanskrit, Greek, and Latin (the non-Germanic languages), all from Proto-Indo-European **p.* While Grimm's Law accounts for the systematic correspondences seen in Table 7.8, nevertheless these are not entirely without exceptions. However, as we will see, these exceptions all have satisfactory explanations. One set of forms which seem to be exceptions to Grimm's Law involves stops

TABLE 7.8: Indo-European cognates reflecting Grimm's Law

Sanskrit	Greek	Latin	Gothic	English
Set Ia: *p > f				
pad-	pod-	ped-	fōtus	foot
páńča [páṇča]	pénte	[quinque] [kʷinkʷe]	fimf	five
pra-	pro-	pro-	fra-	fro
pū-'make clear, bright'	pur	pūrus 'pure'	[OE fȳr]	fire
pitár-	patē´r	pater	fadar [faðar]	father [OE fæder]
nápāt- 'descendant'		nepōs 'nephew, grandson'	[OHG nefo]	nephew [OE nefa]
Set Ib: *t > θ				
trī-/tráyas	treīs/tría	trēs	þrija	three
tv-am	tū (Doric)	tu	þu	thou
-ti-	-ti-	-tis/-sis		-th 'nominalizer'
gátis 'gait'	básis 'going'	mor-tis 'death'		[health, birth, death]
Set Ic: *k, *k̂ > h (or [x])				
śván- [ʃvən-]	kúōn	canis [kanis]	hunds	hound 'dog'
śatám [ʃətóm]	(he-)katón	centum [kentum]	hunda (pl.)	hundred
kravís 'raw flesh'	kré(w)as 'flesh, meat'	cruor 'raw, blood, thick'		raw [OE hrāw] 'corpse'
dáśa [dáʃə]	déka	decem [dekem]	taíhun [tɛxun]	ten

Set IIa: *b > p (*b* was very rare in Proto-Indo-European, and many doubt that it was part of the sound system; some Lithuanian forms are given in the absence of cognates in the other languages)

Sanskrit	Greek	Latin	Gothic	English
		(*Lithuanian*) dubùs	diups	deep [OE dēop]
	kánnabis	(*Lithuanian*) kanapẽs]		hemp (borrowing?)
		Latin lūbricus	sliupan	slip
Set IIb: *d > t				
d(u)vắ-	dúo/dúō	duo	twái [twai]	two
dánt-	odónt-	dent-	tunþus	tooth
dáśa [dáʃə]	déka	decem [dekem]	taíhun [tɛxun]	ten
pad-	pod-	ped-	fōtus	foot
ad-	édō	edō		eat [OE etan]

TABLE 7.8: continued

Sanskrit	Greek	Latin	Gothic	English
'eat'	'I eat'	'I eat'		
véda	woīda	videō	wáit	wit 'to know'
'I know'	'I know'	'I know'	[wait]	
			'I know'	

Set IIc: *g, *ĝ > k

janás	génos	genus	kun-i	kin
			'race, tribe'	
jánu-	gónu	genū	kniu	knee
jnātá	gnōtós	(g)nōtus	kunnan	known
			'to know'	
ájra-	agrós	ager	akrs	acre 'field'
'country'				
mr̥j-	(a-)mélgō	mulgeō	miluk-s	milk
'to milk'	'to squeeze	'I milk'	'milk'	
	out'			

Set IIIa: *bh > b

bhar-	phér-	fer-	baír-an	bear
			[bɛran]	
			'to bear'	
bhrātar	phrátēr	frāter	brōþar	brother
a-bhū-t	é-phū	fu-it	bau-an	be
'he was'	'he grew,	'he was'	[bɔ̄-an]	
	sprang up'		to dwell'	

Set IIIb: *dh > d

dhā-'put'	ti-thē-mi	fē-cī 'I made'		do [OE dō-n]
	'I put'			
dhrs.nóti	thrasús	(fest-)	(ga-)dars	dare
'he dares'	'bold'		'he dares'	
dvār-	thúr-a	for-ēs	daúr-	door
			[dor-]	
vidhávā	ē-wíthewos	vidua	widuwo	widow
	'unmarried			
	youth'			
mádhu	méthu			mead
madhya-	mésos	medius	midjis	mid

Set IIIc: *gh, *ĝh > g

haṁs-á-	khēn	āns-er	Gans [*German*]	goose
[hɔ̄sɔ́]				
'swan, goose'				

TABLE 7.8: continued

Sanskrit	Greek	Latin	Gothic	English
stigh- 'stride'	steíkhō 'I pace'		steigan [stīgan] 'to climb'	
vah- 'carry'	wókh-os 'chariot'	veh-ō 'I carry'	ga-wig-an 'to move, shake'	weigh/wain

in consonant clusters, and examples of these are given in Table 7.9. (OE = Old English; OHG = Old High German.)

TABLE 7.9: Exceptions to Grimm's Law in consonant clusters

	Sanskrit	Greek	Latin	Gothic	English
1.	páś-	[skep-]	spec-	[OHG speh-]	spy (?) 'to see'
2.	(sthiv-)	pū	spu-	speiw-an [spīw-an]	spew 'to spit'
3.	aṣṭáu [əṣṭáu]	oktō	octō [oktō]	ahtau [axtau]	eight
4.	nákt-	nukt-	noct- [nokt-]	nahts [naxts]	night
5.			capt(īvus)	(haft)	[OE hæft] 'prisoner'
6.	-t-	-ti-	-tis/-sis		-t 'nominalizer'
	gátis 'gait'	básis 'going'	mor-tis 'death'		thrift, draught, thirst, flight, drift
7.			piscis [piskis]	fisks	[OE fisc] 'fish'

In these forms, by Grimm's Law, corresponding to the *p* in (1) and (2) of Sanskrit, Greek, and Latin we should expect to find *f* in Gothic and English, not the *p* seen in these forms. (And given the *p* of Gothic and English, the Germanic languages, we expect the correspondence in Sanskrit, Greek, and Latin to be *b*, not the *p* that actually occurs.) In (3–6) we expect Gothic and English to have /θ/ (not the actually occurring *t*) corresponding to the *t* of Sanskrit, Greek, and Latin. And in (7), we would expect Latin *k* to correspond to Germanic *h* (i.e. *x*), not to the *k* of the Gothic and English words in this cognate set. These exceptions are explained by the fact that Grimm's Law was actually a conditioned change; it did not take place after fricatives (*sp* > *sp*, not ✗ *sf*) or after stops (*kt* > *xt*, not ✗ *xθ*; the *k*, the first member of the cluster, does change to *x* as expected by Grimm's Law, but the *t*, the second member, does not change to expected *θ*). In the case of (6), the difference between *thrift, draught, thirst, flight, drift* of Table 7.9 and the *health, birth, death* of Table 7.8 is explained in the same way. The /θ/ forms (spelled with <th>, as in Table 7.8) underwent Grimm's Law (*t* > *θ*); the forms with *-t* (in Table 7.9) are exempt from Grimm's Law because this *t* comes after a fricative in English (what is spelled <gh> in *draught* and *fight* was formerly [x], which was later lost; see Chapter 14). Thus, when Grimm's Law is correctly formulated – written to exclude stops after fricatives and other stops in consonant clusters involving obstruents (environments in which they did not change) – the stops in clusters turn out in fact not to be true exceptions to the sound change.

7.4.2 Grassmann's Law

Another set of forms which earlier had seemed to be exceptions to Grimm's Law is explained by Grassmann's Law (seen already in Chapter 2). In Greek and Sanskrit, Grassmann's Law regularly dissimilated the first of two aspirated stops within a word so that the first stop lost its aspiration, as in the change from Proto-Indo-European *dhi-dheh$_i$-mi 'I put, place' (with reduplication of the root *dheh$_i$-) to Sanskrit da-dhā-mi and Greek ti-thē-mi. As a result of Grassmann's Law, some sound correspondences between Sanskrit, Greek, and Germanic languages do not match the expectations from Grimm's Law, as, for example, in the following cognates:

Sanskrit	Greek	Gothic	English	
bōdha	peutha	biudan	bid	'to wake, become aware'
bandha	—	bindan	bind	'to bind'.

The first is from Proto-Indo-European *bheudha-, the second from *bhendh-; both have undergone dissimilation of the first *bh due to the presence of a second aspirated stop in the word (*dh in this case). This gives the SOUND CORRESPONDENCE in (1):

(1) Sanskrit b: Greek p: Gothic b: English b.

By Grimm's Law, we expect the b of Sanskrit to correspond to p in Germanic (Gothic and English in this case), and we expect Germanic b to correspond to Sanskrit bh and Greek ph. So SOUND CORRESPONDENCE 1 in these cognate sets is an exception to Grimm's Law. The cognate sets with SOUND CORRESPONDENCE 1 (and others for the originally aspirated stops at other points of articulation), then, are not real exceptions to Grimm's Law; rather, their reflexes in Germanic are correct for Grimm's Law, and the Sanskrit and Greek reflexes are not those expected by Grimm's Law only because Grassmann's Law regularly deaspirated the first aspirated stop when it occurred before another aspirated stop later in the word in these languages. That is, SOUND CORRESPONDENCE 1 (and the others like it at other points of articulation) is the result of regular changes, Grimm's Law in Germanic, and Grassmann's Law in Sanskrit and Greek.

7.4.3 Verner's Law

A final set of what had earlier appeared to be exceptions to Grimm's Law is explained by Verner's Law (called *grammatical alternation* in older sources). Some forms which illustrate Verner's Law are seen in the cognate sets of Table 7.10 (OE = Old English; OHG = Old High German).

In cognate set (1), by Grimm's Law we expect the p of Sanskrit, Greek, and Latin to correspond to f in Germanic (Gothic and English), but instead we have

TABLE 7.10: Examples illustrating Verner's Law

	Sanskrit	Greek	Latin	Gothic	English
(1)	saptá	heptá	septem	sibun [siβun]	seven
(2)	pitár-	patɛ́r	pater	fadar [faðar]	OE fæder 'father'
(3)	śatám [ʃətəm]	(he-)katón	centum [kentum]	hunda (pl.)	hundred
(4)	śrutás 'heard'	klutós 'heard'			OE hlud 'loud'
(5)		makrós 'long, slender'	macer [maker]	[OHG magar]	meagre

Gothic *b* ([β]) and English *v*; given Gothic *b*, we expect the correspondence in Sanskrit to be *bh* and in Greek to be *ph*. Similarly, in cognate sets (2–4) we have the correspondence of Sanskrit, Greek, and Latin *t* to Germanic *d*, not the θ expected by Grimm's Law in Germanic (and not the Sanskrit *dh* and Greek *th* we would expect, given Germanic *d*). These apparent exceptions to Grimm's Law are explained by Verner's Law. Verner's Law affects medial consonants; when the Proto-Indo-European accent followed, medial fricatives in a root – both original ones and those resulting from Grimm's Law – became voiced in Germanic, (*)f > β, (*)θ > ð, (*)x > ɣ, and *s > z. Since later in Proto-Germanic the accent shifted to the root-initial syllable, the earlier placement of the accent can only be seen when the cognates from the non-Germanic languages are compared. Thus, in the cognate sets of Table 7.10, we see in the Sanskrit and Greek cognates that the accent is not on the initial syllable but on a later syllable, after the sound that changed, and that the Germanic forms do not match expectations from Grimm's Law in these instances. In (1), we would not expect Gothic *sibun*, but rather something like *sifun*, given the *p* of Sanskrit *saptá* and Greek *heptá*; however, since the accent is on the last syllable in the Sanskrit and Greek forms, Verner's Law gives Gothic β (spelled *b*) in this case. The forms of Table 7.11 show how the forms with the accent later in the word (which undergo Verner's Law, symbolized as . . .C. . .') contrast with forms with the accent before the sound in question (indicated as '. . .C. . ., cases which have undergone Grimm's Law), but where Verner's Law does not apply because they do not fit the environment for it.

It is easy to see why Verner's Law was also referred to as illustrating 'grammatical alternation' (*grammatischer Wechsel* in German). The accent in Proto-Indo-European fell on different syllables in certain grammatically related forms, as seen in the forms compared in Table 7.12 (PIE = Proto-Indo-European; P-Germ = Proto-Germanic). As a result, in grammatical paradigms Germanic languages have different allomorphs which depend upon whether or not Verner's Law applied, and these grammatical alternations further support Verner's Law and its correlation with the place of the accent in the proto-language.

Just as expected by Grimm's Law, the Old English forms in the first two columns have /θ/ (spelled <þ>), where the accent in Proto-Indo-European preceded the original *t* (as illustrated by the accent in the Sanskrit forms). However, in the last two columns, Old English does not have the /θ/ expected by Grimm's Law, but rather has the /d/ of Verner's law because the accent came after this medial *t* in Proto-Indo-European, again as shown by the accent in the Sanskrit forms.

TABLE 7.11: Examples showing the effects of Grimm's Law and further effects of
Verner's Law on medial consonants in different contexts

Grimm's Law	Verner's Law
'. . .C. . .	. . .C. . .'
*p > f	*p > f > β
(1a) OE hēafod 'head'	(1b) Gothic sibun [siβun] 'seven'
Latin cáput [káput]	Sanskrit saptá-
*t > θ	*t > θ > ð
(2a) Gothic brōþar [brōθar] 'brother'	(2b) OE fæder 'father'
Sanskrit bhrãtar-	Sanskrit pitár-
*k > x	*k > x > ɣ
(3a) Gothic taíhun 'ten'	(3b) Gothic tigus 'decade'
Greek déka	Greek dekás

TABLE 7.12: Verner's Law in grammatical alternations

	'I become'	'I became'	'we became'	'became [participle]'
PIE	*wértō	*(we)wórta	*(we)wr̥təmé	*wr̥tonós
Sanskrit	vártāmi	va-várta	vavr̥timá	vr̥tānáh
	'I turn'	'I have turned'	'we have turned'	'turned'
P-Germ	*werθō	*warθa	*wurðum(i)	*wurðan(a)z
OE	weorþe	warþ	wurdon	worden
OHG	wirdu	ward	wurtum	wortan

The Old High German forms subsequently underwent other sound changes of
their own, but the difference between those with /d/ and those with /t/ has its
origin in Verner's Law just as the alternations seen in the Old English cognates
do. The allomorphic variation which resulted, as for example that seen in the
verb paradigm in Table 7.12, illustrates the 'grammatical alternation' that comes
from Verner's Law.

So the Verner's Law cases (as in Tables 7.10, 7.11, and 7.12), which originally
appeared to be exceptions to Grimm's Law, turn out also to be explained by
regular sound change – by Verner's Law, a conditioned change having to do with
the earlier location of the accent within the word.

7.4.4 Sound laws and regularity of sound change

The sound laws just considered played an important role in the history of Indo-
European studies and as a consequence in the overall history of historical linguistics. Grimm's Law, which was published first (in 1822), was quite general and
accounted for the majority of sound correspondences involving the stop series
between Germanic and non-Germanic languages. However, as initially formulated, it did appear to have exceptions. When Hermann Grassmann discovered
his law (in 1862), a large block of these 'exceptions' was explained, and then
Karl Verner through Verner's Law (in 1877) explained most of the remaining

exceptions. This success in accounting for what had originally appeared to be exceptions led the Neogrammarians to have confidence that sound change was regular and exceptionless (see Chapter 2). This is one of the most significant conclusions in the history of linguistics.

7.5 Basic Assumptions of the Comparative Method

What textbooks call the 'basic assumptions' of the comparative method might better be viewed as the consequences of how we reconstruct and of our views of sound change. The following four basic assumptions are usually listed.

(1) The proto-language was uniform, with no dialect (or social) variation. Clearly this 'assumption' is counterfactual, since all known languages have regional or social variation, different styles, and so on. It is not so much that the comparative method 'assumes' no variation as that there is just nothing built into the comparative method which allows it to address variation directly. This means that what is reconstructed will not recover the once-spoken proto-language in its entirety. Still, rather than stressing what is missing, we can be happy that the method provides the means for recovering so much of the original language. This assumption of uniformity is a reasonable idealization; it does no more damage to the understanding of the language than, say, modern reference grammars do which concentrate on a language's general structure, typically leaving out consideration of regional, social, and stylistic variation. Moreover, dialect differences are not always left out of comparative considerations and reconstructions, since in some cases scholars do reconstruct dialect differences to the proto-language based on differences in daughter languages which are not easily reconciled with a single uniform starting point. This, however, has not been common practice outside of Indo-European studies.

Assumptions (2) and (3) are interrelated, so that it is best to discuss them together.

(2) Language splits are sudden.

(3) After the split-up of the proto-language, there is no subsequent contact among the related languages.

These 'assumptions' are a consequence of the fact that the comparative method addresses directly only material in the related languages which is inherited from the proto-language and has no means of its own for dealing directly with borrowings, the results of subsequent contact after diversification into related languages. Borrowing and the effects of subsequent language contact are, however, by no means neglected in reconstruction. Rather, we must resort to other techniques which are not formally part of the comparative method for dealing with borrowing and the results of language contact (see Chapters 3, 9, and 10). It is true that the comparative method contains no means for addressing whether the language of some speech community gradually diverged over a long period of time before ultimately distinct but related languages emerged, or whether a sudden division took place with a migration of a part of the community so far away that there was no subsequent contact between the two parts of the original community, resulting in a sharp split and no subsequent contacts between the groups. (Assumptions (2) and (3) are better seen as the consequence of the family-tree model for classifying related languages, dealt with in Chapter 9, since the tree diagram depicts a parent language splitting up sharply into its daughters.)

(4) Sound change is regular. The assumption of regularity is extremely valuable to the application of the comparative method. Knowing that a sound changes in a regular fashion gives us the confidence to reconstruct what the sound was like in the parent language from which it comes. If a sound could change in unconstrained, unpredictable ways, we would not be able to determine from a given sound in a daughter language what sound or sounds it may have come from in the parent language, or, looking at a particular sound in the parent language, we could not determine what its reflexes in its daughter languages would be. That is, if, for example, an original *p of a proto-language could arbitrarily for no particular reason become f in some words, ə in others, q' in others, and so on, in exactly the same phonetic and other linguistic circumstances, then it would not be possible to reconstruct. In such a situation, comparing, say, a p of one language with a p of another related language would be of no avail, if the p in each could have come in an unpredictable manner from a number of different sounds.

For reconstruction of morphology and syntax, see Chapter 11.

7.6 How Realistic are Reconstructed Proto-languages?

The success of any given reconstruction depends on the material at hand to work with and the ability of the comparative linguist to figure out what happened in the history of the languages being compared as reflected in the extant documentation. In cases where the daughter languages preserve clear evidence of what the parent language had, a reconstruction can be very successful, matching closely the actual spoken ancestral language from which the compared daughters descend. However, there are many cases in which all the daughter languages lose or merge formerly contrasting sounds or eliminate earlier alternations through analogy, or lose morphological categories due to changes of various sorts. We cannot recover things about the proto-language via the comparative method if the daughters simply do not preserve evidence of them. In cases where the evidence is severely limited or unclear, we often miss things or make mistakes in postulated reconstructions. We make the best inferences we can based on the evidence available and on everything we know about the nature of human languages and linguistic change.

A few scholars in the past argued that because we cannot know how things were pronounced in the past, sounds reconstructed by the comparative method have no phonetic value and are instead mere abstract place-holders. Nearly all historical linguists today reject this view and seek phonetic realism in their reconstructions. We do the best we can with what we have to work with. Often the results are very good; sometimes they are less complete.

A comparison of reconstructed Proto-Romance with attested Latin provides a telling example in this case. We do successfully recover a great deal of the formerly spoken language via the comparative method. However, the modern Romance languages for the most part preserve little of the former noun cases and complex tense–aspect verbal morphology which Latin had. Subsequent changes have obscured this inflectional morphology so much that much of it is not reconstructible by the comparative method.

7.7 Temporal Limitation to the Comparative Method

The comparative method does have some real limitations. A principal one is its *temporal limitation*: it is generally acknowledged that there is a limit to how far into the past the comparative method can reach, said by different scholars to be somewhere between 6,000 and 10,000 years ago. This is because so much language change can take place with the passage of time that after a very long time in which so many language changes take place, little that was original in a language may be preserved, and it becomes no longer possible to identify accurately what may have been inherited. For example, vocabulary changes and gets replaced. According to glottochronology (see Chapter 16), after about 14,000 years, nearly all of a language's basic vocabulary will have been replaced, meaning that if we were to compare two related languages which had split up before, say, 15,000 years or more ago, it is unlikely, according to the method, that we would find recognizable cognates. For example, Nichols (1998: 128) reports that 'after 6,000 years of separation, two languages are expected to exhibit only 7% shared cognates, and 7% represents the lowest number of resemblant items that can safely be considered distinct from chance'.

It matters not whether either of these views is correct – certainly there is no reason to believe in the glottochronological date (see Chapter 16 for details); however, they do correctly note that over time vocabulary items are replaced and change. We cannot expect non-replaced cognate vocabulary to survive in languages or to persist in recognizable form for tens of thousands of years. Clearly, after nearly all of the vocabulary of related languages has been replaced or changed so that it is no longer possible to recognize connections, we cannot expect meaningful results from the application of the comparative method. While the temporal threshold may vary from case to case, in the long run, after enough structural change and vocabulary replacement, comparison of only very distantly related languages by the comparative method can cease to be effective.

The amount of change over time is relevant to the many hypotheses of proposed distant genetic relationships. It is quite likely that, for many of these proposals, even if there had ever been a relationship among some of the languages involved, it lies so far in the distant past that the amount of inherited material in recognizable form is so vanishingly small that no effective case for a genealogical relationship among the languages compared can be made. (See Chapter 13.)

7.8 Exercises

Exercise 7.1 Aymaran

Consider the following data from the two major branches of the Aymaran language family (Peru and Bolivia). Focus your attention on the sibilant fricatives (s and š) only (ignore x and χ for this exercise). What will you reconstruct? How many sibilant fricatives do you postulate for Proto-Aymaran? State your evidence.

NOTE: š = IPA [ʃ], č = IPA [ʧ]; χ = voiceless uvular fricative; C' = glottalized [ejective] consonant.

	Central Aymara	Southern Aymara	gloss
1.	saxu	sawu-	'to weave'
2.	sa(wi)	sa(ta)	'to plant'
3.	asa	asa-	'to carry flat things'
4.	usu	usu-	'to become sick'
5.	nasa	nasa	'nose'
6.	aski	hiskʰi	'to ask'
7.	muxsa	muχsa	'sweet'
8.	suniqi	sunaqi	'small spring'
9.	šanq'a	sanqa	'to snuffle'
10.	waša	wasa	'silent place'
11.	iši	isi	'dress'
12.	muši	musi	'to take care (of)'
13.	puši	pusi	'four'
14.	išt'a	hist'a-	'to close'
15.	išapa	isapa-	'to hear, listen'

(based on Cerrón-Palomino 2000: 145–6)

Exercise 7.2 Tulu

Tulu is a Dravidian language (of India) which has several varieties. Consider the following data from two principal varieties. Focus your attention only on the nasals. What will you reconstruct for these for the proto-language that is the parent of these two varieties? How many nasals do you postulate for this proto-language? State your evidence.

NOTE: j = [ĵ], IPA [ʤ]; ṇ = IPA [ɳ].

	Shivalli	Sapaliga	gloss
1.	a:ṇi	a:ni	'male'
2.	uṇi	u:ni	'dine'

	Shivalli	Sapaliga	gloss
3.	manṇi	manni	'soil'
4.	ko:nɛ	ko:nɛ	'room'
5.	e:ṇi	ya:nɨ	'I'
6.	ninɛ	ninɛ	'wick'
7.	ja:nɛ	da:nɛ	'what'
8.	sanɛ	tanɛ	'conceiving'

(Bhat 2001: 11)

Exercise 7.3 Finnic reconstruction

Reconstruct Proto-Finnic based on these cognates in these four Finnic languages. The focus in this exercise is on the velar stops. You need not attempt to reconstruct other sounds, but if you do, assume that if more data were given the correspondences found in a single cognate set here would recur in other sets of cognates. Do not struggle with the vowels, as there is not sufficient information here to reconstruct them adequately. Also, there is not sufficient information to reconstruct all of the consonants of Proto-Finnic in these data.

NOTE: *ä* = IPA [æ]; *č* = IPA [ʧ]; *ž* = IPA [ʒ]. *y* and *ü* are the same; they both represent IPA [y], a high front rounded vowel. Double vowels (*ee, oo,* etc.) represent vowel length, long vowels. Some phonetic details of some of these languages are not present in these forms.

	Finnish	Estonian	Vote	Veps	gloss
1.	käsi	käsi	čäsi	käzʲi	'hand'
2.	käy-	käi-	čäü-	kävu-	'to go, walk'
3.	kivi	kivi	čivi	kivʲi	'stone'
4.	kieli	keel	čeel	kelʲ	'tongue, language'
5.	kylä	küla	čüllä	kylä	'village'
6.	kysy-	küsi-	čüsü-	kyzu-	'to ask'
7.	kala	kala	kala	kala	'fish'
8.	kana	kana	kana	kana	'hen'
9.	kolme	kolm	kilmi-	koume	'three'
10.	kuol-la	kool-ma	kool(-aa)	kou-da	'die'
11.	kutsu-	kutsu-	kuttsu-	kuts-	'call'
12.	kuusi	kuus	kuus	kuzʲ	'six'
13.	kaksi	kaks	kahsi	kaksʲ	'two'
14.	yksi	üks	ühsi	yksʲ	'one'

Excercise 7.4 Proto-Utian

Utian (aka Miwok-Costanoan) is a family of languages in California, with two major branches, Miwokan and Costanoan. Each branch has several languages in it. Here, only the sound correspondences between Proto-Miwokan and Proto-Costanoan are presented. Based on these sound correspondences, reconstruct the sounds of Proto-Utian. In the case of overlapping correspondences, state your reasons for why you choose the reconstruction that you do.

NOTE: *ṭ* and *ṣ* are retroflex sounds; *č* = IPA [ʧ], *y* = IPA [j].

Proto-Costanoan	Proto-Miwokan
*p	*p
*t	*t
*ṭ /__i, e, / i, e __	*č /__i, e, / i, e __
(before or after front vowel)	
*ṭ elsewhere	*ṭ elsewhere
(before or after non-front vowel)	
*č	*č
*s /__high V, / high V__	*k /__high V, / high V__
(before or after a high vowel)	
*k elsewhere	*k elsewhere
(before or after non-high vowel)	
*kʷ /__high V, / high V__	*w /__high V, / high V__
(before or after a high vowel)	
*kʷ elsewhere	*kʷ elsewhere
(after a non-high vowel, that is, after /a/ or /o/)	
*ʔ	*ʔ
*s	*s
*ṣ	*ṣ
*h	*ṣ
*h	*h
*m	*m
*n	*n
*l	*l
*w	*w
*y	*y

(based on Callaghan 2014: 69, somewhat simplified)

Exercise 7.5 Polynesian

The Polynesian languages of the Pacific form a subgroup of the Oceanic branch of the Austronesian family of languages (see Figure 9.3).

1. What sound correspondences are found in these data? What sound do you reconstruct for the proto-language to represent each correspondence set?
2. What sound change or changes have taken place in each of these languages?
3. What is the best reconstruction (proto-form) for examples 6, 16, 20, and 32? Show how your postulated sound changes apply to each of these cases (examples 6, 16, 20, 32) to produce the modern forms.

Note that not all sounds of the proto-language are represented in these cognate sets with their sound correspondences. For example, in one not represented clearly here, Tongan has Ø corresponding to *l* or *r* of the other languages (reflecting what is usually reconstructed as *r* of Proto-Polynesian), distinct from the set in which Tongan has *l* corresponding to *l* or *r* in these sister languages (reflecting Proto-Polynesian *l*). This distinction is not clearly visible in the data presented in this exercise.

NOTE: <ʼ> [ʔ]. Hawaiian <ʻ> (a letter of Hawaiian orthography called ʻokina) is also [ʔ].

	Māori	Tongan	Samoan	Rarotongan	Hawaiian	gloss
1.	tapu	tapu	tapu	tapu	kapu	'forbidden, taboo'
2.	pito	pito	—	pito	piko	'navel'
3.	puhi	puhi	—	puʼi	puhi	'blow'
4.	taha	tafa ʻedge'	tafa	taʼa	kaha	'side'
5.	tae 'trash'	taʼe	tae	tae	kae	'excrement'
6.	taŋata	taŋata	taŋata	taŋata	kanaka	'man, person'
7.	tai	tahi	tai	tai	kai	'sea'
8a.	kaha	kafa	ʼafa	kaʼa	ʻaha	'strong'
8b.	maːrohi-	maːlohi	maːlosi	maːroʼi	—	'strong'
9.	karo	kalo	ʼalo	karo	ʻalo	'dodge'
10.	aka	aka	aʼa	aka	aʻa	'root'
11.	au	ʼahu	au	au	au	'gall'
12.	uru 'tip of weapon'	ʼulu	ulu	uru	ulu 'centre'	'head'
13.	uhi	ʼufi	ufi	uʼi	uhi	'yam'
14.	ahi	afi	afi	aʼi	ahi	'fire'

	Māori	Tongan	Samoan	Rarotongan	Hawaiian	gloss
15.	ɸa:	fa:	fa:	ʼa:	ha:	'four'
16.	ɸeke	feke	feʼe	ʼeke	heʼe	'octopus'
17.	ika	ika	iʼa	ika	iʼa	'fish'
18.	ihu	ihu	isu	puta-iʼu	ihu	'nose'
				'nostril' (*puta* 'hole')		
19.	hau	hau	sau	ʼau	hau	'dew'
	'wind' (*hauku:* 'dew'; *-ku:* 'showery weather')					
20.	hika	—	siʼa	ʼika	hiʼa	'firemaking'
21.	hiku	hiku	siʼu	ʼiku	hiʼu	'tail'
	'fishtail'					
22.	ake	hake	aʼe	ake	aʼe	'up'
23.	uru	huu	ulu	uru	ulu	'enter'
24.	maŋa	maŋa	maŋa	maŋa	mana	'branch'
25.	mau	maʼu	mau	mau	mau	'constant, fixed'
26.	mara	ma:	mala	mara	mala	'fermented food'
	'marinated'	'ensilage'				
27.	noho	nofo	nofo	noʼo	noho	'sit'
28.	ŋaru	ŋalu	ŋalu	ŋaru	nalu	'wave'
29.	ŋutu	ŋutu	ŋutu	ŋutu	nuku	'mouth'
30.	waka	vaka	vaʼa	vaka	waʼa	'canoe'
31.	wae	vaʼe	vae	vae	wae	'leg'
32.	raho	laho	laso	raʼo	laho	'scrotum'
	'testicle'					
33.	rou	lohu	lou	rou	lou	'fruit-picking pole'
	'long forked stick'					
34.	rua	ʼua	lua	rua	lua	'two'

Exercise 7.6 Lencan

Compare the cognates from the two Lencan languages (both of which have recently become extinct: Chilanga was spoken in El Salvador; Honduran Lenca was spoken in Honduras). Work only with the consonants in this problem (the changes involving the vowels are too complex to solve with these data alone).

1. Set up the correspondence sets.
2. Reconstruct the sounds of Proto-Lencan.
3. Find and list the sound changes which took place in each language.
4. Determine what the relative chronology may have been in any cases where more than one change took place in either individual language, if there is evidence which shows the relative chronology.

Some aspects of this exercise present challenges that you may find difficult.

NOTES: *t'*, *k'*, and *ts'* are glottalized (ejective) consonants; *ts'* is a single segment, a glottalized alveolar affricate – it is not a consonant cluster. Also, these data do not provide enough information for you to recover all the consonants of the proto-language, so that it will not be possible to apply steps 5 and 6 here satisfactorily.

š = IPA [ʃ], *y* = IPA [j].

	Honduran Lenca	Chilanga	gloss
1.	pe	pe	'two'
2.	lepa	lepa	'jaguar'
3.	puki	puka	'big'
4.	ta	ta	'cornfield'
5.	tem	tem	'louse'
6.	ke	ke	'stone'
7.	kuma	kumam	'fingernail, claw'
8.	katu	katu	'spider'
9.	waktik	watih	'sandals'
10.	kakma	k'ama	'gourd'
11.	siksik	sisih	'shrimp'
12.	nek	neh	'tooth'
13.	insek	ints'eh	'beak'
14.	taw	t'aw	'house'
15.	tutu	t'ut'u	'flea'
16.	kin	k'in	'road'
17.	kunan	k'ula	'who'
18.	kelkin	k'elkin	'tortilla griddle'
19.	sewe	ts'ewe	'monkey'
20.	say	ts'ay	'five'
21.	musu	muts'u	'liver'
22.	sak-	ts'ih-	'to wash'

	Honduran Lenca	Chilanga	gloss
23.	lawa	lawa	'three'
24.	liwa-	liwa-	'to buy'
25.	tal-	tal-	'to drink'
26.	wala	wala	'raccoon'
27.	was	wal	'water'
28.	asa	alah	'head'
29.	wasan	wila	'urine'

30.	wara	wara	'river'
31.	siri	sirih	'star'
32.	sili	sili	'iron tree' (tree species)
33.	suri-sur	šurih	'squirrel'

[NOTE: *suri-sur* involves reduplications; just compare the *suri-* part of it.]

34.	say-	šey-	'to want'
35.	so	šo	'rain'
36.	suna	šila	'flower'
37.	soko	šoko	'white'
38.	sak	šah	'firewood'
39.	wewe	wewe	'baby'
40.	yet-	yete-	'to laugh'
41.	yuku	yuku	'coyol palm' (palm tree species)
42.	sa	šam	'good'

Exercise 7.7 Uto-Aztecan

1. State the sound correspondences found in these data.
2. Present the sound that you reconstruct for Proto-Uto-Aztecan for each sound correspondence.
3. List the sound changes that you observe in each of the languages.

There are not sufficient examples in the data given here to be able to reconstruct the full set of Proto-Uto-Aztecan sounds. Ignore vowel length, and do not attempt to reconstruct all the vowels for this exercise. However, you may need to consider the presence of particular vowels that condition certain changes in some environments or instances where a vowel is deleted or inserted, as they can affect the conditions of other sound changes involving consonants. Assume that correspondences found in only a single cognate set would recur if more data were present. Given the paucity of forms presented here, you may have to postulate some sound changes on the basis of inconclusive evidence, in hopes of confirming (or disconfirming) them when more data are brought into the picture. It is often the case that the historical linguist must work with incomplete or imperfect data, so the challenge here of attempting to reconstruct with less than complete information is a realistic experience.

NOTE: A few examples have been regularized, slightly modified, in order to avoid complications for the reconstruction.

š = IPA [ʃ], *č* = IPA [ʧ], *y* = IPA [j], *ö* = IPA [ø]. Note that *tl* is a voiceless lateral affricate, a single segment, not a consonant cluster.

Ignore material in parentheses in these cognate sets; mostly they involve morphological material not relevant to this problem.

In 1. Tohono O'odham *wa:pka* 'reed, cane' involves reduplication of the first syllable (wa:-pka < wa:-paka < *pa:-paka).

In 3. these forms for 'three' all come from an earlier /. . .ahi/ after the first consonant.

In 6. Tohono O'odham *wo:g* comes from *woh* > wow > *wo:g*.

In 9. Tohono O'odham *ta:tami* 'tooth' involves reduplication of the first syllable (*ta:-tami*).

In 10. Hopi *timp-* 'edge' is from *tin-pa* 'at the edge'; Comanche *ti:pe* 'mouth' is also from *tin-pa*. Compare only the *tin-* part.

In 13. Comanche *kee* 'no' is from *kay* (compare only the *ka-* part of it).

In 16. ignore the glottal stop (/ʔ/) in some of the forms in this cognate set.

In 21. Tohono O'odham *maččuḍ* is not a straightforward cognate to the forms in the other sister languages; its *uḍ* does not correspond to the final *a* of the others.

	Cupeño	Hopi	Comanche	Tohono O'odham	Huichol	Nahuatl	gloss
1.	paxa(l) 'arrowreed'	pa:qa- 'arrow'	paka 'arrow'	wa:pka	haka	a:ka	'reed'
2.	pa-	pa:(hi)	pa:	wa-	ha:	a:	'water'
3.	pah	pa:y-	pahi-	wai(k)	hai-	e:y	'three'
4.	paxi-	paki		wa:ki	ha:	aki	'enter'
5.	-puš	po:si	pui	wuhi	hiši	i:š	'eye'
6.	pi-	pöhɨ	puʔe	wo:g	hu:ye:	oʔ	'road'
7.	—	pitɨ	pɨhtɨ	we:č	he:te	ete-	'heavy'
8.	tax(wi)	ta:qa	—	—	—	tla:ka	'man, person, body'
9.	tama	tama	ta:ma	ta:tami	tame	tla:n	'tooth'
10.	—	timp- 'edge'	ti:pe	čini	teni	te:n	'mouth'
11.	—	tos-	tusu(ri)	čuhi	tɨsi	tiš	'grind, flour'
12.	—	qa:si	—	kahi(o)	—	ikši	'leg, thigh, foot'
13.	qa(y)	qa	kee		—	ka	'no, not'
14.	qʷaš(i)-	kʷasi	kʷasɨ-	bahi	kʷaši	ikʷši	'cooked, ripe'
15.	qʷaš	kʷasi 'penis'	kʷasi	bahi	kʷaši	—	'tail'
16.	qʷa-	—	—	baʔa	-kʷaʔa	kʷa	'eat'
17.	—	kʷita	kʷita-	bi:t	kʷita	kʷitla	'excrement'
18.	hax(i)	hak(im)	haki	—	—	a:k	'who'
19.	maxa	maqa	maka	ma:k	—	maka	'give'
20.	—	mo:ki	—	mu:ki	mɨki	miki	'die, dead'
21.	mala	mata	—	(maččuḍ)	ma:ta:	matla	'grindstone'
22.	naqa	na:qa	na:ki	na:k	naka	nakas	'ear'
23.	nema	ni:ma	ni:ma	nem	nema	—	'liver'

	Cupeño	Hopi	Comanche	Tohono O'odham	Huichol	Nahuatl	gloss
24.	nemi(n) 'follow'	nima 'go around doing'	nɨmi	—	— 'live, walk about'	nemi	'walk round'
25.	waxe	la:ki	—	gaki	-waki	wa:ki	'dry'
26.	wexi-	lökö	woko	—	huku	oko	'pine'

(based on Stubbs 2011)

Exercise 7.8 Mixe-Zoquean

Mixe-Zoquean is a family of languages spoken in southern Mexico. It has two major branches, Mixean and Zoquean, each reconstructed. Proto-Mixean and Proto-Zoquean are based on comparison of the sister languages in each of these two subgroups (subfamilies). Reconstruct Proto-Mixe-Zoquean based on the following cognate sets in Proto-Mixean and Proto-Zoquean, representing the two branches of the family. Give the sound correspondences you set up together with what you reconstruct for each in Proto-Mixe-Zoquean, and list the sound changes you assume took place in each branch. Try to apply all the steps discussed in this chapter.

NOTES: ts is a single segment (alveolar affricate), not a consonant cluster. š = IPA [ʃ], y = IPA [j]. Note that in example 22 'granary' and 'bed' involve very similar construction in these cultures.

	Proto-Mixean	Proto-Zoquean	gloss
1.	*pahk	*pak	'bone'
2.	*pa:hts	*pats	'skunk'
3.	*panats	*panats	'slippery'
4.	*pahak	*pahak	'sweet'
5.	*pištin	*pistin	'ceiba' (silk-cotton tree)
6.	*pitsi	*pitsi	'nixtamal' (leached corn meal)
7.	*pɨn	*pɨn	'who'
8.	*pɨhk	*pɨk	'skin'
9.	*puhy	*puy	'thigh'
10.	*ta:tsɨk	*tatsɨk	'ear'
11.	*tɨhn	*tin	'excrement'
12.	*tɨhk	*tik	'house'
13.	*tɨhm	*tɨm	'fruit'
14.	*tɨ:hts	*tits	'tooth'
15.	*tɨ:ši	*tisi	'bat'
16.	*to:hts	*tots	'tongue'
17.	*tuka	*tuka	'tortoise'
18.	*tsa:wi	*tsawi	'monkey'

	Proto-Mixean	*Proto-Zoquean*	*gloss*
19.	*tsahy	*tsay	'rope'
20.	*tsiku	*tsiku	'coati' (coatimundi)
21.	*tsihn	*tsin	'pine'
22.	*tseʔš 'granary'	*tseʔs	'bed'
23.	*tsohy	*tsoy	'medicine, remedy'
24.	*tsu:ʔ	*tsuʔ	'night'
25.	*kama	*kama	'corn field'
26.	*ka:na	*kana	'salt'
27.	*kapay	*kapay	'sister-in-law'
28.	*kape	*kape	'reed' (type of bamboo)
29.	*keʔw	*keʔŋ	'spurge nettle'
30.	*kihpš	*kips	'measure, think'
31.	*kuma	*kuma	'palm' (species)
32.	*kunu	*kunu	'Montezuma oropendola' (bird species)
33.	*ša:ka	*saka	'shell'
34.	*ši:kitiw	*sikitiŋ	'cicada'
35.	*šiš	*sis	'meat'
36.	*šɨhk	*sɨk	'bean'
37.	*šɨhw	*siŋ	'fiesta, name, sun'
38.	*šoʔw	*soŋ	'peck, punch'
39.	*mah	*mah	'strength'
40.	*may	*may	'much'
41.	*min	*min	'come'
42.	*mo:hk	*mok	'maize, corn'
43.	*mu:tu	*mutu	'squirrel'
44.	*na:hš	*nas	'earth'
45.	*ni:wi	*niwi	'chilli'
46.	*ni:hts	*nits	'armadillo'
47.	*niʔpin	*niʔpin	'blood'
48.	*noki	*noki	'paper'
49.	*nuʔpu	*nuʔpu	'vulture'
50.	*hahm	*ham	'lime' (caustic alkaline substance)
51.	*hɨ:pak	*hipak	'corncob'
52.	*hohn	*hon	'bird'
53.	*hoko	*hoko	'smoke'
54.	*wahy	*way	'hair'
55.	*wihn 'eye'	*win	'body'
56.	*wɨ:yi	*wɨyi	'mange'
57.	*wo:n	*won	'pull, carry'
58.	*yahk	*yak	'give'
59.	*yeʔp	*yeʔp	'extend, lay out'
60.	*yiʔ	*yiʔ	'this'

	Proto-Mixean	*Proto-Zoquean*	*gloss*
61.	*yu:ʔ	*yuʔ	'hunger'
62.	*aha	*aha	'canoe'
63.	*a:ka	*aka	'cheek, edge'
64.	*eši	*esi	'crab'
65.	*etse	*etse	'dance'
66.	*it	*it	'place'
67.	*oko	*oko	'grandmother'
68.	*uhš	*us	'tremor'
69.	*u:ma	*uma	'dumb' (mute)
70.	*pi:w	*piŋ	'pick up'
71.	*puʔw	*puʔŋ	'to break'
72.	*ka:haw	*kahaŋ	'jaguar'
73.	*ki:w	*kiŋ	'to cook'
74.	*ti:w	*tiŋ	'to be straight, upright, to fall'
75.	*tsow	*tsoŋ	'unite'
76.	*te:ʔn	*teʔn	'to step on, stand up'
77.	*ke:k	*kek	'to fly'

(based on Wichmann 1995, modified slightly)

Exercise 7.9 Jicaquean

Jicaquean is a family of two languages in Honduras. Eastern Jicaque (Jicaque of El Palmar) is extinct; Tol (Jicaque of La Montaña de la Flor) is still spoken by a few hundred people, but has become extinct or nearly so everywhere except in the village of La Montaña de la Flor. Reconstruct Proto-Jicaquean; state the sound correspondences which you encounter in the following cognate sets, and reconstruct a proto-sound for each. State the sound changes that have taken place in each language.

HINT: Your reconstruction should include the following sounds:

p	t	ts	k	ʔ	i	ɨ	u
pʰ	tʰ	tsʰ	kʰ		e		o
p'	t'	ts'	k'			a	
		s					
		l					
m	n						
w	y	j		h			

What happens to each of the proto-sounds that you reconstruct in initial and in final position in these two languages? Can you make hypotheses about an appropriate reconstruction and sound changes to account for sounds in medial positions?

NOTE: The correspondences involving affricates and sibilants are quite complex, and you will need to pay special attention to the possibilities for combining some of the initial correspondence sets with some of the medial ones as reflecting the same proto-sound. The consonants *p'*, *t'*, *ts'*, *k'* are glottalized (ejective). The accent mark on a vowel (for example á) means that it is stressed; this is not relevant to the sound changes, however. In a few cases, a non-initial *h* does not match well in the two languages; ignore this, since it is due to changes which you do not have enough evidence in these data to discover. The hyphen (-) before some words, as in 9 (-*rik*), means that they occur with some other morpheme before them which is not relevant to comparison here and so is not presented.

š = IPA [ʃ], *č* = IPA [ʧ], *y* = IPA [j]. Also, *ts*, *ts'*, and *ts^h* are all single segments (alveolar affricates); they are not consonant clusters.

	Jicaque	*Tol*	*gloss*
1.	pe	pe	'stone'
2.	pit	pis	'meat'
3.	piné	piné	'big'
4.	piga-	piʔa-	'jaguar'
5.	pen	pel	'flea'
6.	kamba	kampa	'far, long'
7.	arba-	alpa	'above'
8.	to-bwe	to-pwe	'to burn'
9.	-rik	-lip	'lip'
10.	kek	kep	'woman'
11.	ik	hip	'you'
12.	huruk	hulup	'grain' (of corn)
13.	huk	hup	'he, that'
14.	nak	nap	'I'
15.	-kuk	-kup	'we'
16.	te	te	'black'
17.	tek	tck	'leg'
18.	tebé	tepé	'he died'
19.	tit	tit'	'louse'
20.	mandi	manti	'vulture'
21.	n-gon	n-kol	'my belly'
22.	harek	halek	'arrow'
23.	mak	mak	'foreigner'
24.	n-abuk	n-ayp^huk	'my head'
25.	kon	kom	'liver'
26.[=6]	kamba	kampa	'far, long'

	Jicaque	Tol	gloss
27.	pirik	pilik	'much'
28.	keré	kelé	'nephew'
29.	mik	mik	'nose'
30.	korok	kolok	'spider'
31.	pʰe	pʰe	'white'
32.	pʰen	pʰel	'arm, shoulder'
33.	-pʰa	-pʰa	'dry'
34.	pʰiya	pʰiya	'tobacco'
35.	m-bat	m-pʰats'	'my ear'
36.	libi-	lipʰi	'wind'
37.	pʰibih	pʰipʰih	'ashes'
38.	urubana	(y)ulupʰana	'four'
39.	ten	tʰem	'boa constrictor'
40.	tut	tʰutʰ	'spit'
41.	peten	petʰel	'wasp'
42.	kun	kʰul	'fish'
43.	ke-ke	(kʰ)ekʰe	'agouti'

NOTE: *keke* is a reduplicated form and should be treated as the root *ke-* repeated, rather than as having an intervocalic *-k-* or *-kʰ-*.

44.	kan	kʰan	'bed'
45.	kere	kʰele	'bone'
46.	to-gon-	to-kʰol	'to grind'
47.	kuyuh	kʰuyuh	'parrot'
48.	pit	p'is	'deer'
49.	m-biy	m-p'iy	'my body'
50.	pičá	p'isá	'macaw'
51.	-te	-t'e	'to cut'
52.[=19]	tit	tit'	'louse'
53.	-tya	-t'ya	'to be late'
54.	mata	mat'a	'two'
55.	kat	ʔas	'blood'
56.	kot	ʔos	'I sit, am'
57.	kaw-	ʔaw-a	'fire'
58.	kona	ʔona	'sour'
59.	kan	ʔan	'zapote' (fruit)
60.[=4]	piga-	piʔa-	'jaguar'
61.	te-ga	te-ʔa	'to give'
62.	čok	sok'	'tail'

	Jicaque	*Tol*	*gloss*
63.	čorin	tsolin	'salt'
64.	ču(h)	tsu	'blue'
65.	čiwiri	-tsiwil-	'to lie'
66.	čigin-	tsikin	'summer'
67.	čo?-	tso?-	'to nurse'
68.	čuba	tsupa	'to tie'
69.	nočot	notsots	'fly'
70.	šeme	ts^{h}eme	'horn'
71.	šiyó	ts^{h}iyó	'dog'
72.	še(w)	ts^{h}ew	'scorpion'
73.	čin	ts'il	'hair, root'
74.	-čun	ts'ul	'intestines'
75.	čoron	ts'olol	'oak'
76.	čih	ts'ih-	'caterpillar'
77.	te-neče	te-nets'e	'to sing'
78.	ločak	lots'ak	'sun'
79.	m-bat	m-phats'	'my ear'
80.	čot	sots'	'owl'
81.	-čɨ	-sɨ	'water'
82.	čok	sok'	'tail'
83.[=2]	pit	pis	'meat'
84.	-mut	mus	'smoke'
85.	hoč(uruk)	hos-	'his heart'
86.[=50]	pičá	p'ɨsá	'macaw'
87.	mon	mol	'cloud'
88.[=25]	kon	kom	'liver'
89.	ma	ma	'land'
90.	wa	wa	'house'
91.	wara	wala	'forehead'
92.	yo	yo	'tree'
93.	he	he	'red'
94.[=22]	harek	halek	'arrow'

(data from Campbell and Oltrogge 1980)

Exercise 7.10 K'ichean languages

K'ichean is a subgroup of the Mayan family. Compare these cognate forms and establish the sound correspondences; propose the most appropriate reconstruction for the sound in the proto-language for each, and write the sound changes which account for the developments in the daughter languages. Are there any cases in any of the individual languages in which it is necessary to state what the relative chronology of changes was?

NOTES: ɓ = voiced imploded bilabial stop; t', ts', č', k', q', m', w' = glottalized consonants. In Uspanteko, the accent mark over the vowel, as in ò:x 'avocado', indicates falling tone. Although the correspondence set in which Q'eqchi' h corresponds to x of the other languages is not found in these data before u, ignore this – this correspondence occurs in general with no restrictions that have anything to do with u. Note also that ts and ts' are not consonant clusters but rather are affricates, single segments. Note that 28. is repeated as 62. and 32. as 64.

y = [j], š = IPA [ʃ], č = IPA [ʧ]; C' = glottalized [ejective] consonant. Also, ts and ts' are both single segments (alveolar affricate); neither is a consonant cluster.

	Kaqchikel	Tz'utujil	K'iche'	Poqomam	Uspanteko	Q'eqchi'	gloss
1.	pak	pak	pak	pak	pak	pak	'custard apple'
2.	pur	pur	pur	pur	pur	pur	'snail'
3.	pim	pim	pim	pim	pim	pim	'thick'
4.	to?	to?	to?	to?	to?	to?	'to help'
5.	tox	tox	tox	tox	tox	tox	'to pay'
6.	ki?	ki?	ki?	ki?	ki?	ki?	'sweet'
7.	ka:?	ka:?	ka:?	ka:?	ka:?	ka:?	'quern' (metate)
8.	k'el	k'el	k'el	k'el	k'el	(k'el)	'parrot'
9.	qa-	qa-	qa-	qa-	qa-	qa-	'our'
10.	qul	qul	qul	—	qul	—	'neck'
11.	q'o:l	q'o:l	q'o:l	q'o:l	q'o:l	q'o:l	'resin, pitch'
12.	q'an	q'an	q'an	q'an	q'an	q'an	'yellow'
13.	si:p	si:p	si:p	si:p	si:p	si:p	'tick'
14.	saq	saq	saq	saq	saq	saq	'white'
15.	tsuy	tsuy	tsuh	suh	tsuh	suh	'water gourd'
16.	uts	uts	uts	us	uts	us	'good'
17.	tsats	tsats	tsats	sas	tsats	sas	'thick'
18.	ts'i?	ts'i?	ts'i?	ts'i?	ts'i?	'ts'i?'	'dog'
19.	če:?	če:?	če:?	če:?	če:?	če:?	'tree, wood'
20.	ču:n	ču:n	ču:n	ču:n	ču:n	ču:n	'lime'
21.	č'o:p	č'o:p	č'o:p	č'o:p	č'o:p	č'o:p	'pineapple'

	Kaqchikel	Tz'utujil	K'iche'	Poqomam	Uspanteko	Q'eqchi'	gloss
22.	xul	xul	xul	xul	xul	xul	'hole, cave'
23.	winaq	winaq	winaq	winaq	winaq	kwinq	'person'
24.	we:š	we:š	we:š	we:š	—	kwe:š	'trousers'
25.	ya:x	ya:x	ya:x	ya:x	ya:x	ya:x	'genitals, shame'
26.	mu:x	mu:x	mu:x	mu:x	mù:x	mu:h	'shade'
27.	o:x	o:x	o:x	o:x	ò:x	o:h	'avocado'
28.	ča:x	ča:x	ča:x	ča:x	čà:x	ča:h	'ashes'
29.	tu:x	tu:x	tu:x	tu:x	tù:x	tu:h	'steam-bath'
30.	q'i:x	q'i:x	q'i:x	q'i:x	q'ì:x	(-q'ih)	'day, sun'
31.	ka:x	ka:x	ka:x	ka:x	kà:x	—	'sky'
32.	čax	čax	čax	čax	čax	čax	'pine'
33.	k'ax	k'ax	k'ax	k'ax	k'ax	k'ax	'flour'
34.	k'o:x	k'o:x	k'o:x	k'o:x	k'o:x	k'o:x	'mask'
35.	6a:y	6a:y	6a:h	w'a:y	6a:h	6a:h	'gopher'
36.	6a:q	6a:q	6a:q	w'a:q	6a:q	6a:q	'bone'
37.	6e:y	6e:y	6e:h	w'e:h	6e:h	6e:h	'road'
38.	si6	si6	si6	sim'	si6	si6	'smoke'
39.	xa6	xa6	xa6	xam'	xa6	ha6	'rain'
40.	xuku:?	xuku:?	xuku:6	xuku:m'	xuku:6	xuku6	'canoe, trough'
41.	a:q'a?	a:q'a?	a:q'a6	a:q'am'	a:q'a6	(a:q'6)	'night'
42.	xal	xal	xal	xal	xal	hal	'ear of corn'
43.	xe:y	xe:y	xe:h	xe:h	xe:h	he:h	'tail'
44.	č'o:y	č'o:y	č'o:h	č'o:h	č'o:h	č'o:h	'mouse, rat'
45.	k'yaq	k'yaq	k'yaq	k'aq	k'aq	k'aq	'flea'
46.	kyaq	kyaq	kyaq	kaq	kaq	kaq	'red'
47.	(i)kyaq'	(i)kyaq'	kyaq'	kaq'	—	—	'guava'
48.	išk'yaq	šk'yaq	išk'yaq	išk'aq	išk'aq	—	'fingernail'
49.	winaq	winaq	winaq	winaq	winaq	kwinq	'person'
50.	šikin	šikin	šikin	šikin	šikin	(šikn)	'ear'
51.	išoq	išoq	išoq	iššoq	—	išq	'woman'
52.	nimaq	nimaq	nimaq	nimaq	nimaq	ninq	'big' (PL)
53.	sanik	sanik	sanik	(sanik)	sanik	sank	'ant'
54.	su?t	su?t	su?t	su?t	sù:t'	(su?ut)	'cloth, kerchief'
55.	po?t	po?t	po?t	po?t	pò:t'	po?ot	'blouse'
56.	pi?q	pi?q	pi?q	pi?q	pì:q'	—	'corncob'
57.	ati?t	ati?t	ati?t	ati?t	atì:t'	ati?t	'grand-mother'
58.	k'ax	k'ax	k'ax	k'ax	k'ax	k'ax	'flour'
59.	k'ay	k'ay	k'ah	k'ah	k'ah	k'ah	'bitter'
60.	k'ay	k'ay	k'ay	k'ay	k'ay	k'ay	'to sell'
61.	mo:y	mo:y	mo:y	mo:y	mo:y	mo:y	'blind' (dark)

	Kaqchikel	*Tz'utujil*	*K'iche'*	*Poqomam*	*Uspanteko*	*Q'eqchi'*	*gloss*
62.	ča:x	ča:x	ča:x	ča:x	čà:x	ča:h	'ashes'
63.	čax	čax	čax	čax	čax	čax	'pine'
64.	č'ax	č'ax	č'ax	—	č'ax	č'ax	'to wash'
65.	č'ay	č'ay	č'ay	č'ay	—	—	'to hit'

For additional comparative reconstruction exercises with solutions, see Blust (2018: 99–148, 297–394).

8

INTERNAL RECONSTRUCTION

Language is the armoury of the human mind, and at once contains the trophies of its past and the weapons of its future conquests.

(Samuel Taylor Coleridge 1817: 26)

8.1 Introduction

Internal reconstruction is like the comparative method but applied to a single language. It is a technique for inferring aspects of the history of a language from what is in that language alone. Lying behind internal reconstruction is the fact that when a language undergoes changes, traces of the changes are often left behind in the language's structure, as allomorphic variants or irregularities of some sort. The things that are compared in internal reconstruction, which correspond to the cognates of the comparative method, are the forms in the language that have more than one phonological shape in different circumstances, that is, the different allomorphs of a given morpheme, such as those found in alternations in paradigms, derivations, stylistic variants, and the like. Internal reconstruction is frequently applied in the following situations where it can recover historical information: (1) on language isolates (languages without known relatives), (2) on reconstructed proto-languages, and (3) on individual languages to arrive at an earlier stage to which the comparative method can then be applied to compare this with related languages in the family. In this chapter, we will learn how to apply internal reconstruction, and we will take its uses and limitations into account.

8. 2 Internal Reconstruction Illustrated

Lying behind internal reconstruction is the assumption that the variants (allomorphs) of a morpheme are not all original, but that at some time in the past each morpheme had only one form (shape) and that the variants known today have come about as the result of changes that the language has undergone in its past. We internally reconstruct by postulating an earlier single form together with the changes – usually conditioned sound changes – which we believe to have produced the various shapes of the morpheme that we recognize in its alternants. Internal reconstruction can also be applied to elements of language larger than single morphemes or words, so long as the entity in question has variant forms.

The language reconstructed by internal reconstruction bears the prefix *pre-* (as opposed to the *proto-* of comparative-method reconstructions). For example, we would call the results of an internal reconstruction of English *Pre-English*. (Note, though, that *pre-* is sometimes used in historical linguistics where it has nothing to do with internal reconstruction; for example, it is possible to read about the 'Pre-Greeks' where what is intended is the Greeks before they appear in recorded history, or about 'Pre-English' which is not reconstructed but refers to a stage of English assumed to have existed before the earliest Old English texts but after the break-up of West Germanic.)

The steps followed in internal reconstruction, broadly speaking, are the following:

> Step 1: Identify alternations, that is, forms which have more than one phonological shape (different allomorphs, variant forms of a construction) in paradigms, derivations, different styles, and so on.
> Step 2: Postulate a single, non-alternating original form.
> Step 3: Postulate the changes (usually conditioned sound changes) that must have taken place to produce the alternating forms. (Where relevant, determine the relative chronology – the temporal sequence in which these changes took place.) As in the comparative method, we use all the information at our disposal concerning directionality of change and how natural or likely (or unexpected and unlikely) the changes we postulate are in order to evaluate the reconstruction and the changes we propose.
> Step 4: Check the results to make certain that the changes we postulated do not imply changes in other entities in the language that they do not in fact undergo. That is, we must guard against proposing changes which might seem to work for certain morphemes but which, if allowed to take place generally, would produce non-existent forms of other morphemes. We must also check to make certain that the postulated reconstructions are typologically plausible and do not imply things that are impossible or highly unlikely in human languages.

In actual practice, these steps are typically applied almost simultaneously and with little attempt to distinguish one step from the other. The best way to gain an understanding of internal reconstruction is through examples of its application, and several follow.

8.2.1 First example

Let us begin with a rather simple example from Tojolabal (Mayan). Compare the following words and notice the variants for the morpheme that means 'I':

(1)	h-man	I buy	man	to buy
(2)	h-lap	I dress	lap	to dress
(3)	h-k'an	I want	k'an	to want
(4)	k-il	I see	il	to see
(5)	k-uʔ	I drink	uʔ	to drink
(6)	k-al	I say	al	to say

In step 1, we identify h- and k- as alternants of the morpheme meaning 'I'; h- is the variant which occurs before consonants, and k- is the form which appears before vowels. In step 2, we attempt to postulate the original form of this morpheme in Pre-Tojolabal. Three hypotheses suggest themselves: (1) *h-, which would presuppose a change *h- > k- before vowels to derive the other form of the morpheme, the k allomorph; (2) *k-, with a change *k- > h- before consonants to account for the h- variant; or (3) possibly some third thing, which would change into h- before consonants and into k- before vowels. The third alternative would require two independent changes and thus would go against the criterion of economy, discussed in Chapter 7, whereas hypotheses (1) and (2) would each need only one change. Therefore we abandon (3) under the assumption that it is less likely that two independent changes took place than it is that only one did. There is no particular phonetic motivation for h- to change into k- before vowels, as presupposed by hypothesis (1) – and if we had more data, we would see that there are many words with initial h- before a vowel, for example, haʔ 'water', hune 'one', hiʔ 'unripe ear of corn', etc. However, a change of k- to h- before consonants is not phonetically unusual, a dissimilation encountered in other languages – and if we had more data, we would discover that there are no consonant clusters in Tojolabal with k- before another consonant. (The general directionality of k > h and not h > k was seen in Chapter 7.) Therefore, we assume that hypothesis (2) with *k- reconstructed is more plausible. In step 3, we postulate that the *k- which we reconstruct for 'I' in Pre-Tojolabal undergoes the change *k- > h- before consonants and that this accounts for the h- variant of this morpheme. So, for example, we would reconstruct *k-man 'I buy', and then the change of *k- to h- before consonants would give modern h-man; for 'I see' we reconstruct *k-il, and since this k- 'I' is before a vowel it does not change, leaving modern Tojolabal with k-il. This reconstruction and the derivation of the modern forms are seen in Table 8.1.

TABLE 8.1: Internal reconstruction and derivation of Tojolabal k-

	'I buy'	'I see'
Pre-Tojolabal:	*k-man	*k-il
Change k > h / __C:	hman	——
Modern Tojolabal:	hman	kil

8.2.2 Second example

In Nahuatl (Uto-Aztecan), a sizeable number of morphemes have two variant shapes, one with an initial i and one without, of the sort illustrated in 'foot', with its two allomorphs, *ikši* when without prefixes and *-kši* when it occurs with prefixes that end in a vowel (as in *ikši-* foot', but *no-kši* 'my foot') (*š* = IPA [ʃ]). In internal reconstruction, we must reconstruct a single form as original and attempt to account for the variants that occur by postulating changes which will derive the variant forms from the single reconstructed form. In this case, the two most likely choices are: (1) to reconstruct **ikši* together with some change that deletes the initial *i* in order to provide for the *kši* variant, as in *no-kši* 'my foot'; (2) to reconstruct **kši* and posit some change that inserts the initial *i* in appropriate contexts to give *ikši*. In Nahuatl there are also many forms with initial *i* that do not lose this vowel when preceded by prefixes, for example, *n-ihti* 'my stomach' – the change in which *no-* becomes *n-* before vowels is a general trait of the language, that is, *o* in prefixes is lost before a vowel in the following morpheme (*o* > Ø /*n*__+V). Therefore, it turns out to be impossible to write a rule that works which assumes the *i* of *ikši* was originally present but got lost due to the presence of the prefix (**no-ikši* > *no-kši* 'my foot'). This would wrongly predict, in step 4, that the non-alternating forms such as *ihti* should also lose their initial *i* (*no-ihti* > *no-hti*), but this does not happen. There is no ✗*no-hti* 'my stomach'; rather, the initial *i* is preserved in the form with the possessive prefix, *n-ihti*. The second hypothesis, however, encounters no such problem. We get the right results if we assume that the initial *i* was not originally present in the morpheme for 'foot' and reconstruct the words **kši* 'foot' and **no-kši* 'my foot', with *i* added to **kši* later by initial epenthesis, **kši* > *ikši* 'foot'. In looking at the phonological pattern of the language, we find that there are no initial consonant clusters and we therefore assume that a change added *i* to the beginning of words which formerly began in a consonant cluster:

Epenthesis change: Ø > i /#__CC

Thus we reconstruct the forms **kši* 'foot' and **no-kši* 'my foot' and then the epenthesis change follows to produce the modern forms as shown in Table 8.2.

TABLE 8.2: Internal reconstruction and derivation of Nahuatl roots with initial *i*

	'foot'	'my foot'	'stomach'	'my stomach'
Pre-Nahuatl:	*kši	*no-kši	*ihti	*no-ihti
Epenthesis:	ikši	—	—	—
Vowel-loss				
(o > Ø / n __ +V):	—	—	—	n-ihti
Modern Nahuatl:	ikši	no-kši	ihti	n-ihti

8.3 Relative Chronology

Sometimes in internal reconstruction when more than one change can apply to a particular form it is necessary to pay attention to the temporal order in which the changes took place in the forms in question. The identification of the temporal sequence of different changes in a language is called *relative chronology* (seen also in Chapters 2, 3, and 7). When more than one change is involved in the reconstruction, it may be necessary to figure out which change or changes took place earlier and which later. There is no hard-and-fast procedure for working out the relative chronology of the changes. However, the criterion of *predictability* is the most useful – determining a chronological sequence of changes which, when applied in reverse order, does not produce any non-occurring forms. This is illustrated in the next example.

8.3.1 Third example: Finnish

Consider the forms in Table 8.3. They provide a straightforward illustration of relative chronology in internal reconstruction (see also the discussion of this example in Chapter 2).

TABLE 8.3: Finnish internal reconstruction

Essive singular		*Nominative singular*	
1. onne-na	'as happiness'	onni	'happiness'
2. sukse-na	'as (a) ski'	suksi	'ski'
3. vete-nä	'as water'	vesi	'water'
4. käte-nä	'as (a) hand'	käsi	'hand'
5. tuoli-na	'as (a) chair'	tuoli	'chair'

(NOTE: /ä/ = [æ]. The *-na* / *-nä* alternation is the result of vowel harmony in Finnish and is not relevant to the discussion here.)

In these data, we note the alternants (allomorphs) of each root: *onne-/onni*, *sukse-/suksi*, *vete-/vesi*, and *käte-/käsi*. In internal reconstruction, we must postulate a unique, single form for each root in Pre-Finnish together with the changes we believe took place to produce the modern alternant forms of each root. We postulate that in examples 1–4 in Table 8.3 the stem-final *e* must have been original and the forms with final *i* (those in the nominative singular case) are derived by the change of final *e* to *i*:

Change 1: e > i / __#

This is clearer in the forms for 'happiness' and 'ski':

Pre-Finnish:	*onne-na	*onne	*sukse-na	*sukse
Change 1:	—	onni	—	suksi
Modern Finnish:	onnena	onni	suksena	suksi

A conceivable alternative solution in which *i* would become *e* when not final (Change X: *i* > *e* / __+ C, or something similar) is impossible, since by this Change X, *tuoli-na* should become ✗*tuole-na*, but that does not happen. If we postulate for Pre-Finnish *tuoli-na* and *tuoli*, then Change 1 simply does not apply to them since there is no *e* in these forms to which it could apply. (Ultimately, *tuoli* 'chair' is a loanword in Finnish, from Swedish *stol* 'chair', but this does not change the results as far as this example is concerned.)

Change 1, then, accounts for the *e/i* alternation in the forms for 'happiness' and 'ski' (and indirectly for the lack of alternation in 'chair'), but for 'water' and 'hand' an additional change is involved:

> Change 2: t > s / __i.

Both Change 1 and Change 2 apply to the forms for 'water' and 'hand'. With Change 1 and Change 2 in the right sequence – Change 1 first, followed later in time by Change 2 – we can account for modern *vesi* and *käsi*, as shown in Table 8.4.

TABLE 8.4: Derivation showing Finnish relative chronology

Pre-Finnish:	*vete-nä	*vete	*käte-nä	*käte
Change 1:	—	veti	—	käti
Change 2:	—	vesi	—	käsi
Modern Finnish:	vetenä	vesi	käte-nä	käsi

However, if we were to imagine that perhaps the changes had taken place in the reverse order, Change 2 earlier and then Change 1 later, we would get the wrong results, as seen in the hypothetical order in Table 8.5.

TABLE 8.5: Hypothetical derivation of Finnish with the wrong relative chronology

Pre-Finnish:	*vete-nä	*vete	*käte-nä	*käte
Change 2:	—	—	—	—
Change 1:	—	veti	—	käti
Modern Finnish:	vetenä	✗veti	käte-nä	✗käti

That is, in this hypothetical application of the changes in reverse order (in Step 4), we end up with the erroneous ✗*veti* 'water' and ✗*käti* 'hand'. Change 2 cannot create the *s* in these words until after Change 1 has created a final *i*, since Change 2 requires an *i* after the *t* for it to become *s* (and in these words the *i* comes into existence only with the prior change in Change 1). In this example, then, we conclude that the relative chronology was that Change 1 (e > i / __#) took place first (**vete* > *veti*, **käte* > *käte* > *käti*) and then later in time Change 2 took place (t > s / __i) (*veti* > *vesi*, *käti* > *käsi*).

8.3.2 Fourth example: Classical Greek

In Classical Greek paradigms, we find alternative forms of morphemes such as:

> genes-si 'race, family (DATIVE PLURAL)'
> gene-os 'race, family (GENITIVE SINGULAR)'

Here we see two variants (allomorphs) of the root: *gene-* when followed by a vowel-initial suffix (as in *gene-os*, with the 'genitive singular' -*os*), and *genes-* when followed by a consonant-initial suffix (as in *genes-si* 'race, family [DATIVE PLURAL]' or *genes-thai* 'be born'). (In later developments, *geneos* changed to end up as *génous* in major dialects, but that does not affect the story here.) Since there is no compelling phonetic motivation for a language to insert precisely an *s* before consonants (not *gene-si* > *genes-si*), we assume that the original form had the root-final *s* and that this *s* was lost between vowels, represented in Change 1:

Change 1 (Deletion of intervocalic *s*): s > Ø /V__V

The reconstruction and the result of this change are seen in the historical derivation presented in Table 8.6.

TABLE 8.6: Derivation showing loss of intervocalic *s* in Classical Greek

	'dative plural'	'genitive singular'
Pre-Greek:	*genes-si	*genes-os
Change (1) (Deletion of intervocalic *s*):	—	geneos
Classical Greek	genessi	geneos

However, in a different set of forms in Classical Greek, we encounter morphemes with different variants (allomorphs) in which *t* and *s* alternate, where *s* is found intervocalically, as in:

ambros-ia 'food of the gods' (that is, 'immortality')/*ambrotos* 'immortal'
pos-is 'drink, beverage/*potēs* 'a drinking, a drink'

In this instance, we might first attempt to reconstruct internally by choosing the variant with *s* as original with a change to *t* under certain circumstances; or vice versa, we might assume that the original forms are to be reconstructed with *t* with a change from this original *t* to *s* in appropriate contexts. The sound change of *s* > *t* before various vowels is extremely rare, and therefore, based on the known directionality of change, the reconstruction which presupposes **s* is unlikely. On the other hand, the change of *t* to *s* before *i* is found in a good number of languages around the world, and in these data we see that the alternant with *s* is always before *i*, which leads us to reconstruct **t* as original and to postulate Change 2:

Change 2: t > s /__i

The reconstruction of these forms and the application of this change to them are illustrated by the historical derivation shown in Table 8.7.

TABLE 8.7: Derivation showing *t* to *s* before *i* in Classical Greek

	'immortality'	'immortal'	'drink'	'drinking'
Pre-Greek:	ambrot-ia	ambrot-os	pot-is	potēs
Change 2 (*t* to *s* before *i*):	ambrosia	—	posis	—
Greek:	ambrosia	ambrotos	posis	potēs

Now that we have postulated two changes which affect Pre-Greek, Change 1 and Change 2, the question of relative chronology comes up: which change took place earlier, which later? If we assume that the relative chronology was that first Change 2 took place and then later Change 1 occurred, we end up with the wrong result for forms such as *ambrosia* and *posis*, as shown in the hypothetical historical derivation of Table 8.8.

TABLE 8.8: Hypothetical derivation showing wrong chronological order in Classical Greek

Pre-Greek:	*ambrot-ia	*pot-is	*genes-os	*genes-si
Change 2 (*t* to *s* before *i*):	ambrosia	posis	—	—
Change 1 (Deletion of intervocalic *s*):	ambroia	pois	geneos	—
Erroneous Greek:	✘ambroia	✘pois	geneos	genessi

Since ✘*ambroia* and ✘*pois* are erroneous, the relative chronology must be that first Change 1 (s > Ø /V__V) took place and then sometime later, after the change in which intervocalic *s* was deleted had run its course, Change 2 (t > s /__i) created new forms with intervocalic *s*, the result of the change *t* > *s* /__*i*, as seen in the correct historical derivation in Table 8.9.

TABLE 8.9: Derivation showing the correct chronological order in Classical Greek

Pre-Greek:	*ambrot-ia	*pot-is	*genes-os	*genes-si
Change 1 (Deletion of intervocalic *s*):	—	—	geneos	—
Change 2 (*t* to *s* before *i*):	ambrosia	posis	—	—
Greek:	ambrosia	posis	geneos	genessi

Often, if comparative evidence from related languages is available, we can check the accuracy of our internal reconstructions. In the case of Greek *geneos* 'race, family (GENITIVE SINGULAR)', which we postulated to be from Pre-Greek *genes-os*, the presence of an original *-s- which we reconstructed for the Pre-Greek form is confirmed by cognates in some of Greek's sister languages, for example in Sanskrit *jánas-as* and Latin *gener-is* (both 'GENITIVE SINGULAR'), which show the -s- that we reconstructed in Pre-Greek *genes- (in Latin the -r- of *gener-is* is due to rhotacism of an earlier intervocalic -s- – *genesis* > *generis*).

8.3.3 Fifth example

Let us look at one more example,[a] also from Classical Greek. Consider first the following forms:

	Nominative singular	Genitive singular	gloss
(1)	aitʰíops	aitʰíopos	'Ethiopian'
(2)	klṓps	klōpós	'thief'
(3)	pʰléps	pʰlebós	'vein'
(4)	pʰúlaks	pʰúlakos	'watchman'
(5)	aíks	aigós	'goat'
(6)	sálpiŋks	sálpiŋgos	'trumpet'
(7)	tʰɛ́s	tʰētós	'serf'
(8)	elpís	elpídos	'hope'
(9)	órnīs	órnītʰos	'bird'
(10)	kórus	kórutʰos	'helmet'
(11)	hrī́s	hrīnós	'nose'
(12)	delpʰī́s	delpʰínos	'dolphin'

Throughout these data, we see the suffixes *-s* 'NOMINATIVE SINGULAR' and *-os* 'GENITIVE SINGULAR'; since they do not have alternate forms, the best that we can do is tentatively reconstruct these to Pre-Greek as *-s and *-os, respectively. In (1), (2), and (4), we also see no alternations in the roots, only the non-alternating morphemes, *aitʰíop-* 'Ethiopian', *klṓp-*'thief', and *pʰúlak-* 'watchman', presumably from Pre-Greek **aitʰíop*, **klṓp*, and **pʰúlak-*, respectively. However, in the other forms, we see alternations: (3) *pʰlep-/pʰleb-*, (5) *aik-/aig-*, (6) *sálpiŋk-/sálpiŋg-*, (7) *tʰɛ́-/tʰɛ́t-*, (8) *elpí-/elpíd-*, (9) *órnī-/órnītʰ-*, (10) *kóru-/kórutʰ-*, (11) *hrī-/hrīn-*, and (12) *delpʰī́-/delpʰīn-*. Internal reconstruction requires us to reconstruct a single original form for each and to postulate changes which derive the variant forms from that single original form. In the case of (3) *pʰlep-/pʰleb-*, two hypotheses suggest themselves. Hypothesis I: reconstruct **pʰlep-* for (3) and assume the *pʰleb-* allomorph is the result of intervocalic voicing, since it is found with *-os* in *pʰleb-ós*. Let's call this Change A:

Change A (intervocalic voicing): p > b /V__V

This hypothesis would give us the derivation in Table 8.10.

TABLE 8.10: Derivation for Hypothesis I for Classical Greek 'vein'

	'nominative singular'	'genitive singular'
Pre-Greek	*pʰlép-s	*pʰlep-ós
Change A (p > b/V__V):	—	pʰleb-ós
Classical Greek	pʰléps	pʰlebós

Hypothesis I would be fine if it only had to account for the alternation in *pʰléps/pʰlebós*. The postulated sound change in Change A would account for the *p/b* alternation in this form, but it makes the further prediction that Pre-Greek *aitʰíop-os* 'Ethiopian (GENITIVE SINGULAR)' should have become *aitʰíobos* by the intervocalic voicing of Change A. However, this is wrong; ✗*aitʰíobos* does not occur – the correct form is *aitʰíopos*. This means that we must abandon (or at least seriously modify) Hypothesis I.

Let us now look at Hypothesis II: reconstruct **pʰleb-* for (3) and assume that the *pʰlep-* allomorph is the result of devoicing before *s*, since it is found with *-s* in *pʰlep-s* (NOMINATIVE SINGULAR). Let's call this Change B:

> Change B (devoicing before *s*): b > p/__s
> Or better: voiced stop > voiceless /__s (since it also applies to give *g* > *k*, and *d* > *t*, as in examples below).

This hypothesis would give the derivation in Table 8.11.

TABLE 8.11: Derivation for Hypothesis II for Classical Greek 'vein'

	'nominative singular'	'genitive singular'
Pre-Greek	*pʰléb-s	*pʰleb-ós
Change B (b > p /__s):	pʰléps	—
Classical Greek	pʰléps	pʰlebós

Hypothesis II accounts for the *p/b* alternation in *pʰléps/pʰlebós*, and does not erroneously predict in (1) that Pre-Greek **aitʰíop-os* 'Ethiopian (GENITIVE SINGULAR)' should become ✗*aitʰíobos* (as the intervocalic voicing of Change A in Hypothesis I does). Rather, in Hypothesis II we reconstruct Pre-Greek *aitʰíop-s and *aitʰíop-os, and since these words have no *b*, nothing will change in Change B, which affects only forms with *b* (that is, voiced stops), such as *pʰlebós / pʰléps*, as illustrated in Table 8.12.

TABLE 8.12: Derivation of **aitʰíop-* 'Ethiopian' in Hypothesis II

	'nominative singular'	'genitive singular'
Pre-Greek	*aitʰíop-s	*aitʰíop-os
Change B (b > p /__s):	—	—
Classical Greek	aitʰíops	*aitʰíopos

Thus, Hypothesis II makes correct predictions, while Hypothesis I makes erroneous predictions; therefore Hypothesis II is accepted and Hypothesis I rejected. Since the forms in (2) follow the same pattern, we reconstruct **klōp-* 'thief' for its root (**klōp-s* 'NOMINATIVE SINGULAR' and *klōp-ós 'GENITIVE SINGULAR').

Turning now to the alternants in the forms in (5) for 'goat', *aík-/aig-*, we follow the pattern in Hypothesis II further, reconstructing Pre-Greek **aig-* 'goat' to which Change B applies (devoicing before *s*) to derive the *aík-* variant found in *aík-s* 'NOMINATIVE SINGULAR'. That is, we reconstruct *aig-s 'goat (NOMINATIVE SINGULAR)' which becomes *aiks* by Change B, and *aig-ós 'goat (GENITIVE SINGULAR)' which remains *aigós*, since no changes apply to it. The two variants of the root in (6), *sálpiŋk-/sálpiŋg-* 'trumpet', follow the same pattern, and we therefore reconstruct **sálpiŋg-s* 'NOMINATIVE SINGULAR' and **sálpiŋg-os* 'GENITIVE SINGULAR' in this case.

If we continue to follow the pattern in Hypothesis II, given *tʰēt-ós* 'serf (GENITIVE SINGULAR)' in (7), we would reconstruct Pre-Greek **tʰēt-ós* and we would expect the nominative singular to be ✘*tʰēt-s*; however, the actually occurring nominative singular form is *tʰēs*. In (8), from *elpíd-os* '(GENITIVE SINGULAR)' we would similarly expect the nominative singular to be the non-occurring ✘*elpits*, that is, a Pre-Greek form **elpid-s* which Change B (devoicing before *s*) would change to ✘*elpits*. However, we do not get *elpits*, but rather *elpís*. Similarly, from *órnūtʰ-os* in (9), *kórutʰ-os* in (10), *hrīn-ós* in (11), and *delpʰîn-os* in (12) we would expect the corresponding nominative singular forms to be ✘*órnūtʰ-s*, ✘*kórutʰ-s*, ✘*hrīn-s*, and ✘*delpʰîn-s*, respectively, not the actually occurring *órnīs*, *kórus*, *hrī:s*, and *delpʰîs*. Unlike the forms in (1–6) whose roots end in labials (*p* or *b*) or velars (*k* or *g*), what the forms in (7–12) have in common is that their root-final consonant has an alveolar (*t, d, tʰ, n*) in the genitive singular forms, which is missing from the nominative singulars. It would not be possible, starting with the nominative singular forms which lack these root-final consonants, to postulate a plausible account to predict just which consonant would be added in each instance to derive the genitive singular forms. Therefore, we reconstruct for Pre-Greek roots the forms reflected in the genitive singulars (as we did for the forms in (1–6) in Hypothesis II), and then derive the nominative singular variants by postulating Change C, deletion of alveolars before *s*:

Change C (alveolar deletion before *s*): t, d, tʰ, n > Ø / __s

Note that in this case we cannot tell whether Change B took place before Change C or whether the historical events happened in the reverse order, since in either sequence we obtain correct results. In the order of Change B followed by Change C, reconstructed **elpid-s* would first be devoiced by Change B, giving *elpits*, and then the *t* would be lost by Change C (alveolar loss before *s*), giving the correct form *elpís* (that is, **elpid-s* > by Change B *elpits* > by Change C *elpís*). In the order with Change C followed by Change B, reconstructed **elpid-s* would become *elpís* by Change C, in which the final alveolar (*d* in this case) is lost before the *-s* of the nominative singular; Change B would then not apply to this form, since there would no longer be a *d* which could be made voiceless (*t*) by this change (that is, **elpid-s* > by Change C *elpís*, with Change B then not applicable; result: Classical Greek *elpís*).

The derivation of the nominative singular forms in the changes from the postulated Pre-Greek to Classical Greek forms is illustrated in Table 8.13.

8.4 The Limitations of Internal Reconstruction

In attempting to apply the method of internal reconstruction, we need to keep in mind the circumstances in which we can expect more reliable results and

TABLE 8.13: Internal reconstruction of Classical Greek 'nominative singular' forms

	Pre-Greek	Rule B (devoicing)	Rule C (alveolar loss before s)	Classical Greek form
(1)	*aitʰíop-s	—	—	aitʰíops
(2)	*klṓp-s	—	—	klṓps
(3)	*pʰléb-s	pʰlép-s	—	pʰléps
(4)	*pʰúlak-s	—	—	pʰúlaks
(5)	*aíg-s	aík-s	—	aík-s
(6)	*sálpiŋg-s	sálpiŋk-s	—	sálpiŋks
(7)	*tʰḗt-s	—	tʰḗs	tʰḗs
(8)	*elpíd-s	elpíts	elpís	elpís
(9)	*órnītʰ-s	—	órnīs	órnīs
(10)	*kórutʰ-s	—	kórus	kórus
(11)	*hrī́n-s	—	hrī́s	hrī́s
(12)	*delpʰī́n-s	—	delpʰī́s	delpʰī́s

those where it is of limited or no value for recovering a language's history. Let us examine some of these limitations.

(1) The strongest limitation is that, while internal reconstruction is often able to recover conditioned changes, *internal reconstruction cannot recover unconditioned changes*. For example, in the unconditioned merger of **e, *o, *a* to *a* in Sanskrit (seen in Chapter 2), these original vowels ended up as *a*. If we attempt to reconstruct internally the Pre-Sanskrit forms of *dánta* 'tooth' or *dva* 'two', we find no alternations in these vowels which would provide clues to the fact that *danta* originally had **e* (Proto-Indo-European **dent-*, compare Latin *dent-*) but that *dva* had **o* (Proto-Indo-European **dwo*, compare Latin *duo*). It is simply impossible to recover via internal reconstruction the unconditioned change which these Sanskrit vowels underwent: if *a* is all we ever see, there is no basis in Sanskrit itself for seeing anything else in the past of the *a* which occurs in these words.

(2) The method may be reliable if later changes have not eliminated (or rendered unrecognizable) the context or contexts which condition the change that we would like to recover as reflected in alternations in the language. We have seen several examples of this in the cases discussed in this chapter. However, internal reconstruction can be difficult or impossible if later changes have severely altered the contexts which conditioned the variants that we attempt to reconstruct. For example, some splits are impossible to recover due to subsequent changes, as illustrated by the case of voiced fricatives in English. We observe in English such forms as *breath/breathe* ([brɛθ]/[brið]) and *bath/bathe* ([bæθ]/[beið]), which suggest an alternation between *θ* and *ð* (voiceless and voiced dental fricatives). Because we can identify alternations, we would like to be able to reconstruct a single original form, but since in these forms both alternants can occur in exactly the same phonetic environments, we have no basis for internal reconstruction. From other sources of information, however, we know that the voiced fricatives in Old English were allophones of the voiceless fricatives in intervocalic position. Remnants of this rule are seen in such forms as *mouths* (with [ð], compare *mouth* with [θ]) and *paths* (with [ð], compare *path* with [θ]), and so on. The problem is

that, due to later sound changes which eliminated certain vowels, these voiced fricatives are no longer intervocalic: these later changes have so altered the context which conditioned the change to voicing of fricatives between vowels that, in spite of the alternations we find which prompt us to attempt to reconstruct, we are unable to do so with any reliability in this case. Moreover, later loanwords have also made the original context which conditioned the alternation no longer clearly visible. For example, in looking at *mother, rather.* and *either* (each with intervocalic [ð]), we might be tempted to see evidence of the former intervocalic voicing (θ > ð /V__V); however, later loanwords such as *lethal, ether, method, mathematics,* and so on, with intervocalic [θ], obscure the former intervocalic voicing beyond recognition, since, after the borrowings entered the language, [θ] and [ð] are both found between vowels, and the former complementary distribution with only [ð] intervocalically and [θ] elsewhere no longer holds. In short, subsequent sound changes and borrowings have rendered the conditioning of the former intervocalic voicing of fricatives in English unrecognizable, making internal reconstruction in this case unsuccessful.

Another example (already considered in a different context in Chapter 2) which illustrates this point is that of such singular–plural alternations as seen in *mouse/mice* and *goose/geese.* Given these alternations, we would like to be able to apply internal reconstruction, but the context which originally produced these variant forms is now totally gone, due to subsequent changes. Though today such plurals are irregular, they came about in a relatively straightforward way. In most Germanic languages (except Gothic), back vowels were fronted (underwent 'umlaut') when followed by a front vowel or glide in the next syllable, and the plural suffix originally contained a front vowel, as in Proto-Germanic **muːs* 'mouse'/**muːs-iz* 'mice' and **goːs* 'goose'/**goːs-iz* 'geese'. So, in the plural, the root vowels were fronted: *muːs-i > myːs-i* and *goːs-i > gøːs-i.* Two later changes took place: this final vowel was lost, and the front rounded vowels *y* and *ø* became unrounded to *i* and *e* respectively, merging with *i* and *e* from other sources. These changes produced the alternations, *miːs* and *geːs* as the plurals, but *muːs* and *goːs* as the singulars. Finally, all these forms underwent the Great Vowel Shift, giving Modern English /maus/ 'mouse', /mais/ 'mice', and /gus/ 'goose', /gis/ 'geese' (see Chapter 2). This sequence of changes is represented in Table 8.14.

TABLE 8.14: Historical derivation of 'mouse', 'mice', 'goose', 'geese'

	'mouse'	*'mice'*	*'goose'*	*'geese'*
Proto-Germanic:	*muːs	*muːs-iz	*goːs	*goːs-iz
Early Pre-English:	muːs	muːs-i	goːs	goːs-i
Umlaut:	—	myːs-i	—	gøːs-i
Loss of -i:	—	myːs	—	gøːs
Unrounding:	—	miːs	—	geːs
Great Vowel Shift:	maus	mais	gus	gis
Modern English:	/maus/	/mais/	/gus/	/gis/

However, since the environment for umlaut was lost in subsequent changes which deleted the *i* which had caused the umlauting, we are unable to recover this history through internal reconstruction, even though the alternations seen in these singular–plural pairs provoke us to imagine that some historical explanation which we cannot recover by this method alone lies behind these different forms of the same root.

Finally, while the examples presented in this chapter deal with sound changes, it is important to mention that internal reconstruction of morphology and aspects of syntax is also possible in favourable circumstances.

8.5 Internal Reconstruction and the Comparative Method

Sometimes it is suggested that internal reconstruction should be undertaken first and the comparative method applied afterwards. In this view, internal reconstruction would help us to see beyond the effects of many recent changes so that we would have access to an earlier stage of the language for use in the comparative method when sister languages are compared with one another. This is often the case. Usually, both internal reconstruction and the comparative method lead in the same direction. However, in reality there is no rigid principle about which method is to be applied first – they can be applied in either order. Often, reconstruction by the comparative method reveals alternations which the proto-language underwent, and it is perfectly legitimate to apply internal reconstruction to these proto-alternations in order to reach even further back in time, to a pre-proto-language. In this event, the sequence would be the comparative method first, followed by internal reconstruction. In any event, it is important to check, when internal reconstruction is applied before the comparative method, that it does not factor out alternations which were present in the proto-language.

A straightforward case from Romance languages illustrates this. Starting in the second century, spoken Latin words that began with a consonant cluster that began with *s* followed by stop (*sp, st, sk*) took on a prothetic short *i*, and this prothetic *i* became *e* in Western Romance languages, as for example in words for 'school' from Latin *scola* [skóla]: Spanish *escuela*, Portuguese *escola*, Catalan *escola*, etc. French, too, underwent the change, but then later lost the *s* in this context: *scola* > *escole* > *école* 'school'. This change left alternations in these languages, forms with and without the prothetic *e*, as in the following cases from Spanish:

escribir 'to write'	inscribir 'to inscribe' (in- + scribir)
espirar 'to exhale'	inspirar 'to inhale, inspire' (in- + spirar)
estimular 'to stimulate, excite'	instimular 'to incite, stimulate'

We can compare corresponding cases in the sister languages such as:

	'to write'	'to inscribe'
Spanish	escribir	inscribir
Portuguese	escrever	inscrever
Catalan	escriure	inscriure
French	écrire	inscrire

This alternation of *e* (when word-initial) with Ø (when preceded by the affix *in-* in this case) would lead us to the internal reconstruction of these forms without the initial *e* – Pre-Spanish **scribir* 'to write' and **in-scribir* 'to inscribe' – plus the change to add the prothetic *e*:

Ø > e /#__sC

with the sequence of:

Pre-Spanish:	*scribir	*in-scribir
Prothetic *e*:	escribir	—
Outcome:	escribir	inscribir

We could repeat this internal reconstruction for the other Western Romance languages, based on similar forms, and in the process end up eliminating the *e* from the internally reconstructed forms of all of these languages. Then if we compare the internally reconstructed forms of these languages (with **sC* initially, but never **esC*) with one another, we find we have factored out the prothetic *e* from the internally reconstructed forms of these languages that each of them has (as in Pre-Spanish **scribir* and **inscribir*), and as a consequence we then fail to understand that their immediate ancestor in fact had the prothetic *e* which alternated with Ø (as it does in each of the languages, as in the Spanish example *escribir/in-scribir*), and because each language has the alternation, it should be reflected in the reconstructed proto-language from which these languages descend.

A case from Finnic illustrates this point well. In Finnic languages we see alternations of the sort exemplified by the words 'leg' and 'legs' in Table 8.15.

TABLE 8.15: Comparison of alternating forms for 'leg' in Finnic languages

	nominative singular	nominative plural
Finnish	jalka	jalat
Estonian	jalg [jalk]	jalad [jalat]
Karelian	jalka	jalla-t
Votic	jalka	jalga-D [jalgat]

(See Laanest 1982: 108.)

If internal reconstruction is applied to Finnish alone, based on the alternation of *jalka/jalat*, we would presumably reconstruct **jalka* 'leg' /**jalka-t* 'legs' for Pre-Finnish, together with the change that **k* was lost in non-initial closed syllables (syllables that ends in a consonant, **k* > Ø /__VC# or /__VCC). In this case the nominative plural case suffix *-t* closes the syllable, causing the change. If we apply internal reconstruction to the other languages, each one has a similar alternation. For Votic, for example, for the alternation of *jalka/jalgat*, we would reconstruct for Pre-Votic **jalka* 'leg' /**jalka-t* 'legs', with a change of **k* to *g* in the closed syllable (**k* > *g* /__C# or /__VCC). Internal reconstruction applied to Estonian and Karelian would again give us the reconstructions **jalka* 'leg' /**jalka-t* 'legs'. Scholars postulate that in Finnish the *k in closed syllables first changed to ɣ and then later was lost (*k > ɣ > Ø). This view is no doubt influenced by the fact that older written documents attest that this is precisely what happened, that the change did go through this intermediate step.

Now, if the comparative method is applied after internal reconstruction, then the cognates that will be compared by the comparative method will be *jalka and *jalka-t in each of the Finnic languages seen here (that is, in Pre-Finnish, Pre-Estonian, and so on) – the evidence of the alternation will have been factored out in the internal reconstruction of each, and therefore it would not show up in the proto-language as reconstructed by the comparative method applied to these internally reconstructed words in these languages.

However, if the comparative method is applied before internal reconstruction, comparing the forms in Table 8.15, the alternation is revealed to have been part of the proto-language, reconstructed to Proto-Finnic as *jalka 'leg' and *jalga-t 'legs'. The moral is clear: internal reconstruction can help by offering forms to be compared in the comparative method which see past the disruptions of many recent changes in individual languages; nevertheless, caution should be exercised so that alternations that should legitimately be reconstructed to the proto-language by the comparative method are not factored out by previous internal reconstruction of related languages and then lost sight of. (See Anttila 1989: 274.)

8.6 Exercises

Exercise 8.1 German internal reconstruction

Compare the following German words; find the variant forms of the roots (do not be concerned with the forms of the suffixes), and apply internal reconstruction to these. Reconstruct a single original form for the morphemes which have alternate forms, and postulate the change or changes which you think took place to produce the modern variants. Present your reasoning; why did you choose this solution?

HINT: The criterion of predictability is important in this case.

German traditional orthography is given in parentheses after the forms, which are presented in phonemic transcription. The orthographic 'e' of the final syllable in these forms is phonetically closer to [ə] in most dialects, though this is not a relevant fact for solving this problem.

1.	ty:p (Typ)	'type'	ty:pən (Typen)	'types'
2.	bo:t (Boot)	'boat'	bo:tə (Boote)	'boats'
3.	lak (Lack)	'varnish'	lakə (Lacke)	'kinds of varnish'
4.	di:p (Dieb)	'thief'	di:bə (Diebe)	'thieves'
5.	to:t (Tod)	'death'	to:də (Tode)	'deaths'
6.	ta:k (Tag)	'day'	ta:gə (Tage)	'days'

Exercise 8.2 Kaqchikel internal reconstruction

Kaqchikel is a Mayan language of Guatemala. Compare the following words; find the forms which have variants; apply internal reconstruction to these forms. Reconstruct a single original form for the morphemes which have alternate forms, and postulate the change or changes that you think must have taken place to produce these variants. Present your reasoning; why did you choose this solution and reject other possible hypotheses?

NOTE: -*ir* is the inchoative suffix, meaning 'to become/turn into', and -*isax* is the causative suffix. *č* = IPA [ʧ].

1.	nax	'far'	naxt-ir-isax	'to distance (to make it become far)'
2.	čox	'straight'	čoxm-ir	'to become straight'
			čoxm-il	'straightness'
3.	war	'sleep'	wart-isax	'to put to sleep (to cause to sleep)'
4.	ax	'ear of corn'	axn-i	'of corn (-*i* 'adjective suffix')'

Exercise 8.3 Sanskrit internal reconstruction

Compare the following forms from Sanskrit. Identify the variants of the various roots and attempt to reconstruct a Pre-Sanskrit form for each root. Note that the reconstructions for the forms in examples 10–16 are not straightforward and may require some creative thinking on your part. What change or changes do you think took place to produce these forms? Why did you choose this particular analysis and not some other one?

NOTE: Consonants with dots underneath are retroflex. *j* is [ɟ] (voiced palatal stop).

	Nominative		*Instrumental*	
1.	śarat	'autumn'	śarad-ā	'by autumn'
2.	sampat	'wealth'	sampad-ā	'by wealth'
3.	vipat	'calamity'	vipad-ā	'by calamity'
4.	marut	'wind'	marut-ā	'by wind'
5.	sarit	'river'	sarit-ā	'by river'
6.	jagat	'world'	jagat-ā	'by world'

	Nominative		*Ablative*	
7.	suhṛt	'friend'	suhṛd-ā	'from friend'
8.	sukṛt	'good deed'	sukṛt-ā	'from good deed'
9.	sat	'being'	sat-ā	'from being'
10.	bhiṣak	'physician'	bhiṣaj-ā	'from physician'

11.	ṛtvik	'priest'	ṛtvij-ā	'from priest'
12.	yuk	'yoke'	yuj- ā	'from yoke'
13.	srak	'garland'	sraj-ā	'from garland'
14.	rāṭ	'king'	rāj-ā	'from king'
15.	iṭ	'worship'	ij-ā	'from worship'
16.	sṛṭ	'creation'	sṛj-ā	'from creation'

(Bhat 2001: 33, 91, 94)

Exercise 8.4 Finnish vowel internal reconstruction

Compare the following words; what happens when the -i 'plural' or -i 'past tense' suffixes are added to these roots? State what the variants (allomorphs) of the roots are; apply internal reconstruction to these forms. Reconstruct a single original form for each root morpheme and postulate the changes which you think must have taken place to produce these variants. Present your reasoning; why did you choose this solution and reject other possible hypotheses?

NOTE: Double vowels, such as *aa*, *yy*, and so on, are phonetically long vowels ([a:], [y:], etc.). Finnish *ä* = IPA [æ], *ö* = [ø].

HINT: Native Finnish words do not have (surface) *oo*, *ee*, or *öö* [øø]; Finnish, however, does have diphthongs *uo*, *ie*, and *yö* [yø] where long mid vowels might be expected. The correct answer for words containing these diphthongs does NOT involve the first vowel being lost when *i* is added (that is, NOT *suo* + *i* > *soi* by loss of *u*).

1.	saa	'gets'	sai	'got'
2.	maa	'land'	mai-	'lands'
3.	puu	'tree'	pui-	'trees'
4.	luu	'bone'	lui-	'bones'
5.	pii	'tooth (of rake)'	pii-	'teeth'
6.	pää	'head'	päi-	'heads'
7.	pyy	'wood grouse'	pyi-	'wood grouses'
8.	täi	'louse'	täi-	'lice'
9.	suo	'grants'	soi	'granted'
10.	suo	'swamp'	soi-	'swamps'
11.	luo	'creates'	loi-	'created'
12.	syö	'eats'	söi	'ate'
13.	lyö	'hits'	löi	'hit'
14.	tie	'road'	tei-	'roads'
15.	vie	'takes'	vei	'took'
16.	talo	'house'	taloi-	'houses'

17.	hillo	'jam'	hilloi-	'jams'
18.	halu	'desire'	halui-	'desires'
19.	hylly	'shelf'	hyllyi-	'shelves'
20.	nukke	'doll'	nukkei-	'dolls'
21.	hölmö	'fool'	hölmöi-	'fools'
22.	sata	'hundred'	satoi-	'hundreds'
23.	pala	'piece'	paloi-	'pieces'
24.	hella	'stove, cooker'	helloi-	'stoves, cookers'
25.	hilkka	'hood'	hilkkoi-	'hoods'
26.	hiha	'sleeve'	hihoi-	'sleeves'
27.	sota	'war'	sotei-	'wars' (soti- in Modern Finnish)
28.	pora	'drill'	porei-	'drills' (pori- in Modern Finnish)
29.	muna	'egg'	munei-	'eggs' (muni- in Modern Finnish)
30.	rulla	'roll'	rullei-	'rolls' (rulli- in Modern Finnish)
31.	tupa	'cabin'	tupei-	'cabins' (tupi- in Modern Finnish)
32.	jyvä	'grain'	jyvei-	'grains' (jyvi- in Modern Finnish)
33.	hätä	'distress'	hätei-	'distresses' (häti- in Modern Finnish)
34.	mökä	'hullabaloo'	mökei-	'hullabaloos' (möki- in Modern Finnish)

Exercise 8.5 Nahuatl internal reconstruction

Nahuatl is a Uto-Aztecan language, spoken by over 1,000,000 people in Mexico; it was the language of the Aztecs and the Toltecs. Compare the following words. Find the forms which have variants; apply internal reconstruction to these forms. Reconstruct a single original form for the morphemes which have alternate shapes, and postulate the changes which you think must have taken place to produce these variants. Can you establish a relative chronology for any of these changes? Present your reasoning; why did you choose this solution and reject other possible hypotheses?

NOTES: *tl* is a single consonant, a voiceless lateral affricate; *kʷ* is a labialized velar stop and is a single segment; *č* = IPA [ʧ]; *š* = IPA [ʃ].) The morpheme which has the allomorphs *-tl*, *-tli*, *-li* is traditionally called the 'absolutive'; it has no other function than to indicate that a noun root has no other prefixes or suffixes attached to it. The *-w* of 11b. is 'inalienable possession'.

1a.	tepos-tli	'axe'	13a.	ikši-tl	'foot'
1b.	no-tepos	'my axe'	13b.	no-kši	'my foot'
1c.	tepos-tlān	'place of axes'	14a.	ikni-tl	'fellow'
2a.	kak-tli	'shoe, sandal'	14b.	no-kni	'my fellow'
2b.	no-kak	'my shoe, sandal'	15a.	isti-tl	'fingernail'
3a.	teš-tli	'flour'	15b.	no-sti	'my fingernail'
3b.	no-teš	'my flour'	16a.	ihti-tl	'stomach'
4a.	mis-tli	'cougar'	16b.	n-ihti	'my stomach'
4b.	mis-tlān	'place of cougars'	17a.	īšte-tl	'eye'
5a.	kal-li	'house'	17b.	n-īšte	'my eye'
5b.	no-kal	'my house'	18a.	ihwi-tl	'feather'
6a.	tlāl-li	'land'	18b.	n-ihwi	'my feather'
6b.	no-tlāl	'my land'	19a.	iskʷin-tli	'little dog'
7a.	čīmal-li	'tortilla griddle'	19b.	n-itskʷin	'my little dog'
7b.	no-čīmal	'my tortilla griddle'	20a.	ička-tl	'cotton'
7c.	čīmal-lān	'place of tortilla griddles'	20b.	no-čka	'my cotton'
			21a.	okič-tli	'male, man'
8a.	mīl-li	'cornfield'	21b.	n-okič	'my husband'
8b.	no-mīl	'my cornfield'	22a.	kaši-tl	'bowl'
8c.	mīl-lan	'place of cornfields'	22b.	no-kaš	'my bowl'
9a.	āma-tl	'paper, fig tree'	23a.	kʷawi-tl	'tree, wood'
9b.	n-āma	'my paper, fig tree'	23b.	no-kʷaw	'my tree, wood'
9c.	āma-tlān	'place of fig trees'	24a.	māyi-tl	'hand'
10a.	e-tl	'bean'	24b.	no-māy	'my hand'
10b.	n-e	'my bean'	25a.	šāmi-tl	'brick'
10c.	e-tlān	'place of beans'	25b.	no-šān	'my brick'
11a.	siwā-tl	'woman'	26a.	pāmi-tl	'flag'
11b.	no-siwā-w	'my wife'	26b.	no-pān	'my flag'
11c.	siwā-tlan	'place of women'	27a.	kōmi-tl	'jug'
12a.	ol-li	'rubber'	27b.	no-kōn	'my jug'
12b.	n-ol	'my rubber'			
12c.	ol-lān	'place of rubber'			

Exercise 8.6 Indonesian internal reconstruction

Identify the morphemes which have more than one variant in the following data from Indonesian (an Austronesian language). Apply internal reconstruction to these forms; reconstruct a single original form for each of the roots and for the prefix, and postulate the changes you think must have taken place to produce these variants. Can you establish a relative chronology for any of these changes? Provide sample derivations which show your reconstruction and how the changes apply to it for both the simple and the prefixed forms in examples 2, 12, 13, 15, 19, and 20. (The prefix in the second column has a range of functions; among them, it places focus on the agent ('doer') of a verb, derives transitive or causative verbs, and derives verbs from nouns.)

HINT: Relative chronology is important to the solution of this problem.

NOTE: *y* = IPA [j]; *č* = IPA [ʧ]; *j* = [ɉ] (IPA [ʤ]); *ɲ* = palatal nasal.

	simple form	prefixed form	gloss
1.	lempar	məlempar	'throw'
2.	rasa	mərasa	'feel'
3.	wakil	məwakil-	'represent'
4.	yakin	məyakin-	'convince'
5.	masak	məmasak	'cook'
6.	nikah	mənikah	'marry'
7.	ŋačo	məŋačo	'chat'
8.	ɲaɲi	məɲaɲi	'sing'
9.	hituŋ	məŋhituŋ	'count'
10.	gambar	məŋgambar	'draw a picture'
11.	kirim	məɲirim	'send'
12.	dəŋar	məndəŋar	'hear'
13.	tulis	mənulis	'write'
14.	bantu	məmbantu	'help'
15.	pukul	məmukul	'hit'
16.	jahit	məɲjahit	'sew'
17.	čatat	mənčatat	'note down'
18.	ambil	məŋambil	'take'
19.	isi	məŋisi	'fill up'
20.	undaŋ	məŋundaŋ	'invite'

Exercise 8.7 Tol (Jicaque) internal reconstruction

Tol (also called Jicaque) is spoken in Honduras. State the variants (allomorphs) of the roots and of the possessive pronominal prefixes; apply internal reconstruction to these forms. Reconstruct a single original form for each root morpheme and write the changes which you think must have taken place to produce these variants. Present your reasoning; why did you choose this solution and reject other possible hypotheses?

Many find this to be a difficult exercise.

HINT: The original form of the possessive pronominal prefixes was: **n-* 'my', **hi-* 'your', and **hu-* 'his'; original **n-* + *h* > *n*. Note that the palatalization and labialization of consonants are due to the former presence of *hi-* and *hu-* prefixes, respectively; the *e* and *o* as the first vowel of some roots (but not others) also has to do indirectly with the former presence of these two prefixes.

Note that what is structurally a labialized *w* is realized phonetically as [wⁱ], but is written as *wʷ* in this problem. This phonetic fact should not affect your analysis; just treat it as labialization as with the other labialized consonants.

NOTE: *č* = IPA [ʧ]; *ǰ* = IPA [dʒ], *y* = IPA [j], including superscript ʸ, which is equivalent to IPA ʲ, the diacritic for palatalization. *tsʰ* and *ts'* are not consonant clusters, rather they are single segments, a voiceless aspirated alveolar affricate and a voiceless glottalized alveolar affricate, respectively.

	my	*your*	*his*	*meaning of the noun root*
1.	mbata	peta	pota	'duck'
2.	mbapay	pepay	popay	'father'
3.	ndaʔ	teʔ	toʔ	'man's brother'
4.	ndarap	terap	torap	'woman's younger sister'
5.	ŋkʰan	kʰen	kʰon	'bed'
6.	nlara	lera	lora	'mouth'
7.	ntsʰam	tsʰem	tsʰom	'foot'
8.	mbe	hepe	pʷe	'rock, stone'
9.	mbep	hepep	pʷep	'fingernail'
10.	mberam	heperam	pʷeram	'tongue'
11.	mpʰel	hepʰel	pʰwel	'arm'
12.	ŋgerew	hekerew	kʷerew	'cousin'
13.	ŋkʰere	hekʰere	kʰwere	'bone'
14.	ŋgiway	hikiway	kʷiway	'woman's brother'
15.	nǰič	hičič	čʷič	'tendon'
16.	nǰipe	hičipe	čʷipe	'paired sibling'
17.	mbomam	pʸomam	hopomam	'chokecherry'
18.	mpʰok	pʰʸok	hopʰok	'cheek'
19.	ŋgol	kʸol	hokol	'belly'
20.	nts'ul	ts'ʸul	huts'ul	'intestines'
21.	mpʰɨya	pʰʸeya	hipʰɨya	'tobacco'
22.	mp'ɨs	p'ʸes	hip'ɨs	'deer'
23.	ndɨm	tʸem	hitɨm	'heel'
24.	mbasas	wesas	wosas	'woman's sister-in-law'
25.	mbɨs	hiwɨs	wʷɨs [wⁱɨs]	'tooth'
26.	mbɨn	hiwɨn	wʷɨn [wⁱɨn]	'toad'
27.	mboyum	wʸoyum	howoyum	'husband'
28.	namas	mes	mos	'hand'
29.	nemen	hemen	mʷen	'neck'
30.	nimɨk	himɨk	mʷɨk	'nose'
31.	nimɨnɨ	mʸenɨ	himɨnɨ	'yam'
32.	namap	hemap	homap	'aunt'
33.	nasunu	hesunu	hosunu	'chest'

Exercise 8.8 Samoan internal reconstruction

Compare words in the two columns. Identify the morphemes which have more than one variant. Reconstruct a single original form for each of the morphemes here, and postulate the changes you think must have taken place to produce these forms. Can you establish a relative chronology for any of these changes? Why did you choose this solution and reject other possible hypotheses?

NOTE: Many roots will have two allomorphs; the suffix also has more than one variant in several of the cases.

HINT: Think 'predictability' and exploit differences involving the behaviour of the consonants that can occur as the last consonant in these words, or differences in where certain consonants can occur.

1.	alofa	'love'	alofaŋia	'loved'
2.	taŋo	'grasp'	taŋofia	'grasped'
3.	fua	'measure'	fuatia	'measured'
4.	au	'reach'	aulia	'reached'
5.	faitau	'read'	faitaulia	'read'
6.	u	'to bite'	utia	'bitten'
7.	ula	'smoke'	ulafia	'smoked'
8.	na	'hide'	natia	'hidden'
9.	fau	'bind'	fausia	'bound'
10.	ʔata	'laugh'	ʔataŋia	'laughed'
11.	inu	'drink'	inumia	'drunk'
12.	taofi	'hold'	taofia	'held'
13.	mu	'burn'	muina	'burned'
14.	tuʔu	'put'	tuʔuina	'put'
15.	faŋa	'feed'	faŋaina	'fed'
16.	sauni	'prepare'	saunia	'prepared'
17.	siʔi	'raise'	siʔitia	'raised'
18.	pisi	'splash'	pisia	'splashed'
19.	ao	'gather'	aofia	'gathered'
20.	ilo	'perceive'	iloa	'perceived'
21.	ʔave	'take'	ʔavea	'taken'
22.	oso	'jump'	osofia	'jumped'
23.	ʔino	'hate'	ʔinosia	'hated'
24.	filo	'mix'	filoŋia	'mixed'
25.	fasioti	'kill'	fasiotia	'killed'
26.	utu	'fill'	utufia	'filled'
27.	ufi	'cover'	ufitia	'covered'
28.	ʔai	'eat'	ʔaiina	'eaten'
29.	afio	'come in'	afioina	'(has) come in'
30.	laʔa	'step over'	laʔasia	'stepped over'

31. mana?o   'want'   mana?omia   'wanted'
32. mata?u   'destroy   mata?utia   'destroyed'
33. milo   'twist   milosia   'twisted'
34. taŋi   'cry'   taŋisia   'cried'
35. vavae   'divide'   vavaeina   'divided'

Exercise 8.9 Nivaclé internal reconstruction

Nivaclé (also called Chulupí) is a Matacoan language of northern Argentina and Paraguay. Compare the forms in the two columns; identify the morphemes which have more than one phonological shape (variant). Attempt to reconstruct a unique form for each of these words in Pre-Nivaclé, and state the changes which have taken place, according to your analysis, in the transition from Pre-Nivaclé to modern Nivaclé. Is there any relative chronology involved in the changes you postulate? If so, state what it is and show sample derivations of at least four word pairs (for instance both words of examples 12, 14, 18, and 20). Do not try to reconstruct the exact nature of the vowel of the plural suffixes. The plural suffixes, in the second column, have several different forms; do not attempt to reconstruct them; the different plural morphemes seen here differ depending in part on gender classification and in part on noun classes in the language.

NOTE: /kl/ is a single segment, both phonemically and phonetically – the velar closure and the lateral articulation are released simultaneously as a single sound; /ts/ is also a single segment, an alveolar affricate, not a consonant cluster. /ɑ/ is a low back vowel, and contrasts with /a/, a low central vowel; ł = voiceless *l*; *C'* = glottalized [ejective] consonant; *š* = IPA [ʃ]; *č* = IPA [ʧ].

Set I

1. xutsax   'vulture'   xutsx-as   'vultures'
2. ɸatsux   'centipede'   ɸatsx-us   'centipedes'
3. snomax   'ash'   snomx-as   'ashes'
4. łtasex   'seed'   łtasx-ey   'seeds'
5. kutsxanax   'thief'   kutsxanx-as   'thieves'
6. yipaset   'my lip'   yipast-es   'my lips'
7. nasuk   'guayacán (tree)'   nask-uy   'guayacans'
8. ɸa?ayuk   'algarrobo (acacia   ɸa?ayk-uy   'algarrobos'
                  tree)'
9. axɑyuk   'mistol (tree)'   axɑyk-uy   'mistols '

Set II

10. inkɑ?p   'year'   inkɑp-es   'years'
11. łu?p   'nest'   łup-is   'nests'
12. k'utxa?n   'thorn'   k'utxan-is   'thorns'

13.	ɬsaʔt	'vein'	ɬsat-ɑy	'veins'
14.	tisuʔx	'quebracho (tree)'	tisx-uy	'quebrachos'
15.	k'utsaʔx	'old man'	k'utsx-as	'old men'

Set III

16.	towɑk	'river'	towx-ɑy	'rivers'
17.	ɸinɑk	'cigarette'	ɸinx-ɑy	'cigarettes'
18.	yituʔk	'my arm'	yitx-uy	'my arms'
19.	tsanuʔk	'duraznillo (tree)'	tsanx-uy	'duraznillos'
20.	namač	'axe'	namx-ay	'axes'
21.	šateč	'head'	šatx-es	'heads'

Set IV

22.	titeč	'plate'	titx-ey	'plates'
23.	k'atseč	'wood chip'	k'atsx-es	'wood chips'
24.	axpɑyič	'your house'	axpɑyx-ey	'your houses'

For additional internal reconstruction exercises with solutions, see Blust (2018: 149–70, 395–416).

9

LANGUAGE CLASSIFICATION AND MODELS OF LINGUISTIC CHANGE

> It may be worth while to illustrate this view of classification, by taking the case of languages ... The various degrees of difference between the languages of the same stock, would have to be expressed by groups subordinate to groups; but the proper or even the only possible arrangement would still be genealogical; and this would be strictly natural.
>
> (Charles Darwin 1859: 422)

9.1 Introduction

How are languages classified? How are family trees established? *Subgrouping*, as the classification of languages with their degree of relatedness to one another in a language family is called, is an important part of historical linguistics, and methods and criteria for subgrouping are treated in this chapter. Language classification relates to 'models of change' as well, also treated in this chapter. When historical linguistics textbooks talk about 'models of change', they typically mean the traditional 'family-tree' model and the 'wave theory'. Both are described here, and the conflict that is assumed to exist between them is reconciled. The contrasting (but actually complementary) approaches taken by dialectologists and Neogrammarians are examined and clarified, sociolinguistic approaches to language change are brought into the picture, and the related notion of 'lexical diffusion' is put in perspective. (Quantitative approaches to language classification are taken up in Chapter 16.)

Let us begin our exploration of language classification by looking briefly at the *language families* of the world.

9.2 The World's Language Families

There are about 398 distinct language families (including language isolates) in the world, listed in Table 9.1. This count, however, is far from definitive, since there are languages about which we do not yet know enough to be able to classify them, and others where reasonable opinions about classification differ. There are also abundant hypotheses about potential but unconfirmed more inclusive groupings which attempt to combine some of these into higher-order language families, thus reducing the overall number of independent language families. Some of the proposals of distant affiliation are more plausible than others; some are controversial (see Chapter 13). It is possible that as research progresses, some of these families and isolates may be shown to be related to others. This is quite possible for some language groups in New Guinea, and for some in Australia and South America. It is unlikely that the total number of independent language families (including isolates) will change much for Europe, most of Asia, or North and Central America. The classification of languages in Africa will probably change, though the number of families there is unlikely to be reduced by much. Also, there are many extinct languages with so little attestation that we will probably never be able to classify them successfully, and there are living languages for which so little information is known that they remain unclassified, at least until better descriptive material for them may be obtained and compared with other languages to determine whether they may belong to particular language families.

TABLE 9.1: Language families of the world, including language isolates

Africa (42)

1. Afro-Asiatic
2. Bangi Me (isolate)
3. Berta
4. Central Sudanic
5. Daju
6. Dizoid
7. Dogon
8. Eastern Jebel
9. Furan
10. Gimojan (Gonga-Gimojan, North Omotic?)
11. Hadza (isolate)
12. Heiban
13. Ijoid
14. Jalaa† (isolate)
15. Kadu (Kadugli-Krongo)
16. Khoe (Khoe-Kwadi?) (Kwadi may be an isolate)
17. Koman
18. Kresh-Aja
19. Kuliak
20. Kunama
21. Kx'a (Ju + ǂHuan)
22. Laal (isolate)
23. Maban
24. Mande
25. Mao
26. Nara (isolate?)
27. Narrow Talodi
28. Niger-Congo (or Atlantic-Congo, i.e. Niger-Congo minus unproven groups often associated with it: Mande, Dogon, Ijoid, Katla, and Rashad languages)
29. Nilotic
30. Nubian (possibly including also Meroitic)
31. Nyimang
32. Rashad
33. Saharan
34. Sandawe (isolate?)
35. Songhay

TABLE 9.1: continued

36. South Omotic (Aroid?)	40. Tegem (Lafofa) (isolate? unclassified? family? member of Niger-Congo?)
37. Surmic	
38. Tama (Taman)	41. Temein
39. Ta-Ne-Omotic	42. Tuu

North America (54)

43. Adai† (isolate)	70. Maiduan
44. Algic	71. Muskogean
45. Alsea† (isolate)	72. Na-dene (Eyak-Athabaskan and Tlingit)
46. Atakapa† (isolate, small family?)	
47. Beothuk† (isolate)	73. Natchez† (isolate)
48. Caddoan	74. Palaihnihan
49. Cayuse† (isolate)	75. Plateau (Plateau Penutian)
50. Chimakuan†	76. Pomoan
51. Chimariko† (isolate)	77. Salinan†
52. Chinookan†	78. Salishan
53. Chitimacha† (isolate)	79. Shastan†
54. Chumashan†	80. Siouan-Catawban
55. Coahuilteco† (isolate)	81. Siuslaw† (isolate)
56. Cochimí-Yuman	82. Takelma† (isolate)
57. Comecrudan†	83. Timucua† (isolate)
58. Coosan†	84. Tonkawa† (isolate)
59. Cotoname† (isolate)	85. Tsimshianic
60. Eskimo-Aleut	86. Tunica† (isolate)
61. Esselen† (isolate)	87. Utian (Miwok-Costanoan)
62. Haida (isolate, possibly a small family?)	88. Uto-Aztecan
	89. Wakashan
63. Iroquoian	90. Washo (isolate)
64. Kalapuyan†	91. Wintuan
65. Karankawa† (isolate)	92. Yana† (isolate)
66. Karuk (Karok) (isolate)	93. Yokutsan
67. Keresan	94. Yuchi (isolate)
68. Kiowa-Tanoan	95. Yukian†
69. Kootenai (Kutenai) (isolate)	96. Zuni (isolate)

Mexico and Mesoamerica (14)

97. Cuitlatec† (isolate)	104. Mixe-Zoquean
98. Guaicurian†	105. Otomanguean
99. Huave (isolate)	106. Purépecha (Tarascan) (isolate)
100. Jicaquean (Tol)	107. Seri (isolate)
101. Lencan†	108. Tequistlatecan
102. Mayan	109. Totonacan
103. Misumalpan	110. Xinkan†

TABLE 9.1: continued

South America (105)

111. Aikanã (isolate)
112. Andaquí† (isolate)
113. Andoque (isolate)
114. Arara do Rio Branco† (Arara do Beiradão, Mato Grosso Arara) (isolate)
115. Arawakan
116. Arawan
117. Atacameño† (Cunza, Kunza) (isolate)
118. Arutani (Awaké, Uruak) (isolate)
119. Aymaran
120. Barbacoan
121. Betoi-Jirara† (isolate)
122. Boran
123. Bororoan
124. Cahuapanan
125. Camsá (isolate)
126. Candoshi (Canndoshi-Sharpa) (isolate)
127. Canichana† (isolate)
128. Cariban
129. Cayuvava† (Cayubaba) (isolate)
130. Chapacuran
131. Charruan†
132. Chibchan
133. Chicham (Jivaroan)
134. Chipaya-Uru
135. Chiquitano (isolate)
136. Chocoan
137. Cholonan†
138. Chonan
139. Chono† (isolate)
140. Cofán (A'ingaé) (isolate)
141. Culli† (Culle) (isolate)
142. Enlhet-Enenlhet (Mascoyan)
143. Esmeralda† (Atacame) (isolate)
144. Fulnio (Yaté) (isolate)
145. Guachí† (isolate)
146. Guaicuruan
147. Guajiboan
148. Guamo† (isolate)
149. Guató† (isolate)
150. Harakmbut-Katukinan
151. Huarpean†
152. Irantxe (Münkü) (isolate)
153. Itonama (isolate)
154. Jêan (Sensu Lato)
155. Jirajaran†
156. Jotí (Yuwana) (isolate)
157. Kakua-Nukak
158. Kapixaná (Kanoé) (isolate)
159. Karajá
160. Karirían†
161. Kaweskaran (Qawasqaran, Alacalufan)
162. Kwaza (Koayá) (isolate)
163. Leco† (isolate)
164. Lule-Vilela†
165. Máko† (Maku) (isolate)
166. Mapudungun (Araucanian)
167. Matacoan
168. Matanawí† (isolate)
169. Mochica† (Yunga) (isolate)
170. Mosetén-Chinamé (isolate)
171. Movima (isolate)
172. Munichi† (isolate)
173. Nadehup (aka Makúan, now considered a pejorative name)
174. Nambiquaran
175. Omurano† (isolate)
176. Otomacoan†
177. Paez (isolate; possibly a small family?)
178. Pano-Takanan
179. Payaguá† (isolate)
180. Pirahã (Muran) (isolate, possibly a small family of closely related languages)
181. Puinave (isolate)
182. Puquina† (isolate)
183. Purí-Coroado† (isolate)
184. Quechuan
185. Sáliban
186. Sapé† (Kaliana) (isolate)
187. Sechura†
188. Tallan
189. Taruma† (Taruamá) (isolate)
190. Taushiro (isolate)
191. Tequiraca† (isolate)
192. Tikuna-Yurí

TABLE 9.1: continued

193. Timotean†
194. Tiniguan†
195. Trumai (isolate)
196. Tukanoan
197. Tupían
198. Urarina (isolate)
199. Waorani (isolate)
200. Warao (isolate)
201. Witotoan
202. Xukurúan(?)
203. Yaghan† (Yámana) (isolate)
204. Yaguan
205. Yanomaman
206. Yaruro (Pumé) (isolate)
207. Yuracaré (isolate)
208. Yurumangui† (isolate)
209. Zamucoan
210. Zaparoan

Europe and Asia (31)

211. Ainu† (isolate)
212. Austroasiatic
213. Basque (isolate)
214. Burushaski (isolate)
215. Chukotko-Kamchatkan
216. Dravidian
217. Elamite† (isolate)
218. Hattic† (isolate)
219. Hmong-Mien (aka Miao-Yao)
220. Hruso (Hruso-Aka) (isolate?)
221. Hurrian (Hurro-Urartean)†
222. Indo-European
223. Japonic
224. Kassite† (isolate)
225. Koreanic
226. Kra-Dai (Tai-Kadai)
227. Kusunda (isolate)
228. Mongolian
229. Nakh-Dagestanian (Northeast Caucasian)
230. Nihali (isolate)
231. Nivkh (isolate, possibly a small family)
232. Northwest Caucasian (Abkhazo-Adyghean)
233. Sino-Tibetan
234. South Caucasian (Kartvelian)
235. Sumerian† (isolate)
236. Tungusic
237. Turkic
238. Tyrsenian† (Etruscan-Lemnian and possibly also Rhaetic)
239 Uralic
240. Yeniseian
241. Yukaghir

Pacific (128)

242. Abinomn (isolate)
243. Abun (isolate)
244. Afra (Usku) (isolate)
245. Amto-Musan
246. Anêm (isolate)
247. Angan
248. Anim
249. Ap Ma (Botin, Kambot, Kambrambo) (isolate)
250. Arafundi
251. Asaba (isolate)
252. Austronesian
253. Awin-Pa
254. Baibai-Fas
255. Baining
256. Baiyamo (isolate)
257. Banaro (isolate)
258. Bayono-Awbono
259. Bilua (isolate)
260. Bogaya (isolate)
261. Border
262. Bosavi
263. Bulaka River
264. Burmeso (isolate)
265. Busa (Odiai) (isolate)
266. Dagan
267. Damal (Uhunduni, Amung) (isolate)
268. Dem (isolate)
269. Dibiyaso (isolate)
270. Doso-Turumsa
271. Duna (isolate)
272. East Bird's Head
273. East Kutubu
274. East Strickland

TABLE 9.1: continued

275. Eastern Trans-Fly
276. Eleman
277. Elseng (Morwap) (isolate)
278. Fasu (isolate)
279. Geelvink Bay (Cenderawasih Bay)
280. Goilalan
281. Great Andamanese
282. Guriaso (isolate)
283. Hatam-Mansim
284. Inanwatan
285. Kaki Ae (isolate)
286. Kamula (isolate)
287. Kapauri (isolate)
288. Karami
289. Kaure-Narau (possibly an isolate)
290. Kayagar
291. Kehu (isolate)
292. Kibiri-Porome (isolate)
293. Kimki (isolate)
294. Kiwaian
295. Koiarian
296. Kol (isolate)
297. Kolopom
298. Konda-Yahadian
299. Kosare (isolate)
300. Kuot (isolate)
301. Kwalean
302. Kwerbic
303. Kwomtari
304. Lakes Plain
305. Lavukaleve (isolate)
306. Left May (Arai)
307. Lepki-Murkim
308. Lower Sepik-Ramu
309. Mailuan
310. Mairasi
311. Manubaran
312. Marori (Moraori)
313. Masep (isolate)
314. Mawes (isolate)
315. Maybrat (isolate)
316. Mombum (family, two languages)
317. Monumbo (family, two languages)
318. Mor (isolate)
319. Morehead-Wasur
320. Mpur (isolate)
321. Namla-Tofanma
322. Ndu
323. Nimboran

324. North Bougainville
325. North Halmahera
326. Onge-Jarawa (Jarawa-Onge)
327. Pahoturi
328. Pauwasi
329. Pawaia
330. Pele-Ata
331. Piawi
332. Powle-Ma (sometimes called Molof)
        (isolate)
333. Purari (sometimes called Namau)
        (isolate)
334. Pyu (isolate)
335. Sause (isolate)
336. Savosavo (isolate)
337. Senagi
338. Sentani
339. Sepik
340. Sko (Skou)
341. Somahai
342. South Bird's Head
343. South Bougainville
344. Suki-Gogodala
345. Sulka (isolate)
346. Tabo (Waia) (isolate)
347. Taiap (isolate)
348. Tambora† (isolate)
349. Tanahmerah (isolate)
350. Taulil-Butam
351. Teberan
352. Timor-Alor-Pantar
353. Tor-Orya
354. Torricelli
355. Touo (isolate)
356. Trans New Guinea
357. Turama-Kikori
358. Ulmapo ('Mongol-Langam')
359. Walio
360. West Bird's Head
361. West Bomberai
362. Wiru (isolate)
363. Yale (Yalë, Nagatman) (isolate)
364. Yareban
365. Yawa
366. Yele (Yélî Dnye) (isolate)
367. Yerakai (isolate)
368. Yetfa-Biksi (isolate)
369. Yuat

TABLE 9.1: continued

Australia (30)

370. Bachamal† (isolate, possibly North Daly family)	386. Northeastern Tasmanian†
371. Bunaban	387. Northern Daly
372. Eastern Daly†	388. Nyulnyulan
373. Gaagudju† (isolate)	389. Oyster Bay†
374. Garrwan	390. Pama-Nyungan
375. Giimbiyu†	391. Southeastern Tasmanian†
376. Gunwinyguan	392. Southern Daly
377. Iwaidjan	393. Tangkic
378. Jarrakan	394. Tiwi (isolate)
379. Kungarakany† (isolate)	395. Umbugarla/Ngurmbur† (isolate or small family?)
380. Limilngan†	396. Wagiman† (Wageman) (Yangmanic?) (isolate)
381. Mangarrayi† (isolate)	
382. Maningrida	397. Wardaman† (isolate or small family)
383. Maran	398. Western Daly
384. Marrku-Wurrugu	399. Worrorran
385. Mirndi (Mindi)	

(† after a language family's name indicates 'extinct', that is, that no language in that language family has any remaining native speakers. ǂ represents a palato-alveolar click.)

It may be helpful to point to a few cases where opinions about classification have differed to give a sense of why the exact number of distinct language families can never be known. The following are cases that are sometimes listed as language isolates and sometimes suggested as belonging to a particular language family, but for which the information available is so scant that no defensible conclusions are warranted: *Kujargé* (on the Chad–Sudan border), long extinct *Meroitic* (from the First Cataract of the Nile to the Khartoum area in Sudan), *Minkin* (in Australia), *Ongota* (aka Birale) (in Ethiopia), *Shabo* (in Ethiopia), *Maratino* (in Mexico), among many others. For example, *Aranama* (aka *Tamique*) shows up often in lists of the language families of North America, reported as a language at the Franciscan mission of Espiritu Santo de Zúñiga, founded in Texas in 1726. The entire corpus of what is known of this language is one single word and one two-word phrase: *himiyána* 'water' and *Himiána tsýi!* 'Give me water!', taken down in 1884 from a native speaker of Tonkawa (another indigenous language from the region). So Aranama must be considered unclassified because obviously the material available on the language is too limited to permit a legitimate classification. Similarly, *Calusa* (in Florida) is known only from about a dozen words obtained from a Spanish captive among the Calusa in 1575 and from fifty or sixty place names. This attestation is too limited to demonstrate any relationship with any other language or to demonstrate that it is an isolate because it has no relationship with any other. It must simply be left as unclassified. *Cañar-Puruhá* (in Ecuador) is often presented as a language family of two members, Cañar (Cañari) and Puruhá. However, both languages are extinct, with extremely little attestation, meaning that the status of this proposed family is uncertain and the classification cannot be embraced (Adelaar and Muysken 2004: 396–7). Some of the Pacific language isolates listed in Table 9.1 could possibly be considered unclassified, rather than true isolates, given the limited information available on them. Cases of unclassified (unclassifiable) languages show why the exact number of language families (including language isolates) cannot be known with certainty (Campbell 2018b).

All the languages of ninety-one of these language families are extinct (marked with † after the name). This means that very close to a quarter (23 per cent) of the linguistic diversity of the world, calculated in terms of independent language families, is gone.

Historical linguistic research has reached an advanced state for only a few of these language families. For example, Sino-Tibetan (c. 300 languages) is an extremely important family, since its languages are spoken by a larger number of people than any other language family in the world except Indo-European. Nevertheless, comparative linguistic research in Sino-Tibetan is actually recent, flourishing only since the early 1980s or so. Its classification has been and continues to be controversial, with many Chinese scholars classifying Sino-Tibetan together with the languages of the Hmong-Mien (aka Miao-Yao) and Kra-Dai (Tai-Kadai) families, where most other scholars limit the family membership to the Sinitic (Chinese) and Tibeto-Burman languages. A few scholars even believe that Sino-Tibetan has not yet been adequately demonstrated as a legitimate language family, that it has not been shown that the Sinitic (Chinese) and Tibeto-Burman branches belong to a single language family. Table 9.1 presents a consensus view of language families, as accepted by most specialists in each region, but by no means by all.

9.2.1 Language isolates and their history

A language isolate is a language which has no known relatives, that is, that has no demonstrable genetic relationship with any other language. Consequently, language isolates are in effect language families with only a single member. The best-known and most often cited are Basque, Burushaski, and Ainu, though there are many others (see Campbell 2018a; 2018b, and see below). Language isolates have often been misunderstood and so it is important to clarify them and their status in language classification schemes.

Language isolates are not very different from language families that have multiple members. Some language isolates may have had relatives in the past which have disappeared without coming to be known, leaving these languages isolated, though if we had information about their lost relatives, the remaining languages would not be isolates but rather members of families of more than one language. For example, Ket in Siberia is the only surviving language of the Yeniseian language family. Nevertheless, there were other Yeneseian languages, now extinct: Arin, Asan, Kott, Pumpokol, and Yugh. If these languages had disappeared without a trace, today Ket would be considered an isolate. However, since data from these other, now extinct Yeniseian languages were registered before the languages disappeared, Ket was not left an isolate; rather it is a member of a family of languages, albeit the only surviving member of that family.

Language isolates and language families are also not so different from one another in another sense. Some languages which were thought to be isolates have turned out not to be; rather, they have proven to be members of small families of related languages as previously unknown relatives became known. For example, Korean was considered a language isolate, but recently it was demonstrated that Jejeou (of Jeju Island) is a separate language, related to Korean. Thus Korean is no longer a language isolate, but a member of the small Koreanic language family. A second example is Etruscan, long thought to be an isolate; however, though this is still disputed, Etruscan appears to be related to Lemnian. Lemnian is known from a stella and ceramic fragments from the Greek island of Lemnos, dating from c. 400 BC. Many scholars also include Rhaetic (a long extinct language of the eastern Alps, attested in a small number of inscriptions) as another relative, though the evidence is less abundant for that. This language family is called Tyrsenian. Thus, Etruscan is no longer considered an isolate by most scholars; it is considered a member of a small language family.

As mentioned, it is necessary to distinguish language isolates from *unclassified* languages, languages so poorly known that they cannot be classified, though some of these are also sometimes called language isolates. An unclassified language is one for which there are not enough data (attestation) available to be able to determine whether it has relatives or not – these languages lack enough data for them to be compared meaningfully with other languages and therefore their possible kinship remains unknown. For language isolates, sufficient data do exist; these languages are not grouped in larger genetic classifications with any other languages because comparisons of these languages, from known data, with other languages do not reveal any confirmable linguistic kinship.

There are two sorts of unclassified languages. To the first belong those extinct languages which are too poorly attested to group with any other language or language group. Some examples include:

Aranama-Tamique, Texas
Camunico, Northeast Italy, to the second half of the first millennium BC
Gamela, Brazil
Ibrerian, Iberian Peninsula, second half of first millennium BC to first half of
    first millennium AD
Kaskean, Northeast Anatolia, second millennium BC
Ligurian, Northeast Italy, few words, 300 BC–AD 100
Minkin, Australia
Mysian, Western Anatolia, before first century BC
Naolan, Tamaulipas, Mexico
Northern Picene, Adriatic coast of Italy, first millennium BC
Pictish, Scotland, seventh to tenth centuries AD, few inscriptions
Quinigua, Northeast Mexico

Sicanian, Central Sicily, pre-Roman epoch
Solano, Texas, Northeast Mexico
Sorothaptic, Iberian Peninsula, pre-Celtic, Bronze Age

The second kind of unclassified language includes still extant languages not classified for lack of data, living languages that are so little known that the data available do not permit them to be compared with other languages in order to determine whether they may be related or not. Examples of this sort of unclassified language include:

In Africa: Bung, Lufu, Kujargé, perhaps Mpre (Mpra), Oropom, Rer Bare, Weyto
In Asia and the Pacific: Bhatola (India), Doso (Papua New Guinea), Kehu (Indonesia Papua), Sentinelese (Andaman Islands), Tirio (Papua New Guinea), Waxianghua (China)
In South America: Amikoana, Ewarhuyana, Himarimã, Iapama, Korubo, Miarrã, Papavô, Potiguara, Tremembé, Wakoná, Wasu, Yarí, and many others.

It should be noted that some of these unclassified languages could also be language isolates, but without better data on them we cannot know. The total number of known language isolates of the world is 157. They are identified in Table 9.1 with 'isolate' in parentheses after their names. Language isolates thus make up 39 per cent of all the c. 398 'language families'. Seen from this perspective, isolates are not at all weird; rather they have as their 'cohorts' more than one third of the world's 'language families'.

How do we explain the general attitude that language isolates are commonly considered highly unusual, so strange that they should be treated with suspicion? How do we account for the frequent sentiment that it is not to be tolerated that there should be languages with no relatives? It may be suspected that these feelings stem from lack of knowledge about how many isolates there are and lack of understanding about how little isolates differ from other language families in their basic character, as seen above.

How can we learn about the history of isolates, languages without relatives? The means that can be employed to learn about the history of language isolates include:

Internal reconstruction (see Chapter 8)
The philological study of the attestations (see Chapter 14)
Evidence from toponyms (see Chapter 15)
Names (personal names, names of rivers, deities, etc.) (see Chapter 15)
Early historical reports about the language (see Chapter 14)
Comparative reconstruction based on dialects (see Chapter 7). Some illustrative examples of the comparison of dialects of isolates to reconstruct older states of the languages include:
Ainu (Vovin 1993)

Basque (Gorrochategui and Lakarra 1996; 2001; Lakarra 1996, Michelena
1988; 1995; Trask 1997)
Huave (Suárez 1975)
Purépecha (Tarascan) (Friedrich 1971).
Evidence from loanwords (see Chapter 3)
Language contact and areal linguistics (see Chapter 10)
Wörter und Sachen techniques (see Chapter 15).

It is important to be aware of these ways of obtaining information about the
history of language isolates, since it has often been asserted that since they have
no known relatives, nothing can be known of their history.

9.3 Terminology

For language classification, it is important to understand the terminology used.
This can be confusing, since the terms are not always used consistently and there
is controversy concerning the validity of some of the kinds of entities which some
labels are intended to identify. Therefore, it is helpful to begin by clarifying this
terminology. In linguistic classification, we need to deal with names for a range
of entities which distinguish language groups of greater and lesser relatedness,
that is, entities with different degrees of internal diversity (time depth), each more
inclusive than the level below it.

Dialect means only a variety (regional or social) of a language, which is mutually intelligible with other dialects of the same language. 'Dialect' is not used in
historical linguistics to mean a little-known ('exotic') or minority language, and
it is no longer used to refer to a daughter language of a language family, though
the word was sometimes used in these senses in the past.

Language means any distinct linguistic entity (variety) which is mutually unintelligible with other such entities.

A *language family* is a group of genealogically related languages, that is, languages which share a linguistic kinship by virtue of having descended from a
common ancestor. Many language families are designated with the suffix -*an*,
as in, for example, *Algonquian, Austronesian, Indo-European, Sino-Tibetan*, and so on.

A *language isolate* is a language which has no known relatives, that is, it is a family
with but a single member (see above).

Traditionally, historical linguists speak of a *genetic* relationship when languages
belong to the same language family, that is, when they descend from the same
proto-language (common ancestor). More recently, some linguists prefer to speak
of *phylogenetic* relationships, perhaps to avoid possible confusion with *genetic* as used
in biology, connected there with *genes* rather than with languages.

Language families can be of different magnitudes; that is, they can
involve different time depths, so that some larger-scale families may include
smaller-scale families (that is, subfamilies) among their members or branches.
Unfortunately, however, a number of confusing terms have been utilized in
attempts to distinguish more inclusive from less inclusive language family
groupings.

Subgrouping is about the internal classification of the languages inside of languages families; it is about the branches of a family tree and about which sister languages are most closely related to one another. The term *subgroup* (also called *subfamily*, *branch*) is relatively straightforward. It is used to refer to a group of languages within a language family that are more closely related to each other than they are to other languages of that family – that is, a subgroup is a branch of a language family. As a proto-language (for example, Proto-Indo-European) diversifies, it develops daughter languages (such as Proto-Germanic, Proto-Celtic, and so on); if a daughter (for instance, Proto-Germanic) then subsequently splits up and develops daughter languages of its own (such as English, German, and so on), then the descendants (English, German, and others, in the case of Germanic) of that daughter language (Proto-Germanic) constitute members of a subgroup (the Germanic languages), and the original daughter language (Proto-Germanic) becomes in effect an intermediate proto-language, a parent of its own immediate descendants (its daughters, English, German, and so on), but still at the same time is a descendant (daughter) itself of the original proto-language (Proto-Indo-European).

A number of terms have also been used for postulated but undemonstrated higher-order, more inclusive families (proposed but as yet unproven distant genetic relationships); these include *stock*, *phylum*, *macrofamily*, and the compounding element '*macro-*' (as in *Macro-Penutian*, *Macro-Siouan*, and the like). These terms have proven confusing and controversial, as might be expected when names are at stake for entities that have been postulated but where agreement is lacking about the validity of the entity to which they refer. In order to avoid confusion and controversy, none of these terms should be used. Since the entities called 'stock', 'phylum', and 'macro-' would be bona fide language families if they could be established (demonstrated) on the basis of the linguistic evidence available, and they will not be accepted families if the proposals which they embody fail to hold up based on the evidence, scholars believe that it is much clearer to refer to these proposed but as yet unsubstantiated relationships as 'proposed distant genetic relationships', 'postulated families', or 'long-range hypotheses'. The question of distant genetic relationships – how to determine whether languages not yet known to be related to one another may be distantly related – is much debated (see Chapter 13). (See Chapter 16 for other terminology, used in quantitative approaches.)

9.4 How to Draw Family Trees: Subgrouping

Subgrouping is the internal classification of language families to determine which sister languages are most closely related to one another, which more distantly. It is common for a language over time to diversify, that is, to split up into two or more daughter languages (with the consequence that the earlier language ceases to be spoken except as reflected in its descendants) – this means that the original language comes to constitute a proto-language. After the break-up of the original proto-language, a daughter language (for example, Western Romance, which split off from Proto-Romance) may itself subsequently diversify into daughters of its own (Western Romance split up into Spanish, Portuguese, French, and others). This gives the first daughter language to branch off (Western Romance in our example) an intermediate position in the family tree – it is a daughter of the original proto-language (Proto-Romance) and it is an ancestor of its own daughters (the parent of Spanish, Portuguese, French, and others). So the languages which branch off from the intermediate language (Western Romance) belong to the same subgroup (Spanish, Portuguese, and French are more immediate daughters of Western Romance, thus belonging to the Western Romance subgroup, which itself belongs to the Romance family, itself a branch of the higher-order Indo-European family).

A subgroup, then, is all the daughters which descend from an ancestor (intermediate proto-language) which itself has at least one sister. To say that certain languages belong to the same subgroup means that they share a common parent language which is itself a daughter of a higher-order proto-language, just as English is a descendant of Proto-Germanic (together with its other Germanic sister languages, such as German, Swedish, Icelandic, and others) and so is a member of the Germanic subgroup, which in turn is a daughter of (branch of) Proto-Indo-European, together with other subgroups (such as Slavic, Italic – to which Romance belongs as a branch – Celtic, Indo-Iranian, and so on, which have their own later daughter languages). Also, after the break-up of the original proto-language, a daughter language may remain unified; such a language which branches off directly from the proto-language and does not later split up into other languages constitutes a subgroup (branch) of the family all by itself, a subgroup with only a single member. The purpose of subgrouping is to determine the family tree for genetically related languages. Its goal is to determine which languages belong to different branches (descendants of intermediate parent languages) and the relationship among branches of the tree.

The only generally accepted criterion for subgrouping is *shared innovation*. A shared innovation is a linguistic change which shows a departure (innovation) from some trait of the proto-language and is shared by a subset of the daughter languages. It is assumed that a shared innovation is the result of a change which took place in a single daughter language which then subsequently diversified into daughters of its own, each of which inherits the results of the change. Thus the innovation is shared by the descendants of this intermediate parent but is not shared by languages in other subgroups of the family. This is because the languages of other subgroups do not descend from the intermediate parent that underwent the change which is inherited from this language by its daughter languages. The fact that these daughter languages share the innovation is evidence which suggests that they were formerly a single, unified language which underwent the change and then subsequently split up, leaving evidence of this change in its descendant languages.

An example of a family tree has already been seen in Chapter 7 in Figure 7.1 for the Proto-Romance family tree. Since examples from the Indo-European and Uralic families are cited frequently in this book, and because so much historical linguistic work has been done on these families, their family trees are presented in

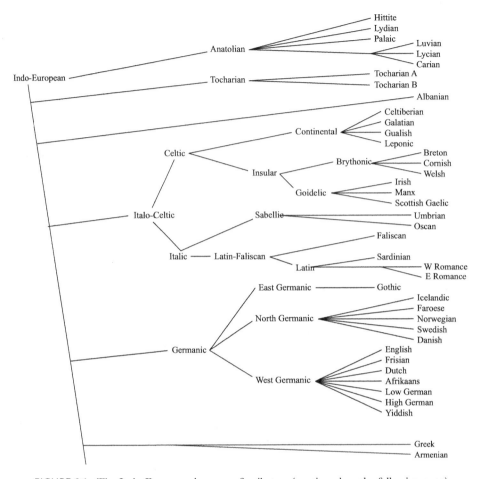

FIGURE 9.1: The Indo-European language family tree (continued on the following page)

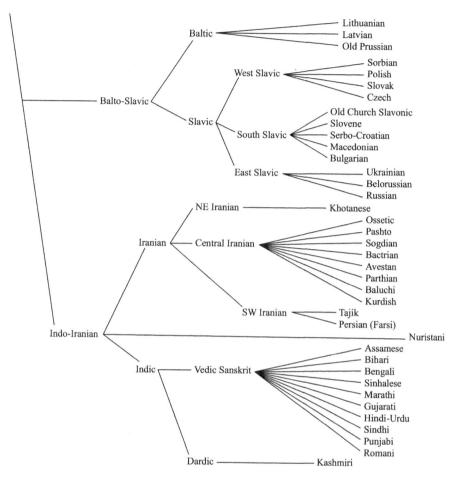

FIGURE 9.1: The Indo-European language family tree

Not all Indo-European languages are present in this figure. For the members of Western Romance and Eastern Romance, see Figure 7.1.

Figures 9.1 and 9.2. The Austronesian family tree is also presented, in Figure 9.3. Frequent examples from Mayan languages are also cited here; the Mayan family tree is given in Figure 9.4.

The particular family trees presented here for Indo-European (in Figure 9.1) and Uralic (in Figure 9.2) are representative, but are not universally agreed upon. In both families, there is general agreement about the major lower-level subgroups (subfamilies), where the evidence is fairly clear. However, there is disagreement about the higher-order branches. In both families, the evidence for the higher branches, those closer to the proto-language, is more limited and sometimes unclear. The most common tree given traditionally for Indo-European usually presents some ten separate subgroups branching directly from Proto-Indo-European with little intermediate branching that would combine any of the higher-order subgroups into a single branch. The Indo-European family tree presented in Figure 9.1 incorporates some hypotheses about higher-order branching, but this is still inconclusive. The position of Albanian,

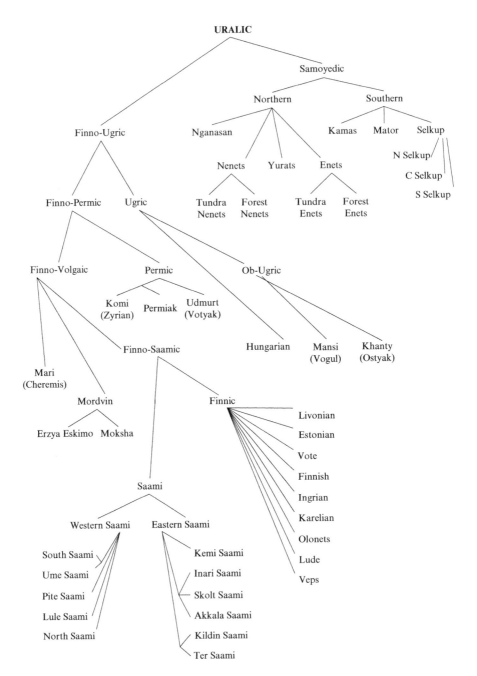

FIGURE 9.2: The Uralic family tree

in particular, is unclear. Other ancient and lesser-known Indo-European lan-
guages should also be included, for example, Phrygian, Thracian, Illyrian,
Messapic, and Venetic, though where they should appear in the tree is not clear.
(For discussion of the classification of Indo-European, see Clackson 2007: 5–15;
Garrett 1999; Jasanoff 2003; Mallory and Adams 1997: 550–6; and Ringe,
Warnow, and Taylor 2002.)

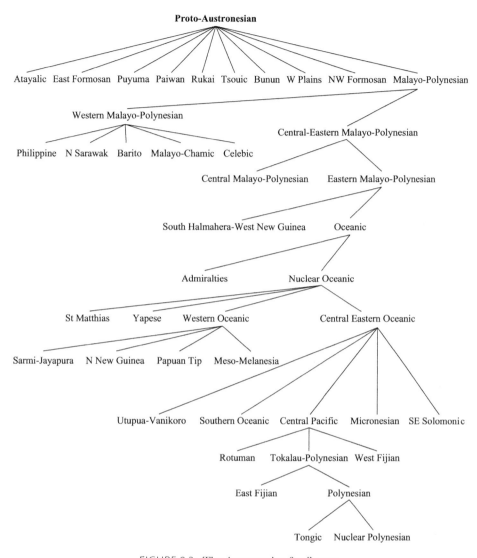

FIGURE 9.3: The Austronesian family tree

The Uralic tree given in Figure 9.2 represents a more traditional classification of the family. This Uralic family tree is representative, though it is not accepted by all Uralic scholars. Some find little support for the branching classification with its higher-order intermediate subgroups. Others are sympathetic to the problems pointed out due to the limited evidence for higher-order internal branches, but nevertheless see sufficient evidence to support much of the branching classification (see Sammallahti 1988). There is general agreement that the former Volgaic branch (not shown here), which would group Mari and Mordvin more closely together, should be abandoned. (See also Abondolo 1998; Häkkinen 1984; 2001; Janhunen 2001; Salminen 2001.)

The Austronesian family tree is given in Figure 9.3. It provides another example of a family tree and the subgrouping that it represents.

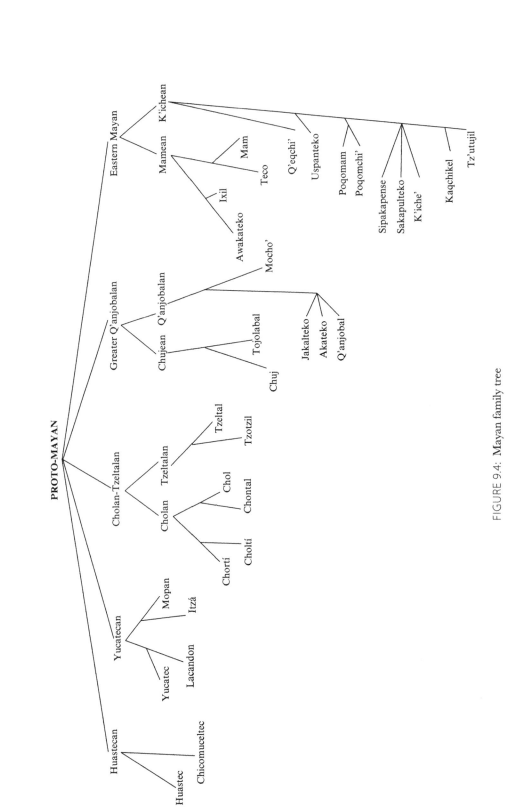

FIGURE 9.4: Mayan family tree

The classification of the Mayan languages will serve as a guided exercise to illustrate how subgrouping is done, and we will examine how shared innovations among these languages determine their subgrouping. Let us look first at the classification which has been established, given in the family tree in Figure 9.4, and then we will consider some of the shared innovations upon which the subgrouping is based.

Given that there are thirty-one Mayan languages and each has undergone several sound changes, we consider only a subset of the many shared innovations to give an idea of how subgroups are established. The following is a list of the major sound changes which are innovations shared among some but not others of the languages of the family. These form the basis for subgrouping languages of the Mayan family.

1. *w > Ø /#__ u, o, i, a (for example, *winaq > Huastec inik 'person')
2. *ŋ > w /#__, h /__# (*ŋe:h > Huastec we:w 'tail', *o:ŋ > Huastec uh 'avocado')
3. *ts, *t̯ > t; *ts', *t̯' > t' (here t̯ represents a fronted 't', perhaps palatalized) (*tseʔ- > Huastec teʔ- 'laugh')
4. *-h > -y (final h became y) (*ɓa:h > Kaqchikel ɓa:y 'gopher')
5. *-ɓ > -ʔ /VCV__# (in polysyllabic forms final imploded ɓ became a glottal stop) (Kaqchikel xuna:ʔ 'year' <*xun + ha:ɓ 'one year')
6. *h > ʔ (*haʔ > Mam ʔaʔ 'water')
7. *r > t (*ri:x > Mam ti:x 'old man')
8. *t > č (*tap > Mam čap 'crab')
9. * č > ç (alveopalatal affricate > laminal retroflex affricate) (*č'am > Mam ç'am 'sour')
10. *-t > -č (word-final t changed to č) (*naxt > Yucatec ná:č 'far')
11. *e: > i, *o: > u (long mid vowels raised to high vowels) (*so:ts' > Chol suts' 'bat')
12. *ŋ > x̯ (velar nasal > a kind of fronted velar fricative) (*ŋa:h > K'iche' xa:h 'house')
13. *t̯ > ć (a fronted t [dental or palatalized] changed to a prepalatal affricate) (*t̯e:ʔ > Mam tse:ʔ, K'iche' *če:ʔ 'tree')
14. *CVʔVC > CVʔC (*xoʔoq > K'iche' xoʔq 'corn husk, maize leaf')
15. ć > č (the prepalatal affricates became palato-alveolar) (*t̯e:ʔ > *će:ʔ > K'iche' *če:ʔ 'tree')
16. *q > k, *q' > k' (the uvular stops became velars) (*saq > Huastec θak, Yucatec sak, Chol sak 'white')
17. *ŋ > n (*ŋe:h > Chol neh 'tail')
18. *ts > s (*tsuh > Q'eqchi' suh 'bottle gourd')

Note that innovations in morphology and syntax are just as important as phonological innovations. Examples involving sound change are utilized here because they require less space to describe than changes in other areas of the grammar usually do, and the phonological innovations are better understood in Mayan languages.

Let us begin by looking at the lower-level groupings (the languages most closely related) for ease of illustration. In the Huastecan subgroup, Huastec and Chicomuceltec share the changes (1), (2), and (3). Other Mayan languages did not undergo these changes. We interpret this to mean that Huastec and Chicomuceltec belong together as members of a single subgroup: while Proto-Huastecan was still a unified language, it underwent these three sound changes (and others not presented here). After having undergone these changes, Proto-Huastecan then split up into its two daughter languages, Huastec and Chicomuceltec. As a consequence of this shared history, when we examine cognates, we see in both Huastec and Chicomuceltec that the cognates show the results of these sound changes, shared innovations, not shared by the cognates in the other Mayan languages. It is because Huastec and Chicomuceltec share these innovations that we postulate that there was an earlier unified Proto-Huastecan language which underwent these changes before it diversified into the two daughter languages, Huastec and Chicomuceltec, of this branch of the family.

Kaqchikel and Tz'utujil share the two innovations (4) and (5), which show that these two languages are more closely related to one another than to the others, since none of the others have evidence of these changes. Here we assume that there was a unified language which underwent the two changes and then later split up into Kaqchikel and Tz'utujil, accounting for why these two languages share the results of these changes. The alternative would require us to assume that these two languages are not closely related but just happened independently to undergo changes (4) and (5). Such a coincidence is not likely.

The four Mamean languages, Ixil, Awakateko, Mam, and Teco, share a series of innovations, (6)– (9) (and others not mentioned here). These include a chain shift (mentioned in Chapter 2) in which Proto-Mayan (PM) *r became t (7), while *t in turn became č (8), while *č in turn changed to Mamean ç (9).

The four Yucatecan languages (Yucatec, Lacandon, Mopan, and Itzá) share the change in (10) (final -t > - č), among others.

The Cholan languages, but no others, share change (11) (raising of long mid vowels, *e: > i, *o: > u).

At higher, more inclusive levels of the classification, all the languages of the K'ichean and Mamean groups share the innovations (12)– (14), showing that they all descend from a common parent language, Proto-Eastern Mayan, which had itself branched off from Proto-Mayan and then later split into two branches, K'ichean and Mamean.

We proceed in this fashion (not all the evidence is presented here) until we have worked out the classification of all the Mayan languages and subgroups to which they belong, both lower-level and higher-order ones, and it is on this basis that we draw the family tree presented in Figure 9.4.

It might be asked: why would just a list of shared similarities not be enough to distinguish more closely related languages from more distantly related ones within a language family? The answer is that not just any similarity provides reliable evidence of closer affinity. For example, it is important to emphasize and keep in mind that *shared retentions* are of practically no value for subgrouping. A shared retention is merely something that different daughter languages inherit unchanged from the proto-language regardless of whether the daughters belong to the same subgroup or not. For example, Huastec, Mam, and Mocho' (which, as seen in Figure 9.4, belong to separate branches of the family) retain the vowel-length contrast, which has been lost in some other languages. However, this is not evidence that these three necessarily belong to a single subgroup of Mayan, sharing a period of common history not shared by the other languages of the family. Rather, since Proto-Mayan had contrastive vowel length, the fact that Huastec, Mam, and Mocho' (and others) share this trait means only that these languages still retain unchanged something that Proto-Mayan had, and they could retain this inherited trait regardless of whether they belonged together in a single subgroup or were members of separate subgroups each of which independently retained this feature of the proto-language, that is, that had not changed this feature that the proto-language had. Shared retentions just do not reveal which languages share a period of common history *after* the break-up of the proto-language.

Although shared innovation is the only generally accepted criterion for subgrouping, not all shared innovations are of equal value for showing closer linguistic kinship. Some shared innovations represent sound changes that are so natural and happen so frequently cross-linguistically that they may take place independently in different branches of a language family and thus have nothing to do with a more recent common history. For example, in Mayan, change (16) (*q > k, *q' > k') took place in all the languages of the Huastecan, Yucatecan, and Cholan-Tzeltalan branches, as well as in some of the Greater Q'anjobalan languages. However, the fact that change (16) seems to be shared by languages of these branches does not necessarily mean that a single change took place in some presumed more immediate ancestor of all of these languages before they split up – it is just as likely that the uvulars (*q* and *q'*) changed to velars (*k* and *k'*) independently in different languages within the family, since uvular stops are more difficult to produce and more difficult for children to learn than velars and thus can easily change to velars, independently. Change (17) (*ŋ > n) took place in the Yucatecan, Cholan-Tzeltalan, and some of the Greater Q'anjobalan languages, but velar nasals (*ŋ*) can easily become alveolar nasals (*n*), a change frequently found in the world's languages. In these two cases (changes (16) and (17)), it is assumed that the branches of Mayan that exhibit these results underwent these very common sound changes independently. These changes merely represent independent, convergent innovations. Obviously, such changes are not as useful for subgrouping as other less expected changes are.

A telling example of this sort is the loss of the vowel-length contrast through the merger of long vowels with their short counterparts in Cholan and in some dialects of Kaqchikel. This is perfectly understandable, since the loss of vowel length is a very common change which languages seem easily to undergo. In this case, it would be ludicrous to imagine that Cholan languages and the Kaqchikel dialects without the length contrast formed one branch of the family while the other Kaqchikel dialects which maintain the contrast belong to a totally distinct branch. Clearly, the seemingly shared innovation of loss of vowel length came about independently in these instances. Very natural, very frequent changes are candidates for convergent development (innovations shared due to independent change rather than by being inherited results from a single change in an earlier parent). These frequent and common changes include the likes of nasalization of vowels before nasal consonants, intervocalic voicing, final devoicing, palatalization before *i* or *j*, and a number of other such changes.

Finally, some sound changes can spread by diffusion among related languages, and this can complicate the subgrouping picture. For example, Q'eqchi', Poqomam, and Poqomchi' share change (18) (*ts* > *s*); however, documents from the sixteenth and seventeenth centuries reveal that this change took place long after these three were independent languages and that the change diffused across language boundaries (see Chapters 3 and 10). Naturally, if the change is borrowed from one language to another after they had become separate languages, this does not reflect a time of common history when a single language underwent a change and then subsequently split up, leaving evidence of that change in its daughter languages. Therefore, borrowed changes, which may appear to be shared innovations, are also not evidence of subgrouping. Fortunately, such changes that diffuse across independent languages are not very common.

While it is clear that shared innovation is the only reliable criterion for subgrouping, it must be kept in mind that the subgrouping can be only as successful as the reconstruction upon which it is based. That is, what constitutes an innovation depends crucially upon what an ancestor language had in it, and thus on what is reconstructed for that ancestor. If the reconstruction is wrong, there is a strong possibility that the subgrouping which depends on that reconstruction will be inaccurate as well. Let's consider an example illustrated by Nootkan (a subfamily of the broader Wakashan family). Nootkan has three member languages, Makah, Nitinat, and Nuu-chah-nulth (Nootka), spoken in the Northwest Coast area of North America). Consider the sound correspondences presented in Table 9.2. (See Haas 1969b; some of the Nootkan correspondences and changes were seen in Chapter 7.)

Let us begin with what is believed to be the best reconstruction and subgrouping before considering the consequences of erroneous alternatives. Proto-Nootkan is reconstructed with **q'* for (1), **χ* (voiceless uvular fricative) for (2),

TABLE 9.2: Some Nootkan sound correspondences

	Makah	*Nitinat*	*Nuu-chah-nulth (Nootka)*	*Proto-Nootkan*
(1)	q'	ʕ	ʕ	*q'
(2)	χ	χ	ħ	*χ
(3a)	b	b	m	*m
(3b)	b'	m̉	m̉	*m̉
(4a)	d	n	n	*n
(4b)	d'	n̉	n̉	*n̉

*m for (3a), * m̓ for (3b), *n for (4a), and ň for (4b) (* m̓ and * ň are the glottalized nasals). Nitinat and Nuu-chah-nulth (Nootka) are subgrouped together, with Makah as a separate branch of the Nootkan subfamily. This interpretation is based on the fact that Nitinat and Nuu-chah-nulth (Nootka) share, for example, the innovation in (1) in which the glottalized uvular stop (q̓) changed to pharyngeal ʕ. While Makah and Nitinat seem to share an innovation (in (3a), (3b), (4a), and (4b)) in which the Proto-Nootkan nasals became corresponding voiced oral stops (b, b', d, and d', respectively), this change came about through diffusion in the linguistic area after Makah and Nitinat had separated. Nitinat and Makah belong to the area of the Northwest Coast of North America where several languages lack nasal consonants. In (2), since only Nootka changed (*χ > ħ), Makah and Nitinat share only the retention of the uvular fricative χ, not evidence for subgrouping. However, suppose now that for (2) we were to reconstruct (erroneously) *ħ (pharyngeal fricative) for Proto-Nootkan; this would presuppose the change of *ħ to χ in Makah and Nitinat, and this would be a shared innovation, seeming evidence to support subgrouping these two together but with Nuu-chah-nulth (Nootka) apart. As this shows, subgrouping is very much at the mercy of how accurate the reconstruction is upon which it is based. In this case, if we did not recognize that the change from nasals to corresponding voiced stops, *m > b, *m̓ > b', and *n > d, *ň > d', was due to areal diffusion and we reconstructed erroneously *b, *b' and *d, *d' instead, with the assumption that Nuu-chah-nulth (Nootka) changed these to nasals, nothing would follow for subgrouping, since Nuu-chah-nulth (Nootka) alone would change and Makah and Nitinat would only share a retention.

The Mayan subgrouping, considered above, provides a final example, though it is simplified here in that we will consider only one of many sound correspondences together with the changes and the reconstruction based on it. In the Mayan family, the lower-level subgroups are well established; these include the Huastecan, Yucatecan, Cholan-Tzeltalan, Greater Q'anjobalan, K'ichean, and Mamean subgroups. Some of these are grouped together in higher-order, more inclusive branches of the family; we must ask what the evidence for these larger subgroupings is and whether it is accurate. Consider the following sound correspondence:

Yucatecan n: Cholan-Tzeltalan n: Q'anjobalan ŋ: K'ichean x̣: Mamean x

The generally accepted reconstruction in this case is Proto-Mayan *ŋ. (Huastecan has h in this correspondence set, but since it is assumed that Huastecan independently changed *ŋ > h (change (2) in the list above), it is left out of the discussion here.) K'ichean and Mamean share the change of *ŋ > x̣ (change (12) above; x̣ then later changed to x in Mamean and in most of the K'ichean languages), and this shared innovation of *ŋ > x̣ (together with others mentioned above) supports subgrouping K'ichean and Mamean together; the group is usually called Eastern Mayan. In this reconstruction for the correspondence set that Proto-Mayan *ŋ is based on, Yucatecan, Cholan-Tzeltalan, and Q'anjobalan each retain the nasal (where it is assumed that the change of ŋ > n is so natural and easy that Yucatecan and Cholan-Tzeltalan each underwent it independently), and since nasality for this sound is a shared retention, nothing follows for whether or not these three groups may have a closer kinship with one another. However, K'ichean and Mamean share the innovation *ŋ > x̣, which is grounds for subgrouping them together. Suppose hypothetically now that this reconstruction were wrong and that Proto-Mayan actually had *x̣ (although this is not really an option). In this case, K'ichean and Mamean would share not an innovation but merely a retention (a velar-like voiceless fricative), and nothing would follow from this for their position within the family tree. However, Yucatecan, Cholan-Tzeltalan, and Greater Q'anjobalan would all share an innovation to a nasal (*x̣ > ŋ, then later ŋ > n in Yucatecan and Cholan-Tzeltalan), and this would be evidence for classifying Yucatecan, Cholan-Tzeltalan, and Greater Q'anjobalan as members of the same subgroup. That is, if the reconstruction of *ŋ is wrong, then the subgrouping based on the shared innovations which depart from that reconstruction is also not supported. If the alternative reconstruction with *x̣ for Proto-Mayan is wrong (which is almost certainly the case), then any subgrouping which presupposes it must also be wrong (unless other shared innovations can be found which do support it).

See Chapter 16 for discussion of subgrouping and classification involving glottochronology and its problems, and of more recent quantitative approaches to the topic.

9.5 Models of Language Change

Models of linguistic change are associated with language classification. When historical linguistics textbooks talk about 'models of change', they typically mean the traditional 'family-tree' model and the 'wave theory'. The discussion usually focuses on the approaches taken by dialectologists and Neogrammarians, typically assumed to conflict with one another, though as we will see, they are actually complementary. (Recent quantitative models are considered in Chapter 16.)

9.5.1 The family-tree model

The family tree (sometimes called *Stammbaum*, its German name) is the traditional model for representing language diversification. The family-tree model attempts to show how languages diversify and how language families are classified (as described above). A family-tree diagram's purpose is to show how languages that belong to the same language family are related to one another. *Linguistic diversification* refers to how proto-languages split up into daughter languages of a language family, to how a single ancestor language (a proto-language) develops dialects which in time through the accumulation of changes become distinct languages (sister languages to one another, daughter languages of the proto-language), and how through continued linguistic change these daughter languages can diversify and split up into daughters of their own (members of a subgroup of the family). The family-tree diagram represents this diversification, being a classification of the languages of a family and of the degree of relatedness among the various languages.

The family-tree model is often associated with August Schleicher (1821– 68), prominent in the history of Indo-European linguistics and teacher of several founders of Neogrammarianism, as well as of well-known opponents to Neogrammarian thinking (see Schleicher 1861–2). This model is typically linked in the literature with the development of the comparative method and eventually with the Neogrammarian notion of regularity of sound change. At the heart of the conflict over models are two of the basic assumptions of the comparative method (discussed in Chapter 7), that sound change is regular (the Neogrammarian hypothesis) and that there is no subsequent contact among the sister languages after the break-up of the proto-language.

The Neogrammarian slogan, *sound laws suffer no exceptions*, was declared virtually as doctrine in the so-called 'Neogrammarian manifesto', in the foreword to Hermann Osthoff and Karl Brugmann (1878), written mostly by Brugmann. It became an important cornerstone of reconstruction by the comparative method (as explained in Chapter 7). There is nothing inherently hostile to language contact and borrowing in the comparative method it is just that there is no provision in the comparative method for dealing directly with borrowings. For this, it is necessary to resort to considerations that are not properly part of the comparative method itself (see Chapters 3 and 10). Nevertheless, this absence of language contact in the comparative method is the source of dispute about which models are assumed most appropriate for dealing with kinds of changes and kinds of relationships among languages. Clearly, genetic relationship, the only thing represented directly in family-tree diagrams, is not the only sort of relationship that exists among languages – for example, languages do also borrow from one another.

9.5.2 The challenge from dialectology and the 'wave theory'

Some scholars, many of them dialectologists, did not accept the Neogrammarian position that sound change is regular and exceptionless, but rather opposed this and the family-tree model. The slogan associated with opponents of the Neogrammarian position was *each word has its own history* ('*chaque mot a son histoire*'). This slogan is often attributed to Jules Gilliéron, author of the *Atlas linguistique de la France* (1902–10), the dialect atlas of France (see Gilliéron 1921; Gilliéron and Roques 1912), although it should be credited to Hugo Schuchardt, a contemporary of the Neogrammarian founders, of whose claims he was critical. The alternative to the family-tree model which was put forward was the 'wave theory' (*Wellentheorie*). The wave theory is usually attributed to Johannes Schmidt (1872), though it, too, was actually developed slightly earlier by Hugo Schuchardt (in 1868 and 1870; see Alvar 1967: 82–5) – Schuchardt and Schmidt were both students of Schleicher, as were several of the prominent Neogrammarians. The 'wave theory' was intended to deal with changes due to contact among languages and dialects. According to Schmidt's wave model, linguistic changes spread outward concentrically like waves, which become progressively weaker with the distance from their central point. Since later changes may cover the same area, there may be no sharp boundaries between neighbouring dialects or languages. Rather, the greater the distance between them, the fewer linguistic traits dialects or languages may share. The dialectologists' slogan, that every word has its own history, reflects this thinking – a word's history might be the result of various influences from various directions, and these might be quite different from those involved in another word's history, hence each word has its own (potentially quite different) history.

The dialectologists believed that their findings contradicted the regularity hypothesis of the Neogrammarians; however, that was not really the case. What is at stake here is, in the traditional view, the difference between regular sound change internal to a particular language or dialect and dialect borrowing, change that can be irregular and comes from outside the particular language or dialect. Labov (2010: 305) describes it well, speaking of the distinction 'between transmission within the speech community and diffusion across communities'. Both types of change are important. The first is subject to 'the normal type of [regular] internal language change; it is termed "change from below" or change from within the system, as opposed to "change from above" or the importation of elements from other systems' (Labov 2010: 307) – or for short, the distinction between transmission and diffusion (see below for further discussion).

To see what is meant, let us consider an instructive example from English dialects. The velar fricative /x/ of earlier English is gone from Standard English, either lost (for example, by the rule that deleted the velar fricative before following consonants, $x > Ø / \_\_C$, as in 'light': /lixt/ > /liːt > lait [by the Great Vowel Shift]) or in some cases x changed to /f/ (as in /trox/ > /trɒf/ 'trough'). However, in southern West Yorkshire, the *Survey of English Dialects* (Orton et al. 1962–71) recorded 'occasional relic forms such as [trɒx] for *trough* (whose RP [British Received Pronunciation] is /trɒf/) and [lɪçt] for *light*' (Wells 1982: 190) ([ç] is the allophone of /x/ which appeared after a front vowel such as the /ɪ/ in *light*). That is, a handful of words, which maintain /x/, appear to be exceptions to this change, though the overwhelming majority of words with original /x/ in this geographical region did undergo the changes, deleting /x/ or turning it into /f/ in relevant contexts.

Some dialectologists took cases such as this one as evidence that the Neogrammarian idea of exceptionless sound change must be wrong. A dialectologist might say that each of these words has its own history. For example, a 'homely' word such as *trough*, characteristic of rural life, might more successfully resist the wave of change affecting /x/ which had spread from other, more prestigious dialects. However, there are two important things to notice about this case. First, we can identify these words as exceptions only if we recognize the sound changes which affected /x/ – without acknowledging the sound changes, it would be impossible to recognize these few words in southern West Yorkshire, found at the time of the *Survey of English Dialects*, as exceptions. While these words are exceptions to the strict exceptionlessness of sound change, we cannot explain their individual histories, that they are exceptions, without reference to the sound changes themselves. Second, it is possible that a situation like this one can tell us something more about how some sound changes take place – in this case apparently through the spread of the prestige norm (without /x/) to more remote locations.

This sort of change is traditionally called *dialect borrowing*. Most importantly, this example shows that neither model – neither the family tree nor the wave theory – is sufficient to explain all linguistic change and all the sorts of relationships that can exist between dialects or related languages. Without recognizing the sound change, we would not be able to identify these dialect forms as exceptional, and without the information from dialectology, our knowledge of how some changes are transmitted or how they diffuse would be incomplete. Clearly, both are needed. This being the case, it will pay us to look more closely at some basic aspects of dialectology. (Other aspects of the explanation of change are deferred until Chapter 12.)

9.5.3 Dialectology (linguistic geography, dialect geography)

Dialectology deals with regional variation in a language. Some concepts of dialectology that it is helpful to understood are the following.

Isogloss: a line on a map which represents the geographical boundary (limit) of regional linguistic variants. By extension, the term 'isogloss' also refers to the dialect features themselves, an extension of the original sense of the word from dealing with a line on a map to reference to the actual linguistic phenomena themselves. For example, in the USA the *greasy/greazy* isogloss is a line roughly corresponding to the Mason–Dixon line which separates the North Midlands from the South Midlands dialects; it runs across the middle of the country until it dives down across southeastern Kansas, western Oklahoma, and Texas (see Map 9.1).

North of the line, *greasy* is pronounced with *s*; south of the line it is pronounced with *z*. Another isogloss has to do with a contrast versus lack of contrast in the vowels in such word pairs as *pin/pen* and *tin/ten*. In these words, [ɪ] and [ɛ] before nasals contrast in other dialects, but in the South Midlands and Southern dialect areas there is no contrast – these vowels have merged before nasals in these dialects. This explains how country-music songs, many of whose writers and singers are from the dialect areas which lack the contrast, can rhyme words such as *win* and *end*, both phonetically with [ɪn] (*end* also loses the final consonant [nd > n]), as in the song, *Heartaches by the Number* (recorded by nearly two dozen well-known singers since 1959), where the last line of the refrain goes: 'I've got heartaches by the number for a love that I can't *win*, but the day that I stop countin' is the day my world will *end*.'

Bundle of isoglosses: several isoglosses whose extent coincides at the same geographical boundary; such bundling of isoglosses is taken to constitute the boundary of a dialect (or dialect area). The two examples of isoglosses just mentioned happen to bundle, both along the Mason–Dixon line, with *greasy* and the *pin/pen* contrast north of the line (for example, in the North Midlands dialect area), and with *greazy* and lack of the vowel contrast south of the line (for example, in the South Midlands dialect area) (see Map 9.1).

Focal area: zone of prestige from which innovations spread outwards.

MAP 9.1: Some major dialect areas in the USA

Relic area (*residual area*): an area (usually small) which preserves older forms that have not undergone the innovations that the surrounding areas have; relic areas are often regions of difficult access for cultural, political, or geographical reasons, and thus resistant to the spread of prestige variants from elsewhere. The southern West Yorkshire area mentioned above which retained *x* in certain words is a relic area.

Lect: some scholars feel the need for a more open-ended term which signifies any linguistic variety, whether defined by its geographical distribution or by its use by people from different social classes, castes, ages, genders, and so on. *Lect* is intended to cover all such varieties (geographical dialect, sociolect, idiolect – the language characteristic of a single individual – and so on).

Mutual intelligibility: when speakers of different linguistic entities can understand one another, these entities are said to be mutually intelligible. This is the principal criterion for distinguishing dialects of a single language from distinct languages (which may or may not be closely related). Entities which are totally incomprehensible to speakers of other entities clearly are mutually unintelligible, and for linguists they therefore belong to separate languages. However, the criterion of mutual intelligibility is often not so straightforward. For example, there are cases of non-reciprocal intelligibility (for instance, many Portuguese speakers understand Spanish reasonably well, while many Spanish speakers do not understand Portuguese well) and of non-immediate intelligibility, where upon first exposure understanding is limited, but after a time intelligibility grows. There are many studies in the sociolinguistic and dialecto-logical literature of cases of various sorts having to do with how to determine to which language various dialects belong, often having to do with the relationship of regional varieties to some standard or *superordinate* language or to their posi-tion within a dialect chain. We cannot get into the details here, though these various relationships among varieties are relevant to linguistic change.

Language: the definition of 'language' is not strictly a linguistic enterprise, but sometimes is determined more by political or social factors. For this reason, Max Weinreich's famous definition is frequently reported: *a language is a dialect which has an army and a navy*. This emphasizes that what is considered a distinct 'language' is not merely a linguistic matter. For example, while speakers of Norwegian and Swedish have little difficulty understanding one another (they are mutually intelligible for the most part), they are considered separate languages for polit-ical reasons. On the other hand, Chinese has several so-called 'dialects' which are so different one from another that their speakers do not easily understand each other. By the criterion of mutual intelligibility, linguists consider these to be separate languages; however, official policy in China regards many of them as representing the same language.

Although the literature on the history of linguistics often disposes us to think that dialectology played an important role in giving us the wave theory, with its slogan 'every word has its own history', in fact the study of dialects also significantly influenced the Neogrammarians and the origin of their slogan, that 'sound laws suffer no exceptions'. The Neogrammarian founders were impressed by Jost Winteler's (1876) study of the Kerenzen dialect of Swiss German, in which he presented phonological statements as processes (following the ancient rules for Sanskrit of Pāṇini, an important Hindu grammarian from around the fifth century BC, which Winteler studied in his linguistic training). The 'regularity' observed in Winteler's (synchronic) rules for the dialect – for example, in Kerenzen every *n* became *ŋ* before *k* and *g* – inspired the Neogrammarian founders to have confidence in the exceptionlessness of sound changes (Weinreich et al. 1968: 115). Of course, as we saw, Gilliéron (1921), who opposed regularity, also based his objections on what he observed in the study of dialects, arguing against the Neogrammarians, with the other slogan, 'every word has its own history'. Ironically, both these famous orientations to historical linguistics were influenced significantly by dialect studies.

The conflict between the Neogrammarians' 'exceptionless sound change' and the dialectologists' 'every word has its own history' is implicated in more recent controversies over how sound change is transmitted. This controversy will be considered presently, but first it will be helpful to have in mind the general frame-work which has been very significant in thinking in this area, that of Weinreich, Labov, and Herzog (1968).

9.5.4 A framework for investigating the causes of linguistic change

The framework presented by Weinreich, Labov, and Herzog (1968) has been very influential in historical linguistic thought concerning 'why' and 'how' linguistic changes take place (see Chapter 12). These authors asked a number of questions, which they also called 'problems', which must be answered (or 'solved') by any theory that hopes to explain language change. These are:

(1) *The constraints problem*: what are the general constraints on change that determine possible and impossible changes and directions of change? For example, among the constraints on change, Weinreich et al. (1968: 100) postulate that 'no language will assume a form in violation of such formal principles as are . . . universal in human languages'. The constraints problem is a central issue in linguistic change for many scholars; it takes the form of a search for the kinds of linguistic change that will *not* take place. The irreversibility of mergers (see Chapter 2) is a good example of such a constraint.

(2) *The transition problem*: how (or by what route or routes) does language change? What intermediate stages or processes does a language go through to get from a state before the change began to the state after the change has taken place? For example, a much-debated question is whether certain kinds of changes must be seen as gradual or abrupt.

(3) *The embedding problem*: how is a given language change embedded in the surrounding system of linguistic and social relations? How does the greater environment in which the change takes place influence the change? That is, the parts of a language are tightly interwoven, often in complex interlocking relationships, so that a change in one part of the grammar may have an impact on (or be constrained by) other parts of the grammar (see Chapter 12). Also, language change takes place in a social environment, where differences in language may be given positive or negative sociolinguistic status, and this sociolinguistic environment plays an important role in change.

(4) *The evaluation problem*: how do speakers of the language (members of a speech community) evaluate a given change, and what is the effect of their evaluation on the change? What are the effects of the change on the language's overall structure? (How does the system change without damage to its function of serving communication?)

(5) *The actuation problem*: why does a given linguistic change occur at the particular time and place that it does? How do changes begin and proceed? What starts a change and what carries it along? The actuation question is the most central, since the other questions relate to it. If we succeed in answering the actuation question, we will be able to explain linguistic change (see Chapter 12).

9.6 Sociolinguistics and Language Change

Changes typically begin with variation, with alternative ways of saying the same thing entering the language. Variation is the specific subject matter of sociolinguistics, and while sociolinguists are also interested in many other things in addition to linguistic change, sociolinguistics is extremely relevant to understanding how and why languages change. Sociolinguistic concerns underlie the questions in Weinreich et al.'s (1968) framework (just considered). Sociolinguistics deals with the systematic co-variation of linguistic structure with social structure, especially with the variation in language which is conditioned by social differences. The most important dimensions which can condition variation have to do with social attributes of the sender (speaker), the receiver (hearer), and the setting (context). Variation in a language can be conditioned by such social characteristics of the speaker as age, gender, social status, ethnic identity, religion, occupation, self-identification with a location or a group, and in fact by almost any important social trait.

Let's consider just a couple of examples of some of these to get a flavour of what is involved. Grammars of Classical Nahuatl report that where Aztec men pronounced *w*, women spoke the same words with *v*. This is linguistic variation conditioned by the gender of the speaker. Since Proto-Uto-Aztecan (Nahuatl's parent language) had *w in these words, it is necessary to conclude that the *w/v* variation in Classical Nahuatl is due to a linguistic change which women adopted, *$w > v$, but men did not. An example reflecting the social status of the speaker is the variation in the Hindi of Khalapur village in India (in Uttar Pradesh) where in words with a stressed vowel in the next syllable, the higher castes contrast /ʊ/ and /ə/, but the lower castes have only /ə/ both in words with /ʊ/ and those with /ə/ in the speech of the higher castes (as seen in, for example, higher caste *dʊtə́i*/low caste *dətə́i* 'blanket'). Here, it appears that there has been a sound change in which ʊ and ə have merged with ə (ʊ, ə > ə) in the language of the low-caste speakers, affecting the language of only a portion of the population, leading to the socially conditioned variation in speech characteristic of the different castes. Many similar examples could be presented for the various other social attributes of speakers. Similarly, social attributes of hearers can condition linguistic variation. This sort of variation is often indicative of changes in progress in a speech community, and this makes the study of such variation and its implications for understanding linguistic change in general extremely important.

Sociolinguistic investigations of change have been of two types: *apparent-time* and *real-time* studies. In apparent-time research, by far the more common, a *variable* (a linguistic trait subject to social or stylistic variation) is investigated at one particular point in time. To the extent that the variation correlates with age, it is assumed that a change in progress is under way and that the variant most characteristic of older speakers' speech represents the earlier stage and the variant more typical of younger speakers' speech shows what it is changing to. The age-gradient distribution shows the change in progress. An example of this sort is the ongoing merger of diphthongs /iə/ (as in *ear, cheer*) and /ɛə/ (as in *air, chair*) in New Zealand English: where in general older speakers maintain the contrast more, most younger speakers merge the two to /iə/, hence jokes based on the homophony of for example 'beer' and 'bear' (see Maclagan and Gordon 1996). Real-time studies compare samples of language from different times; for example, a comparison of recordings from fifty years ago with comparable samples of speech today can reveal changes, as for example in New Zealand English (Gordon et al. 2004). (See Labov 1994 for discussion of several examples.)

Some general claims about linguistic change which have been made based on large-scale sociolinguistic investigations in urban settings include:

1. Women lead most linguistic changes (women accept and help to propagate the linguistic changes earlier than men do).
2. Linguistic changes originate in the intermediate social classes (the upper working class or lower middle class), not in the highest or the lowest socio-economic classes.
3. The innovators of change are usually people with the highest local status who play a central role within the particular speech community.
4. These innovators have the highest density of social interactions within their communication networks and they have the highest proportions of contacts outside the local neighbourhood, as well.
5. Different ethnic groups who newly enter a speech community participate in changes in progress only to the extent that they begin to gain local rights and privileges in jobs and housing, and access to or acceptance in the society. (See Labov 1994, 2001.)

Several of these claims are currently being challenged or refined – for example, there is a range of opinion concerning whether (4) holds up, even in the urban settings for which it is designed. Some of these claims may be appropriate only to modern settings; it is important to determine to what extent these and other claims may be true of changes which take place in languages spoken in societies and social settings with very different social organization, subsistence patterns, and economic practices, less nucleated settlements, and so on.

A number of influential historical linguists (for example, Henning Andersen, Eugenio Coseriu, Brian Joseph, James Milroy) hold that speakers change, and not languages, making all linguistic change social change, rather than language change per se. Some go so far as to deny any language-internal motivation (arising from the structural aspects of the language itself) for language change. Most historical linguists, however, disagree with this, since there is strong evidence that the explanation of some aspects of linguistic change requires appeal to non-social factors. For example, how could the approach which views linguistic change as merely a kind of social change explain why certain changes (for example, intervocalic voicing of stops) recur in language after language, despite the vastly different social settings in which these different languages are used? The explanation of linguistic change is not found solely in conscious change by speakers for social purposes, rather only rarely so. Both internal and external factors are important (explained in detail in Chapter 12).

Different conceptions of linguistic change are often closely linked with the stand taken on the *actuation problem* (mentioned above). For example, James Milroy (1992: 10) stresses network theory's emphasis on language *maintenance*: 'In order to account for differential patterns of change at particular times and places [that is, to solve the actuation problem], we need first to take account of those factors that tend to maintain language states and resist change.' Strong network ties are seen as norm-enforcement mechanisms, a model for maintenance of local language norms against encroaching change from outside the network. However, how can the actuation problem, the question about how changes get started in the first place, be approached with a model based solely on norm maintenance, that is, on resistance to change but not on change itself? In Milroy's view, linguistic change takes place in strong-tie networks only to the extent that they fail in their primary mission of maintaining the network norms and resisting change from outside. If the social network can only resist but not initiate change, with all change entering from without, how could network theory contribute to solving the actuation problem? The origins of these changes in the broader community from where they flow into the strong-tie networks would appear to be more relevant to the actuation problem and generally to understanding how and why languages change.

9.6.1 Historical sociolinguistics

Historical sociolinguistics (also called sociohistorical linguistics) is a relatively new subfield (research concentration) in linguistics, which now has conferences and a journal of its own, in addition to books and articles dedicated to it. It is understood as the application of sociolinguistic methods and models to the study of historical language variation and language change over time. Put differently, it is the study of the interaction of language and society in historical periods and from historical perspectives. Thus, a wide range of areas of linguistic subdisciplines and methodologies are seen in works on historical sociolinguistics. This range of interests and approaches may make historical sociolinguistics seem diffuse and not well-defined; nevertheless, significant results have come from work characterized as historical sociolinguistics. (See for example the chapters of Hernández-Campoy and Conde-Silvestre 2014.)

9.6.2 The issue of lexical diffusion

For the Neogrammarians, the three primary mechanisms of change were regular sound change, analogy, and borrowing. Regularity for them meant that every instance of a sound changes mechanically, irrespective of particular words in which it is found; that is, that it affects every word in which the sound occurs in the same phonetic environment. Cases where a change does not affect all words in the same way at the same time (under the same phonetic conditions) were not seen to be the result of regular sound change, but as due to analogy or to dialect borrowing, as in the case of the variable result of the *x > Ø change in different words in southern West Yorkshire (above) due to the differential impact of dialect borrowing from the prestige variety. This, in essence, constitutes an attempt to answer the transition question of how change is implemented. The concept of *lexical diffusion*, promoted by William Wang and his associates (Wang 1969; see Labov 1994: 421–543; 2020 for an extensive survey and evaluation), challenges Neogrammarian regularity. They do not see sound change as being implemented by mechanically affecting every instance of a sound in stipulated phonetic environments regardless of the particular words in which instances of the sound are found (as in the Neogrammarian position). Rather, they see sound change as affecting the sound in certain words and then diffusing gradually to other words in the lexicon. Fully regular sound changes, in this view, are those in which the change diffuses across the lexicon until it reaches all relevant words. This is like 'dialect borrowing', but with some words borrowing from others in the same dialect. It constitutes a different outlook on the transition problem. It should be kept in mind, however, that in spite of strong claims that lexical diffusion is a more basic mechanism by which sound change is transmitted than Neogrammarian regularity, very few cases of lexical diffusion have actually been reported and most of these are doubtful.

While several cases have been analysed as involving lexical diffusion, most mainstream historical linguists have not been convinced. They see these cases as being better explained as the results of dialect borrowing, analogy, and erroneous analyses. On closer scrutiny, most of these cases prove not to be real instances of lexical diffusion but to be more reliably explained by other means. Often it turns out that the phonetic conditioning environments are quite complex – important phonetic environments were missed in several of the cases for which lexical diffusion was claimed. Detailed studies of the same cases by people aware of the claims for lexical diffusion have found sounds behaving regularly in changes in these environments with no evidence of lexical conditioning. When these environments are understood more fully, Neogrammarian regularity is what is behind many of the changes and not lexical diffusion after all. In the examples from the history of Chinese, which had been considered influential support for lexical diffusion, it turns out that the extent of borrowing from literary Chinese into the varieties of Chinese studied was vastly more extensive than originally thought. That is, like the southern West Yorkshire case, they amounted to just dialect borrowing, which proponents of lexical diffusion later called 'intimate borrowing'; these cases were a misreading of the influence of stylistic choices, language contact, and sociolinguistic conditions in general. (See Labov 1994: 444–71.)

With this background, let us consider again the irregularities often pointed out in the dialect atlases of various languages and the assumed hostility of dialect atlas data to the Neogrammarian regularity hypothesis. The collectors of the dialect atlas data did not take into account the fact that commonly the data collected from local dialects were the result of long interaction between local dialect forms and the dominant prestige or standard language, as in the case of the English forms recorded in southern West Yorkshire. These atlas forms did not come to us recorded with tags identifying which words represent an uninterrupted inheritance from an original form versus which were replaced due to influence from an external source. Also, the methods involved in collecting the data for the atlases were not sufficiently sensitive to different styles and socially conditioned variation and were not geared to looking for complex phonetic conditioning environments. It is little wonder, then, that with dialect atlas evidence alone we seem to see support for the slogan 'each word has its own history'; however, with more detailed information on the social interaction of different varieties/dialects and on phonetic conditioning factors, we find the Neogrammarian regularity more firmly supported. The irregularities seem to develop not internally to a system, but through interaction or interference among systems (Labov 1994: 474). The Neogrammarians with their 'dialect borrowing' account were right all along! In fact, evidence of regular, phonetically conditioned sound change (and not lexical diffusion) in dialect geography turns out to be strong in the cases which have been investigated in detail (Labov 1994: 501; 2020).

Labov has attempted to reconcile the mostly regular changes with the few which seem to involve sound changes which affect some lexical items but not others. He notes that 'earlier stages of change are quite immune to such irregular lexical reactions [as implied in lexical diffusion]; and even in a late stage, the unreflecting use of the vernacular preserves that regularity' (Labov 1994: 453). This he calls 'change from below', that is, below the level of awareness. Only in later stages of a change do speakers become aware of the change and give it sociolinguistic value (positive or negative), and this often involves the social importance of words. Change of this sort is what Labov calls 'change from above'. For him, lexical diffusion can involve only the later stages and change from above, the same changes which are often characterized by dialect mixture and analogical change, by a higher degree of social awareness or of borrowing from another system (Labov 1994: 542–3).

In summary, sound change is regular within its own system, though dialect borrowing and various influences from outside the system can result in changes which are less like regular exceptionless sound change. Consequently, to explain change we need both 'sound laws suffer no exceptions' and 'every word has its own history' – they address different things, both of which are important for the full picture of linguistic change.

Some of the topics of this chapter are considered further in relation to the explanation of linguistic change in Chapter 12. The discussion of distant genetic relationships in Chapter 13 logically also belongs in this chapter on classification. Nevertheless, it is important to consider first other matters, particularly language contact (Chapter 10), that are relevant to understanding issues involved in hypotheses of remote linguistic kinship.

9.7 Exercises

Exercise 9.1 Polynesian subgrouping

There are numerous Polynesian languages, of which the ones in this exercise are only a sample. Polynesian is a branch (subgroup) of the Austronesian family. Consider the two cognate sets from these five Polynesian languages. What sound change has taken place? Observe which languages underwent the change and which ones did not, and on this basis draw all the alternative possible family trees that could account for the subgrouping of these languages. Present your arguments for the tree with the subgrouping you think is most accurate.

HINT: Which languages share an innovation? Which languages share a retention?

NOTE: The medial consonant, spelled <ng> or <g>, is /ŋ/ in these languages.

Proto-Polynesian	*songi 'smell'	*sae 'to tear'
Tongan	hongi [hoŋi]	hae
Niuean	hongi [hoŋi]	hee

Proto-Polynesian	*songi 'smell'	*sae 'to tear'
Samoan	sogi [soŋi]	sae
East Futuna	sogi [soŋi]	sae
Luangiua	songi [soŋi]	sae

(data from Otsuka 2005)

Exercise 9.2 Barbacoan subgrouping

Barbacoan is a small family of languages spoken in Colombia and Ecuador; its members include Awa Pit, Cha'palaachi, Guambiano, Totoró, and Tsafiqui. Consider the following sound changes in the various Barbacoan languages. On the basis of these, draw the most likely family tree which represents the subgrouping of the Barbacoan family. Explain what facts lead you to this decision.

The Proto-Barbacoan vowels were *i, *i, *u, *a.

NOTE: č = IPA [ʧ]; š = IPA [ʃ]. ʦ is a single segment (an affricate), not a consonant cluster.

1. Proto-Barbacoan *t > č /__i (when before i) in Guambiano
2. Proto-Barbacoan *t > č /__i (when before i) in Totoró
3. Proto-Barbacoan *t > š /__i (when before i) in Awa Pit
4. Proto-Barbacoan *t > ʦ elsewhere (when not before i) in Guambiano
5. Proto-Barbacoan *t > ʦ elsewhere (when not before i) in Totoró
6. Proto-Barbacoan *t > s elsewhere (when not before i) in Awa Pit
7. Proto-Barbacoan *š > Ø /__# (lost word-finally) in Guambiano
8. Proto-Barbacoan *š > Ø /__# (lost word-finally) in Totoró
9. Proto-Barbacoan *l > n /#__i (before i) in Guambiano
10. Proto-Barbacoan *l > n /#__i (before i) in Totoró
11. Proto-Barbacoan *l > n /#__i (before i) in Awakateko
12. Proto-Barbacoan *p, *t, *k > Ø /__# (stops lost word-finally) in Cha'palaachi
13. Proto-Barbacoan *p, *t, *k > Ø /__# (stops lost word-finally) in Tsafiqui
14. Proto-Barbacoan *s > h in Cha'palaachi
15. Proto-Barbacoan *s > h in Tsafiqui

(adapted from Curnow and Liddicoat 1998)

Exercise 9.3 Other subgrouping exercises

Return to your reconstructions of Proto-Polynesian (Exercise 7.5), Proto-Uto-Aztecan (Exercise 7.7), and Proto-K'ichean (Exercise 7.10) and, based on your reconstruction and the sound changes that you postulated for each language, attempt to establish the subgroupings in these language families and present the family trees that represent them. Doing the subgrouping of these language families may prove difficult, depending on what you reconstructed and on the number and kind of sound changes that you postulated in each of these reconstruction exercises.

For additional subgrouping exercises with solutions, see Blust (2018: 174–94, 417–72).

10

LANGUAGE CONTACT

Es gibt keine Mischsprache. [There is no mixed language.]

(Max Müller 1871: 86)

Es gibt keine völlig ungemischte Sprache. [There is no totally unmixed language.]

(Hugo Schuchardt 1884: 5)

10.1 Introduction

When historical linguists speak of language contact, they usually mean change in languages caused by interaction among languages. Some prefer to speak of *contact-induced language change*. Sometimes the study of language contact is called 'contact linguistics'. This usually includes borrowing, multilingualism, areal linguistics, pidgin and creole languages, language shift and maintenance, language endangerment, code-switching, sometimes mixed languages, and sometimes also other topics. In this chapter we look at how historical linguists deal with change due to language contact. In particular, we look at what can be borrowed beyond just words, at areal linguistics, pidgin and creole languages, mixed languages, and language endangerment. (See Chapter 3 for loanwords and borrowing generally; the role of language contact in syntactic change is treated in Chapter 11.)

10.2 What Can Be Borrowed besides Just Words?

Not only can words be borrowed, but also sounds, phonological features, morphology, syntactic constructions, and in fact virtually any aspect of language can be borrowed, given enough time and the appropriate sorts of contact situations.

10.2.1 Borrowed sounds used in native lexical items

Foreign sounds can be borrowed – that is, speakers of one language can borrow sounds from another language with which they are familiar. There are two main ways in which non-native sounds can end up in native words: through areal diffusion (see below) and through onomatopoeia and expressive symbolism.

As seen in Chapter 3, foreign sounds can enter a language along with abundant loanwords from another language. Through intense long-term contact, foreign sounds can be borrowed and come to occur even in native, non-borrowed words. A few examples are: the clicks borrowed from so-called Khoisan languages (Khoe and San languages) of southern Africa into some neighbouring Bantu languages (for example, Xhosa, Zulu, Sotho; Proto-Bantu had no clicks); glottalized consonants borrowed into Ossetic and Eastern Armenian from neighbouring languages in the Caucasus linguistic area; and the retroflex consonants of Indo-Aryan languages, which owe their origin to contact with Dravidian languages in the South Asian (Indian) linguistic area (see below; Campbell 1976).

Expressive symbolism is the use of certain phonetic traits to symbolize affectations, heightened expressive value, or the speaker's attitude. An example of a foreign sound which has been extended into native words through onomatopoeia and affective symbolism is the *r* of Chol and Tzotzil (two Mayan languages). Before contact with Spanish, these languages had no *r*; this sound was introduced through Spanish loanwords which contained it, for example Chol *arus* 'rice' < Spanish *arroz* /aros/, and Tzotzil *martoma* 'custodian' < Spanish *mayordomo* 'butler, steward'. After *r* was introduced in loanwords, this new sound – which apparently seemed exotic to the speakers of these languages – came to be employed also in certain native words for onomatopoeic or expressive purposes, for example, Chol *buruk-ña* 'buzzing, humming', *burbur-ña* 'noisily', *porok-ña* 'breathing when there is an obstruction', *sorok-ña* 'bubbling'. Some of the expressive Tzotzil words which now have the *r*, first introduced via loanwords from Spanish that contained *r*, formerly had only *l*; for example, *ner-iš* 'cross-eyed' had *l* earlier; Colonial Tzotzil had only *nel-iš* (compare *nel-* 'crooked, twisted, slanted'). The word **kelem* 'strong young man, male' has split into two in modern Tzotzil: *kerem* 'boy (affective)' and *kelem* 'rooster' – Colonial Tzotzil had only *kelem* 'boy, bachelor, servant' (Campbell 1996).

It should be mentioned that in general the introduction of foreign sounds into native words is quite rare. Most foreign sounds enter a borrowing language along with borrowed words which have the new sounds in them.

10.2.2 Shifts in native sounds

Another kind of change that can take place in language contact situations is the shift in native sounds to approximate more closely to phonetic traits of sounds in neighbouring languages. For example, Creek (a Muskogean language of the southern USA) shifted its ϕ (voiceless bilabial fricative) to *f* (labiodental) under

English influence. Finnish *ð* shifted to *d* under influence from Swedish, due in part to the Swedish reading model with *d* which was imposed in Finnish schools (Campbell 1976).

10.2.3 Elimination of sounds through language contact

Not only can foreign sounds be acquired through diffusion, but language contact can also lead to the elimination of sounds (or features of sounds). Some examples of loss of this sort due to language contact include the merger of /l/ and /ľ/ in Czech to / l/, attributed to German influence in the fashionable speech of the cities (Weinreich 1953: 25), and loss of the emphatic (pharyngealized) consonants and of vowel length in Cypriotic Arabic under the influence of Cypriotic Greek (Campbell 1976). Proto-Nootkan had nasals, as Nuu-chah-nulth (Nootka) still does, but closely related Nitinat and Makah lost nasality – former nasals became corresponding voiced oral stops (*m > *b*, *n > *d*, **m̓* > *b'*, **n̓* > *d'*) – due to diffusion within the linguistic area. Nitinat and Makah are in a region of the Northwest Coast of North America where languages of several different families lack nasal consonants. The lack of nasals in Nitinat and Makah is due to the influence of other nasal-less languages in the linguistic area (see below).

10.2.4 Retention of native sounds due to language contact

In addition to the loss of sounds, language contact can also sometimes contribute to the retention of a sound, even if that sound is lost in other areas where the language is spoken which are not in contact with languages that influence the retention. For example, /ľ/ (IPA [ʎ], spelled <ll>) persists in the Spanish of the Andes region, even though in nearly all other areas of Latin America /ľ/ has merged with *y* (IPA [j]). The area where Spanish in the New World has maintained this contrast coincides closely with the region where Quechuan and Aymaran languages are spoken, which have phonemic /ľ/. Thus, it is due to contact with languages which have the *ľ* that the Spanish of this region preserves /ľ/ in contrast with /y/, a contrast lost in most other varieties of Latin American Spanish.

10.2.5 Borrowed rules

Not only can foreign sounds be borrowed, but foreign phonological rules (constraints) may also be borrowed. For example, the French spoken in Quimper borrowed a rule of final consonant devoicing from Breton, spoken in that region. Several Greek dialects of Asia Minor have incorporated a vowel-harmony rule under influence from Turkish. The rule of first syllable stress diffused among many of the languages in the Baltic linguistic area. The rule which places stress on the vowel before the last consonant (V → V́ /__C(V)#) diffused and came to be shared by several unrelated indigenous languages of southern Mexico and Guatemala. The rule which palatalizes velar stops when followed by a uvular

MAP 10.1: Diffusion of Velar palatalization rule in K'ichean languages (redrawn after Campbell 1977: Map 1)

consonant in the same root (for example, *k'aq* → *kʲ'aq* 'flea'; *ke꞉χ* → *kʲe꞉χ* 'deer') was borrowed from Mamean languages into the adjacent dialects of several K'ichean languages (two distinct subbranches of the Mayan family), as shown in Map 10.1. (See Campbell 1976, 1977.)

10.2.6 Diffused sound changes

Related to borrowed phonological rules is the borrowing of sound changes from one language to another. For example, the change of *k* to *č* (IPA [tʃ]) diffused throughout the languages of a continuous area of the Northwest Coast of North America from Vancouver Island to the Columbia River, affecting languages of several different families. A similar change of *k* to *c* (a laminal palato-alveolar affricate) before front vowels diffused through Telugu, Tamil, Malayalam, some dialects of Tulu (Dravidian languages), and Marathi (Indo-Aryan) (in several of these languages, *c* before front vowels is in complementary distribution with *ts* before back vowels). The sound change of *ts* to *s* diffused after European contact among neighbouring Q'eqchi', Poqomchi', and Poqomam (Mayan languages) (Campbell 1977).

10.2.7 Borrowed bound morphology

It has been widely believed that languages do not borrow bound morphology or that they do so only very rarely. It is true that borrowing of bound morphemes is unusual, but still many cases are attested.

In English alone we have several instances of borrowed suffixes that can be added productively to roots to create new words: *-ess* (< French *-esse*, as in *actress*, *goddess*, *lioness*); *-ee* (< Anglo-French *-é* 'past participle' [used as a noun], *addressee*, *jailee*, *stalkee*, *trustee*); *-esque* < French *-esque* 'like, in the manner of', *Hollywoodesque*, *Tolkienesque*, *vampiresque*); *-ette* (< French *-ette* 'diminutive [FEMININE]', *bachelorette*, *dinette*, *featurette*); *-oid* (< Latinized form from Greek *-oeidēs* 'form', *android*, *factoid*, *opioid*, *planetoid*); *-ism* (< French *-isme* and directly from Latin *-isma/-ismus* 'deriving nouns that imply a practice, system, or doctrine', *racism*, *sexism*, *structuralism*); *-ist* (< French *-iste* and directly from Latin *-ista* 'one who does or makes', *activist*, *capitalist*, *environmentalist*); and *-nik* (first some English words were borrowed from Yiddish words that contained the suffix *-nik*, which is itself borrowed into Yiddish from Russian *-nik* 'person or thing associated with or involved in'; then new English words were created by attaching this foreign suffix to regular existing English words, as in *beatnik*, *peacenik*, *refusenik*).

See Chapter 11 for examples and discussion of syntactic borrowing.

10.3 Areal Linguistics

Areal linguistics is concerned with the diffusion of structural features across languages within a geographical area. This section defines areal linguistics, surveys the features of a few of the better-known linguistic areas of the world, and then addresses issues concerning how areally diffused features are identified and how linguistic areas are established. (See Chapter 13 for the impact areal linguistics has on other aspects of historical linguistics – its implications for subgrouping, reconstruction, and proposals of distant genetic relationship.) Areal linguistics is very important because the goal of historical linguistics is to determine the full history of languages, to find out what really happened. The full history includes understanding both inherited traits (traits shared in genealogically related languages because they come from a common parent language) and diffused features (traits shared because of borrowing and diffusion among neighbouring languages).

10.3.1 Defining the concept

The term *linguistic area* refers to a geographical area in which, due to language contact, languages of a region come to share certain structural features – not only borrowed words, but shared elements of phonological, morphological, or syntactic structure. Linguistic areas are also referred to at times by the terms *Sprachbund*, *diffusion area*, *adstratum*, and *convergence area*. The central feature of a linguistic area is the existence of structural similarities shared among languages of a geographical area (where usually some of the languages are genetically unrelated or at least are not all close relatives). It is assumed that the reason why the languages of the area share these traits is because at least some of the traits are borrowed.

While some linguistic areas are reasonably well established, more investigation is required for nearly all of them. Some other linguistic areas amount to barely more than preliminary hypotheses. Most linguistic areas are defined, surprisingly, by a rather small number of shared linguistic traits.

10.3.2 Examples of linguistic areas

A good way to get a solid feel for linguistic areas and how they are defined is to look at some of the better-known ones. In what follows, some are presented with the more important of the generally accepted traits shared by the languages of each linguistic area considered here.

(1) *The Balkans.* The languages of the Balkans linguistic area are Greek, Albanian, Serbo-Croatian, Bulgarian, Macedonian, and Romanian (to which some scholars also add Romani [the language of the Rom (formerly called Gypsies)] and Turkish). Some salient traits of the Balkans linguistic area are:

1. A central vowel /ɨ/ (or /ə/) (not present in Greek or Macedonian).
2. Syncretism of dative and genitive (dative and genitive cases have merged in form and function); this is illustrated by Romanian *fetei* 'to the girl' or 'girl's' (compare *fată* 'girl'; *ă* represents a short or reduced *a*), as in *am dat o carte fetei* 'I gave the letter to the girl' and *fratele fetei* 'the girl's brother'.
3. Postposed articles (not in Greek); for example, Bulgarian *mɔʒ-ət* 'the man'/ *mɔʒ* 'man'. (In *mɔʒ* the /ʒ/ is phonetically voiceless word-finally, [ʃ].)
4. Periphrastic future (futures signalled by an auxiliary verb corresponding to 'want' or 'have'; not in Bulgarian or Macedonian), as in Romanian *voi fuma* 'I will smoke' (literally 'I want smoke') and *am să scriu* 'I will write' (literally 'I have that[SUBJUNCTIVE] I write').
5. Periphrastic perfect (with an auxiliary verb corresponding to 'have').
6. Absence of infinitives (instead, the languages have constructions such as 'I want that I go' for 'I want to go'); for example, 'give me something to drink' has the form corresponding to 'give me that I drink', as in Romanian *dă-mi să beau*, Bulgarian *daj mi da pija*.
7. Use of a personal pronoun copy of animate objects so that the object is doubly marked, as in Romanian *i-am scris lui Ioan* 'I wrote to John', literally 'to.him-I wrote him John', and Greek *ton vlépo ton jáni* 'I see John', literally 'him.ACCUSATIVE I see the/him.ACCUSATIVE John' (Joseph 1992; Sandfeld 1930).

(2) *South Asia (Indian subcontinent).* This area is composed of languages that belong to Indo-Aryan (a branch of Indo-European), Dravidian, Munda (a branch of the broader Austroasiatic family), and Tibeto-Burman (a branch of Sino-Tibetan). Some traits shared among different languages of the area are:

1. Retroflex consonants, particularly retroflex stops.
2. Absence of prefixes (except in Munda).
3. Presence of a 'dative-subject construction' (that is, dative-experiencer, as in Hindi *mujhe maaluum thaa* 'I knew it' [*mujhe* 'to me' + know + PAST], *mujhe yah pasand hai* 'I like it' [to.me + this + like + Past]).
4. Subject–Object–Verb (SOV) basic word order, including postpositions.
5. Absence of a verb 'to have'.
6. The 'conjunctive or absolutive participle' (tendency for subordinate clauses to have non-finite verb forms and for them to be preposed; for example, relative clauses precede the nouns they modify).
7. Morphological causatives.
8. So-called 'explicator compound verbs' (where a special auxiliary from a limited set is said to complete the sense of the immediately preceding main verb and the two verbs together refer to a single event, as in, for example, Hindi *kho baithanaa* 'to lose' ['lose' + 'sit'], and *le jaanaa* 'to take away' ['take' + 'go']).
9. Sound symbolic (phonaesthetic) forms based on reduplication, often with *k* suffixed (for example in Kota, a Dravidian language: *kad-kadk* '[heart or mind] beats fast with guilt or worry'; *aːnk-aːnk* 'to be very strong [of man, bullock], very beautiful [of woman]').

Some of these proposed areal features are not limited to the Indian subcontinent, but can also be found in neighbouring languages outside the linguistic area. For example, SOV basic word order is also found throughout much of Eurasia and northern Africa, and in languages in many other parts of the world. Some of the traits are not necessarily independent of one another; for example, languages with SOV basic word order tend to have non-finite subordinate clauses too (as in (6)), especially true of relative clauses, and not to have prefixes. (See Emeneau 1980.)

(3) *Mesoamerica.* The language families and isolates which make up the Mesoamerican linguistic area are: Nahua (branch of Uto-Aztecan), Mixe-Zoquean, Mayan, Xinkan, Otomanguean, Totonacan, Purépecha (aka Tarascan), Cuitlatec, Tequistlatecan, and Huave. Five areal traits are shared by nearly all Mesoamerican languages, but not by neighbouring languages beyond this area, and these are considered particularly diagnostic of the linguistic area. They are:

1. Nominal possession of the type *his-dog the man* 'the man's dog', as illustrated by Pipil (Uto-Aztecan): *i-peːlu ne taːkat*, literally 'his-dog the man'.
2. Relational nouns (locative expressions composed of noun roots and possessive pronominal affixes), of the form, for example, *my-head* for 'on me', as in Tz'utujil (Mayan): *(č)r-iːx* 'behind it, at the back of it', composed of *č-* 'at, in', *r-* 'his/her/its' and *-iːx* 'back', contrasted with *č-w-iːx* 'behind me', literally 'at-my-back' (*w-* 'my').
3. Vigesimal numeral systems based on combinations of twenty, such as that of Chol (Mayan): *hun-kʼal* '20' (1 × 20), *čaʔ-kʼal* '40' (2 × 20), *uš-kʼal* '60' (3 × 20),

ho?-k'al '100' (5 × 20), *hun-bahk'* '400' (1 × 400), *ča?-bahk'* '800' (2 × 400), and so on.

4. Non-verb-final basic word order (no SOV languages) – although Mesoamerica is surrounded by languages both to the north and south which have SOV (Subject–Object–Verb) basic word order, languages within the linguistic area have VOS, VSO, or SVO basic order, but not SOV.

5. A large number of loan translation compounds (calques) are shared by the Mesoamerican languages; these include examples such as 'boa' = 'deer-snake', 'egg' = 'bird-stone/bone', 'lime' = 'stone(-ash)', 'knee' = 'leg-head', and 'wrist' = 'hand-neck'.

Since these five traits are shared almost unanimously throughout the languages of Mesoamerica but are found almost not at all in neighbouring languages outside of Mesoamerica, they are considered strong evidence in support of the validity of Mesoamerica as a linguistic area.

Additionally, many other features are shared among several Mesoamerican languages but are not found in all the languages of the area, while other traits shared among the Mesoamerican languages are also found in some languages beyond the borders of the area. Examples of these sorts include:

1. Devoicing of final sonorant consonants (*l, r, w, y*) (K'ichean, Nahuatl, Pipil, Xinkan, Totonac, Tepehua, Purépecha (Tarascan), and Sierra Popoluca), as for example in Nahuatl /no-mi:l/ [no-mi:l̥] 'my cornfield'.

2. Voicing of obstruents after nasals (most Otomanguean languages, Purépecha (Tarascan), Mixe-Zoquean, Huave, Xinkan), as in Copainalá Zoque /n-tik/ [ndik] 'my house'.

3. Predictable stress; most Mesoamerican languages have predictable stress (contrastive stress is rare in the area). Some of the languages share the rule which places the stress on the vowel before the last (right-most) consonant of the word (V́ /__C(V)#) (Oluta Popoluca, Totontepec Mixe, Xinkan, and many Mayan languages; in these Mayan languages, the stress falls on the final syllable, since generally morphemes end in a consonant and do not end in a vowel).

4. Inalienable possession of body parts and kinship terms (in almost all Mesoamerican languages; however, this feature is characteristic of many languages throughout the Americas).

5. Numeral classifiers (many Mayan languages, plus Purépecha (Tarascan), Totonac, Nahuatl, and so on), as in Tzeltal (Mayan) *oš-**tehk** te?* [three plant-thing wood] 'three trees', *oš-**k'as** te?* [three broken-thing wood] 'three chunks of firewood'.

6a. Noun incorporation, a construction where a nominal object can become part of the verb, is found in some Mayan languages (Yucatec, Mam), Nahua, and Totonac. An example is Nahuatl *ni-**tlaškal**-čiwa* [I-tortilla(s)-make] 'I make tortillas'.

6b. Body-part incorporation (Nahuatl, Pipil, Totonac, Mixe-Zoquean, Tlapanec, Purépecha (Tarascan)), a sort of noun incorporation where specific forms for body parts can be incorporated in the verb, usually functioning as instrumentals, though sometimes also as direct objects, as for example in Pipil (Uto-Aztecan): **tan**-*kwa* [tooth-eat] 'bite', **ikši**-*ahsi* [foot-arrive] 'to reach, overtake', *mu*-**yaka**-*pitsa* [REFLEXIVE-nose-blow] 'to blow one's nose'. This type of construction is also found in various languages elsewhere in the Americas.

7. Directional morphemes ('away from' or 'towards') incorporated into the verb (Mayan, Nahua, Tequistlatecan, Purépecha (Tarascan), some Otomanguean languages, Totonac), as in Kaqchikel (Mayan) *y-e-**be**-n-ka-misax* [ASPECT-them-thither-I-kill] 'I'm going there to kill them'.

8. An inclusive–exclusive contrast in first person plural pronouns (Chol, Mam, Akateko, Jakalteko, Chocho, Popoloca, Ixcatec, Otomí, Mixtec, Trique, Chatino, Yatzachi Zapotec, Tlapanec, Huave, several Mixe-Zoquean languages), as, for example, in Chol (Mayan) *honon la* 'we (INCLUSIVE)', *honon lohon* 'we (EXCLUSIVE)'.

9a. 'Zero' copula (no form of the verb 'to be'). An overt copula is lacking from most Mesoamerican languages in equational constructions, as in K'iche' (Mayan) *saq le xaːh* [white the house] 'the house is white'. This feature is also found widely elsewhere in the Americas and beyond.

9b. A pronominal copular construction (Mayan, Nahua, Chocho, Chinantec, Mazatec, Otomí, several Mixe-Zoquean languages). Copular sentences with pronominal subjects are formed with pronominal affixes attached directly to the complement, as in Q'eqchi' (Mayan) *išq-**at*** [woman-you] 'you are a woman', *kwinq-in* [man-I] 'I am a man'; Pipil **ti**-*siwaːt* [you-woman] 'you are a woman' (Campbell, Kaufman, and Smith-Stark 1986).

(In all these examples, *š* = IPA [ʃ], *č* = IPA [tʃ].)

(4) *The Northwest Coast of North America.* As traditionally defined, the Northwest Coast linguistic area includes Tlingit, Eyak, the Athabaskan languages of the region, Haida, Tsimshian, Wakashan, Chimakuan, Salishan, Alsea, Coosan, Kalapuyan, Takelma, and Lower Chinook. This is the best-known North American linguistic area. The languages of this area are characterized by elaborate systems of consonants, which include series of glottalized (ejective) stops and affricates, labiovelars, multiple laterals (*l*, *ɬ*, *tl*, *tlʼ*), and uvular stops and fricatives that contrast with velars. The labial consonant series typically contains fewer consonants than those for other points of articulation; labials are completely lacking in Tlingit and Tillamook, and are quite limited in Eyak and most Athabaskan languages. In contrast, the uvular series is especially rich, with many contrastive phonemes in most of these languages. The vowel systems are limited, with only three vowels (*i*, *a*, *o*, or *i*, *a*, *u*) in several of the languages, and only four vowels in others. Several of the languages have pharyngeals (*ʕ*, *ħ*), and most have glottalized resonants and continuants.

Shared morphological traits include extensive use of suffixes; nearly complete absence of prefixes; reduplication processes (often of several sorts, signalling various grammatical functions, for example iteration, continuative, progressive, plural, collective, and so on); numeral classifiers; alienable/inalienable oppositions in nouns; pronominal plural; nominal plural (distributive plural is optional); verbal reduplication signifying distribution, repetition, and so on; suffixation of tense–aspect markers in verbs; evidential markers in the verb; and locative–directional markers in the verb; masculine/feminine gender (shown in demonstratives and articles); visibility/invisibility opposition in demonstratives; and nominal and verbal reduplication signalling the diminutive. Aspect is relatively more important than tense (and aspect includes at least a momentaneous/durative dichotomy). All except Tlingit have passive-like constructions. The negative appears as the first element in a clause regardless of the usual word order. Northwest Coast languages also have lexically paired singular and plural verb stems (that is, an entirely different lexical root may be required with a plural subject, distinct from the root used with a singular subject).

Some other traits shared by a smaller number of Northwest Coast languages include:

1. A widely diffused sound change of *k > č (IPA [tʃ]) which affected Wakashan, Salishan, Chimakuan, and some other Northwest Coast languages (mentioned above).
2. Tones (or pitch-accent contrasts), found in a number of the languages (Tlingit, Haida, Bella Bella, Upriver Halkomelem, Quileute, Kalapuyan, Takelma, etc.).
3. Ergative alignment in several of the languages (where the subject of intransitive verbs and the object of transitives have similar morphosyntactic marking, while the subject of transitive verbs is marked differently) (Tlingit, Haida, Tsimshian, some Salishan languages, Sahaptin, Chinookan, Coosan).
4. 'Lexical suffixes', found in a number of the languages (Wakashan and Salishan have many of these); lexical suffixes designate such familiar objects (which are ordinarily signalled with full lexical roots in most other languages) as body parts, geographical features, cultural artefacts, and some abstract notions.
5. In the grammar of these languages, one finds a severely limited role for a contrast between nouns and verbs as distinct categories.

The subarea of the Northwest which lacks primary nasals includes the languages Twana and Lushootseed (Salishan languages), Quileute (Chimakuan), and Nitinat and Makah (Nootkan, of the broader Wakashan family). The last two, for example, have changed their original *m > b, *m̓ > b', *n > d, and *n̓ > d' due to areal pressure, but closely related Nuu-chah-nulth (Nootka) has retained the original nasals (Haas 1969b; Campbell 1997a: 333–4) (also mentioned above).

(5) *The Baltic.* The Baltic linguistic area is defined somewhat differently by different scholars. It includes at least Finnic languages (especially Estonian and Livonian) and Baltic languages, and usually also Baltic German. Some scholars have included also all of the following in their treatment of the Baltic linguistic area: the Baltic languages (a branch of Indo-European that includes Lithuanian,

Latvian, Old Prussian, and others); the ten Saamic languages (of the Finno-Saamic [earlier called Early Balto-Finnic] branch of Finno-Ugric, a major division of the Uralic family); Finnic languages (Uralic family) (Finnish, Estonian, Livonian, Vote, Veps, Karelian, etc.); several Germanic languages (Baltic German, Yiddish, High German, Low German, Danish, Swedish, Norwegian); Slavic languages of the region (Russian, Belorussian, Ukrainian, Polish, Kashubian); Romani (Indo-Aryan, branch of Indo-European); and Karaim (Turkic).

The Baltic area is defined by several shared features, some of which are:

1. First-syllable stress.
2. Palatalization of consonants.
3. Tonal contrasts.
4. Partitive case/partitive constructions (to signal partially affected objects, equivalent to, for example, 'I ate (some) apple'), found in Finnic, Lithuanian, Latvian, Russian, Polish, etc.
5. Nominative objects of verbs in a number of constructions when they lack overt subjects (Finnic, Baltic, North Russian).
6. Evidential mood ('John works hard [it is said/it is inferred]': Estonian, Livonian, Latvian, Lithuanian).
7. Prepositional verbs (as German *aus-gehen* [out-to.go] 'to go out'): German, Livonian, Estonian, Baltic, and others.
8. Subject–Verb–Object (SVO) basic word order.
9. Agreement of adjectives in number with the nouns which they modify (in all languages of the area except Saamic languages and Karaim). Adjectives also agree in case in all except the Scandinavian languages (which have lost case distinctions for adjectives); adjectives also agree in gender in Baltic, Slavic, Scandinavian languages, German, Yiddish, and some others.

(For a more complete list of traits which have been attributed to this linguistic area, see Zeps 1962; Dahl and Koptjevskaja-Tamm 2001; and especially Koptjevskaja-Tamm and Wälchli 2001.)

(6) *Ethiopia.* Languages of the Ethiopian linguistic area include: Cushitic (Beja, Awngi, Afar, Sidamo, Somali, etc.), Ethiopian Semitic (Ge'ez, Tigre, Tigrinya, Amharic, etc.), Omotic (Wellamo [Wolaytta], Kefa, Janjero [Yemsa], etc.), Anyuak, Gumuz, and others. Among the traits they share are the following:

1. SOV basic word order, including postpositions.
2. Subordinate clause preceding main clause.
3. Gerund (non-finite verb in subordinate clauses, often inflected for person and gender).
4. A 'quoting' construction (a direct quotation followed by some form of 'to say').
5. Compound verbs (consisting of a noun-like 'preverb' and a semantically empty auxiliary verb).
6. Negative copula.
7. Plurals of nouns not used after numbers.

8. Gender distinction in second and third person pronouns.
9. Reduplicated intensives.
10. Different present tense marker for main and subordinate clauses.
11. The form equivalent to the feminine singular is used for plural concord (feminine singular adjective, verb or pronoun is used to agree with a plural noun).
12. A singulative construction (the simplest noun may be a collective or plural and it requires an affix to make a singular).
13. Shared phonological traits such as *f* but no *p*, palatalization, glottalized consonants, gemination, presence of pharyngeal fricatives (ʕ and ħ).

(See Ferguson 1976; cf. Tosco 2000; see also Thomason 2001: 111–13.)

Some eighty-six linguistic areas have been proposed in the linguistic literature – a surprising number. Not all of these are well established; in fact very few are well accepted by specialists in the languages involved in these various regions.

10.3.3 How to determine linguistic areas

On what basis is it decided that something constitutes a linguistic area? Scholars have at times utilized the following considerations and criteria: the number of traits shared by languages in a geographical area, bundling of the shared traits (clustering at roughly the same geographical boundaries), and the weight of different areal traits (some are counted differently from others on the assumption that some provide stronger evidence than others of areal affiliation).

With respect to the number of areal traits necessary to justify a linguistic area, in general the rule is: the more, the merrier – that is, linguistic areas in which many diffused traits are shared among the languages should be considered to be stronger, better established; however, some argue that even one shared trait is enough to define a very weak linguistic area (Campbell 1985). Regardless of debate over some arbitrary minimum number of defining traits, it is clear that some areas are more securely established because they contain more abundant shared traits, whereas other areas may be weaker because their languages share fewer areal traits. In the linguistic areas considered above, we see considerable variation in the number and kind of traits they share which define them.

With respect to the relatively greater weight or importance attributed to some traits than to others for defining linguistic areas, the borrowed word order patterns in the Ethiopian linguistic area provide an instructive example. Ethiopian Semitic languages exhibit a number of areal traits diffused from neighbouring Cushitic languages. Several of these individual traits, however, are interconnected due to the borrowing of the SOV (Subject–Object–Verb) basic word order patterns of Cushitic languages into the formerly VSO Ethiopian Semitic languages. Typologically, the orders Noun–Postposition, Verb–Auxiliary, Relative Clause–Head Noun, and Adjective–Noun are all correlated with and tend to co-occur with SOV order cross-linguistically. If the expected correlations among these constructions are not taken into account, we might be tempted to count each one as a separate shared areal trait. Their presence in Ethiopian Semitic languages might seem to involve several different diffused traits (SOV counted as one, Noun–Postposition order as another, and so on), and they could be taken as several independent pieces of evidence defining the linguistic area. However, from the perspective of expected word order co-occurrences, these word order arrangements are not independent traits, but can be viewed as the result of the diffusion of a single complex feature: the overall SOV word order type with its various expected coordinated orderings of typologically interrelated constructions. What is important to the point here is that even though the borrowing of SOV basic word order type may count only as a single diffused areal trait, most scholars would rank it as counting for far more than some other individual traits, based on the knowledge of how difficult it is for a language to change so much of its basic word order by diffusion.

With respect to the criterion of the bundling of areal traits, some scholars had thought that such clustering at the boundaries of a linguistic area might be necessary for defining linguistic areas correctly. However, this is generally not the case. Linguistic areas are similar to traditional dialects in this regard (see Chapter 9). Often, one trait may spread out and extend across a greater territory than another trait, whose territory may be more limited, so that their boundaries do not coincide ('bundle'). This is the most typical pattern, where languages within the core of an area may share a number of features, but the geographical extent of the individual traits may vary considerably one from another. However, in a situation where the traits do coincide at a clear boundary, rare though this may be, the definition of a linguistic area based on their shared boundary is relatively secure. As seen earlier, several of the traits in the Mesoamerican linguistic area do have the same boundary, but in most other linguistic areas, the areal traits do not share the same boundaries, offering no clearly identifiable outer border of the linguistic area in question.

In the end, what is important is to try to answer the question, 'What happened?' If we succeed in determining what changes have taken place, and how, when, and where they took place, we will have provided the information upon which linguistic areas depend. If we succeed in finding out what happened, we will know which changes are due to borrowing and which to other factors, and we will know how the changes are distributed in the languages involved. Understanding of the geographical patterning of linguistic areas will be a natural by-product of this fuller historical account. In the end, areal linguistics is not distinct from borrowing; rather, it depends on an understanding of the patterns of borrowing. Therefore, a full account of the linguistic changes in the languages involved, including in particular contact-induced changes, is a sufficient goal, even if in the end the definition of a linguistic area based on these traits may not be entirely clear. It is the borrowed traits that tell us about linguistic areas; linguistic areas are not necessary to understand these traits themselves and to answer the question of what really happened.

Areal linguistics can have consequences for reconstruction, for subgrouping, and for what is considered evidence of distant genetic relationships among languages (see Chapter 13).

10.4 Pidgins and Creoles

Definitions of *pidgin* and of *creole* differ. It is said to be a law of pidgin and creole studies that almost everyone else's definition of a creole sound absurd and arbitrary (DeCamp 1977: 4). A pidgin language is traditionally seen as a minimal contact language, for example used to facilitate trade, though it is not the native language of either trading group; instead, it is often based largely on a simplified version of one of the languages, usually a European one, perhaps mixed with some elements from the other language or languages in the contact situation. Thus, according to one definition, a pidgin 'is a marginal language which arises to fulfill certain restricted communication needs among people who have no common language' (Todd 1974: 1). In contrast, a creole language in the traditional view arises from a pidgin that has become the dominant native language of a group of speakers – it is a pidgin that has acquired native speakers, usually through marriage of individuals who only have the pidgin language in common and whose children grow up with this pidgin as their primary means of communication. In this situation, it is believed that the former pidgin becomes elaborated from its simplified origins and becomes a fuller language able to meet all the communicative needs of its speakers. In this view, while a pidgin is not the native language of its speakers, a creole is the native language of many of its speakers. As we will see shortly, however, this traditional view of how pidgins and creoles arise and the relationship between the two is not universally accepted.

The etymology of *pidgin* is uncertain, but there is no shortage of hypotheses about the origin of the word. Among proposals, many assumed it is derived from a Chinese corruption of English *business*; some think it is a Chinese corruption of Portuguese *ocupação* 'business, occupation'. The etymology of *creole* is clearer, from Portuguese *crioulo* or Spanish *criollo* 'person born in the (American) colonies'.

There are many pidgin and creole languages around the world; a few that are more commonly talked about are:

Bajan Creole (English based, Barbados)
Belizean Creole (English based, Belize)
Bislama (English based, Vanuatu)
Chavacano (Spanish based, Philippines)
Chinese Pidgin English (English based)
Chinook Jargon (Chinuk Wawa) (based on Lower Chinook, Pacific Northwest of North America)
Gullah (English based, sea islands of North Carolina, South Carolina, and Georgia)
Guyanese Creole (English based, Guyana)
Haitian Creole (French based, Haiti)
Hawaiian Pidgin (also called Hawaii Pidgin English, Hawaii Creole English) (English based, Hawai'i)
Hiri Motu (Police Motu) (based on Motu, an Austronesian language of Papua New Guinea)
Jamaican Creole (Jamaican Patois) (English based, Jamaica)

Krio, Sierra Leone Krio (English based, Sierra Leone)
Louisiana Creole (French based, Louisiana)
Mauritian Creole (French based, Mauritius)
Mobilian Jargon (based on Choctaw and Chickasaw, Muskogean languages,
    used as a lingua franca in the Southeastern USA along the Gulf of Mexico)
Ndyuka (English based, Suriname)
Palenquero (Spanish based, Colombia)
Papiamento (Portuguese or Spanish based, Aruba, Bonaire, Curaçao)
Pitcairnese (English based, Pitcairn Island, Norfolk Island)
Réunion Creole (French based, Réunion)
Russenorsk (Russian based, northern Norway and Russian Kola Peninsula)
Saramacca (English based, Suriname, French Guiana)
Seychellois Creole (French based, Seychelles)
Sranan Tongo (English based, with a later layer of words from Dutch,
    Suriname)
Tok Pisin (English based, Papua New Guinea; the name is from *talk pidgin*)

Some of these have remarkable real-life stories. For example, Pitcairnese on Pitcairn Island comes straight out of adventure annals. Pitcairn Island was settled by the mutineers from the *Bounty*, led by Fletcher Christian in 1790 – a story so captivating that it became the subject of five different movies. The group was made up of eight English sailors, their Tahitian and Tubuaian wives, and nine others who were Tahitian or Tubuaian. Most of the males killed each other within a few years, and by 1808 John Adam was the only survivor among the original English sailors. The language developed in isolation; at that time there was no Pidgin English in the Pacific, and Pitcairnese differs in some respects from other pidgins and creoles.

Pidgins and creoles are often looked down upon as not being 'real' languages, or as being corrupt. This attitude is changing. There is strong popular and political support for these languages in some areas, and creoles have become official languages in some countries, for example Haitian Creole in Haiti, Papiamento in Aruba and Curaçao, Sranan Tongo in Suriname, Tok Pisin and Hiri Motu in Papua New Guinea, and Bislama in Vanuatu.

10.4.1 Structural characteristics of pidgins and creoles

Scholars of pidgin and creole languages typically believe that the data of other scholars are messy, or just that the data seen in these languages in general are complex and chaotic, and it is often said that pidgin and creole scholars prefer unruly data. Pidgins are often characterized as contrasting with 'full' or 'normal' (non-pidgin) languages by having the following traits, among others: (1) being simpler, more regular; (2) having fewer resources – a small number of lexical items, sounds, and grammatical constructions; (3) relying almost exclusively on 'content' words – on nouns and verbs, lacking grammatical morphemes; (4) having little if any grammatical morphology; and (5) not differentiating forms of pronouns that are distinguished in their 'lexifier' languages. The lexifier language is the one from which the language takes most of its lexical material. These assumed traits are exemplified in what follows. It should be kept in mind, though, that they are not necessarily accurate.

The idea of *simple phonology* can be seen in comparisons of some pidgins with their lexifier languages. For example, Tok Pisin of Papua New Guinea lacks phonological contrasts that are present in English, its lexifier language, seen in examples such as: *hat* 'hat', 'hard', 'heart', coming from words in English distinguished by several phonological contrasts: *hat, hot, hard, heart*. The lack of the /p/-/f/ contrast is seen in *pis* 'fish' versus *pispis* 'urinate'; the lack of contrast between /ʃ/ and /s/ is also seen in this last pair, and again in *sua* 'sore' versus *sua* 'shore', *sip* 'ship' versus *sipsip* 'sheep'. Simplified phonological structure is seen in the break-up or elimination of consonant clusters, as in Tok Pisin examples where a vowel is inserted to break up a consonant cluster in the corresponding word in the lexifier language, as in *supia* 'spear' and *bokis* 'box', or a sound is lost to simplify the cluster, as in *pain* 'find' (where final *d* was eliminated).

The trait of *limited vocabulary*, with extensive periphrasing, said to characterize pidgins, can be seen in the following from Tok Pisin.

Based on *gras* from *grass* in English originally:

gras bilong ai 'eyebrow', 'eyelash' (literally, 'grass belong eye'; structurally 'eye's grass')
gras bilong dok 'fur (dog's fur)'
gras bilong het 'hair' (cf. 'grass belong head'; structurally 'head's grass')
gras bilong maus 'moustache' (cf. 'grass belong mouth')
gras bilong pisin 'feather' (cf. 'grass belong bird [< *pigeon*]') *gras bilong sipsip* 'wool' (cf. 'grass belong sheep')
gras bilong solwara 'seaweed' (cf. 'grass belong sea [< *saltwater*]')
gras nogut 'weeds' (cf. 'grass no good')

Based on *haus* 'house, building, hut' from English *house*:

haus bilong king 'palace'
haus bilong pisin 'nest' (cf. 'house belong bird [< *pigeon*]')
haus bilong wasim klos 'laundry' (cf. 'house belong wash clothes')
haus mani 'bank' (cf. 'house money')
haus marasin 'pharmacy' (cf. 'house medicine')
haus piksa 'cinema, theatre' (cf. 'house picture [pictures, picture show]')
haus sik 'hospital' (cf. 'house sick')

In support of the notion of *lack of morphology* or very limited grammatical morphology, often examples of the lack of inflectional morphology are cited where bound morphemes of the lexifier language are absent or are signalled by independent words in the pidgin or creole. For example, Tok Pisin grammar uses *bai* for 'future' (etymologically from *by and by*), *bin* 'past tense' (from *been*), and *stap* 'present progressive' as in *kaikai stop* 'is eating' (etymologically from *stop* as in 'stay, continue'). Nevertheless, Tok Pisin does have some inflectional morphology, not parallel to standard English, for example *-im* 'transitive verb' (etymologically from *him*), as in *mi laik wok-im haus* 'I want to build a house' (etymologically *I like work-him house*).

Pronoun under-differentiation is also often pointed out as evidence of limited grammar and of the lack of morphology. This can be illustrated by the single form of a pronoun where in the lexifier language there are distinctions, as for example Tok Pisin *em* for 'he', 'she', 'it', 'him', 'her', as in *em i-save* 'he/she/it knows'; and *mi* for 'I' and 'me', as in *mi lukim yu* 'I see you' versus *yu lukim mi* 'you see me' (*lukim* 'see' etymologically from *look-him*, *-im* 'TRANSITIVE VERB SUFFIX').

Nevertheless, the very common view that pidgins and creoles are maximally simple is inaccurate and so is misleading. For example, we find that Tok Pisin has a complex pronominal system, contrasting singular, dual, trial, and plural pronouns, as seen in those pronouns for which English has only *we*:

> *mitupela* 'we exclusive dual' (he or she and I) (etymologically from English *me-two-fellow*)
> *mitripela* 'we exclusive trial' (both of them and I) (from *me-three-fellow*)
> *mipela* 'we exclusive plural' (all of them and I) (from *me-fellow*)
> *yumitupela* 'we inclusive dual' (you singular and I) (from *you-me-two-fellow*)
> *yumitripela* 'we inclusive trial' (both of you and I) (from *you-me-three-fellow*)
> *yumi* (or *yumipela*) 'we inclusive plural' (all of you + I) (from *you-me, yu-mi-fellow*).

Chinook Jargon, to take another example, has a rather complex phoneme inventory, including glottalized (ejective) stops and affricates, uvular stops and fricatives, voiceless 'l', and a glottalized lateral affricate ([tɬ']), etc. Chinook Jargon is not simple phonologically.

10.4.2 Pidgin and creole origins

There have been a number of different ideas about the origins of pidgin languages, from which creoles were generally assumed to have developed later. As mentioned above, a very common view has been the general notion of pidgins arising as minimal contact languages among groups with no language in common, usually for trading. Another idea, now generally discarded, was that pidgins derive from foreigner talk, a kind of spontaneous simplified communication that might occur any time people lacking a common language have to communicate. This is the sort of baby-talk-like simplification of one's own language a European might use with a taxi-cab driver in some Asian country where the European traveller does not know the local language, for example.

Ideas of origins have also differed in that some have argued for *monogenesis* while most now insist on *polygenesis*. The theory of monogenesis holds that all pidgins and creoles ultimately have a single origin, coming from a pidgin language based on Portuguese that was used aboard ships from the fifteenth to the eighteenth century in the slave trade, often called West African Pidgin or West African Pidgin Portuguese. Supporters of this view believe that this explains why many pidgin and creole languages share a number of grammatical similarities and especially why there are some words of Portuguese origin in many of these languages. A couple of examples from Tok Pisin include *pikinini* 'baby, child' (ultimately from Portuguese *pequenino* 'little, small') and *save* 'know' (seen in the Tok Pisin example above of *em i-save* 'he/she/it knows', ultimately from Portuguese *sabe* 'knows'). These are even found as loanwords into English from creole languages, English *savvy* 'practical knowledge, intelligence, having good judgement, to know, understand' and *pickaninny* 'small black child' (both ultimately from Portuguese, widely found in pidgin and creole languages). The theory of monogenesis is coupled with *relexification*, the idea that the original Portuguese-based vocabulary of these pidgins and creoles came to be replaced by words from another lexifier language without changing the basic grammatical structure. So, for example, the English-based creoles of today, in this view, would mostly be relexified with English vocabulary replacing most of the vocabulary of this assumed original Portuguese pidgin.

Often the theory of monogenesis assumes an even earlier original contact language, called *Sabir* or *Lingua Franca* of the Mediterranean, from which the later Portuguese pidgin and all others are ultimately derived according to this view. Sabir was a pidgin language used in the Crusades (1095 to c. 1450) and in the Mediterranean region from the eleventh to the nineteenth century, with vocabulary mostly from Provençal and Italian in the eastern Mediterranean, and later with more vocabulary from Spanish and Portuguese, especially on the Barbary coast (the Berber lands of north Africa, today's Algeria, Libya, Morocco, and Tunisia), but also with borrowings from Arabic, French, Greek, and Turkish. It was used throughout the Middle East in the Middle Ages (and survived until the nineteenth century) as a language of commerce and diplomacy, and also by slaves and the famous Barbary pirates of this region. In the monogenesis hypothesis, this Lingua Franca was known by Mediterranean sailors, including the Portuguese, who carried it with them in exploring Africa and beyond, and in settling New World colonies.

From this Lingua Franca comes the modern sense of *lingua franca* as any language used by speakers of different languages who have no language in common to be able to communicate with each other, a bridge language among people of different mother tongues. 'Franca' in Romance languages referred to the Franks, the Germanic rulers for whom modern France is named. 'Lingua Franca' meant language of the Franks, but in Arabic and Greek from quite early on Roman Christians and later all Western Europeans were called 'Franks', the source of the word for 'foreigner' in several languages, *faranji* in Arabic, *farang, farangī* in Persian, and borrowed from Persian into a number of languages of the Indian subcontinent, etc. It is also behind the name of the *Ferengi*, a race of extraterrestrials in some of the Star Trek series.

Of course, a serious problem for the monogenesis hypothesis is that there are a number of pidgin or creole languages which are not based on any European language and thus cannot have come about via relexification of a former Portuguese vocabulary, for example Chinook Jargon, Hiri Motu, and Mobilian Jargon.

A different view about the origins of creoles comes from the *bioprogramme* or *language bioprogramme hypothesis*, proposed by Derek Bickerton. He claimed that the structural similarities among various creole languages are not due just to the languages upon which they are based, but rather creolization involves the innate language-learning capacity of children operating on a variable and unstructured pidgin. As a consequence, a pidgin changes – according to this view – into a fully fledged, normal, more elaborated language with a structured grammar that follows the principles of universal grammar built into the children's innate language capacity, assumed to be the explanation for similarities among many creole languages. Many exceptions to this explanation of similarities among creoles have been discussed, and the theory of the bioprogramme for the origin of creoles is now not widely favoured.

Under the more traditional view, it was typically held that creole languages have multiple parents, with most of the lexicon from the lexifier language and much of the grammar due to the 'substrate' languages, for example the West African languages of slaves in the case of Caribbean creoles. This would mean that creoles present a problem for classification, since genetic classification assumes one parent per language, a single ancestor, but creoles in this view seemingly have multiple ancestor languages. Thomason and Kaufman (1988) propose a solution to the problem. They say that only languages which have a single parent qualify for classification into language families, that is, only languages which have normal transmission. Creoles are, they say, not changed forms of some single parent language; they do not arise in direct transmission from one speaker to another, and because of their imperfect transmission, genetic relationship by definition does not apply to them.

The traditional view of the origin of pidgins and creoles and of their relationship to one another is rejected by a number of scholars today, Salikoko Mufwene in particular. They believe, for example, that pidgins and creoles have different origins from one another and arise under different conditions. They do not believe that a creole must evolve from a prior pidgin. In this view, pidgins come about in trade contact among people who keep their native languages for everyday communication. Many creoles, these scholars believe, developed in a different way, namely in colonies where speakers of some European language – often indentured servants who spoke non-standard versions of the European language involved – and non-European slaves interacted intensely. The language they used took on some traits and words from non-European languages, but remained essentially a version of the European language underlying it. The creole that started out in this way would then became the daily language of slaves and workers, not just used for contact with speakers of the non-creole version of the European language lying behind the creole in restricted contexts. According to supporters of this view, each creole has a single ancestor. It is the language of the founder population, speakers of the dominant European language, that predominates in the formation of the creole language and in its content. In this view, creoles present no particular problem for genetic classification; they are classified in the same way as any other language would be. So, for example, Jamaican Creole and Tok Pisin are Germanic languages, closely related to English, and Haitian Creole and Mauritian Creole are Romance languages, closely related to French.

It is perhaps too soon to tell, but it might be suspected that this latter view, in which creoles can be classified as genetically related to the dominant language upon which they are based, may prevail among historical linguists.

10.5 Mixed Languages

In recent years another challenge has arisen to the ability to classify languages according to the families to which they belong, namely *mixed languages*. Until around the early 1980s, most linguists believed that truly mixed languages did not exist. A mixed language is one which has two source languages for different components or parts of its grammar and as a result has no single ancestor; consequently it cannot easily be classified as belonging exclusively to the language family of one or of the other of its source languages. There are very few true mixed languages, which makes linguists believe that probably they can arise only in very limited circumstances. The development of mixed languages seems often to correlate with how newly developed ethnic groups identify themselves.

Unlike pidgins and creoles, in the case of mixed languages both source languages are well known by members of the community involved. Also, mixed languages are not structurally simplified and can have complex morphology.

The best-known cases of mixed languages are the following.

(1) *Gurindji Kriol*, spoken in the Victoria River District, Northern Territory, Australia. Gurindji Kriol continues to be spoken alongside Gurindji and Kriol (the English-based creole widely spoken in the Northern Territory) and is now the first language of all Gurindji people under the age of thirty-five. Its verb phrase grammar is from Kriol; its noun phrase grammar is from Gurindji; its lexicon is from both Gurindji and Kriol. Gurindji Kriol functions to perpetuate Aboriginal identity amid massive cultural incursion from outside.

(2) *Mbugu (Ma'a)*, spoken in Tanzania in two forms; so-called 'normal Mbugu' is fully Bantu, whereas 'inner' Mbugu (Ma'a) has much of its vocabulary from Southern Cushitic, but has Bantu grammar.

(3) *Media Lengua*, spoken in Salcedo, Ecuador (the name is from Spanish meaning 'half language'). It is composed of Spanish lexicon and Quechua morphology and pronunciation. Its speakers give themselves a separate ethnic identity, neither Quechua nor Spanish, but in between.

(4) *Mednyj Aleut* (Copper Island Aleut), originally spoken on Copper Island, from where the population was moved to Bering Island. The original population was made up of Russians who settled there for seal hunting and Aleuts brought there from the Aleutian Island chain by the Russian-American Company in 1826, and of children of Russian men and Aleut women. The language has Russian verbal morphology but mostly Aleut vocabulary.

(5) *Michif*, spoken by the Métis in North Dakota, Manitoba, and Saskatchewan, descendants of mostly Cree women and European fur traders. The nouns, adjectives, and noun phrase syntax are from French and have French lexical items, pronunciation, and morphology (such as agreement, gender marking); verbs and verb phrase grammar are from Plains Cree, with the complex morphology and pronunciation of Cree. (See Meakins 2013.)

As yet there is no generally agreed upon solution to the problem of the mixed ancestry of mixed languages, though there are a few proposals. Their existence constitutes a problem for comparative linguistics, where it is assumed that each language indeed has only a single parent and therefore can be classified as belonging to that parent's language family. If systematic comparisons with other languages sometimes point to correspondences in the language family to which one parent belongs and sometimes to the family of the other parent, reconstruction by the comparative method is frustrated. The directions to which some have looked to solve this difficulty include the following.

(1) They rely on the vocabulary and classify the mixed language with the parent that provides the bulk of the vocabulary. Some have thought that in mixed languages it is usually the mother's language which provides the grammar while the father's supplies the vocabulary. The thinking behind this is that children usually have more access to their mother's language and learn it better, while men in these situations are often immigrants. There are some difficulties with this line of thought, however. First, the number of confirmed mixed languages is so small that it is questionable to what degree accurate generalizations about them are possible. Second, even given the small number of mixed languages, some do not fit the scenario envisaged – Michif has its noun vocabulary and associated grammar from one language, French, that of the original fathers, and its verb vocabulary and associated grammar from Plains Cree, the language of the mothers in the early mix. Mbugu (Ma'a) has two sets of vocabulary, one from Bantu and one in the mixed variety of Mbugu from Southern Cushitic. And worse, Mednyj Aleut has the opposite, not the mothers' grammar, but the mothers' Aleut vocabulary and the fathers' Russian verbal morphology.

(2) They consider the grammar, especially the morphology, to be basic and thus classify the mixed language with the parent language which supplies most of the grammar. There is no agreement among linguists that either the vocabulary or the grammar should be considered somehow basic for language classification purposes. In any event, Michif and Gurindji Kriol would still raise difficulties, with their nominal grammar from one language but their verbal grammar from another.

(3) They consider mixed languages as not truly mixed but as basically having only one parent with exceptionally heavy lexical borrowing. This approach may prove a reliable reflection of how some of these languages were formed – the ones with a split along the lines of the vocabulary from one language and the grammar from another – letting the historical linguist off the hook with respect to the assumed indeterminacy of the genetic classification of these languages. However, this may not be a useful approach to cases where the split is not lexicon vs. grammar but involves verbal vs. nominal grammar and lexicon.

10.6 Endangered Languages and Linguistic Change

Language extinction can be seen as the most extreme outcome of language contact, where typically one language replaces another entirely. The highly accelerated rate of language extinction in recent times has made language endangerment the highest priority for many linguists, a crisis of enormous proportions. Of the world's c. 398 independent language families (including language isolates, language families which have only one member), ninety-one are extinct – no language belonging to any of these ninety-one families has any remaining native speakers – so 23 per cent of the linguistic diversity of the world, calculated in terms of language families, has been lost, forever.

It is clear that language extinction will continue, since many languages in various parts of the world are no longer being learned by children. To understand fully what is possible in human languages, we need reliable descriptions of languages representing the full range of independent language families (including language isolates – families with only a single member). The loss without documentation of a language isolate or of the last language of a language family whose other languages are undescribed is a substantial blow. The loss of a single language with relatives can be compared to the loss of a single species, say the Siberian tiger or the right whale – it would be a blow to biodiversity. However, the loss of whole language families (including isolates) means the loss of complete lineages, analogous to losing whole branches of the animal kingdom. Trying to work out the full range of structural possibilities in human languages and the ways they reflect the history of humankind when undocumented families and isolates have become extinct is analogous to trying to understand the animal kingdom with major branches missing, for example if all the felines or cetaceans were extinct. Language endangerment and extinction are important to historical linguistics for this and several other reasons. (See *The Catalogue of Endangered Languages* at www.endangeredlanguages.com; Campbell and Belew 2018; and Rehg and Campbell 2018.)

CHANGE IN SYNTAX AND MORPHOLOGY

Our speech hath its infirmities and defects, as all things else have. Most
of the occasions of the world's troubles are grammatical.

(Montaigne, *Essays* II, xii)

11.1 Introduction

This chapter is about morphosyntactic change: change in syntax and in morphology. There has been no generally recognized approach to the treatment
of syntactic change or to how morphological change should be presented or talked
about, such as there is for sound change. The study of syntactic change is now
an extremely active area of historical linguistics. While there were some excellent
studies in historical syntax in the nineteenth century and many in the last thirty
years or so, syntactic change was very often not represented (or presented only
superficially) in the textbooks on historical linguistics. The approach in this book
follows that of Harris and Campbell (1995). Many textbooks also do not have
chapters dedicated specifically to morphological change, and in several others
what is labelled morphological change is in fact mostly limited to just analogy (see
Chapter 4). It is easy to understand, however, why this might be the case, since
changes that affect morphology also can involve analogy, sound change, grammaticalization, syntactic change, and lexical and semantic change – indeed, many
aspects of morphological change have already been seen in previous chapters of this
book. In this chapter, we learn about the mechanisms of morphosyntactic change –
reanalysis, extension, and borrowing – and the common pathways that grammatical changes take; that is, we are interested in the more commonly occurring
kinds of syntactic changes found in the world's languages. Grammaticalization, an
approach currently of much interest, is also considered together with its limitations,
and some key concepts that relate to morphological change are discussed. (For a
fuller treatment of morphological change, see Campbell 2013: 247–72.) Finally,
the possibilities for syntactic reconstruction are described and defended.

11.2 Mechanisms of Syntactic Change

There are only three *mechanisms* of syntactic change: *reanalysis, extension*, and *borrowing*. Let us consider these mechanisms in turn, first with a brief characterization of each, followed by additional examples.

11.2.1 Reanalysis

Reanalysis changes the underlying structure of a syntactic construction, but does not modify its surface manifestation (surface form). The *underlying structure* includes (1) constituency, (2) hierarchical structure, (3) grammatical categories, (4) grammatical relations, and (5) cohesion. We will come to examples illustrating changes in each of these shortly. *Surface manifestation* includes (1) morphological marking (for example, morphological case, agreement, gender) and (2) word order.

An important axiom of reanalysis is: *reanalysis depends on the possibility of more than one analysis of a given construction.* The following example from English exemplifies both reanalysis and this axiom. A new construction with a 'future' auxiliary (seen here in (2)) was derived through reanalysis from the construction in (1) which has a main verb (a verb of motion with a purposive sense):

(1) *Brutus is going to kill Caesar.*
     [Structurally: Brutus is going$_{\text{VERB OF MOTION}}$ to kill Caesar]
     (The meaning of (1) is that Brutus is going (moving in the direction) to kill Caesar.)

The purposive *be going (to)* was reanalysed as a 'future auxiliary':

(2) *Brutus is going to kill Caesar.*
     [Structurally: Brutus is going$_{\text{FUTURE}}$ to kill Caesar]
     (The new meaning in (2) is that Brutus will kill Caesar.)

In the reanalysis which produced (2), the surface manifestation remained unchanged – (1) and (2) are identical in form, but are not the same in internal structure (meaning), which changed in the reanalysis. In this case, (1) came to be interpreted as having more than one possible structural analysis – it underwent reanalysis, yielding (2) with its different structural analysis as a new, additional interpretation.

Another example of reanalysis is the development of the 'progressive' in English. It began as a copula (form of the verb *to be*) + *on* (locative preposition) + GERUND (verb made nominal by the suffix *-ing*), as for example in (3):

(3) Tarzan is a-hunt-ing. (*a-* < *on* 'on, at')
     [Structurally: NOUN is PREPOSITION-VERB-GERUND]

This was reanalysed as (4):

(4) Tarzan is a-hunt-ing.
     [Structurally: NOUN is PROGRESSIVE-VERB-PROGRESSIVE]

Later the *a-* (from *on* 'on') was lost, leaving (5), with progressive meaning:

(5) Tarzan is hunting

A vestige of *a-* from the locative preposition is still found in the progressive in some non-standard varieties of English, and it is also preserved, for example, in the familiar nursery rhyme:

> Bye baby bunting,
> Daddy's gone **a-hunting**,
> Gone to get a rabbit skin,
> To wrap the baby bunting in.

For another example, in Finnish, a new postposition (seen here in (7)) was derived through reanalysis from what was formerly an ordinary noun root with a locative case suffix (as in (6)):

(6) *miehe-n rinna-lla*
     man-GENITIVE chest-ADESSIVE   (Adessive case = 'on, by')
     'on the man's chest'   (Original)

(7) *miehe-n rinna-lla*
     man-GENITIVE POSTPOSITION-ADESSIVE
     'beside the man'   (Reanalysed)

In this case there is nothing ambiguous or opaque about (6), and in fact it is still fully grammatical in the language with its original meaning. However, it came to be interpreted as having more than one possible analysis, as a regular noun in locative case (in (6)), but also as a postposition (as in (7)). This new postposition in Finnish is parallel to the development of the preposition *abreast of* in English, which comes historically from *a-* 'on' + *breast*. Such developments are common in English and other languages, as seen in English *beside* < *by* + *side*, *behind* < *by* + *hind*, and so on. In this instance, an original construction with an ordinary lexical noun in a locative case, as in (6), was the basis of the reanalysis which produced the postposition new construction, as in (7). Notice, however, that (6) and (7) are the same except for their internal analysis; that is, though a reanalysis took place to produce (7), the surface manifestation remained unchanged – (6) and (7) are identical in form, but not in their internal structure.

Some kinds of reanalysis have been called *exaptation*. This refers to cases where phonological material takes on a new function, unrelated to its original or obsolete function in the language. Gould and Vrba (1982) coined the term 'exaptation' in biological evolution to refer to the co-opting for new functions of structures originally developed for other purposes, for example the co-opting in the evolution of vertebrates of respiratory and digestive structures for sound production. Roger Lass, who adopted the term for linguistics, characterizes it as the opportunistic renovation of material that was already there but served some other purpose or served no purpose at all, so that both structures in use and 'junk of various kinds' can be exapted (reanalysed) for other purposes (Lass 1997: 316–24). For example, Lass presents as a case in point the changes in *you* versus *thou*. When the number opposition was marginalized (originally *thou* 'singular' versus *you* 'plural'), the then mostly useless opposition was exapted so that *thou* found new uses when it took on senses of affectation and contempt, as for example when in 1603 at the trial of Sir Walter Raleigh, Sir Edward Coke, prosecuting for the crown, insulted Raleigh, saying, 'thou viper, for I thou thee, thou traitor'.

11.2.2 Extension

Extension results in changes in surface manifestation, but does not involve immediate modification of underlying structure. This can be seen in the reanalysis mentioned above in which a new future auxiliary came from 'be going to'. After this reanalysis took place, there was a subsequent extension so that *be going to* as a future auxiliary could appear with new verbs that were not possible earlier. Earlier the *be going to* as a future auxiliary could occur only with verbs which could be the complements in the purposive and motion verb constructions, for example *Brutus is going to eat* (as in, *is going over there to eat* or *is going in order to eat*). However, the new construction was extended so that it could occur with complement verbs which were not possible in the former sense of a verb of motion, for example:

> Brutus is going to go to Rome.
> It is going to rain on Caesar.
> Caesar is going to like Brutus.

Before the reanalysis it would not have been possible to say, for example, *going to go* with *going* in the sense of 'going [over there] in order to go' – *going to go* became possible after the extension with the future meaning.

The other 'future' auxiliary in English, *will*, has a parallel history of reanalysis followed by extension. *Will* was originally an ordinary verb meaning 'want' (as German *will* still does, as in for example, *ich will essen* 'I want to eat'). It went from a stage where *will* meant only 'want', to a second stage where both *will* ['want'] and reanalysed *will* [FUTURE] became possible, and finally to a stage where only the reanalysed *will* [FUTURE] remained possible. We see extension of the reanalysed *will* as FUTURE when *will* as 'future' shows up in cases that were previously impossible. Originally, *will* as 'want' could only occur with animate subjects, with subjects capable of wanting (like, for example, *I want*, *my dog wants*, etc.). Later, however, the reanalysed *will* as FUTURE was extended and appeared in situations previously impossible, with inanimate subjects, as for example:

> It will rain tomorrow.
> Drink will be his downfall.

This is another case where invisible reanalysis was followed by visible extension. The following cases illustrate in more detail the interaction of reanalysis and extension.

11.2.2.1 First example: Spanish reflexive to passive

Another example which shows both reanalysis and extension involves changes in the reflexive in Old Spanish. Old Spanish had only the reflexive as in (8), with none of the other functions that the Spanish *se* later came to have (REFL = reflexive):

> (8) Juanito   **se**   vistió
>   Johnny   **REFL**   dressed
>   'Johnny dressed himself'

A reanalysis of the reflexive took place in which *se* could additionally be interpreted as a passive. In the first stage of this change, certain transitive verbs with *se* and a human subject came to have interpretations as either a reflexive of volitional/consentive action, or a passive, as illustrated in (9) and (10):

> (9)   El   rico   **se**   entierra   en   la   iglesia
>   the   rich   **REFL** bury   in   the   church
> a.   'The rich person has himself buried in the church' (*volitional reflexive*; literally: 'the rich person inters himself in the church')
> b.   'The rich person gets buried/is buried in the church' (*passive*)
>   (from Alfonso de Valdés [1527–8], Lapesa 1981: 402)

> (10) Cum   esto   **se**   vençen   moros   del   campo
>   with   this   **REFL** they.conquer   Moors   of.the   countryside
> a.   'Therefore Moors of the countryside give themselves up for conquered' (*consentive*; literally: 'with this Moors of the countryside conquer themselves')
> b.   'Therefore Moors of the countryside get conquered/are conquered' (*passive*)
>   (from *El Cantar de Mio Cid* [1207?], Lapesa 1981: 216)

In (9) and (10), different interpretations are possible, either reflexive or passive; the surface manifestation is unaltered in the new, reanalysed passive interpretation of these sentences (in (9b) and (10b)). Also, the original reflexive construction (as in (8)) remains grammatical in Spanish. In the next step, the passive interpretation of the former reflexive *se* was extended to include not just human subjects, but also non-animate subjects, where a reflexive interpretation was no longer possible, as in (11) and (12) (PERS = person; PL = plural):

(11) Los vino-s   que   en   esta ciudad se   vende-n ...
      the wine-**PL** that in   this city   **REFL** sell-3rd.**PERS.PL**
      'The wines that are sold in this city ...'
      (from Lazarillo de Tormes [c. 1530], Lapesa 1981: 401)

(12) Cautiváron-**se**   quasi   dos   mil   persona-s
      they.captured-**REFL**   almost   two   thousand   person-**PL**
      'Almost two thousand persons were captured'
      (from Diego Hurtado de Mendoza [1504–75], Lapesa 1981: 401)

In (11) and (12), after the extension, the consequences of the reanalysis are visible, since these sentences are now clearly passive and not reflexive; in (11) the 'wines' cannot 'sell themselves', and in (12) the 'two thousand persons' are not 'capturing themselves'.

11.2.2.2 Second example: change in some Finnish subordinate clauses

Finnish subordinate clauses provide an example of reanalysis followed by extension. Old Finnish had sentences of the form illustrated in (13) (NOTE: orthographic <ä> is phonetically [æ]; ACC = accusative, GEN = genitive, PART = participle, SG = singular):

(13) näe-n   miehe-m   tule-va-m
      see-I   man-ACC.SG   come-PART-.ACC.SG
      'I see the man who is coming'

Here, the noun *miehe-m* 'man' is the direct object of the verb *näen* 'I see', and the participle *tule-va-m* 'coming/who comes' modifies this noun ('man') and agrees with it in case and number (both take the 'accusative singular' suffix *-m*) (literally 'I see the coming man'). Later, Finnish underwent a sound change in which final *-m* > *-n*, and as a result the accusative singular *-n* (formerly *-m*) and genitive singular *-n* became homophonous, both *-n*. After this sound change, the resulting form, shown in (14), was seen as having two possible interpretations, in (14a) and (14b):

(14) näen   miehe-n   tule-van
a.   I.see   man-ACC.SG   come-PART
b.   I.see   man-GEN.SG   come-PART
      'I see the man who is coming'

This led to a change in which the older structural interpretation in (14a) was eventually eliminated and this subordinate clause construction was reanalysed as (14b), with genitive case. That is, *miehe-n* was reinterpreted not as the direct object (in accusative case) of the verb *näen* 'I see' as it had originally been in Old Finnish before the reanalysis (as in the example in (14a), also in (13)), but as the subject (in genitive case) of the participle *tule-van* (as in (14b)). The change is somewhat like starting with the equivalent of *I saw the coming man* and changing it to *I saw the man's coming*. At this stage there is still no visible difference in the surface manifestation; (14a) of older Finnish and (14b) of modern Finnish are in form the same, though different in analysis.

The next phase was the *extension* of the reanalysed structure to other instances where the surface manifestation was visibly changed, as seen in the comparison of Old Finnish (15) with modern Finnish (16):

(15) näin   venee-t   purjehti-va-t
     I.saw   boat-ACC.PL   sail-PART.ACC.PL
     'I saw the boats that sail'

(16) näin   vene-i-den   purjehti-van
     I.saw   boat-PL-GEN   sail-PART
     'I saw the boats that sail'

In Old Finnish, sentence (15), with *venee-t* in the 'accusative plural', did not permit a second interpretation, as (14) did, where the 'accusative singular' was homophonous with the 'genitive singular', both -*n*. However, the reanalysis (from accusative to genitive, that began with the homophonous singular forms) was extended to include the plurals, so that in modern Finnish *venee-t* 'accusative plural' is no longer possible in this construction (as it was in (15) in Old Finnish), but was replaced through extension by *vene-i-den* 'genitive plural', as in (16). Where formerly the singular had two possible interpretations, 'accusative singular direct object of the main verb' or 'genitive singular subject of the participle', after the change had been extended to the plural making it also genitive, the original (accusative) interpretation was no longer available. The extension that changed *veneet* 'accusative plural' in this construction to *veneiden* 'genitive plural' made the change very evident, now visible in the surface manifestation.

11.2.3 Syntactic borrowing

Syntactic borrowing is much more frequent and important than many scholars had thought in the past, though others had gone to the other extreme of assuming that nearly everything not otherwise readily explained in a language's grammar was due to borrowing. It is important to avoid such excesses but also to recognize the proper role of syntactic borrowing in syntactic change.

A good example is seen in the 'after perfect' construction in Irish English, [be + after +VERB-ing], as in (17):

(17) Brutus is after hunting Caesar
     [Meaning: 'Brutus has hunted Caesar']

This construction is due to the influence of a parallel construction in Irish for expressing 'hot news', a case of grammatical borrowing from Irish into Irish English (Hickey 2000).

A grammatical change in French offers another clear case of grammatical bor-rowing, the result of which has parallels in English grammar. Originally French was like other Romance languages that permit sentences without overt subjects. Languages with this feature are called 'null subject' or 'pro-drop' languages. French was like, for example, Spanish, which has sentences such as *viene mañana* 'he/she/it comes tomorrow'. However, under German influence, which requires an overt subject (a non-pro-drop language, like English in this regard), now an overt subject is also required in French, as in *il vient demain* ('he comes tomorrow'), parallel with German ***Er** kommt morgen* 'he comes tomorrow', where the overt subject is required. Compare French *il pleut* and German *es regnet* with the required subject pronouns to Spanish *llueve* (with no subject pronoun), all meaning 'it is raining'.

A straightforward example of syntactic borrowing is found in Pipil (a Uto-Aztecan language of El Salvador), that borrowed its comparative construction from Spanish, as in (18):

(18) ne   siwa:t   **mas**   galá:na   **ke**   taha
      the   woman   **more** pretty   **than**   you
      'That woman is prettier than you are'

Compare the Spanish equivalent in (18'):

(18') esa   mujer   es   **más**   linda   **que**   tú
       that   woman   is   more   pretty   than   you
       'That woman is prettier than you are'

Pipil had several different comparative expressions before its contact with Spanish, but these have been eliminated, replaced by this borrowed comparative construction.

11.3 Generative Approaches

Most work on historical syntax since 1960 has taken the perspective of Generative Grammar (or one of its descendants). Generative linguists gener-ally associate syntactic change with child language acquisition, seeing syntac-tic change as part of what happens in the transition of grammars from one generation to the next. In this view, child language learners hear the output of adults around them and on the basis of these data they must construct their own grammar. The grammar which the children acquire reproduces the output that they hear from the adults' grammar more or less accurately, but it does not necessarily coincide with the internal structure of adults' grammar. After acquiring an optimal grammar as children, adults may later make changes to their grammars which make them no longer optimal. Children of the next generation, hearing the output of this non-optimal adult grammar, restructure it as they construct their own internal grammar, making it more optimal.

We can illustrate this approach with a somewhat hypothetical example, but one that figured in early generative discussions of syntactic change (cf. Klima 1964). Suppose that an earlier generation of English speakers had learned a grammar with the rule that pronouns, including *who*, require an object case marking (*me, him, her, whom*) when they occur as the object of a verb (*Harry saw him/her/me, Whom did Harry see?*) or as the object of a preposition (*to him, to her, to me, to whom*). Let us call this Grammar$_1$, informally characterized as in Table 11.1 (PRO = Pronoun, PREP = Preposition).

TABLE 11.1: Derivation of *whom* in Grammar$_1$

Underlying:	*saw who*	*to who*
	[Verb + Pro]$_{\text{VERB PHRASE}}$	[Prep + Pro]$_{\text{PREPOSITIONAL PHRASE}}$
Rule 1:	*saw whom*	*to whom*
(Case-marking)	[Verb + Pro-Case]$_{\text{VERB PHRASE}}$	Prep + Pro-Case]$_{\text{PREPOSITIONAL PHRASE}}$
Result:	*saw whom*	*to whom*

(Another rule which fronts question words such as *who(m)* gives, for example, *Whom did Harry see?*)

Now suppose that later in life, as adults, speakers of Grammar$_1$ changed their grammar by adding a rule which deletes the case marking with *whom*; let's call this Grammar$_{1a}$, characterized informally as in Table 11.2.

TABLE 11.2: Derivation of *who(m)* in Grammar$_{1a}$

Underlying:	*saw who*	*to who*
	[Verb + Pro]$_{\text{VERB PHRASE}}$	[Prep + Pro]$_{\text{PREPOSITIONAL PHRASE}}$
Rule 1:	*saw whom*	*to whom*
(Case-marking)	[Verb + Pro-Case]$_{\text{VERB PHRASE}}$	[Prep + Pro-Case]$_{\text{PREPOSITIONAL PHRASE}}$
Rule 2:	*saw who*	*to who*
(Delete Case from *whom*)		
Result:	*saw who*	*to who*

The next generation of children learning the language would hear only *who* as the output of the adult grammar, Grammar$_{1a}$, and therefore for their own grammar would simply learn *who* in all contexts, having no need for Rule 2 of adult Grammar$_{1a}$. That is, the adults' non-optimal Grammar$_{1a}$ would have two rules: Rule 1 to add object case marking to pronoun objects of verbs and prepositions, including *to whom*, and Rule 2 to convert *whom* into *who* (deletion of the object case marking from *whom*, making it *who*). The children learning the language, hearing only the output *who*, would not learn Rule 2, but would simply learn to use *who* in all contexts. They would thus construct their grammar with simpler internal structure. They would have no Rule 2 to eliminate case marking from *who*, and their Rule 1 would be modified to apply only to personal pronouns (*me, him, her, us*, etc.) and not to *who*. Let us call this children's grammar Grammar$_2$, which can be characterized informally as in Table 11.3.

TABLE 11.3: Derivation of *who* in Grammar$_2$

Underlying:	*saw who*	*to who*
	[Verb + Pro]$_{\text{VERB PHRASE}}$	[Prep + Pron]$_{\text{PREPOSITIONAL PHRASE}}$
Rule 1:	[Verb + PersPro-Case]$_{\text{VERB PHRASE}}$	[Prep + PersPro-Case]$_{\text{PREPOSITIONAL PHRASE}}$
(Case-marking):	(Not applicable with *who*: *saw who, to who*; but *saw him, to him*)	
Result:	*saw who*	*to who*

The children's grammar (Grammar$_2$) achieves the same output as the adult grammar (Grammar$_{1a}$) but is now more optimal again.

David Lightfoot's (1979; 1991) work has been influential, a major representative of generative views. His scenario for the explanation of syntactic change is that grammatical complexity builds up gradually in a language (through minor changes of little importance) until eventually a sudden, catastrophic and far-reaching restructuring of the grammar takes place which eliminates this complexity that made the language's grammar difficult for children to learn. One criticism of this view is that there is no reliable means of distinguishing the catastrophic changes (which overhaul grammars that become too complex, Lightfoot's major interest) from the gradually accumulating, less significant changes. Another criticism is that catastrophic changes of this sort are extremely rare in the attested history of most languages. For Lightfoot, syntactic changes operate independently of considerations of meaning and use. A central feature of Lightfoot's (1979) treatment is the claim that syntactic change (and syntax in general) is autonomous, meaning that syntactic change takes place independently of semantic relations, pragmatic considerations, discourse functions, or sociolinguistic considerations, with no room for syntactic borrowing. This claim has been much criticized because syntax and syntactic changes do not operate independently of meaning, use, pragmatics, sociolinguistic value judgements, foreign-language influences, and so on.

Central to the generative view of language change is the notion that linguistic change in general, and therefore also syntactic change, takes place in the child language acquisition process and in the transition of grammars from one generation to the next. Many cases of syntactic changes would seem to conform to this view, though others seem at odds with it. This approach assumes that many of the changes that take place are the results of the child language learners just getting it wrong, making mistakes. For example, this view claims for the change in the Finnish participle construction (sentences (13)–(16) above) that in language acquisition children incorrectly assumed that sentence (14) was to be analysed as containing the genitive singular (in (14a)) because they incorrectly perceived what was (formerly) the accusative singular (in (14a)). Then they carried through with this assumption by imposing their new and erroneous genitive interpretation on sentences with the plurals (as in (16)), which were not ambiguous at all as the singulars had been (where the suffix -*n* might be seen as either 'accusative singular' or 'genitive singular'), resulting in a restructuring of the grammar.

However, this view is simply not available for many kinds of syntactic change where, after the change, the original construction still remains grammatical and unchanged alongside the innovative construction that the change is based on; the development of the *be going to* future in English and of the new Finnish postposition (in (7) above) are such cases. In such changes, the original construction remains but in effect gains additional interpretations, that is, multiple analyses. The same is true of the changes involving the Spanish reflexive above and the new passive construction derived from it (in (8)–(12). In the development of the new Finnish postposition, the source construction (in (6)) and the new postpositional construction based on it (in (7)) both survive. In these changes, there is nothing which requires the assumption that the child language learner got it wrong so that a different grammar with a different construction (a new and different analysis of the old construction) resulted, one that eliminates the original interpretation of the construction from the grammar. Adult speakers could just as easily initiate the new analyses alongside the pre-existing ones. If these changes did begin with adults, their results would be part of the language which the next generation would hear around them, and consequently the children would simply learn these new, additional constructions together with any others that happened to be around as part of the grammar which they acquire – if adults added things to their grammars, it would not be children who initiated the change in imperfect learning of what they heard. This, then, challenges the claim that generative approaches make that child language acquisition is the crucial locus of all syntactic change.

11.4 Grammaticalization

Grammaticalization is a topic of extensive recent and current interest. The famous French Indo-Europeanist Antoine Meillet (1912: 132) introduced the term 'grammaticalization' with the meaning of 'the attribution of a grammatical character to a formerly independent word', where an independent word with independent meaning may develop into an auxiliary word and, if the process continues, ends up as a grammatical marker or bound grammatical morpheme. Jerzy Kuryłowicz's (1965: 52) much-cited definition is: 'Grammaticalization consists in the increase of the range of a morpheme advancing from a lexical to a grammatical or from a less grammatical to a more grammatical status.' In grammaticalization, two related processes are the typical objects of investigations: (1) changes of the lexical-item-to-grammatical-morpheme sort, which can involve phonological reduction and exhibit change from independent word to clitic or affix; and less commonly (2) the discourse-structure-to-morphosyntactic-marking sort, the fixing of discourse strategies in syntactic and morphological structure (Traugott and Heine 1991: 2). In both kinds, grammaticalization is typically associated with *semantic bleaching* and *phonological reduction* (to which we return below). Thus, Heine and Reh (1984: 15) define grammaticalization as 'an evolution whereby linguistic units lose in semantic complexity, pragmatic significance, syntactic freedom, and phonetic substance'.

A frequently cited example is English *will* (seen above), which originally meant 'want', as its German cognate, *will*, still does. We can see remnants of the former 'want' meaning in such things as *have the will* [= desire], *if you will* [= if you want to], and *good will* [= wishes, desires]. English *will* became semantically bleached (lost its sense of 'want') and was grammaticalized as a 'future' marker. Grammaticalized forms are also often associated with 'phonetic erosion' (reduction of fuller forms to phonologically shorter ones). In this example, grammaticalized *will* 'future' can also be reduced in form, as in contractions such as *I'll, she'll, my dog'll do it*, and so on.

Meillet presented a parallel example in Greek of the grammaticalization of a verb 'to want' as a future marker, though its history is more complex than the change in English and is coupled with the loss of infinitives in Greek. Modern Greek *θa* 'future marker' began life as the Classical Greek main verb *thélei* 'want'. Greek lost its original infinitive construction and replaced it with a subordinate clause construction: *thélō hina gráphō* 'I want to write' (literally 'I want that I write'), *thélei hina gráphei* 'he/she wants to write' ('he/she wants that he/she writes'). Though *thélei* continued as a main verb meaning 'want', it also came to mean 'will' (future), so that *thélō hina gráphō*, for example, could mean either 'I want to write' or 'I will write'. Later, the 'future' became restricted to the 'third person' form only, /θeli/ (from *thélei*), and eventually the combination of /θeli hina/ changed to /θa/, going through the steps: /θeli hina/ > /θeli na/ > /θe na/ > /θa na/ > /θa/, giving Modern Greek /θa ɣráfo/ 'I will write' (Joseph 1990).

Another example is the frequent grammaticalization of lexical 'go' to 'future', as with English *be going to* which originally referred only to the verb of motion, but then acquired a sense of 'future'/'future intention', which can now be reduced phonologically to *gonna* in spoken language.

Many cases of grammaticalization involve morphological change, where a former lexical item becomes a bound grammatical morpheme. This is seen, for example, in the change in Romance languages where the independent auxiliary 'to have' became bound to infinitive forms to become the new 'future', as in Spanish *cantaré* 'I will sing' < *cantar* + *hé* [to.sing + I.have]. A couple of other examples that illustrate this are:

French -*ment* 'adverb' (like English -*ly*), as in *absolument* 'absolutely' < Latin *absoluta mente* 'in absolute mind', from the ablative of *mens* 'mind'.

Swedish -*s* 'passive, impersonal' < *sig* 'third person accusative reflexive pronoun' (see Old Norse *sik*), originally like English *self*, as in *hoppa-s* 'it is hoped, one hopes', and *dörren öppna-s* 'the door opens'.

11.4.1 Examples of typical grammaticalization changes

It will be helpful to mention some of the sorts of grammaticalization changes, and the pathways they typically take, that are seen to have taken place in various languages around the world.

1. Auxiliary < main verb (as in English *will* 'future auxiliary' < 'want').
2. Case suffixes < postpositions (as in Estonian -*ga* (/-ka/) 'comitative case' suffix < **kansak* 'with' postposition (as in Estonian *poja-ga* /poya-ka/ 'with the boy'); related Finnish preserves the postposition, *poja-n kanssa* [boy-GENITIVE with] 'with the boy').

3. Case marking < serial verbs.
4. Causatives < causal verb ('make, have, get, cause, force') + Clause with another verb.
5. Classifiers (numeral and noun) < concrete nouns ('man', 'woman', 'child', 'animal', 'tree', etc.).
6. Complementizer/subordinate conjunction < 'say'; demonstrative, relative clause markers.
7. Coordinate conjunction ('and') < 'with'.
8. Copula ('to be') < positional verbs 'stand', 'sit', or 'give', 'exist' (Spanish *estar* 'to be' < Latin *stāre* 'to stand'; some Quechua varieties *tiya-* 'to be' < **tiya-* 'to sit'). Note that Spanish *ser* 'to be' comes from a blending of Latin *sedēre* 'to sit' and *esse* (*essere* in Vulgar Latin) 'to be'.
9. Dative case marker < 'give'.
10. Definite article < demonstrative pronoun.
11. Direct object case markers < locatives, prepositions (for example, a dative marker has become an accusative marker in Spanish, Kwa, Bemba, and others; compare Spanish *Brutus mató **a** César* [Brutus killed HUMAN.OBJECT. MARKER Caesar] 'Brutus killed Caesar' with *Brutus lo dio **a** César* [Brutus it gave TO Caesar] 'Brutus gave it to Caesar').
12. Dual < 'two'.
13. Durative, habitual, iterative < 'stay'; durative aspect < 'remain, stay, keep, sit'.
14. Existential/presentational constructions < 'have', 'be' (often with no inflection or only third person present inflection allowed), or < locative pronoun (for a example, Spanish *hay* 'there is/are' < *haber* 'to have'; French *il y a* < *y* 'there' + *a* 'has'; English *there is/are*).
15. Future < 'want', 'have', 'go', 'come' (English *will* 'future auxiliary' < 'want'); adverbs ('quickly', 'tomorrow', 'then', 'afterwards').
16. Grammatical gender < noun (masculine < 'man, male, boy'; feminine < 'woman, female, girl').
17. Hortative < 'come', 'go', 'leave (abandon)'.
18. Impersonal/agentless verb forms: the following constructions are interrelated in many languages and changes frequently go from one to another among these, though directionality is not strongly determined in most cases: reflexive ~ reciprocal ~ spontaneous/automatically occurring ~ potential ~ honorific ~ plural ~ detransitivizing constructions ~ middle/medio-passive/pseudo-passive ~ passive ~ defocusing ~ non-agent topicalization ~ impersonal verb ~ first person plural imperative/hortatory ~ causative ~ transitive (for example, *Don Jr had/got his rifle stolen*) ~ stative/resultative ~ perfect ~ ergative. A directionality is frequently attested in which reflexive > reciprocal > passive > impersonal (where reflexive > passive, or reflexive > impersonal are possible and occur with frequency).
19. Indefinite article < 'one' (English *a(n)* comes from 'one').
20. Indefinite pronoun < 'person', 'man', 'body', 'thing'; 'one'; 'you'; 'they' (as with English *somebody*, *anybody*, which incorporate *body*).
21. Infinitive < 'to', 'for' (purpose).

22. Locative constructions < body-part terms (compare English *at the head of, at the foot of, abreast of, beside*, etc.).
23. Negative < negative intensifiers (for example, French *ne pas*, originally 'not a step', where *pas* was a negative intensifier much as English *not a bit* is today; similar changes are attested in many languages).
24. Quotative < 'say'.
25. Obligation < 'need', 'necessity', 'owe' (for example, English *ought (to)* < Old English *āhte*, past tense of *āgan* 'to owe').
26. Obligation < copula (for example, *you are to go to the doctor today*).
27. Passive < 'get', 'obtain', 'receive'; 'they'.
28. Perfect(ive) < 'finish', 'complete', 'have/possess', 'end'.
29. Preposition/postpositions < verb (preposition < VO; postposition < OV).
30. Progressive < locative + non-finite verb (English, for example, *is hunting* < *is a-hunting* < *is on hunting*; Pennsylvania German and Cologne German *ist am Schreiben* [is on.the to.write] 'is writing').
31. Progressive/habitual < durative verbs ('keep'), 'do', copula, positional verb.
32. Reflexive pronoun < body-part noun ('body', 'head', 'belly', 'person') + possessive; 'reciprocal' < 'body'.
33. Relative pronouns < *wh*-question words/interrogative pronouns (compare English relative pronouns *who, which* with question words *who?, which?*).
34. Relative clause markers < demonstratives.
35. Third person pronoun < demonstrative, 'man', 'person'.
36. *Wh*-questions < cleft or pseudo-cleft (equivalent to 'what did she do?' < 'what is it that she did?'

These are just a few of the many. Also, these are not the only paths by which several of these elements can develop. (For actual examples of these and others, see especially Kuteva et al. 2019; also Harris and Campbell 1995; Hopper and Traugott 2003.)

11.4.2 The status of grammaticalization

Some argue that grammaticalization has no independent status of its own, that there is nothing special or unique about it, that it merely involves other kinds of linguistic changes which are well understood and not inherently connected with grammaticalization: sound change, semantic change, and reanalysis.

Most scholars agree that grammaticalization is not a mechanism of change in its own right, but relies on the other mechanisms, primarily on reanalysis, but also sometimes on extension and borrowing. There are, however, many reanalyses which do not involve grammaticalization, for example those involving word-order changes, affixes becoming independent words (which is rare, but a number of examples are known from various languages), changes from one syntactic structure to another, and so on – that is, any reanalysis which does not involve lexical items shifting towards having a more grammatical status, or discourse structure becoming more fixed morphosyntactically.

Grammaticalization is often associated with 'semantic bleaching' (also called *fading, weakening*). Semantic bleaching, however, is best seen as just semantic change in action (see Chapter 6). Semantic bleaching in grammaticalization is rather unremarkable, since it is essentially part of the definition of grammaticalization, a shift from more lexical meaning to more grammatical content. The types of semantic change involved in grammaticalization are primarily narrowing, sometimes coupled with metaphor, metonymy, and others (see Chapter 6). Also, the emphasis on semantic loss or weakening is perhaps misleading, since in the process of grammaticalization forms also take on new meanings, such as in the case of 'future' from *will* and *gonna*. Also, it is not necessarily the case that lexical meaning is lost, since often the source of the grammaticalization remains in the language with its original meaning alongside the new grammaticalized form, as with *be going to*, where the original directional verb remains in the language alongside the new 'future' meaning acquired in the grammaticalization. The semantic bleaching (the semantic change) in grammaticalization is just part of semantic change in general.

The phonological reduction ('erosion' of form) which many associate with grammaticalization is also not inherent in grammaticalization, but rather involves normal phonological change. Phonological reduction processes apply to items of the appropriate phonological character generally in a language, not just to certain items which happen to be involved in processes of grammaticalization. Reduction often follows grammaticalization because it is at that stage that the conditions favourable to phonological reduction changes first come about, for example where the grammaticalized forms come to be in relatively unstressed positions, which favour phonological reduction.

In short, grammaticalizations involve reanalysis, but reanalysis is not limited to or coextensive with grammaticalization. Sound change and semantic change apply to all sorts of things in addition to grammaticalizations. For this reason, many find grammaticalization derivative, with no independent explanatory status of its own. (For general treatments of grammaticalization, see Heine 2003; Hopper and Traugott 2003; Kuteva et al. 2019; Narrog and Heine 2011; for critiques of grammaticalization as an explanatory theory, see the articles in Campbell 2001.)

11.5 Reconstruction of Morphology and Syntax

Reconstruction of the grammar of a proto-language is possible. Reconstruction of morphology is generally considered more straightforward, while opinions about syntactic reconstruction have varied. Let's look into both, beginning with reconstruction of morphology.

11.5.1 Morphological reconstruction

Basically, the reconstruction of morphology follows directly from normal lexical reconstruction by the comparative method (as in Chapter 7), with morphological analysis applied to reconstructed lexical items that happen to be composed of more than one morpheme. Lexical reconstruction based on the sequence of sound correspondences in cognate words can result in the reconstruction of pol-ymorphemic words. Morphological analysis of these reconstructed proto-words provides the reconstructed morphology free, so to speak. This can be illustrated in a comparison of some cognate verb forms in Romance languages, each of which contains more than one morpheme, in Table 11.4, where a paradigm with the infinitive and forms from the present indicative conjugation are given.

TABLE 11.4: Comparison of some verb morphology in some Romance languages

	Spanish	Portuguese	French	Italian	
Infinitive	amar	amar	aimer	amare	'to love'
Present indicative	amo	amo	aime	amo	'I love'
	amas	amas	aimes	ami	'you love'
	ama	ama	aime	ama	'(he/she/it) loves'
	amamos	amamos	aimons	amiamo	'we love'
	aman	amam	aiment	amano	'(they) love'

For the 'infinitive' form, we would presumably reconstruct *amare, based on sound correspondences. The vowels of French aimer [εmé] reflect the sound change of *a > ε (as seen in Chapter 7). The m and r correspond across all these languages, reconstructed as *m and *r. As for the final e of Italian, it is more likely that Western Romance (Spanish, Portuguese, and French) lost the final e than that Italian added it. Comparison with Classical Latin amāre 'to love' confirms this.

The reconstruction of *ama for third person singular 'he/she/it loves' is also straightforward, where the reflexes of the sound correspondences in each of the languages, a of the others to French /ε/ (aime [εm(ε)], and m in all the languages, allow for the reconstruction of *ama. The other forms in Table 11.4 allow reason-ably clear reconstruction, but not all are completely straightforward.

The amo of Spanish, Portuguese, and Italian would seem to suggest reconstruc-tion of *amo based on the straightforward sound correspondences reflecting *a and *m just seen. These correspondences also account for the /εm/ of the begin-ning of French aime 'I love'. However, the final orthographic <e> of French aime in contrast to the o of the first person singular forms of the other languages sug-gests something has changed in the individual history of French, since the ending of French aime does not fit the expected correspondences with o seen in the other languages (see Chapter 7). On the basis of majority wins, we can still reconstruct *amo 'I love', and seek an explanation for the difference in the separate history of French. We might hypothesize, for example, that the unexpected French form has to do with Watkins' Law: that third person verb forms tend to take over other parts of verbal paradigms, in this case making the first person singular and third person singular forms essentially the same in shape (both aime).

We would be tempted to reconstruct *amas 'you love' for 'second person singular', based on the regular sound correspondences, if we could leave Italian ami 'you love' out of the picture. This Italian word does not fit the expected reflexes, where amas might otherwise be expected. Again, we would seek an explanation for this difference in the separate history of Italian. However, it is not straightforward, since Spanish, Portuguese, and French are all members of a single branch, Western Romance, while Italian is a member a different branch of Romance. It could be the case that Italian innovated in some special way and the other three reflect the original form of the 'second person singular' verb form, or it could be that Western Romance changed (leaving the same reflex in Spanish, Portuguese, and French), meaning that Italian would reflect a truer picture of the original Proto-Romance suffix for this form. This may be a case where the data we have to compare do not easily allow us to come to a definitive conclusion. Nevertheless, when we compare these with Classical Latin *amās* 'you love', the reconstruction with **amas* seems vindicated, and an explanation for the change to *-i* in Italian needs to be sought.

The original 'first person plural' form of this verb is less clear. Once we take into account sound changes in the individual languages, the endings *-mos, -mo,* and *-ons* in the different languages reflect **-mos,* and we would reconstruct **amamos* 'we love' based on the other sound correspondences already seen. However, we need to look further for an explanation of why Italian *amiamo* has an unexpected *i*. Though opinions differ, it is agreed that the *i* in Italian *amiamo* started with Latin subjunctives *-iamus* and *-eamus* in first person plural forms (the two found in different conjugation classes), as for example in Latin *sapiamus* 'let us be wise, understand' > Italian *sappiamo* 'let us know', and the *i* of *-iamo* eventually extended from there to indicative forms throughout the paradigm by analogy (cf. Maiden 1995: 128). The reconstruction **amamos* receives support again from the external comparison with Classical Latin *amāmus* 'we love'. In our reconstruction we appear to miss the vowel length of the *ā* and we reconstruct *o* rather than *u*, but in fact for later Common Romance (or Vulgar Latin), the reconstruction with **amamos* is actually accurate.

Finally, the reconstruction is also not straightforward for 'third person plural', but it is not difficult to propose a reasonable hypothesis. The forms we compare are Spanish *aman*, Portuguese *amam* [amã], French *aiment* [ɛmã/ɛmãt-], and Italian *amano*. The Portuguese final nasalized vowel (/ã/) comes from /an/, taking us to earlier *aman*, just as in Spanish. French third person plural verb endings are slightly complicated; in the colloquial language the pronominal suffix is present in the spelling but is not pronounced, although it is present in formal French and historically was pronounced. As seen in Chapter 7 and again here, the French /ɛ/ corresponds to /a/ in the other languages and comes from **a*. The nasalized vowel [ã] (/ɛmã/ is from /ɛn/, another case of French /ɛ/ corresponding to *a* of the other languages, from **a*. This takes us to earlier *aman*; however, what of the final <t> in the spelling of *aiment.*? This can be pronounced [ɛmãt] if followed by a word or clitic beginning in a vowel, as in the question, *aiment-ils* 'do they love?', seen in *Les Français aiment-ils le futur?* 'Do the French like the future?' This final *t* presents a problem, since the forms in the other languages do not have anything corresponding to it. We could imagine it was somehow added in the separate history of French, reconstructing **aman*, or we could imagine it was originally present, from **amant*, and the other languages lost it. Since there is no easy phonetic explanation for why French might have added a *t* here, perhaps the best hypothesis is to reconstruct the form with **t* and propose that final *t* after *n* was lost in the other languages. While this is not entirely satisfying, the external comparison with Classical Latin *amant* reveals that the reconstruction with *t* was in fact the correct conclusion. Italian *amano* requires explanation. Italian lost final *-t*, so *amant* > *aman*, as in Spanish and Portuguese. As a result of this change and of a change of final *m* > *n*, Latin *sunt* 'they are' and *sum* 'I am' became homophonous in Italian, both *son*. By analogy, the first person singular ending *-o* (as in *amo* 'I love') was added to *son* 'I am', to give *sono*. However, because *son* 'they are' was identified with *son* 'I am', when *son* 'I am' became *sono* by analogy with other first person singular verb forms, then *son* 'they are' also became *sono* based on analogy with *sono* 'I am'. Then by analogy with *sono* 'they are', the final *o* was added to other third person plural verb forms, resulting in *amano* (see Maiden 1995: 130–1). After sorting through the various sound changes and changes by analogy, we reconstruct **amant* '(they) love', which matches Classical Latin *amant*.

These verb forms were reconstructed just as we reconstruct ordinary lexical items based on the sound correspondences that they exhibit and the phonemes postulated to reconstruct each of the sounds, as in Chapter 7. If, however, we compare the reconstructed verb forms with one another, we can do a standard morphological analysis just as we would for any other language. Thus, comparing the reconstructed words, contrasting the parts that recur with the parts that have different meanings, we come up with a morphological analysis where what is after the hyphen (-) reflects the reconstructed bound morphemes:

> *ama-re* 'to love' (*-re* 'infinitive')
> *am-o* 'I love' (*-o* 'first person singular indicative')
> *ama-s* 'you love' (*-s* 'second person singular indicative')
> *ama* 'he/she/it loves' (*-Ø* 'third person singular indicative')
> *ama-mos* 'we love' (*-mos* 'first person plural indicative')
> *ama-nt* '(they) love' (*-nt* 'third person plural indicative').

That is, a standard morphological analysis of the reconstructed words based on the cognate forms in the related languages gives this proto-morphology.

This look at part of the verb paradigm compared in some Romance languages gives a good sense of how bound grammatical morphemes can be reconstructed and of some of the kinds of problems such morphological reconstruction can encounter. Morphological reconstruction faces difficulties that mean that it is not always as straightforward or as easy as lexical reconstruction. For instance, when some of the bound morphemes have been lost or have changed their function in all or most of the sister languages, it may be impossible to recover those earlier affixes. For example, Classical Latin had a 'future' verbal affix as seen in *amābō* 'I will love', *amābis* 'you will love', *amābit* 'he/she/it will love', *amābimus* 'we will love', etc. This 'future' morpheme, however, did not survive in the modern Romance languages and thus simply cannot be reconstructed from a comparison of future forms in the languages we have looked at. Also, if languages add new grammatical affixes through grammaticalization, that can complicate reconstruction, particularly if related languages undergo parallel grammaticalization after they have split up into separate languages. If the related languages have clear phonological reflexes of sounds in a particular bound morpheme but its function has changed dramatically across the languages, it may be impossible to reconstruct what the original function (meaning) of the affix was. Again, if different languages in the family have a grammatical morpheme with the same function across the related languages, but the phonological shapes of the morphemes are different in the different languages, it can be impossible to reconstruct an original morpheme with this function. Still, enough of the original phonetic form and comparable function is often preserved across related languages so that it is possible to reconstruct aspects of the proto-language's morphology with confidence. In general, the further back in time we go, the more opportunity related languages have had to undergo changes which can make it harder to recover past morphology by comparative reconstruction.

Some of these difficulties are evident in the examples presented here in Table 11.5, a comparison of some forms from the conjugation of the verb 'to bear, carry' in several branches of Indo-European, far more distantly related to one another than the Romance languages compared in Table 11.4.

Without going into details, it is clear that there are similarities among the related forms in Table 11.5, but there are also considerably greater differences among them than seen the comparison of Romance verb forms in Table 11.4, which makes reconstruction of the affixes of Proto-Indo-European more difficult. Nevertheless, forms of the thematic present of the PIE verb *bher- 'bear, carry' have been reconstructed, with sound changes and analogical reformations to explain the divergent forms in the individual languages:

*bhér-o-h₂ 'first person singular'
*bhér-e-si 'second person singular'
*bhér-eti 'third person singular'
*bhér-o-me 'first person plural'
*bhér-e-te(-) 'second person plural'
*bhér-o-nti 'third person plural'

(For the reconstructions with sound changes and analogical reformations to explain the divergent forms in the individual languages, see Fortson 2004: 89.)

TABLE 11.5: Comparison of some verb forms in some Indo-European languages

Sanskrit	Greek	Latin	Gothic	Old Church Slavonic	
bhárāmi	phérō	ferō	baíra	berǫ	1st person singular
bhárasi	phéreis	fers	baíris	bereši	2nd person singular
bhárati	phérei	fert	baíriþ	beretŭ	3rd person singular
bhárāmas	phéromen	ferimus	baíram	beremŭ	1st person plural
bháratha	phérete	fertis	baíriþ	berete	2nd person plural
bháranti	phérousi	ferunt	baírand	berǫtŭ	2nd person plural

(based on Fortson 2004: 89)

11.5.2 Syntactic reconstruction

Opinions have differed sharply concerning whether syntax is reconstructible by the comparative method at all or to what extent. Nevertheless, the evidence available for comparison is often sufficient for successful reconstruction of many aspects of the syntax of a proto-language. To understand why there has been doubt about reconstruction of syntax and to see the real potential for successful reconstruction in this area, we need to look at some of the obstacles to such reconstruction that are sometimes mentioned and at ways of surmounting the difficulties which they raise. However, we begin with consideration of some things that are thought to aid syntactic reconstruction.

11.5.2.1 Morphological reconstruction as clues to syntactic reconstruction

To the extent that morphology can be reconstructed, some aspects of the proto-syntax are clear as a consequence of the reconstructed proto-morphology. As just seen in the example involving verbs of Romance languages, the techniques used for lexical reconstruction (Chapter 7), based on the sequence of sound correspondences in cognate words, can frequently be used to reconstruct polymorphemic words. The morphological analysis of these reconstructed proto-words often provides reconstructed grammatical morphemes that signal syntactic properties of the proto-language. An example of this sort is seen in Table 11.6, involving polymorphemic cognate words in the paradigm of the verb 'to read' in some Finnic languages.

TABLE 11.6: Finnic comparative verbal morphology

Finnish	Vote	Estonian	Proto-Finnic
1. luen 'I read (indicative)'	lugən	loen	*luɣe-n
2. olen lukenut 'I have read' (first person perfect indicative)	ələn lukənnu	olen lugenud	*ole-n luke-nut
3. luettiin '(it) was read' (past passive)	lugəti:	loeti [loetti]	*luɣe-ttiin
4. lukemaan 'third infinitive'	lukəma:	lugema [lukema]	*luke-ma-han
5. lukeva 'reading' (present active participle, basis of relative clauses)	lukəva	lugev [lukev]	*luke-va?

The 'third infinitive' is an infinitival form (formerly nominal), used especially with verbs of motion.

From just these few compared words, we see such aspects of Proto-Finnic morphosyntax as tenses and aspects, indicative vs. impersonal passive, embedded clauses with the third infinitive, and the present participle (which is also used in one kind of relative clause). This is enough to illustrate how the technique of reconstructing the proto-morphology can reveal aspects of the proto-syntax.

While in some situations this technique can recover a considerable amount of the proto-syntax, it works less well where the cognate grammatical morphemes have undergone functional or positional shifts or have been lost due to other changes in the languages. Successful reconstruction here, as with phonological and lexical reconstruction, depends on the nature of the evidence preserved in the languages being compared. For example, when we compare the modern Romance languages, we are able to recover less when it comes to some parts of the original verbal morphology because much has been lost in the various languages. This being the case, the technique of morphological reconstruction which worked well for aspects of Proto-Finnic syntax provides less for some aspects of Proto-Romance syntax.

11.5.2.2 Directionality

Just as knowing the characteristic direction of various sound changes provides clues to the best reconstruction in phonology, the directionality of a number of grammatical changes is also known, and this provides clues for the best grammatical reconstruction. An example of this involves typical changes that can affect postpositions. Postpositions frequently become attached to roots and lose their independent status, becoming case suffixes; however, case suffixes only very rarely become independent postpositions. With the directionality Postposition > Case in mind, consider the comparisons of forms meaning 'with' in Table 11.7, where POSTP = Postposition; COM = Comitative case ('with').

TABLE 11.7: Comparison of Finnic 'with' forms

Finnish	Karelian	Veps	Estonian	Vote	Livonian	Proto-Finnic
kanssa	kanssa	-ka	-ga [-ka]	ka:sa	ka:zu	*kans(s)a?
(Postp)	(Postp)	(Com)	(Com clitic)	(Postp)	(Postp)	(Postp)

In this example, given the known directionality of Postposition > Case, it is incumbent upon us to reconstruct the postposition as original and to postulate that the comitative case endings that are the cognates in Veps and Estonian are due to a grammatical change, 'postposition' > 'comitative' case or clitic.

11.5.2.3 Archaisms

An *archaism* (also often called *relic*) is something characteristic of a past form of a language, a vestige, which survives chiefly only in special circumstances. The archaisms of most interest tend to be the ones that are in some way exceptional or marginal to the language in which they are found. They are most commonly preserved in certain kinds of language such as proverbs, folk poetry, folk ballads, nursery rhymes, legal documents, prayers and religious texts, very formal genres or stylistic variants, and so on. A straightforward example is English *pease* for 'pea', an archaism preserved in the nursery rhyme *Pease Porridge Hot*, which goes, 'Pease porridge hot, pease porridge cold, pease porridge in the pot nine days old'. It contains the older *pease* before it was changed to *pea* by back formation on analogy with other nouns that have *s* as their plural (mentioned in Chapter 4). As an example of archaisms in English more relevant to historical grammar, we might mention the verb forms with the *-eth* third person and *-st* second person agreement markers, seen also in the auxiliary forms *hath, hast, art, doth (doeth)*, and the archaic second singular pronoun forms, *thou, thee, thy, thine*. These are all archaic and no longer productive in Modern English. Some examples are:

> Hell **hath** *no fury like a woman scorned.* (Proverb)
> *What therefore God* **hath** *joined together, let not man put asunder.* (Marriage ceremony, Biblical, from Matthew 19:6)
> *The lady* **doth** *protest too much, methinks.* (*Hamlet*)
> *O Romeo, Romeo! wherefore* **art thou** *Romeo?* (*Romeo and Juliet*)

Several of these are illustrated in the 23rd Psalm, oft repeated in literature, poetry, and song:

> *The Lord is my shepherd . . . He* **maketh** *me to lie down in green pastures; He* **leadeth** *me beside the still waters. He* **restoreth** *my soul; he* **leadeth** *me in the paths of righteousness . . . for* **thou art** *with me;* **thy** *rod and* **thy** *staff they comfort me.* **Thou preparest** *a table . . .* **thou anointest** *my head . . . my cup* **runneth** *over.*

As exceptions, archaisms have somehow been bypassed or exempted from the general changes which the language has undergone. Grammatical archaisms are favoured in syntactic reconstruction – some scholars believe them to be the single most useful source of evidence for reconstructing syntax. Naturally, if we can tell what is archaic – by definition 'old' – it affords us valuable information for historical reconstruction.

A difficulty with using archaisms (relics) for reconstruction is that it can be difficult to tell whether we are dealing with a legitimate archaism or something that is exceptional for other reasons but is not particularly old. Another difficulty comes from the frequent situation in which we easily identify exceptions, but where the archaism, nevertheless, provides too little information to guide reliable reconstruction.

For illustration's sake, let's look at a slightly more complicated example. As we saw above, Proto-Finnic had a participle construction in which the logical subject of the participial verb was originally a direct object in accusative case of the main verb, as in examples (13), (14a), and (15), but this was reanalysed in Finnish so that the noun phrase came to be interpreted as the subject (in genitive case) of the participle, as in (14b) and (16). This reanalysis was made possible by the homophony of the accusative and genitive singular case endings, both *-n* in the singular. Finnish archaisms preserve evidence of the construction before the change from accusative to genitive marking. For example, in folk poems there are instances of relics such as (19a) (ACC = 'accusative', PASS = 'impersonal passive', PL = 'plural', PART = 'participle'):

(19a) kuul-tihin   kala-**t**   kute-van,
hear-PAST.PASS   fish-ACC.PL   spawn-PART
lohenpursto-**t**   loiskutta-van
salmon.tail-ACC.PL   splash-PART
'the fish were heard spawning, salmon-tails splashing'
(from the *Kanteletar* volume II, line 252.)

Instead of the form with the accusative plural of 'fish' (*kala-t*) and 'salmon-tails' (*lohenpursto-t*), modern Standard Finnish requires the genitive plural for these, as in (19b) (GEN = 'genitive'):

(19b) kuul-tiin   kalo-**j-en**   kute-van,
hear-PAST.PASS   fish-PL-GEN   spawn-PART
lohenpursto-**j-en**   loiskutta-van
salmon.tail-PL-GEN   splash-PART
(same meaning as (19a))

The relic contained in this folk poem provides additional support for the reconstruction with the accusative pattern in this subordinate construction which was securely established on the basis of comparative evidence from the related Finnic languages (presented just below in section 11.5.2.4). However, if other supporting evidence from these related languages were not available, this archaism alone would be insufficient for a reliable reconstruction. We would not be certain whether this was in fact an archaism (and thus evidence of a former state of the grammar) or perhaps just some exception to the normal pattern for, say, expressive or poetic purposes, or just a mistake.

11.5.2.4 Reanalysis as an obstacle to reconstruction

Instances of traditional analogy sometimes pose obstacles in phonological and lexical reconstruction. Reanalysis in syntactic change, like analogy, can make syntactic reconstruction difficult. However, in instances where analogy changes the form in one language so that it does not fit the forms seen in the related languages with which it is compared, we seek an explanation for the non-fitting form, and often we find the analogical reformation which caused the form to deviate, as in the following cognate set from Germanic:

English	German	Gothic	Old Norse	
adder	*natter*	*nadr-*	*naðra*	'adder'/'snake'

The weight of the evidence in German, Gothic, and Old Norse suggests an initial **n-* in the proto-form, and this bids us seek an explanation for why the reflex of this *n-* is missing in the English cognate. In seeking an explanation, we eventually discover that the pattern of the English indefinite article with *a* before words beginning in a consonant (as in *a plum*) and *an* before vowel-initial words (as in *an apple*) suggests analogical reinterpretation, from *a nadder* to *an adder* (compare Old English *næddre* 'snake'). In a situation such as this one, the analogical change is not devastating to lexical reconstruction, and it is precisely the comparative method and the evidence from the other languages which help us to unravel the complication. We reconstruct initial *n- and posit an analogical change based on the behaviour of a/an to account for the deviance of the English cognate in this set.

Using the same procedure, in many instances where one of the languages being compared has undergone reanalysis in some particular construction, we can discover the reanalysis and explain it so that it no longer prevents us from reconstructing the syntactic pattern in question. Earlier, we saw the example in which a Finnish participle construction was reanalysed so that the noun that had originally been an accusative direct object of the main verb (as in (13) and (15)) came to be interpreted as the genitive subject of the participle (as in (14b) and (16)). If we compare cognate constructions among the Finno-Saamic languages, we soon discover that Finnish stands out as not fitting the pattern of the other languages, as seen in the following examples (ACC = accusative, GEN = genitive, PART = participle):

(20a) Finnish: näin   häne-**n**   tule-van [GENITIVE]
                I.saw   he-GEN   come-PART
                'I saw him coming/that he comes'

  b. Estonian: nägin   te-**da**   tule-va-t [ACCUSATIVE]
                I.saw   he-ACC   come-PART-ACC
                'I saw him coming/that he comes'

  c. Vote: näin   me:s-**sä**   tuɭə-va-a   te:tämö [ACCUSATIVE]
            I.saw man-ACC   come-PART-ACC   street along
            'I saw a man coming/who is coming along the street'

Compare the modern Finnish equivalent in (20d) to (20c) in Votic:

(20d) näin   miehe-**n**   tule-van   tietä   pitkin [GENITIVE]
      I.saw   man-GEN   come-PART   road   along
      (same meaning as (20c))

  e. North Saami: son   oaidná   bohccu-i-**d**   vuolgá-n [ACCUSATIVE]
                   he/she sees   reindeer-PL-ACC leave-PERFECTPART
                   'he/she sees that the reindeer have left'

Compare the equivalent to North Saami (20e) in modern Finnish (20f):

(20f) hän   näkee   poro-j-**en**   lähte-neen [GENITIVE]
      he   sees   reindeer-PL-GEN   leave-PAST.PART
      (same meaning as (20e))

These cognate constructions in Finno-Saamic languages, except for Finnish, have a noun phrase that plays the dual role syntactically of being the subject of the subordinate clause and simultaneously the direct object of the verb of the main clause, marked accordingly by the accusative case to show its role as direct object of the verb in the main clause. However, in modern Finnish, this noun phrase is marked in the genitive case to show its role as subject of the participle, the verb of the subordinate clause, and does not take the accusative case. This difference in Finnish from what its close relatives have demands an explanation. In seeking an explanation, we soon discover that the accusative singular and genitive singular cases are both signalled by -*n* in Finnish, allowing for multiple interpretations. Given this and the difference between Finnish and the other languages with respect to this construction, we encounter little difficulty in determining that Finnish has undergone a reanalysis (from accusative to genitive marking) and does not reflect the original form (with accusative marking). We reconstruct the construction as reflected in the other Finno-Saamic languages with the noun phrase in accusative case marked as the object of the main verb, and point out the changes of reanalysis and extension that have caused Finnish to depart from this structure and end up with genitive marking signalling subject of the subordinate verb, the participle.

In short, though reanalysis and analogy can complicate reconstructions in syntax, often the weight of the corresponding structures in related languages helps us to see past these complicating changes and gives clues about what might be behind their difference.

11.5.2.5 Borrowing as an obstacle to syntactic reconstruction

Just as borrowing can complicate lexical reconstruction, it can be an obstacle to syntactic reconstruction as well. However, the techniques for identifying lexical borrowing (in Chapter 3) can often help to identify syntactic borrowing and thus help us get beyond the obstacle. For example, a comparison of the words for 'mother' across Uralic languages reveals reflexes of **ema* 'mother' in most of them; however, Finnish has *äiti* 'mother' instead, and this difference turns out to be the result of borrowing. Closer investigation reveals that Finnish did indeed borrow this word from Germanic 'mother' (see Gothic *aiþei* [ɛ̄θī], Old High German *eidī* Proto-Germanic **aiθī*). Since Finnish *äiti* is borrowed, it is not a legitimate witness of what the form in the proto-language may have been; to determine that, we rely rather on the information available from the other languages which did not replace the original cognate word through borrowing.

In syntactic reconstruction, we do the same thing. For example, in most varieties of Finnish, verbal constructions involving obligation require the subject to be in the genitive case and the verb to be in a third person singular form (that is, the verb does not agree with this genitive subject), as in the following example from Standard Finnish (GEN = genitive, SG = singular, PERS = person, PRES = present):

(21a) minu-**n**   täyty-y   mennä
      I-GEN   must-3RD.PERS.SG.PRES   to.go
      'I must go'

    b. minu-**n**   pitä-ä   mennä
       I-GEN   must-3RD.PERS.SG.PRES to.go
      'I have to go'

However, Western Finnish has different case marking in this obligation construction. It has borrowed its construction from neighbouring Swedish, now with a subject in nominative case and with the verb agreeing in person with this subject, as in the following examples ((21c) and (21d) are Western Finnish; NOM = nominative):

    (21c) mä   täydy-n   mennä
          I   PERS.SG.PRES to.go
          'I must go'

      d. mä   pidä-n   mennä
          I.NOM must-1ST.PERS.SG.PRES to.go
          'I have to go'

Compare Swedish:

    (21e) Jag   måste   gå
          I.NOM   must   go
          'I must go'

If it were parallel to Standard Finnish, it would have *min måste gå*, where *min* 'my' is possessive, but this is ungrammatical in Swedish.

    When we compare the many regional varieties of Finnish (exemplified in (22) and (23)), Western Finnish (in (21c)–(21d)) with its nominative subjects and verb agreement in this construction stands out as inconsistent with the others, which take genitive subjects and have no verb agreement. This is illustrated here with an example from just two of the many dialects spread from Norway to Russia, here from Vermland (in Sweden, (22a)) and Koprina (Inkeri, Russia, (23a)) (PL = plural, PART = participle):

    (22a) nii-j-**en**   ois   pitän-nä   lahata
             oamuśe-lla
          these-PL-GEN would.have must-PAST.PART to.slaughter
             morning-on
          'they should have slaughtered in the morning'

Compare Standard Finnish:

    (22b) nii-**den**   olisi   pitä-nyt   lahdata
             aamu-lla
          these-PL.GEN would.have must-PAST.PART to.slaughter
             morning-on
          (same meaning as (22a))

(23a) sulhaśe-**n**   pitj   antaa   kolme   ruplaa   pojil
        viinarahaa
        bridegroom-GEN   had   to.give   three   roubles   boys.to
        wine.money
        'The bridegroom had (was supposed) to give three roubles to the boys
        for drinking money'

Compare Standard Finnish:

(23b) sulhase-n   piti   antaa   pojille   kolme   ruplaa
        viinarahaa
        bridegroom-GEN   had   to.give   boys.to   three   roubles
        wine.money
        (same meaning as (23a))

Given that all other varieties of Finnish have the genitive subject and non-agreeing third person verb form in verbal obligation constructions, we reconstruct this pattern and we explain the Western Finnish one with nominative subjects and verbs that agree in person with their subjects as a later change due to borrowing from the Swedish model, with nominative subjects and verbs that agree with these subjects. The evidence from other varieties shows that Western Finnish is inconsistent, and further research reveals that this is due to borrowing. Therefore, in spite of the borrowing in this case, we are able successfully to reconstruct the older stage of the language, with genitive subjects and non-agreeing verbs, based on the weight of the comparative evidence from the other varieties compared.

That is, in syntactic reconstruction, again, the weight of the shared forms in related languages can often help us see past the effects of grammatical borrowing on particular languages.

11.5.3 What can be successfully reconstructed

Another way of appreciating the possibilities for successful syntactic reconstruction is by evaluating the results of attempts to reconstruct the syntax of various language families. For example, the application of the comparative method to languages of the Uralic family reveals a proto-language with the following grammatical features. There were three contrasting grammatical numbers, 'dual' (*-kV), 'plural' (*-t and *-j), and 'singular' (Ø). Direct objects of finite verbs were marked by the 'accusative' case (*-m), but the objects of an imperative verb bore no accusative marker. Case and definiteness were related; the genitive and accusative cases implied definiteness, while indefinite nouns took no marking (that is, in form they were not distinct from the nominative case). The 'genitive' case not only marked the possessor but also served to signal an adjective attribute before its head noun. Proto-Uralic verb suffixes included: *-j 'past', *-ś(A)- 'past', *-pA 'active participle', -k '2nd person imperative', and -mA, -jA, and -ntA 'non-finite verb forms' ('A' denotes vowel harmony with the attached root). There was a negative verb, *e-. Sentences minimally had a nominal subject and a predicate (verbal or nominal); the subject could be signalled by personal pronominal suffixes attached to the predicate. The predicate agreed with its subject in person and number. The copula *woli- 'be' was also an auxiliary verb. The predicate of embedded clauses was in form a verbal noun, where a genitive suffix was used to signal its nominal subject, and personal possessive pronominal suffixes to signal its pronoun subject (that is, the equivalent of 'I see that the dog is running' was in form equal to 'I see the dog's running', and 'the dog sees that I run' was equivalent to 'the dog sees my running'). The role of the embedded clause in the overall sentence was shown by case-markings on the verbal noun (a nominalization) which was the core of the embedded clause. Proto-Uralic had no overt conjunctions or relative pronouns; embedded verbal nouns, nominalizations, were the only means of showing subordination.

In brief, the application of the comparative method to the reconstruction of Proto-Uralic morphosyntax has proven quite successful and this case shows that, at least in some instances, we are capable of syntactic reconstruction (Aikio 2020, Janhunen 1982; Campbell 1990). For some other examples of syntactic reconstruction and discussion, see Barðdal and Eythórsson 2012; Gildea 1998; Harris 2008; Harris and Campbell 1995; Kroeber 1999; Walkden 2014.

In summary, there are many obstacles to successful morphosyntactic reconstruction, but many of these are like the obstacles encountered in phonological and lexical reconstruction, and often it is possible to see beyond the obstacles given the weight of the comparative evidence from related languages. Reliance on the known directionality of many grammatical changes helps, and reconstructed morphology and archaisms can provide very valuable grammatical information. In short, while morphosyntactic reconstruction can be very difficult, it is clearly possible.

11.6 Exercises

Exercise 11.1 Syntactic change in Panare

Consider the following from Panare (a Cariban language of Venezuela). State the syntactic changes that have affected *kah* and *nah*. Explain the historical development of these items as best you can using the terms and mechanisms presented in this chapter.

NOTE: y = IPA [j], $ñ$ = IPA [ɲ], $č$ = IPA [ʧ]. The basic word order is verb first and subject final. When the subject is 'I' or 'you', no copula (form of the verb 'to be') is required in the present tense, as in:

(1) maestro yu   (2) maestro amən
    teacher   I   teacher   you
    'I am a teacher'   'You are a teacher'

However, with a third person subject, a copula is obligatory. With an inanimate subject, the copula is *mən*, as in (3):

(3) eʔčipen   **mən**   manko
    fruit   mən   mango
    'Mango is a fruit'

For this exercise, examples with inanimate subjects are not so relevant. However, with an animate subject, the copula is either *kəh* or *nəh*, with a difference in meaning. Sentences (4) and (5) show that sentences with third person subjects but with no copula are ungrammatical (here ✗ means ungrammatical):

(4) ✗maestro   eʔñapa
    teacher   Panare
    'The Panare is a teacher'

(5) ✗eʔčipen   manko
    fruit   mango
    'Mango is a fruit'

Sentences (6), (7), and (8) illustrate the *kəh* and *nəh* copulas and their difference:

(6) maestro   **kəh**   eʔñapa
    teacher   kəh   Panare
    'This Panare here is a teacher'

(7) eʔčipen   **mən**   manko
    fruit   mən   mango
    'Mango is a fruit'

(8) maestro   **nəh**   eʔñapa
    teacher   nəh   Panare
    'That Panare there is a teacher'

Now consider some demonstratives. The demonstratives *məh* 'this person whom I can see now' and *kən* 'that person whom I can't see now' at first glance appear to behave straightforwardly, as in (9) and (10):

(9) maestro   **kəh**   məh
    teacher   kəh   this.guy
    'This guy is a teacher here'

(10) maestro   **nəh**   kən
     teacher   nəh   that.guy
     'That guy is a teacher there'

But consider the additional Panare copular sentences in (11)–(14). (Note here that /y/ changes to /č/ after /h/, so that *yu* 'I' in this example is *ču* in this context.)

(11) maestro   **nəh**   məh
     teacher   nəh   this.guy
     'This guy was a teacher'

(12) maestro   **nəh**   ču
     teacher   nəh   I
     'I was a teacher'

(13) maestro   **nəh**   amən
     teacher   nəh   you
     'You were a teacher'

(14) maestro   **kəh**   kən
     teacher   kəh   that.guy
     'That guy is being a teacher right now' (that is, he is off somewhere performing his teaching duties at this very moment)

Though originally it was not possible, notice that *kəh* and *nəh* now can also occur with ordinary verbs, as in (15)–(18) (the question mark indicates a sentence which sounds strange to native speakers):

(15) ə?púmanəpəh   **kəh**   Toman   (16)   ? ə?púmanəpəh   **nəh**   Toman
     be.falling   *kəh*   Thomas   be.falling   *nəh*   Thomas
     'Tom is falling'   'Tom is falling (I can't see him)'

(17) yɨupúmən   **kəh**   Toman   (18)   yɨupúmən   **nəh**   Toman
     fall   *kəh*   Thomas   fall   *nəh*   Thomas
     'Tom is going to fall!'   'Tom is going to fall one day'
                                                 or 'Tom fell'

(based on Gildea 1993)

Exercise 11.2 Syntactic change in Estonian

Compare the sentences in this exercise, which represent different stages of Estonian (a Uralic language). Explain what changed and identify the kinds of changes or the mechanisms involved. (NOTE: GEN = 'genitive', INDIR = 'indirect/inference', NOM = 'nominative', PART = 'participle', PRES = 'present indicative'.)

Stage I: Estonian had two alternative constructions for subordinate clauses involving the complements of speech-act and mental-state main verbs, illustrated in (1) and (2):

(1) sai   kuulda,   et   seal   üks   mees   ela-b
     got   to.hear   that   there   one.NOM   man.NOM   live-3rd.PRES
     'he/she came to hear that a man lives there'

(2) sai   kuulda   seal   ühe   mehe   ela-vat
     got   to.hear   there   one.GEN   man.GEN   live-PART
     (same meaning as (1))

Stage II: (1) and (2) remain possible, but the construction in (3) also became possible (from a new additional meaning of the construction in (2) (note that 'participle' became 'indirect/inference'):

(3) sai   kuulda,   (et)   seal   üks   mees   ela-vat
     got   to.hear   (that)   there   one.NOM   man.NOM   live-INDIR
     'he/she came to hear that they say a man lives there', 'he/she
     came to hear that reportedly a man lives there'

Stage III: (1), (2), and (3) are all possible now, but forms formerly found only in subordinate clauses, as in (3), came to be found also in main clauses, as in (4):

(4)   ta   tege-vat   töö-d
      he.NOM   do-INDIR   work-PARTITIVE
      'they say he is working', 'reportedly he is working'
      (based on Campbell 1991)

Exercise 11.3 The development of perfect auxiliaries in Spanish

In the following, the stages in the development of perfect auxiliaries in Spanish from their Latin origins are described and illustrated. On the basis of this information, compare the stages and attempt to determine the changes that took place and to identify the kinds of changes or the mechanisms involved. (NOTE: ACC = 'accusative', FEM = 'feminine', MASC = 'masculine', PART = 'participle', PL = 'plural', PPP = 'past passive participle', SG = 'singular'.)

Stage I: Latin used expressions with 'past passive participle' (PPP) in combination with the verbs *tenēre* 'hold', *habēre* 'keep, hold', and others meaning 'hold, possess, own', to represent something as ready or kept in a completed condition, as in (1):

(1)   Late Latin
      Metuō   enim   nē   ibi   vos   habeam   fatigā-tō-s
      fear.I truly   lest   there   you   have.I   fatigue-PPP.MASC-PL
      'I fear that I have you tired'/'that I have tired you'/'that you are tired'

This construction with 'past passive participle' was quite limited in its occurrence in Classical Latin, but became associated with 'perfect' aspect in combination with the development of *habēre* as an auxiliary. Originally this construction had *habēre* 'keep, hold, have' (a main verb) with the 'past passive participle' form as an adjective which modified the direct object (both the logical and surface object) of this main verb (*habēre*), which agreed in number and gender with this object as its head:

(2) a. [habe-ō]   [litter- ā -s   scrip-t-ā-s]
        have-I   letter-FEM-PL.ACC   write-PPP-FEM-PL.ACC
        'I have written letters' = ('I have letters which are written')

    b. [habe-ō]   [scrip-tum   libr-um]
        have-I   write-PPP.MASC.ACC.SG   book-MASC.ACC.SG
        'I have (a) written book'

As seen here, the past passive principles *scriptās* in (2a) and *scriptum* in (2b) are declined as adjectives that agree in case, gender, and number with the head nouns, *litterās* in (2a) and *librum* in (2b). The past passive principle is not part of the main verb (*habeō* 'I have, hold' in this example), but functions as an adjective modifying the noun (*litterās* in (2a) and *librum* in (2b)).

Stage II: In Old Spanish, *haber* (spelled *aver* in Old Spanish, from Latin *habēre* 'to have, hold') in such constructions began to lose its possessive meaning and to consolidate the auxiliary function, resulting in compound tenses, but still with agreement in gender and number between the participle and the direct object until the mid-sixteenth century, as illustrated in (3) (where the *-o-s* 'masculine plural' of *hechos* 'made' agrees with the *-o-s* 'masculine plural' of *enemigos* 'enemies'):

(3) Los   había. . .hech-*o-s*   enemig-*o-s*   de estotros
     them had   make.PAST.PART-MASC-PL enemy-MASC-PL of these.others
     'He had made enemies of these others' (from Hernán Cortés 1522)

Stage III: Gradually, the *haber* + PPP construction changed, eliminating the requirement that 'past passive participle' must agree in number and gender with the noun that it modified, losing its passive sense, with the verb *haber* becoming the 'perfect auxiliary', and Modern Spanish no longer permits agreement between the participle and the object, as in (4):

(4) Hemos   escri-to   cart-a-s
     have.we   write-PAST.PART   letter-FEM-PL
     'We have written letters'

The adjectival participle source with number and gender agreement still survives in other contexts (but not in the perfect construction with forms of the verb *haber*), for example:

(5) Tenemos cart-**a-s**   escri-t-**a-s**   en tint-a   roj-a
     have.we letter-FEM-PL write-PAST.PART-FEM-PL in ink-FEM.SG red-FEM.SG
     'We have letters written in red ink'.

In the series of changes described here, the meaning is no longer 'X possesses that which has been done', but 'X has done', and is accompanied by the structural change of *haber* from main verb to an auxiliary.

Stage IV: Additional changes in connection with the new 'perfect' construction also came about. First, the verb *ser* 'to be' had formerly also been an auxiliary used with certain intransitive verbs (especially verbs of motion) (as in (6a) and (7a)), but this was replaced by the auxiliary *haber*, as seen in the Modern Spanish equivalents in (6b) and (7b):

(6a) Old Spanish   ella   *es*   naci-d-*a*
                        she   is   be.born-PAST.PART-FEM

(6b) Modern Spanish ella   ha   naci-do
                        she   has   be.born-PAST.PART
                        'she has been born'

(7a) Old Spanish   ellos   *son*   i-d-*o-s*
                        they   are   go-PAST.PART-MASC-PL

(7b) Modern Spanish   ellos   *han*   i-do
                        they   have   go-PAST.PART
                        'they have gone' (Lapesa 1981: 212)

Second, the word order changed, placing the participle closer to the auxiliary, for example from the equivalent of 'I **have** a letter **written**' (as in (2)) to 'I **have written** a letter' (as in (4)).

Exercise 11.4 Finding examples of grammaticalization

The following are some of the most common pathways of grammaticalization (that is, lexical sources which often become grammatical morphemes as a result of grammaticalization changes). Attempt to find examples from English or from other languages you may be familiar with which illustrate these processes. (A few which are extremely common around the world are also included even though English alone may not offer examples.) As an example, for 'go to' > FUTURE, you might list English 'going to' > FUTURE as in 'Brutus is going to stab Caesar.'

(1)   Allative ('to') > complementizer (for example, marker of infinitives)
(2)   'come' > future
(3)   Copula ('to be') > obligation (such as 'must', 'should')
(4)   Demonstrative pronoun (such as 'this', 'that') > definite article (such as 'the')
(5)   'get' > passive
(6)   'have' (possession) > obligation
(7)   'have' (possession) > perfect or completive aspect
(8)   'keep' ('hold', 'grasp') > continuous
(9)   'keep' > possession ('have')
(10) 'man' > indefinite pronoun
(11) 'need' > obligation
(12) 'one' > indefinite pronoun, indefinite article
(13) 'owe' > obligation
(14) 'say' > quotative
(15) 'say' > conditional
(16) 'want' > future
(17) *Wh*-question word (such as 'what?', 'which?', 'who') > relative pronoun, relative clause marker.

12

EXPLANATION OF LANGUAGE CHANGE

These phonetic changes [in Grimm's Law] have, it is true, been brought about by the influence of climate, food, laziness or the reverse, analogy, and fashion; but we are still ignorant of the relative power of these causes, and the precise manner in which they affect the phonology of a language.

(Sayce 1874: 16)

12.1 Introduction

This chapter is concerned with the explanation of linguistic change or, perhaps better said, with attempts that linguists have made towards explaining why languages change as they do. The explanation of linguistic change is usually understood as the search for causes. It is central to the study of language change, though it is a topic of much debate and considerable disagreement. In this chapter, we see how linguists have attempted to explain linguistic change and whether the different kinds of explanations that have been proposed provide a foundation for understanding why languages change. Until the early 1970s, it was common to find statements in historical linguistic works to the effect that we should be concerned with 'how' languages change, but that the question of 'why' languages change could not be answered and therefore should be avoided. For example, in Lehmann's introduction to historical linguistics, we were told: 'A linguist establishes the facts of change, leaving its explanation to the anthropologist' (1962: 200). What is behind the comment about leaving explanation to the anthropologist is the once widely shared notion that linguistic changes were like changes in fashion – in one year new cars might have fins and in another not, or the hemlines of women's dresses might be higher in one year and lower in another. So the driving force behind language change was held to be cultural, to do with social choices, and thus outside of the structure of language itself and hence not primarily even a linguistic concern.

However, not everyone had such a dismissive view. Many causal factors in linguistic change had been identified and discussed earlier, and in the last few decades much has been done to consolidate what we know about the causes of linguistic change. In this chapter, the term *causal factors* is used to designate both factors which always bring about change and those that create circumstances which are known to facilitate change although change is not always obligatory when the factors are present. Here, we examine some of the better-known efforts in the direction of explaining linguistic change. We begin with a brief look at some of the earlier and less successful claims about why languages change – the ones we can safely eliminate from any theory of linguistic change.

12.2 Early Theories

Almost anything affecting humans and their language has at one time or another been assumed to be behind some change in language. Some of these today seem hilarious, for example, nearly all the 'causes' mentioned by Sayce in the quote at the head of this chapter; some are socially or morally disturbing; but fortunately some seem pointed, if only vaguely, in the right direction.

Climatic or *geographical determinism* was thought by some to lie behind some linguistic changes. A revealing example is the claim that the consonantal changes of Grimm's Law were due to life in the Alps, where all that running up and down mountains caused huffing and puffing which led to the voiceless stops becoming fricatives (the changes *p* > *f*, *t* > *θ*, *k* > *h*). Examples of similar changes are known in languages not found in mountainous regions, and in many other languages found in mountains no change of this sort has taken place. Therefore the suggested cause is neither necessary (given the existence of such changes in non-mountain languages) nor sufficient (given the lack of change in other mountain languages). In any case, the Alps were not the homeland of Proto-Germanic speakers – now thought to be in southern Scandinavia.

In another case from even as distinguished a linguist as Henry Sweet (1900: 32) we read:

> The influence of climate may be seen in the frequency with which (a) is rounded in the direction of (o) in the northern languages of Europe – as in English *stone* from Old English *stān* – as compared with the southern languages, in which it is generally preserved; this rounding of (a) is doubtless the result of unwillingness to open the mouth widely in the chilly and foggy air of the North.

We now know that geographical determinism plays no significant role in language change.

Etiquette, *social conventions*, and *cultural traits*. Many have speculated concerning cultural motivations for certain linguistic changes. For example, Wilhelm Wundt (a famous psychologist and linguist, writing in 1900) believed that the reason why Iroquoian languages have no labial consonants is because according to Iroquoian etiquette, so he reported, it is improper to close the mouth while speaking.

Apparently the only evidence for this principle of Iroquoian etiquette was the fact that the Iroquoian languages lack labials. The same absence of labial consonants from Aleut, Tlingit, and some languages of African has at times been attributed to labrets (plugs, discs inserted in holes cut into the lips, an important part of personal adornment and ornamentation in some societies). However plausible this idea might seem to some, it has the disadvantage of not being testable. If a group is found who lack labials but who also do not use labrets, it could be claimed that at some former time they must have used the lip devices and this led to the loss of labial consonants, and then sometime subsequently they just stopped using labrets. Or, if a language possessing labial consonants were found spoken among a group which did wear labrets, it might be claimed that the lip-ornament fashion must not yet have been in vogue long enough to lead to the loss of labials. That is, again, the proposed account for the loss of labials due to the wearing of labrets is neither a sufficient nor a necessary explanation.

In general, we find no evidence that kinds of cultures or kinds of societies lead their speakers to particular sorts of language changes or to particular sorts of languages. (See Campbell and Poser 2008: 350-62 for discussion.)

Indolence. A particularly common assumption, especially among lay people, is that language change is the result of laziness – young people or particular social groups who are seen to be changing their speech in ways disapproved of are assumed to be just too slothful to pronounce correctly or to produce the full or distinct grammatical forms.

Ease and *simplification.* A common assumption has been that language speakers tend towards 'ease of articulation', which leads to language change. 'Simplification' became an important part of the generative linguists' approach to linguistic theory and consequently also to their views of linguistic change. We will need to look at this in more detail, and at the physical reasons behind it, as we explore plausible explanations for why languages change. Movement towards ease of production, of course, may involve many factors other than sheer laziness.

Foreign influence (substratum) – borrowing. Languages do change through borrowing, indisputably (as seen in Chapters 3 and 10), though often language contact has been exaggerated and abused in attempts to explain particular changes. Often, any change whose cause is otherwise not understood, or any exception to otherwise general accounts, has been attributed to influence from other languages, in spite of lack of any evidence in the neighbouring languages that might support such a view. For more practical views of the role of borrowing in linguistic change, see Chapters 3 and 10.

Desire to be distinct and *social climbing.* It is sometimes proposed that groups of people changed their language on purpose to distinguish themselves from other groups. A pervasive notion was that members of lower classes purposefully change their speech by imitating society's elite in order to improve their own social standing, and that as a consequence the upper class changes its language in order to maintain its distance from the masses – the social-climbing masses in hot linguistic pursuit of society's fleeing elite. Sociolinguistic study of language change reveals that group identity can be an important factor in many changes, but not in the simplistic way of former thinking. Rather, it reveals that the more typical pattern is for the middle classes to initiate linguistic change and for the highest and lowest social classes to change only later, if at all (see Labov 1994, 2001; see Chapter 9).

External historical events. It is sometimes asserted that particular historical events are the cause of certain linguistic changes. A typical example is the proposed correlation between the expansion of the Roman Empire and certain linguistic changes. Otto Jespersen correlated the Black Death (the Great Plague) and the wars and social disruption of the later Middle Ages in England and France with rapid linguistic change. Romance linguistics has had a tradition of more tolerance for explanations of linguistic changes involving external history; however, external history has not been accorded as much attention in the Germanic historical linguistics tradition, which has dominated in the general historical linguistics of today. Perhaps there should be more tolerance for it, but appeal to external historical factors should not be abused – there are many examples in past scholarship of assumed external causes presented without evidence of causal connections between the linguistic change and the external history asserted to be involved.

12.3 Internal and External Causes

Modern literature on linguistic change often distinguishes *internal* and *external* causes of change. The internal causes are based on what human speech production and perception are and are not capable of – that is, the internal causes are determined for the most part by the physical realities of human biology, by limitations on control of the speech organs and on what we humans are able to distinguish with our hearing or are able to process with our cognitive make-up.

Thus, *internal* causes include physical and psychological factors. An example of a *physical* factor, involving the physiology of human speech organs, is seen in the typical sound change which voices stops between vowels (let us symbolize this as VpV > VbV). This change is in some sense explained by the limitations of human muscle control, which tends to maintain the vibration of the vocal cords (the voicing, which is inherent in vowels) across the intervening consonant. That is, it is much easier to allow the vocal cords to continue to vibrate right through the V-p-V sequence (resulting in *VbV*) than it is to have the vocal cords vibrating for the first vowel, then to break off the voicing for the stop, and then to start up the vibration of the vocal cords once again for the second vowel (to produce *VpV*). Phonetic factors are behind most sound changes. For example, motor control is involved in the frequent partial overlap in the timing of adjacent sound, resulting in the anticipatory gestures that contribute to assimilations and changes to secondary articulations.

Psychological or *cognitive* explanations involve the perception, processing, and learning of language. For example, the change in which nasalized vowels are lowered (let us symbolize this as $\tilde{\imath} > \tilde{e}$), found so frequently in languages with contrastive nasalized vowels, is explained by the fact that, with nasalization, vowel height tends to be perceived as lower. Thus [ɛ̃] tends to be perceived as [æ̃], for example, and this perception leads to changes in what speakers think the basic vowel is. This is illustrated, for example, by changes in French nasalized vowels:

ẽ > ã (in the eleventh century), as in *pendre* > [pãdr(e)] 'to hang'
ĩ > ẽ (in the thirteenth century), as in *voisin* > [vwaˈzẽ] 'neighbour'
ỹ > œ̃ (thirteenth century), as in [brỹ] (spelled *brun*) > [brœ̃] 'brown'.

(Some of these nasalized vowels underwent further lowerings later in time.)

External causes of change involve factors that are largely outside the structure of language itself and outside the human organism. They include such things as expressive uses of language, positive and negative social evaluations (prestige, stigma), the effects of literacy, prescriptive grammar, educational policies, political decree, language planning, language contact, and so on. The following are a few examples of changes which illustrate external motivation.

(1) Finnish changed *ð* to *d* (for example, [veðen] > [veden] 'water (GENITIVE SINGULAR)') due to spelling pronunciation based on the Swedish reading model which dominated in Finland and was imposed in Finnish schools – though pronounced [ð], this sound was spelled <d>, which educators assumed must be pronounced as in Swedish, as [d].

(2) Teotepeque Pipil (of El Salvador) changed *š* to *r* (a voiceless retroflex fricative became a trilled 'r') because local Spanish has *š* as a stigmatised variant of its *r*. In this case, Spanish is the dominant national language and the negative attitudes about variant pronunciations of its /r/ were transferred to this variety of Pipil, the minority language, leading to a change in its native phoneme which originally in Pipil had nothing to do with different pronunciations of /r/ – native Pipil has no 'r' sound of any sort.

The many cases of sound changes and morphosyntactic changes due to language contact involve external causes (see Chapter 10).

12.4 Interaction of Causal Factors

Change in one part of a language may have consequences for other parts. There is a trade-off between the phonological needs and the semantic/functional needs of a language. A change in sound may have deleterious effects on aspects of the meaning side of language, and a change in meaning/function can have consequences for the sound system. At the crux of much debate concerning the explanation of linguistic change is thinking about the outcome of cases where a change in one component of a language has consequences for another component of the language.

To understand the sort of causal factors that have been proposed and the debate over explanation of linguistic change, it will be helpful to begin with some examples which illustrate what is debated, and then to return to the proposed explanations themselves afterwards with the examples as a basis for understanding the claims. Let us begin with well-known (putative) examples of morphological conditioning of sound change.

12.4.1 Classical Greek loss of intervocalic **s** and morphological conditioning

A sound change is said to be morphologically or grammatically conditioned when it takes place regularly except in a certain morphological context, or, in another sense, when it takes place in a particular morphological environment rather than in strictly phonologically determined contexts. A well-known example illustrating morphological conditioning is the loss of intervocalic *s* in Classical Greek except in certain 'future' and 'aorist' verb forms, where the *s* was not lost. In this case, loss of *s* by regular sound change would have eliminated the 'future' morpheme in these verbs. One view of this set of circumstances is that this sound change was prevented from obliterating intervocalic *s* in just those cases where the meaning distinction between 'future' and 'present' would have been lost, intervocalic *s* being morphologically conditioned, that is, not lost when the *s* in question represented the 'future' in these verbs.

However, the *s* of the 'future' was freely lost with verb stems ending in a nasal or a liquid, where the future/present distinction could be signalled formally by the *e* which these future stems bear. Thus in *poié-**s**-ō* 'I will do', the *s* of the 'future' was maintained, since otherwise it would be identical with the 'present' *poié-ō* 'I do' and it would not be possible to distinguish the 'present' from the 'future'. However, in *mén-ō* 'I remain'/*mené-ō* [< *mene-s-ō] 'I will remain', the *s* was lost, since the 'future' could be distinguished from the 'present' based on the difference in the stems, *mén-* in 'present' versus *mené-* in 'future'.

Compare the following two sets of verbs, where Set I retains *s* in the 'future' and Set II – the *l*-stem or *n*-stem verbs with *e* in the future stem – loses the *s*:

Set I:

páu-ō	'I stop, cease'	páu-s-ō	'I will stop, cease'
poié-ō	'I do'	poié-s-ō	'I will do

Set II:

stéllō	'I send'	steléō [< *stele-s-ō]	'I will send'
mén-ō	'I remain'	mené-ō [< *mene-s-ō]	'I will remain'

It is said in this case that the need of the meaning side of language to be able to distinguish 'future' from 'present' prevented the sound change from occurring in Set I verbs where the 'future' would have been lost (with the deletion of intervocalic *s* by sound change), but the sound change was allowed freely to delete intervocalic *s* even of the 'future' in Set II verbs where the contrast between 'future' and 'present' could be signalled by other means. With the verb stems ending in a nasal or a liquid, in Set II, where the distinction between 'present' and 'future' could still be signalled by the presence of the *e* of 'future' stems, the *s* of 'future' was freely lost. (Compare Anttila 1989: 99.)

Not all scholars agree that morphologically conditioned sound changes are possible; some believe instead that such changes involve restoration by analogy after the regular sound change took place. In the Greek case, in verb roots that end in a consonant (other than liquids and nasals) the *s* 'future' was not threatened, since it was not between vowels, for example *trép-**s**-ō* 'I will turn' (contrast *trép-ō* 'I turn'). In this view, forms such as *poié-s-ō* 'I will do' are seen as actually at one time having lost the intervocalic *s* which marked 'future' by the regular sound change, but later in time, the *s* 'future' was restored to these verbs by analogy based on the s 'future' of consonant-final verb stems such as in *trép-s-ō*; thus, *poié-s-ō* > *poié-ō* by regular sound change, and then *poié-ō* > *poié-s-ō* by analogy, restoring the *s* 'future'.

The first view, favouring morphological conditioning (the blocking of the sound change in just those cases where it would have negative effects on important meaning distinctions), sees *prevention* for functional reasons (to maintain important meaning distinctions) as the explanation behind this example. Supporters of the second view, which favours analogical restoration after the initial loss by regular sound change, see post-operative *therapy* as the explanation, the fixing-up of the negative consequences of sound change for meaning distinctions after the fact by other means. Let us look at some additional examples that illustrate these notions.

12.4.2 Estonian loss of final *-n*

A change in Estonian, similar to that in Classical Greek, is also well known (compare Anttila 1989: 79, 100). Northern Estonian and Southern Estonian dialects are quite different from one another. In Estonian, final *n* was lost; however, in Northern Estonian the *-n* of 'first person singular' verb forms was exempted from this otherwise regular sound change, while in Southern Estonian the change took place without restrictions, as illustrated in Table 12.1. Loss of both *ʔ* and *n* in Northern Estonian would have left the 'first person singular' and 'imperative' forms indistinct; prevention of loss of final *n* in the 'first person singular' forms maintained this distinction. In Southern Estonian, where *ʔ* was not lost, these verb forms remained distinct and so final *n* could also freely be lost in 'first person singular' verb forms without distress to the meaning difference.

TABLE 12.1: Estonian verb forms after certain sound changes

Northern Estonian	Southern Estonian	Proto-Finnic
kannan	kanna	*kanna-n 'I carry'
kanna	kanna?	*kanna-ʔ 'Carry!'

Those who favour analogical restoration after the regular sound change must rely, in this case, on variation in an early stage of the change. Earlier, final *n* was lost when the next word began with a consonant or when there was no following word, but *-n* was not yet lost when the next word began in a vowel. Those favouring loss followed by analogical restoration would say that, based on the instances of final *n* before a following vowel, *-n* was also restored before a following consonant and word-finally (that is, in all instances) when it served to signal the 'first person' in Northern Estonian, but that *-n* was lost completely in all contexts in Southern Estonian (including before following vowel-initial words) (that is, also now lost before an initial vowel of a following word).

12.4.3 Estonian compensation for lost final *-n*

The loss of final *n* in Estonian was not blocked in all instances where its loss would have resulted in the loss of meaning distinctions. For example, the 'accusative singular' suffix was also -*n*, but this was entirely lost in the sound change which deleted final -*n*. Rather than the sound change being 'prevented' from damaging the accusative's ability to be signalled, the change also deleted the final -*n* of the accusative singular. In this case, however, the damage to the meaning side of the language was *compensated* for by other means in the language. In many nouns, the nominative and accusative forms could still be distinguished by other means after the loss of the -*n* 'accusative singular'. Final vowels were lost in an earlier Estonian sound change in words where the preceding syllable had a long vowel or was closed by a consonant (the first of a consonant cluster), and many roots underwent what is called consonant gradation, essentially a change in stops in closed syllables (syllables that terminate in a consonant). Thus, for example, the 'nominative' and 'accusative' of a noun such as *kand* [kant] 'heel' could be signalled in spite of the lost *n* of the accusative case: *kand* (< *kanta) 'nominative singular', *kanna* (< *kanna-n < *kanta-n) 'accusative singular', where the difference between *kand* and *kanna* continues to signal the distinction between nominative and accusative that was formerly indicated by Ø 'nominative singular' versus -*n* 'accusative singular'. On the other hand, in nouns such as *kala* 'fish', consonant gradation (which did not apply to *l*) and final-vowel loss (which applied in other contexts, but not this one) could not compensate for the lost -*n* of 'accusative' to signal the difference: *kala* (<*kala) 'nominative'/ *kala* (<*kala-n) 'accusative'. However, a different sort of therapy came to be called upon to help fix the negative consequences of the sound change for the accusative case suffix, namely in instances such as *kala* 'nominative' vs. *kala* 'accusative', where nothing in the phonological form can function to distinguish the two: the particle *ära* 'up' could be used in partial compensation for the lost 'accusative', as in *söön kala ära* 'I eat the fish (up)'.

12.4.4 Avoidance of pernicious homophony

Discussions of explanation of change often include the concept of *avoidance of homophony* and refer to examples attributed to it. While scholars opposed to functional explanations of linguistic changes have never been friends of avoidance of homophony as an explanation of certain changes, instances of such avoidance are nevertheless well documented. Avoidance of homophony can take several forms.

Lexical replacement and loss. The best-known cases involve lexical replacement or loss. A famous example comes from France, where in Gascony reflexes of Latin *gallus* 'rooster' (commonly *gal* in southern France) were replaced in exactly those varieties in the area where a sound change took place in which original *ll* changed to *t*, where *gallus* 'rooster' would have ended up as *gat*, leaving *gat* 'rooster' homophonous with *gat* 'cat'. This homophony was avoided by the replacement of 'rooster' by other words which formerly meant 'pheasant' or 'vicar', and this allowed 'cat' and 'rooster' to be signalled by phonetically distinct forms. Without appeal to avoidance of homophony, it would be difficult to explain why it is precisely and only in the area where the sound change would have left 'rooster' and 'cat' homophonous that this lexical replacement has taken place (Gilliéron 1921; Gilliéron and Roques 1912; seen in Map 12.1).

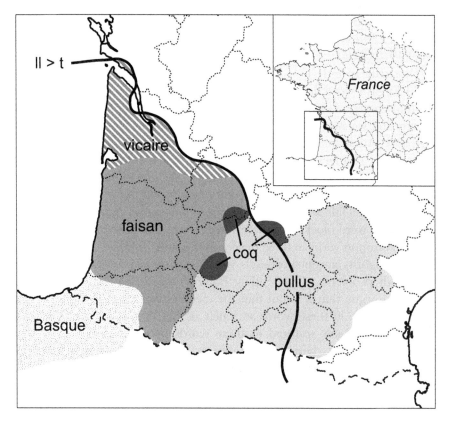

MAP 12.1: Distribution of the names for 'rooster' in the southwest of France
(Redrawn after Ilari 2001: 27)

It will be helpful to look at a few other examples attributed to the avoidance of homophony.

(1) A much-cited example involves the fact that English had two words, *quean* 'disreputable woman, prostitute' and *queen*, but the former has disappeared nearly everywhere because of homophonic clash after Middle English [ɛ:] (of *quean*) and [e:] (of *queen*) merged, especially in East Midlands and Southeast English dialects. However, in the southwestern area, the two vowel sounds remained distinct and both words, *quean* and *queen*, still survive there, where they are not homophonous, but *quean* did not survive elsewhere where the two became homophonous – it was intolerable that the word for the queen should sound exactly like the word for a prostitute (Menner 1936: 222–3).

(2) In Standard German, *Fliege* [fliːgə] 'fly' and *Flöhe* [fløːə] 'fleas' are phonetically distinct, but in certain German dialects the two would have become homophonous through regular sound changes (loss of intervocalic *g* and changes in the vowels). Here, *Fliege* for 'fly' was replaced by *Mücke*, which had originally meant 'gnat, mosquito', as it still does in Standard German (Bach 1969: 168).

(3) In southern French dialects, reflexes of the Latin word *serrāre* 'to saw' survive today only in a few scattered areas. It has disappeared because it became homophonous with the French reflexes of Latin *serāre* 'to close'. In these areas

where *ser(r)āre* 'to saw' disappeared, 'to saw' has been replaced by words which come from Latin *sectāre* 'to cut', *secāre* 'to cut, divide', *resecāre* 'to cut back, curtail' (Palmer 1972: 331).

(4) Due to the sound change in which initial *h* was lost before other consonants, the Old English word *hrūm* 'soot' was left homophonous with *rūm* 'room' after this sound change; consequently, the word *hrūm* was simply dropped from the language, and *soot* now exclusively carries that meaning.

Prevention. Avoidance of homophony can also sometimes block otherwise regular sound changes from taking place in certain forms. For example, in some German dialects, regular sound changes (the loss of intervocalic *g* and the unrounding of *ü* [IPA *y*]) would have left *liegen* [liːgən] 'to lie (down)' and *lügen* [lyːgən] 'to lie (tell falsehoods)' homophonous, but sound changes that were otherwise regular were blocked in these words to preserve the distinction between these two common verbs in these dialects (Öhmann 1934).

Not all linguists accept proposals which call upon prevention as a way of dealing with problems of impending homophony. In this German example, some would argue that it is not that the changes were blocked and prevented from taking place in these words so much as that the changes took place and the sounds were later restored to these words by analogy based on related verb forms in which these sounds appear, or due to influence from other, more prestigious dialects (dialect borrowing). (See Anttila 1989: 182 for other examples.)

Deflection. Another way by which some languages have avoided certain uncomfortable homophonies is through irregular or spontaneous changes in one or more of the homophonous forms, the result of which maintains a formal distinction between the forms that clash. A simple example that illustrates how such deflection can come about is seen in the euphemistic *fudge!* as an expletive to avoid the stronger obscene expletive which begins with the same sounds but ends with a different consonant. A change of this sort involving the homophonous *quean/ queen* pair of words (cited above) took place in some locations. In some northern English dialects, an initial *wh* [ʍ] was substituted for *qu* [kw] in *quean* (but not in *queen*), and both words survive there; the homophonic conflict is avoided through this special, sporadic change. The Middle English form for 'rabbit', variously spelled as *cony*, *coney*, or *cunny*, was considered too close in pronunciation to a phonetically similar obscenity and so was changed by deflection to *bunny*. If in its history English *shut*, from Old English *scyttan*, had not been deflected, it would have become *shit* by regular sound change, a homophony too pernicious to abide – from **skuttjan* 'obstruct', *u > y* (umlaut because of /j/ in the next syllable), *sk > (/ʃ/, y > i* (unrounding of front rounded vowels), so *skuttjan > skytt- > shyt*; to avoid homophony with *shit*, as would be expected by the regular sound changes, *shyt* was deflected to *shut*.

12.4.5 Loss (neglect)

As is well known, many cases of homophony are not prevented, deflected, or replaced; in these, the sound changes create homophonous forms that remain in the language. We see this in English in such sets of words as *sun/son*, *eye/I*, *rock* (stone)/*rock* (move undulatingly), *to/too/two*, and so on. An example from German illustrates a change in which neither blocking nor direct therapy was exercised. In it, the earlier partitive construction was lost from the grammar due to the phonological changes which resulted in the merger of neuter adjectives marked with *-es* 'genitive' and *-ez* 'nominative/accusative'. After the merger, the old *-es* ('genitive') with partitive interpretation was seen as 'accusative' and so was interpreted as full direct objects in these instances. The outcome was that the partitive object construction was simply lost from German as a result of the phonological merger which left the genitive and accusative undifferentiated – neither prevention nor compensation occurred to rescue it. (Ebert 1978: 52.)

As the discussion of these examples (several of them well known in the literature) shows, a broad view will be required in order to explain linguistic change, a view which must include internal factors, external factors, the structure of the language as a whole and how different parts of the language interact with one another, the communicative and social functions of the language, the role of the individual, the role of society/the speech community, and more – that is, the complex interaction and competition among a large number of factors. Let us look at some views of what it means to 'explain' linguistic change, with the examples just considered as background for the discussion.

12.5 One Form, One Meaning

The principle of 'one form, one meaning' (which has also been called Humboldt's Universal and the Principle of Isomorphism) is often thought to be an important explanatory principle of language change. It claims that there is a tendency for languages to change in ways that maximize the one-to-one relationship between form and meaning, where each form (the phonological shape of a morpheme or word or construction) has only one meaning and each meaning has only one phonological shape, a single form. This principle assumes that languages disfavour forms that have multiple meanings or functions, so, for example, *-s* should not function to signal both noun plurals (as in the *s* of *rats*) and possession (as in the *s* of *Gandalf's staff*, and *Fodor's ring*). Similarly, it assumes that cases are disfavoured in which a single meaning (or function) is signalled by more than one form, so that the past participle of English should not be marked by *-ed* (as in *waited*) sometimes and by *-en* (as in *eaten*) other times. These cases illustrate violations of the principle of 'one form, one meaning'. It is thought that something about general human cognition underlies this tendency.

Cases of linguistic changes that conform to the principle are abundant, seen especially in changes that bring earlier violations in line with the principle. For example, the cases of analogical levelling (seen in Chapter 4) conform to and illustrate the principle, reducing multiple forms of a morpheme to one-to-one matches of form and meaning. Formerly there were multiple forms for the possessive pronouns *my* and *thy*, with *mine* and *thine* before nouns beginning in a vowel (as in *mine eyes*) but with *my* and *thy* before nouns beginning in a consonant (as in *my teeth*); with the loss of the final *n* of these forms, they were brought into conformity, with only one form to match a single meaning – no longer two forms, *my* and *mine*, for a single meaning of 'my' before nouns. Originally, English *will* meant 'want', as it still does in German; in the grammaticalization of *will* to 'future' at one stage, *will* meant both 'want' and 'future', *I will eat* for 'I want to eat' and 'I will eat', but the 'want' meaning was eliminated, leaving *will* 'future' in conformity with the one-form-one-meaning principle – the multiple meanings for the form *will* were reduced to a single meaning.

While there are far too many conforming examples in languages everywhere to discard the principle, nevertheless, this tendency is not overpowering. It is easy to find examples of changes where new instances of multiple forms for one meaning or of multiple meanings for one form are created – for example, many sound changes create new allomorphs (morphemes with multiple shapes), and analogical extensions result in new instances not conforming to the principle of 'one form, one meaning'.

12.6 Explanation and Prediction

The recognition of a large number of interacting and competing causal factors in language change means that at present we are unable fully to predict linguistic change. Some scholars conclude from this that it is impossible to explain linguistic change, since they equate 'explain' with 'predict', as required in some approaches to the philosophy of science. These scholars believe that the need to postulate competing principles and multiple causes renders law-like explanations of the sort sought in physics and chemistry impossible in historical linguistics. Others are more optimistic, believing that the current unpredictability may ultimately be overcome through research to identify causal factors and to understand the complex ways in which these factors interact. This more optimistic approach hopes for prediction (for law-like explanations) in the future, to the extent that they may be possible. On the other hand, some scholars recognize that absolute predictability may not be an appropriate requirement, since, for example, evolution by natural selection in biology is almost universally recognized as a scientifically legitimate explanation, though it does not 'predict' the evolutionary changes that it explains.

In the view held by many historical linguists, the overall outcome of changes is usually (though not always) in the direction of maintaining or achieving the language's functional needs (a loose but hopefully useful notion about languages being able to serve the communicative needs of speech communities). These functional needs may be served in some cases by preventing or deflecting certain changes in order to avoid their detrimental effects on the language, or by permitting the disruptive changes to take place but then following them with subsequent compensatory (therapeutic) changes which help to rectify the damage. Of course, not all historical linguists agree; some insist that 'languages do not practice prophylaxis [no prevention or blocking], only therapy' (first said by Hermann Paul in the late nineteenth century, and reasserted by linguists such as Paul Kiparsky (1982: 190), William Labov (1994), and David Lightfoot (1979: 123)). That is, they accept the compensatory changes – therapy after a change that has had negative consequences – but reject the interpretations which involve prevention and deflection in the examples considered above.

From the point of view of scholars who insist on predictability for explanation, it might be objected that appeal to such things in the examples above as prevention (prophylaxis, to counteract the ill effects of some changes) and compensation (therapy, to fix things up after deleterious changes) cannot predict when such changes will take place, what exact form they may take, or when they may fail to occur even though the appropriate condition may have been present. It is important to distinguish what is impossible to predict (for example, that a change will occur, which change will occur, when a change will occur, and so on) from what is possible to predict (the nature of the changes that do occur, the conditions under which they can occur, what changes cannot occur).

Certain predictions may in fact already be possible, though these are not necessarily the mechanistic causal or deterministic kind known from physics which some scholars would insist on for any scientific explanation in any field to be considered valid. For example, to use an analogy (from Wright 1976), given certain circumstances, we may be able to determine in an objective manner that a rabbit will flee from a pursuing dog and that the paths that the rabbit follows are indeed appropriate for attempting to escape the dog, but we may not be able to predict the particular escape route which the rabbit will follow. Similarly, given certain conditions, we may be able to predict that a language (or more accurately, its speakers) may resort to one of a variety of alternative means for resolving the conflicting consequences of changes, though we may not be able to predict the particular 'escape route' that will be taken, be it prevention of sound change (as claimed in the morphological-conditioning view of the Greek and the first Estonian example above and for some of the cases of avoidance of homophony), or compensation (as in the second Estonian case), or deflection (as in some of the instances of homophony avoidance). That is, there are different kinds or degrees of prediction: weak prediction (something is likely to happen), strong prediction (something will happen, though when and where is unclear), and absolute prediction (something will happen at a specifiable time and place) (Aitchison 1987: 12). We may be able to obtain some degree of predictability without needing to insist on the strongest absolute sort of prediction.

That more than one cause is frequently involved in a particular change also makes prediction difficult. Change within complex systems (languages, living organisms, societies) involves many factors which are interrelated in complex ways. Given that multiple causes frequently operate simultaneously in complex ways to bring about particular linguistic changes, to explain linguistic change we must investigate the multiple causes and how they jointly operate in some cases and compete in others to determine the outcomes of linguistic changes.

Because we do not yet understand fully the complex interactions among the causal factors, we cannot predict all outcomes. The internal causal factors (mentioned above) rely on the limitations and resources of human speech production and perception, physical explanations of change stemming from the physiology of human speech organs, and cognitive explanations involving the perception, processing, or learning of language. These internal explanations are largely responsible for the natural, regular, universal aspects of language and language change. However, even well-understood internal causal factors can compete in their interactions in ways which make prediction difficult and for the present out of reach.

Consider another analogy, that of a car smashed against a tree, where the following conditions obtain: it is dark and foggy (poor visibility), the road is narrow and covered with ice (poor driving conditions), the driver is intoxicated and suffers from several physical disabilities (driver impaired), the car was in poor operating condition (worn tyres, bad brakes, loose steering), the driver was exceeding the speed limit and not watching the road at the time of the accident (poor judgement), and finally, the tree happened to be situated at just the spot where the vehicle left the road (chance). In such a situation, it would not be possible to determine a unique cause (or even a joint interaction of causes) of the accident with sufficient precision to allow us to predict the crash. Linguistic changes are often like this crash, where competing or overlapping causal factors may be at play, but precise prediction of whether a change will take place (will the car in fact crash?) or when and how a change (a crash) will be realized is not fully possible. Still, it would be foolish to dismiss the probable or potential contributing causal factors as irrelevant to the event (a car crash, a linguistic change). From the study of many other crashes, we may be certain that each of these factors is capable of contributing to automobile accidents.

At this stage of our understanding, we cannot ignore any potential causal factor, such as prevention or therapy in the examples above, and thus cut off inquiry before we arrive at a fuller picture of how and why changes occur. It will only be through further extensive investigation of the interaction of the various overlapping and competing factors that are suspected of being involved in linguistic changes that we will come to be able to explain linguistic change more fully.

Moreover, even if mechanistic (internal) explanations were more readily available for linguistic change, that would not necessarily invalidate other sorts of explanations. There are different kinds of legitimate explanation. Consider one more analogy (from Wright 1976: 44). To answer the question 'why did the window break?' with 'because John slammed it' is a completely adequate answer/explanation, even if shock waves and molecular structure may lie behind the breaking at some other level of interpretation. There are contexts in which an answer of 'because of a certain causal factor x' is correct and adequate, even if there may be deeper, more mechanistic causal things which one could mention. For example, consider the constraint 'no language will assume a form in violation of such formal principles as are postulated to be universal in human languages' (Weinreich et al. 1968: 100) (mentioned in Chapter 9). That languages cannot undergo changes which would violate universals is an adequate explanation in certain contexts of inquiry even if we discover the aspects of human physiology and cognition (mechanistic, internal factors) which explain the universals themselves. The existence of the underlying internal explanation of universals at some level does not invalidate explanations such as 'because languages do not undergo changes which would violate universals' at some other level. Even if we may ultimately come to understand more fully the aspects of human cognition which underlie avoidance of homophony or therapeutic compensation in the wake of other disruptive changes, and the like, at another level these factors remain potentially valid in explanations for the changes that they deal with.

13

DISTANT GENETIC RELATIONSHIP

De Laet [1643], speaking of Hugo Grotius' methods:
Si literas mutare, syllabas transponere, addere, demere velis, nusquam
non invenies quod ad hanc aut illam similitudinem cogas: sed hoc pro
indicio originis gentium habere, id vero mihi non probatur.

[If you are willing to change letters, to transpose syllables, to add and
subtract, you will nowhere find anything that cannot be forced into
this or that similarity; but to consider this as evidence for the origin of
peoples – this is truly not proved as far as I am concerned.]

(Metcalf 1974: 241)

13.1 Introduction

A topic of extensive interest is that of distant genetic relationships, and both the
methods and the hypothesized distant family relationships have been much
debated. Postulated remote relationships such as Amerind, Nostratic, and Proto-
World have been featured in newspapers, popular magazines, and television doc-
umentaries, and yet these same proposals have been rejected by most mainstream
historical linguists. How is one to know what to believe? How can claims about
very remote linguistic relationships be evaluated? This chapter addresses these
questions by surveying the various methodological principles, criteria, and rules of
thumb that are considered important in attempts to establish genealogical relatedness of languages. The goal here is to prepare the reader to be able to see past the
controversies by explaining the methods and their limitations. Armed with these,
you should be able to evaluate proposals of remote linguistic affinity for yourself.
As Antoine Meillet, a famous Indo-Europeanist well known for his common sense
discussions of historical linguistic methods, cautioned, excessive zeal for long-
range relationships can lead to methodological excesses: 'The difficulty of the task
of trying to make every language fit into a genetic classification has led certain

eminent linguists to deprive the principle of such classification of its precision and its rigour or to apply it in an imprecise manner' (1948 [1914]: 78). The comparative method has always been the basic tool for establishing family relationships among languages, though it is necessary to discuss a number of particular aspects of how it is applied in work on distant genetic relationships and to address approaches which have sometimes been advocated as competitors of the comparative method.

In order to give an idea of what is at issue, a list of some of the better-known hypotheses that would group together languages which are not yet known to be related is presented here. None of the proposed genetic relationships in this list has been demonstrated, though some are repeated frequently, even in encyclopaedias and textbooks. Many other unconfirmed proposals of distant genetic relationship (not listed here) have also been made.

Altaic (proposed grouping of Turkic, Tungusic, and Mongolian, to which some proposals also add Japanese and Korean, and others)

Amerind (Joseph Greenberg's (1987) proposal which would lump into one large group all the 170 or so language families of the Americas except Eskimo-Aleut and so-called Na-Dene)

Austric (Austro-Asiatic with Austronesian) Austro-Tai (Japanese-Austro-Thai)

Basque-Caucasian

Basque-SinoTibetan-Na-Dene

Chitimacha-Totozoquean (Chitimacha [language isolate of Louisiana] with Totonacan and Mixe-Zoquean families of Mexico)

Dene-Sino-Tibetan (Athabaskan [or Na-Dene] and Sino-Tibetan

Dene-Yeniseian (groups the Yeniseian family of Siberia with Athabaskan and Tlingit)

Dravidian-Japanese

Dravidian-Uralic

Eskimo and Indo-European

Eskimo-Uralic

Eurasiatic (Greenberg's (2000) grouping of Indo-European, Uralic, Eskimo-Aleut, Ainu, and several other otherwise unaffiliated languages)

Hokan (in various versions which group many American Indian families and isolates)

Indo-European and Afroasiatic

Indo-European and Semitic

Indo-Pacific (Greenberg's (1971) grouping of all the non-Austronesian languages of the Pacific, including all Papuan families, languages of Tasmania, and the languages of the Andaman Islands)

Indo-Uralic (Indo-European and Uralic)

Japanese-Altaic

Japanese-Austronesian

Khoisan (the African families with clicks, except the Bantu languages which borrowed clicks; much of Khoisan is now considered to be more an areal grouping than a genetic one)

Macro-Siouan (Siouan, Iroquoian, Caddoan, sometimes also Yuchi)

Maya-Chipayan (Mayan, Uru-Chipayan of Bolivia)

Na-Dene (Eyak-Athabaskan, Tlinglit, Haida – Haida is now considered a language isolate, not related to these other languages)

Niger-Kordofanian (Niger-Congo) (Africa, Greenberg's (1963) grouping which includes Mande, Kru, Kwa, Benue-Congo [of which Bantu is a branch], Gur, Adamawa-Ubangi, Kordofanian, and others)

Nilo-Saharan (large number of African families; Greenberg's (1963) grouping which contains most of the leftover African languages not otherwise classified as belonging to one of his other three groupings)

Nostratic (various versions; the best-known groups Indo-European, Uralic, Altaic, South Caucasian (Kartvelian), Dravidian, and Afroasiatic; some add also Chukchi-Kamchatkan, Eskimo-Aleut, Sumerian, and Nivkh (Gilyak))

Penutian (various versions; groups a number of American Indian families and isolates)

Proto-Australian (all twenty-six or so of the Australian families)

Proto-World (Global Etymologies)

Ural-Altaic (Uralic and 'Altaic')

Ural-Altaic and Eskimo-Aleut

Yukaghir-Uralic

(See the less controversial classifications in Table 9.1, Chapter 9.)

Two outlooks can be distinguished in hypotheses for new, previously unknown language families. The first is like a scouting expedition. In it, the intention is to call attention to a possible but as yet untested connection between languages not known to be related to one another. In this approach, a wide net is often cast in order to haul in as much potential preliminary evidence as possible. The second outlook comes into play typically when the intention is to test a hypothesis of relatedness that has been made. In it, those forms considered initially as possible evidence are submitted to more careful scrutiny. Unfortunately, the more laissez-faire setting-up type hypotheses of the first approach are not always distinguished from the more cautious hypothesis-testing type of the second.

Let us look in more detail at the methods and criteria that have been used in research on distant genetic relationships. (These are treated in detail in Campbell and Poser 2008.)

13.2 Lexical Comparison

Throughout history, word comparisons have been employed as evidence of language family relationship, but, given a small collection of likely-looking potential cognates, how can we determine whether they are really the residue of common origin and not the workings of pure chance or some other factor? It turns out that lexical comparisons by themselves are seldom convincing without additional support from other criteria, except in very obvious cases. Because lexical comparisons have typically played the major role in hypothesized distant genetic relationships, we begin by considering the role of basic vocabulary and lexically based approaches.

13.2.1 Basic vocabulary

Most scholars insist that basic vocabulary should be part of the supporting evidence presented in favour of any hypothesis of distant family relationship. Basic vocabulary is usually not defined rigorously but is understood generally to include terms for body parts, close kinship, frequently encountered aspects of the natural world (mountain, river, cloud, and the like), and low numbers. Basic vocabulary is in general resistant to borrowing, and so similarities found in comparisons involving basic vocabulary items are unlikely to be due to diffusion and hence stand a better chance of being evidence of distant genetic relationships, of being inherited from a common ancestor, than other kinds of vocabulary. Of course, basic vocabulary can also be borrowed – though this happens less frequently – so that its role as a safeguard against borrowing is not fool-proof (see examples below, see Chapter 16).

13.2.2 Glottochronology

Glottochronology, which depends on basic, relatively culture-free vocabulary, has been rejected by most linguists, since all its basic assumptions have been challenged. Therefore, it warrants little discussion here. Suffice it to repeat that it does not find or test distant genetic relationships, but rather by ticking off similarities it *assumes* that the languages compared are related and merely proceeds to attach a date based on the number of core-vocabulary words that are considered similar among the languages compared. This, then, is no method for determining whether languages are related. (See Chapter 16 for more details about glottochronology.)

   Glottochronology's focus on vocabulary replacement over time does draw attention indirectly to a serious problem concerning lexical evidence in long-range relationships. Related languages that separated from one another long ago may have undergone so much vocabulary replacement that insufficient shared original vocabulary will remain for an ancient shared linguistic kinship to be detected. This constitutes a serious problem for detecting really ancient language family connections.

13.2.3 Multilateral (or mass) comparison

The best-known of the approaches which rely on inspectional resemblances among lexical items is that advocated by Joseph Greenberg, called 'multilateral (or mass) comparison'. It is based on 'looking at . . . many languages across a few words' rather than 'at a few languages across many words' (Greenberg 1987: 23). The lexical similarities determined by superficial inspection which are shared 'across many languages' alone are taken as evidence of genetic relationship. This approach stops where others begin, at the assembling of lexical similarities. These inspectional resemblances must be investigated to determine why they are similar, whether the similarity is due to inheritance from a common ancestor (the result of a phylogenetic relationship) or to borrowing, chance, onomatopoeia, sound symbolism, nursery formations, and the various things which we will consider in this chapter. Since multilateral comparison does not do this, its results are controversial and rejected by most mainstream historical linguists.

In short, no technique which relies on inspectional similarities in vocabulary alone has proven adequate for establishing distant language family relationships.

13.3   Sound Correspondences

It is important to emphasize the value and utility of sound correspondences in the investigation of linguistic relationships. Nearly all scholars consider regular sound correspondences strong evidence for genetic affinity. Nevertheless, while sound correspondences are fundamental to most approaches to determining language families, they can be misused, and it is important to understand how this can be.

First, it is systematic sound correspondences that are crucial, not mere similarities; sound correspondences do not necessarily involve similar sounds. The sounds which are equated in proposals of remote relationship are typically very similar, often identical, although such identities are not so frequent among the daughter languages of well-established, non-controversial older language families. The sound changes that lead to such non-identical correspondences often result in cognate words being so changed that their cognacy is not readily apparent. These true but non-obvious cognates are missed by methods, such as multilateral comparison, which seek only inspectional resemblances. They miss such well-known true cognates as French *cinq*/Russian *pʲatʲ*/Armenian *hing*/English *five* (all derived from original Indo-European **penkʷe-* 'five'); French *boeuf*/English *cow* (from Proto-Indo-European **gʷou-*); French /nu/ (spelled *nous*) 'we, us'/English *us* (both ultimately from Proto-Indo-European **nos-*; English from Germanic **uns* < **n̥s*); and French *feuille* /føj/ 'leaf'/Spanish *hoja* /oxa/ 'leaf', cognates that come from Latin *folia* 'leaf'. The words in these cognate sets are not visually similar to each other, but most exhibit regular sound correspondences among the cognates.

There are a number of ways in which the criterion of sound correspondences can be misapplied. Sometimes regularly corresponding sounds may also be found in loanwords. For example, it is known from Grimm's Law (Chapter 7) that real French–English cognates should exhibit the correspondence *p* : *f*, as in *père*/*father*, *pied*/*foot*, *pour*/*for*. However, French and English also appear to exhibit the correspondence *p* : *p* in cases where English has borrowed from French or Latin, as in *paternel*/*paternal*, *piédestal*/*pedestal*, *per*/*per*. Since English has many such loans, examples illustrating this bogus *p* : *p* sound correspondence are not hard to find. In comparing languages not yet known to be related, we must use caution in interpreting sound correspondences to avoid the problem of apparent correspondences found in undetected loans. Generally, sound correspondences found in basic vocabulary warrant the confidence that the correspondences are probably legitimate, since, as mentioned above, terms for basic vocabulary are borrowed infrequently. However, even here we have to be careful, since items of basic vocabulary can also be borrowed, though more rarely. For example, Finnish *äiti* 'mother' and *tytär* 'daughter' are borrowed from Indo-European languages; if these loans were not recognized, one would suspect a sound correspondence of *t* : *d* involving the medial consonant of *äiti* (compare Old High German *eidī*) and the initial consonant of *tytär* (compare Germanic **duhtēr*) based on these basic vocabulary items (found also in other loans).

Some non-genuine sound correspondences can also come from accidentally similar lexical items among languages. Languages share a certain amount of similar vocabulary by sheer accident. A few examples that show this are: Proto-Jê **niw* 'new'/English *new*; Kaqchikel dialects *mes* 'mess, disorder, garbage'/English *mess*; Jaqaru *aska* 'ask'/English *ask*; Māori *kuri* 'dog'/English *cur*; Lake Miwok *hóllu* 'hollow'/English *hollow*; Gbaya *be* 'to be'/English *be*; Seri *kiʔ*/French *qui* (/ki/) 'who?'; Yana *t'inii-* 'small'/English *tiny, teeny*; and the famous handbook examples of Persian *bad*/English *bad*, and Malay *mata* 'eye'/Modern Greek *mati* 'eye'.

Other cases of unreal sound correspondences may turn up if one permits wide semantic latitude in proposed cognates, so that phonetically similar but semantically disparate forms are equated. For example, if we were to compare Pipil (Uto-Aztecan) and Finnish (Uralic) words such as Pipil *teki* 'to cut' : Finnish *teki* 'made', *te:n* 'mouth' : *teen* 'of the tea', *tukat* 'spider' : *tukat* 'hairs', *tila:n* 'pulled' : *tilaan* 'into the space', *tu:lin* 'cattails, reeds' : *tuulin* 'by the wind', and so on, we would note a recurrence of a *t* : *t* correspondence, among others. However, the phonetic correspondence in these words is due to sheer accident, since it is always possible to find phonetically similar words among languages if their meanings are ignored. With too much semantic liberty among compared forms, it is easy to come up with spurious correspondences such as the Pipil–Finnish *t* : *t*. Unfortunately, wide semantic latitude is frequently a problem in proposals of remote relationship (see below). Additional non-inherited phonetic similarities crop up when onomatopoeic, sound-symbolic, and nursery forms are compared. A set of proposed cognates involving a combination of loans, chance enhanced by semantic latitude, onomatopoeia, and such factors may exhibit false sound correspondences. For this reason, some proposed remote relationships that are purportedly based on regular sound correspondences nevertheless fail to be convincing.

Most linguists find sound correspondences strong evidence, but many do not trust them fully. Most linguists are happier when additional evidence from comparative morphology and grammar also supports the hypothesis.

13.4 Grammatical Evidence

Scholars throughout linguistic history have considered morphological evidence important for establishing language families. Many favour 'shared aberrancy' (talked about sometimes as 'submerged features', 'morphological peculiarities', 'arbitrary associations'), as illustrated, for example, by the corresponding irregularities in forms of the verb 'to be' in branches of Indo-European in Table 13.1 (PERS = person, PL = plural, SG = singular; OCS = Old Church Slavonic).

For example, the Algonquian–Ritwan hypothesis, which groups Wiyot and Yurok (two languages of California) with the Algonquian family, was

TABLE 13.1: Forms of the verb 'to be' in some Indo-European languages

	3rd pers sg	3rd pers pl	1st pers sg
Hittite	estsi	asantsi	—
Sanskrit	ásti	sánti	asmi
Greek	estí	eisí	eimí
Latin	est	sunt	sum
OCS	jestı	sãntı	jesmı
Gothic	ist	sind	im

controversial, but morphological evidence such as that in the following comparison of Proto-Central Algonquian (PCA) and Wiyot helped, along with other evidence, to prove the relationship:

PCA   *ne + *ehkw- = *netehkw 'my louse'
Wiyot   du + híkw   =   dutíkw 'my louse'. (Teeter 1964: 1029)

In Proto-Central Algonquian, a -t- is inserted between a possessive pronominal prefix and a vowel-initial root, while in Wiyot a -t- is inserted between possessive prefixes and a root beginning in hV (with the loss of the h in this process). Sapir (1913) had proposed that Wiyot (and also Yurok) of California were related to the Algonquian family; this proposed relationship was controversial, but evidence increased, including that presented here, which ultimately demonstrated the validity of the hypothesis to the satisfaction of all.

There is no clear phonetic motivation for a language to add a t in this environment (between vowels or between a vowel and hV), and this is so unusual that it is not likely to be shared by borrowing or by accident. Inheritance from a common ancestor which had this peculiarity is more likely, and this hypothesis of distant genetic relationship is confirmed by other evidence shared by these languages; this broader language family (that includes Wiyot, Yurok, and Algonquian) is called Algic.

An often-repeated example of shared aberrancy is the agreement between English good/better/best and German gut/besser/best, said to be 'obviously of enormous probative value' for showing that languages are related (Greenberg 1987: 30).

Morphological correspondences of the 'shared aberrancy'/'submerged features' type, just like sound correspondences, are generally thought to be an important source of evidence for distant genetic relationships. Nevertheless, caution is necessary here as well. There are impressive cases of apparent idiosyncratic grammatical correspondences which in fact have non-genetic explanations. Since some languages do share some seemingly submerged features by accident, caution is necessary in the interpretation of morphological evidence. Clearly, then, the strongest hypotheses of remote linguistic kinship are those which have evidence of several sorts: recurrent sound correspondences in basic vocabulary and multiple examples of grammatical evidence of the sort just discussed.

13.5 Borrowing

Diffusion is a source of non-genetic similarity among languages. It can complicate evidence for remote relationships. Too often, scholars err in not eliminating
loans from consideration as possible evidence of wider relationship. An example
which was presented as evidence of the now rejected 'Chibchan–Paezan' genetic
grouping (involving several South American language families) illustrates this
problem. For the proposed cognate set meaning 'axe', forms from only four of
the many languages involved were cited, two of which are loanwords: Cuitlatec
navaxo 'knife', borrowed from Spanish *navajo* 'knife, razor', and Tunebo *baxi-ta*
'machete', borrowed from Spanish *machete* (in Tunebo [x] alternates with [ʃ];
nasal consonants do not occur before oral vowels; the last two vowels of the
Tunebo form are expected substitutes for Spanish *e*) (Greenberg (1987: 108).
Clearly, because two of the four pieces of evidence are borrowings, the putative
'axe' cognate is not good evidence for the hypothesis. Among compared forms
cited as support for the controversial Nostratic hypothesis (which would join
Indo-European, Uralic, Altaic, South Caucaisan (Kartvelian), and for some
scholars also Dravidian and Afroasiatic into one large superfamily), some involve
known loanwords (for example, those for 'practice witchcraft'), and others have
been claimed to involve loans, for example those for 'vessel', 'honey', 'birch',
'bird-cherry', 'poplar', 'conifer', and so on (see Campbell 1998; 1999).

Since it is not always possible to recognize loanwords without extensive
research, it is frequently suggested (as mentioned above) that the problem
of borrowing can be made less severe by sticking only to comparisons of
basic vocabulary and avoiding words with cultural content. By this rule of
thumb, the Nostratic forms which have been questioned as possible loans
would all be set aside. While this is good practice, it must be remembered (as
mentioned above and shown in Chapter 3) that even basic vocabulary can
sometimes be borrowed. Finnish borrowed from its Baltic and Germanic neighbours various terms for basic kinship and body parts, for example 'mother',
'daughter', 'sister', 'tooth', 'navel', 'neck', 'thigh', 'fur', and so on. English has
borrowed from French or Latin the basic vocabulary items *stomach, face, vein,
artery, intestine, mountain, navel, pain, penis, person, river, round, saliva*, and *testicle*; from
Scandinavian languages English borrowed *egg, leg, sister, skin, sky, they*, and others.
The problem of loans and potential loans is very serious for distant genetic
relationships.

13.6 Semantic Constraints

It is dangerous to present phonetically similar forms with different meanings as
potential evidence of remote genetic relationship under the assumption that semantic shifts have taken place. Of course meaning can shift, as seen in Chapter 6 (for
example, Albanian *motër* 'sister', from Indo-European 'mother'), but in hypotheses
of remote relationship the assumed semantic shifts cannot be documented. When
semantically non-equivalent forms are compared, the possibility that chance
accounts for the phonetic similarity is greatly increased, as in the Pipil–Finnish

examples above (cf. Ringe 1992). Even within families where the languages are known to be related, etymologies are not accepted unless an explicit account of any assumed semantic changes can be provided. The advice often given is to count only exact semantic equivalences. The problem of semantic permissiveness is one of the most common and most serious in long-range proposals. The following are a few of the many examples from various proposals of long-range relationships, presented just for illustration's sake (only the glosses of the various forms compared are cited). Among evidence cited for Nostratic, we find proposed cognate sets whose words differ in meaning in the following ways: 'lip'/'mushroom'/'soft outgrowth'; 'grow up'/'become'/'tree'/'be'; 'crust'/'rough'/'scab' (see Kaiser and Shevoroshkin 1988). In the proposed global etymology for 'finger, one' (in the Proto-World hypothesis) we find, for example, 'one'/'five'/'ten'/'once'/ 'only'/'first'/'single'/'fingernail'/'finger'/'toe'/'hand'/'palm of hand'/'arm'/ 'foot'/'paw'/'guy'/'thing'/'to show'/'to point'/'in hand'/'middle finger' (Ruhlen 1994: 322–3). In forms from the Amerind hypothesis (which proposes that nearly all the languages of the Americas belong to a single macrofamily), we find semantic equations such as 'body'/'belly'/'heart'/'skin'/'meat'/'be greasy'/'fat'/'deer'; 'child'/'copulate'/'son'/'girl'/'boy'/'tender'/'bear'/'small'; 'field'/'devil'/'bad'/'underneath'/'bottom' (Greenberg 1987). It is for reasons like this that these proposals of remote linguistic relationship are not generally accepted.

13.7 Onomatopoeia

Onomatopoeic words imitate the real-world sounds associated with the meaning of the words, such as *bow-wow* for the noise that dogs make when barking, *cockadoodledoo* for roosters' crowing, and so on. Sometimes the connection to the sounds in nature is strong enough to inhibit onomatopoeic words from undergoing otherwise regular sound changes. For example, English *peep* /pip/, from earlier *pīpen*, would have become /paip/ by regular sound change (via the Great Vowel Shift; see Chapter 2) if not for the influence of onomatopoeia, to keep the word sounding more like the sound in nature that it refers to (Anttila 1989: 86). Onomatopoeic forms may be similar in different languages because they have independently imitated the sounds of nature, not because they share any common history. Examples involving onomatopoeia must be eliminated from proposals of distant genetic relationship. A way to reduce the sound-imitative factor is to omit from consideration words which cross-linguistically are often imitative in form, for example, words meaning 'blow', 'breathe', 'suck', 'laugh', 'cough', 'sneeze', 'break/cut/chop/split', 'cricket', 'crow' (and many bird names in general), 'frog/toad', 'lungs', 'baby/ infant', 'beat/hit/pound', 'call/shout', 'choke', 'cry', 'drip/drop', 'hiccough', 'kiss', 'shoot', 'snore', 'spit', and 'whistle', among others. Unfortunately, examples of onomatopoeic words are found very frequently in proposals of distant genetic relationships.

13.8 Nursery Forms

It is generally recognized that nursery words (the 'mama–nana–papa–dada–caca' sort of words) should be avoided in considerations of potential linguistic relationships, since they typically share a high degree of cross-linguistic similarity which is not due to common ancestry. Nevertheless, examples of nursery words are frequently presented as evidence for distant genetic relationship proposals. The forms involved are typically those meaning 'mother', 'father', 'grandmother', 'grandfather', and often 'brother', 'sister' (especially elder siblings), 'aunt', and 'uncle', and have shapes like *mama, nana, papa, baba, tata, dada*, where nasals are found more in terms for females, and stops for males, but not exclusively so.

Roman Jakobson explained the cross-linguistic non-genetic similarity among nursery forms which enter adult vocabulary. In his view, the sucking activities of a child are accompanied by a nasal sound, which can be made while nursing, and this nasal sound first associated with nursing is reproduced to show a desire to eat or impatience for missing food or the absent nurse/mother. Since the mother dispenses the food, most of the infant's longings are addressed to her, and the nasal form is turned into a parental term. Then comes a transitional period when *papa* means whichever parent is present while *mama* signals a request for need-fulfilment, and eventually the nasal–mother, oral–father association becomes established (1962 [1960]: 542–3). This helps to explain frequent spontaneous, symbolic, affective developments, seen when inherited *mother* in English is juxtaposed to *ma, mama, mamma, mammy, mommy, mom, mummy, mum*, and *father* is compared with *pa, papa, pappy, pop, poppy, da, dad, dada, daddy*. Similarities among such nursery words do not provide reliable support for distant genetic proposals.

13.9 Short Forms and Unmatched Segments

How long proposed cognates are and the number of matched sounds (segments) within them are important, since the greater the number of matching segments in words compared in a proposed cognate set, the less likely it is that accident accounts for the similarity. Monosyllabic morphemes composed of a single consonant and vowel (or even a single vowel or a single consonant) may be true cognates, but they are so short that their similarity to forms in other languages could also easily be due to chance. Likewise, if only one or two sounds of longer forms are matched (and other sounds are left unmatched, unaccounted for), then chance remains a strong candidate for the explanation of any perceived similarity. Such comparisons will not be persuasive; all the sounds of whole words must be accounted for. (See Ringe 1999.)

13.10 Chance Similarities

Chance (accident) is another possible explanation for similarities among compared languages, and it needs to be avoided in questions of deep family relationships. Conventional wisdom holds that 5–6 per cent of the vocabulary of any two compared languages may be accidentally similar. Also, phoneme frequency within a language plays a role in how often one should expect chance matchings involving particular sounds to come up in comparisons of words from that language with ones from other languages. For example, about 15 per cent of English basic vocabulary begins with *s*, while only about 7.5 per cent begins with *w*; thus, given the greater number of initial *s* words in English, one must expect a higher possible number of chance matchings for *s* than for *w* when English is compared with other languages. The potential for accidental matching increases dramatically when one leaves the realm of basic vocabulary, or when one increases the pool of words from which potential cognates are sought, or when one permits the semantics of compared forms to vary (Ringe 1992: 5).

Cases of non-cognate words which are similar in related languages are well known, for example French *feu* 'fire' and German *Feuer* 'fire' (French *feu* < Latin *focus* 'hearth, fireplace' [-k- > -g- > -Ø-; o > ø]; German *Feuer* < Proto-Indo-European **pūr* 'fire', Proto-Germanic **fūr-i*; compare Old English *fȳr*). As is well known, these cannot be cognates, since French *f* comes from Proto-Indo-European **bh*, while German *f* comes from Proto-Indo-European **p* (by Grimm's Law). The phonetic similarity which these basic nouns share is due to the accidental convergence resulting from sound changes that they have undergone, not to inheritance from any common word in the proto-language. That originally distinct forms in different languages can become similar due to sound changes is not surprising, since even within a single language originally distinct forms can converge, for example, English *son/sun*, *eye/I*, and *lie/lie* (Proto-Germanic **ligjan* 'to lie, lay'/**leugan* 'to tell a lie').

13.11 Sound–Meaning Isomorphism

A generally accepted principle (advocated by Antoine Meillet) permits only comparisons which involve both sound and meaning together. Similarities in sound alone (for example, the presence of tonal systems in compared languages) or in meaning alone (for example, grammatical gender in the languages compared) are not reliable, since they can develop independently of genetic relationship, due to diffusion, accident, and typological tendencies (see Greenberg 1963).

13.12 Only Linguistic Evidence

Another valid principle permits conclusions to be based only on linguistic information, with no non-linguistic considerations as evidence of distant genetic relationship permitted. As Gabelentz (1891: 157) put it, 'the only sure means for recognizing a [genetic] relationship lies in the languages themselves.' (See also Greenberg 1963.) Shared cultural traits, mythology, folklore, and biological traits must be eliminated from arguments for linguistic family relationship. The wisdom of this principle becomes clear when we take into account the many strange proposals based on non-linguistic evidence. For example, some earlier African classifications proposed that Ari (Omotic) belongs to either Nilo-Saharan or Sudanic 'because the Ari people are Negroes', that Moru and Madi belong to Sudanic because they are located in central Africa, or that Fula is Hamitic because its speakers herd cattle, are Moslems, and are tall and Caucasoid (Fleming 1987: 207). Clearly, language affinities can be independent of cultural and biological connections.

13.13 Erroneous Morphological Analysis

Where compared words are analysed as being composed of more than one morpheme, it is necessary to show that the segmented morphemes (roots and affixes) in fact exist in the grammatical system. Unfortunately, unmotivated morphological segmentation is found frequently in proposals of remote relationship. Often, a morpheme boundary is inserted in forms where none is justified, as for example the arbitrarily segmented Tunebo 'machete' as *baxi-ta* (a loanword from Spanish *machete*, as mentioned above, which contains no morpheme boundary but rather is a single morpheme). This false morphological segmentation makes the form appear more similar to the other forms cited as putative cognates, Cabecar *bak* and Andaqui *boxo-(ka)* 'axe' (Greenberg 1987: 108).

Undetected morpheme divisions are also a frequent problem. An example of this, taken from the Amerind hypothesis, compares Tzotzil *tiʔil* 'hole' with Lake Miwok *talokʰ* 'hole', Atakapa *tol* 'anus', Totonac *tan* 'buttocks', and Takelma *telkan* 'buttocks' (Greenberg 1987: 152). However, the Tzotzil form is *tiʔ-il*, from *tiʔ* 'mouth' + *-il* 'indefinite possessive suffix', meaning 'mouth, lip, edge, border, outskirts', but not 'hole'. The appropriate comparison *tiʔ* bears no particular resemblance to the other forms in this comparison set. (For other examples, see the discussion of Amerind, below.)

13.14 Non-cognates

Another problem is the frequent comparison of words which are not cognates even within their own family with words from other languages as evidence of distant genetic relationship. Often, unrelated words from related languages are joined together in the belief that they might be cognates and then this set is compared further with forms from other language families as evidence for even more distant linguistic affinities. However, if the words are not even cognates within their own family, any further comparison with forms from languages outside the family is untrustworthy.

Examples from the Maya–Chipayan hypothesis (Olson 1964; 1965) illustrate this difficulty. Tzotzil *ay(in)* 'to be born' comes from Proto-Tzotzilan **ay-an* 'to live, to be born', which in turn is from Proto-Mayan **ar-* 'there is/are'. However, this is not cognate with Olson's *yaʔ* (*yah*) 'pain' in the other Mayan languages that he joins in this putative Mayan cognate set; those *yah* 'pain' forms are from Proto-Mayan **yah* 'pain, hurt', an entirely different etymon from the **ar-* 'there is/are', although the grouping together of these otherwise unrelated Mayan cognates makes Mayan comparisons seem more like Chipaya *ay(in)* 'to hurt'. (*y* = IPA [j] in these examples.) Yucatec Maya *čal(tun)* 'extended (rock)' is compared to non-cognate *čʼen* 'rock, cave' in some other Mayan languages; the true Yucatec cognate is *čʼeʔen* 'well' (and 'cave of water') (from Proto-Mayan **kʼeʔn* 'rock, cave'). Yucatec *čal-tun* means 'cistern, deposit of water, porous cliff where there is water' (from *čal* 'sweat, liquid' + *tun* 'stone', which is from Proto-Mayan **to:ŋ* 'stone'). The non-cognate *čaltun* suggests greater similarity to Chipaya *çara* 'rock (flat, long)' with which the set is compared than the **k'e?n* cognates do (Campbell and Poser 2008: 207-8). (*č* = IPA [ʧ] in these examples; *ç* = retroflex affricate.)

13.14.1　Words of limited distribution

Often in proposals of distant genetic relationship, an isolated word from some language with no known cognates in other languages of its family is compared to forms in languages from other families. However, a word which has cognates in its own family stands a better chance of perhaps having an even more remote connection with words of languages that may be distantly related than an isolated word which has no known cognates in other languages in its family, and hence offers no prima facie evidence of potential older age. Inspectionally resemblant lexical sets of this sort are not convincing. Meillet's principle for established families is just as important – even more so – when considering proposals of distant genetic relationship, where the languages are not yet known to be related:

> When an initial 'proto language' is to be reconstructed, the number of witnesses which a word has should be taken into account. An agreement of two languages . . . risks being fortuitous. But, if the agreement extends to three, four or five very distinct languages [of the same family], chance becomes less probable. (Meillet 1966: 38, Rankin's 1992: 331 translation)

13.14.2　Neglect of known history

It is not uncommon in proposals of distant genetic relationship to encounter forms from one language which exhibit similarities to forms in another language where the similarity is known to be due to recent changes in the individual history of one of the languages. In such cases, when the known history of the languages is brought back into the picture, the similarity disintegrates. An example of this sort is seen in the set of lexical comparisons labelled 'dance' in the Amerind hypothesis which compares Koasati (a Muskogean language) *bit* 'dance' with Mayan forms for 'dance' or 'sing': K'iche' *bis* (actually *b'i:š* [IPA ɓiːʃ] 'sing'), Huastec *bisom* and so on (Greenberg 1987: 148). However, Koasati *b* comes from Proto-Muskogean **kʷ*; the Muskogean root was **kʷit-* 'to press down', where 'dance' is a semantic shift in Koasati alone, applied to stomp dances (Kimball 1992: 456). Only by neglecting the known history of Koasati (that *b < *kʷ*, and that the original meaning was not 'dance') could the Koasati form be seen as similar to Mayan.

13.15　Spurious Forms

Another problem is that of non-existent 'data', that is, difficulties that have to do with the 'bookkeeping' and 'scribal' errors which result in spurious forms being compared. For example, among the forms presented as evidence for the

Mayan–Mixe-Zoquean hypothesis (Brown and Witkowski 1979), Mixe-Zoquean words meaning 'shell' were compared with K'iche' (Mayan) *sak'*, said to mean 'lobster', but which actually means 'grasshopper' – a mistranslation of the Spanish gloss *langosta* found in a K'iche'–Spanish dictionary, where *langosta* in Guatemala means 'grasshopper' in this context. While a 'shell'–'lobster' comparison is a semantic stretch to begin with, it is not as fully implausible as the comparison of 'shell'–'grasshopper', which makes no sense. Errors of this sort can be very serious. Such a case is that of the words given as Quapaw in the Amerind hypothesis (Greenberg 1987) where in fact none is from the Quapaw language, but rather all are from Biloxi and Ofo (other Siouan languages, not closely related to Quapaw; see Rankin 1992: 342). Skewed forms also often enter proposals due to philological mishandling of the sources. For example, in the Amerind evidence, the <v> and <e> of the Creek source of the data were systematically mistransliterated as *u* and *e*, although these represent /a/ and /i/ respectively. Thus <vne> 'I' is presented as *une* rather than the accurate *ani* (Kimball 1992: 448). Such spurious forms skew the comparisons.

13.16 Areal Linguistics and Proposals of Distant Genetic Relationship

Unfortunately, it is not uncommon to find cases of similarities among languages which are in reality due to areal diffusion but which are mistakenly taken to be evidence of a possible distant family relationship among the languages in question. For example, much of the evidence upon which the Altaic hypothesis was based when it was originally formed turns out to be traits diffused in the linguistic area, and this is one of the main reasons why specialists have not found Altaic convincing. Failure to distinguish areal linguistic traits is a considerable obstacle to the Altaic hypothesis. (The various problems for the proposal are considered in the discussion of Altaic below.)

From such examples, it is easy to see why the identification of areal traits is so important in historical linguistics, where failure to recognize the areal borrowings can lead to erroneous proposals of genetic relationship.

13.17 Some Examples of Long-range Proposals

It will be helpful to look briefly at a few well-known but disputed proposals of distant genetic relationship to see why most mainstream historical linguists are sceptical about them.

13.17.1 Altaic

The Altaic hypothesis (just seen, above) would group Turkic, Mongolian, and Tungusic together, and some versions also include Korean and Japanese. While 'Altaic' continues to be included in numerous basic reference works, most leading 'Altaicists' have abandoned the hypothesis. The most serious problems for the Altaic proposal are the extensive lexical borrowings among the languages involved, lack of significant numbers of convincing cognates, extensive areal diffusion, and typologically commonplace traits presented as evidence of relationship. The 'Altaic' traits shared among the languages of these language families that are typically cited include vowel harmony, relatively simple phoneme inventories, agglutination, suffixing with no prefixes, (S)OV word order, postpositions, no verb 'to have' for possession, no articles, no grammatical gender, and non-finite verb forms for subordinate clause constructions. These shared features are not only commonplace traits which occur with frequency in unrelated languages of the world, they are also areal traits, as mentioned above, shared by a number of languages in northern Eurasia whose structural properties were not well known when the hypothesis was first framed. Proposed cognates for Altaic languages include very little basic vocabulary; for example, most body-part terms and low numbers are lacking. Criticisms also involve problems with the putative sound correspondences that have been suggested among the 'Altaic' languages.

In short, most scholars are not convinced by the evidence that has been presented for the 'Altaic' hypothesis. (See Campbell and Poser 2008.)

13.17.2 Nostratic

The Nostratic hypothesis as advanced in the 1960s by Vladislav Illich-Svitych groups Indo-European, Uralic, Altaic, South Caucasian (Kartvelian), Dravidian, and Hamito-Semitic (later reformulated as Afroasiatic), though other versions of the hypothesis would include various additional language groups. The sheer number of languages and the many proposed cognates might seem to make it difficult to evaluate Nostratic. Nevertheless, assessment is possible. With respect to the many putative cognate sets, assessment can concentrate on those cases considered the strongest by proponents of Nostratic (see Dolgopolsky 1986; Kaiser and Shevoroshkin 1988). Campbell (1998) shows that these strongest cases do not hold up well and that the weaker sets are not persuasive. It is also relatively easy to determine that several of the proposed reconstructions violate typological expectations, that sounds in various proposed cognate sets do not actually fit the proposed Nostatic sound correspondences, that numerous proposed cognates involve excessive semantic latitude, and that onomatopoeia, forms too short to deny chance, nursery forms, and the like are involved in several cases.

Illich-Svitych's (henceforth IS) version of Nostratic exhibits the following methodological problems (as seen, for example, in Illich-Svitych 1990).

(1) *'Descriptive' forms*. IS is forthright in labelling 26 of his 378 forms – 7 per cent of the total – as 'descriptive', meaning onomatopoeic, affective, or sound-symbolic. There are 16 additional onomatopoeic, affective, or sound-symbolic forms, not so labelled, giving a total of about 11 per cent.

(2) *Questionable cognates*. IS himself indicates that 57 of the 378 sets (15 per cent) are questionable, signalling them with a question mark. However, this number should be much increased, since in numerous forms IS signals problems with proposed cognates in other ways, with slanted lines (/ /) for things not conforming to expectations, with question marks, and with upper-case letters in reconstructions to indicate uncertainties or ambiguities.

(3) *Sets with only two families represented.* One of IS's criteria was that only cognate sets with representatives from at least three of the six 'Nostratic' families would be considered as supportive. Nevertheless, 134 of the 378 sets (35 per cent) involve forms from only two families, questionable by IS's own criteria.

(4) *Non-conforming sound correspondences.* Frequently the forms presented as evidence of Nostratic do not exhibit the proposed sound correspondences, that is, they have sounds at odds with those that would be required according to the claimed Nostratic sound correspondences. Campbell (1998), looking mostly only at stops and only at the Indo-European and Uralic data, found twenty-five sets that did not follow the proposed Nostratic correspondences. There is another way in which IS's putative sound correspondences are not consistent with the standard comparative method. Several of the putative reconstructed Nostratic sounds are not reflected by regular sound correspondences in the languages. For example, 'in Kartv[elian] and Indo-European, the reflexes of Nostratic [**]p are found to be unstable' (IS 1990: 168); Nostratic forms beginning in **p reveal that both the Indo-European and the South Caucasian (Kartvelian), forms arbitrarily begin with either *p or *b. However, this is not regular and is not sanctioned by the comparative method. Similarly, glottalization in Afroasiatic is said to occur 'sporadically under other conditions still not clear' (IS 1990: 168). In the correspondence sets, several of the languages are listed with multiple reflexes of a single Nostratic sound, but with no explanation of conditions under which the distinct reflexes might appear.

(5) *Short forms.* Of IS's 378 forms, 57 (15 per cent) involve short forms (CV, VC, C, or V), too short to deny chance as an alternative explanation.

(6) *Semantically non-equivalent forms.* Some 55 cases (14 per cent) involve comparisons of forms in the different languages that are fairly distinct semantically.

(7) *Diffused forms.* Given the history of central Eurasia, with much language contact, it is not at all surprising that some forms turn out to be borrowed. Several of the putative Nostratic cognate sets have words which have been identified by others as loans, including words for 'sister-in-law', 'water', 'do', 'give', 'carry', 'lead', 'do'/'put', and 'husband's sister', to which we can add the following as probable or possible loans: 'conifer, branch, point', 'thorn', 'poplar', 'practise witchcraft', 'deer', 'vessel', 'birch', 'bird cherry', 'honey', and 'mead'.

(8) *Typological problems.* Nostratic as traditionally reconstructed is typologically problematic. Counter to expectations, few Nostratic roots contain two voiceless stops; glottalized stops are considerably more frequent than their plain counterparts; and Nostratic affricates change to a cluster of fricative + stop in Indo-European.

(9) *Evaluation of the strongest lexical sets.* An examination of the Nostratic sets held by proponents to be the strongest reveals serious problems with most. These include Dolgopolsky's (1986) fifteen most stable lexemes. Most are questionable in one way or another according to the standard criteria for assessing proposals of remote linguistic kinship. In the Nostratic sets representing Dolgopolsky's fifteen most stable glosses, four have problems with phonological correspondences; five involve excessive semantic difference among the putative cognates; four have representatives in only two of the putative Nostratic families; two involve problems of morphological analysis; IS himself listed one as doubtful; and finally, one

reflects the tendency to rely too heavily on a form from Finnish which is not supported by the historical evidence. All but two cases are challenged, and for these two the relevant forms needed for evaluation are not present. These 'strong' cases are not sufficiently robust to support the proposed genetic relationship.

Once again, it is for reasons such as these that most historical linguists reject the Nostratic hypothesis. (See Campbell 1998; 1999; Campbell and Poser 2008 for details.)

13.17.3 Amerind

Joseph Greenberg's Amerind hypothesis, represented principally in his book *Language in the Americas* (1987), contends that all indigenous languages of the Americas, except the 'Na-Dene' and Eskimo-Aleut languages, belong to a single macrofamily, 'Amerind', based on multilateral comparison. Amerind is rejected by virtually all specialists in Native American languages and by the vast majority of historical linguists. They maintain that valid methods do not at present permit reduction of Native American languages to fewer than about 170 independent language families and isolates. Amerind has been criticized, on various grounds. Specialists find extensive inaccuracies in Greenberg's data: 'the number of erroneous forms probably exceeds that of the correct forms' (Adelaar 1989: 253). Greenberg assembled forms which on superficial inspection are similar among the languages which he compared and declared them to be evidence of common heritage. However, as mentioned earlier, where Greenberg's method stops, after having assembled the similarities, is where other linguists start. Since similarities can be due to a number of factors – accident, borrowing, onomatopoeia, sound symbolism, nursery words, and universals – for a plausible proposal of remote relationship one must attempt to eliminate all other possible explanations, leaving a shared common heritage the most likely. Greenberg made no attempt to eliminate these other explanations, and the similarities he amassed appear to be due mostly to accident and a combination of these other factors. In various instances, Greenberg compared arbitrary segments of words, equated words with very different meanings (for example, 'excrement'/'night'/'grass'), misidentified numerous languages, failed to analyse the morphology of some words and falsely analysed that of others, neglected regular sound correspondences entirely, failed to eliminate loanwords, and misinterpreted well-established findings. The Amerind 'etymologies' proposed are often limited to a very few languages of the many involved. (For details and examples, see Adelaar 1989; Berman 1992; Campbell 1988b; 1997a; Kimball 1992; McMahon and McMahon 1995; Poser 1992; Rankin 1992; Ringe 1992; 1996.) Finnish, Japanese, Basque, and other randomly chosen languages fit Greenberg's Amerind data as well as or better than any of the American Indian languages do; Greenberg's method has proven incapable of distinguishing implausible relationships from Amerind generally.

Critics of the hypothesis point out problems of various sorts. Greenberg introduced some *language names* into his classification which are not languages at all – for example, *Membreño*, which Greenberg classified as a Lencan language, is a person's name, a reference (Membreño 1897). There are numerous examples that involve *borrowing*, some mentioned above. Some examples of *excessive semantic latitude*, with only the meanings compared, include 'ask/wish/seek/pleasure'; 'bitter/to rot/sour/sweet/ripe/spleen/gall'; 'body/belly/heart/skin/meat/be greasy/fat/deer'; 'child/copulate/son/girl/boy/tender/bear/small'; 'earth/sand/sweepings/mud/dirty'; 'field/devil/bad/underneath/bottom'; 'earth/island/forest/mud/village/town/dust/world/ground'; 'hole/mouth/ear/listen/chin/nose/smell/blow nose/sniff'; and so on. Such semantic permissiveness increases the probability that chance explains the compared forms. Numerous forms involved *onomatopoeia*; one example is the set with *pui, puhi, phu-* for 'blow'(Greenberg 1987: 196). Undetected *morpheme divisions* can make forms seem more similar than they actually are. Greenberg has a number of these, including Rama *mukuik* 'hand' as "cognate" with other American Indian languages with forms like *ma* or *makV*; however, 'hand' in Rama is *kwi:k*; the *mu-* is the 'second person possessive' prefix; the root *kwi:k* 'hand' bears no significant resemblance to Greenberg's **ma(-kV)*. Similarly, several examples involve *insertion of morpheme boundaries* where none is justified. Poser (1992) showed that of Greenberg's Salinan and Yurumanguí forms, eleven of twenty-six cited have specious morphological analyses. Berman (1992: 232) noted 'there is not a single Tualatin [Kalapuya] word in which Greenberg segments any of these prefixes correctly.' Other examples are mentioned above. There are numerous *spurious forms*, scribal errors, etc. For example, as mentioned, none of the Quapaw entries in Greenberg (1987) is from Quapaw; rather they are from Biloxi or Ofo.

In short, it is with good reason that Amerind has been rejected.

(For evaluations of the Dene-Yeniseian and the Chitimacha-Totzoquean hypotheses that show that the evidence presented in their favour is not adequate to sustain these proposed distant genetic relationships, see Campbell 2011; 2016.)

13.18 Methodological Wrap-up and Looking to the Future

Given the confusion that certain claims regarding proposed distant genetic relationships have caused, the methodological principles and procedures involved in the investigation of possible distant genetic relationships are extremely important. Principal among these are reliance on regular sound correspondences in basic vocabulary and patterned grammatical (morphological) evidence involving 'shared aberrancy' or 'submerged features', with careful attention to eliminating other possible explanations for similarities noted in compared material (for example, borrowing, onomatopoeia, accident, nursery forms, and so on). Research on possible distant genetic relationships that does not heed the methodological recommendations and cautions of this chapter will probably remain inconclusive. On the other hand, investigations informed and guided by the principles and criteria surveyed here stand a good chance of advancing understanding, by either further supporting or disconfirming proposed family connections.

Many proposals of distant genetic relationship have not stood up well when the evidence presented for them has been subjected to the methodological considerations surveyed in this chapter. This fact might seem to cast a doubt on the likelihood of demonstrating new, as yet unproven language family relationships.

However, we can take encouragement from the number of success stories of previously unknown or disputed relationships which subsequently have come to be demonstrated since the beginning of the twentieth century, and which satisfy the methodological recommendations presented in this chapter. A few examples are: Hittite and the other Anatolian languages demonstrated to be Indo-European; the Uto-Aztecan family demonstrated to the satisfaction of all; the Otomanguean family proven, and then later the demonstration that Tlapanec belongs to Otomanguean (not to 'Hokan' as previously believed); Algic demonstrated to the satisfaction of all (that Yurok and Wiyot of California and the Algonquian family belong to a more inclusive family); Sino-Tibetan established. Indeed, in recent years a number of new families have been recognized and the membership of others has been extended to include additional languages, in Australia (Pama-Nyungan in general, and that Western Torres Island belongs with Pama-Nyungan), in southeast Asia (Austroasiatic, with Munda and Mon-Khmer), and in Latin America with the recent establishment of the families Harakmbut-Katukinan (Harakmbut with Katukinan), Pano-Takanan (the two former families of Panoan and Takanan), Tikuna-Yuri (joining Tikuna and Yuri), Lule-Vilelan (with Lule and Vilela), and the demonstration that Rama belongs to Chibchan. Future demonstrations of linguistic relatedness can be expected if proper methodological procedures are followed. (See Campbell and Poser 2008 for detailed discussion.)

13.19 Exercises

Exercise 13.1 The Xinka–Lenca hypothesis

Handbooks and encyclopaedias continue to report the claim that 'Xinca' (Xinka) and Lenca are related to one another and belong in a single language family. Essentially all the evidence ever published for this hypothesis is presented below. Evaluate this proposed evidence based on the criteria and considerations discussed in this chapter. What do you conclude about the strength of the supporting evidence?

Background: 'Xinca' (Xinka, pronounced [ˈʃiŋka]) is actually a language family, called Xinkan, of four languages in southeastern Guatemala. These languages no longer have any mother-tongue speakers, though there is a programme to awaken one of these dormant languages. Lenca is also a small language family, Lencan, composed of two languages, Chilanga (Salvadoran Lenca) and Honduran Lenca, both recently extinct. Walter Lehmann (1920: 767) suggested that the two families are linked, though he also included other languages in his comparison, some as far away as California, a fact now long forgotten. Lehmann's evidence for the proposed 'Xinca–Lenca' relationship is reproduced here (with the form from Guazacapán Xinka in parentheses). Observations that may be relevant in your deliberations are also included as notes below the forms.

Xinka   *Lenca*
1. 'one'   ical (ik'ał)   etta, ita
2. 'two'   bi-al, pi-ar, pi (pi?)   pe
3. 'three'   vuaal-al, hual-ar (wał, wała)   laagua, lagua
4. 'four'   iri-ar ((h)irha)   heria, erio (also sa, aria, eslea)

[NOTE: Words for numbers higher than 'two' are widely borrowed in languages of this part of Central America; these include forms similar to those for 'two', 'three', and 'four' in these languages.]

5. 'water'   uÿ (uːy)   cuy 'winter'
6. 'night'   suma (sa-siʼma 'in the dark')   ts'ub 'night'
7. 'dark,   ts'ama (siʼma)   ts'ana-uamba 'morning
      black'   (to dawn)'
8. 'shade'   ti-tzuma (ti-siʼma 'in   saba
                  the dark')

[NOTE: The Xinkan forms in 6, 7, and 8 all involve the same root, /siʼma/ 'dark, black'.]

9. 'dog'   xusu (<x> = [š] (IPA [ʃ]))   shushu (<sh> = [š] (IPA [ʃ]))

[NOTE: These languages in effect have no alveopalatal affricate č (IPA [ʧ]); note also that the most common word for 'dog' in colloquial Spanish of the area is *chucho*.]

10. 'cough'   ojo [<j> = [x]] (oho)   hoo, oiguin
11. 'maize   au, aima (ayma)   ama, aima

[NOTE: Forms similar to *aima, ama, ayma, eima* for 'maize' are found widely in other languages of this region; they involve borrowings.]

12. 'bean'   xinak (šiʼnak)   shinag

[NOTE: Mayan languages border Xinkan territory and are close to Lencan territory. Cf. Cholan-Tzeltalan (Mayan) *čenek'* 'bean', from Proto-Mayan *kinaq'* 'bean'. Terms for 'bean' are borrowed from Mayan in some other languages of this part of Central America.]

Exercise 13.2 An 'Amerind' putative 'etymology'

Greenberg and Ruhlen (1992) presented the forms given here as one of the strongest examples of a putative cognate set to support their 'Amerind' hypothesis. Evaluate these data on the basis of the criteria and considerations discussed in this chapter.

Background: Joseph H. Greenberg's (1987) 'Amerind' hypothesis would group all the language families and isolates of the Americas except Eskimo-Aleut and Na-Dene. Most specialists in American Indian linguistics believe there are about 170 independent language families (including language isolates), not just one big family – that is, they believe the evidence available today is insufficient to reduce this number of language families by much, though it may be possible that in the remote past they were related, just so long ago that the evidence available to us is no longer sufficient to demonstrate it.

Nootka (Nuu-Chah-Nulth)	t'an'a	'child'
Yuchi	tane	'brother'
Totonac	t'ána-t	'grandchild'
Coahuilteco	t'an-pam	'child'
Proto-Uto-Aztecan	*tana	'daughter, son'
Miskito	tuk-tan	'child, boy'
Warrau [Warao]	dani-	'mother's sister'
Aymara	tayna	'firstborn child'
Masaca	tani-mai	'younger sister'
Urubu-Kaapor	ta'ïn	'child'
Pavishana	tane	'my son'
Lengua	tawin	'grandchild'
Tibagi	tog-tan	'girl'
Yurok	tˢin	'young man'
Mohawk	-'tˢin	'male, boy'
Molale	pēn-t'in	'my elder brother'
Yana	t'inī-si	'child, son, daughter'
Cuicatec	'díínó	'brother'
Changuenga	sin	'brother'
Millcayac	tzhœng	'son'
Tehuelche	den	'brother'
Tiquie	ten	'son'
Mocochi	tin-gwa	'son, boy'
Yagua	dēnu	'male child'
Tacana [Takana]	u-tse-kwa	'grandchild'
Guato	china	'older brother'
Coeur d'Alene	tune	'niece'
Yuchi	tˢ'one	'daughter, son'
Central Sierra Miwok	tūne-	'daughter'
Salinan	a-t'on	'younger sister'
Taos	-t'út'ina	'older sister'
Cayapa	tˢuh-ki	'sister'
Tehuelche	thaun	'sister'
Tiquie	ton	'daughter'
Morotoko	a-tune-sas	'girl'
Nonuya	-tona	'sister'

| Tacana [Takana] | -tóna | 'younger sister' |
| Pikobyé | a-ton-kä | 'younger sister' |

Exercise 13.3 Macro-Panoan distant genetic relationship

All of the evidence presented by Greenberg (1987: 74–8) for his proposed Macro-Panoan hypothesis (part of his larger Amerind proposal) is repeated here. Evaluate it based on the criteria and considerations in this chapter. What other possible explanations (other than that of cognates inherited from some common ancestor) do you see for some of the similarities among the lexical items compared from the different languages? What kinds of problems do you notice? List the problems involved with each lexical set. (Pay attention also to the number of languages from which potential evidence is cited in comparison to the total number of languages hypothesized to belong to this group.) After you have set aside forms that potentially have other, non-genetic explanations, what evidence (if any) do you find that might support a possible genetic relationship among the languages compared here?

Greenberg's Macro-Panoan hypothesis would group several South American language families and isolates: Panoan, Takanan (demonstrated as belonging to a single family, Pano-Takanan), Mosetén, Mataco[an], Guaicuru[an], Charruan, Lule, Vilela (now recognized as Lule-Vilelan), and Mascoy[an] (Enlhet-Enenlhet). Clarification of some of the names and some of the forms not included in Greenberg's data are given below in brackets, as [. . .].

1. BE ABLE [Mascoyan:] Lengua *wan(-či)*, *wan(-kje)*. Mataco[an]: Chulupi [Nivaclé] *ha-wanaia* [no such form exists; *xa-* 'first person pronoun'].
2. ANIMAL Guaicuru[an]: Toba-Guazu *sigiak*. [Mascoyan:] Lengua *askok*. Mataco[an]: Vejoz [Wichí] *łokue* [no such word exists in Wichi; *łokwe* is 'jug'; *lo* is the classifier for possessed domestic animals].
3. ANSWER (v.) Mataco[an]: Choroti *kamtini* 'speak'. Panoan: Cazinaua *køma*. Cavineña *kiema*.
4. ANUS Guaicuru[an]: Caduveo *-auio* 'buttocks'. Mataco[an]: Choroti *i-we*, Vejoz [Wichí] *wex* ['tail, backside']. Mosetén *jive* 'buttocks, anus'. Panoan [Pano-Takanan]: Caripuna *wahaa* 'open'. Takanan [Pano-Takanan]: Huarayo *wexa* 'opening', Chama *wexa* 'hole'.
5. AWAKE Charruan: Chana *inambi*. Guaicuru[an]: Toba-Guazu *tom* 'awake, dawn'. Mataco[an]: Vejoz [Wichí]: *nom* (intransitive) [*n-om* 'come, arrive', *n-* 'directional']. Panoan: Proto-Panoan **nama* 'to dream'.
6. BACK [Mascoyan:] Lengua *ak-puk*, *(eja-)puk* 'behind'. Panoan: Shipibo *puika*. Takanan: Cavineña *ebekakwa*, Chama *kiibaaxaxe* 'behind'.
7. BAD Guaicuru[an]: Guachi [Guachi is not a Guaicuruan language, though there is a hypothesis that it may be related] <oetcho> 'devil'.

Mataco[an]: Nocten [Wichí], Vejoz [Wichí] *tsoi* 'devil'. Mosetén *ači-tui* 'make dirty'. Takanan: Takana *ači*. Cf. Lule *ičelo* 'devil'.

8. BAT   Guaicuru: *kahit (h < s)*. Panoan: Proto-Panoan **kaši*.

9. BE   Lengua [Mascoyan]: Mascoy *h-*. [Matacoan:] Mataco [Wichí] *ihi, hi* [*i-* 'to be', *i-hi* 'be-LOCATIVE'].

10. BEAR (v.)   Guaicuru[an]: Mocovi *koo*, Toba-Guazu *koe*. Lule *kaa* 'born'. [Matacoan:] Mataco [Wichí] *ko*, Vejoz [Wichí] *ko*. Panoan: Proto-Panoan **kai* 'to bear, mother', Chacobo *ko* 'born'. Takanan: Chama *kwaja* 'be born'.

11. BEFORE   Lengua [Mascoyan]: Lengua, Mascoy *nanič*, Lengua *nahno, nahtu* 'mucho anteo' [*anteo* is unclear in Spanish, perhaps *mucho antes* 'much earlier, long before' was intended?]. Mataco[an]: Chulupi [Nivaclé] *naxeš* 'forward' [no such form exists; possibly from *nax-* 'to end, terminate'; probably a mixture of *nayiš* 'road' and the verb derived from it, *nayi-n* 'to anticipate, prepare, be first, go on ahead', where one translation in Spanish is *adelantarse* 'to go ahead, to go forward', which is similar to *adelante* 'ahead, forward, in front of, before'], Payagua [not Matacoan, sometimes hypothesized as belonging to Guaicuruan or to proposed Macro-Guaicuruan with Guaicuruan, Matacoan, Payaga, Guachi, but not demonstrated] *inahi*. Mosetén <yno>, *xinoje*.

12. BLOOD   Guaicuruan: Toba *t-auo*, Lule *ewe*. Mataco[an]: Chunupi [Nivaclé] *woi* [*woʔy*]. Takanan: Chama *woʔo* 'red'.

13. BODY   Lule *toip* [*-p* 'third person possessive pronoun']. Mataco[an]: Mataco [Wichí]: *tape* [*t-* 'third person possessive pronoun']. Takanan: Cavineña *etibo* 'trunk' [*e-tibu: e-* 'pronoun', *tibu* 'base'].

14. BREAK   Lengua [Mascoyan]: Mascoy *pok-* (intransitive). Mataco[an:] Mataco [Wichí] *puhʷoje* [*pux-u* 'break, explode'], Suhin [Nivaclé] *poktoče* (intransitive) [*pakxet-ši: pakxet* 'break' + *-ši* 'indefinite direction or location']. Mosetén *fok*.

15. BREAST   Lengua [Mascoyan]: Lengua *namakuk*, Kaskiha *neme* 'nipple'. Lule *ineme* 'milk'.

16. BROTHER   Charruan: Charrua *inčala*. Lule *kani* 'younger brother'. Mataco[an:] Mataco [Wichí] *čila* 'older brother' *[kʸila]*, *činix* 'younger brother' [*kʸinix*], Choroti *kiili* 'older brother', *kiini* 'younger brother'. Vilela *ikelebepe*. (Perhaps two related roots for older and younger brother [definitely two different lexical items in the Matacoan languages cited].)

17. CLOSE (v.)   Mataco[an:] Choroti *pone, pione* 'close, cover', Vejoz [Wichí] *ponhi* 'imprison', Towothli [Maká] *aponik* 'cover'. Takanan: Cavineña *pene* ['cover, protect'].

18. COLD[1]   [Mascoyan]: Lengua *math(-kaiyi)* 'be cold'. Panoan: Proto-Panoan **matˢi* 'be cold'.

19. COLD[2]   Lule *kei*. Mataco[an:] Enimaga [Maká] *koija*, Chunupi [Nivaclé] *kui* [k'uy].

20. CUT   Lengua [Mascoyan]: Guana *čečet* 'cut up'. Mataco[an]: Suhin [Nivaclé] *siči* [note that Nivaclé has ten distinct verbs which translate 'to

cut'; probably intended is *se?x* 'to cut up', perhaps *se?x-ši* 'cut up-indefinite location or direction'], Choroti *esita, ešita*. Panoan: Proto-Panoan **šaʔté*.

21.   DARK   Guaicuru[an]: Toba, Mocovi *epe, pe* 'night'. Mataco[an]: Choroti *pe* 'shadow'. Takanan: Chama *kea-apo* 'night', Takana *apu-* 'dark'.

22.   DIG   Mataco[an]: Vejoz [Wichí] *tih*, Mataco [Wichí] *tiho* [*tix-i* 'dig']. Takanan: Chama *teo*.

23.   DOG   Mataco[an]: Suhin [Nivaclé] *nuu*, Choropi [Nivaclé] *nuux*. Panoan: Proto-Panoan **ʔino, *ʔnaka*.

24.   DOOR   Lule *atˢiki-* <aciqui-p> 'hole'. Panoan: Proto-Panoan **šikʷé* 'doorway'. Takanan: Proto-Takanan **tˢekʷe* 'door, doorway'. [Note that Panoan and Takanan belong to Pano-Takanan.]

25.   DRESS (v.)   Lule *tala* 'clothing', *talaks*. Mataco[an:] Mataco [Wichí] *tula* 'clothing' [form unknown].

26.   DRY   [Mascoyan:] Lengua *jima(-gjaji)* 'be dry'. Mataco[an:] Mataco [Wichí] *jém* 'dry up' [Wichí has no *é*], Suhin, Chulupi [Nivaclé] *jim*, Macca [Maká] *iim*. Mosetén *jiñ* 'bone'.

27.   EMPTY   Lule *em-p*. Mataco[an:] Mataco [Wichí] *jim*, Chulupi [Nivaclé] *jimši* [*yim-ši* 'to dry up, to end', *yim* 'dry' + *-ši* 'indefinite direction or location'. Same root as in 26].

28.   FEAR[1] (v.)   Guaicuru[an]: Toba-Guazu *nahi*. Mataco[an]: Vejoz [Wichí] *nowai* [the root is *oway*, *n-* 'middle voice marker']. Mosetén *nojii* 'frighten'. Panoan: Cashibo *noo* 'frighten', Nocaman *no* 'enemy', Panobo, Shipibo *nawa* 'enemy'.

29.   FEAR[2] (v.)   Lule *lako* 'be ashamed'. Panoan: Proto-Panoan **rakʷé*.

30.   FINISH   Lule *tum-p* 'be finished'. Mataco[an]: Choroti *temi*, Suhin [Nivaclé] *timš* [*im* 'to end, run out'; perhaps based on *xa-t-im-ši* "IACTIVE-VERBALIZER-end-INEFINITE.LOCATIVE']; cf. Takanan: Cavineña *tupu* 'enough'.

31.   FLY (v.)   Mosetén *naj*. Panoan: Proto-Panoan **noja*.

32.   GREEN   Lule <za>. Mosetén <za>. Panoan: Proto-Panoan **šoo* 'green, not ripe'. Takanan: Proto-Takanan **zawa*. [Note that Panoan and Takanan are members of the Pano-Takanan family.]

33.   HANG   Mosetén *pina* 'hammock'. Panoan: Conibo *panea* 'be hung', *pani* 'hang up', Shipibo *panni* 'hang up'.

34.   HATE   Guaicuru[an]: Abipone *n-paak* 'hated'. Mosetén *fakoj, fakin* 'be angry'.

35.   HORN   Lengua [Mascoyan]: Guana *taša*. Mosetén *daš* <dasc>.

36.   KNEAD   [Matacoan:] Mataco [Wichí] *pʔon*. Mosetén *puñe* 'knead, mud'.

37.   KNOW   Mataco[an]: Vejoz [Wichí] *hanex* [*han-* 'to know', *-ex* 'applicative'], Choroti *hane* 'know, be able'. Mosetén *(am)-xeñ* ('no se puede' [it is not possible]). Panoan: Proto-Panoan **onã* 'know, be able', Shipibo *huna*.

38.   LEAF   Guaicuru[an]: Toba: *l-awe*. [Mascoyan:] Lengua *wa*.

39.   LEAVE (ABANDON)   Guaicuru[an]: Toba-Guazu *jane*. Lengua [Mascoyan]: Mascoy *jiño*. Panoan: Proto-Panoan **éné*. Vilela *jane*.

40.   LOOK   Charruan: Chana *sola*. Guaicuru[an]: Pilaga *čelage*, Toba-Guazu *silaha*.

41. LOSE   Mosetén *moñi* 'perish, lose, err'. Panoan: Cashibo *mano* 'forget', Cashinahua *manu* 'miss'. Takanan: Proto-Takanan **manu* 'die'.

42. MAKE   Guaicuru[an]: Toba-Guazu *uo*. Panoan: Proto-Panoan **wa, *ʔa*. Takanan: Proto-Takanan **a* 'make, say'.

43. MANY   Guaicuru[an]: Toba-Guazu *lamai*. [Mascoyan:] Lengua *łamo*. Mataco[an]: Payagua [not a Matacoan language] *lehmi* 'all'.

44. MEAT   Guaicuru[an]: Pilaga *niiak* 'fish.' [Mascoyan:] Lengua *nohak* 'wild animal'. Takanan: Chama *noe*, Tiatinagua, Huarayo *noči*. Vilela *nuhu* 'fish'.

45. MOSQUITO   Lengua [Mascoyan]: Mascoy *p-aija*. Mataco[an]: Choroti *eji*, Suhin [Nivaclé] *iya* [(*y*)*iyaʔ*].

46. MOTHER   Mataco[an]: Macca [Maká] *nana*. Takanan: Proto-Takanan *nene* 'aunt'. Vilela *nane*.

47. MOUSE   Guaicuru[an]: Toba-Guazu *mekahi* 'bat'. Mosetén *meče* 'rat'. Panoan: Proto-Panoan **maka* 'rat, mouse'. Cf. Mataco[an]: Mataco [Wichí], Suhin [Nivaclé], Chulupi [Nivaclé] *ama* [am?ɑ 'rat'], Vejoz [Wichí] *ma*.

48. NECK[1]   Mosetén *tetˢ* <tez>. Panoan: Proto-Panoan **téšo*.

49. NECK[2]   Lule *u(-p)*. Mataco[an]: Mataco [Wichí], Choroti, etc. *wo*. Mosetén <huh> 'throat'.

50. OLD   Guaicuru[an]: Guachi [Guachi is not a Guaicuruan language] *seera*. Mataco[an]: Payagua [Payagua is not a Matacoan language] *aheri* 'old woman'. Panoan: Proto-Panoan **šéné*. Takanan: Proto-Takanan **ziri*.

51. RED   Guaicuru[an]: Toba, Mocovi *tok*. [Mascoyan:] Lengua *eteig-ma*. Mataco[an]: Macca [Maká] *tek* 'blood' [no such form exists in Maká; see *-athits* 'blood', *-atxuʔ* 'to bleed', *siyixiʔ* 'red']. Takanan: Proto-Takanan **čiaka*.

52. RIB   Guaicuru[an]: Mocovi <emeneh>. Mosetén *mana*.

53. ROTTEN   [Mascoyan:] Lengua *abik*. Lule *poko* 'to rot'. Mosetén *fokoi*.

54. SHOUT   Lule *se* 'cry'. Panoan: Shipibo *sei*, Conibo *sije*, Cashinahua *sa*. Takanan: Proto-Takanan **tˢea*.

55. SIDE   Guaicuru[an]: Toba-Guazu *ai, aji*, Mocovi *ai* 'side', Abipone *uii*. Lule *je*.

56. SMALL   Lengua [Mascoyan]: Mascoy *etkok*. Mataco[an]: Churupi [Nivaclé] *tikin* [*tik'in*], Suhin [Nivaclé] *tika* [no such form exists, perhaps a mistake for *tik'in*]. Towothli [Maká] *taake* 'short.' Panoan Culino *tukuča* 'short'.

57. SON   Charruan: Chana, Guenoa *ineu*. Guaicuru[an]: Guachi [Guachi is not a Guaicuruan language] *inna*. Vilela *ina-hmi* (Pelleschi [source]), *ina-ke* 'son, daughter' (Gilij [source]), *hina-kis* (Fontana [source]).

58. SOUR   Mataco[an]: Choroti *paši* <paxhi>. Mosetén *pase*. Panoan: Proto-Panoan **paša* 'sour, raw, uncooked', Takanan: Proto-Takanan **patˢe*.

59. SWIM   Guaicuru[an]: Pilaga *ubogai*. Mosetén <vigi>. Takanan: Proto-Takanan **betˢa*.

60. THIN   Lule *kam*. Mosetén *kum*. Cf. Mataco[an]: Vejoz [Wichí] *čemsa-* 'small'.

61. URINE   [Mascoyan:] Lengua *jis(-weji)* 'urinate'. Lule <ys> 'urinate'. Mataco[an]: Suhn [Nivaclé] *yuł*, Churupi [Nivaclé] <yius, yiusl> 'urinate'

(*sl* probably represents the voiceless lateral fricative *ł*) [both are from the root *-ul* 'urine, to urinate', *y-ul* 'he/she/it urinates', *y-* 'third person pronoun']. Panoan: Proto-Panoan **isõ*, **istõ*.

62.   WEAK   Lengua [Mascoyan]: Mascoy *jil, jel-k*. Mataco[an]: Mataco [Wichí] *jel* 'weak, tired' [*y-* 'third person pronoun', root *-el* 'to tire'].

14

WRITING AND PHILOLOGY: THE ROLE OF WRITTEN RECORDS

Philologists, who chase
A panting syllable through time and space
Start it at home, and hunt it in the dark,
To Gaul, to Greece, and into Noah's Ark.

(William Cowper [1731–1800], *Retirement*, 691)

An ounce of documents is worth more than a peck of artifacts.

(Thompson 1970: xiii)

14.1 Introduction

This chapter is about writing, writing systems, and philology. Philology has to do primarily with the use of written attestations of earlier stages of languages, and with how the information from written forms of a language can be used to determine aspects of that language's history – with the methods for extracting historical linguistic information from written sources. The investigation of written records has always been important in historical linguistics.

14.2 Writing and the History of Writing Systems

We hardly need a formal definition of writing, since everybody reading these words has some sense of what writing is. Still, a definition might be helpful as we consider the development of writing systems and how written records can contribute to historical linguistic interests. Therefore, writing, defined, is visual (or tactile) signs used to represent language; it is a visual (or tactile) code for recording and communicating information. We add 'tactile' to the ordinary definition, which is usually limited to 'visual' signs, in order to allow for writing for the blind, in particular Braille, devised by Louis Braille, a blind Frenchman, in 1821. Each Braille character or cell is made up of six dot positions, arranged in a rectangle containing two columns of three dots each. Its signs are distinct from one another in form and are generally alphabetic, so that sighted persons could also read the system if they knew what to look for. While the definition of writing offered here is intended to include writing for the blind, it is the visual signs we concentrate on in this chapter.

It is useful to point out at the beginning of this chapter that the notation < > is often used to enclose written attestations in order to indicate that the material is presented exactly as found in the source.

14.2.1 Kinds of writing systems

Some writing systems are called *hieroglyphic* (from Greek *hieros* 'sacred' + *glyphein* 'to carve'). These are usually mixed systems with signs representing logograms (whole words) as well as some phonetic and other signs (see below). A number of early scripts were *cuneiform* ('wedge-shaped', from Latin *cuneus* 'wedge'). Some are *syllabaries*, and many are *alphabetic*. Some of these are described below as we consider how writing systems developed.

Some better-known writing systems include the following:

Akkadian cuneiform (2500 BC to AD 100)

Anatolian hieroglyphics (called 'Hittite' hieroglyphics, though representing the Luwian language, c. 1400 to 700 BC)

Aztec writing (c. AD 1400 to 1600, logographic with syllabic signs)

Brahmi script (syllabary, 400 BC to AD 300), ancestor of many South Asian and other scripts, for example those used for Burmese, Thai, and Tibetan, including Devanagari, used to write Sanskrit and numerous languages of India

Cherokee syllabary (AD 1821 to present)

Chinese (1500 BC to present, logographic) – Chinese kanji was influential in the writing that developed for several other East Asian languages

Coptic (100 BC to present, adopted from Greek with five letters added from Egyptian hieroglyphics)

Cree 'syllabics' (syllabary, AD 1840 to present)

Cyrillic alphabet (AD 800 to present, based on the Greek alphabet)

Egyptian hieroglyphics (3100 BC to AD 400)

Elamite (c. 3300 to 500 BC)

Epi-Olmec script (hieroglyphic, c. 70 BC to AD 500)

Hittite cuneiform (1650 to 1200 BC)

Japanese writing (400 BC to present, first based on Chinese *kanji* logographic characters, to which *hiragana* and *katakana* syllabaries were added, based on Chinese signs used to represent sounds)

Korean Hangul (AD 1443 to present)

Linear A (Cretan, Minoan, 1800 to 1400 BC), remains undeciphered

Linear B (Mycenaean Greek) (1500 to 1200 BC)

Maya hieroglyphic writing (by 400 BC to AD 1600, logographic with syllabic signs)

Mixteca (Mixteca-Puebla, AD 1200 to 1600)

Ogham (AD 200 to 500), recording Old Irish

Runic writing (called 'Futhark', AD 150 to 1600, in two forms: Anglo-Frisian Futhorc and earlier Continental Germanic Futhark)

Semitic family of scripts (Phoenician)

Sumerian (3300 to 100 BC, hieroglyphic), evolved into cuneiform

Tibetan (AD 600–700 to present; its ultimate ancestor was the Brahmi script)

Zapotecan script (hieroglyphic, c. 500 BC to AD 1000)

Several alphabets:

    Proto-Sinaitic (Proto-Canaanite) consonantal alphabet (1700 BC, perhaps as early as 1900 BC, which evolved into the Phoenician script)

    Phoenician consonantal alphabet (1100 to 300 BC)

    Greek (eighth century BC to present, adopted from Phoenician)

    Etruscan (700 BC to AD 100, adapted from Greek)

    Latin (Roman) (seventh century BC to present, modified version of Etruscan alphabet), source of most European alphabets (though some are closer to Greek in origin).

Note that the Indus 'script' or Indus Valley 'writing' (c. 2600 to 1900 BC), which is often listed as an undeciphered writing system, is disputed and may not be writing at all (Farmer et al. 2004).

14.2.2 Origins of writing

It is often thought that the earliest writing systems evolved out of tally systems for economic purposes, to keep track of inventories and transactions, for example, the 'sheep' sign ⊕ in Sumerian writing associated with keeping track of transactions involving sheep. However, scholars of writing systems today tend to believe that tally systems had origins which are distinct from true writing. It has also been proposed that some writing systems develop out of iconographic representations – sets of conventionally recognized symbols, often with religious motivations. However, there seems to be little reason to believe that the representations of linguistic features in true writing developed from earlier pictorial elements. The beginning of writing systems seems generally to be independent of numeral systems and art. For example, in modern English, we use the Roman alphabet alongside Arabic numerals, two separate systems with independent origins. Also, letters of our alphabet can be traced back to signs that were more pictorial in origin; for example, the letter 'A' once looked like an ox head (rotated 180°), and its name referred to 'ox' – 'A' is from Latin *alpha*, taken from Greek *alpha*, itself a borrowing from Phoenician *'aleph* 'ox'. However, there is no evidence that portraits of oxen predated the use of this sign to represent the associated sound. (See below for more on the origin of this alphabet.)

The bar and dot notation for numbers in Mesoamerican tally systems was used in conjunction with writing. A dot is for 'one', so two dots is 'two', three dots 'three', etc. A bar is for 'five'. A combination of four dots (1×4) and three bars (3×5), thus, is 'nineteen'. An example with 'four' in the Maya system is seen in Figure 14.3a.

In the past some scholars supported the hypothesis of *monogenesis*, believing that all writing had a single origin, that it was invented only once in the world, and then spread. There are (or have been) many writing systems in the world, and some well-known writing systems that probably had independent origins include Chinese, Egyptian, and Sumerian, among others. For certain the writing systems of ancient Mesoamerica are completely independent of Old World writing, meaning that the notion of monogenesis for the origin of all writing is incorrect, even if many Old World scripts developed from other scripts before them.

14.2.3 Generalizations about writing and its origins

An interesting question is: to what do we owe similarities among many ancient writing systems? Proposed explanations have been offered, to which we now turn.

(1) *Reading order* (direction of reading and writing). Top-to-bottom reading or writing order is often thought to have developed due to close association with the vertical axis of the dominant figures in the pictorial scenes that writing often accompanied. Since the associated depiction of a person or animal or scene from nature is typically scanned from the head or top downward, the direction of writing naturally followed the same direction. Left-to-right order is favoured in scripts that developed in the context of painting or recording in clay, that is, when the writing was on materials that smudge easily. A reason for this seems to be that, since most scribes are right-handed, if they write from left to right in the direction away from the symbols they write, they do not smear what they have just written. The etymological origin of the word 'to write' in a good number of languages is 'to paint', for example Proto-Mayan **ts'ihb'* 'paint', later 'write', Proto-Aztecan **(tla)hkʷilowa* 'to paint, to stripe', later 'to write'. In contrast, English *write* is from Germanic **wrītan* 'to cut, scratch, tear', calling to mind the carving of runes in wood or on stone; compare the German cognate *reissen* 'to tear', and Old English *wrītan* 'to score, outline, draw the figure of', and then later 'to write'. The earliest writing for Germanic peoples involved carving or cutting marks on wood, etc. When writing came to be done with pen and ink, the term for writing carried over.

These terms for writing are sometimes connected with the material upon which these writing systems were typically written. For example, English *book* derives from *beech*, presumably reflecting a wooden surface used on which to scratch or carve the earliest runes; Old English *bōc*, from which we get *book*, meant any written document. Similarly, in some Slavic languages, such as Russian and Bulgarian, the word for 'letter', *bukva*, is similar to English 'beech', reflecting the same medium for writing. Also, Latin *liber* 'book' originally meant the 'inner bark of a tree', used for writing. This Latin word is behind the origin of words for 'book', in French *livre*, Italian and Spanish *libro*, and is ultimately behind English *library*. The Proto-Mayan word **huʔŋ* originally meant a kind of 'fig tree' but also came to mean 'bark paper' and 'book'; the word for a kind of 'fig tree' also means 'paper' and 'book' in several other Mesoamerican languages, for example Nahuatl *āmatl*, for the books and paper of the Aztecs – reflecting the fact that early Mesoamerican writing was painted on perishable media, not carved in stone. In English, *paper* comes from Latin *papȳrus*, which got it from Greek *pápuros* 'papyrus', a wetland reed once abundant in the Nile Delta of Egypt and used in ancient Egypt and throughout the Mediterranean region as a writing material. A second Greek word for 'papyrus' was *búblos*, perhaps derived from *Byblos*, the name of a famous Phoenician city, used in a more restricted sense for certain products made of papyrus, including writing material. This is seen in the origin of such English words as *Bible, bibliography*, and *bibliophile*, and of French *bibliothèque*, German *Bibliotek*, Italian and Spanish *biblioteca* 'library', with similar forms in several other languages.

Though the left-to-right reading order may be very common, it is by no means universal. There are scripts which are written right-to-left, those used for writing Arabic, Hebrew, and Persian being well-known examples. In some situations, writing was in both directions, left-to-right and right-to-left, called *boustrophe-don*, from Greek *boustrophēdon* 'ox-turning' (*bous* 'ox' + *strophē* 'turn'). The name suggests an ox drawing a plough across a field and turning at the end of each furrow to return in the opposite direction; this is because in boustrophedon every other line of writing reversed the direction of reading. Some archaic Greek stone inscriptions are written in boustrophedon, as are some scripts such as Safaitic and Sabaean.

(2) *Orientation of signs or characters*. Signs or characters tend to face left. Since most writing is from left to right, the signs thus face the direction from which the reader would read or from which the scribe would write. More precisely, in pictorially based scripts, figures universally face the direction in which one reads. Thus, consistency in sign orientation mostly amounts to consistency in reading order, where a consistent orientation of signs makes reading easier to process for the reader. Thus, where the direction of writing is left-to-right, characters face left. In boustrophedon writing, characters switch their orientation in alternate lines to face the direction in which the line is read.

(3) *Part-for-whole (pars pro toto) principle*. This principle refers to the depiction of a part of something to represent the whole of what is indicated. This is not found universally in writing systems. In fact it is rare in Old World scripts, which tend to emphasize wholes not parts of what is depicted; however, it is common to the formation of all Mesoamerican scripts, where some part of animals or humans, particularly the head, is used to represent the entire object, as illustrated by the signs in Figure 14.1.

(4) *Columns*. Writing when it is in columns is read from top to bottom (see above), rather than in rows. This too is not universal. Column format is common in several early scripts, for example Sumerian, Chinese, and most Mesoamerican systems. When writing develops in a context of iconography, the vertical axis corresponds to the orientation of dominant figures in scenes.

14.2.4 Kinds of signs and their evolution in writing systems

The kinds of signs employed in different writing systems are not universal, of course, though there are often common patterns of how the signs in writing systems evolve over time. This can be illustrated with a brief look at Maya

FIGURE 14.1a: Maya HIX (/hiš/) 'feline' head

FIGURE 14.1b: Maya HIX (/hiš/) 'feline' ear

FIGURE 14.1c: Maya *ka* syllable, fish body (from *kay* 'fish')

FIGURE 14.1d: Maya *ka* syllable, fish fin (from *kay* 'fish')

FIGURE 14.1e: Aztec TSINAKAN 'bat' body

FIGURE 14.1f: Aztec TSINAKAN 'bat' head

hieroglyphic writing. Egyptian writing evolved in parallel fashion, and also illustrates these stages in the development of signs in a writing system.

(1) *Iconography* is conventionalized symbolic representation, not language per se. For example, images of crosses, † ✝ ⛨, have conventional meanings in Christian religions, though they are not considered writing. Any symbolic representation with direct connection to language is of interest for how writing develops; however, writing systems appear not to have originated directly from iconography.

(2) *Pictograms.* It was thought that writing systems begin with pictographic symbols in their early stages – symbols which broadly represent ideas or concepts which could be interpreted relatively independently of any particular language.

Some examples of pictograms in use today include road signs, danger signs, airport signs, a heart for 'love', smiley faces, and symbols of a man or woman on lavatory doors. Such signs may be used in combination with writing, but true writing is not divorced from the language of the writers and readers. Most scholars no longer believe that pictograms have any significant role in the development of writing. The notion of 'ideographic' writing, as systems such as Chinese writing are sometimes called, is also misleading, since no ideographic writing system has ever existed in the sense intended where the signs represent pure ideas rather than linguistic units of some sort.

(3) *Logograms*. Logographic signs represent whole words (or morphemes). Some examples of logographic signs in use today, which represent whole words not spelled out alphabetically, are: $, %, &, +, @, 1, 2, Ø, etc. These can be interpreted in various languages, so that the logogram *2* in an English text would be read as 'two', in a Spanish text as 'dos', and in German as 'Zwei', for example. Nevertheless, these signs are indeed interpreted as representing those words in those languages.

Many Maya logographic signs are undoubtedly pictorial in origin. The sign B'AHLAM 'jaguar' is a portrait of a jaguar, for example (seen in Figure 14.4a–1, below); however, it serves no purpose to call this a 'pictogram' because it does not convey the concept JAGUAR independently of the word for jaguar itself in the language represented. Not all Maya logograms are pictorial in origin. Some are abstract or stylized signs for ritual products, foodstuffs, gods, etc. It is not their origin but their behaviour that defines logograms: logograms represent real words in the language that is written.

Some examples of logograms in the Maya and Aztec scripts were seen in Figure 14.1 (above), and other examples are illustrated in Figure 14.2. Figure 14.2a is the logogram for 'jaguar'. Similarly, Figure 14.2b is the Maya logogram for 'stone', Figure 14.2c for 'mountain', and Figure 14.2d for 'sun'. Figures 14.2e–h are the Aztec logograms for 'ocelot', 'stone', 'mountain', and 'sun', respectively. These can be compared with the Maya logograms in Figures 14.2a–d to see similarities but also considerable differences.

(4) *Rebus*. The name 'rebus' comes from Latin *rēbus* 'by means of objects' (the ablative plural of *rēs* 'thing, object'). Rebus signs are in effect logograms which have been pressed into phonetic service, sometimes seen as the first steps towards signs coming to represent phonological aspects of the language of a writing system in a more direct fashion. Rebus signs involve morphemes which are not easy to depict graphically. In such cases, sometimes signs for words or morphemes that are easier to depict graphically can be used to represent other words or morphemes that are difficult to depict but which sound like the ones that are easier to draw – like a visual pun. These signs that exploit homophonic or nearly homophonic words are called rebus signs; for example, in English the picture of an 'eye' to represent 'I', as in rebus 'spelling' of the phrase with 'eye' '(tin)can' C U for 'I can see you', or the more conventional rebus spelling of IOU for 'I owe you'. Another example is the series of pictures '2' 'bee' 'oar' 'knot' '2' 'bee' to represent 'To be or not to be'. Many coats of arms (family crests) involved rebus symbols, called 'canting arms'. A famous example is the

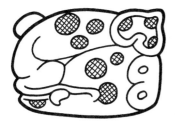

FIGURE 14.2a: Maya B'AHLAM 'jaguar'
logogram

FIGURE 14.2b: Maya TUN 'stone'
logogram

FIGURE 14.2c: Maya WITS 'mountain'
logogram

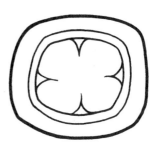

FIGURE 14.2d: Maya K'IN 'sun'
logogram

FIGURE 14.2e: Aztec OSELO- 'ocelot' logogram

FIGURE 14.2f: Aztec TE- 'stone'
logogram

FIGURE 14.2g: Aztec TEPE- 'mountain'
logogram

FIGURE 14.2h: Aztec TONATIW- 'sun'
logogram

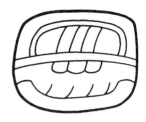

FIGURE 14.3a: Maya
ČAN 'four'

FIGURE 14.3b: Maya
ČAN 'snake'

FIGURE 14.3c: Maya
ČAN 'sky'

coat of arms of the English queen mother, born Elizabeth Bowes-Lyon. Her crest has depictions of bows and lions, a rebus representation of the Bowes and Lyon family names.

Some examples of rebus signs in Maya hieroglyphic writing include the interchange of several signs that represent words pronounced /čan/ (IPA [tʃ]) in Cholan (a subgroup of Mayan): ČAN 'four', ČAN 'snake', and ČAN 'sky', seen in Figures 14.3a–c.

Occasionally Maya scribes utilized one of the logographic signs in Figure 14.3 to represent the meaning of one of the other words that sounded like it, for instance writing the 'snake' sign to represent 'sky', or writing either 'snake' or 'sky' in contexts where 'four' was intended. The fact that these signs could be interchanged in this way is an indication that Cholan was the Mayan language in which they were written, since words for these things were homophonous in Cholan. The cognate words in Yucatec Maya, once thought by some to be the language of the hieroglyphic texts, are not homophonous: *kan* 'four', *kàan* 'snake', and *káʔan* 'sky'. The Maya codices, written much later, are in Yucatec Maya, but the glyphic texts from the earlier monuments are written in Cholan.

(5) *Phonetic complements*. Logograms can be ambiguous, where the thing depicted may correspond to more than one possible word in the language. Phonetic complements were used in some writing systems to help disambiguate the forms represented. It is sometimes thought that logograms with a particular pronunciation in the language could be used in association with other ambiguous logograms to specify some aspect of the pronunciation of the latter in order to make the intended referent clear and to distinguish between multiple possible interpretations of the logogram in question. However, phonetic complements do not necessarily need to develop from earlier independent logograms, but can serve the role played by signs in other scripts which just have some phonetic content, as in the case of the *nd* in *2nd* for 'second' in English. Several examples with phonetic complements to logograms are seen in the images in Figures 14.4a and Figure 14.4b.

Phonetic complements were used in other scripts which employed logograms, for example in Akkadian, Egyptian, Japanese, and Sumerian writing. In nearly all these scripts, the phonetic complements are selected from words with the phonetic shape CVC, where the final consonant is phonetically weak, for example in Mayan *h*, *ʔ*, and more rarely also *w* and *y*, as in Figures 14.1c–d, where the

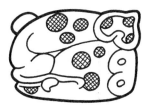

FIGURE 14.4a-1: Maya B'AHLAM 'jaguar' logogram

FIGURE 14.4a-2: Maya B'AHLAM 'jaguar' logogram + *ma* complement

FIGURE 14.4a-3: Maya /b'ahlam/ 'jaguar' spelled out with phonetic signs *ba* + *la* + *ma*

FIGURE 14.4a-4: Maya /b'ahlam/ 'jaguar' spelled differently with phonetic signs *ba* + *la* + *ma*

FIGURE 14.4b-1: Maya PAKAL 'shield' logogram

FIGURE 14.4b-2: Maya PAKAL 'shield' logogram with *la* phonetic complement

syllabic sign *ka* is derived from *kay* 'fish', with weak final *y*. In other writing systems, sometimes the final consonant that was considered weak also included liquids (*l* and *r*) and nasals, though this is not the case in Maya writing.

(6) *Syllabic signs.* In Maya and Egyptian writing, and in other similar systems, a set of signs developed that could be employed as phonetic complements and could be used in combination to 'spell' out words or morphemes 'syllabically', using these signs for their constant phonetic values, independent of the meaning of words from which the symbol may have been derived originally. The phonetic complements, when they come to be able to represent phonetic content alone, are called 'syllabic' signs (or 'syllabograms'), and a writing system composed primarily of them is called a *syllabary*, as for example Japanese *hiragana* and the Cherokee and Cree syllabaries in North America, and Linear B (Mycenaean Greek). In syllabaries, some signs only approximate syllables but are not

FIGURE 14.4b-3: Maya / pakal/'shield' spelled out with phonetic signs *pa + ka + la*

FIGURE 14.4b-4: Maya / pakal/'shield' spelled differently with phonetic signs *pa + ka + la*

FIGURE 14. 4b-5: Maya / pakal/'shield' spelled out again with phonetic signs *pa + ka + la*

necessarily identical to syllables of the language they represent. In many writing systems that use syllabic signs the signs are restricted mostly to those which phonetically correspond only to CV (a consonant and a vowel) or CVC syllables ending in a weak C (as mentioned above).

Mayan root morphemes are mostly monosyllabic and of the shape CVC, and can be spelled syllabically by two syllabic signs together, where the V of the second sign is silent, that is, a spelling of <CV-CV> with two syllabic signs which together represent /CVC/. Typically when the vowel of the root is not accompanied by vowel length or by *h* or *ʔ* – not in syllables of the form CV:C, CVhC, or CVʔC – and is not followed by a grammatical affix, the two V's of the two syllabic signs are the same (harmonic) (though the second vowel is not pronounced). There are, however, numerous exceptions.

In Maya writing, words could be and sometimes were spelled out using only these syllabic signs, though the writing system remained a mixed one, just as in ancient Egyptian writing, where a form could be represented sometimes by only a logogram, sometimes by a logogram in combination with a phonetic complement, sometimes with multiple phonetic complements, and sometimes by only combinations of syllabic signs without a logogram at all. This kind of variation of representation in Maya writing is exemplified in Figures 14.4a and 14.4b.

Figure 14.4a–1 is the Maya logogram for 'jaguar' with no phonetic complements. Figure 14.4a–2 has the Maya 'jaguar' logogram plus the phonetic complement *ma* beneath it. In Figure 14.4a–3, the word for 'jaguar', *b'ahlam*, is spelled out phonetically with a combination of the syllabic signs *ba + la + ma*: it has a large *ba* sign, with *la* following *ba* to the right and with *ma* below the *la* sign. Figure 14.4a–4 also spells out *b'ahlam* 'jaguar' with a combination of *ba + la + ma*: the large main sign on the left represents *ba*, the sign with two circles below the *ba* sign is for *la*, and the sign to the right of *ba* is for *ma*.

Figure 14.4b presents different ways in which /pakal/ 'shield' was written in Maya writing.

Because *pakal* not only meant 'shield' but also was the name of a powerful ruler of Palenque, a prominent Maya archaeological site, representations of *pakal* show up prominently in the glyphic texts. Figure 14.4b–1 is the logogram PAKAL 'shield' by itself; it depicts a shield. Figure 14.4b–2 has the logogram PAKAL 'shield' with the phonetic complement *la* below the logogram. Figures 14.4b-3–5 represent alternative ways of spelling out *pakal* with syllabic signs. In 14.4b–3, the first sign, to the left, with cross-hatching, is *pa*, the large sign is *ka* (fish sign), and the sign below *ka* is *la*. In 14.4b–4, the large sign with the cross-hatching is *pa*, the *ka* sign (representing the fish fin) is below, and the *la* sign is to the right. In 14.4b–5, *pa* is at the top, *ka* is in the middle below *pa*, and *la* is at the bottom.

(7) '*Mixed*' *scripts*. Mixed scripts, such as Maya and Egyptian hieroglyphic writing – sometimes called 'logosyllabic' scripts – can use combinations of signs as seen above, mixtures of logograms, phonetic complements, and syllabic signs, and are thus able to represent the same words or morphemes in varying forms. The kinds of alternative representations available to Maya writing are seen in examples in Figure 14.4.

14.2.5 The organization of Maya writing

Maya writing is organized according to the following principles.

(1) *Columns*. Maya glyphic texts are read top-to-bottom usually in pairs, two columns at a time, rather than in rows. The reading order begins with the first two columns (on the left), the first pair read together left-to-right, then the second pair below the first, and so on from top to bottom – the first two columns are read together top to bottom, then the next two top to bottom, and so on to the end. If there is a single column left over after the columns are read in pairs, it is read as a single unpaired column, top to bottom. Let us assume that Figure 14.5 represents abstractly a Maya hieroglyphic text, where each box corresponds to a glyph block, with columns under the letters and rows across corresponding to the numbers.

Reading begins A1 then B1, then A2 and B2, then A3–B3, and so on to the bottom of the first pair of columns (ending in A5–B5 here). Then the reading proceeds to the next pair of columns, C and D, reading them from top to bottom, C1–D1, C2–D2, and so on to C5–D5. Then, since E is a single leftover column, it is read straight from top to bottom, E1, then E2, then E3, to the bottom at E5.

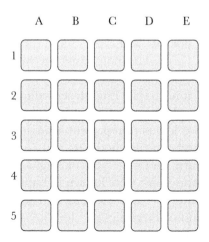

FIGURE 14.5: Illustration of reading order in Maya hieroglyphic texts

(2) *Glyph blocks.* Maya scribes used aesthetic principles to govern how they arranged signs within glyph blocks, with a preference for logograms, if present, to be dominant, represented as the largest sign in a group – what scholars called the main sign in earlier work. The glyph blocks can be composed of a larger sign in combination with smaller signs, called in earlier times affixes. The position of a smaller sign (affix) before (to the left) or above the large sign was functionally equivalent (formerly called prefixes), and similarly the smaller sign (affix) after (to the right) or below the larger sign generally had the same function (called postfixes in earlier terminology). J. Eric S. Thompson's (1962) catalogue of Maya glyphs has 842 glyphs, which reduces to about 750 when duplications are eliminated; Alan Gardner's (1957) Egyptian grammar has 603 signs, which expands to 734 when numbers and ligatures are added.

14.2.6   Alphabetic writing

As seen in the list of writing systems mentioned above, many Old World alphabets have a common ancestor, a much abbreviated pedigree of which is: the Proto-Sinaitic script begot the Phoenician alphabet, which begot the Greek alphabet, from whence the Etruscan alphabet, which lies behind the Latin (Roman) alphabet, from whence the alphabets of most western European languages, including English. The name 'alphabet' betrays some of this origin. It comes from a combination of the name of the first two letters of the Greek alphabet, *alpha* and *beta*. These letter names, however, are not Greek in origin, but reflect their Phoenician origin, which represented consonants but not vowels. The first is from Phoenician *'aleph* 'ox' and represented a glottal stop, the first sound in the word for 'ox' for which this letter was named; the sign represents an ox head – the <A> of modern alphabets now seemingly upside down, with the top originally depicting the ox's snout and the two lines at the bottom representing its horns. Since Greek had no phonemic glottal stop, it took the symbol to represent the first vowel of the word instead, <A> /a/, as in the English alphabet today. The second name in 'alphabet' is from the second letter of the Phoenician alphabet, *beth* 'house'.

Anglo-Saxon scribes used the Latin (Roman) alphabet to write Old English, but added some letters: (1) <æ>, called 'ash' after the runic letter *æsc*; (2) the runic letter <þ> 'thorn' (for /θ/ and /ð/); (3) the runic letter <ƿ> 'wynn' (for /w/); and (4) <ð> 'edh', a modification based on the Latin letter *d*, alternating with 'thorn' to represent this sound. With the Norman conquest of 1066, Norman French scribes came to spell English according to French orthographic practices. The non-Latin letters used to write Old English were dropped. Digraphs – the use of two letters to represent a single sound – came into use, <ch> for /č/ (IPA [ʧ]) and <th> for both /θ/ and /ð/, the sounds earlier represented by the <þ> 'thorn' and <ð> 'edh' of Anglo-Saxon writers. The combinations <ph>, <th>, and <ch> were known in Latin and French spellings of words of Greek origin, and <h> came to be used in other digraphs to represent sounds unfamiliar in Latin or French, <gh> for /x/ (see below), <sh> for /ʃ/, and <wh> for /ʍ/ (so-called 'voiceless' or 'aspirated' *w*, as in *which, where, white,* etc.).

The letters <i> and <j> were not originally distinct from one another; *j* was just the longer curved variant of *i* used for writing the last *i* in Latin words that ended in double *i*, as in <filij> for *filii* 'sons'. For English scribes <y> was the version of <j> used for the second *i* in these cases and for the last *i* of words generally; this explains such differences in spelling as *holy* with *y* but *holiest* and *holiday* (from *holy day*) with *i*, and *carry* but *carried*, *pretty* but *prettier*, *worry* but *worrier*, and so on. The dot over *i* and *j* was not originally used, and is still lacking from capital (upper-case) *I* and *J*. It owes its origin to a small sloping line that came to be placed above the very slim letter *i* to distinguish it from letters composed of more strokes such as *m*, *n*, and *u*, often difficult to distinguish in the hand-writing of scribes, and the dot was extended to *j* (then a variant of *i*). The lack of distinction between <I> and <J> is illustrated well in the '*INRI*' caption on Roman Catholic representations of crucifixes and paintings of the crucifixion of Christ (seen often also in religious paintings). It is an abbreviation of the title Pontius Pilate was reported to have had written on the cross of Jesus Christ, *Iesvs Nazarenvs Rex Ivdaeorvm*, or in more conventional modernized spelling, *Jesus Nazarenus Rex Judaeorum* 'Jesus of Nazarus, King of the Jews'. Association of <j> with an affricate [ʤ]) is due to later developments in French, where initial *j* (/y/, IPA [j]) inherited from Latin had become [ʤ] word-initially, due to sound change, though still spelled <j>, and this was the Norman French convention that was used to write English after the Norman conquest. Thus French loans in English from an earlier period reflect the earlier pronunciation with [ʤ] in words written with <j>, as for example, *jolly*, *journey*, *juice*, and so on. Later, this [ʤ] in French changed further to [ʒ], but after the orthographic value of [ʤ] for <j> had been established for English spelling. Thus, these French words, the source of the English loans, in modern French are *joli* [ʒoli] 'pretty', *journée* [ʒuʀne] 'day' ('day's earnings, day's travel'), and *jus* [ʒy] 'juice'.

The letters *u*, *v*, and *w* have a similar history. In Latin spelling, which persisted in earlier French spelling practice, *u* and *v* were interchangeable, used for either /u/ or /w/. Later, in the early Christian era, Latin /w/ changed to /v/, though the two letters continued in use essentially interchangeably for either the vowel /u/ or the consonant /v/. The letter *w* was originally formed from a doubling of *u*, as the name 'double u' suggests, or from a double *v* in shape, which was not distinct from *u* in its function, and then *v* later came to be considered a different letter for a different sound, no longer valid for the vowel /u/. The *u* shape of the letter came to be associated with vowels and the *v* shape with consonants, and so considered distinct letters.

Additionally, in some contexts, some cases that are today spelled in English with *o* should actually have *u* according to expectations. In cases with the sequence /uv/ (or /ʊv/), the convention was to close the *u* in writing, making it into an *o*, in order to distinguish /uv/ from sequences of letters difficult to identify in squiggled handwriting involving *m*, *n*, *u*, *v*, *w*. Thus <love> 'love', from Old English *lufu*, never had the pronunciation usually associated with the *o* of the spelling, but rather was meant to represent /lʊv/.

14.3 Philology

Philology is understood in different ways. Sometimes it is taken to be merely the study of some classical or older language – in this sense we see university departments and professional journals dedicated to Classical philology, English philology, Germanic philology, Nordic philology, Romance philology, and so on. Sometimes philology is understood to mean historical linguistics as practised in the nineteenth century; what today is called historical linguistics was earlier often referred to as 'philology', as in 'Indo-European philology'. In another sense of the word, philology is understood as the scholarly activity that attempts to get systematic information about a language from written records. Definitions of *philology* range across these varied notions: the intensive study of texts, especially old ones; the humanistic study of language and literature, considering both form and meaning in linguistic expression, combining linguistics and literary studies; the history of literature and words; the systematic study of the development and history of languages; and the study of written records to determine their authenticity, original form, and meaning. Definitions of *philologist* involve these notions, meaning a collector of words and their etymologies; a humanist specializing in classical scholarship; and a person who engages in philology (historical linguistics).

One aim of philology is to get historical information from documents in order to learn about the culture and history of the people behind the text; another aim is to examine and interpret older written attestations with the goal of obtaining information about the history of the language (or languages) in which the documents are written. This second aim is the most common in historical linguistics today, and it is in this sense that the term *philology* is used in this book.

In the use of philology for historical linguistic purposes, we are concerned with what linguistic information can be obtained from written documents, with how we can get it, and with what we can make of the information once we have it. The philological investigation of older written attestations can contribute in several ways, for example by documenting sound changes that have taken place, distinguishing inherited from borrowed material, dating changes and borrowings, and helping to understand the development and change in writing systems and orthographic conventions, among others. Results of these studies can have implications for claims about scribal practice, subgroup classification, causes of changes, the reconstruction of a proto-language, borrowed changes, the identification of extinct languages, decipherment of writing systems, and the historical interpretation of many changes within the languages investigated in this way.

14.3.1 Examples of what philology can contribute

The following examples illustrate some of the kinds of information that can be retrieved through philological investigations and the implications such information can have for historical linguistic understanding of the languages involved. Examples abound from Indo-European and ancient Near Eastern languages. Here, cases from the history of English are presented first because they are easier for speakers and readers of English to understand, but also, in order to illustrate the general applicability of philological notions, cases are selected from the rich written attestations in various Mayan languages since the 1500s and from Maya hieroglyphic writing. It is often believed, erroneously, that Native American languages lack older written sources and that therefore little can be gained from philological investigation of them. The examples presented here are interesting both for what they reveal and because they show the applicability of philology to American Indian languages.

(1) Proto-Mayan contrasted *x [velar fricative] and *h [glottal fricative], as several of the thirty-one Mayan languages still do; however, in Yucatec Maya these both merged to h (*x, *h > h). Nevertheless, some colonial sources show that the contrast survived until after European contact. For example, in the Motul Dictionary of Yucatec Maya from c. 1590 the two sounds were distinguished with lexical entries under the heading of 'loud H' (< *x) and others under the heading of 'simple H' (< *h), though both were written with <h>. (The orthography of this and following cases is based on that of Spanish at the time that the documents were written.) Some example dictionary entries that illustrate the contrast are seen in Table 14.1.

This example shows that through philological investigation we can sometimes recover information about sound changes in the language under investigation, in this case about a merger in Yucatec Maya, and information about the relative date when the change took place. In this case the merger of x, h > h took place sometime after the Motul Dictionary was written in c. 1590.

(2) Huastec, another Mayan language, has contrastive kw (labialized velar stop) and $k^{w'}$ (glottalized labialized velar stop), though no other Mayan language has these sounds. Based on the correspondence sets of Huastec k^w : other Mayan languages k, and Huastec $k^{w'}$: others' k', some had thought Proto-Mayan must be reconstructed with *k^w and *$k^{w'}$. However, written attestations from the eighteenth century show that the labialized velars in Huastec are the results of a recent change. In words which originally had a velar stop (k or k') followed by rounded back vowel (u or o) followed by a glide (w, y, h, or ?) followed by a vowel, the velars were labialized and the rounded vowel together with the following glide was lost (y = IPA [j] here):

$$\begin{Bmatrix} k \\ k' \end{Bmatrix} \begin{Bmatrix} u \\ o \end{Bmatrix} \begin{bmatrix} w \\ y \\ h \\ ? \end{bmatrix} V > \begin{Bmatrix} k^w \\ k^{w'} \end{Bmatrix} V$$

TABLE 14.1: Contrastive h and x in Classical Yucatec Maya

Under 'simple H' ([h])	*Under 'loud H' ([x])*
haa [Proto-Mayan *ha?] 'water'	haa [xa?] 'to scrape, file'
hel- [Proto-Mayan *hil] 'rest'	hel [Proto-Mayan *xel] 'succeed, exchange'
halab- [halaɓ-] 'thing said or sent'	halab- [Proto-Mayan *xal] 'weaving stick'

TABLE 14.2: The origin of Huastec labialized velars

Colonial Huastec	Modern Huastec
<cuyx> [kuwi(:)š] 'vulture'	kʷi:š 'vulture'
<coyen> [koyen] 'mass'	kʷen 'piled together'
<cohuych> [kowi(:)č] 'tamale'	kʷi:č 'tamale'

Some examples are seen in Table 14.2.

This philological evidence shows that Huastec k^w and $k^{w'}$ are the results of later sound change and therefore do not require these sounds to be reconstructed to Proto-Mayan. This case shows how philological information can be relevant to the reconstruction of proto-languages, as well as to determining the source of certain sounds and the sound changes that brought them about. It also reveals something about when the change took place, in this case some time after these eighteenth-century sources were written.

(3) Poqoman, Poqomchi', and Q'eqchi', three neighbouring Mayan languages, have all undergone the sound change *ts > s. Some scholars had thought this shared innovation (see Chapter 9) was evidence that the three should be grouped together in a subgroup of languages more closely related to one another than to other languages of the family. However, philological evidence shows that the change *ts > s is not in fact a shared innovation reflecting a change in some immediate ancestor of these three languages at a time before they split up. Rather, the earliest written attestations in these languages reveal that the change was under way after European contact and that the change diffused later through these three languages. For example, the Zúñiga Poqomchi' Dictionary (c. 1608) has entries such as: *vatz* [w-ats], *vaz* [w-as] 'older brother' [modern Poqomchi' *w-as* 'my older brother'; *azeh* [as-ex], *atzeh* [ats-ex] 'to treat as a brother, to take an older brother' – the dictionary entry says 'some say it with *tz* atzeh, and others with only *z*, azeh; say it as you please. Most say azeh, with *z*, and some with *tz*' (from Proto-Mayan *-ats* 'elder brother'). Some other examples from this dictionary are:

tzab, zab	'addition, balancing weight'
tzeel, zeel	'laugh' (Proto-Mayan *tseʔl)
tzinuh, zinuh	'oak'
tzub, zub	'the profit from what is sold'

The Morán Poqomam Dictionary (c. 1720) has examples such as:

ah itz	'witch, sorcerer' (modern Poqomam *ax is* (< Proto-Mayan *ax i:ts* 'witch, sorcerer'; cf. *i:ts* 'witchcraft')
ah zeel, ah tzeel	'laughter' (Proto-Mayan *tseʔl)
alaz, alaatz	'descendants'
azvez, atzvez	'elder brother' (modern Poqomam *as-w'es*) (< Proto-Mayan *-ats*)

Other sources show that this change was complete in Poqomchi' and Poqomam shortly after these dictionaries were written, but that it diffused to Q'eqchi' only later. For example, the Morales Q'eqchi' Grammar (1741) shows most forms still with <tz> ([ts]), though in Modern Q'eqchi' these are now with /s/:

tzimaj	'bow, arrow' (modern Q'eqchi' *simax*)
tzuc	'gnat' (modern Q'eqchi' *suq*)

A very few of the words cited in this dictionary show the beginnings of the change, for example:

tzununk, sununk	'smell' (modern Q'eqchi' *sunu:nk*)

The philological information derived from this example shows that the change **ts > s* in these three languages took place after European contact and spread among these already independent languages. This means that this change is not support for subgrouping these languages together as more closely related. This case shows how philological evidence can be relevant for subgrouping, as well as for determining the date when changes took place.

(4) Philological information can also document grammatical changes. Modern Kaqchikel (Mayan) has affixes that mark tense, but Old Kaqchikel, recorded in numerous colonial documents from the late 1600s and 1700s, did not have tense markers. Tense markers in this language are the result of rather recent change involving aspect prefixes. Colonial sources reveal a Kaqchikel aspect system with:

<x-> (/š-/ [IPA /ʃ-/]) 'completive' (perfective)
<t-> (/t-/) 'incompletive' (imperfective) for transitive verbs
<c-> or <qu-> (/k-/) 'incompletive' (imperfective) for intransitive verbs (where, following Spanish orthographic conventions for /k/, <c-> occurred before *a, o, u*, and <qu-> before *i* and *e*).

The present tense developed from the verbs in incompletive aspect when they followed the adverb <tan> 'now'. The combination of <tan> and incompletive aspect marker changed; *tan + t-* was ultimately reduced to *nd-* or *n-* in modern dialects, for example <tan t-in-ban> 'I am doing' [now INCOMPLETIVE.TRANSITIVE, first person singular ERGATIVE -do] > /n-in-b'an/. The verbs with *tan + k-* 'incompletive intransitive' > *ng-, ny-, y-* in different modern dialects. The 'completive' <x-> was reinterpreted as 'past' *š-*, since completive (completed) actions typically take place in the past. Earlier, these morphemes did not mark tense; 'completive' (perfective) could involve non-past events, as in English equivalents such as 'I did it', 'I have done it', 'I will have done it (by tomorrow)', and incompletive equivalents as in 'I am doing it', 'I was doing it', 'I will be doing it'.

The ample documentation in colonial texts attests the change from the former aspect system with no tense morphology to the modern tense system.

(5) Philological information which can be derived from Maya hieroglyphic writing helps to identify the language in which the hieroglyphic texts (c.

400 BC to AD 1600) were written and demonstrates that certain sound changes had already taken place by the date of writing. The language of the script is Cholan, and it had already undergone such distinctive Cholan sound changes as *k > č (IPA [ʧ]) and e: > i. (Note, there is some difference of opinion among specialists about which Cholan language or languages may be involved, but no disagreement that the hieroglyphic texts on the earlier monuments represent some form of Cholan.) The change *k > č is seen in the images in Figure 14.3, where forms interchanged as rebuses in that figure are all pronounced /čan/ in Cholan (ČAN 'four', ČAN 'snake', and ČAN 'sky'). As pointed out above, that these signs could be interchanged in this way shows that Cholan was the language of the writing, since in Yucatec Maya the cognate words are not homophonous as they are in Cholan. Figure 14.6 shows not only that Cholan was the language of the script, but also that two Cholan sound changes had already taken place by the time of the writing, *k > č and e: > i. Figure 14.6 presents the syllabic spelling of 'deer', written <či-xi> for čix – the first syllabic sign is či, the second xi.

'Deer' in Proto-Mayan was *kehx, and is ké:h in Yucatec. The syllabic spelling shows the results of the two Cholan sound changes, *k > č and e: > i, and is seen in Cholan čix 'deer' (see modern Chol čih), not the form in cognates for 'deer' in Yucatecan or the other subgroups of Mayan. The <či> glyph is used in hieroglyphic spellings of other words that have /či/ in them, but never for words with /ki/ or /ke/.

These brief examples from Maya hieroglyphic writing show how the philological investigation of these written records contributes by showing which language the hieroglyphic script was written in, and that the changes *k > č and e: > i took place at a time before the texts were written. (For other examples from Maya hieroglyphic writing, see Campbell 1984; Justeson et al. 1985.)

The examples cited in this section show that findings from philological investigation can have implications for, among other things, (1) documenting former

FIGURE 14.6: Cholan 'deer' spelled syllabically či-xi /čix/

contrasts now lost and sound changes that have taken place; (2) refining and clarifying the reconstructions of proto-phonology; (3) distinguishing borrowed changes from legitimate shared innovations; (4) clarifying evidence for subgrouping; (5) documenting grammatical changes; (6) identifying ancient, sometimes extinct, languages, and deciphering writing systems; and (7) establishing the relative age of changes. In effect, if the right kind of information is preserved in the written sources, the philological investigation of written records can contribute insight and understanding to most areas of linguistic change.

14.4 The Role of Writing

The relationship of writing to reconstruction by the comparative method has sometimes been misrepresented but needs to be understood. Since reliance on written languages had been important in Indo-European linguistics, some scholars came to believe that it was impossible to do reliable historical linguistic investigation without written records from earlier stages of the languages investigated. This belief continued to be repeated by some scholars in spite of the fact that the comparative study of unwritten, so-called 'exotic' languages has had a long and successful history. Leonard Bloomfield disproved once and for all the assertion that a proto-language could not be reconstructed successfully in the absence of written records from earlier stages of the languages. Bloomfield's (1925; 1928) famous proof of the applicability of the comparative method in unwritten languages was based on the assumption that sound change is regular. This meant that different sound correspondence sets among Algonquian languages that could not be explained away required different proto-sounds to be reconstructed. Bloomfield's decision to reconstruct *çk for one sound correspondence set, even though it contained only sounds found in other correspondence sets but corresponding to different sounds in the different daughter languages, was confirmed by the discovery of Swampy Cree, which contained distinct sounds as the reflexes in these sound correspondences.

Bloomfield's proof of the applicability of the comparative method to unwritten languages is considered a major contribution to historical linguistics. It means that while we are happy to have the testimony of written records for earlier periods when we can get it, written attestations are by no means necessary to comparative reconstruction. Moreover, it must be recalled that written records have to be interpreted – which is one of the roles of philology – and the records' value is limited to our ability to interpret the sound system underlying them.

Hittite illustrates this point. While Hittite has radically revised our understanding of Indo-European phonology, it was written in an imprecise cuneiform syllabary on clay tablets from 1650 to 1200 BC, and several aspects of its phonetic interpretation are still in dispute. For example, did Hittite have four or five vowels? Did it have an [o]? Did Hittite have contrastive vowel length, or what does the doubling of vowels in the texts mean? What do the frequent double signs for stop consonants in the orthography represent? Clearly, then, Hittite writing provides much useful information, but it also has limitations for the historical interpretation of the language.

Since Bloomfield's proof, the proto-languages representing many language families whose languages are mostly unwritten have been reconstructed and the historical developments in the languages have been investigated, in cases such as Algonquian, Athabaskan, Austronesian, Bantu, Chibchan, Mixe-Zoquean, Muskogean, Saamic, Samoyedic, Tupían, Uto-Aztecan, etc. In short, the existence of an old written tradition with older texts is by no means necessary for the comparative method to be applicable, and in any case, the written records are only as valuable for historical linguistic interests as our ability to interpret them and to determine accurately the phonetic and structural properties of the language they represent.

14.4.1 Getting historical linguistic information from written sources

The techniques employed and the sort of information one can expect to obtain from written records vary greatly from case to case, depending on the circumstances. For example, how we investigate texts written in a logographic writing system (where signs represent whole words) will differ markedly from how we treat texts written in syllabaries (with symbols based on properties of syllables) or in alphabetic scripts. However, in general, in philology we can use anything that provides information helpful for interpreting the phonetic, phonemic, semantic, and grammatical contents of the language which the written records represent, so that this information can be put to use in unravelling further the history of the language involved.

Very often, what information we can derive for interpreting the structure of the language at the time when the texts were written and extrapolating from that for understanding the history of the language is a matter of luck, a matter of what happens to show up in the sources available. In the best cases, we may have descriptions of or commentaries about the pronunciation at the time the texts were written, and these can be immensely helpful. For example, in the case of Sanskrit, fortunately ancient Sanskrit grammarians provided reasonably detailed descriptions of pronunciation and grammar (Fortson 2004: 6). In most situations, however, we are not so fortunate as to have worthwhile, readily interpretable phonetic descriptions from the past. Other valuable sources of phonetic information include rhymes, metre, occasional spellings, transliterations of forms in other languages whose phonology is better known, aid from translations from texts known in other languages, and clues from related languages and dialects. Old written texts can also provide insights into grammatical changes. Let us consider some of these briefly.

(1) *Rhymes and the testimony of poetry*. For example, the word 'night' was spelled variously <niht>, <nyʒt>, <nyght>, and <nicht> in Middle English texts. For various reasons it is assumed that the consonant before the final *t* represented in these various spellings (especially by <gh> and <ʒ>) of the word for 'night' and others like it was /x/, a voiceless velar fricative, even though that sound is gone from Modern English /nait/ 'night'. Some of the evidence for concluding that

it represented /x/ in Middle English comes from the fact that in Middle English poetic texts, words spelled with <gh> and <ʒ>, with the postulated /x/, rhyme only with other words spelled in this way and never with words which contain the same vowel but lack a spelling of the sound we believe to have been /x/. For example, Chaucer rhymes *knight* with *wight* 'strong' but not with *white* (Lass 1992: 30).

(2) *Occasional spellings.* An indirect source of knowledge about changing pronunciation is the variant spellings (and misspellings) that sometime provide clues concerning what was changing and when the change took place. In the history of English, spelling conventions were starting to regularize in the 1600s, as printers more and more used uniform spelling, but standard spelling was far from fixed. Occasional spellings (not the more expected ones) from the period show change in pronunciation. For example variants such as *ceme/came* 'came', *credyll/cradel* 'cradle', and *teke/take* 'take' show that former /a/ had changed to something closer to modern /e(i)/ in these words. Examples such as *symed/semed* 'seemed', *stypylle/stepel* 'steeple', reflect the /e:/ > /i:/ of the Great Vowel Shift. Spellings of *marcy/mercy* 'mercy', *sarten/certein* 'certain', *parson/persoun* 'person', and so on, show that /er/ changed to /ar/ in the pronunciation of the writers of these forms. This change was fairly general, though sociolinguistically conditioned, and it was ultimately reversed, but left behind such doublets in English as *clerk/clark*, *person/parson*, *vermin/varmint*, and *university/varsity*.

In Latin, the earlier diphthong spelled <ae> changed to a monophthong *e* shortly before the beginning of the Christian era. Occasional Roman (mis-) spellings of, for example, <etate> for older <aetate> 'age' show the onset of this change in the language (Fortson 2004: 6).

(3) *Interpretation from material from foreign languages.* For example, the principal source of information on Gothic is Bishop Wulfila's (311–82) translation of the Bible, part of which has survived. The Gothic orthography used was based on that of Greek at the time Wulfila wrote. The spellings with <ai> and <au> are interpreted as representing /ɛ:/ and /ɔ:/, respectively, based on the value of <ai> and <au> in Greek spelling at the time. This interpretation is supported by the Gothic spellings of foreign names and words known to have had *e(:)* and *o(:)* in the source languages, for example *Ailisabaiþ* 'Elizabeth', *Nazaraiþ* 'Nazareth', *praúfetus* 'prophet', *Gaúmaúrra* 'Gomorrah', and *Naúbaímbaír* 'November'. This gives greater confidence in the interpretation of the phonetic value of Gothic <ai> and <au> (Krause 1968: 67).

Greek loanwords borrowed into Latin in the first century BC that had Greek phi (<φ>) were spelled with <ph> in Latin (for example, *phasma* 'ghost' < Greek *pʰasma* 'apparition, phantom'; *philosophia* 'philosophy' < Greek *pʰilosopʰía* 'love of knowledge'; *physica* 'physics' < Greeek *pʰusiké* 'nature, natural sciences'). It is argued that at that time, Greek had not yet changed its aspirated /pʰ/ to the /f/ it later came to have and that Latin scribes chose <ph> to represent it, knowing that the Greek sound matched neither Latin's unaspirated /p/ nor its fricative /f/. By bishop Ulfilas' time, fourth century AD, Greek had undergone the change (*pʰ > f*), seen in his writing of <f> for Greek names in Gothic, as in

Filippus 'Philip' < Greek *phílippus*, and *Fareisaius* 'Pharisee' < Greek *pharisaios* (see Fortson 2004: 6).

(4) *Clues from related languages.* In the case of texts in languages which are less well known, sometimes clues to the interpretation of the writing can be obtained from related languages. For example, in the case of Middle English <gh> / <ȝ> (above), although 'night' in Modern English has no /x/, we can be more assured of our /x/ interpretation of the phonetic value based on the fact that English's closest relatives have /x/ in cognate words for 'night', as in Dutch *nacht*, Frisian *nacht*, and German *Nacht* ([naxt]) (Lass 1992: 30).

An example which shows how both translated texts and clues from related languages can help comes from Chicomuceltec, an extinct Mayan language, closely related to Huastec. Very little is known directly about Chicomuceltec, just limited word lists (no more than 500 words) and one short text from before it became extinct. The text is a *Confesionario* (confessional) from 1775 with about ten lines in Chicomuceltec corresponding to the adjacent Spanish text. The orthography is based on Spanish, and by having recourse to the Spanish translation of the text for possible meanings in the Chicomuceltec version and by comparing forms that correspond in Huastec, it is possible to work out much of the contents of the text, as seen in the following lines:

Chicomuceltec: ixcataton tan Domingo?
Spanish: Has trabajado los Domingos?

The Spanish line means 'Have you worked on Sundays?' and we believe that the Chicomuceltec version has the same meaning. In the Spanish orthography at the time, <x> represented [š] (IPA [ʃ]); Spanish /š/ changed to a velar fricative [x] in the early 1700s, which is spelled today primarily with <j>. In comparing Huastec material, we postulate that the Chicomuceltec text contains *ixca-* [iška-] 'you-PAST' (containing within it *-a-* 'you-SINGULAR') + *-t'ohn-* 'work', *tan* 'in', and the Spanish loanword *Domingo* 'Sunday'.

Without access to related Huastec forms and corresponding translation of the same text in Spanish, we would have no basis for segmenting the morphemes or guessing what this line meant. Without reference to Huastec forms, we would not be able to recover the word 'to work' or to postulate that it contained a glottalized *t'* as in the Huastec cognate, since the glottalized stops are not distinguished from plain ones in the Spanish-based orthography of the Chicomuceltec text. Together, the corresponding translation in a better-known language (Spanish in this case) and comparison with a closely related language (Huastec) provide for a fairly successful philological interpretation of this text in an otherwise very poorly known extinct language (Campbell 1988a: 202–7).

There are also many potential pitfalls and sources of error in attempts to interpret older written sources, and it is important to keep in mind the many ways in which well-meaning interpretations can go astray. Sometimes the writing system just underrepresents the contrasts that existed in the language at the time it was written, and so information is simply not available for a full interpretation. In the Chicomuceltec example, this is illustrated by the lack of distinction in the

Spanish-based orthography between plain /t/ and glottalized /t'/ which we assume to have been present in the language based on corresponding words in closely related Huastec which have the glottalized sound. In early attestations of other Native American languages, contrastive tones, glottal stops, and long vowels, for example, are simply not represented in the documents. Other problems can come from the difficulty of interpreting variations in the writing, from cases where different dialects with different features are represented, and from the tendency for writing systems to be conservative and thus to preserve representations of features which have been lost or much changed in the spoken language, long after the language has changed – witness the <gh> still written in Modern English *night*. The needs of poetic form (especially metre) may distort the written language, for example in cases of poetic licence using word orders not normally found in the spoken language. Old texts which are translations of texts in other languages, such as the Bible in Gothic based on Greek, or in English based on translations from Latin, often lead to grammatical distortions, loan translations or calques, and so on, which were not actually part of the spoken language.

(5) *Grammatical change.* The Kaqchikel example above shows how information about grammatical change in a language can be obtained. Many examples in other languages also illustrate this.

In summary, in many cases, exercising appropriate caution, we can obtain much information through the philological investigation of older written attestations of value to the historical interpretation of languages. This is a very important source of historical linguistic information, useful in the arsenal of tools the historical linguist uses to recover the history of languages.

14.5 Exercises

Exercise 14.1 Philological analysis of Latin *Appendix Probi*

The *Appendix Probi* ('Appendix of Probus') was compiled in the third to fourth century AD. It lists 227 Latin words in what the scribe considered both 'correct' and 'incorrect' form. It was devised to aid scribes with the spelling, but the forms listed also illustrate some phonological and analogical changes that were taking place or had already taken place in spoken Latin at that time. Compare the following examples from the list and attempt to formulate the changes that they appear to reflect. These examples are of the form *X non Y*, that is, *X not Y*, where the scribe considers the 'X' form 'correct' and the 'Y' form 'incorrect', as in *masculus non masclus*, meaning '*masculus* ['male'] not *masclus*', or more precisely, 'write *masculus*; do not write *masclus*'. For this exercise, assume that the forms on the left of *non* represent conservative and thus older pronunciations, and that the forms that follow *non* on the right either correspond to later pronunciations which result from changes in the language or represent alternative, non-standard pronunciations that represent changes in progress.

HINT: In instances where some forms seem to change in the opposite direction to others, consider the possible role of hypercorrection.

	Appendix Probi	*Conventional Classical Latin spelling and gloss*

Set I

1. masculus non masclus — māsculus 'male, manly'
2. vetulus non veclus — vetulus 'little old, poor old'
3. vitulus non viclus — vitulus 'calf, foal'
4. vernaculus non vernaclus — vernāculus 'native, of home-born slaves'
5. articulus non articlus — articulus 'joint, knuckle, limb'
6. angulus non anglus — angulus 'angle, corner'
7. oculus non oclus — oculus 'eye'
8. tabula non tabla — tabula 'board, plank'
9. calida non calda — calida 'warm, hot'
10. frigida non fricda — frīgida 'cold'
11. viridis non virdis — viridis 'green'

Set II

12. vacua [vakua] non vaqua [vakwa] — vacua 'empty, void'
13. equs [ekwus] non ecus [ekus] — equus 'horse'
14. coqus [kokwus] non cocus [kokus] — coquus 'cook'
15. rivus [rīwus] non rius [rius] — rīvus 'stream, brook'
16. avus [awus] non aus — avus 'grandfather'
17. flavus [flāwus] non flaus [flaus] — flāvus 'yellow, golden'

Set III

18. passim non passi — passim 'here and there, at random'
19. pridem non pride — prīdem 'long ago, long'
20. olim non oli — ōlim 'once, at the time, at times'
21. idem non ide — īdem, idem 'the same, likewise'
22. numquam non numqua — numquam 'never'
23. triclinium non triclinu — trīclīnium 'dining-couch, dining room'

Set IVa (the more common direction of change)

24. ansa non asa — ānsa 'handle'
25. mensa non mesa — mēnsa 'table, meal'
26. Capsensis non Capsessis — Capsensis 'from Capsitanus'

Set IVb (occasional examples)

27. Hercules non Herculens — Herculēs
28. occasio non occansio — occāsiō 'opportunity, convenient time'

Appendix Probi	*Conventional Classical Latin spelling and gloss*

Set *Va* (the more common direction of change)

29. vinea non vinia   vīnea 'vineyard'
30. cavea non cavia   cavea 'cage, coop, hive'
31. lancea non lancia   lancea 'lance, spear'
32. balteus non baltius   balteus 'belt, girdle, sword-belt'
33. cochlea non coclia   coclea, cochlea 'snail'

Set *Vb* (occasional examples)

34. ostium non osteum   ōstium 'door, entrance'
35. noxius non noxeus   noxius 'harmful'
36. alium non aleum   ālium 'garlic'

Set *VI*

37. vapulo non baplo   vāpulō 'be beaten, flogged'
38. alveus non albeus   alveus 'hollow, trough, bathtub'
39. tolerabilis non toleravilis   tolerābilis 'bearable, tolerable'

Set *VII*

(The more common direction of change was <x> [ks] becoming <s> [s]. In light of this, how would you explain the following?)

40. miles non milex   mīles 'soldier'
41. aries non ariex   ariēs 'ram'
42. poples non poplex   poples 'knee'
43. ocuples non locuplex   locuplēs 'rich, reliable'

(from Baehrens 1922)

Exercise 14.2 Greek philological comparison

The short text in line (1) is from Mycenaean Greek (before 1200 BC), given in the conventional transliteration for the Linear B syllabary. Roots for the words in this text are compared in line (2) with Attic Greek (Classical Greek from Athens, end of the fifth century BC), and then in line (3) with Modern Greek. Each is given with its phonetic equivalents, well understood from a variety of sources of information.

Compare the Greek from these three different times and attempt to specify sound changes that can be detected in these data. (Do not struggle attempting to match the suffixes between these versions, as they differ in several instances.)

NOTE: FOOTSTOOL is represented by a logogram, where the sign signals the whole word and it is not spelled out in the syllabary. NOM = nominative; INST = dative-instrumental. 'Octopus' is literally 'many-foot' (*polu-/poly-* 'many' + *pod-* 'foot'). The word for 'griffin' (glossed as 'phoenix' in Modern Greek) also means 'palm tree'. This text means 'One footstool inlaid in ivory with a man and a horse and an octopus and a griffin / palm tree.'

(1) Linear B (c. 1400 BC):

Ta-ra-n	a-ja-me-no	e-re-pa-te-jo	a-to-ro-qo	i-qo-qe	po-ru-po-de-qe	po-ni-ke-qe FOOTSTOOL
[tʰrâ:nus	aia:ménos	elepʰanteío:i	antʰró:kʷo:i	híkkʷo:i-kʷe]	polupódei-kʷe	pʰoiní:kei-kʷe X]
stool.NOM	inlaid.NOM	ivory.INST	man.INST	horse.INST-and	octopus.INST-and	griffin.INST-and X

(2) Attic Greek (c. 400 BC):

θρανίον	ελεφάντινος	ἄνθρωπος	ἵππος	πολύπους	φοίνιξ
[tʰra:níon	elepʰántinos	ántʰro:pos	híppos	polýpu:s	pʰoíni:ks]

(3) Modern Greek (c. AD 2000):

θρανίο	ελεφάντινος	άνθρωπο-	ιππο-	πολύποδ-	φοίνικαξ
[θranío	elefá(n)dinos	ánθropos	ípos	polípoðas	finikas]
'desk/form'	'made.of.ivory'	'man'	'horse'	'polyp/ polypod'	'phoenix/ palm tree'

(from Horrocks 2014: 2–3)

Exercise 14.3 Spanish philological interpretation

The epic poem *Cantar de Mio Cid* is one of the oldest texts in Spanish, from about 1140 AD. A fragment of the poem is given here and compared with the modern equivalent in Latin American Spanish (as, for example, spoken in Mexico or Central America). Each line is given with broad phonetic equivalents. There is an English translation of the six lines, together, following the modern equivalent.

Compare the two versions. What lexical changes do you note? What other changes have taken place in this variety of modern Spanish? Assume for present purposes that any non-lexical, non-grammatical phonetic difference between the two versions represents a general change even if only one example appears in these data. What conclusions can you draw about the history of some of these changes?

NOTE: ñ = palatal nasal, IPA [ɲ]; [s̪] = dental 's' (which in modern Peninsular Spanish became [θ]); [s̺] = apical postalveolar 's'. Here. OBJ = marker of human specific object; REFL = reflexive. *nosotros* < *nós* 'we' + *otros* 'others'; *do* = modern *donde* 'where'.

I Original form from Cantar de Mio Cid

(1)	Nós	çercamos	el	escaño	por	curiar	nuestro	señor,
	[nos̺	s̪erkamos̺	el	es̪kaño	por	kuriar	nuestro	s̺eñor]
	we	surrounded	the	bench	for	to.guard	our	lord,

(2) fasta do   desperto mio Cid, el que Valencia gañó;
     [faṣta do   deṣperto mio ṣid el ke   valenṣia gañó]
     until where awoke   my   Cid he who Valencia won

(3) levantós del escaño   e   fos   poral   león;
     [levantó-ṣ del eṣkaño   e   fo-ṣ   por-al   león]
     got.up-REFL from.the bench and went-REFL for.the lion;

(4) el   león   premió la   cabeça, a   mio Cid   esperó,
     [el león   premió la   kabeṣa, a   mio ṣid   eṣperó]
     the lion   lowered the   head,   for my   Cid   waited

(5) dexósle   prender al   cuello e   a   la   red le metió.
     [deʃó-ṣ-le   prender al   kueľo   e   a   la   red le metió]
     allowed-REFL-him to.take to.the neck   and to the net it put

II Modern equivalent

(1) Nosotros rodeamos   el   escaño para custodiar a   nuestro señor,
     [nosotros rodeamos   el   eṣkaño para kustodiar a   nuestro señor]
     we   surrounded the   bench   for   to.guard OBJ our   lord,

(2) hasta que se   desperto mi Cid, el que ganó Valencia;
     [asta ke   se   desperto mi sid   el ke   ganó balensia
     until that REFL   awoke   my Cid   he who won   Valencia;

(3) se   levantó del   escaño y   se   fue   por el   león;
     [se   lebantó del   eṣkaño i   se   fue   por el   león]
     REFL   got.up   from.the bench   and REFL went   for the lion;

(4) el   león   bajó   la   cabeza, esperó a   mio Cid,
     [el león   baxó   la   kabesa, esperó a   mi   sid]
     the lion   lowered the   head,   waited for my   Cid

(5) se   le   dejó   coger por el cuello y   meter-lo en la jaula.
     [se   le   dexó   koxer por el kueyo   i   meterlo   en la xaula]
     REFL him allowed to.take by the neck   and put-it   in the cage

(1) 'We surrounded the bench to guard our lord,
(2) until my Cid awoke, he who conquered Valencia;
(3) he got up from the bench and he went for the lion;
(4) the lion lowered its head, [and] waited for my Cid;
(5) it allowed him to take it by the neck and put it in the cage.'

15

LINGUISTIC PREHISTORY

Language, too, has marvels of her own, which she unveils to the inquiring glance of the patient student. There are chronicles below her surface, there are sermons in every word.

(Müller 1866: 12–13)

15.1 Introduction

Linguistic prehistory has been called linguistic palaeontology and linguistic archaeology (though 'linguistic palaeontology' also often has a more restricted meaning). Linguistic prehistory has a long (and sometimes chequered) history, though in recent years it has again come into focus. Broadly speaking, linguistic prehistory uses historical linguistic findings for cultural and historical inferences. Linguistic prehistory correlates information from historical linguistics with information from archaeology, ethnohistory, history, ethnographic analogy, and human biology in order to obtain a clearer, more complete picture of the past. Thus, the comparative method, linguistic homeland and migration theory, cultural inventories from reconstructed vocabularies of proto-languages, loanwords, place names, classification of languages, internal reconstruction, dialect distributions, and the like can all provide valuable historical information useful to linguistic prehistory. How these methods can contribute to a fuller picture of prehistory is the focus of this chapter. What linguistic prehistory is about is illustrated by a few well-known and informative cases. At the same time, it is also important to be aware of the limitations of linguistic prehistory and of the possible pitfalls and problems which can be encountered in attempts to correlate historical linguistic information with the findings in other fields. This is the subject of the last section of this chapter.

15.2 Indo-European Linguistic Prehistory

To get started, it is helpful to look briefly at some of the findings and claims about the prehistory of Indo-European-speaking peoples as reflected in linguistic evidence. This is an instructive case study.

By the mid-1800s, comparative Indo-European linguistics had advanced sufficiently for it to be possible to say how most of the Indo-European languages had diversified, and to make reasonably informed hypotheses about the material culture and social structure of the Proto-Indo-Europeans (the speakers of Proto-Indo-European) and about their homeland – all based solely on linguistic findings (see Kuhn 1845; Pictet 1859–63; Schrader 1883 [1890]). However, crucial archaeological and other information was not yet available at that time, and the first archaeological data that did become available seemed to clash with the most probable linguistic interpretations. For example, according to an early hypothesis based on linguistic evidence, the Indo-European homeland (the place where Proto-Indo-European was originally spoken, from where Indo-European languages diversified and spread out, ultimately to their current locations) was located in the steppes to the north of the Black Sea; however, it was objected that no likely archaeological culture was known from this area at that time. In fact, supportive archaeological evidence did not appear until some 100 years later, with Marija Gimbutas' (1963) work on the Kurgan culture of the Pontic and Volga steppes.

The correlation between Proto-Indo-European and the Kurgan archaeological culture is attractive but has also generated debate (see Mallory 1989; Mallory and Adams 1997; Anthony and Ringe 2015). In Gimbutas' view, the expansion of Kurgan culture corresponds in time and area with the expansion of Indo-European languages outwards from this homeland, and correlates with the arrival in these areas of such typically Indo-European things as horses, wheeled vehicles, double-headed axes, small villages, pastoral economy, and patriarchal society. The Kurgan tradition was very broad, covering a series of cultures of the Black Sea–Volga area. Some see it as thus imprecise to equate Kurgan culture with Proto-Indo-European culture and homeland. Some prefer an association with some more specific culture of the Pontic Steppe, a subculture of Kurgan.

Reconstruction by the comparative method has provided a fairly clear view of important aspects of Proto-Indo-European culture, including valuable information on the original homeland, social structure, kinship, subsistence, economy, law, religion, environment, technology, and ideology. As Calvert Watkins observed,

> When we have reconstructed a protolanguage, we have also necessarily established the existence of a prehistoric society . . . the contents of the Indo-European lexicon provide a remarkably clear view of the whole culture of an otherwise unknown prehistoric society.
>
> The evidence that archaeology can provide is limited to material remains. But human culture is not confined to material artifacts. The

reconstruction of vocabulary can offer a fuller, more interesting view of a prehistoric people than archaeology because it includes nonmaterial culture. (2011: xx)

Aspects of Proto-Indo-European's cultural inventory can be recovered from the reconstructed vocabulary of Proto-Indo-European, as seen in the list below, which is based upon Mallory and Adams (1997) and Watkins (2011), amplified and interpreted by Michael Weiss. (I thank Michael Weiss for his very extensive work preparing and presenting these Indo-European forms and for his help in this section generally.) The traditional Indo-Europeanist notation used here requires some explanation, and it will be helpful to have some information on Proto-Indo-European (PIE) sounds as background before we present the vocabulary that reflects PIE culture.

Most Indo-Europeanists recognize three sounds called laryngeals, though their number and phonetic values are still disputed. They are represented conventionally as: $*h_1$ ('neutral', perhaps /h/ or /ʔ/); $*h_2$ ('a-colouring', perhaps /x/ or /ħ/); and $*h_3$ ('o-colouring', perhaps /ʕ/). Undisputed consonantal reflexes of these survive only in Hittite and the other Anatolian languages. The laryngeals are gone from the other Indo-European (IE) languages, but not without a trace. The evidence of their earlier presence is seen primarily in their effect on vowels in these languages, changing the quality of both preceding and following vowels, and lengthening any vowel preceding them. In addition a number of languages provide other bits of evidence involving reflexes of the Proto-Indo-European laryngeals.

Indo-Europeanists normally reconstruct three distinct series of velars: the palatovelars ($*\hat{k}, \hat{g}, \hat{g}^h$), the plain velars ($*k, *g, g^h$), and the labiovelars ($*k^w, *g^w, *g^{wh}$). Until recently, it was generally believed that no single language preserved distinct reflexes of all three series (western subfamilies tended to have velars and labiovelars where eastern subgroups tended to have palatovelars and velars); this allowed us to think that Proto-Indo-European had only two series in contrast and that those eastern branches had shifted plain velars to palatovelars and labiovelars to velars. However, it has now been shown that the Anatolian language Luvian has in fact kept the reflexes of all three series apart, requiring all three to be reconstructed for Proto-Indo-European.

The position of the accent in Proto-Indo-European is reconstructible for many lexical items. However, in many forms the accent could move depending on the morphology of the words involved, and in many cases the crucial testimony from the limited number of branches which preserve direct or indirect traces of the Proto-Indo-European accent (Balto-Slavic, Indo-Iranian, Greek, Germanic, and Anatolian) is missing. For these reasons the accent is generally not indicated in the following reconstructions.

Verbal roots are cited with an inserted *e* vowel (the so-called *e*-grade), which appear in certain morphological categories. Most nouns are cited in a stem form without case endings. (The exceptions are neuter nouns, which are cited in the nominative–accusative form, and those nouns for which a stem cannot be reconstructed with certainty. These are cited as mere roots.)

The reconstructed cultural lexicon of Proto-Indo-European includes the following words. Note that here in Indo-European words, the symbols <l̥, r̥, m̥, n̥> stand for syllabic liquids and nasals.

15.2.1 Agriculture

'grain'
- *yewo- 'a grain, particularly barley'
- *gr̥h₃nom (younger than *yewo-, perhaps meaning 'ripened grain', which replaced *yewo- in most of the west and centre of the IE world and competes with it in Iranian)

CROP

'fruit'
- *seso- (occurred on the margins of the IE world if derived from the root *seh₁-'sow'; the reconstruction could be *sesh₁o- or *sh₁eso-)

'barley'
- *ĝʰrV(s)d(h)- (a very problematic reconstruction)
- *bʰaros (confined to the northwest of the IE world)

'wheat'
- *puh₂ro-
- *ga/ondʰ- (southern and eastern peripheries of the IE world)

'rye'
- *rugʰi- (confined to the northwest of the IE world)

'ear of grain, chaff'
- *h₂eḱos (from *h₂eḱ- 'point, sharp')

LAND

'field'
- *h₂eĝro- (probably derived from *h₂eĝ- 'to drive', hence originally 'pasture'; Vedic ájra- still just means 'plain')
- *h₂erh₃ur ~ *h₂erh₃wo- (derived from *h₂erh₃- 'to plough', at least late PIE in the west and centre of the IE world)

'piece of land/garden'
- *ḱeh₂pos / *ḱeh₂péh₂

'enclosure/garden'
- *gʰorto- (connection with the root *gʰer- 'take' is uncertain)

FIELD PREPARATION AND PLANTING

'to plough'
- *h₂erh₃-

'plough'
- *h₂erh₃trom (widespread derivative of *h₂erh₃-)

'ploughshare'
- *wogʷʰni- (at least west and centre of the IE world)

'furrow'
- *le/oiseh₂- (west and centre of the IE world)

'harrow'
- *h₂okete₂-

'hoe'
  *mat- (root only)
'sow'
  *seh$_1$-
HARVESTING
'harvest'
  *(s)kerp-
'mow'
  *h$_2$meh$_1$-
'sickle'
  *sr̥po-/eh$_2$-
GRAIN PROCESSING
'thresh'
  *peis- (earlier meaning 'stamp, crush')
  *wers- (earlier meaning perhaps 'sweep')
'winnow'
  *neik- (at least late PIE)
'grind'
  *melh$_2$- (agreement in various European subgroups on the agricultural
    sense of 'grind')
  *g^{h}rend(h)- 'grind' (a somewhat problematic reconstruction; younger than
    * melh$_2$-; west and centre of the IE world)
'quern'
  *g^{w}réh$_2$won- ~ *g^{w}erh$_2$nu- 'quern' (from suffixed form of *g^{w}erh$_2$-
    'heavy')

15.2.2 Domestic animals and animal husbandry

'livestock'
  *peḱu ('livestock', 'moveable wealth' > 'wealth')
'herdsman'
  *westor- (though not widely attested, the distribution (Anatolian and
    Iranian) suggests great antiquity in IE probably derived from the
    following)
'graze'
  *wes-
'guard, protect'
  *peh$_2$- (to describe the herdsman's activities)
'dog'
  *ḱ(u)won-
'horse'
  *h$_2$eḱwo-
'larger domestic animal'
  *steuro-
'pig'
  *suh$_x$-

'boar'
  *h_1epero- (at least west and centre of the IE world)
'piglet'
  *$por\hat{k}o$-
'sheep'
  *h_2owi-
'ram/fleece'
  *$moiso$-
'ewe'
  *$h_2owikeh_2$-
'lamb/kid'
  *h_1er- (root only)
'lamb'
  *$h_2eg^{w}no$- (at least west and centre of the IE world; some prefer the
    reconstruction $h_2eg^{wh}no$-)
  *$wr̥(h_x)en$- (centre and east of the IE world)
'goat'
  *$h_2ei\hat{g}$- (centre and east of the IE world)
  *g^haido- (northwest region)
'he-goat'
  *$b^hu\hat{g}o$- (also male animal of various kinds, stag, ram)
  *$kapro$-
  *$h_2e\hat{g}o$- (centre and east of the IE world)
'bovine'
  *g^wou-
'bull'
  *$uksen$-
  *$tauro$- (possibly also 'aurochs')
'cow'
  *$wakeh_2$-
'cowherd'
  *$g^wouk^wolh_1o$- (at least west and centre of the IE world, based on *g^wou- 'cow'
    + *k^wolh_1o- 'one who turns, moves' from *k^welh_1- 'turn, move around')
DAIRY PRODUCTION
  'to milk'
    *$h_1mel\hat{g}$-
  'milk'
    *$g(a)lakt$
  'coagulated milk'
    *$d^hed^hh_1e$ (at least centre and east of the IE world)
  'curds'
    *tuh_xro/i- (at least centre and east of the IE world)
  'whey'
    *$ksih_xrom$ (centre and east of the IE world)
  'buttermilk'
    *$tenklom$ ~ $tn̥klom$ (from *$temk$- 'congeal')

'butter'

*h_3eng^wn (from *h_3eng^w- 'anoint')

'rich in milk'

*$pipih_xusih_2$- (at least centre and east of the IE world; a feminine perfect participle of the root *$peih_x$- 'swell')

15.2.3 Foods

'salt'

*sal-

'honey'

*melit (also *melit-ih_2- 'honey bee')

'mead'

med^{h}u

'beer'

*h_2elut- or *alut- (northwest of the IE world with an outlier in eastern Iranian; at least late IE in date)

'wine'

$wih_x Vno$- ~$woih_x no$- ~ $wih_x nom$ (related to words for wine in non-Indo-European Georgian and West Semitic; the ultimate relationship between these forms is unclear)

'apple'

*$h_2eb Vl$- (late PIE?)

*meh_2lom (or any seed- or pit-bearing fruit)

'cherry'

$kr̥nes$- ~ *$kr̥nom$ 'cornel cherry'

'fruit/berry'

*h_2ogeh_2-

*h_xoiweh_2- (at least west and centre of the IE world)

'blackberry, mulberry'

*morom

'bean'

*$b^hab^heh_2$- (at least west and centre of the IE world with variant *b^ha-un in Germanic)

'porridge'

*$pl̥t$- ~ polto- (late IE of the west and centre?)

'broth'

*yuh_x- 'broth'

15.2.4 Economy and commerce

'exchange'

*mei- (extended form *meit -'to change, go, move'; with derivatives referring to the exchange of goods and services within a society as regulated by custom or law) 'to sell'

    *$perh_2$- (at least of late IE status)

'to buy'

    *wes-

'purchase'

    *wVs-no- (derived from the above)

'payment, prize'

    *$h_2elg^{wh}o$-/eh_2- (derived from *h_2elg^{wh}- 'to earn, be worth')

'gift'

    *deh_3rom (derived from *deh_3- 'give')

'apportion, get a share'

    *b^hag-

'wealth'

    *h_3ep-

15.2.5 Legal terms

'law'

    *d^heh_1ti- 'thing laid down or done, law, deed' (derived from *d^heh_1- 'to
      set, put')

    *yewos 'religious law, ritual, norm'

'plead a case'

    *$(h_1)arg^w$-

'guilty'

    *h_1sont- (literally 'being', the present participle of the verb *h_1es-
      'be')

'penalty'

    *k^woineh_2- (derived from *k^wei- 'to pay, atone, compensate')

'make whole'

    *serk- (legal expression 'to pay for damages')

15.2.6 Transport

'yoke'

    *yugom (derived from *yeug- 'to yoke')

'wagon'

    *we/o$\hat{g}^hno$- (derived from *$we\hat{g}^h$- 'to go, transport in a vehicle')

'wheel'

    *$h_2wr̥g$- (root only; reflexes in Hittite and Tocharian suggest antiquity,
      derived from *h_2werg- 'turn')

    *$roteh_2$- (derived from *ret- 'to run, roll'; old PIE word for 'wheel', deriv-
      atives came to mean 'wagon' or 'war-chariot' in a number of eastern
      subgroups)

    *k^wek^wlom (probably from the root *k^welh_1- 'turn)

'axle'

    *$h_2e\hat{k}s$-

'shaft' (of a cart or wagon)

*$h_2/_3eih_1os$ ~ *$h_2/_3(e)ih_1so$-

'pole/peg'

*d^hur- 'pivot of door or gate, axle of a chariot, harness, means of harnessing a horse to a cart, pole, yoke, peg of axle'

'reins'

*$h_2ensiyo$-/eh_2- (the equivalence in form and meaning in Greek and Irish is evidence of PIE antiquity)

'boat'

*neh_2us derived from the verb *neh_2- 'float'

*h_xoldhu- '(dugout) canoe, trough' (probably late PIE)

'row'

*h_1erh_1-

15.2.7 Technology (other tools and implements)

'craftsman'

*d^hab^hro- (from *d^hab^h- 'to fit together')

'craft'

*$kerdos$

'metal'

*$h_2ey(o)s$ (often specialized as 'copper' or 'bronze')

'gold'

*h_2eusom

'silver'

*$h_2erĝntom$ 'white (metal), silver' (based on *$h_2erĝ$- 'white')

TOOLS

'axe'

*$(h_1)adhes$- or *h_1odhes-?

'spit, spear'

*g^heru (presence in Avestan, Celtic, and Italic strongly suggests it was once widespread in PIE)

'auger'

*$terh_1trom$ (derived from *$terh_1$- 'to rub, turn') 'awl'

*h_2oleh_2- 'whetstone'

*$ k̂oh_xno$- ~ *$k̂oh_xini$- (limited distribution, from PIE *$k̂eh_x(i)$ sharpen, hone', which is widespread)

'net'

*h_1ekt-

15.2.8 House and building(s)

'to build'

*$demh_2$-

'carpenter'

*$tetk̂$-on- (derived from *$tek̂$- 'create')

'house'

*dom-

*domh$_2$o- (both derived from *demh$_2$- 'build')

'hearth'

*h$_2$eh$_x$seh$_2$-

'door'

*dʰwor-

'doorjamb'

*h$_2$enh$_x$t(e)h$_2$

'roof'

*(s)tegos (derived from *(s)teg- 'cover')

*h$_1$rebʰ- 'cover with a roof'

'room'

*ket- (root only)

'beam/plank'

*bhelh$_2$ĝ- (at least west and centre of the IE world)

*kl̥h$_2$ro- (late IE)

'dwelling, settlement'

*wastu, *wāstu- (not related to *h$_2$wes- 'spend the night')

*treb- (west and centre of the IE world)

HOUSEHOLD

'cauldron'

*kʷeru-

'dish'

*potr̥

'plate'

*tek̂steh$_2$- (an Iranian–Italic match)

'cup'

*peh$_3$tlom (derived from *peh$_3$(i)- 'to drink')

'bed'

*legʰos ~ *logʰo- (derived from *legʰ- 'to lie, lay')

15.2.9 Clothing and textiles

'wool'

*h$_2$wl̥h$_1$neh$_2$-

'comb'

*kes- (early meaning probably 'put in order')

*kars- (the meaning 'comb (wool)' is found only in European languages)

'spin'

*sneh$_1$- 'twist fibres together to form thread; occupy oneself with thread'

*spenh$_1$- (earlier meaning 'stretch'; the specialization of 'working with thread' must be at least late IE)

'braid'

*plek̂-

'plait'
  *resg-
'twist'
  *weih$_x$-
'weave'
  *h$_x$eu-
  *web^h- 'weave' (in later PIE)
  *tek(s)-
'sew'
  *syeuh$_x$-
'fasten'
  *(s)ner- 'fasten with thread or cord' (a late PIE word at least)
  'thread'
  *dek- (root only; probably the oldest which can be reconstructed whose
     meaning subsumes 'thread')
'sinew'
  *g^{wh}ih$_x$slo- 'wear'
  *wes-
'skin bag'
  *b^{h}olĝ^{h}i- (derived from *b^{h}elĝ^h- 'to swell')

15.2.10 Warfare and fortification

'war-band'
  *koryo- ~ koro- (at least west and centre of the IE world)
'hold/conquer'
  *seĝ^h-
'citadel'
  *pelh$_x$- (centre and east of the IE world, at least)
'hillfort'
  *b^{h}r̥g^h- (derived from *b^{h}erg^h- 'high')
'fort'
  *wriyo-/eh$_2$-
'booty'
  *soru (particularly men, cattle, and sheep)
'sword'
  *h$_{2/3}$n̥si-
'spear'
  *ĝ^{h}ais-o-
'spear-point'
  *ḱel(h$_x$)- (root only)

15.2.11 Social structure and social interaction

'master'
  *poti-

'housemaster'

    dems-pot(i)-

'household/village'

    * k̂oimo-* (west and centre of the IE world)

'member of a household'

    k̂eiwo-

'group'

    wik̂- (a settlement unit composed of a number of extended families which was later extended to the complex of buildings they occupied and, later still, to the sociopolitical unit) derived from PIE *weik̂-* 'to settle')

'groupmaster'

    wik̂-pot(i)- (at least centre and east of the IE world)

'family'

    ĝenh₁os (derived from *ĝenh₁-* 'to give birth, beget')

'people'

    teuteh₂-

'member of one's group'

    (h₁)aro- ~ *(h₁)aryo-* 'self-designation of the Indo-Iranians' (perhaps derived from *(h₁)ar-* 'to fit')

'dear'

    prih$_x$o- (in west of IE world 'free'; from *preih$_x$-* 'delight')

'king'

    h₃rḗ ĝs (derived from *h₃reĝ-* 'to move in a straight line' with derivatives meaning 'to direct in a straight line, lead, rule')

'rule'

    welh$_x$- (earlier meaning 'be strong')

    med- 'to apply the appropriate measures' (sometimes specialized in medical sense)

'free'

    h₁leud^{h}ero- 'free born' (derived from *h₁leud^h-* 'to mount up, grow')

'stranger, guest/host'

    g^{h}osti- 'someone with whom one has reciprocal duties of hospitality' (an outsider could be considered both guest and potential foe)

'servant'

    h₂entb^{h}i-k^{w}olh₁o- (compound, *h₂entb^{h}i-* 'on either side, around' + *k^{w}olh₁o-*, from *k^{w}elh₁-* 'turn, move round in a circle')

'dowry'

    h₂wed-mno- (west and centre of the IE world)

'one's own custom'

    swed^h- 'custom, characteristic, individuality' (connected in particular to reciprocal and contractual relationships, including poet–patron relations and other gift exchanges; from *swe-* 'third person pronoun and reflexive', appearing in various forms referring to the social group as an entity)

'fame'

    k̂lewos- (literally 'what is heard', derived from *k̂leu-* 'to hear')

'poet/seer'
> *weh₂t- (as 'poet' confined to west of the IE world) (Greek and Indo-Iranian provide evidence of a PIE *wekʷos tetk̂on- 'fashion speech')

15.2.12 Religion and beliefs

'holy'
> *ish₁ro-
> *sakro- (derived from *sak- 'to sanctify')
> *kwen(to)-
> *noibʰo-

DIVINITIES

'god'
> *deiwo- (derivative of *dyeu- 'sky, day, (sun)god', itself a derivative of the root *dei- 'shine')

'sky-father'
> *dyeusph₂ter [VOCATIVE], *dyeu-ph₂ter 'o father Jove' (cf. *Jupiter, Zeus*) (compound of *dyeu-* 'Jove, god of the daylight sky, head of the Indo-European pantheon' + *ph₂ter* 'father')

PRAYER

'pray'
> *prek̂-
> *meldʰ-
> *gʷʰedʰ-

'speak solemnly'
> *h₁wegwh-

'call/invoke'
> *ĝʰeuhₓ- (perhaps English *god* < *ĝʰu-to- 'that which is invoked', but derivation from *ĝʰu-to- 'libated' from *ĝʰeu- 'libate, pour' is also possible)

'priest, seer/poet'
> *kowhₓei-

CULT PRACTICE

'worship'
> *hₓiaĝ-

'consecrate'
> *weik- (earlier meaning perhaps 'to separate')

'handle reverently'
> *sep-

'libate'
> *spend-
> *ĝʰeu-, *ĝʰeu-mn̥ 'libation'

'sacrificial meal'
> *dapnom derived from *dap- 'to apportion (in exchange)'

'meal'
> *tolko/eh₂- (at least late PIE)

'sacred grove'
>   *nemos* (west and centre of the IE world)

'sacred enclosure'
>   *werbʰ-* (attestation in Anatolian, Tocharian, and probably Italic suggests antiquity)

SUPERNATURAL

'magical glory'
>   *keudos*

'sorcery'
>   *(h₁)alu-*

'phantom'
>   *dʰrougʰo-* (from *dʰreugʰ-* 'deceive')

'dragon'
>   *dr̥k̂ont-* (from *derk̂-* 'see', from the dangerous, potentially lethal, gaze of dragons)

The implications of Indo-European linguistic research were seldom ignored by archaeologists working in the area; they frequently took linguistic hypotheses into account in framing their own research. Archaeology and linguistics have contributed reciprocally in famous cases of Old World ancient history where, for example, archaeology brought forth the tablets and documents from such places as Boğazköy (in modern Turkey), Knossos (on Crete), Tel el-Amarna (in Egypt), and so on, and then scholars with linguistic skills deciphered and translated them, pushing back the recorded history in this part of the world by several millennia. Such decipherments also contributed to the picture of which languages were spoken, when and where they were spoken, and how they are classified. For example, the picture of the Indo-European language family was radically revised by the addition of the languages of the Anatolian branch (in which Hittite is of major importance), which came to light through these discoveries and decipherments. Successful interaction to the mutual benefit of both archaeology and linguistics is perhaps not surprising for cultures with ancient writing systems, which provide written documentation of ancient history. However, linguistic prehistory is also able to contribute significantly in cases that lack writing, and indeed it has contributed much to the interpretation of the prehistory of many other regions of the world.

15.3 The Methods of Linguistic Prehistory

Virtually any aspect of linguistics which renders information with historical content or implications for historical interpretations can be valuable in linguistic prehistory. Let's consider some of these and see how they work in specific examples.

15.3.1 The cultural inventory of reconstructed vocabulary

As we saw in the Indo-European case study (above), much information about the culture and society of the speakers of a proto-language can be recovered from the reconstructed vocabulary. Not only do individual reconstructed lexical items provide us with information valuable for interpreting a people's past, but comparative reconstruction can and often does also give us whole complexes of terms interconnected in particular semantic domains that reflect a people's past culture, as, for example, the several reconstructed terms involving Proto-Indo-European livestock (seen above).

Here we look at a few other cases, where the cultural inventory of the reconstructed vocabulary has been investigated. In these cases, only the glosses of the items that have been reconstructed in these proto-languages are given. (For the actual forms and details of the studies, see the references cited after each case.)

15.3.1.1 Proto-Finno-Ugric and Proto-Uralic culture

Uralic is a language family of about forty-four languages spoken across northern Eurasia. Uralic is generally but not universally held to have two major branches, Finno-Ugric and Samoyedic. It includes the various Samoyedic Selkup languages, Saamic languages, Finnish, Estonian, Hungarian, and several others (see Map 15.1 and Figure 9.2: The Uralic Family tree, in Chapter 9). Studies have dealt with both older Proto-Uralic culture and subsequent Proto-Finno-Ugric culture based on the reconstructed vocabulary, though these are difficult to separate based on the evidence available. We look at each, in turn.

15.3.1.1.1 Proto-Uralic culture

Kaisa Häkkinen (2001) finds in the vocabulary reflecting Proto-Uralic culture thirty-one animal and animal-related terms, seventeen terms for transport, traffic, and motion, five for water and water systems, nine hunting and fishing terms, six for buildings, constructions, and equipment, two for foodstuffs and four for dishes and food preparation, sixteen for family and personal relationships, twenty-two for tools, work, and work implements, and two for clothing. Analysis of the cultural inventory of reconstructed Proto-Uralic vocabulary (based on Sammallahti's 1988 rigorously constrained reconstructions) reveals aspects of the life of a Stone Age hunting and gathering people. Bearers of Proto-Uralic culture knew and presumably utilized the following things which reflect their culture:

> *Hunting, fishing, and food terms*: bow, arrow, bowstring, knife; egg, fish, berry, bird-cherry, hare, to pursue/hunt, track.
> *Other tools, implements, clothing and technology*: needle, belt, glue, birch-bark, drill, cord/rope, handle, (lodge)pole, bark/leather, enclosure/fence, metal, to braid, shaft, to cook.
> *Travel and transport*: ski, to row, fathom, cross-rail (in boat).
> *Climate and environment*: snow, lake, river, wave, summer/thaw, water.
> *Commerce*: to give/sell.
> (Cf. Sammallahti 1988; Janhunen 1981.)

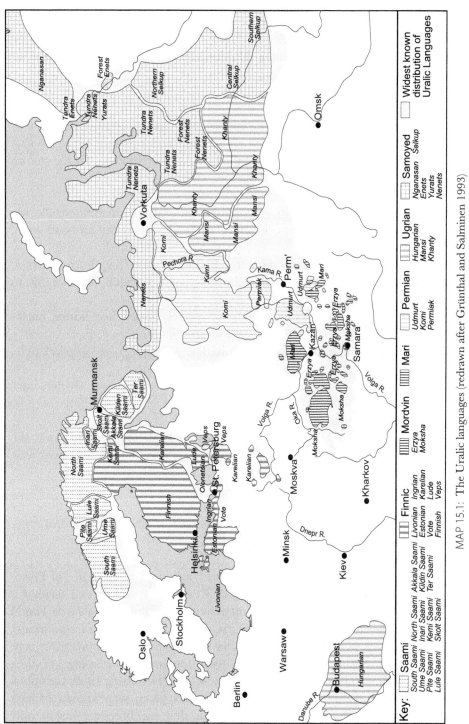

Key:

Saami	Finnic	Mordvin	Mari	Permian	Ugrian	Samoyed
South Saami	Livonian	Erzya		Udmurt	Hungarian	Nganasan Selkup
Ume Saami North Saami	Estonian Ingrian	Moksha		Komi	Mansi	Enets
Pite Saami Inari Saami	Vote Karelian			Permiak	Khanty	Yurats
Lule Saami Kemi Saami	Finnish Lude					Nenets
Akkala Saami Kildin Saami	Veps					
Skolt Saami Ter Saami						

Widest known distribution of Uralic Languages

MAP 15.1: The Uralic languages (redrawn after Grünthal and Salminen 1993)

From such evidence, Péter Hajdú (1975: 51–9) concluded that the Proto-Uralic people were engaged in hunting and fishing, with close connections to water. Their food was mostly fish and game. They travelled in boats, on skis, and in sleighs. Hajdú doubted they were involved in reindeer breeding, since reindeer breeding is fairly recent, but believed, rather, that wild reindeer was 'one of the most important prizes for the hunter' (Hajdú 1975: 54; see also various papers in Fogelberg 1999; Campbell 1997b).

15.3.1.1.2 Proto-Finno-Ugric culture
The reconstructed Proto-Finno-Ugric vocabulary is more extensive than that of its parent, Proto-Uralic, and provides a somewhat wider picture of the cultural inventory of its speakers. It inherited all that was in found in Proto-Uralic culture (the items listed above) and also had the following:

> *Fishing*: spawn, net, to fish with a net, gill/mouth, raft/loft, netting needle, ide (fish species), tench (fish species), fish skin/scales, cross-rail (in boat), loon, duck, wall/dam.
> *Hunting and animal foods*: spear, drive, track/trace, to skin/flay, horn, marrow, (domestic) animal, grouse, tallow, hunting party, to catch, to shoot/hit, to rut, goose/bird.
> *Plant and other foods*: broth/soup, two berry species, honey, bee, butter, mushroom.
> *Technology* (tools and implements): birch-bark vessel, knife, rope, to grind, pole, (soft) metal, gold, to sew, knife, pot, rope, needle, net.
> *Building and household items*: canopy, bed, house/hut, scoop, pot, shelter, hut/house, board, to cook, pole.
> *Clothing*: sleeve, glove, to sew.
> *Climate and environment*: ice crust, frost, ice, to melt, sleigh (sled), to snow, ski, winter, summer, autumn, bog, to sink, lake/flood, flood soak, downriver, stream.
> *Social structure and society*: lord, orphan.
> *Religion and beliefs*: soul, spirit, ghost, idol/village.
> *Commerce*: to buy, value/price/worth, to give/sell.
> (Cf. Sammallahti 1988.)

There is no evidence of agriculture in Proto-Uralic and its existence in Proto-Finno-Ugric culture is generally doubted. Reasonably widespread terms for 'wheat' and 'grain' are encountered, though mostly as diffused loanwords. Hajdú (1975: 57) believed that Proto-Finno-Ugric speakers did not know agriculture, based on the lack of reconstructible names for implements and processes connected with agriculture; for example, no word for 'sowing', 'reaping', 'scythe', 'hoe', and so on can be traced to Proto-Finno-Ugric (Fogelberg 1999; Campbell 1997b). Hajdú thought that 'pig' and probably also 'sheep' were known through contact with Indo-European neighbours, but that pig breeding began only later. In the realm of religion, Hajdú thought that ancestor worship and gods in natural phenomena were typical (Hajdú 1975: 58). He found animism suggested by cognates for: (1) 'evil spirit', 'lord (of underworld)', 'giant' (with compounds found in disease names), and (2) 'spirit, fall into a trance', though not all of these are accepted as legitimate cognates. (Cf. Campbell 1997b.)

15.3.1.2 Proto-Mayan culture

Mayan is a family of thirty-one languages, argued to have begun to separate at around 2200 BC. Both the linguistic and the non-linguistic prehistory of Mayan-speaking peoples has been intensively investigated, perhaps because of the romantic appeal of ancient Maya civilization. The cultural inventory reflected in the reconstructed vocabulary of Proto-Mayan includes the following:

Maize complex (maize was at the centre of Mesoamerican cultures): maize, corncob, ear of corn, roasting ear, atole (a corn drink), to sow, to harvest, to grind, metate (grindstone for corn), to roast (grains), flour, lime (used to soften kernels of corn for grinding).

Other food plants: avocado, chilli pepper, sapodilla, custard apple, sweet manioc, squash, sweet potato, bean, achiote (bixa, a food-colouring condiment), century plant, cotton, tobacco, cigar.

Animals: dog, jaguar, opossum, mouse, gopher, armadillo, cougar, squirrel, deer, weasel, coyote, skunk, fox, bird, crow, vulture, hummingbird, owl, bat, hawk, flea, bee, honey, fly, gnat, ant, louse, spider, tick, butterfly, bumblebee/wasp, scorpion, toad, fish, worm, snake, snail, crab, alligator, monkey, quetzal.

Trees and other plants: nettle, vine, willow, oak, cypress, pine, palm, silk-cotton tree (ceiba).

Religion and ritual: god/holy, evil spirit/witch, priest, sing/dance, drum/music, rattle, tobacco (used ritually), writing, paper.

Social structure: lord, slave/tribute.

Implements (and other technology): water gourd, trough/canoe, bench, cord, mat, road, house, home, whetstone, axe, toy, hammock, sandals, trousers, to sew, spindle.

Economy and commerce: to pay, to lose, to sell, poor, market, town.

(Cf. Campbell and Kaufman 1985; Kaufman 1976; 2003.)

15.3.1.3 Proto-Mixe-Zoquean culture

Mixe-Zoquean is a family of some twenty languages spoken in southern Mexico in the region across the Isthmus of Tehuantepec. It is assumed to have been unified until about 1500 BC, and is considered to be of great cultural significance in the region, since it is argued that bearers of the Olmec archaeological culture (the earliest civilization of the Mesoamerican region) were speakers of Mixe-Zoquean languages (see below). The reconstructed vocabulary reveals the following cultural inventory:

Maize complex: corn field, to clear land, to sow, to harvest, seed, maize, to grind corn, leached corn, corncob, corn gruel, to grind grains, to shell corn, lime (used to soften kernels of corn for grinding).

Other cultivated plants (and food plants): chilli pepper, bean, tomato, sweet potato, manioc, a tuber (species); chokecherry, custard apple, avocado, sapote, coyol palm, guava, cacao.

Animals and procurement of animal resources: deer, rabbit, coati-mundi, honey, bee, fish, crab, to fish with a hook, to fish with a net, canoe.

Religion and ritual: holy, incense, knife-axe (used in sacrifice), to write, to count/ divine/adore, to dance, to play music, ceremony, year, twenty, bundle of 400, tobacco, cigar, to smoke tobacco (tobacco was used ceremonially).

Commerce: to sell, to pay, to cost, to buy.

Technology: to spin thread, agave fibre, to twist rope/thread, hammock, cord, water gourd, gourd dish, ladder, house, house pole, adobe wall, rubber, ring, arrow, bed, to plane wood, sandals, remedy-liquor.

(Cf. Campbell and Kaufman 1976; Justeson et al. 1985.)

15.3.1.4 Cautions about reconstructed vocabulary

Textbooks are fond of repeating warnings about anachronistic reconstructions, which can complicate cultural interpretation based on the reconstructed vocabulary. For example, Bloomfield, in his reconstruction of Proto-Central Algonquian, found cognates which seemed to support reconstructions for a couple of items which were unknown before contact with Europeans, for example 'whisky'. It turns out that the different languages had created names based on the same compound, 'fire' + 'water' (for example, Cree *iskote:w-a:poy*, composed of *iskote:w* 'fire' + *a:poy* 'water, liquid'), and this 'firewater' compound found in each of the languages looked like a valid cognate set to support the reconstruction, although the similarity in words for 'whisky' is due either to independent parallel formation of the compound in the related languages or to diffusion of a loan translation (calque) among these languages. We have no secure guarantees against such anachronisms entering our cultural interpretations of the past based on reconstructed vocabulary, although we rely on clues from our knowledge of what things were introduced by Europeans and on the criterion which we will see directly (below), namely that the age of analysable terms (ones with multiple morphemes) is not as secure as that of unanalysable terms (those composed of but a single morpheme). In actual cases, this problem comes up rarely; that is, it is not as serious as it might at first appear to be.

15.3.2 Linguistic homeland and linguistic migration theory

A question which has been of great interest in the study of many language families, and especially of Indo-European, is that of the geographical location of the speakers of the proto-language. Two different techniques have been utilized in attempts to determine where speakers of proto-languages lived, that is, where the linguistic 'homeland' (*Urheimat*) of the family was located. We consider each in turn.

15.3.2.1 Homeland clues in the reconstructed vocabulary

The first technique seeks geographical and ecological clues from the reconstructed vocabulary which are relevant to the location of where the proto-language was spoken, especially clues from reconstructed terms for plants and animals. In this approach, attempts are made to find out what the prehistoric geographical distributions were of plants and animals for which we can successfully reconstruct terms in the proto-language, and then these are plotted on a map. The area where the greatest number of these reconstructible plants' and animals' ranges intersects is taken to be the probable homeland of the language family. We see how this works in the examples considered below.

For the prehistoric geographical distributions of the plants and animals involved, the information which palaeobotany, biology, or other fields can provide is relied on. Due to climatic changes and other factors during the last few thousand years, the range of plants and animals is often not the same today as it was in former times. For example, earlier it was argued, based on the reconstruction of *$bherh_{1}\acute{g}$*- 'birch', that the Proto-Indo-European homeland lay north of the 'birch line' (where birches grow) which today runs roughly from Bordeaux (France) to Bucharest (Romania). However, this interpretation failed; the birch has shifted its habitat significantly over time and formerly extended considerably to the south, and furthermore birch has always been present in the Caucasus region (Friedrich 1970: 30). That is, to locate the birch's distribution during Proto-Indo-European times, we must rely on the results of palynology (the study of ancient pollens). While the case of the birch's earlier distribution is clear, matters can be difficult, since palynological information may not be available for some of the regions in question. Also, in many cases we may have only the roughest of estimates concerning the time when the proto-language was spoken. It is difficult to correlate the distribution of ancient plants based on palynology and of languages without some idea of the period of time at which their respective distributions are being correlated (Friedrich 1970).

15.3.2.2 Linguistic migration theory

The other technique for getting at linguistic homelands – called *linguistic migration theory* – looks at the classification (subgrouping) of the family and the geographical distribution of the languages, and, relying on a model of maximum diversity and minimum moves, hypothesizes the most likely location of the original homeland. The underlying assumption is that when a language family splits up, it is more likely for the various daughter languages to stay close to where they started out and it is less likely for them to move very far or very frequently. Therefore, turning this process around, if we look at today's geographical distribution of related languages, we can hypothesize how they got to where they are now and where they came from. This procedure deals not just with the geographical spread of the languages of the family, but rather with the distribution of members of subgroups within the family. The highest-order branches on a family tree (the earliest splits in the family) reflect the greatest age, and therefore the area with the greatest linguistic diversity – that is, with the most representatives of the higher-order subgroups – is likely to be the homeland. This is sometimes called the *centre of gravity* model (after Sapir 1949 [1916]: 455). Lower-level branches (those which break up later) are also important, because they may allow us to postulate the direction of later migration or spread of members of the family. In this model, we attempt to determine the minimum number of moves which would be required to reverse these migrations or spreads to bring the languages back to the centre of gravity of their closest relatives within their individual subgroups, and then to move the various different subgroups back to the location from which their distribution can be accounted for with the fewest moves. In this way, by combining the location of maximum diversity and the minimum moves to get languages back to the location of the greatest diversity of their nearest relatives, we hypothesize the location of the homeland.

Let's look at some of the better-known cases in which these two techniques have been employed in order to get a feel for how they work.

15.3.2.3 Proto-Indo-European homeland

There is a very large literature on the question of the Proto-Indo-European homeland (see Mallory 1989; Mallory and Adams 1997: 290–9; 2006: 442–63; Anthony and Ringe 2015; Pereltsvaig and Lewis 2015). While there are a number of competing hypotheses, most mainstream historical linguists favour the view which places the Proto-Indo-European homeland somewhere in the Pontic steppes–Caspian region. The evidence for this comes from linguistic migration theory, interpretation of geographical and ecological clues in the reconstructed vocabulary of the proto-language, loans and the location of their neighbours from whom they borrowed, and attempted correlations with archaeology and human genetics (though the archaeological and human genetic interpretations are subject to dispute).

Proto-Indo-European tree names have been at the centre of some homeland considerations, and Proto-Indo-European *$bheh_2\hat{g}o$ 'beech' has been given much weight. It was thought that beech did not grow to the east of a line running from Königsberg (in East Prussia, now Kaliningrad, Russia) to Odessa (in Crimea, Ukraine). This would seem to place constraints on the location of the Proto-Indo-European homeland, locating it essentially in Europe. However, there are various difficulties with this. There are doubts about the original meaning of the word; the cognates do not all refer to the same tree; Greek *phēgós* means 'oak' and the Slavic forms mean some sort of 'elder', as for example Russian *buziná* 'elder(berry)'; and no reflexes are known from Asiatic Indo-European languages. If *$bheh_2\hat{g}o$ did not originally mean 'beech', then arguments based on the distribution of beeches in Proto-Indo-European times would not be relevant. There are phonological problems in that the sounds in the putative cognates for 'beech' in some branches of the family do not correspond as they should.

Finally, two species of beech are involved and the eastern or Caucasian beech was (and still is) present in the Caucasus and extended to the east. Therefore, many Indo-European groups would have been familiar with it, not just those of Europe west of the infamous Königsberg–Odessa line (Friedrich 1970: 106–15). The problem with the arguments for the homeland based on the distribution of 'birch' has already been mentioned above; the current distribution of birches is not the same as it was in Proto-Indo-European times, and this weakens the original argument.

Another participant in the discussion has been Proto-Indo-European *lokŝ- 'salmon', which was formerly thought to have a limited distribution, involving rivers which flowed into the Baltic Sea – this was seen as indicating a Northern European homeland. However, the original meaning of the word appears to include not only 'salmon' but species of salmon-like trout found in a very wide distribution which also includes the Pontic steppes and Caspian region, the current best candidate for the homeland.

The centre of gravity model, when applied to Indo-European, also suggests this area. (For details and criticism of the Anatolian hypothesis and other hypotheses for the Indo-European homeland, see Anthony and Ringe 2015; Mallory and Adams 1997: 290–9; 2006: 442–63; Pereltsvaig and Lewis 2015.)

15.3.2.4 Proto-Algonquian homeland

Frank Siebert (1967) found some twenty Proto-Algonquian terms for plants and animals whose distributions overlap in southern Ontario. The animal and plant terms reconstructed for Proto-Algonquian include: golden eagle, pileated woodpecker, oldsquaw, common raven, quail, ruffed grouse, kingfisher, common loon, nighthawk, sawbill duck, seal, raccoon, lynx, squirrel, flying squirrel, moose, porcupine, skunk, fox, bear, woodchuck (groundhog), buffalo (bison), caribou, buck, fawn, beaver, muskrat, weasel, mink, black bass, lake trout, northern pike, brown bullhead, white spruce, tamarack (larch), white ash, conifer–evergreen tree, elm, alder, basswood (linden), sugar maple, beech, willow, and quaking aspen. From this Siebert concluded that the original Algonquian homeland lay between Lake Huron and Georgian Bay and the middle course of the Ottawa River, bounded by Lake Nipissing and the northern shore of Lake Ontario.

Dean Snow (1976) reconsidered the Proto-Algonquian homeland focusing on only the names of species whose ranges were most sharply defined; these included five tree names and six animal terms. This resulted in a broader homeland than Siebert had deduced, a homeland defined most clearly by the overlap in the territories of the 'beech' and 'tamarack' – the Great Lakes lowlands east of Lake Superior, the St Lawrence valley, New England, and Maritime Canada. This was bounded on the west by the Niagara Falls in order to accommodate the reconstructed word for 'harbour seal'. This constitutes a large hunting and trapping zone for nomadic bands.

However, Ives Goddard (1994: 207) finds that the terms which Siebert reconstructed are 'consistent with the homeland of Proto-Algonquians being somewhere immediately west of Lake Superior', but Goddard points out the circularity of the method. Words for 'harbour seal' would typically only survive in languages in areas where harbour seals are found, leaving out languages (and hence regions) to the west which lacked a cognate for this word. In fact, Goddard concluded that the Proto-Algonquians were located more to the west based on other information, especially the distribution of the languages and the nature of the innovations which they share.

15.3.2.5 Proto-Uto-Aztecan homeland

For the Uto-Aztecan family, the results are interesting but not definitive. Early work on the Proto-Uto-Aztecan homeland had suggested the region between the Gila River in Arizona and the northern mountains of northwest Mexico, though later work showed that not all the items upon which this conclusion was based could actually be reconstructed for Proto-Uto-Aztecan. Terms which can be reliably reconstructed include, among others, 'pine', 'reed/cane', and 'prickly pear cactus', and these have received considerable attention. Based on nine certain reconstructions and eighteen less secure but likely reconstructed terms, Fowler (1983) interpreted the Proto-Uto-Aztecan homeland to be in 'a mixed woodland/grassland setting, in proximity to montane forests', and this fits a region across southeastern California, Arizona, and northwestern Mexico (see Map 15.2).

   The results for the Proto-Numic homeland, however, are much more precise. Numic is a subgroup of Uto-Aztecan (to which Shoshone, Comanche, and Ute

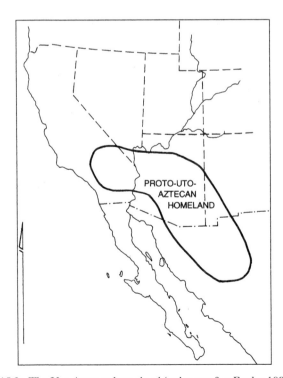

MAP 15.2: The Uto-Aztecan homeland (redrawn after Fowler 1983: 233)

belong, as well as several other languages, from southern California to Oregon and across the Great Basin into the Great Plains). Catherine Fowler (1972: 119) found that

> The homeland area for Proto-Numic . . . must have been diverse in elevation, allowing for stands of pine and pinyon, but also for such mid- to low-altitude forms as cottonwood, oaks, chia, cholla, and tortoises; two, the homeland area was probably in or near desert zones capable of supporting prickly pear, chia, lycium, ephedra, cholla, tortoise, . . . three, based on the presence of proto-forms for cane, crane, heron, mud-hen, tule [reeds], cattail, and fish, the area probably contained marshes or some other substantial water sources.

Fowler concludes that the Proto-Numic homeland was in southern California slightly west of Death Valley.

15.3.2.6 Uralic and Finno-Ugric homeland

Much research has been done on the Proto-Uralic and the Proto-Finno-Ugric homelands, and their identification is held to be on a firmer footing than that of Proto-Indo-European (Mallory 2001: 345). These homeland studies often do not distinguish between Proto-Uralic and Proto-Finno-Ugric (one of the two branches of Proto-Uralic), and many scholars place the homeland of both in the same location. Information from linguistics, archaeology, human genetics, and other areas of knowledge has been correlated, generally interpreted in more or less consistent ways, but in hypotheses that differ in their details. For example, the Uralic peoples today have no common culture and are genetically diverse – all Uralic-speaking peoples have received cultural and human genetic traits from several directions, in several cases sharing more with non-Uralic neighbours than with other Uralic groups.

Study of the Finno-Ugric homeland has an ample history, though earlier proposals assigning the homeland to central Asia, southern Europe, and the like now have extremely few supporters. The main candidates differ from one another mostly according to the size assumed for the area of the original homeland. They include: (1) the region of the middle course of the Volga River and its tributaries; (2) the region of the northern Urals on both sides of the mountains; (3) the central and southern Urals on both sides; (4) rather eastward on the Asian side of the Urals; (5) rather westward on the European side; and (6) the broad area between the Urals and the Baltic Sea. There is actually considerable agreement in these views, since the areas represented are near one another and partially overlapping (Korhonen 1984; Suhonen 1999; see Map 15.1).

Plant and animal terms have been presented as supporting evidence for hypothesis (1), which is widely held, namely that the homeland was in the region of the Middle Volga. In view (4), also widely held, the homeland would have been further east and north, between the Urals and the Volga–Kama–Pechora area or on both sides of the Urals. Supporters of candidate (6) believe that the Proto-Uralic population, at least in its final phases, and perhaps also the Proto-Finno-Ugric population, may have occupied a wide area from the Urals to the Baltic Sea, based on the notion that hunting and fishing groups need to exploit wide territories for their subsistence. Ethnographic analogies from subarctic peoples of both the Old and New Worlds have been called upon for supporting evidence, with examples of some reindeer and caribou hunters who travel over 1,000 kilometres twice yearly as they follow the migrating herds of deer (Sammallahti 1984; Mallory 2001). Mikko Korhonen (1984: 63) was of the opinion that while hunting societies typically exploit wide ranges, the proto-language could not have remained unified for long if the speakers were spread from the Urals to the Baltic. For Korhonen, such a picture could be true, if at all, only briefly at the very end of the unified Finno-Ugric period – the earlier homeland would need to be sought in a smaller area. Pekka Sammallahti (1984: 153), on the other hand, points out that a journey from Lake Ladoga (in the Baltic region) to the Urals (c. 1,200 km) is no longer than from one extreme of Saami territory to the other (c. 1,500 km), and he therefore supposes that a Proto-Uralic or Proto-Finno-Ugric population could have lived in the area between Finland and the Urals and still have maintained a relative linguistic unity (see also Mallory 2001). Hajdú argues that fishing kept the Finno-Ugric people to relatively fixed bases, and so that 'their manner of life offers no reason for extending their homeland as far as the Baltic' (1975: 38).

In any event, most scholars assume that the relative homogeneity of the family was broken up by the introduction of Neolithic techniques and agriculture from areas south of the Proto-Uralic and Proto-Finno-Ugric homeland, and that the onset of farming and cattle herding – factors contributing to sedentarism – probably contributed to diversification of the family. Sammallahti points to the uniformity of practically all the palaeolithic cultures between the Baltic Sea and the Urals, which might suggest a linguistic unity, with all the languages of the area perhaps members of a single language family. As long as there were no surplus-producing cultures anywhere nearby, communication among groups was confined to a common ecological (and perhaps cultural) zone, and unity may have been maintained over wide areas by marriage patterns in which spouses as well as linguistic innovations moved from one community to another. However, with the emergence of surplus-producing cultures to the south of the Uralic area, communication was reoriented from latitudinal change to longitudinal change. Longitudinal communication (and weaker latitudinal exchange) caused the ultimate disintegration of the Proto-Uralic area into a series of areas with their own identity and with relatively little interaction, human genetic or linguistic, with others. (See also Carpelan 2001.)

Paavo Ravila (1949), employing the techniques of linguistic migration theory, noticed that the Finno-Ugric-speaking groups are spread geographically today in a way that reflects their linguistic relationships (degree of relatedness), as though the modern situation was created by movements of these groups to settle in the economically most favourable sections of their former overall territory. Indeed, the region around the middle course of the Volga River with its Oka and Kama tributaries appears to be a Finno-Ugric centre of gravity; speakers of Mordvin,

Mari (Cheremis), and Udmurt (Votyak) live in this region as neighbours, though they represent diverse branches of the family.

Proto-Finno-Ugric vocabulary offers clues for delimiting the homeland; some plant and animal names and some culture words have been considered relevant. The words for 'honeybee' (*mekši*) and 'honey' (*meti*) have been emphasized. These were borrowed into Proto-Finno-Ugric from Indo-European. The area where such contact could have taken place is thought to be the region of the middle course of the Volga River, where apiculture was practised from early times. The honeybee was unknown in Siberia, Turkestan, Central Asia, Mongolia, and most of the rest of Asia, but was found in eastern Europe west of the Urals. This area of bee-keeping is often considered one of the clues to the Proto-Finno-Ugric homeland, though this is not without controversy. That the terms refer to wild bees and honey collecting is not ruled out as a possibility (Häkkinen 2001: 176).

There is a sizeable number of reconstructed Proto-Finno-Ugric plant names, but most of these are found in a wide area and are thus not very helpful for delimiting the homeland. However, reconstructed tree names have been vigorously discussed in this regard along with five principal trees that have played a role: 'spruce' (*Picea obovata*), 'Siberian pine' (*Pinus sibirica*), 'Siberian fir' (*Abies sibirica*), 'Siberian larch' (*Larix sibirica*), and 'brittle willow' (*Salix fragilis*)/'elm' (*Ulmus*) (outside the Finnic subgroup the cognates mean 'elm' (*Ulmus*); compare Finnish *salava* 'willow' and Hungarian *szil* 'elm'). According to Hajdú (1969; 1975), the Finno-Ugric homeland could be located only in an area where all these trees were found at the appropriate time. The only place which fits temporally and geographically is from the Middle Urals towards the north, including the lower and middle course of the Ob and the headwaters of the Pechora river in the area of the northern Urals. Not everyone, however, accepts this interpretation.

Other sorts of vocabulary have also played a part. Cognates for 'hedgehog' have also been taken as evidence for the Finno-Ugric homeland (compare Estonian *siil*, archaic Hungarian *szül-* [syl-] (cf. *sün-* [ʃyn-]); hedgehogs are not found east of the Urals, but do extend as far north as 61° latitude. A word that has given rise to much speculation is 'metal', with cognates in nearly all Uralic languages meaning 'copper, iron, ore, metal' (reconstructed as *wäśkä* for Proto-Uralic, seen in Finnish *vaski* 'copper', Hungarian *vas* 'iron', Nenets *veś* 'iron, money', etc.). Since Uralic dates to the Stone Age, such an ancient term for metal is interesting. Some suggest this means the presence of copper trading or cold working of crude copper, but not metallurgy. A metal term of similar shape is also found in various Indo-European languages (for example, Tocharian A *wäs* 'gold') and in other languages, so that it may be an old, widely borrowed word (Joki 1973: 339–40). It also been argued that the lack of old terms for 'sea' ('ocean') in Finno-Ugric languages points to a landlocked original homeland (for example, Finnish *meri* 'sea' is a loanword from Baltic (Indo-European)). There are, however, abundant freshwater terms in the Finno-Ugric vocabulary. Of course, arguments from negative evidence can never be fully persuasive, although this one has been popular.

Salminen (2001) believes the reconstructed plant and animal names are not specific enough in their distribution to warrant a conclusion of anything more than that the homeland was far from the sea, in the deep forests rather than in a tundra or steppe environment, though he sees the distribution of the languages as better support for locating the homeland in the traditional area between the Volga River and the Urals.

Evidence for the original homeland has also been sought in contacts with other languages. Finno-Ugric has a significant number of loans that are Proto-Indo-European in origin, and more that come from Indo-Iranian. If we knew the location of Proto-Iranian, perhaps it would help us locate more precisely the Proto-Finno-Ugric homeland. Some scholars argue for even older Indo-European loans in Uralic, though this is controversial, and some others imagine that the loans were all younger but spread across the Finno-Ugric area by diffusion. Aikio (2020: 51-2) reports that 'there are obviously some very old Indo-European and specifically Indo-Iranian loanwords in Uralic, but they are unlikely to reflect a direct contact of Proto-Uralic with Proto-Indo-European or its descendant Proto-Indo-Iranian'. That is, the testimony of loans may be helpful, but it is not conclusive. Nevertheless, many scholars believe Proto-Finno-Ugric and Proto-Indo-European were neighbours. (See Joki 1973; Campbell 1997b; Häkkinen 2001; Koivulehto 2001; Sammallahti 2001.)

15.3.2.7 Cautions concerning linguistic homelands migration theory

In linguistic migration theory, the homeland of a language family is inferred to be in the area represented by the greatest diversity (largest number of subgroups) for which the minimum number of moves (migrations) would be required to bring the speakers of the diverse languages back to one place. On the whole, the inferences afforded by this method are strong, and few documented cases fail to conform. In principle, however, it is not difficult to imagine rather straightforward situations in which linguistic migration theory would fail to produce reliable results. For example, suppose a language family with a number of subgroups had once been found in one particular geographical area, but something forced all the speakers of all the languages of those subgroups to abandon that area, say a volcanic eruption, a drought, an epidemic, or the onslaught of powerful aggressors. In such a case, it is possible that many of the migrating speakers of the different subgroups could end up relocated near each other in a new area, particularly if driven until they encountered some serious obstacle such as insurmountable mountains, an ocean, inhospitable lands without sufficient subsistence resources, or other peoples who prevented entry into their territory. It is also possible that, rather than being driven, several groups speaking languages of the same family might independently be attracted to the same general area (or nearby areas), for example to take advantage of better resources available there, to forge alliances with other groups of the area, and so on. In such scenarios, it is in principle possible that we might find that the greatest linguistic diversity would in fact not be in the original homeland, but in the new area where the groups come to be concentrated. Another problem for linguistic migration theory would be the possible situation in which all the languages of a family in the former area of greatest diversity were lost with no trace (where the speakers were annihilated by war or pestilence or whatever), or where the inhabitants remained but their languages were replaced by some other unrelated language or languages. In such a situation, what may appear to be a language family's area of greatest diversity today may not have been that in former times.

The fact that such counterexamples could exist means that the conclusions which we draw from linguistic migration theory can never be absolute, but rather remain inferences, warranted by the available evidence but not proven. In our attempts to understand the past, we accept that migration theory has a stronger probability of being correct than any random guess we might make which is not based on these principles. That is, all else being equal, in the absence of other information to help us answer the question, our inference about the original homeland based on linguistic migration theory has a better chance of being right than anything else we might have to go on.

There are similar problems in relying on clues from reconstructed vocabulary for determining the most likely location of the homeland. One is that groups may migrate to geographical zones where certain flora or fauna of the homeland area are no longer found and as a result lose the words which refer to those items. In such a case, those languages lack the sort of evidence upon which we typically rely to infer the homeland. It is possible that in some cases so many languages have left the homeland region, and as a result lost the relevant vocabulary, that these items could not be reconstructed in the proto-language and therefore the evidence for inferring the homeland would be inadequate, as Goddard concluded with respect to some of the arguments for the Proto-Algonquian homeland, mentioned above.

Another problem has to do with instances where the original word is not lost, but its meaning has shifted. Sometimes in such cases it is not sufficiently clear what the proto-meaning may have been to be able to make inferences about the geographical location of the proto-language. For example, as mentioned, tree names have played an important role in identifying the Proto-Indo-European and the Proto-Finno-Ugric homelands. If we know what tree names the proto-language had and if we can figure out the geographical distribution of these trees during the time when the proto-language was spoken, we can narrow the homeland down to an area where the distributions of all the trees known in the proto-language intersect. However, semantic shift in some of the tree names, to accommodate the fact that the original tree is not found in the new areas to which some groups have migrated, or to accommodate new kinds of trees found in the new areas, severely complicates this sort of research. For example, in Proto-Finno-Ugric, the tree name *sala- is reconstructed on very solid evidence from across the family; however, as mentioned earlier, it means 'willow' in Finnish and its closer relatives but 'elm' in Hungarian and its closer relatives. That is, we cannot be certain what the testimony of *sala- is for the location of the homeland of Proto-Finno-Ugric, since the distribution of 'elms' and of 'willows' is quite distinct. Presumably one of these is not the original sense, but rather was acquired as the languages moved out of the territory where the original tree name was known. To take an Indo-European example, even *$bherh_{\hat{g}}$- 'birch', which is one of the best supported of Proto-Indo-European tree names, shifted its meaning to 'ash' in Latin and to 'fir, pine, larch' in Albanian, and is absent in Greek (Friedrich 1970: 29–30; Mallory 1989: 161).

Semantic shifts need not always be a serious problem; in fact, in some cases they can provide additional evidence of homeland and migrations away from it. For Proto-Algonquian, a term for 'woodland caribou' is reconstructed based on abundant evidence across many of the branches of the family. This term has shifted its meaning in a few of the languages whose speakers have moved south of the caribou's range. It has come to mean 'bighorn sheep' in the Arapahoan branch and 'deer' in some Eastern Algonquian languages. Because the reconstruction with the meaning 'caribou' is secure on other grounds (the distribution across branches of the family), the instances where it has shifted meaning to something else are additional evidence that Arapahoan and those Eastern Algonquian languages involved have moved away from the homeland area where the woodland caribou was found (Goddard 1994).

A problem of a different sort with linguistic homeland models is that they typically imagine a proto-language spoken in a rather restricted region from which groups spread out or migrated to fill up more territory later on. When we go through the exercise of reversing these movements or spreads to bring the languages back to the assumed homelands of various proto-languages, we often find that large blank areas are left between homelands of different language families. The linguistic model seems to imply that these areas were simply not occupied at the time, but archaeology typically finds evidence of human occupation both in the homeland areas and throughout the zones left blank in the linguistic homeland interpretations. These conflicting results need to be accounted for. One possibility is that we have fully misunderstood the nature of how the languages expanded and the territory of the homelands in some cases, though we would like to be able to maintain faith in these methods. Another possibility is that we do correctly recover the homelands for the most part with our techniques, and that the evidence of human presence in the areas left blank represents languages which have become extinct or been replaced.

15.3.3 Borrowing: cultural inferences from loanwords

Loanwords by their very definition provide evidence of contacts among peoples speaking different languages. The semantic content of loanwords often reveals a great deal about the kinds of contacts that took place and thus about the social relationships among different peoples. The following examples reveal something of the nature and range of historical information that can be retrieved from loanwords in different situations.

A rather straightforward example which illustrates the point about loanwords contributing historical information involves wine-making terms in German, most of which are borrowed from Latin, for example German *Wein* 'wine'< Latin *vīnum*; *Most* 'new wine, cider, must' < *mustum*; *Kelter* 'wine-press' < *calcātūra* 'stamping with the feet'; and so on. On the basis of these loans, the inference is drawn that very probably German-speaking people acquired knowledge of viticulture and wine production from the Romans (compare Polenz 1977: 23).

Another example which illustrates the sort of cultural information that can be derived from loanwords comes from the 'Western American' or 'cowboy' vocabulary in English, a large portion of which is borrowed from Spanish: *adobe* 'sun-dried bricks, a structure made of adobe bricks' < *adobe*; *arroyo* 'a water-carved gully in a dry region' < *arroyo* 'brook, small stream'; *bronco* < *bronco* 'rough, rude'; *buckaroo* < *vaquero* 'cowhand'; *burro* < *burro* 'burro', 'donkey'; *calaboose* 'jail, prison' < *calabozo* 'prison cell, dungeon'; *canyon* < *cañón* 'ravine, gorge, canyon'; *chaps* [ʃæps] < *chaparreras* 'open leather garment worn by riders over their trousers to protect them'; *cinch* 'saddle-girth' < *cincha* 'belt, sash, cinch'; *corral* < *corral*; *coyote* < Spanish *coyote* (ultimately from Nahuatl *koyōtl* 'coyote'); *desperado* 'a man ready for deeds of lawlessness or violence' < older Spanish *desperado* 'without hope, desperate' (compare Modern Spanish *desesperado* 'without hope'); *lariat* < Spanish *la reata* 'the rope, lasso'; *lasso* < *lazo* 'knot, bow, lasso'; *mesa* 'flat-topped hill with steep sides' < *mesa* 'table', 'plateau'; *mustang* < *mestenco* 'lacking an owner'; *palomino* 'horse with pale cream-coloured or golden coat and cream-coloured to white mane and tail' < *palomino* 'dove-like', see Mexican Spanish *palomo* 'pale cream-coloured horse'; *pinyon* (*pinyon pine*) < *piñón* 'pine nut, kind of pine'; *pinto* 'a paint (horse), a mottled horse' < *pinto* 'painted, mottled'; *quirt* 'a horseman's short whip' < *cuarta* 'a quarter, fourth' (a quarter of a *vara* 'a rod' [measurement]); *ranch* < *rancho* 'hut or house in the country', *rancher* < *ranchero* 'farmer, rancher'; *remuda* 'herd of horses from which ranch hands select their mounts' < *remuda* 'a change of something'; *renegade* < *renegado* 'disowned, turncoat, renegade'; rodeo < *rodeo* 'a round-up' (from *rodear* 'to go round'); *stampede* < Mexican Spanish *estampida* 'crash, uproar'; *vamoose* < *vamos* 'let's go!, we go'; and *vigilante* < *vigilante* '(one who is) vigilant' (from *vigilar* 'to watch, keep an eye on'). Given the large number of loanwords in this semantic domain, we infer that the culture and economy of the Old American West were highly influenced by contact with Spanish speakers there.

Another example comes from Xinkan (in southeastern Guatemala), which borrowed most of its terms for cultivated plants from Mayan languages. This leads us to the inference that Xinkan speakers were not agriculturalists until their contact with Mayan groups and that they acquired knowledge of agriculture from their Mayan neighbours.

A very revealing case is that of the Romani ('Gypsy') migrations. A good deal is known about the identity, origins, migrations, and history of Romani speakers (the Rom). Historical linguistics is the main source of that information, and much of it comes from loanwords. The comparative method demonstrates that Romani belongs to the Indo-Aryan languages (also called 'Indic', a branch of Indo-European) of northern and central India.

Romani started in north central India. While there, the language borrowed some Sanskrit words (words meaning 'believe', 'thirst', etc.). The *first move* was to northwest India (before the second century BC), where words from Dardic languages (another branch of Indo-Aryan) were borrowed, for example words for 'man, male', 'whip', 'to arise', 'six', etc. Because of the known history of sound changes and of the break-up of Indic languages, we know that Romani could not have left India later than c. AD 1000.

The *second* move was to Iran (Persia) before AD 650, where Romani borrowed many words from Persian, 'bag', 'blind', 'breath', 'bridge', 'chicken', 'church', 'donkey', 'fortress, town', 'friend', 'goat', 'handful', 'handle', 'honey', 'linen', 'mule', 'pear', 'saddle', 'silk', 'sin', 'sock', 'spur', 'star', 'wax', 'wool', 'worm', and from Kurdish, 'axe', 'forest', 'garlic', 'honey', 'landlord, host', 'nut', 'steel', 'raise', etc. From here the Rom split, with one branch going southwest into the eastern Mediterranean region, the other towards the east and north. There are Arabic loans in all the languages in regions where Islam arrived. Since there are no Arabic loans in European Romani, we infer that they migrated from Iran before the Muslim conquest of AD 650.

The *third* move, if indeed there was one, is less clear. Some scholars hypothesize that Romani moved to the Caucasus region during the Armenian Trebizond Empire, on the Black Sea, before c. AD 1040, where Romani borrowed from languages of the region, from Armenian ('bewitch', 'button', 'co-parent-in-law', 'deep', 'dough', 'flax', 'forehead', 'hair', 'heart', 'honour', 'horse', 'leather', 'melon', 'oven', 'piece', 'tin'); from Georgian ('eyelash', 'plum', 'tallow', etc.); and from Ossetic ('boot', 'sock', 'wagon'). One branch of Romani remained in Armenia. However, other scholars point out that contact with these languages may have been possible in eastern and central Anatolia, eliminating the need to postulate a separate movement into the Caucasus region (Matras 2002: 25).

The invasion of the Seljuk Turks in c. 1040 is thought to have brought about the *fourth* move, to the Byzantine Empire in Anatolia (Turkey), during which time Romani came under Greek influence, taking on some grammatical patterns and borrowing many Greek words: 'anvil', 'bell', 'bone', 'buckle', 'cherry', 'crow', 'dew', 'embrace', 'flower', 'grandmother', 'hour', 'kettle', 'key', 'lead', 'market', 'nail', 'nine', 'road', 'seven', 'Sunday', 'tent', 'town', 'tablecloth', etc. Since Romani shows no Turkish loans (though Seljuks may have used Persian as their lingua franca), it appears that the European Romani speakers left Anatolia before the Turkish invasions, pushed perhaps by both the Black Death (which reached western Anatolia in 1347) and the invasion of the Ottoman Turks (Ottomans arrived 1265–1328, Byzantium was sacked, and Constantinople fell in 1453).

In their *fifth* move, actually a series of waves, Romani speakers arrived in southeastern Europe, in the Balkans by c. AD 1350, where they came under the influence of Serbo-Croatian and other South Slavic languages, borrowing many words, for example from Serbo-Croatian (perhaps also from Bulgarian and Macedonian) 'bean', 'bed', 'body', 'boot', 'cloak', 'dear', 'green', 'gun', 'hut', 'ice', 'inn', 'king', 'mountain', 'old woman', 'onion', 'paper', 'rat', 'room', 'sand, dust', 'sin', 'sheet', 'stable', 'street', 'thick', 'world', 'time', 'vein', 'wild', etc. After this, the European Romani do not share a common history.

In the *sixth* move, or wave, documented in historical sources, Romani spread throughout Europe during the fourteenth century. Documentary history establishes Romani as present in Ragusa (Dubrovnik) in 1362, in Hildesheim (Germany) in 1407, in Brussels in 1420, and in Bologna in 1422. (See Hancock

2006; Igla 1997; Kaufman 1973; Matras 2002; and see Pereltsvaig and Lewis 2015: 164-7 for somewhat different views of details about some of the stages in Romani migrations.)

This case shows how on the basis of historical linguistic information, and primarily on the evidence of loanwords, we are able to recover a remarkable amount of the history of the identity and migrations of the Romani, ironically the truest 'Aryans' in Europe (despite Nazi views to the contrary).

15.3.3.1 Turkic loans in Hungarian

Hungarian contains many loans, perhaps up to 35 per cent of the vocabulary, and the earliest stratum of these loans is from Turkic ('Chuvash-type'), many of them borrowed before the arrival of the Hungarians in present-day Hungary. The Turkic loans in Hungarian involve chiefly cattle breeding, agriculture, social organization, technology and implements, dress, and religion. These demonstrate that there was extensive contact with Chuvash-type Turkic and that this led to important economic and social changes. Even the name of 'Hungary' appears to be a Turkish loan in origin (Róna-Tas 1988; Hajdú 1975).

15.3.3.2 The Olmec–Mixe-Zoquean hypothesis

The Olmec civilization was the earliest in Mesoamerica (c. 1200–400 BC) and it had a huge impact on the languages and cultures of the region. Based primarily on loanwords, the Olmecs have been identified as Mixe-Zoquean-speaking, at least in large part. The geographical distribution of Olmec archaeological sites and the Mixe-Zoquean languages (spoken across the narrowest part of Mexico and in adjacent areas) coincides to a large degree, which initially suggested the hypothesis that if speakers of Mixe-Zoquean were there during Olmec times, perhaps the Olmecs spoke a Mixe-Zoquean language. This hypothesis is supported by the many loanwords from Mixe-Zoquean languages found far and wide among other languages of the Mesoamerican area. Several of these loans are of significant cultural content, including many terms for things which are diagnostic of the Mesoamerican culture area. Therefore, Mixe-Zoquean speakers had to be involved in a culture important enough to contribute on an extensive scale to others during Olmec times when the culture area was being formed. Examples of Mixe-Zoquean borrowings into the various other languages of the area include the following (glosses only given).

Maize complex: 'to grind corn', 'nixtamal (leached corn for grinding)', 'tortilla', 'corn dough', and others.

Other cultivated plants: 'cacao', 'gourd', 'small squash', 'pumpkin', 'tomato', 'bean', 'sweet potato', as well as 'guava', 'papaya', 'sweet manioc', and others.

Ritual and calendric terms: 'incense', 'to count, divine' (into Q'eqchi and Poqomchi' 'twenty-year period', 'twenty', into Yucatec 'calendar priest', into K'iche' and Kaqchikel 'calendar'), 'day names in various calendars of the region', 'sacrifice'/'axe', 'woven mat' (which functioned as 'throne' for rulers), 'paper', and so on.

Other terms: 'turkey', 'salt', 'pot', 'tortilla griddle', 'ripe', 'fog'/'cloud', 'child'/'infant' (a central motif in Olmec art), 'iguana', 'rabbit', 'opossum', among others.

Based on these loans, it is concluded that the Olmecs spoke a Mixe-Zoquean language (Campbell and Kaufman 1976). This example shows how loanwords can contribute to hypotheses about the ethnolinguistic identity of past cultures and their influence on others.

15.3.3.3 Cautions about interpreting loans

Some cautions are necessary, too, in the cultural interpretation of loanwords, since some loans may not come immediately from the original donor language but rather via some intermediate language which borrowed the form first. For example, in the case of English *coyote*, which is borrowed from Spanish *coyote*, which originally borrowed the word from Nahuatl *koyō-tl* 'coyote', it would be wrong to propose a direct cultural contact between English and Nahuatl based on the fact that English has a word which is ultimately Nahuatl in origin. English has several other loans which have this history, borrowed from Spanish, but being originally from Nahuatl, first borrowed into Spanish and then later from Spanish to English, for example *avocado, chilli, chocolate, guacamole, ocelot, tomato*, and so on. Also, some loans can come into a recipient language in spite of limited contact between speakers of the respective languages, for instance English *yak* from Tibetan *gyag* 'yak'.

15.3.4 Wörter und Sachen

Wörter und Sachen means 'words and things' in German and has to do with historical cultural inferences that can be made from the investigation of words. The idea is that the etymology of words should be studied in close association with or in parallel with the study of the artefacts and cultural concepts which those words denote (or have denoted).

For example, one *Wörter und Sachen* technique is based on the 'analysability of words'. It is assumed that words which can be analysed into transparent parts (multiple morphemes) tend to be more recently created in their language than words which have no internal analysis. This technique gives a rough relative chronology for different sorts of vocabulary, but more importantly, it is assumed that cultural items named by analysable terms were also acquired more recently by the speakers of the language and that those expressed by unanalysable words represent older items and institutions. For example, by this technique, we would reason that *skyscraper* – analysable into the pieces *sky* and *scraper* – is a newer term in English and hence a more recent acquisition in the culture than *house* or *barn*, which, since they are unanalysable today, must be older in the language and in the associated culture. As Edward Sapir said, we know, for instance, that the objects and offices denoted in English by the words *bow, arrow, spear, wheel, plough, king,* and *knight,* belong to a far more remote past than those indicated by such words as *railroad, insulator, battleship, submarine, percolator, capitalist,* and *attorney-general.* (1949 [1916]: 434–5)

Of course, this kind of inference does not always work out. Sometimes languages borrow words from other languages which result in unanalysable terms coming into the language to represent newly acquired cultural items. For example, in English, *palace* is unanalysable (monomorphemic), but is a loan (from Old French *palais*) and yet is younger than *house* and *barn* (compare their Old English sources, *hūs* 'house, dwelling' and *bere-ern* 'barley-storage'). Sometimes older unanalysable names for things are replaced for various reasons by later names which are analysable. For example, replacement of names of things due to taboo and euphemism can result in older items and institutions coming to have analysable names, such as older *toilet* which is replaced later by analysable *restroom, bathroom,* or *washroom* in North America.

Another *Wörter und Sachen* technique involves deriving historical information from cultural items whose names have visibly undergone a change in meaning. Sapir (1949 [1916]: 439) cites *spinster* 'unmarried female of somewhat advanced age' as an example, since it comes originally from 'one who spins', which suggests that the specialized meaning of 'spinster' is the result of a change and that 'the art of spinning was known at an early time and that it was in the hands of the women'. The age of the form is further suggested by the fact that the suffix *-ster* for someone who does something is no longer a productive one, seen frozen in such names as *Bayesian,* originally 'baker', and *Webster,* 'weaver'. To be completely reliable, this technique requires fairly explicit comparative evidence from related languages.

As in the *spinster* example, another technique infers that vocabulary items which have morphological forms that are no longer productive refer to things that are older in the culture. Thus, *ox, calf,* and *sheep* must be reasonably old cultural items in English, since they have non-productive plural forms that new nouns in the language today do not have, *oxen* with the archaic *-en* plural, *calves* with the no-longer-productive *f /v* alternation, and *sheep* with no marker at all for plural. The collection of terms such as these is considered evidence of a greater age for the possession of livestock. Sapir said such irregularities 'are practically always indicative of the great age of the words that illustrate them and, generally speaking, of the associated concepts'. He cited the example in Nootka (Nuu-chah-nulth) of *haʔwiƛ* 'chief' and *qoːƛ* 'slave' having the irregular, non-productive plural forms *haʔwiːh* 'chiefs' and *qaqoːƛ* 'slaves', from which we infer a relatively remote antiquity for an office of chief, the institution of slavery, and some degree of social stratification (Sapir 1949 [1916]: 441).

Another *Wörter und Sachen* strategy has already been encountered in the investigation of the cultural inventory revealed in the reconstructed vocabulary of a proto-language. Related to this is the assumption that cultural items which are represented by terms that have cognates widely spread across the languages in the language family are older in the associated cultures than terms which lack such a wider distribution among the related languages.

15.3.5 Toponyms (place names)

Linguistic aspects of place names very often permit historical inferences about languages and the people who spoke them. A well-known example is that of place names in England whose distribution and linguistic content reflect aspects of history. For example, the English place names which end in -*caster*, -*cester*, and -*chester* reflect Latin *castra* 'camp' (originally 'military post') borrowed into Old English as *ceaster*, as in *Lancaster, Gloucester, Chester, Dorchester, Winchester*, and so on. These names provide information on the history of Roman occupation in England. The area with heavy settlement from Scandinavia during Old English times (called the 'Danelaw', north and east of a line running roughly from Chester to London) has over 2,000 place names of Scandinavian origin (see Map 15.3), and these reflect the invasion and impact of Scandinavians on the history of England.

. Parish names of Scandinavian origin
— Southern limit of the Danelaw

MAP 15.3: Distribution of place names of Scandinavian origin in England
(redrawn after Wakelin 1988: 24)

The names of Scandinavian origin are recognized from linguistic elements of Scandinavian origin such as **-by**, from Old Norse *by* 'settlement' ('village, town'), as in *Busby, Derby, Grimsby, Kirby, Rugby*; **-thorp**, from Old Norse *þorp* 'village', as in *Gunthorpe, Scunthorpe, Winthorp*; and **-waite/-thwaite**, from Old Norse *þveit* 'clearing', as in *Curthwaite, Linthwaite, Micklethwaite, Seathwaite*. In the region south of the Danelaw, names with analysable Anglo-Saxon (Old English) elements predominate, for example Old English **-hām** 'home' (used also in the sense of 'town, village', as in *hamlet*), seen in places with *-ham*, as in *Birmingham, Buckingham, Chatham, Durham, Nottingham*, etc.; and **-tūn** 'enclosure, village, farmstead', seen in the *-ton* of *Arlington, Burton, Kensington, Southampton*, and so on.

The evidence from place-name etymology shows that although in historical times Xinkan speakers were relegated to a very small area near the coast in southeastern Guatemala, in former times Xinkan territory was much larger. This is demonstrated by place names found in the region which have an etymology in Xinkan but not in any other language. A few examples, with their probable Xinkan sources, are:

Ayampuc: *ay-* 'place of' + *ampuk* 'snake' (Ayampuc is on a snake-like ridge)
Ipala: *ipal'a* 'bath' (the volcano of Ipala has a crater lake)
Sanarate: *šan-* 'in, at' + *aratak* 'century plant'
Sansare: *šan-* 'in, at' + *šar-* 'flats, coast'.

It is interesting in this case that J. Eric S. Thompson, the famous Maya archaeologist and explorer, concluded from place names ending in *-agua, -ahua, -gua*, and *-hua* that there had been what he called an '*Agua* people' in the region, a non-Mayan people who were displaced by invading lowland Maya (Chortí speakers) (1970: 98–9). On closer inspection, however, many of Thompson's *-agua* place names appear to be based on Xinkan *šaʋɨ* 'town, to dwell'. Note that Spanish <hu> before a vowel and <gu> before a non-front vowel basically represent [w]. Some of the place names involved are: Xagua, Jagua, Anchagua, Sasagua, Eraxagua (*ɨra-* 'big'), Conchagua, Comasahua, and Manzaragua. When Spanish speakers began to record these names, since Spanish had no equivalent of the Xinkan retroflex laminal fricative /š/, Spanish speakers rendered it as <s>, <x> (/š/ [IPA /ʃ/] in Guatemalan Spanish), or <r>. Later, Spanish *š* (originally spelled <x>) changed to /x/ (velar fricative), spelled <j> in modern Spanish. Thus, these place names appear to contain reasonable renditions of Xinkan *šaʋɨ* 'town'; Thompson's *Agua* people appear to have been Xinkan speakers.

An often-mentioned but less reliable approach to obtaining information from place names is the same as the *Wörter und Sachen* technique involving the analysability of vocabulary terms, where it is assumed that names which are not analysable are older and that toponyms which can be analysed into component morphemes are younger. Sapir (1949 [1916]: 436) explained the logic of this: 'the longer a country has been occupied, the more do the names of its topographical features and villages tend to become purely conventional and to lose what descriptive meaning they originally possessed'. From this we infer that the place names *London, Paris*, and *York*, which are otherwise meaningless today, are older than those with more transparent analyses such as *New York, St Louis, New Orleans,* and *Buffalo.*

15.4 Limitations and Cautions

So far, we have considered the various historical linguistic sources of information and how they might be applied to contribute to greater understanding of prehistory. All these things reflect historical events and connections. However, we need also to consider potential problems and limitations that we may encounter in attempting to recover the past of a people through historical linguistic evidence.

Very often, a principal criterion for determining ethnic identity is the language which a group speaks, and anthropologists and linguists often use language as the most important marker of ethnicity. However, it is well understood that language, culture, and human genetics need not coincide and frequently do not. There are many cases where a single culture involves speakers of various languages, where a single language involves diverse cultures, and where human population genetics does not correspond in a straightforward fashion to either cultural identity or linguistic identity. The genetic make-up of speakers of Indo-European languages varies considerably; there is a significant difference between the genes of speakers of the Indo-European languages in northern India and those of Iceland. Similarly, Finno-Ugric languages are spoken by Finns whose genes are composed predominantly of western elements and by Khanty (Ostyaks) and Mansi (Voguls) who have very high incidences of eastern genetic elements. Multicultural language groups and multilingual cultural groups (societies) exist, both with and without a relatively fluid gene pool. Language is often a symbol of identity, but it is not the only such symbol, and speaking a different language does not necessarily mean a difference in ethnicity. Ethnic identity can be based on various things other than language, for example on shared cultural tradition (heritage), kinship or perceived genealogy, religion, territory, national origin, even ideology, values, and social class.

All this notwithstanding, most of the correlations between linguistics and other sources of information in linguistic prehistory assume a more or less clearly identifiable correlation between language and culture, and between language and human genetics, through time. This raises important questions which call for caution in research in linguistic prehistory. To what extent do a shared cultural tradition and a common language tend to coincide? To what extent does the correlation, when it does exist, tend to last? Unfortunately, on the whole, cultural change and linguistic change are very different in nature. In particular, a group can change its material culture substantially in a relatively short period of time, but a language's structure changes much more slowly. This means that a lack of correlation between language and non-linguistic culture can develop relatively easily.

Similarly, it is too frequently assumed in work seeking correlations between languages and genes that the genetic classification of human groups may help answer questions about the classification of the languages. However, the frequent expectation of a direct association between language and genes (the assumption of parallel descent) is incorrect. Work comparing findings in linguistics with those in human genetics needs to take seriously into account (1) that while a person has only one set of genes (for life), a person can be multilingual, representing multiple languages, and (2) that individuals (and communities) can abandon one language and adopt another, but people do not abandon their genes or adopt new ones – language shift (language replacement) is a common fact of linguistic life; there is no deterministic connection between languages and gene pools. Languages become extinct in populations that survive genetically, language replacement and extinction being frequent. We cannot assume, a priori, that linguistic history and human biological history will correlate well. Since human genetic and linguistic lines of descent very often do not match, it cannot be assumed that the non-linguistic facts from human biology can be either reliable evidence of genealogical relationships among languages or directly relevant to determining the historical trajectory that the language may have followed.

It is important to acknowledge these problems, but it does not defeat the overall enterprise of linguistic prehistory. Some scholars seem to fear that, if linguistic identity and ethnic identity do not coincide through history, then we can say nothing about prehistory from linguistic data. However, this is short-sighted. We have many sorts of information from 'language history' that tell us about the past: place names, information on contacts from borrowings, cultural inventory from reconstructed proto-languages, and evidence of language spread or migration. This remains historical information regardless of whether there was continuity in the linguistic-ethnic identity. This could be turned around. We cannot always know from material culture whether the language remained constant, whether new genes filtered into the population, whether a trait of material culture spread across ethnic and language boundaries, or spread with the expansion of its bearers into territory formerly associated with other cultural and linguistic groups. The whole point of research in prehistory is to take as much evidence from as many lines as possible to try to answer questions such as these. Knowing from linguistic evidence that speakers of Proto-Indo-European had horses, cows, wagons, tribal kings, and so on is historical information regardless of whether we know their precise ethnic and genetic identity or who their present-day lineal descendants might be, and it would be foolish to ignore such information when trying to come to grips with a fuller picture of prehistory.

Attempts to correlate language with material culture may be complicated by the fact that a single cultural tradition may not be continuous in time, since it may change radically through contact with other cultures. Language, too, can change and even be replaced due to contact with other languages. Thus, how successful can we be when we look at the cultures and languages which we know about today and attempt to project back in time to the human groups with whom each may have been associated in the past? We cannot always know, and for that reason it is very important that the lines of evidence be investigated independently before correlations are attempted. However, when independently established sources of evidence point to the same sorts of conclusions, we can be happier about the likelihood of the conclusions which we reach about prehistory. Linguistic prehistory has an important role to play in prehistory in general.

15.5 Exercises

Exercise 15.1 Proto-Chibchan cultural inventory

Chibchan is a language family of more than twenty languages spoken in southern Central America and northern South America. What do the following reconstructed Proto-Chibchan vocabulary items reveal about the culture of Proto-Chibchan speakers?

1. *dihke 'to sow'
2. *ta^l 'cultivated clearing'
3. *ike 'manioc'
4. *tuʔ 'tuber, yam'
5. *apì 'pumpkin, squash'
6. *e, *ebe 'maize'
7. *du, *dua^l 'tobacco'
8. *tã^l 'gourd rattle'
9. *toka 'gourd cup'

(data from Constenla Umaña 2012)

Exercise 15.2 Proto-Tupían cultural inventory

Tupían is a large language family of South America with about seventy languages, spoken in Argentina, Bolivia, Brazil, Colombia, French Guiana, Paraguay, Peru, and Venezuela. (Tupí-Guaranían is a large subgroup of this family.) Examine the following reconstructed Proto-Tupían vocabulary items. What are you able to say about the culture of the speakers of Proto-Tupían based on these reconstructed terms?

NOTE: č = IPA [ʧ].

1.	*awai 'yam (*Dioscorea sp.*)'	11.	*eʔe 'to grate'
2.	*čekʷ 'to pound'	12.	*iɟu 'basket'
3.	*čit 'to bake'	13.	*iʔa 'calabash (gourd)'
4.	*čʔam 'rope'	14.	*kuɾua 'pumpkin'
5.	*čét 'digging stick'	15.	*mani 'manioc'
6.	*ekʷ 'house'	16.	*mõj 'to cook'
7.	*ekʷat 'village patio'	17.	*ŋo/ŋe 'cultivated field'
8.	*ekʷen 'door'	18.	*pe 'tobacco'
9.	*ekʷʔép 'arrow'	19.	*ɾɟuku 'achiote (*Bixa orellana*)'
10.	*ẽri 'hammock'	20.	*tʔap 'thatch'

21. *upap 'bed, lying place'   25. *wet^ji̧k 'sweet potato'
22. *wamu/wamuã 'shaman'   26. *wi 'ax'
23. *waʔẽ 'ceramic pot'   27. *wip 'to cook, bake'
24. *wekẽʔa 'fish trap'

(from Rodrigues and Cabral 2012)

Exercise 15.3 Proto-Muskogean environment

Languages of the Muskogean family include Choctaw, Chicasaw, Creek, Mikasuki, and others, once spoken widely in the southeastern US. What can you say about the Proto-Muskogean speakers' knowledge of their environment and possibly about the Proto-Muskogean homeland based on the fact that terms for the following can be reconstructed to Proto-Muskogean? (Only the glosses of the reconstructed items are given.)

1. apple (crab-apple or persimmon)	29. grape
2. bat	30. grasshopper
3. bee	31. hackberry
4. beetle	32. haw
5. bluejay	33. heron
6. briar	34. hickory
7. briar (blackberry)	35. hoe/plough
8. buckeye	36. honey locust
9. buffalo	37. hoot owl
10. chestnut	38. horned owl
11. chicken snake	39. hornet/wasp
12. chickenhawk	40. horsefly
13. chigger	41. hummingbird
14. chipmunk	42. katydid
15. clam/spoon	43. lamb's quarters (*chenopodium*)
16. copperhead	44. leech
17. corn (maize)	45. lightning bug
18. cotton	46. lizard
19. crane (whooping crane)	47. locust/cicada
20. crawfish	48. louse
21. cricket	49. martin
22. deer	50. milkweed
23. dove	51. mole
24. duck	52. moss
25. falcon	53. mountain lion
26. flea	54. muddauber
27. frog	55. mulberry
28. goose	56. muscadine grape

57.	mushroom
58.	oak (three kinds)
59.	onion
60.	opossum
61.	palmetto
62.	pear
63.	perch
64.	pigeon
65.	pokeweed
66.	potato
67.	prickly
68.	pumpkin
69.	quail
70.	rabbit
71.	redbud
72.	redheaded woodpecker
73.	screech owl
74.	skunk
75.	slippery elm
76.	snake
77.	spider
78.	squirrel,
79.	stinging plant (poison ivy?)
80.	tadpole
81.	thrush
82.	trout
83.	turtle
84.	turtle (soft-shelled)
85.	walnut
86.	water lily
87.	whippoorwill
88.	wildcat
89.	woodpecker
90.	worm
91.	wren
92.	yellowhammer

(from Broadwell 1992)

Exercise 15.4 Proto-Uto-Aztecan cultural inventory

Uto-Aztecan is a large language family with languages stretching from Oregon to Nicaragua. Examine the following reconstructed Proto-Uto-Aztecan terms. What can you say about the culture of the speakers of Proto-Uto-Aztecan? What might you be able to say about the probable homeland of Proto-Uto-Aztecan?

NOTE: N = nasal of undetermined point of articulation; C = consonant of undetermined phonetic features.

1. *aCta   'bow, atlatl'
2. *amu   'agave (yucca plant)'
3. *amu   'hunt'
4. *ayaw   'gourd, squash'
5. *ayo   'turtle'
6. *hulapɨ   'badger'
7. *huma   'flour, meal'

8. *hutsa   'arrow'
9. *kakV   'crow'
10. *kimal   'blanket'

11. *koloka 'beads, necklace'

12. *kuma   'tool (for poking, cutting), knife'
13. *kuna   'sack, bag'
14. *kusa   'bag, sack'
15. *kwika   'sing'
16. *kwisa   'eagle'
17. *maCta   'grinding stone (for seeds, grains), mortar'
18. *motoʔo 'squirrel'
19. *muCta   'cholla cactus'
20. *naka   'mountain sheep (meat)'
21. *osa   'paint, draw'

22. *pakaN 'read'
23. *paʔtsi 'seed'
24. *piŋa 'grind'
25. *pipa 'tobacco'
26. *pitsɨN 'duck'
27. *piʔa 'gather, pick'
28. *pona 'play music, play drum'
29. *pota 'cottonwood tree'
30. *putsi 'seed, pit'
31. *sayo 'enemy'
32. *sikuli 'peyote'
33. *taka 'fruit'
34. *tapi 'hawk'
35. *tɨkpa 'cutting tool, obsidian, knife'

36. *tisoli 'quail'
37. *topi 'cottontail rabbit'
38. *toptu 'dance'
39. *tsal 'loincloth'
40. *tsik 'basket'
41. *tsɨka 'duck'
42. *tuʔi 'grind, flour'
43. *tuʔtsa 'hummingbird'
44. *wa(s)sa 'crane'
45. *wi-talo 'roadrunner'
46. *wika 'digging stick'
47. *wiki 'rope, string'
48. *wipula 'belt, sash'
49. *wokoN 'pine, pine tree'
50. *yawa 'dance'

(from Stubbs 2011)

QUANTITATIVE APPROACHES TO HISTORICAL LINGUISTICS AND TECHNICAL TOOLS

> In the end, the things that count are the things that you can't count.
>
> (Proverb)

16.1 Introduction

The topic of this chapter is the use of quantitative methods in historical linguistics. Quantitative approaches have not traditionally played a large role in historical linguistics, and those that were proposed have been controversial. Thus the topic has not received much attention in most introductory textbooks on historical linguistics. However, quantitative approaches addressed to historical linguistic questions have gained prominence in recent years, and therefore it is important to consider them here. There were earlier attempts to apply quantitative tools to historical linguistic questions. Some were better and some were worse, now mostly discredited, but all have in common that they have had little enduring impact. (See Embleton 1986 for a good survey of this work.) Glottochronology is the best-known of these, and we begin this chapter with a scrutiny of it. Following this, we turn to more recent approaches, many of them based on models, statistical methods, and software packages that were originally developed for evolutionary biology. In this chapter we also explore aspects of the relatively new subdiscipline of historical corpus linguistics.

Although historical linguistics has no generally accepted quantitative or statistical methodology, it is clear that appropriate computer applications could increase the ability to investigate historical linguistic data, providing the possibility for research on large datasets in ways that would be impossible for humans without computer assistance. In recent years, quantitative methods have been applied to a number of historical linguistic topics, to subgrouping (the internal classification of languages of a language family), to issues of detecting relationships among languages or to evaluating proposals of distant genetic relationships, to dating the split-up of related languages, to finding or quantifying similarities among languages, to detecting cognates, to finding sound correspondences, to determining which lexical items are more resistant to replacement based on their meanings, and to questions of linguistic prehistory such as probable homelands and migrations, among others. The principal quantitative applications to historical linguistics are considered in this chapter.

It has been asserted that adoption of quantitative methods, particularly those derived from evolutionary biology, would have many advantages for historical linguistics. It is also often repeated that the new quantitative methods are not seen as alternatives to traditional historical linguistic methods, especially the comparative method, but rather are intended to supplement the traditional methods – although some scholars do argue that their models have the potential to replace traditional historical linguistic methods. Cautions are also called for. For the task of working out family trees (phylogeny), no matter how sophisticated the numerical processing tools, if the task of turning language data into numbers is not done meaningfully and representatively, the outcomes will be neither useful nor convincing (Heggarty 2006: 186).

We turn first to glottochronology, which has had a prominent history in linguistics, and we will see why most linguists reject it.

16.2 Glottochronology

Glottochronology is a well-known method which is still sometimes used but which has been rejected by most historical linguists. Its founding is closely associated with American linguist Morris Swadesh (1909–67). It is sometimes likened to ^{14}C ('carbon14') dating in archaeology. It turned out to be particularly misleading and it is important to understand why. (Models employing similar methods have also been rejected in biology.)

The names *glottochronology* and *lexicostatistics* are often used interchangeably, though there is a difference and in more recent times scholars have called for the two to be distinguished. Glottochronology is defined as a method with the goal of assigning a date to the split-up of some language into daughter languages, whereas lexicostatistics is defined as the statistical manipulation of lexical material for historical inferences (not necessarily associated with dates) (Hymes 1960). McMahon and McMahon (2005: 33) define lexicostatistics as 'the use of standard meaning lists to assess degrees of relatedness among languages'. In this view, lexicostatistics is a prerequisite to glottochronology.

16.2.1   Basic assumptions

There are four basic assumptions of glottochronology, all of which have been challenged. We look at each in turn.

(1) *Basic vocabulary*. The first assumption is that there exists a basic or core vocabulary which is universal and relatively culture free, and thus is less subject to replacement than other kinds of vocabulary. Swadesh proposed well-known

lists of basic vocabulary, his 100-word list and his 200-word list. The *Swadesh 100-word list* of basic vocabulary is:

1.	all	35.	grease	69.	root
2.	ash(es)	36.	green	70.	round
3.	bark (of tree)	37.	hair	71.	sand
4.	belly	38.	hand	72.	say
5.	big	39.	head	73.	see
6.	bird	40.	hear	74.	seed
7.	bite	41.	heart	75.	sit
8.	black	42.	horn	76.	skin
9.	blood	43.	hot (of weather)	77.	sleep
10.	bone	44.	I	78.	small
11.	breasts	45.	kill	79.	smoke
12.	burn	46.	knee	80.	stand
13.	claw	47.	know	81.	star
14.	cloud	48.	leaf	82.	stone
15.	cold	49.	lie (recline)	83.	sun
16.	come	50.	liver	84.	swim
17.	die	51.	long	85.	tail
18.	dog	52.	louse	86.	that
19.	drink	53.	man	87.	this
20.	dry	54.	many	88.	tongue
21.	ear	55.	moon	89.	tooth
22.	earth (soil)	56.	mountain	90.	tree
23.	eat	57.	mouth	91.	two
24.	egg	58.	name	92.	walk
25.	eye	59.	neck	93.	water
26.	feather	60.	new	94.	we
27.	fire	61.	night	95.	what?
28.	fish	62.	nose	96.	white
29.	flesh	63.	not	97.	who?
30.	fly (verb)	64.	one	98.	woman
31.	foot	65	path	99.	yellow
32.	full	66.	person	100.	you
33.	give	67.	rain		
34.	good	68.	red		

The *Swadesh 200-word list* is:

1.	all	7.	bad	13.	to bite
2.	and	8.	bark (of a tree)	14.	black
3.	animal	9.	because	15.	blood
4.	ashes	10.	belly	16.	to blow (wind)
5.	at	11.	big	17.	bone
6.	back	12.	bird	18.	to breathe

19.	to burn (intransitive)	65.	hair	111.	person
20.	child (young)	66.	hand	112.	to play
21.	cloud	67.	he	113.	to pull
22.	cold (weather)	68.	head	114.	to push
23.	to come	69.	to hear	115.	to rain
24.	to count	70.	heart	116.	red
25.	to cut	71.	heavy	117.	right (correct)
26.	day (not night)	72.	here	118.	right (hand)
27.	to die	73.	to hit	119.	river
28.	to dig	74.	hold (in hand)	120.	road
29.	dirty	75.	how	121.	root
30.	dog	76.	to hunt (game)	122.	rope
31.	to drink	77.	husband	123.	rotten (log)
32.	dry (substance)	78.	I	124.	rub
33.	dull (knife)	79.	ice	125.	salt
34.	dust	80.	if	126.	sand
35.	ear	81.	in	127.	to say
36.	earth (soil)	82.	to kill	128.	scratch (itch)
37.	to eat	83.	know (facts)	129.	sea (ocean)
38.	egg	84.	lake	130.	to see
39.	eye	85.	to laugh	131.	seed
40.	to fall (drop)	86.	leaf	132.	to sew
41.	far	87.	left (hand)	133.	sharp (knife)
42.	fat (substance)	88.	leg	134.	short
43.	father	89.	to lie (on side)	135.	to sing
44.	to fear	90.	to live	136.	to sit
45.	feather (large)	91.	liver	137.	skin (of person)
46.	few	92.	long	138.	sky
47.	to fight	93.	louse	139.	to sleep
48.	fire	94.	man (male)	140.	small
49.	fish	95.	many	141.	to smell (odour)
50.	five	96.	moon	142.	smoke
51.	to float	97.	mother	143.	smooth
52.	to flow	98.	mountain	144.	snake
53.	flower	99.	mouth	145.	snow
54.	to fly	100.	name	146.	some
55.	fog	101.	narrow	147.	to spit
56.	foot	102.	near	148.	to split
57.	four	103.	neck	149.	to squeeze
58.	to freeze	104.	new	150.	to stab (stick)
59.	fruit	105.	night	151.	to stand
60.	to give	106.	nose	152.	star
61.	good	107.	not	153.	stick (of wood)
62.	grass	108.	old	154.	stone
63.	green	109.	one	155.	straight
64.	guts	110.	other	156.	to suck

157.	sun	171.	to tie	186.	where
158.	to swell	172.	tongue	187.	white
159.	to swim	173.	tooth (front)	188.	who
160.	tail	174.	tree	189.	wide
161.	that	175.	to turn (veer)	190.	wife
162.	there	176.	two	191.	wind (breeze)
163.	they	177.	to vomit	192.	wing
164.	thick	178.	to walk	193.	wipe
165.	thin	179.	warm (weather)	194.	with (accompanying)
166.	to think	180.	to wash	195.	woman
167.	this	181.	water	196.	woods
168.	thou/you singular	182.	we	197.	worm
		183.	wet	198.	ye
169.	three	184.	what	199.	year
170.	to throw	185.	when	200.	yellow

These are not really lists of 'words' per se, but rather of meanings for which relevant words with the corresponding meanings are sought in the languages investigated. Actually, different versions of these lists exist, with small variations, especially versions of the Swadesh 200-word list, because one or another word on the list was considered problematic by different linguists at different times. The two lists given here is representative.

Swadesh refined his 100-word list of basic vocabulary several times in attempts to arrive at a list of words that were universally found in all languages and relatively culture-free. An earlier version had 200 words, but it was discovered that some of these were not universal or culture-free, and eventually Swadesh arrived at his basic 100-word list. It was thought the 100-word list would be more reliable; however, the 200-word list has had something of a revival, since some who utilize quantitative techniques find the 100-word list too small for their methods to work effectively.

To apply glottochronology, the most natural, neutral translation of each of the basic semantic concepts from the word list is sought for the languages in question and the words on the lists are compared. In one common version, the forms which are deemed phonetically similar among the languages in the compared lists receive a check mark (tick) to indicate probable cognates, and the date when these languages separated from one another is calculated based on the number of the checked/ticked items that they share. In a different version, scholars constrain the method to require that only forms in related languages known to be real cognates from historical linguistic research be counted, rather than mere 'look-alikes' among languages compared, as in the more common approach. The two practices differ in that the second, which requires actual cognates, depends on the prior application of the comparative method to determine the cognates, whereas the first does not, requiring only a judgement of phonetic similarity. This lexical inspection approach to glottochronology has been criticized:

All that these pretty numbers represent is the proportion of arbitrary resemblances between the languages by which the authors are prepared to be impressed. Such work constitutes an abuse of lexicostatistics: guess-work wrapped up in numbers expressed to any number of decimal places is still guesswork. (Trask 1996: 362)

(2) *Constant rate of retention through time.* The second assumption is that the rate of retention of core vocabulary items is relatively constant through time, that a language will retain about 86 per cent of the words of the 100-word list each 1,000 years (or 80.5 per cent, rounded to 81 per cent, retention for the 200-word list).

(3) *Constant rate of loss cross-linguistically.* The third assumption is related to the second; it claims that the rate of loss of basic vocabulary is approximately the same for all languages. It is assumed that languages everywhere lose about 14 per cent of the 100-word list, that is, that some 14 words from the 100-word list will be lost (and thus some 86 of the basic 100 words will be retained) in each 1,000-year period throughout their history.

(4) *Calculation of the date of divergence.* The fourth assumption is that when the number of 'cognates' in the basic vocabulary list shared by related languages is known, the number of centuries since the languages split from an earlier common ancestor can be computed. This is perhaps less of an 'assumption' and more a formula following from assumptions (3) and (4). The time depth is computed with the formula:

$$t = \frac{\log C}{2 \log r}$$

where t is 'time depth' in millennia (1,000-year periods); C is 'percentage of cognates'; and r is 'retention rate' (the percentage of cognates assumed to remain after 1,000 years, that is, 86 per cent for the 100-word list). *Log* means 'logarithm of'.

16.2.2 Historical background of glottochronology

Glottochronology was invented by the American linguist Morris Swadesh in the 1950s. Swadesh began by trying to determine whether there were broad trends involving vocabulary change within particular language families. He reported being surprized to discover that not only were there constant trends within particular language families, but the rate of change turned out, so he said, to be the same across languages, regardless of their family affiliations. This claim constitutes one of the basic assumptions of the method, and it has been vigorously criticized (see below).

The development of glottochronology was based on thirteen test cases – languages with long-attested histories where vocabulary change could be checked against written evidence. In these 'test cases' modern versions of English, German, and Swedish (Germanic languages) were compared with older attested stages of each language (for example, Modern English with Old English).

Catalan, French, Italian, Portuguese, Romanian, and Spanish (Romance languages) were compared with Latin. Athenian Greek and Cypriotic Greek were compared with Classical Greek; Coptic was compared with Middle Egyptian (its ancestor); and modern Mandarin Chinese was compared with Ancient Chinese. (See Lees 1953.) However, only two of these thirteen (Coptic and Mandarin) are non-Indo-European languages, and this has some raised doubts about the method. The strong geographical bias also raised questions, with only Mandarin and Coptic from outside Europe. From later tests with control cases involving Kannada, Japanese, Arabic, Georgian, Armenian, and Sardinian, the claim of a constant rate of retention has been challenged (see below).

16.2.3 Criticisms of glottochronology

16.2.3.1 Problems with the assumption of basic vocabulary

There are serious problems with the assumption of a universal, culture-free basic vocabulary. One is that many of the items on the lists are not culture-free, but rather are found borrowed for cultural reasons in numerous languages. Examples of borrowed terms for items on the list are found for each item of the 100-word list in some language somewhere. A few examples of such loans are mentioned here to illustrate the problem. In several Mayan languages *winaq* 'person' was replaced by a loanword, *krištian* (or something similar), from Spanish *cristiano* 'Christian', colloquially 'person, living being'. In the early colonial period, Spanish contrasted Christianized Indians (the *cristianos*) with pagans. When ultimately all had been 'pacified' (converted), by default all were then called *krištian* 'person', resulting in the elimination from the vocabulary of former *winaq* 'person'. In the case of 'dog', while native peoples of Central America had dogs before the coming of the Spanish, their dog was small, hairless, barkless, and served as food. The big, hairy, noisy dogs that arrived with Europeans were sufficiently different from these native dogs for a number of groups (Pipil, Lencan, Xinkan, etc.) to borrow the foreign name for 'dog' and eventually lost their native term for 'dog'. Thus, for example, 'dog' in Pipil (Uto-Aztecan) is *pe:lu*, borrowed from Spanish *perro* 'dog' (Pipil has no *r*). Forms for 'sun' and 'moon' are widely borrowed among many languages of Southeast Asia and the Andes, due to their central roles in religion and cosmology. In fact, if we just look at the English glosses among the items of the 100-word list, we see that the following are borrowings: *die, egg, give, skin* (Scandinavian loanwords), *grease, mountain,* and *person* (from French), among others. From the 200-word list, we see a considerable number of additional borrowings in English: *animal, vomit* (Latin loans), *count, flower, fruit, lake, river* (French loans), and *sky* (Scandinavian loan). 'Fish' is borrowed in several South American languages from Quechua, and the term for 'fish' is diffused among some highland Guatemalan Mayan languages. 'Tooth' is borrowed in Finnish from Baltic (Indo-European).

Borrowing is a serious problem for the assumption that there is a relatively culture-free basic vocabulary. On the other hand, it is certainly true that the Swadesh lists are, broadly speaking, more universal and culture-free than any randomly selected list of other words would be, and more resistant to borrowing than non-basic vocabulary. For example, Bowern et al. (2011) find in their survey of hunter-gatherer and small-scale cultivator languages that few languages had borrowed more than 10 per cent of their 204-word list of basic vocabulary. (See Haspelmath and Tadmor 2009 for discussion of borrowability.)

Another problem is that glottochronology assumes there will be a direct, one-to-one matching between each word (meaning) on the Swadesh list and a word of each language. However, this is often not the case. For many of the items on the list, languages often have more than one neutral equivalent. For example, for 'I', many languages of Southeast Asia have several forms all meaning 'I' whose use depends on the relative social status of the person spoken to. Similarly, 'you' even more frequently than 'I' has multiple forms, depending on social status and degree of intimacy, for example the familiar versus polite pronouns, Spanish *tu* and *usted*, German *du* and *Sie*, French *tu* and *vous*, Finnish *sinä* and *te*, K'iche' *at* and *la:l*, and earlier English *thou* and *ye* (*you*), to mention just a few, where one form is not more basic than the other. For 'we', many languages have distinct forms for 'inclusive' (includes the addressee) versus 'exclusive' (excludes the addressee) first person plural pronouns. Some Slavic languages have no unique word for 'cloud', but rather have separate words, as for example in Russian *tuča* (IPA [tuʃa]) 'dark storm cloud' and *oblako* 'light cloud'. Navajo and its close sister languages have no unique word for 'water'; rather they have several different words, for 'stagnant water in a pool', 'rain water', 'drinking water', etc. For 'burn', many languages have more than one equivalent; for example, Spanish *arder* 'burn' (intransitive) and *quemar* 'burn' (transitive), or several K'ichean (Mayan) languages *-k'at* 'burn' (accidental) and *-por* 'burn' (purposeful). For 'hot' several K'ichean languages have two equally common forms: *k'atan* 'hot' (of weather, water, a room, etc.) and *meq'en* 'hot' (of food, drinks, fire, etc.). The same is true for 'cold': *te:w* 'cold' (of weather, wind, people, ice, etc.) and *xoron* 'cold' (of food, water, etc.). K'ichean languages have as many as seven different terms for 'to eat'; for example, K'iche' *-waʔ* 'eat (bread-like things)', *-tix* 'eat (meat)', and *-loʔ* 'eat (fruit-like things)' are equally common and none of them is more neutral or basic than the others. For 'not', some languages have no single form, but rather have conjugated negative verbs with several forms; compare Finnish *en* 'I.NEGATIVE' (first person singular negative [like 'I don't']), *et* 'you.NEGATIVE', *ei* 'he/she/it.NEGATIVE', *emme* 'we.NEGATIVE', *ette* 'you.PLURAL.NEGATIVE', *eivät* 'they.NEGATIVE'. For 'all', some languages have different terms depending on whether the meaning is 'all' = 'each member of a group', or 'all' = 'the entire amount'.

Similar examples can be cited for most of the other words in the list. Pereltsvaig and Lewis (2015: 74) list twenty-nine cases (14.5 per cent) from the Swadesh 200-word list where Russian does not have 'a single obvious, unambiguous "common, everyday equivalent".'

Not only do many of the items from the 100-word list have more than one natural, neutral equivalent in many languages, some have no equivalent at all – or better said, in a number of cases, some languages make no distinction between two separate items on the list. For example, 'man' and 'person' are homonymous in many languages. Many languages do not distinguish 'bark' from 'skin' or 'feather' from 'hair', where 'bark' is just '(tree) skin', and 'feather' is just '(bird) hair'. Some indigenous languages of Latin American do not distinguish 'root' from 'hair', where 'root' is equivalent to '(tree) hair'. Work on colour universals has shown that, while all languages have an equivalent (more or less) for 'white' (or light) and 'black' (or dark) and most have a term for 'red', it is not at all uncommon for languages to lack basic colour terms for 'green' and 'yellow' (Berlin and Kay 1969), though these colour terms are on Swadesh's basic vocabulary list.

In instances where a language has more than one word which is equivalent to a single item on the basic vocabulary list or where a single term in a language covers more than one item on the list, the results can be skewed. For example, two languages will appear less closely related than in fact they are if both have, for example, two equivalents for 'hot', but the one meaning 'hot of weather' turns up checked/ticked on one language's list and the one meaning 'hot of food' gets checked/ticked on a related language's list. Similarly, if related languages make no distinction between 'feather' and 'hair', then the same word will turn up twice, as the equivalent of these two separate items in the list, making the languages seem to share more and therefore appearing to be more closely related than would be the case if only distinct items were compared. Such skewing is a problem for the method.

Some 'basic vocabulary' appears to change rather easily for cultural reasons in addition to just borrowing, for example terms for 'head' in various languages. Proto-Indo-European *kaput 'head' gave Proto-Germanic *haubidam/*haubudam (hence Old English hēafod > head) and Proto-Romance *kaput. However, several Germanic and Romance languages no longer have cognates of these terms as their basic equivalent of 'head'. For example, German Kopf 'head' originally meant 'bowl'; the cognate from *kaput is haupt, which now means basically only 'main', 'chief', as in Hauptbahnhof 'main/central train station' (haupt 'main' + Bahnhof 'train station'). French tête and Italian testa both meant originally 'pot'; the French cognate from Latin *kaput is chef, but this now means 'main, principal, chief', not a human head. The Italian cognate capo now means 'top, chief, leader'. Pipil (Uto-Aztecan) tsuntekumat 'head' comes from tsun- 'top, hair' (in compound words only) + tekumat 'bottle gourd', and has replaced Proto-Nahua *kʷāyi- for 'head'. It is a problem for the method that some items on the list seem to be replaced more frequently and more easily than others (more on this below).

Finally, it has been pointed out that taboo has resulted in the replacement of considerable vocabulary, particularly in some languages in Australia, New Guinea, and places in the Americas, where words similar to the names of recently deceased relatives are avoided and substitutions or circumlocutions are used instead. Some of these result in permanent vocabulary replacement, including items in the basic vocabulary. For example, as mentioned in Chapter 6, in dialects of K'iche' and Tz'utujil (Mayan languages), ts'ikin 'bird' has been replaced by čikop (originally 'small animal') due to taboo. In Latin American Spanish, pájaro 'bird' means also 'penis' and is obscene; for that reason many Spanish speakers avoid it and substitute pajarito 'small bird' or something else instead. Because Spanish is the dominant language where Mayan languages are spoken, speakers of some Mayan languages have transferred the obscenity associated with 'bird' in Spanish to the term for 'bird' in their native languages and for that reason replaced the vocabulary item. (See section 6.2.5 of Chapter 6 for other examples.)

Facts such as these show that there is no universal, culture-free vocabulary for which a one-to-one translation equivalent exists in all languages. Still, proponents of glottochronology would respond to this criticism that something must account for the portion of the vocabulary which is lost, and it may be borrowing, taboo, and so on which bring about that loss.

16.2.3.2 Problems with assumptions (2) and (3)

Since the assumption of a constant rate of retention through time and of a constant rate of loss cross-linguistically are related, criticisms of these two assumptions are considered together.

To begin with, common sense would call these assumptions into question. There are good reasons why sound change might be regular, based on what is known about the structure and limitations of human speech-organ physiology and auditory capacity; however, there is nothing inherent in the nature of vocabulary or in the organization of the lexicon which would lead us to suspect any similar sort of regular pattern to lexical change, certainly not that basic vocabulary should be replaced everywhere at the same rate – vocabulary changes for many reasons, including for social and cultural reasons (as seen in Chapters 5 and 6), and there is no reason to expect the rate of change to behave in a law-like fashion. Additional control cases published after Swadesh's work show that this is indeed the case, that there really is no constant rate of loss or retention across languages or through time. Icelandic retained 97.3 per cent, Faeroese over 90 per cent, Georgian and Armenian about 95 per cent each, but English only 67.8 per cent, during the time that these languages have had written attestations. The large difference between Icelandic's 97.3 per cent and English's 67.8 per cent gives us little confidence in the claim of an expected 86 per cent retention, regardless of what the range of error (standard deviation) permitted by the statistical calculation might be. That is, these control cases show that the rate is neither constant across time nor the same for all languages.

16.2.3.3 Problems in calculating dates of separation

Since the split-up of language families (or subgroups) is usually not sudden, the notion of attaching a precise date to such gradual diversifications seems unrealistic – it is difficult to date a language split. Also, subsequent contact among the sister languages after a split is common, but the method as most usually applied does not distinguish loans that are the result of such contact from directly inherited cognates. For example, English *skin* and Norwegian *skinn* 'animal skin' are similar because English borrowed this word under the influence of Scandinavian. This means that in calculating how long ago English and Norwegian separated from one another, the date is skewed towards a more recent break-up because of this basic vocabulary item, which is shared due to contact after they split up.

It is also telling that the basic assumption about being able to calculate the date of separation has been vigorously challenged, that is, the statistical model upon which glottochronology is based has been severely criticized, although others defend it or try to refine it.

In short, the underlying assumptions of glottochronology are problematic.

16.2.4 Purported uses of glottochronology

The principal use to which glottochronology has been put, besides dating when languages split up, is that of subgrouping language families. It is sometimes thought that glottochronological calculations of when languages split up into daughter languages provide a fast and easy means for arriving at the internal classification of a language family, with no need to undertake the more difficult and time-consuming determination of subgrouping based on shared innovations (see Chapter 9). However, since glottochronology is unreliable and is rejected by most historical linguists, it should not be thought of as a substitute for the traditional means of subgrouping. It is simply not reliable for that purpose.

On the other hand, some have found glottochronology a useful starting point in beginning to classify large families, such as Austronesian, with a great number of languages (c. 1,200). Since it would be difficult at the outset to compare all the languages of large families with each other to determine shared innovations among them all, some suggest that a preliminary application of glottochronology may give an idea of the more promising hypotheses, which can then be checked by traditional means. Even so, Dyen's (1965) work of this sort on Austronesian got numerous things about the classification wrong. More importantly, it should be recalled that glottochronology used in this way does not find or demonstrate subgrouping relationships, but merely points in directions where other sorts of research prove more fruitful. The other research is still necessary before the true groupings can be determined, and such preliminary classifications based on glottochronology may well have to be seriously revised or abandoned.

Some suggest that while the dates offered by glottochronology are not reliable, they nonetheless provide a relative chronology which more or less corresponds with what linguists know in many actual cases. That is, some scholars who reject glottochronology and its dates are still willing to entertain the results as a rough guide to the relative age of relationships. In the absence of other information which can help establish linguistic dates, this might seem helpful to some. Still, it must be remembered that many glottochronologically calculated dates are known to be inaccurate.

Finally, some have thought that glottochronology might help to establish distant genetic relationships among languages. However, glottochronology cannot find or demonstrate remote relationships; rather, in the most common kind of application of the method for this purpose, forms which are phonetically similar in the languages being compared are checked/ticked as possible cognates and then, based on the number of checked/ticked words, a date is calculated for when the languages split up. That is, the method does not find or test distant genetic relationships, but rather as soon as any item is checked/ticked the assumption of a relationship is built in, an automatic consequence of ticking the forms, and the method proceeds to attach a date. This is illegitimate for research on possible remote linguistic relationships (see Chapter 13).

Glottochronology has given linguistics a bad reputation with some other prehistorians. For example, many archaeologists initially embraced dates from glottochronology and frequently proposed interpretations of the prehistory of different peoples and areas that relied on glottochronological dates. However, as archaeologists came to find out about the problems of the method and the unreliability of the dates, some felt deceived and came to believe that linguistics had nothing to offer them. This is unfortunate, for though glottochronology proved misleading, historical linguistics has an important role to play and much to offer in the study of prehistory in general (as seen in Chapter 15).

In summary, glottochronology is rejected by most linguists for good reason; all its basic assumptions have been severely criticized. (For references and discussion, see Blust 2000; Campbell 1977: 62–5; Embleton 1986; McMahon and McMahon 2005.)

16.3 Word Lists, Stability, and Replacement Rates

An area which has received considerable recent attention is the nature of words in word lists (actually, lists of meanings) and how retentive or how subject to replacement individual words might be. Several people have attempted to develop lists of words (that is, meanings) that they hold to be more stable, more resistant to replacement, more likely to show up among words reconstructed for proto-languages. Most of these lists are short, between fifteen and forty items. All suffer from the problems already seen. Each has some words that are in fact found as loanwords in various languages (*dog, fish, give, mountain, moon, name, person, salt, skin, star, sun, tooth*). Some have words (meanings) that frequently involve onomatopoeia ('to spit', 'tongue', 'wind'); some have terms that are typically nursery forms ('mother'). (See Lohr 1999; Starostin 1991; McMahon and McMahon 2005; Pagel 2000; Pagel, Atkinson, and Meade 2007; Wichmann and Holman 2009; among others. For discussion and criticism see Campbell 2013: 459-64, Greenhill 2011; Heggarty 2010; Kessler 2001.)

16.4 Other Recent Quantitative Approaches

In recent years, there has been something of an explosion of quantitative work aimed at historical linguistic questions. These methods have been claimed to have the following potential value for historical linguistics:

1. Objectivity and replicability: helping avoid possible research bias in the kind of data dealt with (however, see below for accusations of biases in the selection and weighting of the elements compared).
2. Speed, and ability to handle large volumes of data.

3. Seeking patterns in the data, in particular detecting patterns of diffusion.
4. Giving historical linguistics a greater feel of respectability to scholars in other fields who rely on quantitative approaches in their own disciplines.
5. Providing alternative models for representing relationships among languages – for example, not only family trees but also networks are useful for representing dialect continua and the outcomes of language contact; bringing new ways to visualize and quantify relations among languages.
6. Comparing and quantifying evidence for possible alternative family tree classifications (subgroupings).

16.4.1 Some terminological prerequisites and preliminaries

It is important to clarify some terminology commonly encountered in works that take inspiration from evolutionary biology. It is helpful to be aware of the following terms, together with their linguistic equivalences, though their full significance may become clear only when seen in actual contexts. The terms are listed alphabetically, though some make reference to other terms defined only later in the list; terms which are defined later in the list are underlined.

> *Autapomorphy* (from Greek *auto-apo-morph-* 'self-away-form'): a derived trait possessed by a species or clade (a particular taxon) that is shared with no other species or clade; a unique innovation not shared by others.
>
> *Character*: a feature or trait selected for comparison. With respect to language, a character is a linguistic attribute on which languages that are compared can agree or differ; languages are assigned the same character state if they agree, a different state if they differ. Characters are equivalent in a broad sense to how the term *comparanda* – the things compared – is used in some linguistic literature.
>
> *Character set*: the set of items that are compared; a collection of characters grouped together for a specific purpose, for example for grouping languages.
>
> *Clade* (from Greek *klados* 'branch'): signifies a single 'branch' on the genealogical tree, a group composed of a single ancestor and all its descendants; a set of species or languages derived from a common ancestral species or language, a group of species or languages that share features inherited from a common ancestor.
>
> *Cladistics*: evolutionary genealogy; a system of classification based on historical (chronological) sequences of divergence from a common ancestor.
>
> *Homology* (from Greek *homologia* 'agreement'): defined in biology originally as 'the same organ in different animals under every variety of form and function' (for example, the human hand, a cat's paw, a seal's flipper, and a bat's wing), and having a common underlying structure and an assumed common origin. *Homologous* traits are assumed to be inherited, to be due to the sharing of a common ancestor. *Homologous* is comparable to *cognate* in linguistics. This contrasts with *analogous* traits, which involve similarities among organisms that were not present in the last common ancestor of the

organisms being compared, but rather evolved independently, for example bat wings and bird wings.

Homoplasy (from Greek *homo-plasis* 'same mould'): a similarity not thought to be due to inheritance from a common ancestor; parallel, independent development (convergent evolution), the acquisition of the same trait in unrelated lineages. Homoplasy is a correspondence between the parts of different species acquired as the result of parallel evolution or convergence, not common origin. (It includes '*look-alike*' or *accidental similarity* in linguistics, but also other sorts of non-inherited similarities, for example due to borrowing, onomatopoeia, nursery forms, etc.)

Horizontal transfer (horizontal transmission, lateral gene transmission): the process in which an organism incorporates genetic material from another organism without being the offspring of that organism (not uncommon in bacteria). Horizontal transfer contrasts with *vertical transfer*, the transfer of genetic material down a lineage, that is, by inheritance. It is equivalent to *diffusion, borrowing, contact-induced language change* in linguistics.

Network: a representation of how tree-like or net-like the relationships among a given set of species or languages is. Network methods deal with cases where more than one genetic history may be possible. For parts of the genetic history where only one history is possible, the graphic representation looks tree-like; however, in cases where multiple historical sequences are possible (or where there may not be a true tree because language lineages do not necessarily diverge uniquely in all cases), network analysis draws a box shape, a reticulation or cell within a web, which shows that the data are compatible with more than one tree, if they are tree-like.

Phylogenetic: the study of evolutionary relatedness among various groups of organisms or languages. (See phylogeny.) It is equivalent to the use of *genetic* in linguistics, as in *genetic relationship*. As confusion with biological *genetics* has become more possible, some linguists have been tending to substitute *phylogenetic* or *genealogical* for *genetic* in reference to relationships among languages.

Phylogeny (or *phylogenesis*) (from Greek *phulon* 'tribe, race' + *geneia* 'producing, origin' < *genes* 'birth'): describes how species or languages are related, the evolutionary history of an organism or a language; the sequence of events involved in the development of a species, language, or taxonomic group of organisms, languages, etc. The taxa are often illustrated in a family tree.

Rooted tree: involves a root, descendants, and the time dimension – a root in the case of related languages is usually a proto-language, the ancestral language from which daughter languages descend. In a rooted tree one of the taxa is specified as the (assumed) common ancestor of all the others.

State, character state: the specific value taken by a character in a specific taxon or sequence (for example, blue eyes as a specific state in the character set 'eye colour').

Symplesiomorphy (from Greek *sun-plesio-morph-* 'together-origin-form'): a shared ancestral character, a trait shared between two or more taxa due to inheritance from a common ancestor. It is equivalent to *shared retention* in linguistics.

Synapomorphy (from Greek *sun-apo-morph-* 'together-away-form'): a character or trait that is shared by two or more <u>taxonomic</u> groups and is derived by change from the original ancestral form. It is equivalent to *shared innovation* in linguistics.

Taxon (plural *taxa*): a classificatory group of (one or more) organisms or items, judged to be a unit. Usually the taxon is given a name and a rank, so a taxon is any named group of items or organisms, any named unit of comparison, a category used in classification, for example phylum, species, genus, family, etc. While in principle taxa could be based on various criteria, usually in works about phylogenetics the taxa refer to groups established specifically in terms of shared ancestry. In this context, the terms *taxon* and *taxa* are typically taken to refer to groupings in this sense, thus effectively equivalent to clades, groups whose members have a closer shared ancestry than other groups. It is common for *taxa* to be used to refer to the individual species or languages being compared to one other.

Taxonomy: a classification of organisms or items into groups based on similarities of structure or origin, etc.

Unrooted tree: a phylogenetic tree that shows which entities that are classified (languages in our case) are closer to one another, without, however, selecting a single root as the source from which all the other compared entities later descend. That is, in our case, it does not select a single proto-language from which all the other later languages descend. Thus, an unrooted tree is said not to be directed with respect to time.

Many approaches are concerned with investigating family trees (genetic relationships, phylogenetics, cladistics) computationally, and several of the approaches utilize methods adopted from biology and applied to language. Each of the algorithms relies on a different model of how phylogenetic divergence can best be handled. We turn to these shortly.

16.4.2 Probability approaches

Several other approaches, not just glottochronology, have also involved probability calculations applied to language comparison. Oswalt's (1970) shift (or permutation) test is considered excellent for detecting chance similarities, and has been applied by several scholars, (Lohr 1999; Baxter and Manaster Ramer 2000; Kessler 2001). In it, languages are compared for similarities on a standard word list, for example the word for 'person' in Language$_1$ is compared with the word for 'person' in Language$_2$, the word for 'fish' in Language$_1$ with the word for 'fish' in Language$_2$, and so on. Then the comparison of the lists in the two languages is undertaken again, this time with the meaning slots shifted by one word in one of the languages but not the other, so, for example, the word for 'person' in Language$_1$ this time is compared with the word for 'fish' in Language$_2$, and the word for 'fish' in Language$_1$ is compared with 'bird' (the next item on the list) in Language$_2$, and so on. In languages that are not related, we expect the results for the first comparison of the forms with equivalent meanings not to be significantly different from the later comparisons with shifted, non-equivalent meanings, while for related languages we expect a clear difference between the comparisons among items of equivalent meaning and the shifted comparisons. Kessler (2001) shows that this approach may distinguish historical connections from sheer chance, but may not distinguish a relationship due to common ancestry from connections due to borrowing.

In another approach, Ringe (1992; 1996; 1998; 1999) calculated the probability of chance resemblances and challenged the method of multilateral comparison because of its inability to deal appropriately with chance similarities. He showed that statistical tests are needed to indicate the degree of confidence warranted and whether the result is significant, that is, whether it is greater than expected by sheer chance. He concluded that the distant genetic hypotheses of Amerind and Nostratic, among others, do not hold up.

16.4.3 Methods inspired by evolutionary biology

Historical linguistics and evolutionary biology share a number of interests (Atkinson and Gray 2005). Since language diversification and linguistic change are seen as similar to speciation and biological evolution, respectively, methods developed in biology to address historical questions may potentially be relevant for language change. Biology and linguistics are both interested in answering such questions as: how are similarities among languages or among species explained? How do species or languages arise and diverge? How are languages related to one another and how can species be related to each other? In both, it is asked, are similarities among languages or among species found because they share common ancestry, or are they similar due to diffusion (horizontal transmission), to parallel but independent development, to sheer accident, or to other reasons? Both linguists and biologists have a variety of techniques and tools with which to attempt to answer these questions. In recent years, methods used in biology have been applied to linguistic issues. Nevertheless, language change and biological evolution are also different in fundamental ways, and it is from these differences that some significant problems arise for methods from evolutionary biology when they are applied to languages.

The extensive attention some of this work has received shows that these methods and their application to historical linguistic issues are considered significant. However, reactions from historical linguists to the methods imported from biology have been mixed, and we will see why. It is important to understand how these methods may contrast with or complement the traditional tried-and-true methods of historical linguistics, which typically draw on a broader range of linguistic data than those used in the quantitative approaches, several of which rely on lexical data alone. Most historical linguists will be unwilling to get behind an approach which seems to suggest to them that relatively short lists of lexical items can substitute for the whole of the language when it comes to addressing questions of relatedness and language history – a language does not live by words alone. These linguists hold that morphology and phonology provide better evidence when it comes to descent and relatedness (see, for example, Ringe et al. 2002: 65). Traditionally, linguists' decisions about language relatedness have been made based on sound correspondences, shared innovations, morphological agreements, etc. (as described in Chapter 13). Scholars who apply modern quantitative approaches to questions of language change may view this differently. They might be aware of the rest of the structure of language and of linguists' preference for using structural traits to arrive at family trees, but they wish to explore to what extent some questions about language change might be answered based on basic vocabulary. The opinions, then, are very different. Linguists distrust lexical evidence alone and employ other kinds of data and methods, while the quantitatively oriented scholars have faith that lexical evidence will be sufficient to answer some questions, or that their quantitative methods will be adequate eventually for moving beyond lexical evidence alone to dealing with other sorts of linguistic data.

16.4.3.1 Background

The family tree model plays an extremely important role in historical linguistics, just as in evolutionary biology. The idea of constructing trees for linguistic groupings and for biological taxa was not new, though the application of computer-assisted tree-building algorithms for generating a range of trees compatible with the data, and for choosing one tree over another, was new (McMahon and McMahon 2003). In the inference of evolutionary histories from molecular data in biology, effort has focused on the development of software tools and algorithms for reconstructing phylogenies by means of these models. Many scholars believe that these computational phylogenetic methods have revolutionized evolutionary biology (Levinson and Gray 2012: 167), and indeed there has been an exponential growth in the use of these methods. The result has been a whopping amount of software for reconstructing phylogenies from such data. Some of these phylogenetic approaches have been applied to linguistic data – mostly to lexical information, though nothing in the methods limits their application to lexical items – in order to investigate subgrouping relationships among languages already known to be members of a particular language family.

Scholars attempting to adapt methods developed in evolutionary biology to linguistics initially believed that it would be relatively easy to identify homologous characters in languages (that is, cognates and correspondences among linguistic elements), which, like homologous biological structures, would serve as evidence for inheritance from a common ancestor. The thought was that processes of mutation (change) operate on linguistic characters (traits, features, elements) just as they do on genes. The diversification of languages into language families and subgroups matches biological cladogenesis, where a single lineage splits into two or more new species. Often, in both linguistics and biology, such splits are due to geographic isolation or migration. There is also horizontal gene transfer in some bacteria, some plants, and a few amphibians, comparable to linguistic borrowing and change due to language contact. At first, the biology-inspired methods

TABLE 16.1: Parallels between biological evolution and linguistic change

Biological evolution	Linguistic change
Discrete character	Lexical item (sometimes phonological or morphosyntactic trait)
Homology	Cognate
Mutation	Innovation, change
Natural selection	Social evaluation of forms, causes of change generally
Cladogenesis	Diversification (subgrouping)
Horizontal gene transfer	Borrowing, language contact
Hybrid (plants)	Mixed language (very rare)
Geographic cline, ring species	Dialects, dialect chain/continuum
Fossil	Relic, archaism
Extinction, dormancy	Language death, extinction, dormancy

ignored horizontal transfer, and then later admitted the lateral transfer (borrowing) of words, though they mostly continue to ignore change in other aspects of linguistic structure due to language contact.

Several conceptual parallels between biological evolution and linguistic change are listed in Table 16.1, though different scholars have at times taken some of the particular linguistic concepts as matching other biology terms, different from those listed here.

It is, nevertheless, important not to overemphasize the seeming analogies between the two. Some linguists feel that neglecting the differences and overstating the commonalities has given non-linguistic scholars unwarranted confidence that their methods can be applied directly to languages (see below). For example, cognates – lexical items – in linguistic change are not equivalent to genes in biological evolution. Words come to be shared in unrelated languages often (due to borrowing) but genes only extremely rarely come to be shared by unrelated biological species; borrowing of loanwords and horizontal gene transfer are very different. Moreover, words can be lost or changed for many reasons in many ways, but genes do not tend to get lost and mechanisms that can result in gene mutation are very limited in number. Languages function in social contexts that make them subject to numerous influences that are irrelevant and unknown in biological evolution. Independent, parallel development (homoplasy) is common in linguistics but much less so in biological evolution. Independent languages can come to share linguistic traits as a result of common directionality of some changes motivated by constraints on speech organs or on human perception, or as a result of conforming to general typological tendencies and language universals. There is no parallel in biology to linguistic areas, where phylogenetically very divergent languages can come to share lots of linguistic traits; biological species in a geographical area do not come to share lots of traits through contact with other species in the area. As Pereltsvaig and Lewis (2015: 153) point out, 'vastly less sharing occurs across biological lineages [than across lineages of languages]'. And a biological counterpart to multilingualism is unthinkable (Pereltsvaig and Lewis (2015: 155) although multilingualism is the norm in much of the world.

Various approaches to linguistic questions based on biological methods have been involved (see below); some assumptions shared by a number of the approaches are:

There are significant similarities between linguistic change and biological evolution which allow the same methods to be applied for determining phylogenetic arrangements.

Borrowing is rare (particularly in basic vocabulary).

The distribution of cognate sets among the languages compared can be used to model linguistic evolution in a phylogenetic tree.

Linguistic characters generally develop without homoplasy, that is, without independent parallel development (convergent evolution) and without acquisition of the same trait in unrelated lineages (branches) (counterfactual in that such cases in language change are not that infrequent and constitute significant problems in language classification).

16.4.3.2 Reactions

The application of new techniques from biology to historical linguistics has met with mixed reactions, ranging from excitement on the part of some non-linguists and journalists to outright hostility from a number of linguists. Some non-linguists had thought that the value of these phylogenetic methods for investigating the history of languages should be obvious, and so were shocked by the reticence and negative reactions of many linguists. To many historical linguists it seemed that those applying these new methods were unaware of how complex languages and language change truly are and of how much was being missed as non-linguists applied their tools to linguistic questions (on this point, see also Heggarty 2006). On the other hand, those involved in constructing the models and applying the new methods see it differently. They do not deny the complexity of language and language change, but, as in other fields, they attempt to construct models to deal with limited aspects of the whole. It is standard behaviour in modelling to make simplifying assumptions in order to attack some of the complexity without having to take on everything all at once, and then hopefully to move on later to deal with more complexity as progress is made.

Rather than being simple and straightforward, the language data relevant for addressing historical linguistic questions are vastly more complex than was initially assumed in much of the earlier quantitative work. It was clear to linguists that unless these complications and complexities were taken into account in the application of quantitative methods, the results would not be useful for the purposes intended. Many linguists, aware of the inadequacies of glottochronology and multilateral comparison (see above and Chapter 13), are understandably cautious. They say that if a solution can be provided by standard linguistic methods, then what is the need for the mathematical solution in the first place?

Moreover, different encoding procedures and algorithms were contested among biologists. The debate in biology did nothing to give linguists confidence in the biologists' quantitative methods. However, in more recent times there has come to be more agreement on the value of Bayesian methods in evolutionary biology. Disagreements about molecular clocks and dating seemed especially intense, though relaxed clock methods are being explored (cf. Gray, Atkinson, and Greenhill 2011).

Linguists got the impression that scholars from outside of their field assumed that there is little to knowing about human language and how languages change and that therefore untrained outsiders could jump in and tell the linguists how to do their job properly. Linguists took this as naive arrogance. The linguists' doubts were made worse by publications which ignored linguistic facts or which got the linguistic facts wrong in well-understood cases. Linguists viewed the way the language data were handled in some publications as a tacit if not deliberate rejection of tried-and-true historical linguistic methods. To linguists it seemed that the massive relevant, successful literature of their field was being ignored or deliberately cast aside.

The application of techniques developed in evolutionary biology to language classification is almost certainly inadequate in several ways, since, despite the parallels mentioned above, there are significant differences between languages and biological species and how each changes (evolves). Language is not inherited biologically, but learned. Languages are subject to many kinds of changes that do not affect biological species. Biological and linguistic diversification happen on very different timescales. The genetic (phylogenetic) classification of languages reaches back in time reliably only as far as the oldest confirmed language families, less than 10,000 years, barely a beginning for most phylogenies (family trees) in biology. Textbooks such as this one list many kinds of linguistic change and the explanations behind them that have no biological basis and no obvious counterpart in biology, but rather are motivated by a range of social, cognitive, and other factors.

Thus, considerable care is necessary when methods from biology are applied to linguistic questions. We need to ask: to what extent may things in linguistic data actually match things in biological data? The models adopted from biology do not fit or do not take into account many aspects of language change known to be significant, for example analogical change, chain shifts, directionality of many changes, how entities are constrained by and dependent upon other elements in particular language subsystems, sociolinguistic conditioning of change, impacts of language contact, reanalysis, grammaticalization, avoidance of homophony, aspects of semantic change and neologisms, taboo, and on and on. Clearly, say many linguists, if those employing methods inspired by evolutionary biology hope to find approbation of their efforts from linguists, then attention to the various other things that linguists know to be important for explaining linguistic change is called for. Those modelling aspects of change using quantitative approaches, however, would say it is not necessary to attack all of this at once to get some positive outcomes. Biological evolution is very complex, too, but such approaches are employed there to address specific questions without needing to contend with the entirety of the complexity all at once.

16.4.4 Phylogenetic methods

The quantitative phylogenetic methods attempt to determine the classification and aspects of the history of languages using certain kinds of language data. This information is generally coded in a database, based on distance or on characters, and the methods are grouped as *distance-based methods* or *character-based methods*. As mentioned, these usually involve lexical evidence alone, considered by linguists to be the least reliable data for determining phylogenetic affiliation.

Phylogenetic trees are called *unrooted* when they represent only relationships among languages but not the ancestor behind the relationships (for examples of unrooted trees, see Figures 16.1, 16.4, 16.5, and 16.6, below). They are *rooted* when a common ancestor is identified for them (for examples of rooted trees, see Figures 16.3 and 16.7). To oversimplify: when a method gives more than one tree having the same best score, a *consensus tree* has to be calculated. Put more specifically, the method may produce many hundreds of trees not all with the same score, but all are taken into account to combine into the single consensus tree.

Although tree diagrams are standard for representing language taxonomies (internal relationships among the languages of a language family, that is, sub-grouping), those resulting from the biologically inspired methods do not represent the full story of language affinity that may emerge when phonological and morphosyntactic traits are taken into account, and when the causes of linguistic change are understood. This raises the question, then: how far can the imported models be trusted? Since models only approximate natural phenomena, they are inherently inexact. The question is: are the models imported from biological phylogenetics overly unrealistic with respect to the aspects of linguistic change they attempt to model, or can they contribute to answering questions about linguistic history?

Several studies have relied on large databases that have been established. The Dyen, Kruskal, and Black (1992) database of Swadesh 200-word lists for ninety-five Indo-European languages has been widely used. Ringe, Warnow, and Taylor's (2002) database is similar to the one by Dyen et al. (1992); it has information on twenty-four Indo-European languages including, in addition to the lexical information, twenty-two phonological characters (traits) and fifteen morphological characters. Gray and Atkinson's (2003) database of Indo-European, modified from Dyen et al. (1992), has eighty-seven languages. Other databases have been created for Austronesian (see Greenhill, Blust, and Gray 2008; Austronesian Basic Vocabulary Database, http://language. psy.auckland.ac.nz/austronesian), Bantu, Mayan (Mayan Basic Vocabulary Database, http://language.psy.auckland.ac.nz/mayan), Paul Heggarty's database of Andean languages (http://www.arch.cam.ac.uk/~pah1003/ quechua/Eng/Cpv/DataSamples.htm), and the Automated Dating of the World's Language Families based on Lexical Similarity (ASJP) database (http://email.eva.mpg.de/~wichmann/ASJPHomePage.htm#), among others. A large database of a different sort is the World Loanword Database (WOLD) (http://wold.livingsources.org). It provides vocabularies of 1,000–2,000 entries for forty-one languages from around the world, with information about the loanword status of each borrowed word, about source words and about donor languages, and also makes it possible to compare loanwords across these languages.

Let us take a look at some of the specific approaches. Both the choice of the method for inferring phylogenetic trees and the selection of the data to be investigated significantly impact the result.

16.4.5 Distance methods

A common class of distance-based methods consists of *clustering algorithms* that apply an algorithm to a distance matrix in order to produce a phylogenetic tree. The distance matrix simply denotes the total *distance* between each pair of languages, usually by some method such as summing the total number of cognates shared. These methods are fast but their value is disputed. Two standard clustering algorithms extensively used in computational biology are the Unweighted Pair Group Method with Arithmetic Mean and neighbour joining.

The *Unweighted Pair Group Method with Arithmetic Mean (UPGMA)* algorithm, a distance-based method, is designed to work when changes obey the assumption of a *lexical clock* – of constant rates of change. This is the method used in glottochronological analyses. Phylogenies (family trees) constructed using these methods have often been challenged by linguists, and phylogenies from distance-based methods such as the UPGMA, when used in lexicostatistics (glottochronology) and neighbour joining, are much less accurate than phylogenies based on character-based methods (such as maximum parsimony, weighted maximum parsimony, weighted maximum compatibility, etc.).

Neighbour joining (in several variants) is widely used for tree-like representation of language classifications (phylogenies). Neighbour joining is fast and useful for dealing with a large number of species or languages (taxa); it is, however, considered crude, finding but one tree even if alternatives might be possible, and the tree it finds is unrooted. McMahon and McMahon (2005) applied neighbour joining to ninety-five Indo-European languages, based on 200 lexical items. The unrooted tree they obtained shows the ten branches generally recognized for Indo-European languages (see Chapter 9), but no clear relationship appears among the branches.

Neighbour joining is illustrated in Figure 16.1 for the K'ichean subfamily of Mayan languages (prepared by Simon J. Greenhill based on the Mayan Basic Vocabulary Database).

16.4.6 Character-based methods

Character-based methods include maximum parsimony, maximum compatibility (with 'perfect' phylogenies, outgrowths of maximum parsimony), and

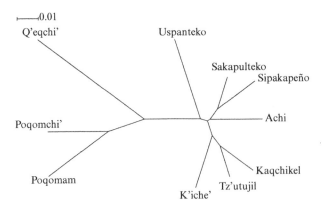

Q'eqchi'   Uspanteko

                                      Sakapulteko
                                        Sipakapeño

                                              Achi

Poqomchi'

                                          Kaqchikel
Poqomam   Tz'utujil
              K'iche'

FIGURE 16.1: Neighbour joining for K'ichean languages

The scale bar here and in subsequent figures that have such a bar in this chapter indicates
difference between languages, where longer branches (lines) mean greater differences.

model-based methods. Character-based methods use the character data to evaluate a phylogeny (family tree). Multi-state characters are coded not as necessarily
binary, but as potentially having representatives of multiple values for each of the
alternative states in the character. For example, the set of words with the basic
meaning 'hand' can be chosen as a character. Among Indo-European languages,
those with cognates of English *hand* (Dutch *hand*, English *hand*, German *hand*,
Swedish *hand*, Gothic *handus*, Old Norse *hönd*) are all assigned a single state of the
'hand' character, while languages that exhibit cognates of Spanish *mano* 'hand'
(Spanish *mano*, Portuguese *mão*, French *main*, Italian *mano*) are given a second
state, and so on for each different cognate set with the meaning 'hand'.

Once the characters are selected and the dataset is encoded, the next step is
analysis of the data. For this, the approach taken needs to specify how the changes
between the character states should be counted.

A matrix with binary coding is illustrated in Figure 16.2, of the cognates of
'father' in a selection of Austronesian languages (prepared by Simon J. Greenhill,
based on the Austronesian Basic Vocabulary Database).

Language	'father'	Cognate set (multi-state value)	Equivalent binary value for cognate set 1	Equivalent binary value for cognate set 2
Paiwan	tjama	A	1	0
Itbayaten	qamaq	A	1	0
Mangarrai	ema	A	1	0
Motu	tama-na	A	1	0
Fijian (Bau)	tama-na	A	1	0
Tongan	tama i	A	1	0
Rarotongan	*metua*	B	0	1
Māori	*matua*	B	0	1

FIGURE 16.2: Binary coded matrix of Austronesian languages

Determining which characters to select is an important part of the procedure. The characters selected should reflect language change, but judgements about what linguistic information to select for this purpose and about how to interpret that information have been subject to debate. (More on this below.)

For *encoding* and *representation*, many of these models involve the following:

1. Compiling a list of basic vocabulary items (most often a Swadesh 200-word list, since the 100-word list is sometimes thought to be too short to give good results).
2. Finding the equivalents of the items on the word list in the languages to be investigated.
3. Searching the language entries for cognates. Some approaches search just for similarities among the words compared. Many others rely on true cognates as already identified by linguists. (See below.)
4. Converting the data from cognate judgements into multi-state or binary form representations. They are converted into a binary matrix where each cognate set is coded for presence (1) or absence (0) of the cognate (a character) in the languages; or, alternatively, cognates are coded as multi-state characters, with as many possible values being coded as there are alternative states available to the character.
5. Using the software to construct a phylogenetic tree (subgrouping) which explains the distribution of cognate sets.

These approaches convert patterns involving correspondences in a dataset into a tree or network diagram that best fits those patterns. For *interpretation*, how representative of real history these diagrams may be depends heavily on the kind of data selected for coding, and on the model of divergence inherent in the algorithm. Eventually, in the interpretation stage, the significance of the identified components has to be assessed. As mentioned, judgements about what linguistic information to select for this purpose and about how to interpret it have been subject to much debate.

16.4.6.1 Maximum parsimony

Maximum parsimony is a statistical method whose target is to find an unrooted tree that requires the minimum number of changes to describe the observed data; its goal is to find the tree or set of trees with the minimal number of character state changes. Maximum parsimony methods were among the first used in modern phylogenetics and are still in use, though most scholars have moved beyond these to likelihood methods. Parsimony methods allow the possibility of constraining an algorithm so that it can reflect tendencies for changes among individual characters, though maximum likelihood and Bayesian methods (below) do this better. Parsimony analyses are valuable for assessing assumptions about assigning different weighting to different characters or about directionality of change. However, assigning more weight to some characters than to others is tricky, because it opens the calculation up to the charge of bias, that is, that the researchers' choice of particular traits to be characters and the differential weighting given to these traits/characters may bring into the picture preconceived ideas of what the researchers expect to find, biasing the results.

Gray and Jordan (2000) did a parsimony analysis of lexical characters to find an optimal tree for seventy-seven Austronesian languages. Holden (2002) applied maximum parsimony to seventy-five Bantu and Bantoid languages, arguing that the most parsimonious tree follows the expansion of farming in sub-Saharan Africa. Rexova, Frynta, and Zrzavy (2003) performed a maximum parsimony analysis of Indo-European lexical items. Their results match all the known major branches of the Indo-European family, but with much uncertainty with regard to higher-order branches. These authors note that the basic vocabulary of Indo-European is strikingly tree-like, but this is hardly surprising, since their dataset was a pre-established set of cognates among Indo-European languages, thus with all the borrowings that could be identified by standard linguistic methods already removed. Dunn et al. (2005) applied a maximum parsimony analysis to a set of structural (morphosyntactic and phonological) features in a set of Oceanic languages which are known to be related.

In biological phylogenetics there has been a gradual shift away from parsimony analysis to likelihood models and Bayesian inference of phylogeny. The reason for this is that there are several problems with maximum parsimony, among them that it does not give good estimates about the uncertainty in the data.

16.4.6.2 Compatibility methods

The computational cladistics project at the University of Pennsylvania (Ringe, Warnow, and Taylor 2002), based on computational mathematics, used compatibility methods to infer an Indo-European language tree. Ringe et al. did not rely exclusively on lexical characters, as many others do, but included, in addition to 333 lexical characters, 22 phonological and 15 morphological characters among Indo-European languages. The University of Pennsylvania project scholars proposed to construct perfect phylogenetic networks by transforming a maximum parsimony tree into a network. (See also Nakhleh, Ringe, and Warnow 2005; Nakhleh et al. 2005.)

Maximum compatibility is a non-parametric method (that is, it cannot be described using a finite number of parameters) which aims at finding an unrooted tree that presents the maximum number of compatible characters to illustrate the observed data. Being compatible here means evolving without any homoplasy, that is, without back mutation or parallel evolution.

A *perfect phylogeny* is a phylogenetic tree that is fully compatible with all of the data. Techniques for using multi-state characters have been devised which suggest that the majority of linguistic characters, if chosen and coded correctly, should be compatible on the true tree. The goal of recovering the evolutionary history of a set of languages becomes the search for a tree on which all of the characters in the dataset are compatible; such a tree, if it exists, is called a perfect phylogeny. Much earlier work was focused on developing the model of perfect phylogenies. In this approach, all (or at least the great majority) of the characters selected are compatible with a single phylogenetic tree. This means that cases of borrowing, parallel but independent change, and changes back to an earlier state (back mutation) are excluded. A character is compatible with a particular tree if all the languages that form a single group (branch) share a particular state for that character. If a single state is shared by languages that fall on different branches of the tree, then the character is not compatible with that tree. If there is not a perfect phylogeny, the best trees will be the ones consistent with most of the data.

One possible explanation for situations where it is not possible to find perfect phylogenies is that the changes involved are not tree-like, that is, that some contact between lineages (languages, branches) must be inferred in order to explain the data that do not fit well. Non-tree-like development can definitely happen, since words can be borrowed across languages and branches of a family tree. This approach is not reliable for understanding the history of language families where there has been much diffusion across branches or where dialect continua are involved. In those cases, a tree model may be less appropriate, and the developments may be represented better in a network model.

16.4.6.3 Model-based methods

Maximum likelihood (ML) methods are based on explicit parametric models (ones that can be described using a finite number of parameters) of character evolution, and they aim to estimate (hypothesize, propose) the tree and the parameters of that model which maximize the likelihood of producing the observed data. That is, ML methods aim to find the tree that best explains the data, under a given model. ML is thought generally to produce good estimates of the tree phylogeny in a robust statistical framework.

Figure 16.3 shows an ML tree for the K'ichean subgroup of Mayan languages (prepared by Simon J. Greenhill based on the Mayan Basic Vocabulary Database).

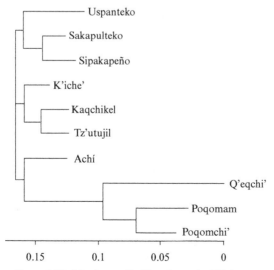

Figure 16.3: Maximum likelihood tree for K'ichean

Automated distance measures, originally introduced by dialectologists, have recently become popular among some scholars who classify forms of speech that are not considered dialects of one another, but rather are distinct languages. This operates with automated pairwise comparison of words for the same concept from a standardized list of basic meanings, such as the Swadesh list (see glottochronology and ASJP, above).

16.4.7 Network methods

Most scholars involved in the phylogenetic analysis of language data agree that a *network* or a *web* rather than trees alone can provide a more appropriate representation of what is seen in the data. Network methods show how much support or lack of support there is for particular branchings in the data that are compared. A network that looks tree-like shows that many of the data compared support tree-like splits or branching. For a network that is not tree-like but instead looks like a web, there are multiple possible hypotheses to represent the relationships among the languages or species compared (the taxa). Networks address the problem of how characters change when distinct but related languages remain in contact with one another. Trees do not represent this kind of change well; networks help to reveal contact and diffusion (horizontal transmission) across branches and across languages. The network is, however, an analysis of trees (cladistic analysis), so that only changes relevant to constructing trees are applicable, equivalent to shared innovations in standard linguistic subgrouping (see Chapter 9). Characters that do not change are ignored. Network approaches have involved both character-based and distance-based methods. (See McMahon and McMahon 2005: 141.) Some scholars think that network approaches are more flexible and revealing than approaches based on trees alone, dealing with both shared divergence from a common ancestor and change due to language contact (McMahon and McMahon 2005: 174, 178). Others point out the difficulty of interpreting the results, the temptation to see in the networks what one wants to see, and the absence of tools to make inferences from them about processes of language change.

16.4.7.1 Neighbour-Net

Neighbour-Net uses an algorithm similar to neighbour joining that decomposes the data into a set of 'splits' (that is, groups of languages supported by some subset of the data). It is particularly useful for visual representation of the results, whether they are more tree-like or less so. The network is not concerned with finding an optimal tree. Instead, alternative trees are suggested. The visual layout and interpretation of a neighbour net show how the relationships between different languages in a language family can be represented geometrically (as seen in Figures 16.4–16.6, below).

   The Neighbour-Net program calculates the possible ways of splitting the data and scores them with confidence levels. In the networks, the lengths of the branches are proportional to the amount of divergence between languages.

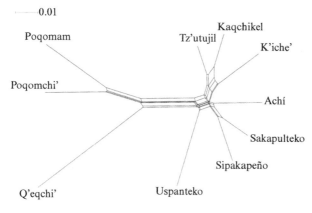

FIGURE 16.4: Neighbour-Net of the K'ichean subfamily of Mayan languages

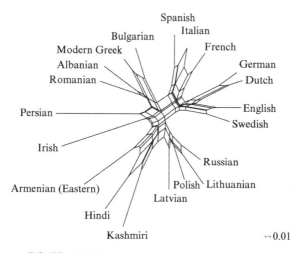

FIGURE 16.5: Neighbour-Net tree of Indo-European

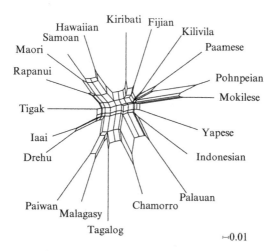

FIGURE 16.6: Neighbour-Net tree of Austronesian

Box-like structures represent the conflicting signals when features support incompatible language groupings. If the languages split rather cleanly without a lot of subsequent interaction after the splits, we would expect the groupings in the network to reflect this and contain few boxes reflecting conflicting signals. In contrast, if the characters (linguistic elements) involve diffusion among adjacent languages, we would expect to see a network with more boxes and clusters reflecting the results of language contact. The extent to which the data are tree-like can be quantified by these methods.

Neighbour-Net trees are illustrated in Figures 16.4–16.6. The tree in Figure 16.4 is of the K'ichean subfamily of Mayan languages (prepared by Simon J. Greenhill based on the Mayan Basic Vocabulary Database). Figure 16.5 is a Neighbour-Net tree based on 200 items of basic vocabulary from twenty Indo-European languages. The Neighbour-Net tree in Figure 16.6 is based on 200 items of basic vocabulary from twenty Austronesian languages. (Figures 16.5 and 16.6 are from Greenhill et al. 2010.)

16.4.7.2 Bayesian methods

Bayesian methods are based on explicit parametric models of character evolution (change), and are generally held to produce good estimates (hypotheses) of the phylogeny (genealogical tree classification). This set of approaches is largely an extension of the maximum likelihood approach within a Bayesian statistical framework. Bayesian analysis involves dataset construction, maximum likelihood modelling, and the search for the most probable evolutionary trees. Bayesian analysis is now at the forefront of phylogenetic algorithm development. Bayesian methods are thought to be valuable whenever there is a need to extract information from data that are uncertain or subject to error or noise. Bayesian inference allows uncertainties to be estimated in a natural way, and prior beliefs about parameters to be made explicit. It permits both quantification of uncertainty and the investigation of conflicting phylogenetic signals. It is difficult to evaluate the accuracy of its results because the history of most language families is not known.

Gray and Atkinson's (2003) well-known study combined a likelihood model of lexical change with Bayesian inference of phylogeny to determine the most probable trees for the Indo-European language family. Greenhill, Drummond, and Gray (2010) found that their phylogeny of 400 Austronesian languages matches well the classification by historical linguists based on the comparative method. These authors believe this argues for the reliability of the method. Algorithm and software development in computational phylogenetics using Bayesian inference has been applied to a number of other linguistic topics. Greenhill, Currie, and Gray (2009) performed computer simulations to quantify the effect of undetected borrowing, concluding that Bayesian phylogenetic methods are good at getting revealing results even with high levels of borrowing. These authors see this as a test of the approach because Austronesian is known for its variation and complexity, which resulted in Dyen's (1965) unreliable classification of the family based on lexicostatistics.

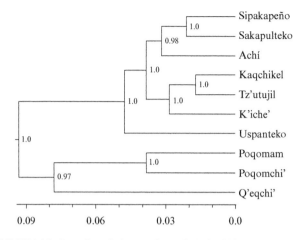

FIGURE 16.7: Bayesian phylogenetic analysis for K'ichean languages

Figure 16.7 (prepared by Simon J. Greenhill based on the Mayan Basic Vocabulary Database) illustrates Bayesian analysis; it is a maximum-clade credibility tree summary of a Bayesian phylogenetic analysis of the K'ichean languages, a subgroup of Mayan. The values on the nodes represent the posterior probability of the subgrouping.

16.4.8 What counts as data, how is it dealt with?

As mentioned, many of the studies which apply quantitative methods to linguistics rely exclusively on lexical data despite the fact that historical linguists generally consider lexical items the least reliable kind of evidence of linguistic relationship, easily replaced or borrowed. As seen above, several of the quantitative techniques rely on mere observed similarity among lexical items. Such techniques are used with the hope that the simpler and faster analyses will correlate sufficiently with true phylogenetic history. However, methods that investigate only superficial similarity among compared lexical items are known to be very unreliable, multilateral comparison being a most notorious example (see Chapter 13). For example, Forster and Toth (2003) did not use cognates in coding their data, but instead coded their data according to judgements of superficial similarity among the forms compared. They attempted to investigate Celtic and Romance languages, grouping together words which look similar even if they are known by linguists to have different origins, and treated as separate other words which are known to be cognates. ASJP (Automated Dating of the World's Language Families based on Lexical Similarity) attempts to calculate similarity automatically, without regard for whether true cognates are involved (Holman et al. 2011).

Similarity, as we have seen, can be due to several things – borrowing, accident, onomatopoeia, sound symbolism, nursery formation, etc. – and inheritance from a common ancestor (phylogenetic relationship) is only one of the possibilities. A straight coding of similarity among lexical items – 'characters' that are words – is not adequate. One familiar problem is that lexical items (as characters) are known to be particularly vulnerable to borrowing. Careful application of the comparative method and techniques for finding loanwords can detect most borrowing and thus can significantly reduce this problem for approaches that rely on lexical characters, but they do not eliminate all cases of borrowing. To get true cognate sets without the complications of borrowing requires application of tried-and-true historical linguistic techniques, especially the comparative method. It has also been assumed that word lists based on basic vocabulary will have most of the borrowings filtered out, since basic vocabulary tends to be resistant to borrowing. However, borrowing of basic vocabulary, while less frequent, is still quite common, as seen above in the loans in English involving items on the Swadesh word lists, *animal, count, die, egg, flower, fruit, give, grease, lake, mountain, person, river, skin, sky,* and *vomit.* Most of the phylogenetic tools from biology were unconcerned with the problem of borrowing because they worked only with pre-established cognate sets, which presuppose that the loanwords have already been removed. However, Greenhill, Currie, and Gray (2009) and Nelson-Sathi et al. (2010) show that Bayesian methods deal well with undetected borrowings. Also, it is often difficult to determine whether compared lexical items are true cognates if they have undergone a significant amount of sound change which leaves them so different in the different languages as to be unrecognizable (as seen in examples in Chapter 13). These cases require careful application of the comparative method with attention to recurrent sound correspondences.

To linguists, methods that depend on linguists identifying cognates in advance make it appear that standard linguistic methods are required to do the heavy lifting, to find the cognates, to eliminate the loanwords, and to deal with the many other complicating factors, just to get the data to a point where they are usable by the quantitative methods. This view is reflected in Donohue et al.'s (2012: 544) criticism that Gray and Atkinson's (2003) method 'uses the results of the comparative method to weakly emulate comparative method results'. Many of the quantitative approaches appear to linguists to depend on the results of the prior application of linguistic methods, made to masquerade as numbers and algorithms. Practitioners of the quantitative methods would see this differently, as ways to quantify uncertainty in hypotheses, putting numbers hopefully to help end or clarify debates.

In any event, character choices can also raise questions about the adequacy of the sample as well as of the analysis of the data, because of both what is included and what is left out. For example, if only lexical items are chosen as characters, crucial information is neglected. Dealing with datasets based on cognates that require expert linguistic input fails to take into account the whole backdrop of what historical linguists have to do to determine cognacy: find sound changes, be aware of the directionality of change, sort shared innovations, ascertain semantic change and determine plausible semantic shifts, recognize recurrent sound correspondences, identify borrowings and contact-induced changes, eliminate forms which are similar due to analogical changes, etc. In short, very complex information and procedures go into the decisions about what forms are cognates.

To do it right, it would seem that the techniques brought in from evolutionary biology must build into their procedures these various things that linguists know and do. As McMahon and McMahon (2005: 36) say, 'mathematical models and methods are not a substitute for careful and reasoned linguistic investigations, though that has not prevented attempts to use them in this way'. Methods that include more realistic views of language change must form the basis for worthwhile inferences about linguistic history. (See Kessler 2001 on the limits of statistical techniques applied to lexical items.)

Some have attempted to include characters based on sound changes, morphology, and typological traits also, and others profess interest in moving in that direction. Linguists have recommended that these approaches take phonological and morphosyntactic data into account, as well as contact-induced language change and the various other things necessary for fuller understanding of how language change affects the data. When phonological and morphological characters are included, the results may improve significantly, but, as mentioned, this can introduce new problems, such as the charge of bias in character selection that might influence the results towards expected or desired outcomes. Linguists have also asked that more standard linguistic criteria for subgrouping be taken into account, for example shared innovations involving sound changes, shared morphological traits, etc. However, these are the things that historical linguists do anyway, so that models taken from biology and applied to the results of historical linguistic methods seem secondary, perhaps risking more than is gained because they deal with these crucial aspects of language beyond the lexicon less fully and less successfully than linguists already do.

To most traditional historical linguists, the scholars who have invested in quantitative approaches to historical linguistic questions have appeared to progress by gradually reinventing the wheel. That is, they appear to (re)discover complicating factors that force them to revise and refine their approaches, complications that linguists already knew about, such as that raw similarities among lexical items do not provide a reliable basis for classifying languages, that often lexical items alone are not sufficient, that phonological and morphological characters are important for determining phylogenetic status, that borrowing exists (that we are not dealing with perfect phylogenies), that homoplasy exists (both independent parallel evolution and back mutation), and so on. It seems these scholars have had to 'discover' aspects of the complexity of language and the unaddressed challenges of language change by being dragged through problems as they arose in their analyses, though even now many have not taken into account the full weight of the problems, and those who do acknowledge them have typically not dealt with them well. For example, the value of shared innovation as a diagnostic of subgrouping – the gold standard in linguistic phylogenetic classification – is not implemented in any significant way in most of the quantitative approaches. Some believe that the level to which cognates are reconstructible on branches of phylogenetic trees reveals shared innovations, but shared innovation among lexical items is not accorded much weight by linguists, since lexical items can change in volatile ways and can be shared for many reasons in addition to inheritance from a common ancestor. This, then, is why many linguists have been and remain sceptical, some even disdainful, of much of the quantitative work in this area.

This is, however, not a fair view of those applying quantitative methods to historical linguistic questions, or at least not of all of them. It is of course a common practice in mathematics and numerous sciences to make simplifying assumptions about some complex phenomenon in order to model it, and then, with progress, gradually to add attention to complications as needed. A problem is that many scholars do not make their simplifying assumptions explicit, and what would be needed to test the models is usually not made sufficiently rigorous and plainly clear. It is also important to ask whether the simplifying idealizations called for in the models are too unrealistic to yield useful results.

Those interested in exploring the possibilities of dating in linguistics might respond that they are definitely not reinventing linguistic wheels, since linguists have just given up on dating. Here, opinions from the two camps diverge. The traditional linguists' response is, predictably, not of optimism, rather of scepticism – the newer dating methods, though more sophisticated than glottochronology, are subject to the limitations and liabilities resulting from relying on lexical lists, which the linguists believe incapable of revealing a sufficient range of linguistic change, of how, why, and when language change happens.

Though a very positive development, incorporation of other sorts of characters beyond just lexical ones can bring with it additional complications, as mentioned above. Borrowing can make phylogenetic classification difficult, except when the amount of borrowing is low. So characters that are resistant to borrowing are more useful in a phylogenetic analysis. Structural characters are valuable because they are more resistant to borrowing than lexical items – though structural borrowing is also not uncommon (see Chapters 10 and 11). Heggarty, Maguire, and McMahon (2010) used divergence in phonetics, advocating network-type phylogenetic methods. Some studies have attempted to use typological features, but their use is controversial (Dunn et al. 2005; Dunn, Levinson, and Lindström 2008; Wichmann and Saunders 2007). Typological traits have been employed not only for internal classification (subgrouping) of languages already known to be related, but also in attempts to address possible remote relationships among languages. It is claimed that the inclusion of typological features may help resolve issues about higher-order relationships where the available lexical data are relatively uninformative.

Dunn et al. (2005), based on typological traits, claimed to be able to detect historical signals among some Papuan languages (not known to be related to one another) that reach beyond the limits of the comparative method, to around 10,000 years ago. These authors ask whether a phylogenetic signal can be identified in the absence of identifiable lexical cognates. They based their study on a broad selection of abstract typological categories as characters which languages of the region might be expected to have, without regard for their form (the sounds that signal them), but rather with concern only for the presence of particular grammatical categories (shared functions or meanings alone). This, however, violates the principle that permits as evidence of linguistic relatedness only comparisons which involve both sound and meaning together (see Chapter

13; Campbell and Poser 2008). Since Dunn et al. compare only similarities in the functions of the typological traits selected for characters, independent of the form (sounds) that signal them, their conclusions would be ruled out on the basis of this standard principle. (See Donohue and Musgrave 2007 for criticisms based on other grounds.)

Typological traits selected as characters can also reflect language contact and geographical distribution of traits rather than phylogenetic relationships among the languages compared. For example, in a comparison of French, Spanish, and German, many characters shared by French and Spanish may actually be inherited and reflect the fact that they belong to the Romance languages. However, traits shared by French and German (the latter a member of the Germanic branch) may reflect some traits shared only because of language contact among these two neighbouring languages. Thus, French and German share several traits which Spanish lacks: uvular r, front rounded vowels (/y, ø/), and requirement of an overt subject – French is not a null subject (pro-drop) language as Spanish is, where verbs in independent clauses can lack an explicit subject. Since Dunn et al. are not able to distinguish typological traits that are shared due to language contact (such as these French–German shared traits) from those that may be inherited and thus reflect a phylogenetic relationship among languages (such as the French–Spanish shared traits in this example), many linguists do not believe that Dunn et al.'s method of comparing raw typological traits to attempt to see into the distant linguistic past can offer reliable results.

Wichmann and Saunders (2007) also used typological features as characters. They attempted to identify features least likely to involve diffusion, parallel changes, and back mutation, which can frustrate attempts to get accurate phylogenetic results. They tried to choose the features that tend to be more stable, least amenable to change due to areal influence. A serious problem for this approach is the difficulty of identifying stable typological features. Also, typological features exhibit relatively high rates of homoplasy (parallel but independent evolution). Moreover, there is the problem of limited possible typological states. For example, the choice of noun–adjective versus adjective–noun word order as a character is of little value for showing phylogenetic relationships, since by chance alone, one would expect a 50 per cent possibility of a match between languages' sharing of one or sharing the other particular order. Some studies find substantial non-tree-like signals in typological data and a poor fit among some languages known to belong to particular language families.

16.4.9 Applications

The various quantitative methods have been applied to a variety of historical linguistic questions, some of which are described briefly in what follows.

16.4.9.1 Subgrouping

Most of the quantitative work in historical linguistics is not aimed at establishing new phylogenetic relationships among languages, but rather deals with internal classification (subgrouping) of the languages that belong to already established families. Applications to the Indo-European family of languages are especially abundant. Traditionally, subgrouping of languages that belong to a family of languages relies on the comparative method and on shared innovations (see Chapter 9). Methods designed to create phylogenetic trees should be good at providing subgroup classification of languages. In the studies that rely on only lexical similarities, no distinction is made between shared innovations and shared retentions, and these approaches are typically less accurate than the traditional method of linguistic subgrouping.

16.4.9.2 Distant genetic relationships

Some scholars have attempted to evaluate particular proposals of distant genetic relationship, or have used related techniques to propose even more wide-reaching groupings (see Chapter 13). As seen above, these proposals have not been found persuasive.

16.4.9.3 Dating

In addition to methods to build more accurate trees, new quantitative approaches have been developed to try to provide estimates for the dates of language diversification, and one of the earliest applications of new phylogenetic methods from biology to linguistics was to dating (Gray and Atkinson 2003; Atkinson and Gray 2006). These approaches do not assume that there is a single rate of lexical change, as was assumed in glottochronology. Sanderson (2002) developed the rate-smoothing approach to allow biologists to infer divergence times without having to assume a constant molecular clock. This requires calibration points – places where nodes (branching points) on the trees can be matched to known dates of historical events. These known ages of nodes are combined with information about branch length to estimate rates of change across the whole tree.

The penalized likelihood rate-smoothing approach (Gray and Atkinson 2003), as well as newer dating methods that can relax the clock, have been employed. The penalized likelihood model allows rates to vary across the tree. Gray and Atkinson (2003) and Atkinson and Gray (2006) attempted to date the divergence among branches of Indo-European. Gray and Atkinson (2003) dated fourteen nodes of their Indo-European trees based on external historical information for calibration points, and applied the rate-smoothing algorithm. Their consensus tree is compatible with the trees linguists produce with conventional subgrouping procedures. Gray and Atkinson arrived at a date for the initial break-up of the Indo-European family at around 8700 BP (before present). Most historical linguists disagree, finding this date too early, as the reconstructed vocabulary appears to reflect a date of c. 6500–4500 BP (Anthony and Ringe 2015; Chang et al. 2015; Clackson 2007: 18–19; Mallory and Adams 1997: 296). (In work yet to be published, Russell Gray and a large team of over two dozen scholars associated with the Department of Linguistic and Cultural Evolution, of the Max Planck Institute for the Science of Human History in Jena, Germany, have arrived at a revised date for the time depth of Proto-Indo-European of 8300 BP.)

Holman et al. (2011) propose Automated Dating of the World's Language Families based on Lexical Similarity (ASJP). They attempt a global survey of linguistic divergence, but their method of measuring divergence is not grounded in any reasonable model of linguistic change. The results gave many wrong or unlikely ages. As seen above, there is nothing to suggest constancy in how words change or how they are organized in the lexicon.

16.4.9.4 Contributions to prehistory

Various studies claim their outcomes have relevance for resolving issues in prehistory. For example, Gray and Atkinson (Gray and Atkinson 2003; Atkinson and Gray 2006) believe their results test the so-called Kurgan and Anatolian hypotheses for the homeland or origin of the Indo-European languages (see Chapter 15), and they argue that the Anatolian view is supported. This hypothesis holds that the original homeland of Proto-Indo-European was in Anatolia, and it links the dispersal of Indo-European languages with the Neolithic spread of agriculture from Anatolia to Europe c. 9000 BP. Gray and Atkinson dated the start of the spread of the Indo-European family to around 8700 BP, as mentioned above. Their analysis does not, they say, agree with the Kurgan (or Steppe) hypothesis, which holds that the spread started around 6000 BP from the steppes of the Ukraine or southern Russian. However, regardless of what date Gray and Atkinson may believe representative of Proto-Indo-European time depth, it still does not follow that Anatolian farmers win out over Kurgan horsemen for locating the homeland. Gray and Atkinson provided a proposed date, but no specific location, so that Proto-Indo-European could have been spoken anywhere at the time indicated and not necessarily in Anatolia. In any case, most linguists think their date is too early and that the Anatolian location is unlikely, based on the geographical and lexical evidence (see Anthony and Ringe 2015; Chang et al. 2015; Pereltsvaig and Lewis 2015). (For discussion of alternative hypotheses of the Indo-European homeland, see Mallory and Adams 2006: 460–3; Anthony and Ringe 2015.)

Phylogenetic methods have also been applied to other questions about linguistic prehistory (see for example Gray and Jordan 2000; Greenhill and Gray 2005; Gray, Drummond, and Greenhill 2009; Greenhill, Blust, and Gray 2008; Greenhill, Drummond, and Gray 2010).

16.4.9.5 Probability of cognacy

Work has been done to develop algorithms to determine the probability that lexical characters are cognate (Heeringa, Nerbonne, and Kleiweg 2002; Kondrak 2001; Covington 1996).

Kessler (2001) estimates the likelihood of chance phonemic correspondences using permutation statistics. Kondrak (2002) develops algorithms to detect cognates and sound correspondences. He proposes computer program methods for detecting and quantifying three attributes of cognates important for historical linguistics: phonetic similarity, recurrent sound correspondences, and semantic affinity. This approach combines novel algorithms developed for these tasks with algorithms adapted from biology and natural language processing. These algorithms can process large numbers of data very rapidly that would otherwise take weeks to do by hand. Kondrak, Beck, and Dilts (2007) apply these techniques to identifying cognate sets and sound correspondences, with the object of providing tools for the rapid construction of comparative dictionaries. There have also been some efforts to detect cognates automatically rather than needing to rely on the judgements of expert linguists (Mackay and Kondrak 2005). Ben Hamed, Darlu, and Vallée (2005) and Bouchard-Côté et al. (2007) developed models for phonological data and use them to attempt to identify language families.

McMahon and McMahon (2005) and Nakhleh, Ringe, and Warnow (2005) apply phylogenetic techniques to comparative reconstruction. Ellison and Kirby (2006) suggest means of detecting relationships which do not depend on word-by-word comparisons. Ellison (2007) combines Bayes' theorem with gradient descent in a method for finding cognates and correspondences. Michael Cysouw and Hagen Jung (2007) use an iterative process of alignment between words in different languages in an attempt to identify cognates.

16.4.9.6 Dialectology

Several quantitative publications examine language change from the point of view of dialectology. Hans Goebl, with quantitative analysis of linguistic varieties, also applies his dialectometric techniques to comparisons across related languages (see for example Goebl 2006; Heeringa, Nerbonne, and Kleiweg 2002; Nerbonne and Heeringa 2009). Some dialectometrical techniques have been used for subgrouping of related languages. Quite different quantitative approaches to dialects are found in McMahon et al. (2007) and Maguire et al. (2010), for example.

16.5 Historical Corpus Linguistics

In recent decades corpus linguistics has developed as a very active subfield in linguistics, and historical corpus linguistics is an important part of corpus linguistics. For linguists, a *corpus* is a body of texts or other specimens of a language that are representative of that language. In corpus linguistics, the corpora (the plural of *corpus*) are usually stored as an electronic database and used for linguistic analyses. *Corpus linguistics* is understood roughly as the study of linguistic phenomena through large collections of machine-readable texts, and the analysis of data obtained from a linguistic corpus. In recent years there has been a large surge in work labelled as *historical corpus linguistics* (sometimes thought of as 'corpus philology'): the building of corpora for historical purposes and the investigation of these texts for historical linguistic purposes. Corpora have been investigated for historical linguistic purposes since long before the age of computers. However, the advent of computers changed the study of corpora for historical linguistic purposes dramatically, making possible investigations that, if performed manually, would be hugely time-consuming, so daunting as to seem impossible in many cases.

There are now more than thirty historical corpora collections available, a number for English, but also other historical corpora for other modern languages, for example German, French, Spanish, and Portuguese.

The Helsinki Corpus of English Texts (often just called 'the Helsinki Corpus') is the best known and most widely used (at http://www.helsinki.fi/varieng/ CoRD/corpora/HelsinkiCorpus/). The aim of the Helsinki Corpus is to facilitate access to an extremely large collection of data on the structure and development of the English language via computer-based corpus linguistics. It contains texts organized periodically from the Old, Middle, and Early Modern English periods, containing more than 1.5 million words. It also involves a number of associated (collaborative) projects: the Helsinki Corpus of Older Scots, the Corpus of Early American English, the Brooklyn-Geneva-Amsterdam-Helsinki Parsed Corpus of Old English, the Penn-Helsinki Parsed Corpus of Middle English, and the Penn-Helsinki Parsed Corpus of Early Modern English.

Investigations based on the Helsinki Corpus have contributed substantially to understanding changes in various linguistic features of English through time, and these illustrate the value of historical corpus linguistics for historical linguistics. For instance, Peitsara (1993) calculated the frequencies of different prepositions introducing agent phrases (for example, in passives such as . . . *plundered **by** the men* . . .) in four subperiods from the Helsinki Corpus. She found that the most common prepositions of this type were *of* and *by*, which were of almost equal frequency at the beginning of the period, but by the fifteenth century *by* was three times as common as *of*, and by 1640 *by* was eight times as common.

ARCHER (A Representative Corpus of Historical English Registers) is a multi-genre historical corpus of British and American English covering the period 1600–1999 (at (http://www.manchester.ac.uk/archer/). The corpus has been designed as a tool for the analysis of language change and variation in a range of written and speech-based registers of English.

The Penn Parsed Corpora of Historical English (at https://www.ling. upenn.edu/hist-corpora/) includes the Penn-Helsinki Parsed Corpus of Middle English (PPCME2), the Penn-Helsinki Parsed Corpus of Early Modern English (PPCEME), and the Penn Parsed Corpus of Modern British English (PPCMBE2). They contain running texts and text samples of British English prose from the earliest Middle English documents to World War I. There are tree forms of texts: simple text, part-of-speech tagged text, and syntactically annotated text. The syntactic annotation (parsing) allows for searching not just for words and sequences of words, but also for syntactic structures. These corpora are especially useful for investigation of the historical syntax of English.

Corpus linguistic study of language change is not without some difficulties. There is the temptation to believe that a corpus may warrant conclusions about an entire period of a language without keeping in mind the corpus' limitations with respect to the genres surveyed and gaps in the coverage (in what is included), difficulties from spelling inconsistency and variation, problems of searchability of the corpus due to the kinds of annotations that have been employed in the corpus, and, related to this, problems in comparability between different corpora.

16.6 Conclusions

As seen here, the quantitative approaches that have been applied to historical linguistics have generated both much enthusiasm and considerable debate. New tools and techniques are clearly welcome to the extent that they may help resolve continuing uncertainties, contribute with more efficient means of achieving results, provide new insights or discoveries, help correlate findings from other fields, or give linguistics more credibility with scholars in other disciplines – though this should not be needed; historical linguistics has been a successful science for a very long time and does not need to be overhauled to make it appear more scientific. Clearly, computational methods can make it possible to process and analyse quantities of data not imaginable by traditional means. And new approaches can perhaps provide us with more illuminating visual means of representing language relationships and changes, for example as Neighbour-Net and Bayesian analyses promise. However, as we have seen, approaches that do not move beyond lexical data alone, or that do not provide for the various ways that characters (traits) can be similar beyond just inheritance from a common ancestor (phylogenetic explanation), tend to find less favour among historical linguists. Glottochronology was rejected for good reasons. On the other hand, quantitative investigations have discovered or at least hold out promise for ways of investigating the possible significance of frequency of usage of particular words, which basic lexical items (meanings) tend to be replaced more often and which retained more.

The value of corpus historical linguistics is well established. Many historical linguists are likely, however, to remain sceptical or to maintain a wait-and-see attitude about attempts to find and evaluate phylogenetic trees, to establish subgrouping, to date changes and the diversification of language families, to see into the distant past beyond the scope of the comparative method, or to detect distant genetic relationships.

BIBLIOGRAPHY

Abondolo, Daniel, 'Introduction', in Daniel Abondolo (ed.), *The Uralic Languages* (London: Blackwell, 1998), pp. 1–42.

Adelaar, Willem F. H., 'Review of *Language in the Americas* by Joseph H. Greenberg', *Lingua* 78 (1989), 249–55.

Adelaar, Willem F. H. and Pieter Muysken, *The Languages of the Andes* (Cambridge: Cambridge University Press, 2004).

Aikio, Ante [Luobbal Sámmol Sámmol Ánte], 'Proto-Uralic', in Marianne Bakró-Nagy, Johanna Laakso, and Elena Skribnik (eds.), *The Oxford Guide to the Uralic Languages* (Oxford: Oxford University Press, 2020), pp. 1–60.

Aitchison, Jean, 'The language lifegame: prediction, explanation and linguistic change', in Willem Koopman, Frederike van der Leek, Olga Fischer, and Roger Eaton (eds), *Explanation and Linguistic Change* (Amsterdam: John Benjamins, 1987), pp. 11–32.

Aitchison, Jean, *Language Change: Progress or Decay?*, 3rd edn, Cambridge Approaches to Linguistics Series (Cambridge: Cambridge University Press, 2001 [1st edn: London: Fortuna, 1981]).

Alvar, Manuel, *Lingüística románica*, reworked and heavily annotated; originally by Iorgu Iordan (Madrid: Ediciones Alcalá, 1967).

Anderson, James M., *Structural Aspects of Language Change* (London: Longman, 1973).

Anthony, David and Don Ringe, 'The Indo-European homeland from linguistic and archaeological perspectives', *Annual Review of Linguistics* 1 (2015), 199–219.

Anttila, Raimo, 'The relation between internal reconstruction and the comparative method', *Ural-Altaischer Jahrbücher* 40 (1968), 159–73.

Anttila, Raimo, *An Introduction to Historical and Comparative Linguistics* (New York: Macmillan, 1972 [2nd edn: Current Issues in Linguistic Theory, 4, Amsterdam: John Benjamins, 1989]).

Arlotto, Anthony, *Introduction to Historical Linguistics* (Boston: Houghton Mifflin, 1972 [reprinted: Washington, DC: University Press of America, 1981]).

Atkinson, Quentin D. and Russell D. Gray, 'Curious parallels and curious connections?

Phylogenetic thinking in biology and historical linguistics', *Systematic Biology* 54 (2005), 513–26.

Atkinson, Quentin D. and Russell D. Gray, 'Are accurate dates an intractable problem for historical linguistics?', in C. P. Lipo, M. J. O'Brien, M. Collard, and S. J. Shennan (eds), *Mapping our Ancestors: Phylogenetic Approaches in Anthropology and Prehistory* (New Brunswick: Aldine, 2006), pp. 269–98.

Atkinson, Quentin, Geoff Nicholls, David Welch, and Russell Gray, 'From words to dates: water into wine, mathemagic or phylogenetic inference?', *Transactions of the Philological Society* 10 (2005), 193–219.

Bach, Adolph, *Deutsche Mundartforschung*, 3rd edn (Heidelberg: Winter, 1969).

Baehrens, W. A., *Sprachlicher Kommentar zur vulgärlateinischen Appendix Probi* (Halle an der Saale: Max Niemeyer, 1922) [reprinted: Groningen: Bouma's Boekhuis, 1967]).

Barðdal, Jóhanna and Thórhallur Eythórsson, 'Reconstructing syntax: construction grammar and the comparative method', in Hans C. Boas and Ivan Sag (eds), *Sign-Based Construction Grammar* (Stanford: CSLI Publications, 2012), pp. 257–308.

Baxter, William H. and Alexis Manaster Ramer, 'Beyond lumping and splitting: probabilistic issues in historical linguistics', in Colin Renfrew, April McMahon, and Larry Trask (eds), *Time Depth in Historical Linguistics* (Cambridge: McDonald Institute for Archaeological Research, 2000), pp. 167–88.

Beekes, Robert S. P., *Comparative Indo-European Linguistics: An Introduction* (Amsterdam: John Benjamins, 1995).

Ben Hamed, M., P. Darlu, and N. Vallée, 'On cladistic reconstruction of linguistic trees through vowel data', *Journal of Quantitative Linguistics* 12 (2005), 79–109.

Berlin, Brent and Paul Kay, *Basic Color Terms: Their Universality and Evolution* (Berkeley: University of California Press, 1969).

Berman, Howard, 'A comment on the Yurok and Kalapuya data in Greenberg's *Language in the Americas*', *International Journal of American Linguistics* 58 (1992), 320–48.

Bhat, D. N. S., *Sound Change* (Delhi: Motilal Banarsidass Publishers, 2001).

Bloomfield, Leonard, 'On the sound system of Central Algonquian', *Language* 1 (1925), 130–56.

Bloomfield, Leonard, 'A note on sound-change', *Language* 4 (1928), 99–100.

Bloomfield, Leonard, *Language* (New York: Holt, Rinehart and Winston, 1933).

Blust, Robert, *The Austronesian Languages* (revised edn) (Canberra: Asia-Pacific Linguistics, 2013).

Blust, Robert, *101 Problems and Solutions in Historical Linguistics* (Edinburgh: University of Edinburgh Press, and Cambridge, MA: MIT Press, 2018).

Bogaya, Robert, 'Why lexicostatistics doesn't work: the "universal constant" hypothesis and the Austronesian languages', in Colin Renfrew, April McMahon, and Larry Trask (eds), *Time Depth in Historical Linguistics* (Cambridge: McDonald Institute for Archaeological Research, 2000), pp. 311–31.

Börjars, Kersti and Nigel Vincent, 'The pre-conditions for suppletion', in Alexandra Galani, Glyn Hicks, and George Tsoulas (eds), *Morphology and its Interfaces* (Amsterdam: John Benjamins, 2011), pp. 21–48.

Bouchard-Côté, Alexandre, Percy Liang, Thomas L. Griffiths, and Dan Klein, 'A probabilistic approach to diachronic phonology', in *Proceedings of the 2007 Joint Conference on Empirical Methods in Natural Language Processing and Computational Natural Language*

Learning (EMNLP/CoNLL) (Prague: Association for Computational Linguistics, 2007), pp. 887–96.

Bowern, Claire, Patience Epps, Russell Gray, Jane Hill, Keith Hunley, Patrick McConvell, and Jason Zentz, 'Does lateral transmission obscure inheritance in hunter-gatherer languages?', *PLoS ONE* 6.e25195 (2011), <https://www.ncbi.nlm.nih.gov/pmc/arti cles/PMC3181316> (last accessed 23 May 2020).

Broadwell, George Aaron, 'Reconstructing Proto-Muskogean language and prehistory: preliminary results', <http://citeseerx.ist.psu.edu/viewdoc/download?doi=10. 1.1.72.4700&rep=rep1&type=pdf> (last accessed 2 June 2020).

Brown, Cecil H. and Stanley R. Witkowski, 'Aspects of the phonological history of Mayan-Zoquean', *International Journal of American Linguistics* 45 (1979), 34–47.

Bybee, Joan, *Language Change* (Cambridge: Cambridge University Press, 2015).

Bynon, Theodora, *Historical Linguistics* (Cambridge: Cambridge University Press, 1977).

Callaghan, Catherine A., *Proto Utian Grammar and Dictionary with Notes on Yokuts* (Berlin: Mouton de Gruyter, 2014).

Callaghan, Catherine A. and Geoffrey Gamble, 'Borrowing', in Ives Goddard (ed.), *Handbook of North American Indians*, vol. 17 (Washington, DC: Smithsonian Institution, 1997), pp. 111–16.

Campbell, Lyle, 'Language contact and sound change', in William M. Christie Jr (ed.), *Current Progress on Historical Linguistics: Proceedings of the Second International Conference on Historical Linguistics* (Amsterdam: North-Holland, 1976), pp. 111–94.

Campbell, Lyle, *Quichean Linguistic Prehistory*, University of California Publications in Linguistics, 81 (Berkeley and Los Angeles: University of California Press, 1977).

Campbell, Lyle, 'The implications of Mayan historical linguistics for glyphic research', in John Justeson and Lyle Campbell (eds), *Phoneticism in Mayan Hieroglyphic Writing*, Institute for Mesoamerican Studies, Pub. 9 (Albany: State University of New York, Institute for Mesoamerican Studies, 1984), pp. 1–16.

Campbell, Lyle, 'Areal linguistics and its implications for historical linguistic theory', in Jacek Fisiak (ed.), *Proceedings of the Sixth International Conference of Historical Linguistics* (Amsterdam: John Benjamins, 1985), pp. 25–48.

Campbell, Lyle, *The Linguistics of Southeast Chiapas*, Papers of the New World Archaeological Foundation, 51 (Provo: New World Archaeological Foundation, 1988a).

Campbell, Lyle, 'Review article on *Language in the Americas*', *Language* 64 (1988b), 591–615.

Campbell, Lyle, 'Syntactic reconstruction and Finno-Ugric', in Henning Andersen and Konrad Koerner (eds), *Historical Linguistics 1987* (Amsterdam: John Benjamins, 1990), pp. 51–94.

Campbell, Lyle, 'Some grammaticalization changes in Estonian', in Elizabeth C. Traugott and Bernd Heine (eds), *Approaches to Grammaticalization, vol. I: Theoretical and Methodological Issues* (Amsterdam: John Benjamins, 1991), pp. 285–99.

Campbell, Lyle, 'On sound change and challenges to regularity', in Mark Durie and Malcolm Ross (eds), *The Comparative Method Reviewed: Regularity and Irregularity in Language Change* (Oxford: Oxford University Press, 1996), pp. 72–89.

Campbell, Lyle, *American Indian Languages: The Historical Linguistics of Native America* (Oxford: Oxford University Press, 1997a).

Campbell, Lyle, 'On the linguistic prehistory of Finno-Ugric', in Raymond Hickey and

Stanislaw Puppel (eds), *Language History and Linguistic Modelling: A Festschrift for Jacek Fisiak on his 60th Birthday* (Berlin: Mouton de Gruyter, 1997b), pp. 829–61.

Campbell, Lyle, 'Nostratic: a personal assessment', in Brian Joseph and Joe Salmons (eds), *Nostratic: Sifting the Evidence* (Amsterdam: John Benjamins, 1998), pp. 107–52.

Campbell, Lyle, 'Nostratic and linguistic palaeontology in methodological perspective', in Colin Renfrew and Daniel Nettle (eds), *Nostratic: Evaluating a Linguistic Macrofamily* (Cambridge: McDonald Institute for Archaeological Research, 1999), pp. 179–230.

Campbell, Lyle (ed.), *Grammaticalization: A Critical Assessment*, special issue of *Language Sciences* 23:2–3 (2001).

Campbell, Lyle, 'Review of *The Dene–Yeniseian Connection* ed. by Kari, James and Ben A. Potter', *International Journal of American Linguistics* 77 (2011), 445–51.

Campbell, Lyle, *Historical Linguistics: An Introduction*, 3rd edn (Edinburgh: Edinburgh University Press, and Cambridge, MA: MIT Press, 2013).

Campbell, Lyle, 'Comparative linguistics of Mesoamerican languages today', in Joaquín Gorrochategui, Carlos García Castillero, and José M. Vallejo (eds), *Franz Bopp and his Comparative Grammar Model (1816–2016)*, special issue of *VELEIA* 33 (2016), 113–34.

Campbell, Lyle, 'Language isolates and their history', in Lyle Campbell (ed.), *Language Isolates* (Abingdon and New York: Routledge, 2018a), 1–18.

Campbell, Lyle, 'How many language families are there in the world?', in Joseba A. Lakarra and Blanca Urgell (eds), *Homenaje a Joaquín Gorrochategui, Anuario del Seminario de Filología Vasca 'Julio de Urquijo'* 52 (2018b), 133–52.

Campbell, Lyle and Anna Belew (eds), *Cataloguing of Endangered Languages* (London: Routledge, 2018).

Campbell, Lyle and Verónica Grondona, 'Who speaks what to whom? Multilingualism and language choice in Misión La Paz – a unique case', *Language in Society* 39 (2010), 1–30.

Campbell, Lyle and Terrence Kaufman, 'A linguistic look at the Olmecs', *American Antiquity* 41 (1976), 80–9.

Campbell, Lyle and Terrence Kaufman, 'Mayan linguistics: where are we now?', *Annual Review of Anthropology* 14 (1985), 187–98.

Campbell, Lyle, Terrence Kaufman, and Thomas Smith-Stark, 'Mesoamerica as a linguistic area', *Language* 62 (1986), 530–70.

Campbell, Lyle and Ronald Langacker, 'Proto-Aztecan vowels', parts 1–3, *International Journal of American Linguistics* 44:2 (1978), 85–102, 44:3 (1978), 197–210, 44:4 (1978), 262–79.

Campbell, Lyle and Mauricio Mixco, *Glossary of Historical Linguistics* (Edinburgh: Edinburgh University Press, and Salt Lake City: University of Utah Press, 2007).

Campbell, Lyle and Martha Muntzel, 'The structural consequences of language death', in Nancy Dorian (ed.), *Investigating Obsolescence: Studies in Language Death*, Studies in the Social and Cultural Foundations of Language 7 (Cambridge: Cambridge University Press, 1989), pp. 181–96.

Campbell, Lyle and David Oltrogge, 'Proto-Tol (Jicaque)', *International Journal of American Linguistics* 46 (1980), 205–23.

Campbell, Lyle and William J. Poser, *Language Classification: History and Method* (Cambridge: Cambridge University Press, 2008).

Canfield, Lincoln D., *Spanish Pronunciation in the Americas* (Chicago: University of Chicago Press, 1982).

Carpelan, Christian, 'Late palaeolithic and Mesolithic settlement of the European north: possible linguistic implications', in Christian Carpelan, Asko Parpola, and Petteri Koskikallio (eds), *Early Contacts between Uralic and Indo-European: Linguistic and Archaeological Considerations*, Mémoires de la Société Finno-Ougrienne 242 (Helsinki: Finno-Ugrian Society, 2001), pp. 37–53.

Cavna, Michael, 'Quote of the week: Persepolis's Marjane Satrapi, on the profound power of words', *Washington Post* 28 April 2012.

Cerrón-Palomino, Rodolfo, *Lingüística quechua*, Biblioteca de la tradición oral andina, 8 (Cuzco: Centro de Estudios Rurales Andinos 'Bartolomé de las Casas', 1987).

Cerrón-Palomino, Rodolfo, *Lingüística aimara* (Cuzco: Centro de Estudios Regionales Aninos 'Bartolomé de Las Casas', 2000).

Chang, Will, Chundra Cathcart, David Hall, and Andrew Garrett, 'Ancestry-constrained phylogenetic analysis supports the Indo-European steppe hypothesis', *Language* 91 (2015), 194–244.

Clackson, James, *Indo-European Linguistics: An Introduction* (Cambridge: Cambridge University Press, 2007).

Coleridge, Samuel Taylor, *Biographia Literaria, or Biographical Sketches of My Literary Life and Opinions* (London: S. Curtis, 1817).

Collinge, N. E., *The Laws of Indo-European* (Amsterdam: John Benjamins, 1985).

Constenla Umaña, Adolfo, 'Chibchan languages', in Lyle Campbell and Verónica Grondona (eds), *The Indigenous Languages of South America: A Comprehensive Guide* (Berlin: Mouton de Gruyter, 2012), pp. 391–440.

Covington, Michael A., 'An algorithm to align words for historical comparison', *Computational Linguistics* 22 (1996), 481–96.

Croft, William, *Explaining Language Change: An Evolutionary Approach* (Harlow: Longman, 2000).

Crowley, Terry and Claire Bowern, *An Introduction to Historical Linguistics*, 4th edn (Auckland: Oxford University Press, 2010).

Curnow, Timothy J. and Anthony J. Liddicoat, 'The Barbacoan languages of Colombia and Ecuador', *Anthropological Linguistics* 40 (1998), 384–408.

Cysouw, Michael and Hagen Jung, 'Cognate identification and alignment using practical orthographies', *Proceedings of Ninth Meeting of the ACL Special Interest Group in Computational Morphology and Phonology* (Prague: Association for Computational Linguistics, 2007), pp. 109–16.

Dahl, Östen and Maria Koptjevskaja-Tamm (eds), *The Circum-Baltic Languages: Typology and Contact* (Amsterdam: John Benjamins, 2001).

Darmesteter, Arsène, *A Historical French Grammar* (London: Macmillan, 1922).

Darwin, Charles, *On the Origin of Species by Means of Natural Selection, or, The Preservation of Favoured Races in the Struggle for Life* (London: J. Murray, 1859).

DeCamp, David, 'The development of pidgin and creole studies', in Albert Valdman (ed.), *Pidgin and Creole Linguistics* (Bloomington: Indiana University Press, 1977), pp. 3–20.

Dolgopolsky, Aaron, 'A probabilistic hypothesis concerning the oldest relationships among the language families', in Vitaly V. Shevoroshkin and Thomas L. Markey (eds), *Typology, Relationship and Time: A Collection of Papers on Language Change and Relationship by Soviet Linguists* (Ann Arbor: Karoma, 1986), pp. 27–50 [English trans. of Aaron Dolgopolsky, 'Gipoteza drevnejsego rodstva jazykovyx semej Severnoj Evraziji s verojatnostnoj tochki zrenija', *Voprosy Jazykoznanija* 2 (1964), 53–63].

Donohue, Mark, Tim Denham, and Stephen Oppenheimer, 'New methodologies for historical linguistics? Calibrating a lexicon-based methodology for diffusion vs. sub-grouping', *Diachronica* 29 (2012), 505–22.

Donohue, Mark and Simon Musgrave, 'Typology and the linguistic macrohistory of Island Melanesia', *Oceanic Linguistics* 46 (2007), 348–87.

Dunn, Michael, Stephen C. Levinson, and Eva Lindström, 'Structural phylogeny in historical linguistics: methodological explorations applied in island Melanesia', *Language* 84 (2008), 710–59.

Dunn, Michael, Angela Terrrill, Ger Reesink, Robert A. Foley, and Stephen C. Levinson, 'Structural phylogenetics and the reconstruction of ancient language history', *Science* 309 (2005), 2072–5.

Dyen, Isidore, *A Lexicostatistical Classification of Austronesian Languages*, International Journal of American Linguistics Memoir 19 (Bloomington: University of Indiana, 1965).

Dyen, Isidore, Joseph B. Kruskal, and Paul Black, *An Indo-European Classification: A Lexicostatistical Experiment*, Transactions of the American Philosophical Society 82, part 5 (Philadelphia: American Philosophical Society, 1992).

Ebert, Robert Peter, *Historische Syntax des Deutschen* (Stuttgart: Sammlung Metzler, 1978).

Ellison, T. Mark, 'Bayesian identification of cognates and correspondences', *Proceedings of Ninth Meeting of the ACL Special Interest Group in Computational Morphology and Phonology* (Stroudsburg, PA: Association for Computational Linguistics, 2007), 15–22.

Ellison, T. Mark and Simon Kirby, 'Measuring language divergence by intralexical comparison', *Proceedings of the 21st International Conference on Computational Linguistics and the 44th Annual Meeting of the Association for Computational Linguistics, Sydney, Australia* (Stroudsburg, PA: Association for Computational Linguistics, 2006), pp. 273–80.

Embleton, Sheila, *Statistics in Historical Linguistics* (Bochum: Brockmeyer, 1986).

Emeneau, Murray B., *Language and Linguistic Area: Essays by Murray B. Emeneau*, selected and introduced by Anwar S. Dil (Stanford: Stanford University Press, 1980).

Farmer, Steve, Richard Sproat, and Michael Witzel, 'The collapse of the Indus-script thesis: the myth of a literate Harappan civilization', *Electronic Journal of Vedic Studies* 11 (2004), 19–57.

Ferguson, Charles, 'The Ethiopian language area', in M. L. Bender, J. D. Bowen, R. L. Cooper, and C. A. Ferguson (eds), *Language in Ethiopia* (Oxford: Oxford University Press, 1976), pp. 63–76.

Fisher, John H. and Diane Bornstein, *In form of speche is chaunge: Readings in the History of the English Language* (Englewood Cliffs: Prentice Hall, 1974).

Fleischman, Suzanne, 'The Romance languages', in William Bright (ed.), *International Encyclopedia of Linguistics*, 4 vols (Oxford: Oxford University Press, 1992), vol. 3, pp. 337–43.

Fleming, Harold C., 'Towards a definitive classification of the world's languages' [review of *A Guide to the World's Languages* by Merritt Ruhlen], *Diachronica* 4 (1987), 159–223.

Fogelberg, Paul (ed.), *Pohjan poluilla: Suomalaisten juuret nykytutkimuksen mukaan* [On paths of the north: the roots of the Finns according to current research], Bildrag till kännedom av Finlands natur och folk 153 (Helsinki: Finnish Society of Science and Letters, 1999).

Forster, Peter and Alfred Toth, 'Toward a phylogenetic chronology of ancient Gaulish, Celtic, and Indo-European', *Proceedings of the National Academy of Sciences* 100 (2003), 9079–84.

Fortson, Benjamin W., IV, *Indo-European Language and Culture: An Introduction* (Oxford: Wiley-Blackwell, 2004).

Fowler, Catherine S., 'Some ecological clues to Proto-Numic homelands', in D. D. Fowler (ed.), *Great Basin Cultural Ecology: A Symposium*, Desert Research Institute Publications in the Social Sciences, 8 (Reno: University of Nevada, 1972), pp. 105–21.

Fowler, Catherine S., 'Some lexical clues to Uto-Aztecan prehistory', *International Journal of American Linguistics* 49 (1983), 224–57.

Friedrich, Paul, *Proto-Indo-European Trees: The Arboreal System of a Prehistoric People* (Chicago: University of Chicago Press, 1970).

Friedrich, Paul, 'Dialectal variation in Tarascan phonology', *International Journal of American Linguistics* 37 (1971), 164–87.

Gabelentz, Georg von der, *Die Sprachwissenschaft: ihre Aufgaben, Methoden, und bisherigen Ergebnisse* (Leipzig: T. O. Weigel Nachfolger, 1891).

Gardner, Alan, *Egyptian Grammar: Being an Introduction to the Study of Hieroglyphs*, 3rd edn (Oxford: Griffith Institute, 1957).

Garrett, Andrew, 'A new model of Indo-European subgrouping and dispersal', in Steve S. Chang, Lily Liaw, and Josef Ruppenhofer (eds), *Proceedings of the Twenty-Fifth Annual Meeting of the Berkeley Linguistics Society* (Berkeley: Berkeley Linguistics Society, 1999), pp. 146–56.

Gildea, Spike, 'The development of tense markers from demonstrative pronouns in Panare (Cariban)', *Studies in Language* 17 (1993), 53–73.

Gildea, Spike, *On Reconstructing Grammar: Comparative Cariban Morphosyntax* (Oxford: Oxford University Press, 1998).

Gilliéron, Jules, *Pathologie et thérapeutique verbales* (Paris: Champion, 1921).

Gilliéron, Jules and Mario Roques, *Étude de géographie linguistique* (Paris: Champion, 1912).

Gimbutas, Marija, 'The Indo-Europeans: archaeological problems', *American Anthropologist* 65 (1963), 815–36.

Goddard, Ives, 'Review of *Language in the Americas* by Joseph H. Greenberg', *Current Anthropology* 28 (1987), 656–7.

Goddard, Ives, 'The West-to-East cline in Algonquian dialectology', in William Cowan (ed.), *Actes du vingt-cinquième congrès des algonquinistes* (Ottawa: Carleton University, 1994), pp. 187–211.

Goebl, Hans, 'Recent advances in Salzburg dialectometry', *Literary and Linguistics Computing* 21 (2006), 411–35.

Gordon, Elizabeth, Lyle Campbell, Jennifer Hay, Margaret Maclagan, Andrea Sudbury, and Peter Trudgill, *New Zealand English: Its Origins and Evolution* (Cambridge: Cambridge University Press, 2004).

Gorrochategui, Joaquín and Joseba Lakara, 'Nuevas aportaciones a la reconstruccíon del protovasco', in Francisco Villar and José d'Encarnação (eds), *La Hispania prerromana: Actas del VI Coloquio sobre lenguas y culturas de la Península Ibérica* (Salamanca: Ediciones Universidad de Salamanca, 1996), pp. 101–45.

Gorrochategui, Joaquín and Joseba Lakara, 'Comparación lingüística, filología y reconstrucción del protovasco', in Francisco Villar and José d'Encarnação (eds), *Religión, lengua y cultura prerromanas de Hispania: Actas del VIII Coloquio sobre lenguas y culturas de la Penísula Ibérica* (Salamanca: Ediciones Universidad de Salamanca, 2001), 407–38.

Gould, Stephen Jay and Elisabeth S. Vrba, 'Exaptation: a missing term in the science of form', *Paleobiology* 8 (1982), 4–15.

Gray, Russell D. and Quentin D. Atkinson, 'Language-tree divergence times support the Anatolian theory of Indo-European origin', *Nature* 426 (2003), 435–9.

Gray, Russell D., Quentin D. Atkinson, and Simon J. Greenhill, 'Language evolution and human history: what a difference a date makes', *Philosophical Transactions of the Royal Society B*, 366 (2011), 1090–100.

Gray, Russell D., A. J. Drummond, and Simon J. Greenhill, 'Language phylogenies reveal expansion pulses and pauses in Pacific settlement', *Science* 323 (2009), 479–83.

Gray, Russell D. and F. M. Jordan, 'Language trees support the express-train sequence of Austronesian expansion', *Nature* 405 (2000), 1052–5.

Greenberg, Joseph H., *Languages of Africa*, Publications of the Research Center in Anthropology, Folklore, and Linguistics, 25 (Bloomington: Indiana University Press, 1963).

Greenberg, Joseph H., 'The Indo-Pacific hypothesis', in Thomas A. Sebeok (ed.), *Current Trends in Linguistics 8: Linguistics in Oceania* (The Hague: Mouton, 1971), pp. 807–71.

Greenberg, Joseph H., *Language in the Americas* (Stanford: Stanford University Press, 1987).

Greenberg, Joseph H., *Indo-European and its Closest Relatives: The Eurasiatic Language Family* (Stanford: Stanford University Press, 2000).

Greenberg, Joseph H. and Merritt Ruhlen, 'Linguistic origins of Native Americans', *Scientific American* 267 (1992), 60–5.

Greenhill, Simon J., 'Levenshtein distances fail to identify language relationships accurately', *Computational Linguistics* 37 (2011), 689–98.

Greenhill Simon J., Quentin D. Atkinson, Andrew Meade, and Russell D. Gray, 'The shape and tempo of language evolution', *Proceedings of the Royal Society, B* 277 (2010), 2443–50.

Greenhill, Simon J., Robert Blust, and Russell Gray, 'The Austronesian Basic Vocabulary Database: from bioinformatics to lexomics', *Evolutionary Bioinformatics* 4 (2008), 271–83.

Greenhill, Simon J., T. E. Currie, and Russell Gray, 'Does horizontal transmission invalidate cultural phylogenies?', *Proceedings of the Royal Society B* 276 (2009), 2299–306.

Greenhill, Simon J., A. J. Drummond, and Russell D. Gray, 'How accurate and robust are the phylogenetic estimates of Austronesian language relationships?', *PLoS ONE*, 5.3:e9573 (2010).

Greenhill, Simon J. and Russell D. Gray, 'Testing population dispersal hypotheses: Pacific settlement, phylogenetic trees and Austronesian languages', in R. Mace, C. J. Holden, and S. Shennan (eds), *The Evolution of Cultural Diversity: Phylogenetic Approaches* (London: University College London Press, 2005), pp. 31–52.

Grimm, Jakob and Wilhelm Grimm, *Deutsches Wörterbuch* (Leipzig: Hirzel, 1854).

Grünthal, Riho and Tapani Salminen (eds), *Geographical Distribution of the Uralic Languages* [map] (Helsinki: Finno-Ugrian Society, 1993).

Haas, Mary R., *The Prehistory of Languages* (The Hague: Mouton, 1969a).

Haas, Mary R., 'Internal reconstruction of the Nootka-Nitinat pronominal suffixes', *International Journal of American Linguistics* 35 (1969b), 108–24.

Hajdú, Péter, 'Finnougrische Urheimatforschung', *Ural-Altaische Jahrbücher* 41 (1969), 252–64.

Hajdú, Péter, *Finno-Ugric Languages and Peoples* (London: André Deutsch, 1975).

Häkkinen, Kaisa, 'Wäre es schon an der Zeit, den Stammbaum zu fallen? Theorien über die gegenseitigen Verwandtschaftsbeziehungen der finnisch-ugrischen Sprachen', *Ural-Altaische Jahrbücher* 4 (1984), 1–4.

Häkkinen, Kaisa, 'Prehistoric Finno-Ugric culture in the light of historical lexicology', in Christian Carpelan, Asko Parpola, and Petteri Koskikallio (eds), *Early Contacts between Uralic and Indo-European: Linguistic and Archaeological Considerations*, Mémoires de la Société Finno-Ougrienne 242 (Helsinki: Finno-Ugrian Society, 2001), pp. 169–86.

Hancock, Ian, 'On Romani origins and identity', Romani Archives and Documentation Center, University of Texas, Austin (2006), <https://www.oocities.org/romani_life_society/indexpics/HistoryOrigins.pdf> (last accessed 20 May 2020).

Harris, Alice C., 'Reconstruction in syntax: reconstruction of patterns', in Gisella Ferraresi and Maria Goldbach (eds), *Principles of Syntactic Reconstruction* (Amsterdam: John Benjamins, 2008), pp. 73–95.

Harris, Alice C. and Lyle Campbell, *Historical Syntax in Cross-Linguistic Perspective* (Cambridge: Cambridge University Press, 1995).

Haspelmath, Martin and Uri Tadmor, *Loanwords in the World's Languages: A Comparative Handbook* (Berlin: Mouton de Gruyter, 2009).

Heeringa, Wilbert, John Nerbonne, and Peter Kleiweg, 'Validating dialect comparison methods', in W. Gaul and G. Ritter (eds), *Classification, Automation, and New Media* (Berlin, Heidelberg, and New York: Springer, 2002), pp. 445–52.

Heggarty, Paul, 'Interdisciplinary indiscipline? Can phylogenetic methods meaningfully be applied to language data – and to dating language?', in Peter Forster and Colin Renfrew (eds), *Phylogenetic Methods and the Prehistory of Languages* (Cambridge: McDonald Institute for Archaeological Research, 2006), pp. 183–94.

Heggarty, Paul, 'Beyond lexicostatistics: how to get more out of "word list" comparisons', *Diachronica* 7 (2010), 301–24.

Heggarty, Paul, Warren Maguire, and April McMahon, 'Splits or waves? Trees or webs? How divergent measures and network analysis can unravel language histories', *Philosophical Transactions of the Royal Society B* 365 (2010), 3829–43.

Heine, Bernd, 'Grammaticalization', in Brian D. Joseph and Richard D. Janda (eds), *The Handbook of Historical Linguistics* (Oxford: Blackwell, 2003), pp. 575–601.

Heine, Bernd and Mechthild Reh, *Grammaticalisation and Reanalysis in African Languages* (Hamburg: Buske, 1984).

Hernández-Campoy, Juan M. and J. Camilo Conde-Silvestre (eds), *The Handbook of Historical Sociolinguistics* (Oxford: Wiley-Blackwell, 2014).

Hickey, Raymond, 'Models for describing aspect in Irish English', in Hildegard Tristram (ed.), *The Celtic Englishes II* (Heidelberg: Winter, 2000), pp. 97–116.

Hock, Hans Henrich, *Principles of Historical Linguistics* (Berlin: Mouton de Gruyter, 1986).

Hock, Hans Henrich and Brian D. Joseph, *Language History, Language Change, and Language*

Relationship: An Introduction to Historical and Comparative Linguistic, 2nd edn (Berlin: Walter de Gruyter, 2009).

Hogg, Richard M., 'Phonology and morphology', in Richard M. Hogg (ed.), *The Cambridge History of the English Language, vol. 1: The Beginnings to 1066* (Cambridge: Cambridge University Press, 1992), pp. 67–167.

Holden, Clare J., 'Bantu language trees reflect the spread of farming across sub-Saharan Africa: a maximum-parsimony analysis', *Proceedings of the Royal Society B* 269 (2002), 793–9.

Holman, Eric W., Cecil H. Brown, Søren Wichmann, André Müller, Viveka Velupillai, Harald Hammarström, Sebastian Sauppe, Hagen Jung, Dik Bakker, Pamela Brown, Oleg Belyaev, Matthias Urban, Robert Mailhammer, Johann-Mattis List, and Dmitry Egorov, 'Automated dating of the world's language families based on lexical similarity', *Current Anthropology* 52 (2011), 841–75.

Hopper, Paul J. and Elizabeth Closs Traugott, *Grammaticalization*, 2nd edn (Cambridge: Cambridge University Press, 2003).

Horrocks, Geoffrey, *Greek: A History of the Language and its Speakers*, 2nd edn (Oxford: Wiley-Blackwell, 2014).

Hymes, Dell H., 'Lexicostatistics so far', *Current Anthropology* 1 (1960), 3–44.

Igla, Birgit, 'Romani', in Hans Goebl, Peter H. Nelde, Zdenek Stary, and Wolfgang Wölck (eds), *Contact Linguistics: An International Handbook of Contemporary Research* 14 (Berlin: Mouton de Gruyter, 1997), pp. 1961–71.

Ihalainen, Ossi, 'The dialects of England since 1776', in Robert Burchfield (ed.), *The Cambridge History of the English Language, vol. 5: English in Britain and Overseas: Origins and Development* (Cambridge: Cambridge University Press, 1994), pp. 197–274.

Ilari, Rodolfo, *Lingüística Românica*, 3rd edn (São Paulo: Editora Ática, 2001).

Illich-Svitych, Vladislav M., 'The Nostratic reconstructions of V. Illich-Svitych, translated and arranged by Mark Kaiser', in Vitaly Shevoroshkin (ed.), *Proto-Languages and Proto-Cultures: Materials from the First* (Bochum: Brockmeyer, 1990), pp. 138–67.

Jakobson, Roman, 'Why "Manchu" and "papa"?', in Bernard Kaplan and Seymour Wapner (eds), *Perspectives in Psychological Theory* (New York: International Universities Press, 1960), pp. 21–9 [reprinted: *Roman Jakobson: Selected Writings*, vol. 1: *Phonological Studies* (The Hague: Mouton, 1962), pp. 538–45]).

Janhunen, Juha, 'Uralilaisen kantakielen sanastosta' [On the vocabulary of the Uralic proto-language], *Journal de la Société Finno-Ougrienne* 77 (1981), 219–74.

Janhunen, Juha, 'On the structure of Proto-Uralic', *Finno-Ugrische Forschungen* 44 (1982), 23–42.

Janhunen, Juha, 'On the paradigms of Uralic comparative studies', *Finno-Ugrische Forschungen* 56 (2001), 29–41.

Janson, Tore, *Speak: A Short History of Languages* (Oxford: Oxford University Press, 2002).

Jasanoff, Jay H., *Hittite and the Indo-European Verb* (Oxford: Oxford University Press, 2003).

Jeffers, Robert J. and Ilse Lehiste, *Principles and Methods for Historical Linguistics* (Cambridge, MA: MIT Press, 1979).

Jespersen, Otto, *Language, its Nature, Development, and Origin* (New York: W. W. Norton, 1964).

Joki, Aulis J., *Uralier und Indogermanen*, Suomalais-ugrilaisen Seuran toimituksia 151 (Helsinki: Suomalais-ugrilaisen Seura, 1973).

Joseph, Brian, *Morphology and Universals in Syntactic Change: Evidence from Medieval and Modern Greek* (New York: Garland Publishers, 1990).

Joseph, Brian, 'Balkan languages', in William Bright (ed.), *International Encyclopedia of Linguistics*, 4 vols (Oxford: Oxford University Press, 1992), vol. 1, pp. 153–5.

Joseph, Brian D. and Richard D. Janda (eds), *The Handbook of Historical Linguistics* (Oxford: Blackwell, 2003).

Justeson, John S., William Norman, Lyle Campbell, and Terrence Kaufman, *The Foreign Impact on Lowland Mayan Languages and Script*, Middle American Research Institute 53 (New Orleans: Tulane University, 1985).

Kaiser, Mark and Vitaly Shevoroshkin, 'Nostratic', *Annual Review of Anthropology* 17 (1988), 309–30.

Kaufman, Terrence, 'Gypsy wanderings and linguistic borrowing', unpublished paper (University of Pittsburgh, 1973).

Kaufman, Terrence, 'Archaeological and linguistic correlations in Mayaland and associated areas of Meso-America', *World Archaeology* 8 (1976), 101–18.

Kaufman, Terrence (with the assistance of John Justeson), *A Preliminary Proto-Mayan Etymological Dictionary*, <www.famsi.org/reports/01051/pmed.pdf, 2003> (last accessed 20 May 2020).

Kessler, Brent, *The Significance of Word Lists* (Stanford: CSLI Publications, 2001).

Kettunen, Lauri, *Suomen murteet II: Murrealueet* [Finnish dialects II: dialect areas] (Helsinki: Suomalaisen Kirjallisuuden Seura, 1930).

Kettunen, Lauri, *Suomen murteet III: Murrekartasto* [Finnish dialects III: dialect atlas], 3rd 'abridged' edn (Helsinki: Suomalaisen Kirjallisuuden Seura, 1969).

Kimball, Geoffrey, 'A critique of Muskogean, "Gulf", and Yukian material in *Language in the Americas*', *International Journal of American Linguistics* 58 (1992), 447–501.

Kiparsky, Paul, *Explanation in Phonology* (Dordrecht: Foris, 1982).

Klima, Edward, 'Relatedness between grammatical systems', *Language* 40 (1964), 1–20.

Koch, Harold, 'Pama-Nyungan reflexes in the Arandic languages', in Darrell Tryon and Michael Walsh (eds), *Boundary Rider: Essays in Honour of Geoffrey O'Grady*, Pacific Linguistics C-136 (Canberra: Research School of Pacific Studies, Australian National University, 1997), pp. 271–301.

Koivulehto, Jorma, 'The earliest contacts between Indo-European and Uralic speakers in the light of lexical loans', in Christian Carpelan, Asko Parpola, and Petteri Koskikallio (eds), *Early Contacts between Uralic and Indo-European: Linguistic and Archaeological Considerations*, Mémoires de la Société Finno-Ougrienne 242 (Helsinki: Finno-Ugrian Society, 2001), pp. 235–63.

Kondrak, Grzegorz, 'Identifying cognates by phonetic and semantic similarity', in *Proceedings of the Second Meeting of the North American Chapter of the Association for Computational Linguistics (NAACL-2001)* (Pittsburgh: Association for Computational Linguistics, 2001), pp. 103–10.

Kondrak, Grzegorz, *Algorithms for Language Reconstruction* (University of Toronto, PhD dissertation, 2002).

Kondrak, Grzegorz, David Beck, and Philip Dilts, 'Creating a comparative dictionary of Totonac-Tepehua', in *Proceedings of Ninth Meeting of the ACL Special Interest Group in Computational Morphology and Phonology* (Prague: Association for Computational Linguistics, 2007), pp. 134–41.

Koptjevskaja-Tamm, Maria and Bernhard Wälchli, 'The Circum-Baltic languages: an areal-typological approach', in Östen Dahl and Maria Koptjevskaja-Tamm (eds), *The Circum-Baltic Languages: Typology and Contact* (Amsterdam: John Benjamins, 2001), pp. 615–761.

Korhonen, Mikko, 'Suomalaisten suomalais-ugrilainen tausta historiallisvertailevan kielitieteen valossa' [The Finno-Ugric background of the Finns in the light of comparative-historical linguistics], in Jarl Gallén (ed.), *Suomen väestön esihistorialliset juuret*, Bidrag till kännedom av Finlands natur och folk, Utgivna av Finska Vetenskaps-Societeten 131 (Helsinki: Finska Vetenskaps-Societeten, 1984), pp. 55–71.

Krause, Wolfgang, *Handbuch des Gotischen*, 3rd edn (Munich: Beck, 1968).

Kroeber, Paul D., *The Salish Language Family: Reconstructing Syntax* (Lincoln: University of Nebraska Press, 1999).

Kuhn, Franz Felix Adalbert, *Zur* ältesten *Geschichte der indogermanischen Völker* (Berlin: Berliner Real-Gymnasium, 1845).

Kuryłowicz, Jerzy, 'Zur Vorgeschichte des germanischen Verbalsystems', in *Beiträge zur Sprachwissenschaft, Volkskunde und Literaturforschung: Wolfgang Steinitz zum 60. Geburtstag* (Berlin: Akademie-Verlag, 1965), pp. 242–7.

Kuteva, Tania, Bernd Heine, Bo Hong, Haiping Long, Heiko Narrog, and Seongha Rhee, *World Lexicon of Grammaticalization*, 2nd edn (Cambridge: Cambridge University Press, 2019).

Laanest, Arvo, *Einführung in die ostseefinnischen Sprachen* (Hamburg: Buske, 1982).

Labov, William (ed.), *Locating Language in Time and Space* (New York: Academic Press, 1980).

Labov, William, *Principles of Linguistic Change: Internal Factors* (Oxford: Blackwell, 1994, 2001).

Labov, William, *Principles of Linguistic Change: Cognitive and Cultural Factors* (Oxford: Wiley-Blackwell, 2010).

Labov, William, 'The regularity of regular sound change', *Language* 96 (2020), 42–59.

Labov, William, Sharon Ash, and Charles Boberg, *The Atlas of North American English* (Berlin: Mouton de Gruyter, 2006).

Lakarra, Joseba A., 'Reconstructing the pre-Proto-Basque root', in José Ignacio Hualde, Joseba A. Lakarra, and R. L. Trask (eds), *Towards a History of the Basque Language* (Amsterdam: John Benjamins, 1995), pp. 189–206.

Lapesa, Rafael, *Historia de la lengua española*, 9th edn (Madrid: Gredos, 1981).

Lass, Roger, *On Explaining Language Change* (Cambridge: Cambridge University Press, 1980).

Lass, Roger, 'Phonology and morphology', in Norman Blake (ed.), *The Cambridge History of the English Language, vol. 2: 1066–1476* (Cambridge: Cambridge University Press, 1992), pp. 23–155.

Lass, Roger, *Historical Linguistics and Language Change* (Cambridge: Cambridge University Press, 1997).

Lees, Robert B., 'The basis of glottochronology', *Language* 29 (1953), 113–27.

Lehmann, Walter, *Zentral-Amerika* (Berlin: Museum für Völkerkunde zu Berlin, 1920).

Lehmann, Winfred P., *Historical Linguistics: An Introduction* (New York: Holt, 1962).

Levinson, Stephen C. and Russell D. Gray, 'Tools from evolutionary biology shed new light on the diversification of languages', *Trends in Cognitive Sciences* 16 (2012), 167–73.

Lightfoot, David, *Principles of Diachronic Syntax* (Cambridge: Cambridge University Press, 1979).

Lightfoot, David, *How to Set Parameters: Arguments from Language Change* (Cambridge, MA: MIT Press, 1991).

Lohr, Marisa, *Methods for the Genetic Classification of Languages* (University of Cambridge, PhD dissertation, 1999).

Lord, Robert, *Comparative Linguistics*, 2nd edn (London: English Universities Press, 1974).

Mackay, Wesley and Grzegorz Kondrak, 'Computing word similarity and identifying cognates with Pair Hidden Markov Models', in *Proceedings of the 9th Conference on Computational Natural Language Learning (CoNLL)* (Morristown,: Association for Computational Linguistics, 2005), pp. 40–7.

Maclagan, Margaret A. and Elizabeth Gordon, 'Out of the AIR and into the EAR: another view of the New Zealand diphthong merger', *Language Variation and Change* 8 (1996), 125–47.

Maguire, Warren, Paul Heggarty, April McMahon, and Dan Dediu, 'The past, present and future of English dialects: quantifying convergence, divergence and dynamic equilibrium', *Language Variation and Change* 22 (2010), 69–104.

Maiden, Martin, *A Linguistic History of Italian* (London and New York: Longman, 1995).

Maiden, Martin, *The Romance Verb: Morphomic Structure and Diachrony* (Oxford: Oxford University Press, 2018).

Mallory, J. P., *In Search of the Indo-Europeans: Language, Archaeology, and Myth* (London: Thames and Hudson, 1989).

Mallory, J. P., 'Uralics and Indo-Europeans: problems of time and space', in Christian Carpelan, Asko Parpola, and Petteri Koskikallio (eds), *Early Contacts Between Uralic and Indo-European: Linguistic and Archaeological Considerations*, Mémoires de la Société Finno-Ougrienne 242 (Helsinki: Finno-Ugrian Society, 2001), pp. 345–66.

Mallory, J. P. and D. Q. Adams, *Encyclopedia of Indo-European Culture* (London: Fitzroy Dearborn, 1997).

Mallory, J. P. and D. Q. Adams, *The Oxford Introduction to Proto-Indo-European and the Proto-Indo-European World* (Oxford: Oxford University Press, 2006).

Martinet, André, *Économie des changements phonétiques: traité de phonologie diachronique*, 3rd edn (Berne: A. Francke, 1970) [1st edn: 1955].

Masica, Colin P., *The Indo-Aryan Languages* (Cambridge: Cambridge University Press, 1991).

Matras, Yaron, *Romani: A Linguistic Introduction* (Cambridge: Cambridge University Press, 2002).

McMahon, April, Paul Heggarty, Robert McMahon, and Warren Maguire, 'The sound patterns of Englishes: representing phonetic similarity', *English Language and Linguistics* 11 (2007), 113–42.

McMahon, April and Robert McMahon, 'Linguistics, genetics and archaeology: internal and external evidence in the Amerind controversy', *Transactions of the Philological Society* 93 (1995), 125–225.

McMahon, April and Robert McMahon, 'Finding families: quantitative methods in language classification', *Transactions of the Philological Society* 101 (2003), 7–55.

McMahon, April and Robert McMahon, *Language Classification by Numbers* (Oxford: Oxford University Press, 2005).

Meakins, Felicity, 'Mixed languages', in Peter Bakker and Yaron Matras (eds), *Contact Languages: A Comprehensive Guide* (Berlin: Mouton de Gruyter, 2013), pp. 159–228.

Meillet, Antoine, 'L'évolution des formes grammaticales', *Scientia* 12:26 (1912) [reprinted: *Linguistique historique et linguistique générale* (Paris: Champion, 1948), pp. 130–48]).

Meillet, Antoine, *La Méthode comparative en linguistique historique* (Oslo: H. Aschehoug, 1925a).

Meillet, Antoine, *The Comparative Method in Historical Linguistics* [English trans. of *La Méthode comparative en linguistique historique* (Oslo: H. Aschehoug, 1925b), reissued 1966] (Paris: Champion, 1967).

Meillet, Antoine, *Linguistique historique et linguistique générale*, Société Linguistique de Paris, Collection Linguistique 8 (Paris: Champion, 1948).

Membreño, Alberto, *Hondureñismos: vocabulario de los provincialismos de Honduras*, 2nd edn (Tegucigalpa: Tipografía Nacional, 1897).

Menner, Robert, 'The conflict of homonyms in English', *Language* 12 (1936), 229–44.

Metcalf, George J., 'The Indo-European hypothesis in the sixteenth and seventeenth centuries', in Dell Hymes (ed.), *Studies in the History of Linguistics: Traditions and Paradigms* (Bloomington: Indiana University Press, 1974), pp. 233–57.

Michelena [Mitxelena], Luis [Koldo], *Sobre historia de la lengua vasca*, ed. Joseba A. Lakarra, Suplementos del *Anuario del Seminario de Filología Vasca 'Julio de Urquijo'* 10, 2 vols (Donastia and San Sebastian: Diputación Foral de Guipúzcoa, 1988).

Michelena [Mitxelena], Luis [Koldo], 'The ancient Basque consonants', in José Ignacio Hualde, Joseba A. Lakarra, and R. L. Trask (eds), *Towards a History of the Basque Language* (Amsterdam: John Benjamins, 1995), pp. 101–35.

Millar, Robert McColl and Larry Trask, *Trask's Historical Linguistics* (London: Routledge, 2015) [2nd edn of R[ichard] L[arry] Trask, *Historical Linguistics* (London: Arnold, 1996)].

Milroy, James, *Linguistic Variation and Change: On the Historical Sociolinguistics of English* (Oxford: Blackwell, 1992).

Minis, Cola, 'Friedrich Maurer, Leid: Studien zur Bedeutungs- und Problemgeschichte, besonders in den großen Epen der staufischen Zeit (besprochen von Cola Minis)', *Euphorion* 46 (1952), 107–9.

Müller, Max, *Lectures on the Science of Language* (New York: Charles Scribner, 1866).

Müller, Max, *On the Philosophy of Mythology: Selected Essays* (London: Longmans, Green, 1871 [1811]).

Mutaka, Ngessimo N., *An Introduction to African Linguistics* (Munich: Lincom Europa, 2000).

Nakhleh, Luay, Don Ringe, and Tandy Warnow, 'Perfect phylogenetic networks: a new methodology for reconstructing the evolutionary history of natural languages', *Language* 81 (2005), 382–420.

Nakhleh, Luay, Tandy Warnow, Donald Ringe, and S. N. Evans, 'A comparison of phylogenetic reconstruction methods on an Indo-European dataset', *Transactions of the Philological Society* 103 (2005), 171–92.

Narrog, Heiko and Bernd Heine (eds), *The Oxford Handbook of Grammaticalization* (Oxford: Oxford University Press, 2011).

Nelson-Sathi, Shijulal, Johann-Mattis List, Hans Geisler, Heiner Fangerau, Russell D. Gray, William Marti, and Tal Dagan, 'Networks uncover hidden lexical borrowing in Indo-European language evolution', *Proceedings of the Royal Society B* 278 (2010), 1794–803.

Nerbonne, John and Wilbert Heeringa, 'Measuring dialect differences', in J. E. Schmidt and P. Auer (eds), *Language and Space: Theories and Methods* (Berlin: Mouton de Gruyter, 2009), pp. 550–67.

Newman, Paul, 'Comparative linguistics', in Bernd Heine and Derek Nurse, *African Languages: An Introduction* (Cambridge: Cambridge University Press, 2000), pp. 259–71.

Nichols, Johanna, 'The origins and dispersal of languages: linguistic evidence', in Nina Jablonski and Leslie Aiello (eds), *The Origin and Diversification of Language* (San Francisco: California Academy of Sciences, 1998), pp. 127–70.

Öhmann, Emil, 'Über Homonymie und Homonyme im Deutschen', *Suomalaisen Tiedeakatemian Toimituksia*, series B, 32 (1934), 1–143.

Olson, Ronald D., 'Mayan affinities with Chipaya of Bolivia I: Correspondences', *International Journal of American Linguistics* 30 (1964), 313–24.

Olson, Ronald D., 'Mayan affinities with Chipaya of Bolivia II: Cognates', *International Journal of American Linguistics* 31 (1965), 29–38.

Orton, Harold, Eugen Dieth, P. M. Tilling, and Wilfrid J. Halliday, *Survey of English Dialects*, 4 vols (Leeds: Arnold, 1962–71).

Osthoff, Hermann and Karl Brugmann, *Morphologische Untersuchungen auf dem Gebiete der indogermanischen Sprachen* (Leipzig: S. Hirzel, 1878).

Oswalt, Robert L., 'The detection of remote linguistic relationships', *Computer Studies in the Humanities and Verbal Behavior* 3 (1970), 117–29.

Otsuka, Yuko, 'History of the Polynesian languages', *Linguistics* 345 (2005), 267–96, <www.Otsuka/70a981f22679f5fb5a49214d574923a80971458d> (last accessed 20 May 2020).

Oxford English Dictionary, 2nd edn (Oxford: Oxford University Press, 1989) [1st edn: 1971].

Pagel, Mark, 'Maximum-likelihood models for glottochronology and for constructing linguistic phylogenies', in Colin Renfrew, April McMahon, and Larry Trask (eds), *Time Depth in Historical Linguistics* (Cambridge: McDonald Institute for Archaeological Research, 2000), pp. 189–207.

Pagel, Mark, Quentin D. Atkinson, and Andrew Meade, 'Frequency of word-use predicts rates of lexical evolution throughout Indo-European history', *Nature* 449 (2007), 717–20.

Palmer, Leonard R., *Descriptive and Comparative Linguistics: A Critical Introduction* (London: Faber & Faber, 1972).

Paul, Hermann, *Prinzipien der Sprachgeschichte*, 5th edn (Tübingen: Max Niemeyer, 1920) [1st edn: 1880].

Peitsara, Kirsti, 'On the development of the by-agent in English' in Matti Rissanen, Merja Kytö, and Minna Palander-Collin (eds), *Early English in the Computer Age: Explorations through the Helsinki Corpus* (Berlin: Mouton de Gruyter, 1993), pp. 219–33.

Pereltsvaig, Asya and Martin W. Lewis, *The Indo-European Controversy: Facts and Fallacies in Historical Linguistics Languages* (Cambridge: Cambridge University Press, 2015).

Pictet, Adolphe, *Les Origines indo-européennes, ou, les Aryas primitifs: essai de paléontologie linguistique* (Paris: J. Cherbuliez, 1859–63).

Polenz, Peter von, *Geschichte der deutschen Sprache* (Berlin: Walter de Gruyter, 1977).

Poplack, Shana, *Borrowing: Loanwords in the Speech Community and in the Grammar* (Oxford: Oxford University Press, 2018).

Poser, William J., 'The Salinan and Yurumangui data in *Language in the Americas*', *International Journal of American Linguistics* 58 (1992), 202–9.

Rankin, Robert L., 'Review of *Language in the Americas*, by Joseph H. Greenberg', *International Journal of American Linguistics* 58 (1992), 324–51.

Ravila, Paavo, 'Suomen suku ja suomen kansa' [The Finnish stock and the Finnish people], in Arvi Korhonen (ed.), *Suomen historian käsikirja I* [Handbook of the history of Finnish I] (Porvoo: Werner Söderström, 1949).

Ravila, Paavo, *Johtadus kielihistoriaan* [Introduction to language history] (Helsinki: Suomalaisen Kirjallisuuden Seura, 1966; 4th edn, 1975).

Rehg, Kenneth and Lyle Campbell (eds), *Handbook of Endangered Languages* (Oxford: Oxford University Press, 2018).

Rexova, K., D. Frynta, and J. Zrzavy, 'Cladistic analysis of languages: Indo-European classification based on lexicostatistical data', *Cladistics* 19 (2003), 120–7.

Ringe, Donald A., Jr, 'On calculating the factor of chance in language comparison', *Transactions of the American Philosophical Society* 82 (1992), 1–110.

Ringe, Donald A., Jr, 'The mathematics of "Amerind"', *Diachronica* 13 (1996), 135–54.

Ringe, Donald A., Jr, 'Probabilistic evidence for Indo-Uralic', in Brian Joseph and Joe Salmons (eds), *Nostratic: Sifting the Evidence* (Amsterdam: John Benjamins, 1998), pp. 153–97.

Ringe, Donald A., Jr, 'How hard is it to match CVC-roots?', *Transactions of the Philological Society* 97 (1999), 213–44.

Ringe, Donald A., Jr, 'Inheritance versus lexical borrowing: a case with decisive sound-change evidence', *Language Log* (2009), <https://languagelog.ldc.upenn.edu/nll/?p=1012> (last accessed 20 May 2020).

Ringe, Donald A., Jr, Tandy Warnow, and Ann Taylor, 'Indo-European computational cladistics', *Transactions of the Philological Society* 100 (2002), 59–129.

Rodrigues, Aryon Dall'Igna and Ana Suelly Arruda Câmara Cabral, 'Tupían', in Lyle Campbell and Verónica Grondona (eds), *The Indigenous Languages of South America: A Comprehensive Guide* (Berlin: Mouton de Gruyter, 2012), pp. 59–166.

Róna-Tas, András, 'Turkic influence on the Uralic languages', in Denis Sinor (ed.), *The Uralic Languages: Description, History, and Foreign Influences* (Leiden: Brill, 1988), pp. 742–80.

Ruhlen, Merritt, *On the Origin of Languages: Studies in Linguistic Taxonomy* (Stanford: Stanford University Press, 1994).

Salminen, Tapani, 'The rise of the Finno-Ugric language family', in Christian Carpelan, Asko Parpola, and Petteri Koskikallio (eds), *Early Contacts between Uralic and Indo-European: Linguistic and Archaeological Considerations*, Mémoires de la Société Finno-Ougrienne 242 (Helsinki: Finno-Ugrian Society, 2001), pp. 385–96.

Sammallahti, Pekka, 'Saamelaisten esihistoriallinen tausta kielitieteen valossa' [The prehistorical background of the Saami in the light of linguistics], in Jarl Gallén (ed.), *Suomen väestön esihistorialliset juuret*, Bidrag till kännedom av Finlands natur och folk, Utgivna av Finska Vetenskaps-Societeten 131 (Helsinki: Finska Vetenskaps-Societeten, 1984), pp. 137–56.

Sammallahti, Pekka, 'Historical phonology of the Uralic languages: with special reference to Samoyed, Ugric, and Permic', in Denis Sinor (ed.), *The Uralic Languages: Description, History, and Foreign Influences* (Leiden: Brill, 1988), pp. 478–554.

Sammallahti, Pekka, 'The Indo-European loanwords in Saami', in Christian Carpelan, Asko Parpola, and Petteri Koskikallio (eds), *Early Contacts between Uralic and Indo-European: Linguistic and Archaeological Considerations*, Mémoires de la Société Finno-Ougrienne 242 (Helsinki: Finno-Ugrian Society, 2001), pp. 397–415.

Sanderson, M. J., 'Estimating absolute rates of molecular evolution and divergence times: a penalized likelihood approach', *Molecular Biology and Evolution* 19 (2002), 101–9.

Sandfeld, Kristian, *Linguistique balkanique: problèmes et résultats* (Paris: Champion, 1930).

Sapir, Edward, 'Wiyot and Yurok, Algonkin languages of California', *American Anthropologist* 15 (1913), 617–46.

Sapir, Edward, 'The concept of phonetic law as tested in primitive languages by Leonard Bloomfield', in S. Rice (ed.), *Methods in Social Science: A Case Book* (Chicago: University of Chicago Press, 1931), pp. 297–306 [reprinted: David Mandelbaum (ed.), *Selected Writings of Edward Sapir in Language, Culture, and Personality* (Berkeley and Los Angeles: University of California Press, 1949), pp. 73–82]).

Sapir, Edward, 'Time perspective in aboriginal American culture: a study in method', in David Mandelbaum (ed.), *Selected Writings of Edward Sapir in Language, Culture, and Personality* (Berkeley: University of California Press, 1949), pp. 389–467 [original edn: Department of Mines, Geological Survey, Memoir 90, Ottawa: Government Printing Bureau, 1916]).

Sayce, Archibald Henry, *The Principles of Comparative Philology* (London: Trübner, 1874).

Schleicher, August, *Compendium der vergleichenden Grammatik der indogermanischen Sprachen: Kurzer Abriss einer Laut- und Formenlehre der indogermanischen Ursprache* (Weimar: Hermann Böhlau, 1861–2).

Schmidt, Johannes, *Die Verwandtschaftsverhältnisse der indogermanischen Sprachen* (Weimar: Böhlau, 1872).

Schrader, Otto, *Sprachvergleichung und Urgeschichte: Linguistisch-historische Beiträge zur Erforschung des indogermanischen Altertums* (Jena: Costenoble, 1883) [English trans.: *Prehistoric Antiquities of the Aryan Peoples: A Manual of Comparative Philology and the Earliest Culture* (London: C. Griffin, 1890)].

Schuchardt, Hugo, *Vokalismus*, vol. 3 (Leipzig: Teubner, 1868).

Schuchardt, Hugo, *Dem Herrn Franz von Miklosich zum 20. November 1883: Slawo-Deutsches und Slawo-Italienisches* (Graz: Leuschner & Lubensky, 1884).

Siebert, Frank T. Jr, 'The original home of the Proto-Algonquian people', Contributions to Anthropology: Linguistics 1, *National Museum of Canada Bulletin* 214 (1967), 13–47.

Snow, Dean R., 'The archaeological implications of the Proto-Algonquian Urheimat', in William Cowan (ed.), *Papers of the Seventh Algonquian Conference* (Ottawa: Carleton University, 1976), pp. 339–46.

Starostin, Sergei, *Altajskaja Problema i Proisxozhdenie Japonskogo Jazyka* [The Altaic problem and the origin of the Japanese language] (Moscow: Nauka, 1991).

Stubbs, Brian, *Uto-Aztecan: A Comparative Vocabulary* (Blanding: Shumway Family History Services and Rocky Mountain Books and Productions, 2011).

Suárez, Jorge, *Estudios Huaves*, Colección Científica, Lingüística 22 (México: Departamento de Lingüística, Instituto Nacional de Antropología e Historia, 1975).

Suhonen, Seppo, 'Uralilainen alkukoti' [The Uralic homeland], in Paul Fogelberg (ed.), *Pohjan poluilla: Suomalaisten juuret nykytutkimuksen mukaan* [On paths of the north:

the roots of the Finns according to current research], Bildrag till kännedom av Finlands natur och folk 153 (Helsinki: Finnish Society of Science and Letters, 1999), pp. 240–4.

Sweet, Henry, *The History of Language* (London: J. M. Dent, 1900).

Sweetser, Eve, *From Etymology to Pragmatics: Metaphorical and Cultural Aspects of Semantic Structure* (Cambridge: Cambridge University Press, 1990).

Teeter, Karl V., 'Algonquian languages and genetic relationship', in Horace G. Lunt (ed.), *Proceedings of the 9th International Congress of Linguists* (The Hague: Mouton, 1964), pp. 1026–33.

Thomason, Sarah G., *Language Contact: An Introduction* (Edinburgh: Edinburgh University Press, 2001).

Thomason, Sarah Grey, and Terrence Kaufman, *Language Contact, Creolization, and Genetic Linguistics* (Berkeley: University of California Press, 1988).

Thompson, J. Eric S., *A Catalogue of Maya Hieroglyphics* (Norman: University of Oklahoma Press, 1962).

Thompson, J. Eric S., *Maya History and Religion* (Norman: University of Oklahoma Press, 1970).

Todd, Loreto, *Pidgins and Creoles* (London: Routledge and Kegan Paul, 1974).

Tosco, Mauro, 'Is there an "Ethiopian Language Area"?' *Anthropological Linguistics* 42 (2000), 329–65.

Trask, R[ichard] L[arry], *Historical Linguistics* (London: Arnold, 1996).

Trask, R[ichard] L[arry], *History of Basque* (London: Routledge, 1997).

Trask, R[ichard] L[arry], *The Dictionary of Historical and Comparative Linguistics* (Edinburgh: Edinburgh University Press, 2000).

Traugott, Elizabeth Closs, 'On the rise of epistemic meanings in English: an example of subjectification in semantic change', *Language* 65 (1989), 31–55.

Traugott, Elizabeth Closs and Richard B. Dasher, *Regularity in Semantic Change* (Cambridge: Cambridge University Press, 2002).

Traugott, Elizabeth Closs and Bernd Heine, 'Introduction', in Elizabeth Closs Traugott and Bernd Heine (eds), *Approaches to Grammaticalization*, Typological Studies in Language 19 (Amsterdam: John Benjamins, 1991), pp. 1–14.

Traugott, Elizabeth Closs and Ekkehard König, 'The semantics-pragmatics of grammaticalization revisited', in Elizabeth Closs Traugott and Bernd Heine (eds), *Approaches to Grammaticalization*, Typological Studies in Language 19 (Amsterdam: John Benjamins, 1991), vol. 1, pp. 189–218.

Vendryes, Joseph, *Le langage: introduction linguistique à l'histoire* (Paris: La Renaissance du Livre [re-edn: 1968]).

Vovin, Alexander, *A Reconstruction of Proto-Ainu* (Leiden: Brill, 1993).

Wakelin, Martyn, *The Archaeology of English* (Totowa: Barnes & Noble, 1988).

Walkden, George, *Syntactic Reconstruction and Proto-Germanic* (Oxford: Oxford University Press, 2014).

Wang, William, 'Competing sound changes as a cause of residue', *Language* 45 (1969), 9–25.

Watkins, Calvert, *The American Heritage Dictionary of Indo-European Roots* (Boston: Houghton Mifflin, 1985) [2nd edn: 2000, 3rd edn: 2011]).

Weinreich, Uriel, *Languages in Contact: Findings and Problems*, Publications of the Linguistic

Circle of New York 1 (New York: Linguistic Circle of New York, 1953) [9th printing: The Hague: Mouton, 1979].

Weinreich, Uriel, William Labov, and Marvin Herzog, 'Empirical foundations for a theory of language change', in Winfred P. Lehmann and Yakov Malkiel (eds), *Directions for Historical Linguistics* (Austin: University of Texas Press, 1968), pp. 95–195.

Wells, John C., *Accents of English*, 3 vols (Cambridge: Cambridge University Press, 1982).

Wessén, Elias, *Språkhistoria I: ljudlära och ordböjningslära* (Stockholm: Almqvist & Wiksell, 1969).

Wichmann, Søren, *The Relationship among the Mixe-Zoquean Languages of Mexico* (Salt Lake City: University of Utah Press, 1995).

Wichmann, Søren and Eric W. Holman, 'Population size and rates of language change', *Human Biology* 81 (2009), 259–74.

Wichmann, Søren and Arpiar Saunders, 'How to use typological databases in historical linguistic research', *Diachronica* 24 (2007), 373–404.

Winteler, J., *Die Kerenzer Mundart des Kantons Glarus in ihren Grundzügen dargestellt* (Leipzig: Winter, 1876).

Wright, Larry, *Teleological Explanation* (Berkeley: University of California Press, 1976).

Wundt, Wilhelm, *Völkerpsychologie: Eine Untersuchungder Entwicklungsgesetze von Sprache, Mythus und Sitte, vol. 1: Die Sprache* (Leipzig: W. Engelmann, 1900).

Zeps, Valdis, *Latvian and Finnic Linguistic Convergence*, Uralic and Altaic Series 9 (Bloomington: Indiana University Press, 1962).

Zvelebil, Kamil V., *Duna Linguistics: An Introduction* (Pondicherry: Pondicherry Institute of Linguistics, 1990).

INDEX